Gardens and Gardening in Papal Rome

# Gardens and Gardening

# in Papal Rome

*by*

# David R. Coffin

PRINCETON UNIVERSITY PRESS

PRINCETON, NEW JERSEY

MCMLXXXXI

*Library of Congress Cataloging-in-Publication Data*
Coffin, David R.
Gardens and gardening in papal Rome / David R. Coffin.
p. cm.
Includes bibliographical references.
Includes index.
ISBN 0-691-04089-3 (alk. paper)
1. Gardens—Italy—Rome—History. 2. Gardens—Italy—
Rome—Design—History. 3. Landscape architecture—
Italy—Rome—History. I. Title.
SB466.I82R636 1991
712'.0945'632—dc20      90-37355

# CONTENTS

# ILLUSTRATIONS

# PREFACE

This study is to parallel my previous work on Roman villas, but to carry the material to the late eighteenth century, when the English mode of gardening replaced the previous principles of classical gardening and often destroyed Italianate gardens. The study is meant to attempt to consider every aspect of the classical garden in Rome and, therefore, is not organized on a chronological formal development. There is a slight chronological organization in some of the separate chapters as they proceed from the universal mediaeval *hortus conclusus* to a consideration of ancient statuary decoration, waterworks, and classical allusions and iconography, which define the characteristic Roman garden of the sixteenth to the eighteenth century. A consideration of Roman gardening in the seventeenth and early eighteenth centuries is important to understand the gradual departure from the Renaissance principle enunciated by the sculptor Bandinelli in the mid-sixteenth century that "built things should be the guide and dominate those things that are planted." The great garden parks of the Borghese and the Pamphili villas proclaim the art of landscaping and gardening as an independent art in which architecture, like sculpture, plays only an incidental role.

As in my book on Roman villas, Rome is defined geographically as "the land surrounding the city which is owned by persons whose political, religious, commercial, or social activities are centered within it," or roughly the modern region of Latium or Lazio.

Chapter 14 on the public and Roman gardens has appeared previously in a somewhat different form in the *Journal of Garden History*, II, 1982, pp. 201–32,

and is republished with permission of the editor, John Dixon Hunt. The occasional references to access to gardens of other countries in the original publication have been omitted here.

This study has percolated for many years parallel with my consideration of Roman villas. Numerous colleagues and former students have contributed material or ideas which I have ingested, sometimes unwittingly, but particular thanks are offered to Lynette Bosch, Sharon Cather, Tracy Cooper, Sabine Eiche, Meredith Gill, David Gobel, Edward Harwood, Claudia Lazzaro, Robert McVaugh, John Shearman, and David Wright. The librarians and staff of the Biblioteca Apostolica Vaticana, the Biblioteca Estense at Modena, the American Academy at Rome, and Marquand Library of Princeton University have been most helpful and kind in their aid during extensive periods of research, as have the directors and staff of the state archives at Florence, Modena, Parma, and Rome. The Department of Art and Archaeology of Princeton University has generously supported this project through its Spears research and publication funds. I particularly wish to thank Elizabeth Powers of the Princeton University Press for her gracious encouragement and direction of the editing of the work; Brian R. MacDonald for his impeccable and exacting copy editing; Cynthia Arbour for her enthusiastic guidance of the work through the intricacies of the Press; and Mike Burton, the designer, for his skill in ordering the whole.

JUNE 5, 1990
PRINCETON, N.J.

# Gardens and Gardening in Papal Rome

# *Hortus Conclusus*

For the Renaissance Italian, the garden was primarily an outdoor room, where the enjoyment of the colors and fragrances of flowers, the cool shade of trees, and the melodious splash and murmur of water augment the pleasures of dining, social conversation, or amorous dalliance. To dine in a garden court with the possible accompaniment of music or even dance was an ancient custom in the Mediterranean region. The Roman lexicographer Nonius Marcellus, when he defined "courts" (*chortes*) as "the spaces within the walls of villas," cited Varro's lost *Life of the Roman People* where the latter noted that "in winter and in the cold they were accustomed to dine by the hearth, in summer in an open place: in the country in the court [*in chorte*], in the city on the balcony [*in tabulino*]."[1] To understand, however, the sensuous appeal of the garden to the ancient Roman as a center for relaxed, domestic life, one must turn to the letter of Pliny the Younger describing his Tuscan villa (v, 6) or, for the restorative power of garden dining for a weary traveler, to the anonymous Vergilian poem on the tavern keeper (*Copa*).[2] So, almost a millennium and a half later, the Italian architect Alberti differentiates the various dining rooms of the villa: "some are for summer, some for winter, others, as is said, for in-between seasons. Summer dining rooms principally require water and the greenery of gardens, those of winter warmth and a fireplace" (v, xvii). Similarly in the next century the Spaniard Antonio de

Guevara, in his treatise extolling country life, paraphrases Varro: "Oh, fortunate villa, where in winter you eat near the fire; in summer before the entrance; in the garden if there are guests, under the loggia if it is too hot."[3] The well-to-do and the powerful then plan their residences with such garden settings for their summer dining. So in the description in 1510 by Paolo Cortese of an ideal cardinal's palace, "the main dining room overlooks a covered walk [*xystus*] and a garden [*topiarium*] so that their cheerful aspect will make dining [*accubatio*] the more pleasant."[4]

As a private, or at least semiprivate, domestic space, the Roman garden of the late Middle Ages and early Renaissance was a walled-in, usually rectangular, area, adjacent to the house and generally at the rear; it was entered directly from the dwelling, although there was often a locked portal in one of the exterior walls for the services of the gardener. The mediaeval documents of the sale or lease of houses in Rome, after briefly defining the building, follow the statement almost inevitably with the notarial formula "with garden behind it" (*cum orto post se* or *horto retro eam*).[5] As late as 1593, Tempesta's map of

[1] Nonius Marcellus, *De conpendiosa doctrina libros XX*, ed. W. M. Lindsay, Leipzig, 1903, I, p. 117.

[2] *Appendix Vergiliana*, ed. R. Ellis, Oxford, 1907; for the archaeological evidence, see W. F. Jashemski, *The Gardens of Pompeii*, New Rochelle, N.Y., 1979, esp. pp. 89–113.

[3] Antonio de Guevara, *Menosprecio de corte y alabaza de aldea*, 1539; quoted from the Italian translation, *Aviso de favoriti et dottrina de cortigiani*, trans. V. Bondi, Venice, 1544, p. 143.

[4] K. Weil-Garris and F. D'Amico, *The Renaissance Cardinal's Ideal Palace: A Chapter from Cortesi's De Cardinalatu*, Rome, 1980, p. 83.

[5] A sampling of such documents is presented in *ASRSP*, XXII, 1899, pp. 25–107, 383–447, 489–538; XXIII, 1900, pp. 66–128, 171–237, 411–47; XXIV, 1901, pp. 159–96; XXV, 1902, pp. 169–209, 273–354; E. Carusi, *Cartario di S. Maria in Campo Marzio (986–1199)*, Rome, 1948, pp. 45–46, 103; L. Cavazzi, *La diaconia di S. Maria in Via Lata e il monastero di S. Ciriaco*, Rome, 1908,

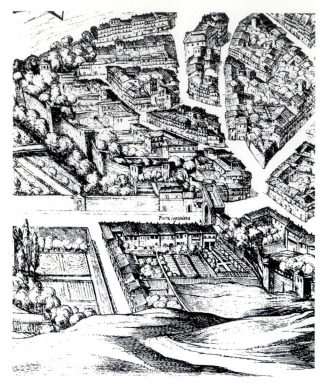

1. Rome, Tempesta Map of 1593, detail of the Trastevere

Rome still suggests the quantity of these small gardens with a few trees rising behind houses lining the streets of even such relatively dense areas as the Via Giulia and the Via del Pellegrino, the Trastevere, or around the Piazza Colonna (Fig. 1). The cold legal documents naturally tell us nothing about the conditions of such gardens. A few accounts of the tenth and eleventh centuries note the existence of a pergola in the garden, and many gardens are described as containing fruit trees (*arbores pomarum*), fig trees in at least one example, and olive trees in two others.[6] The lack of such features in the later mediaeval documents is probably due to the constriction of the notarial formula rather than to the actual disappearance of these features, although a house purchased in 1448 is described as having a garden of bitter-orange trees.[7]

As the garden developed at Rome in the later Renaissance, acquiring other features and values, its an-

cient function as an outdoor living space never diminished, and most of the small gardens, particularly in the more crowded sections of the city, did not differ from their mediaeval predecessors. Roman architecture of the fifteenth and sixteenth centuries was also quite distinctive in incorporating belvederes and upper-story loggias into even the most modest town houses where potted vines and flowers would suggest a garden setting, thus returning to the ancient Roman urban tradition noted by Varro of eating during the summer on balconies or roof terraces (*tabulina*), as is still done by the modern Romans. Even the great classical gardens of the sixteenth century, such as the Villa Medici in Rome (Fig. 35) or the Villa d'Este at Tivoli (Fig. 66), retain adjacent to the residence within their huge settings a small, secluded, walled-in garden (*giardino segreto*) as the private retreat of the owner.

The garden was, therefore, a restricted area set aside by the townspeople from the abundance of their environment to offer them pleasure and contentment in their daily life. Mankind had always retained the image of a place of pleasure, gardenlike in its setting, which existed either during the Golden Age of classical antiquity or in the biblical Garden of Eden. Now with his Fall from Grace man had to labor to create a garden, but by walling it off from the world of nature, as the monk did in his cloister, he might capture an imperfect reminder of that lost world.

The idea of Rome as a city of gardens was even more dramatically enhanced by the monastic establishments that dominated the city, for each monastery generally had at least one cloister planted as a garden. The monastic cloister had preserved the concept of the walled-in garden and the horticultural knowledge of plants and flowers throughout the dark moments of the early Middle Ages, until acquaintance with the wonders of the Middle Eastern gardens of Syria and Constantinople during the Crusades expanded the lure of the garden. The monastic cloister with its inevitable rectangular regularity, defined by porticoes on four sides, presented a clear formal image of the garden, which was undoubtedly lacking in secular examples, but the cloister and its garden were also endowed with a wealth of religious associations.

Solomon's Song of Songs in the Old Testament offered an abundance of complex references to the garden and to plants, which the church fathers from Origen to St. Bernard reveled in explicating in Christian terms. St. Bernard noted in one of his sermons on the Song of Songs that Solomon mentioned flowers in

pp. 247, 356–58; L. M. Hartmann, *Ecclesia S. Mariae in Via Lata Tabularium*, Vienna, 1895; P. Adinolfi, *Roma nell'età di mezzo*, II, Rome, 1881, p. 108; and P. Adinolfi, *La Via Sacra del Papa*, Rome, 1865, pp. 114, 121, 148–50.

   [6] Hartmann, *Ecclesia S. Mariae in Via Lata*, pp. 33, 102, and *ASRSP*, XXIII, 1900, p. 183.

   [7] Adinolfi, *La Via Sacra*, p. 80.

three locations—in the field, in the garden, and in the bedchamber.[8] The garden shares its growing nature with that of the uncultivated fields, but it is a secluded, enclosed area, the *hortus conclusus* of Solomon, created by man's handiwork and his art, as is the bedchamber in which nature only exists as plucked flowers. So the flower of the field symbolizes martyrdom, for martyrs are exposed to the mockery of all, and the flower of the garden is virginity, for it is modest and shuns the public. The cut flowers of the bedchamber must be constantly renewed and, thereby, suggest good works.

The association of the flowers of the enclosed garden with virginity became a common image of the later Middle Ages as the cult of the Virgin Mary swept across Europe. Albertus Magnus in the mid-thirteenth century devoted the last book of his treatise, *De Laudibus Beatae Mariae Virginis*, to the hortus conclusus as her symbol. For him God is the gardener (*hortulanus*) who sows the plants, the herbs, and the trees that symbolize the virtues of Mary, and the garden is both the Church and Paradise, just as those faithful in the Church and the virtues of their souls are symbolized by the herbs and trees.[9] He then goes on to define the virtues symbolized by the specific plants and trees. Shortly thereafter, William Durandus in his *Rationale* on the meaning of the church building and the divine offices similarly believes that the cloister signifies celestial Paradise and "the contemplative state, into which the soul betaking itself, is separated from the crowd of carnal thoughts and meditateth on celestial things only."[10] The garden of trees and herbs planted within the cloister then represents the virtues.

The church fathers were able, therefore, to sublimate the overt sexuality and erotic imagery of Solomon's Song to the ideals of the Christian church. Although every cleric might not be aware of all the interpretations of the garden offered by the church writers, the garden, and especially that of the cloister, would be identified in his mind with moral and religious values. When St. Catherine of Siena urged the pope in 1378 to reform the Church, she wrote of the "garden of the holy Church with its fragrant flowers which should bear the odor of virtue" and his need to "reform again the garden of the Spouse [that is, the Virgin Mary or the *sponsa* of Solomon's Song] with good and virtuous plants, taking care to choose a group of very holy men in whom you find virtue and who do not fear death."[11]

The cloister gardens were often luxuriantly provided with exotic plants and trees, for the monks were members of worldwide orders with sister houses and corresponding brothers on the Mediterranean islands and in the Levant, who would exchange seeds and plants. The bitter-orange tree (*melangolo*), whose golden fruit evoked in the minds of the friars the sanctuaries of the Holy Land and recalled to incipient classicists the Golden Apples of the Hesperides, was the most striking feature of many of the cloistered and secular gardens. One tree in particular attracted the attention of pilgrims and visitors to Rome. Soderini in his treatise on trees written toward the end of the sixteenth century comments on the long life of the bitter-orange tree and offers as proof the one in the monastery of Santa Sabina on the Aventine, which he alleges was planted by St. Dominic in the early thirteenth century.[12] Earlier the German Johann Fichard recorded in the account of his visit in 1536 being shown a tree at Santa Sabina planted by St. Dominic, but he describes it as "an oak, I think" (*puto quercus*). He adds that a memorial altar stood below the tree, as it does today. Fichard's comment suggests that the legend dates at least from the early sixteenth century, although his tentative identification of the type of tree is inaccurate.[13]

In 1600 Ottavio Panciroli in his guide to the sacred treasures of the city of Rome briefly mentions the orange tree planted by St. Dominic in the cloister of Santa Sabina, but then at the Franciscan monastery of San Francesco a Ripa Panciroli recites at greater length the same story about an orange tree in the cloister "which the Seraphic Francis planted with his own hands."[14] The existence of the two identical leg-

[8] St. Bernard de Clairvaux, *Opera*, II: *Sermones super Cantica Canticorum*, ed. J. Leclerq, C. H. Talbot, and H. M. Rochais, Rome, 1958, sermo XLVII, pp. 62–64.

[9] Albertus Magnus, *Opera omnia*, ed. A. Borgnet and E. Borgnet, XXXVI, Paris, 1898, pp. 600, 603.

[10] W. Durandus, *The Symbolism of Churches and Church Ornaments*, ed. J. M. Neale and B. Webb, London, 1893, p. 29.

[11] Caterina da Siena, *Lettere di Santa Caterina*, ed. N. Tommaseo, Rome, 1973, letter LXXV, pp. 379–83.

[12] G. Soderini, *Il trattato degli arbori*, ed. A. B. Della Lega, Bologna, 1904, p. 96. For the history of the tree, see J. J. Berthier, *L'Eglise de Sainte-Sabine à Rome*, Rome, 1910, pp. 477–82; J. J. Berthier, *Le Couvent de Saint-Sabine à Rome*, Rome, 1912, pp. 93–96; and F. Darsy, *Santa Sabina*, Rome, 1961, p. 140.

[13] J. Fichard, "Italia," *Frankfurtisches Archiv für ältere deutsche Litteratur und Geschichte*, III, 1815, p. 38.

[14] O. Panciroli, *I tesori nascosti nell'alma città di Roma*, Rome, 1600, pp. 318–19, 739. Ten years later Felini, obviously following Panciroli, offers the same two legends, [P. M. Felini,] *Trattato*

ends reflects the rampant rivalry between the two religious orders.

The Dominican version, however, eventually dominated. In 1604 François de Sales drew inspiration from the tree in Santa Sabina to write the Baroness de Chantal that it recalled to him "the tree of the desire to sanctity that Our Lord has planted in your soul."[15] By the seventeenth century the tree of St. Dominic was a favorite Roman object of devotion with its fruit generally reserved for the pope. Already in 1378 St. Catherine of Siena had sent from Rome candied fruit of a bitter-orange tree to Pope Urban VI with her usual homily in which she notes that the bitterness of the soul is washed away by the blood of Christ.[16]

For most Romans, irrespective of their social conditions or economic means, the garden was an essential element of life. The modest gardens of the average Roman, however, can only be dimly perceived in the reticent legal documents, the occasional poetic eulogies with which some literary men celebrated their friends' gardens, or the generalized comments by chroniclers, such as the mid-fourteenth-century account of the Prati at Rome by Giovanni Cavallini: "with lovely gardens filled with a quantity and variety of flowers, trees, fruit, and herbs."[17] The importance of such gardens to a fifteenth-century Italian is succinctly expressed in a letter of the humanist Lorenzo Valla in 1449 to a friend at Rome requesting his aid in locating a suitable residence for Valla in anticipation of his joining the Papal Curia. Valla's main concern is that the house must have a pleasant garden "in which I can refresh my eyes, in which sometimes in summer you can dine with me. Believe me, if I obtain it, I shall consider Augustus to have conferred no more on Vergil than Pope Nicholas on me."[18] Although the existence of these gardens and their role in the life of the Romans must never be forgotten, it is the lavish gardens created for the popes, the cardinals, and the noble families fostered by them that express the intellectual concepts necessary for the consideration of the garden as a work of art.

. . .

At the Vatican Pope Nicholas III (1277–1280) in the first year of his pontificate had enlarged the small, towered palace built by Pope Innocent III (1198–1216) next to St. Peter's by adding a large wing to the north and east of the earlier building, as well as a wing to the west. The most striking feature of the addition by Nicholas was a three-story loggia on the eastern facade of his palace facing the present Cortile di San Damaso.[19] In May of the following year, 1278, Nicholas III purchased vineyards on Mons Geretulus to the north and west of his palace.[20] There he laid out a great garden or walled park, called the *pomerium* in the inscription, now in the Museo dei Conservatori, that originally stood in the garden: "And in the second year of his pontificate he ordered to be made the walled enclosure of this garden [*pomerii*]."[21] The great defensive wall erected by Pope Leo IV (846–855) to protect St. Peter's and the Vatican ran along just outside the northern facade of the Palace of Nicholas III and his new pomerium lay outside of the wall on the hillside, now occupied by the Belvedere Court and the gardens northwest of it. An early chronicle relates that Nicholas III "enclosed a small meadow next to the [palace] and commissioned a fountain to flow there, the great garden adorned with various trees being surrounded by walls and towers,"[22] and the pomerium is still visible in the background of Benozzo Gozzoli's fresco of *St. Augustine Leaving Rome for Milan* (1465) in S. Agostino at San Gimignano (Fig. 2). Unfortunately most of the documents are very vague, using apparently interchangeably the terms *viridarium, ortus, pratum,* and *vinea*. In later documents, however, there is an occasional differentiation between a "large garden" (*ortus magnus*) and a "small garden" (*ortus parvus*), and the

*nuovo delle cose maravigliose dell'alma Città di Roma . . . 1610,* ed. S. Waetzoldt, Berlin, 1969, pp. 48, 143. See also M. Escobar, *Le dimore romane dei santi,* Bologna, 1969, pp. 68–69.

[15] St. François de Sales, *Oeuvres de Saint François de Sales,* vol. XII, *Lettres,* vol. ii, Annecy, 1902, no. CCXVI, p. 264.

[16] Caterina da Siena, *Lettere,* letter XCVI, pp. 487–90.

[17] G. Cavallini, *Polistoria de virtutibus et dotibus Romanorum,* in *Codice topografico della città di Roma,* ed. R. Valenti and G. Zucchetti, Rome, 1953, IV, p. 37.

[18] L. Barozzi and R. Sabbadini, *Studi sul Panormita e sul Valla,* Florence, 1891, p. 121.

[19] D. Redig de Campos, "Bramante e il Palazzo Apostolico Vaticano," *Rendiconti della Pontificia Accademia Romana di Archeologia,* XLIII, 1970–1971, pp. 288–92.

[20] F. Ehrle and H. Egger, *Der Vaticanische Palast in seiner Entwicklung bis zur Mitte des XV Jahrhunderts* (Studi e documenti per la storia del Palazzo Apostolico Vaticano, II), Vatican City, 1935, p. 40.

[21] D. Redig de Campos, "Les Constructions d'Innocent III et de Nicolas III sur la collini vaticane," *Mélanges d'archéologie et d'histoire,* LXXI, 1959, pp. 365–76.

[22] Ehrle and Egger, *Vaticanische Palast,* p. 39.

ELOQVII SACRI DOCTOR PARISINVS ET INCENS
GEMIGNANIACI FAMA DECVSQVE SOLI
HOC PROPRIO SVMPTV DOMINICVS ILLE SACELLVM
INSIGNEM IVSSIT PINGERE BENOTIVM · M·CCCC·LXV·

2. Benozzo Gozzoli, *St. Augustine Leaving Rome*, S. Agostino, San Gimignano, detail

chronicle's mention of the "large garden" (*iardinus magnus*) may imply the existence of a smaller garden. The discovery of the eastern loggia elevation of the palace where a century later there existed a smaller, secluded garden suggests that Nicholas III also had such a small garden outside of the loggia in front of his apartment. If so, then the Papal Palace had already in the late thirteenth century the traditional garden layout that was prevalent throughout Trecento Italy at princely palaces. Next to the residence would be a small, walled-in garden open from the building through a loggia. This garden would serve as an outdoor room, particularly for dining in the shade of the loggia. Beyond the "secret garden" (*giardino segreto*) would be a larger, walled-in meadow (*prato*) planted with trees and vines, which would be available for entertainment and enjoyment by other members of the court.

The best description of such a garden is in Pier de'

Crescenzi's slightly later treatise (ca. 1304–1309) on agriculture and gardening.[23] In the chapter on the gardens of kings and lords, a flat area of at least twenty acres is enclosed by walls and the northern part planted with a wood where wild animals could hide. Toward the south would be an open meadow with a fishpool. Rows of trees would be planted from the palace to the wood with walks and pergolas nearby for human pleasure. Along the walls would be fruit trees or elms and willows. At the Vatican, because of the restriction of open land within the old Leonine walls, the two garden areas were separated, with the larger garden outside the main defensive walls, but with its own protective enclosure.

With the Avignon papacy, the gardens at the Vati-

[23] Piero de' Crescenzi, *Trattato della agricoltura*, Milan, 1805, and L. Frati, "Pier de' Crescenzi e l'opera sua," *Atti e memorie della R. deputazione di storia patria per le provincie di Romagna*, ser. 4, IX, 1919, pp. 146–64.

can were neglected, so in November 1365 when Pope Urban V was preparing for his return to Rome, orders were sent from Avignon to have the gardens replanted.[24] Immediately after the arrival of Urban in Rome in October 1367 extensive work took place in the gardens, including the planting, presumably in the large garden (*viridarium*), of trees and vines sent from Marseilles, and the payment to a mason for crenellations (*merletti*) for the wall surrounding the small garden (*viridarium parvum*).[25] One account book alone is devoted to payments from November 1368 to December 1369 "for making a vineyard, garden and fishpond," which at one time, in December 1368, employed almost seven hundred men. According to an account in November 1368 the gardener in charge of the planting was a friar, Fra Guillermus. Already in November 1367, soon after the pope's arrival in Rome, the doge of Genoa sent a leopard as a gift to the pope. The leopard was probably housed in the large pomerium, since it was common in the Trecento for Italian princes to have large animal parks, the ancestors of our zoological gardens, where domestic and even exotic animals lived, as is also suggested by Pier de' Crescenzi.

With the continuation of the Avignon papacy and the schism, the gardens probably fell again into neglect, although the Neapolitan pope Boniface IX (1389–1404) seems to have shown a personal interest in the vineyard there. Vespasiano da Bisticci in his life of Cosimo de' Medici, when he remarks on Cosimo's pruning vines at his villa at Careggi, claims that Cosimo was imitating "Pope Boniface IX, who would prune certain vines in the vineyard of the papal palace at Rome every year in due season."[26] Vespasiano adds that Boniface's pruning knife was still preserved at Naples as a memorial to the pope.

With the accession of Pope Nicholas V (1447–1455) there was a great plan to expand and to rebuild the Vatican Palace and its gardens, as well as the church of St. Peter's and the entire Vatican Borgo, the suburb between the church and the Tiber River. Just before the formulation of this project Giovanni Rucellai of Florence described the Papal Palace during

his visit to Rome in the spring of 1449 "with large and small gardens and with a fishpool and fountains of water and a rabbit warren [*conigliera*]."[27] These would be still the gardens as they were laid out in the Middle Ages. The plan to revise the Vatican was probably instigated by the money and interest occasioned by the Jubilee Year of 1450. Other than some building accounts for the work begun in rebuilding St. Peter's and the great round tower east of the present palace, the only evidence for the project proposed at this time is a description of it in Manetti's life of the pope. The grandeur of the scope of the plan and some of the details for the new urban layout for the Vatican Borgo suggest that the great fifteenth-century architect, Leon Battista Alberti, who was then a member of the papal court, may have been involved in at least some aspects of the project. Presumably in place of the old mediaeval, private garden just east of the palace was to be a new, larger, walled-in garden stretching from the palace down to new walls separating it from the Borgo. Manetti suggests that it was to be "planted with all types of herbs and fruit trees and irrigated by live fountains whose water [the pope] would have brought from the top of the hill by subterranean aqueducts."[28] This garden, however, would no longer be a private garden for the personal use of the pontiff, as it was to contain three large, new buildings: a theater, a chapel, and a council hall with adjacent treasury. The garden then, rather than being a mediaeval retreat, would have been a splendid setting for the ceremonies of the court, but Manetti's description of it as "this most perfect space of Paradise" retains the mediaeval garden imagery.[29] Unfortunately the death of the pope in 1455 prevented any work on this part of the plan, but the ideas expressed in Nicholas's project would inspire the next two centuries of papal building at the Vatican. The old imagery of Paradise recurs with the election in 1455 of Pope Calix-

[24] A. Theiner, *Codex Diplomaticus Domini Temporalis S. Sedis*, II, Rome, 1862, p. 430, no. CCCCVIII.

[25] Ehrle and Egger, *Vaticanische Palast*, p. 76. The detailed documentation is given in J. P. Kirsch, *Die Rückkehr der Päpste Urban V und Gregor XI von Avignon nach Rom*, Paderborn, 1898, pp. XLI and passim.

[26] Vespasiano da Bisticci, *Renaissance Princes, Popes, and Prelates*, trans. W. George and E. Waters, New York, 1963, p. 225.

[27] A. Perosa, ed., *Giovanni Rucellai ed il suo zibaldone* (Studies of the Warburg Institute, 24), London, 1960, p. 72. A *conigliera* is normally a rabbit warren, but in the fifteenth century it could still retain the mediaeval idea of a garden area or meadow where rabbits could sport; see C. W. Westfall, *In This Most Perfect Paradise*, University Park, Penn., and London, 1974, p. 147. In 1453 a monk, Fra Giacomo di Giovanni of Gaeta, served as prefect of the gardens with a monthly stipend of twelve florins; see M. Dykmans, "Du Monte Mario à l'escalier de Saint-Pierre de Rome," *Mélanges d'archéologie et d'histoire*, LXXX, 1968, p. 571.

[28] T. Magnuson, *Studies in Roman Quattrocento Architecture*, Stockholm, 1958, p. 132.

[29] Westfall, *In This Most Perfect Paradise*, considers in detail this concept as applied to the entire program of Nicholas V.

tus III, when the orator of the Florentine embassy of homage likens the setting of their reception at the Vatican to the "house of the Lord and gate of heaven, . . . the enclosed garden [*hortus conclusus*], . . . Paradise with fruit trees."[30]

For the remainder of the fifteenth century the Vatican gardens underwent only minor changes and additions. Pope Pius II (1458–1464), who of all the fifteenth-century popes loved most the countryside and nature, so that he was rarely in residence at the Vatican, nevertheless built in the summer of 1461 a stone and wooden garden pavilion in the "vineyard" (presumably the pomerium of Nicholas III) and in 1462 and 1463 paid for work on a wooden pergola in the "garden" (probably the giardino segreto).[31] In his memoirs, the *Commentari*, Pius affords a glimpse of the role of the gardens, at least in his life at the Vatican. So he recounts how his dog fell into a water cistern in the summer of 1463, while he was receiving ambassadors in the garden, and he adds that he dined in that same garden, presumably the giardino segreto, on the following day. The Gozzoli fresco at San Gimignano (Fig. 2), dating in 1465, depicts a garden at this location with shrubbery, a tree, a fountain, and a pyramidal structure on the new round tower of Nicholas V, which has been identified as either an aviary or a pergola.

The Colonna family, one of the two leading families that dominated the politics of the city, owned a group of impressive gardens near the Quirinal Hill. In antiquity the gigantic Temple of Serapis, sometimes identified as the Temple of the Sun, stood on the western edge of the Quirinal Hill with a great flight of steps mounting the hillside up to the temple. The remains of the temple and stairway, known in the Middle Ages and early Renaissance as either the "Tower of Nero" or the "House of Maecenas," served as a quarry for later building. In fact, the steep flight of steps built in the mid-fourteenth century in front of the church of Sta. Maria d'Aracoeli on the Capitoline was created from the ancient stairway. Below the hill and the ancient remains of the temple, Pope Martin V

(1417–1431) built the Colonna Palace with at least one enclosed garden court whose main feature was a large elm tree.[32] This is apparently the first known example at Rome of one of the typical Renaissance horticultural topoi, the "Court of the Elm," which will occur later at least at the villa of Cardinal Carpi on the Quirinal and the villa of Cardinal Poggio on Monti Parioli. A larger garden, sometimes called the "Garden of the Tower of Nero," stood, probably even in the mid-fourteenth century,[33] on the hillside behind the Colonna Palace amid the remnants of the ancient temple. Flavio Biondo in his *De Roma Instaurata* (1444–1446) mentions that Cardinal Prospero Colonna, about 1440, improved and cleaned up the garden, which Biondo identifies as the ancient one of Maecenas, and laid out a varicolored, tessellated, marble path to the top of the garden.[34] The results, according to Biondo, appropriately rivaled the ancient garden of Maecenas, which he located here, and that of Sallust, which had stood nearby. Similarly in a letter of 1446 to the marchese of Ferrara, Biondo described a dinner offered by the cardinal "in the gardens of Maecenas" to Sigismondo Malatesta of Rimini.[35] Other than the glowing adulation of Biondo nothing is known about the gardens, which later were completely refashioned along with the Colonna Palace. A sixteenth-century drawing by Heemskerck depicts the brick walls of the ancient stairs climbing up the steep hillside to the remains of the Temple of Serapis, and two other drawings of this period show the great fragment of the pediment of the temple in the garden and a contemporary loggia built within some of the antique remains.[36]

About 1485 Cardinal Giuliano della Rovere, the

[30] O. Raynaldus, *Annales ecclesiastici ab anno MCXCVIII*, n.d., ed. J. D. Mansi, Lucca, 1753, X, pp. 28–29: Anno 1455, no. XXI.

[31] E. Müntz, *Les arts à la cour des papes pendant le XVᵉ et le XVIᵉ siècles*, pt. 1, Paris, 1878, pp. 275–77, and E. Casanova, "Un anno della vita privata di Pio II," *Bullettino senese di storia patria*, n.s., II, 1931, p. 23. A supervisor of the giardino segreto, a custodian of the vineyard, and a gardener are listed on the 1460 role of Pius II's *famiglia*, see [G. L. Marini,] *Degli archiatri pontifici*, Rome, 1784, II, pp. 154–55.

[32] R. Lanciani, "Il patrimonio della famiglia Colonna al tempo di Martino V (1417–1431)," *ASRSP*, XX, 1897, pp. 379–80, and doc. XXIII on p. 410. As late as 1591 the Colonna owned a "palace or house known as that of the elm tree," behind SS. Apostoli; see R. Lanciani, *Storia degli scavi di Roma*, II, Rome, 1903, pp. 214–15.

[33] The fragmentary chronicle of Monaldesco, published in L. A. Muratori, *Rerum Italicarum Scriptores*, XII, Milan, 1728, col. 535, relates that at the time of a bullfight at the Colosseum in 1332 a young Colonna daughter could not attend "perchè si era rotto un piede al giardino della Torre di Nerone." The authenticity of the account, however, has been doubted; see R. Lanciani, *ASRSP*, XX, 1897, p. 379.

[34] F. Biondo, *Roma instaurata*, in *Codice topografico della città di Roma*, ed. R. Valentini and G. Zucchetti, Rome, 1953, IV, pp. 283–84.

[35] F. Biondo, *Scritti inediti e rari di Biondo Flavio* (Studi e testi, 48), Rome, 1927, pp. 159–60.

[36] C. Huelsen and H. Egger, *Die Römischen Skizzenbücher von*

3. Rome, Palace of San Marco, Palazzetto, court

later Pope Julius II, built behind his church of the SS. Apostoli near the old Colonna Palace a small residence called the Palazzina.[37] The ground floor consisted only of an arcaded loggia of seven bays opening south onto its garden. Above the loggia was a file of rooms with cruciform-mullioned windows. The Palazzina with its adjacent garden must have served as a summer garden casino to supplement the older episcopal palace of the cardinals Bessarion and Riario on the south side of the church and the other new palace erected by Cardinal della Rovere north of the church. In 1507 Pope Julius gave his Palazzina to his niece on her marriage to Marcantonio Colonna and the building was later incorporated into the expanded Colonna Palace, but traces of it are visible on the north side of the second garden courtyard of the later palace. It must have been in this Palazzina that Julius II in May 1504, after mass at the church of the Apostoli, retired to dine, as described by Burchard: "In the garden loggia he took dinner at a square table in the middle next to the wall near the door of the rooms on a square podium, one priest at his right; along the wall was placed a long table at which twelve cardinals sat and ate."[38] Like the Vatican Palace, the Colonna complex then had a combination of one or more small, walled-in gardens, such as the "Court of the Elm" or the garden and Palazzina of Cardinal della Rovere, and a larger, probably less formal, garden on the hillside of the Quirinal.

When Pope Paul II built his Palace of San Marco below the Capitoline Hill in the heart of the city, there was no room for an extensive garden like the pome-

*Marten van Heemskerck*, II, Berlin, 1916, fols. 81v–82r, and H. Egger, *Römische Veduten*, Vienna, 1932, II, pls. 86, 87.

[37] P. Tomei, *L'Architettura a Roma nel Quattrocento*, Rome, 1942, pp. 211–14, and T. Magnuson, *Studies in Roman Quattrocento Architecture*, Stockholm, 1958, pp. 315–27.

[38] J. Burchard, "Liber Notarum," ed. E. Celani, in *Rerum Italicarum Scriptores*, XXXII, pt. 1, vol. II, Città di Castello, ed. L. A. Muratori, n.d., p. 449, May 1, 1504.

rium of Nicholas III at the Vatican or the Colonna "Garden of Maecenas" on the Quirinal, but he did create a unique giardino segreto. In 1455 before his election as Pope Paul II, Cardinal Pietro Barbo had begun a small palace next to his church of S. Marco, but on his elevation to the papacy in 1461 he started to expand the palace, whose construction would continue for almost a half century. At the southeast corner of the palace nearest the Capitoline Hill he built a walled garden for which plants and seed were purchased in May 1466,[39] and which was probably complete by the fall of 1468 when painters were paid to decorate the ceiling of the upper portico (Fig. 3). Unlike other giardini segreti in Rome, which were merely walled-in gardens, this one was surrounded on all four sides by a two-story portico opening onto the garden like a monastic cloister. The structure was actually in three stories, as the basement, composed of long corridors under the upper porticoes, was used as a stable. The interior garden level was about five meters above ground level so that Fra Mariano in the early sixteenth century described it as a "hanging garden above the horses' stables."[40] Unlike a monastic

cloister, however, the upper two stories of porticoes had large, arched windows in their exterior walls opening onto the city (Fig. 4). On the exterior there were entrances to the basement stables, but the only major access to the garden was a door into the upper portico from the pope's private apartment in the southeast corner of the palace, so that it was designed to be a private garden for the pontiff.

According to a sixteenth-century account, the garden was grassed with a central, cistern fountain surrounded by bitter-orange trees, laurels, and cypresses, and Soderini later in the century, after describing the cypresses planted above the Tomb of Augustus, adds "as are seen planted today above the stables of the Palace of San Marco where there are numerous vines and trees above the masonry vaults."[41] The charm of the garden, as well as the ample accommodations of the large palace, made the Palace of San Marco one of the favorite Roman residences for summer relaxation or *villeggiatura* of the sixteenth-century popes, until the expansion of the Cardinal of Ferrara's villa on the Quirinal Hill offered superior accommodations. In the later nineteenth century the construction of the monument to King Vittorio Emanuele II at the

[39] G. Zippel, "Per la storia del Palazzo di Venezia," *Ausonia*, II, 1907, p. 127, n. 3.

[40] Fra Mariano, *Itinerarium Urbis Romae*, ed. E. Bulletti, Rome, 1931, p. 210.

[41] E. Albèri, *Relazioni degli ambasciatori veneti al senato*, ser. 2, III, Florence, 1846, p. 106, and G. Soderini, *Il trattato della cultura degli orti e giardini*, ed. A. Bacchi della Lega, Bologna, 1903, p. 33.

4. Rome, Palace of San Marco, Palazzetto, exterior, engraving

edge of the Capitoline Hill caused the destruction of the walled garden of the Palace of San Marco. In order to create an unimpeded vista of the nineteenth-century monument along the Corso the walled garden was dismantled in 1911 and reerected at the southwest corner of the palace. In its rebuilding the central garden was reduced by the addition of rooms around it, transforming it into the present Palazzetto di Venezia.

Unlike the fifteenth-century palaces of Florence, the large Roman palaces of the period were rarely organized about a central, enclosed court with the regularity of plan that prevailed in Florence. Many fifteenth-century Roman palaces consisted of two or three wings with rear porticoes and walls to close the palace off from the streets of the city. In some locations at the edge of the city where there was ample space, gardens were created at the rear of the palaces. One of the finest was the palace of Cardinal Domenico della Rovere, now known as the Palazzo dei Penitenzieri, in the Vatican Borgo. Constructed in at least two separate building campaigns, the earlier part, probably begun soon after the appointment of the cardinal in 1478 and in use in 1484, forms the east wing of the present palace on the Via Scossacavalli.[42] By 1490 the building was expanded with its main block in four stories toward the north on the present Via della Conciliazione and another wing at the west. The final building was, therefore, U-shaped with its court open toward the rear where a retaining wall defined the court and separated it from a raised garden terrace (Fig. 5). The rear garden terrace at the level of the piano nobile of the palace was flanked on its east and west sides by three-story wings with ground-floor porticoes opening onto the garden, so that one might walk out into the garden from the piano nobile. At the back of the garden a wall with a garden portal set between the wings of the palace shut the garden off from the street passing behind the palace. Since there was no access from the lower, more public courtyard, the rear garden still functioned as a giardino segreto available primarily to the owner and his guests at the level of the main apartments of the palace. It is no longer, however, a completely walled-in entity. The garden complements the lower court so that spatially there is the suggestion of an axis running from the entrance to the rear garden portal, emphasized by a well set against the center of the retaining wall between the court and garden. This organization along

[42] Magnuson, *Studies*, pp. 332–37.

5. Rome, Della Rovere Palace, court

an axis with terraced levels modestly foreshadows sixteenth-century garden design, particularly Bramante's innovative design for the Belvedere Court of the Vatican, except that at the Vatican there will be physical access between the terraces by means of great flights of stairs.

The Roman fifteenth-century garden was, therefore, a small, walled one, often formally organized about a fountain or well at the center, which would be surrounded by grass plots or flower beds shaded by a few trees, usually laurel and cypress, and with some bitter-orange trees to lend an exotic note. Unlike Florence, where great sculptors such as Donatello or Verrocchio provided the gardens with fountains and decorative features, there is no evidence of important contemporary garden sculpture in Rome at this time. Conceived as a secluded outdoor room, the garden would usually have a loggia or portico opening onto it for dining and social intercourse or a wooden pergola covered with vines, or espaliered trees might serve as a substitute or supplement the loggia. Except for the occasional incorporation of classical fragments and sculpture, to be discussed later, the Roman garden was no different from the hortus conclusus that prevailed throughout northern Europe and the rest of Italy in the late Middle Ages and early Renaissance. Where there was sufficient free land a second, walled-in area on a larger scale and with little formal planting would feature vines and woods for bird hunting. It too might have a well, a fountain, or a fishpool, and, in the open area, a vine-covered pergola or even a garden pavilion for afternoon repose. Here birds and animals were usually left free, except for a possible rabbit warren where game could be raised before its release into the woods.

Already in the late fifteenth century, a few Roman

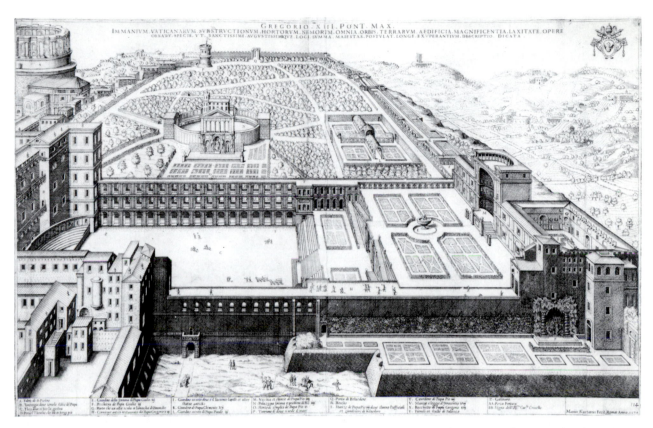

6. Rome, Vatican Palace, Belvedere Court, engraving, 1574, Avery Architectural and Fine Arts Library, Columbia University

gardens, such as that of Cardinal Giuliano della Rovere at SS. Apostoli, were assuming with their collections of ancient sculpture a more typically Roman character. The magnificent additions at the Vatican Palace of the Belvedere Court and its statue garden designed by Bramante in the early sixteenth century for Cardinal della Rovere in his new exalted position as Pope Julius II would dramatically proclaim the importance of this relatively new concept of gardening. Nevertheless even the Vatican continued to create later in the century several prominent examples of the hortus conclusus. During the reign of the Medici pope Clement VII (1523–1534), a new garden was designed along the northern bastions of the Vatican west of the Villa Belvedere.[43] Lacking contemporary documentation, the garden is only identified in a much later (1574) engraving of the Vatican (Fig. 6) as

[43] J. S. Ackerman, *The Cortile del Belvedere* (Studi e documenti per la storia del Palazzo Apostolico Vaticano, III), Vatican City, 1954, p. 57.

that of Clement VII. Originally a loggia set along the western wall of the statue court at the Belvedere opened onto a small cypress wood whose soaring forms are visible rising over the surrounding walls west of the Villa Belvedere in Perino del Vaga's paint-

7. Rome, Castel S. Angelo, fresco of Belvedere Court with naumachia

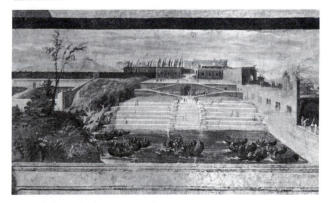

8. Rome, Vatican Palace, Garden of Paul III

ing of the Belvedere Court as the scene of a *naumachia* (Fig. 7) and in the copy of Heemskerck's drawing of the villa. It was beyond this small wood that the new formal garden was created for Clement VII. With the destruction of the cypress grove for the erection of the Cortile degli Archivi designed by Ligorio for Pope Pius IV in 1563, the garden of Clement was left isolated beyond the archives as seen in Cartaro's engraving. As in a mediaeval castle, the garden was defined on its northern edge by the fortified walls of the precinct, but toward the south it was separated from the Vatican hillside or *barco* west of the Belvedere Court by a tall hedge set on a long terrace (Fig. 6). The Cartaro engraving depicts a long alley, flanked by parterres outlined by low hedges, bisecting the center of the garden. The garden must have served as a giardino segreto for the Villa Belvedere, where the pope or visitors to the villa might enjoy the exercise of walking free from the publicity of the Belvedere Court or viewing over the wall the magnificent prospect of Monte Mario in the distance. Indeed, it may be the

enforced withdrawal of Clement VII to the seclusion of the Villa Belvedere during the plagues of 1524 and 1525 that suggested the creation of this new garden.

It was for Clement's successor, Pope Paul III, that the last important example of a hortus conclusus was created in Rome. In November 1535 early in the pontificate of Paul the first payment was made for the commencement of leveling the ground for a "new garden" just outside the western corridor of Bramante's Belvedere Court and adjacent to the earlier garden of Clement VII (Fig. 8).[44] The work was under the direction of the papal architect, Jacopo Meleghino, whose name appears frequently in the accounts, including one in July 1537 that lists the reimbursement for cord and twine to lay out the ditches (*fosse*) in the new garden. The major work was concerned with excavating and leveling the terrain, since the garden was sunk into the hillside of the Vatican. Rectangular in shape,

[44] Documents published in L. Dorez, *La cour du Pape Paul III*, Paris, 1932, I, pp. 214–16 and II, passim.

9. Rome, Vatican Palace, corridor between Garden of Paul III and Garden of Clement VII

about 90 meters wide by about 131 meters, the south-eastern corner was at the original ground level, but the rear or western side, because of the slope, was from 6 to 9 meters below ground level with huge retaining walls. This required extensive excavation and only in November 1538 was recorded payment for leveling the last compartment (*l'ultimo quadro*). Meanwhile, the other principal expense was for the procurement of trees for the garden. So in September 1537, Don Giovanni Aloysi, gardener of the Belvedere, was reimbursed for going to Naples to obtain orange and other citrus fruit trees, and in November transportation was paid for 1,500 citrus trees from Naples. Again in February 1538 the gardener returned to Naples for orange and myrtle trees. It is only in December 1543 that the accounts begin to mention pergolas or espaliers for the garden, so in March through July 1544 a carpenter was paid for chestnut beams and semicircular bows for the great pergola. By 1932, with the completion of the new Vatican Picture Gallery across the northern portion of

the garden, the latter was destroyed, except for a portion of the great excavated area.

The Cartaro print of 1574 (Fig. 6) depicts the garden of Paul III completely enclosed by a wall and divided into four compartments by a cross pergola with a light, domed vault over the crossing. In each of the compartments Cartaro indicates a garden bed surrounded by a low hedge, just as he does for the upper terraces of the Belvedere Court and for the garden of Clement VII, which may be merely his graphic formula for a garden. The cross pergola and the inner walls of the garden are completely covered with espaliered trees, confirmed by the documents of 1544 which mention the woodwork "of the orange tree espaliers" (*spalliere de melangoli*). In the center of the north wall at the end of the cross axis of the pergola was a portal entering a subterranean corridor (Fig. 9) under the terrace and hedge separating the new garden from the older one of Clement VII. This corridor joining the two gardens was created late in 1537, since Meleghino was authorized in February 1538 to pay for the work "in excavating the earth under the vault which leads from the new garden of the Belvedere into the old one" and in October the painter Jacomo was paid for decorating the vault of the passageway.[45] At the southeast corner, where the garden was at ground level, another portal led directly into the garden (Fig. 10). In the center of the south wall at the other end of the cross axis of the pergola opposite the underground corridor, another portal entered onto a double flight of stairs on the inside of the wall, leading down to the level of the garden. On the exterior this portal, which still stands, is framed by a pair of pilasters with richly carved shafts and capitals, bearing a lintel inscribed: "Pius IIII. Pontifex. Maxim" (Fig. 11). The inscription suggests that the portal was created at the time that the Casino of Pius IV was completed on the hillside south of the garden and an alley was laid down from the garden to the northern gateway of the casino complex. The older garden of Paul III then could serve as a *giardino segreto* for the new casino.

The original garden of Paul III was very traditional in concept and design. Although huge, it was only another late mediaeval hortus conclusus, whose appeal was the color and fragrance of the fruit trees espal-

45 The plan and two views in G. Gromort, *Jardins d'Italie*, Paris, 1922, I, pls. 10, 11, before the garden was cut up, give the clearest indication of its organization.

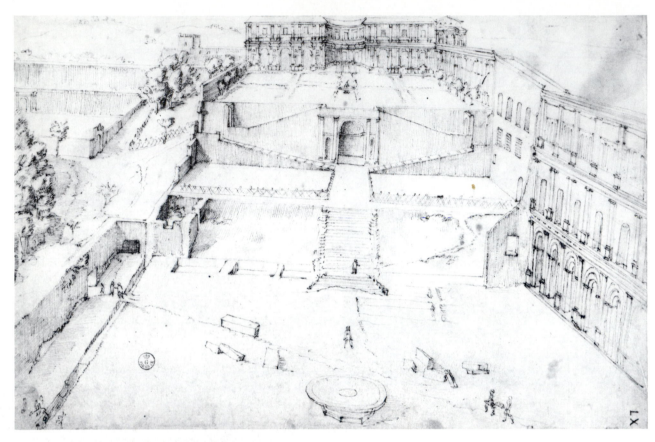

10. Rome, Vatican Palace, Belvedere Court, Dosio drawing, Uffizi 2559A

11. Rome, Vatican Palace, Garden of Paul III, gateway

iered over and along the walkways. Its isolation on the hillside, removed from the Vatican buildings, enhanced its character almost symbolically as a hortus conclusus, which in the history of sixteenth-century Roman gardening is further emphasized by its almost complete disregard for the topography of its site.

# Statuary Gardens

Many of the mediaeval *vigne* or vineyards and courtyards of Rome contained as accidental decoration fragments of ancient statues, architectural pieces, or ancient sarcophagi used as water basins, but it is only in the second half of the fifteenth century that ancient remains were consciously collected as garden decoration. Cardinal Prospero Colonna, who developed the so-called "Gardens of Maecenas" behind his palace at Rome in the 1440s, had an important collection of ancient statues, including a torso of Hercules and the group of the Graces now in Siena,[1] but his antiquities were apparently exhibited in his palace. Poggio Bracciolini, the Florentine chancellor who had earlier been employed at the papal court, was the first to collect ancient statues to adorn a garden. Already in 1427 Poggio owned several marble heads, which he said were "to decorate my Valdarno Academy," that is, his villa at Terranuova in the Valdarno. Later he recounts in his dialogue *De Nobilitate* how Lorenzo de' Medici, seeing the busts in the garden, jokingly accused him of seeking nobility by exhibiting portraits of the ancients rather than images of his own ancestors.[2]

The earliest collection of antiquities to decorate a country residence in Rome probably comprised the forty-two stone, classical inscriptions or inscribed altars that Pomponio Leto gathered in the 1470s in the vestibule and garden of his modest vigna on the Quirinal Hill, near the ruins of the Baths of Constantine.

There, emulating his ancient hero Cato the Censor and following the horticultural precepts of the ancient agricultural treatises of Columella and Varro, which he edited, Leto cultivated his own garden. Because of the life and teaching of Leto, the virtues of ancient Republican Rome founded on an agricultural society pervaded much of the intellectual life of late-fifteenth-century Rome. Even Leto's neighbor, the very wealthy Neapolitan Cardinal Carafa, adorned his great vigna on the western brow of the Quirinal Hill, probably in the 1480s, with images of the *scriptores rei rusticae* such as Cato, Columella, and Varro, accompanied by modern inscriptions with brief quotations of their most pungent horticultural precepts, as well as with a few ancient inscriptions.[3]

Most of the fifteenth-century collections of antiquities consisted of small, portable objects: coins, gems, small bronzes, marble busts, or inscriptions, which could be safely housed in the residence of their owner for the admiration of his friends. Ancient statues, on the other hand, or marble altars and sarcophagi, whose size diminished the threat of theft, could find a more suitable exhibition in the open courtyards of palaces or their adjacent private gardens. Already in the late fifteenth century, the man who at the beginning of the next century would change completely the atmosphere and concept of the garden was gathering for display some notable ancient Roman statues. Cardinal Giuliano della Rovere, nephew of Pope Sixtus IV and later to be Pope Julius II, had a choice collection of a few ancient statues in the garden court of the

---

[1] R. Lanciani, *Storia degli scavi di Roma*, I, Rome, 1902, p. 107.

[2] E. Müntz, *Les arts à la cour des papes pendant le XVe et le XVIe siècles*, pt. 2, Paris, 1879, p. 167, and Poggio Bracciolini, *Opera omnia*, ed. R. Fubini, I, Turin, 1964, p. 65.

[3] L. Schrader, *Monumentorum Italiae*, Helmstadt, 1592, p. 218.

palace he rented next to the church of the Santi Apostoli.[4] The outstanding piece was the Apollo Belvedere, probably discovered at the end of the century on land held by the cardinal near Grottaferrata on the road to Marino. There also may have been a group of Hercules and Antaeus and possibly a figure of Venus Felix, all of which later, when joined by the Laocoön and other statues, formed the nucleus of the magnificent collection exhibited in the Statue Court of the Belvedere at the Vatican built for the cardinal after his election as Pope Julius II.[5]

Late fifteenth- and early sixteenth-century Rome had a wealth of sculpture courts and sculpture gardens, for many of the cardinals or the wealthy bankers and merchants wished to partake of the notoriety and splendor of antique collecting, but the life of most of these collections was rather brief as more wealthy or powerful collectors bought them during the middle to late sixteenth century. Some collections were merely put on exhibition in older palace courtyards, such as that of the Della Valle on the Via Papale or that of the Sassi on the Via del Governo Vecchio. Others were in gardens attached to the palaces, as at the Mattei residence in the Trastevere where at the end of the fifteenth century Fra Giocondo identified "in the garden" thirty-three inscriptions of ancient religious cults.[6] Similarly the Maffei family had at the end of the century a collection of inscriptions recorded by Fra Giocondo as "in the house or garden" of their palace bought in 1491 in the rione Pigna near the church of SS. Quaranta di Calcarario, now S. Francesco delle Stimmate. As Giocondo was only interested in inscriptions, it is possible that the ancient statuary, including a group of Pan and Eros identified later by Aldrovandi as "in the little garden," were also part of the fifteenth-century collection.[7]

One of the early collections, that of Cardinal Giuliano Cesarini at his palace on the Via Papale, was organized as a museum open to a limited public, but there is little evidence about the setting for the exhibition of his antiquities except the charming dedicatory inscription: "Giuliano Cesarini, cardinal deacon of Sant'Angelo, has dedicated this statuary pavilion [*dietam statuariam*] to his studies and to the decorous pleasure [*voluptati honestae*] of his countrymen [*gentilibus*] on his thirty-fourth birthday, the thirteenth Kalends of June [May 20] of the eighth year of Pope Alexander VI, of the fifteen-hundredth of our Lord, and of the two thousand and two hundred and fifty-third year of the founding of the city."[8] The use of the Latin word *diaeta* to describe the housing of the collection suggests a garden pavilion, as Pliny the Younger in the letters describing his villa employs the word for a separate, small apartment in his gardens, and about twenty years after Cesarini's inscription a garden room at the Villa Madama was identified by Raphael with the same Latin word. Fifty years later Aldrovandi records some statues in the home of Giuliano Cesarini "in the street of the Cesarini," inherited from Cardinal Giuliano, and adds that "in the garden of Signor Giuliano, which is not very far from the house," are four caryatids and numerous other pieces.[9]

Although there is no further evidence regarding Cardinal Cesarini's collection, the Dutch artist Heemskerck, who visited Rome between 1532 and 1535, made drawings of several statue gardens, such as the one near S. Lorenzo in Damaso owned by Jacopo Galli, who commissioned the young Michelangelo about 1497 to carve a statue of Bacchus. In Heemskerck's drawing (Fig. 12) the Bacchus stands rather forlornly with a broken right arm in a court littered with ancient sarcophagi and fragments, while behind him other pieces, including a sphinx, line the retaining wall to a small, upper garden.[10] Similarly Cardinal Giovanni de' Medici, later Pope Leo X, bought a palace in 1505 near the Piazza Navona, the present Palazzo Madama, with a large, groin-vaulted loggia opening upon a small garden walled off on the west side from the Via dei Straderari. In the center of the garden was a circular fountain basin on a tall pedestal, and ancient statues stood among the columns of the loggia.[11] These statue gardens are merely later ex-

[4] D. Brown, "The *Apollo Belvedere* and the Garden of Giuliano della Rovere at SS. Apostoli," *Journal of the Warburg and Courtauld Institutes*, XLIX, 1986, pp. 235–38.

[5] A. Michaelis, "Geschichte des Statuenhofes in Vaticanischen Belvedere," *Jahrbuch des kaiserlich deutschen archäologischen Instituts*, V, 1890, pp. 5–72, and H. H. Brummer, *The Statue Court in the Vatican Belvedere*, Stockholm, 1970, pp. 44–47, 123, 139–41.

[6] Lanciani, *Storia*, I, pp. 111–12.

[7] Lanciani, *Storia*, I, pp. 109–10, and C. Huelsen and H. Egger, *Die römischen Skizzenbücher von Marten van Heemskerck*, I, Berlin, 1913, fol. 3v.

[8] R. Lanciani, *Storia*, I, pp. 12, 133–35, but Lanciani confuses the two Cesarini collections; see C. Huelsen, review of *Le statue di Roma*, by P. G. Hübner in *Göttingische gelehrte Anzeigen*, no. 176, 1914, p. 292. The inscription is preserved in Ms 1729 of the Biblioteca Angelica, Rome, fol. 12v.

[9] U. Aldrovandi, *Delle statue antiche*, Venice, 1558, pp. 221–23.

[10] Huelsen and Egger, *Die römischen Skizzenbücher von Marten van Heemskerck*, I, fol. 72r.

[11] Ibid., fol. 5r, and II, fol. 48r.

12. Rome, House of Jacopo Galli, statue garden, drawing by Heemskerck, 79 D 2 Kupferstichkabinett SMPK, Berlin, fol. 72r

amples of the *hortus conclusus* decorated with antique sculpture or inscriptions like the fifteenth-century ones at the house of Pomponio Leto on the Quirinal or that of Cardinal Giuliano della Rovere at his palace next to SS. Apostoli.

The election in 1503 of Cardinal della Rovere as Pope Julius II marks a dramatic step in the development of the Roman garden, for a year later he commissioned the architect Bramante to design and build the Belvedere Court at the Vatican (Fig. 6). In part of the area covered by the pomerium of Pope Nicholas III on the hillside that climbed up from the north side of the Vatican Palace to the Villa Belvedere erected by Pope Innocent VIII on the brow of Monte S. Egidio, Bramante constructed a tremendous, rectangular court connecting the palace and the villa, to be discussed later. As the villa was set askew to the northern end of the Belvedere Court another architectural space, the so-called Statue Court, was set behind the eastern half of the great exedra to serve as a link between the disparate structures. From its design and location the Statue Court would seem to be a *giardino segreto* for the old villa, but, in fact, it was an outdoor museum of antiquities. To exhibit the papal collection of statuary, niches were provided in the corners of the Statue Court and in the center of each of its walls. Unlike a *giardino segreto*, whose use was limited to the enjoyment of the owner and his friends, the Statue Court of the Belvedere was to be open to a more general public whose access was provided by Bramante's addition of his famous spiral stairway at the eastern side of the Villa Belvedere. This stairwell permitted the public to reach the Statue Court without penetrating the Belvedere Court or the Vatican Palace.

The Statue Court was basically completed by the time of Bramante's death in 1514, although a few statues were added later. Already in 1512 Giovanni Francesco Pico della Mirandola mentions the "colossal image of the Tiber" set in a "most fragrant grove of orange trees,"[12] but the most complete description is that by one of the Venetian ambassadors come to pay homage to the new Pope Hadrian VI in 1523. In the niches in the four corners of the court were the Apollo Belvedere, Venus Felix, the river god Tigris, and the so-called Cleopatra. The latter two statues, set in niches against the southern wall of the older Villa, were converted into fountains, the figures reclining in rustic niches above water basins. In the niches in the center of each of the four walls were statues identified as Commodus in the guise of Hercules, Antinous, Dionysus, and the famous Laocoön group discovered in 1506 and immediately purchased by the pope for his collection (Fig. 13). Several of the statues, certainly the Apollo Belvedere, and possibly the group of Hercules and Antaeus and the Venus Felix, had previously been part of the collection assembled by the pope at his palace next to SS. Apostoli. Some doors in the western wall of the court entered into a loggia along the outer wall of the court opening onto the woods to the west of the court. At one end of the loggia a fountain supplied a small canal running down the center of the loggia and then irrigated the trees in the court. The Venetian ambassador adds that "half of the very lovely garden is filled with fresh grass and with laurel trees, mulberry trees and cypresses; the other half is paved in squares of terracotta laid on edge and from each square of the paving issues a very lovely orange tree of which there is quite a number arranged in perfect order." In the ambassador's description the grassed area with cypresses and other trees is the portion of the old pomerium of Nicholas III west of the Statue Court onto which the loggia opened. The court itself was, therefore, paved, but had numerous orange trees, the *nemus odoratissimum citriorum* of the younger Pico della Mirandola, growing among the paving stones. In the center of the court was a small fountain on an antique triangular base, and two huge statues of reclining river gods, the Tiber and the Nile, were set freestanding in the center of the northern and southern halves of the court.

[12] The descriptions are gathered in a catalogue in J. S. Ackerman, *The Cortile del Belvedere* (Studi e documenti per la storia del Palazzo Apostolico Vaticano, III), Vatican City, 1954.

13. Rome, Vatican Palace, Belvedere Statue Court, Laocoön group, drawing by Francisco D'Ollanda

The completed Statue Court of the Belvedere, therefore, translated the form of the traditional hortus conclusus into a most charming and fragrant setting for the collection of papal antiquities, a *locus amoenissimus* in the words of the Renaissance poets and humanists, emulating Vergil and the classical writers. That many of the statues bore symbolic overtones is demonstrated by the writers of the period.[13] Certainly the sculpture was not acquired to accommodate a preconceived overall program, but various pieces evoked in contemporary poets reflections of the political power and achievements of Pope Julius II. Undoubtedly the garden was to suggest the classical concept of a villa and its garden, and perhaps even the more specific idea of the Garden of Hesperides

[13] Brummer, *The Statue Court in the Vatican Belvedere*, pp. 216–51.

protected by Hercules, who won the golden apples, since the orange tree, which was the major horticultural feature of the Statue Court, was often equated with the Tree of the Hesperides, and the figure of Commodus as Hercules stood guard at the entrance to the court. Certainly the inscription, *Procul Este Profani*, paraphrasing Vergil's *Aeneid* (VI, 258), which, according to Albertini, accompanied the statue, implies the idea of the garden court as a sacred precinct.

The completion of the Belvedere Statue Court soon inspired the creation of several other important sculpture gardens at Rome. The most architecturally perfect example was the "hanging garden" or *hortus pensilis* of Cardinal Andrea della Valle (Fig. 14). The Della Valle family owned a cluster of palaces between the Via Papale and the Sapienza, and in one owned by the cardinal, near the present Teatro Valle, the architect-sculptor Lorenzetto, who belonged to the circle of Raphael, designed a statue court, according to Vasari, early in the 1520s. The work was interrupted by the Sack of Rome in 1527 and not complete at the cardinal's death in 1534, so that his nephew Camillo Capranica had to finish it. The court stood above the stables on the piano nobile or second floor, hence its designation as a hortus pensilis, with a flight of stairs from the ground floor entering first into the end of a loggia, which in turn opened onto the court at right angles to the stair. The rectangular court was about twelve meters wide by seventeen meters long with a loggia at each end. From the loggias, which were lined with statue niches and supported toward the court by a pair of Corinthian columns, there was a step down into the open court. Along the base of the two long side walls of the court were raised garden beds with relief sculpture decorating the faces of the low retaining walls. The side walls were in two stories with the lower one alternating sculpture niches with garden trellises. The upper story in two bands had statue niches below alternating with large reliefs and large antique masks above alternating with modern inscriptions. As a result both walls were almost completely covered with ancient sculpture either in niches or applied to the walls as reliefs, and the antiquities were very carefully organized into the entire decorative scheme, even to the symmetrical placing of male and female figures.

The cardinal's garden court was again an outdoor living room surrounded by other rooms. At the end of the left wall a door led to a bathroom decorated,

14. Rome, Della Valle Palace, sculpture garden, drawing by Francisco D'Ollanda

according to a contemporary account, with "most lascivious pictures of nude bathing girls"[14] and in the center of the rear wall of the farther loggia was a portal to the cardinal's dining room. Also behind the left wall was an aviary whose birds could be glimpsed through three small windows, which were later walled up as statue niches. An engraving, probably after a drawing by Heemskerck, depicts low-growing plants, presumably flowers, in the garden beds and small trees and vines espaliered on the trellises against the walls, and identified in a slightly later account as "orange trees, pomegranates, citrons, and other exotic trees" (*mali Medicae, Punicae et Cedri, aliaque arbores peregrinae*). The Della Valle garden court was a perfect setting for a life of elegant and intellectual leisure or *otium*, as the eight epigrams inscribed on marble panels along the top of the side walls proclaimed.[15] One inscription noted that the garden was

"dedicated to honorable leisure [*honesti otii*] and household convenience." While Cardinal Carafa had dedicated the gardens of his vigna on the Quirinal Hill to the enjoyment of his friends, Cardinal della Valle broadened the concept into the first full enunciation of the *Lex Hortorum*, dedicating his garden "to the enjoyment of friends and to the pleasure of citizens and strangers." With overtones of the Garden of the Muses, even the artists were included: "A living garden of antiquities and aid to painters and poets."

The most interesting feature of the Della Valle court is the subservience of the ancient sculpture, despite the size and importance of the collection, to the design of the garden court. It is as if the sculpture had been made to decorate the garden and no piece of statuary was more important than a tree or vine in the garden in contrast to the Belvedere Statue Court where the freestanding sculptural groups and figures dominated both the architectural and horticultural settings. In this respect the Della Valle court begins a long and important tradition of villa and garden decoration in Rome. The ancient sculpture of the Villa

---

[14] C. Huelsen and H. Egger, *Die römischen Skizzenbücher von Marten van Heemskerck*, II, Berlin, 1916, p. 57.

[15] See Appendix IV, no. 5.

Giulia of Pope Julius III in the middle of the century will be similarly related to the decoration of the entire complex. Also Ligorio's Casino of Pius IV in the Vatican with its program of modern stucco relief and ancient sculpture belongs to this tradition, followed by the Villa Medici late in the century and the Villa Borghese and Villa Pamphili of the seventeenth century. In fact, some of the Della Valle sculpture will be reused in a similar fashion. In 1577 Cardinal Ferdinando de' Medici, who was refashioning the villa formerly of Cardinal Ricci on the Pincian Hill, opened negotiations with the Capranica family, who inherited the Della Valle court, for the purchase of the collection. Finally in 1584, as the new Villa Medici was nearing completion, the purchase was consummated and most of the Della Valle antique sculpture was moved to the Pincian, where the great relief panels and some of the busts were incorporated into the garden facade of the Villa Medici.

As the Roman collections of antiquities expanded in the 1540s with the increase in the excavation of works of art and the acquisition of earlier collections, their settings enlarged beyond the scope of courtyards and garden courts. A large collection, which survived the sixteenth century, was that of the Cesi family in the Vatican Borgo. About 1517 Paolo Emilio Cesi, who had just been appointed cardinal by Leo X, bought a palace begun before 1505 by Cardinal Alessandrino south of the old piazza in front of St. Peter's. Next to the Porta dei Cavalleggeri behind the palace was a vineyard on the lower slope of Monte di Sto. Spirito protected toward the south by the old Leonine Wall. Here Cardinal Cesi and his successors laid out their sculpture garden. The collection of antiquities that decorated the palace and garden was probably begun in the 1520s, for Mazzochi's collection of inscriptions of 1521 records none for the Cesi, but during the Sack of Rome in 1527 the cardinal was rightly afraid for his collection, since the imperial troops broke into the city behind his garden, and one account claims that the constable of Bourbon was killed in the garden.

When Cardinal Paolo Emilio Cesi died in 1537, his brother Federico inherited the property, and immediately gave Pope Paul III some of the antiquities in the palace.[16] Federico, however, who was also made a cardinal in 1544, soon expanded the collection and added new features in the garden. With the protection afforded by the construction beginning in 1534 of new city bastions by Sangallo, Cardinal Federico was able to incorporate additional vineyards to the east and south of the palace garden into the complex, converting a small palace garden into the type usually associated with a suburban villa. At his death in 1565, the garden continued in the possession of the family and probably remained unchanged until 1622 when many of the antiquities were sold to Cardinal Ludovico Ludovisi to decorate his tremendous villa and park on the Pincian Hill. When Bernini in the middle of the century erected the great, semicircular arms of his colonnade in front of St. Peter's, the entire front block of the palace was cut away in a curve and part of the giardino segreto beside the palace on the east was destroyed. Finally in 1941 the palace and its gardens were completely leveled.

The Dutch artist Hendrik van Cleef, who was in Rome in the middle of the sixteenth century, later painted a view of Cardinal Cesi's palace and garden (Fig. 15), as well as offering a distant glimpse of them in a panorama of the Vatican Hill dated 1550.[17] However, most of Van Cleef's depictions of Roman topography are not factually accurate in some of their details, and the sculpture inventories and descriptions of the Cesi garden preserved in Aldrovandi and Waelscapple[18] indicate a similar arbitrariness in Van Cleef's painting of the Cesi palace.

In the 1550s, at the fullest moment of the development of the gardens, there was a typical, small, walled-in giardino segreto at the east side of the palace planted with trees and flowers and decorated with fragments of antiquities. A large portal at the south or rear of the giardino segreto opened into a wide alley that ran along the east side of the larger, formal garden behind the palace and terminated at the rear at the ramp that led up the hillside to the Antiquarium. The formal garden, which could also be entered on its central axis from the rear portal of the palace, was about eighteen meters square and divided by cross alleys into four garden beds edged with low hedges and twenty-two herm figures. It was these herms that in 1566 during the stringent papacy of

---

[16] F. de Navenne, *Rome, le palais farnèse et les Farnèse*, Paris, n.d., p. 457.

[17] M. van der Meulen, "Cardinal Cesi's Antique Sculpture Garden: Notes on a Painting by Hendrick van Cleef III," *Burlington Magazine*, CXVI, 1974, pp. 14–24.

[18] C. Huelsen, "Römische Antikengärten des XVI Jahrhunderts," *Abhandlungen der Heidelberger Akademie der Wissenschaften: Philosophisch-historische Klasse*, IV, 1917, pp. 36–42.

15. Rome, Cesi Palace and Sculpture Garden, painting by Heemskerck, National Gallery, Prague

Pius V worried Bishop Agustin for their lascivious effect upon the prudish Northerners.[19] In the center of each bed was an ancient statue of a standing deity, Bacchus, Neptune, and Apollo, and in the southwest bed a Fountain of Silenus with a three-legged antique basin decorated with Bacchic reliefs in the center of which Silenus poured water from a wineskin. At the southwest corner was a fountain with a small boy pouring water from an urn on his shoulder into a granite basin. Beside the fountain the remains of a round tower of the Porta del Cavalleggeri in the south wall were converted presumably by Cardinal Federico Cesi, since Heemskerck's drawing still shows it in ruins,[20] into a small loggia for summer dining. At the other end of the south wall just before the stepped ramp to the Antiquarium and, therefore, serving as a visual accent at the end of the wide alley along the east side of the garden, was a group of *Roma Triumphans*, consisting of a colossal seated female figure restored as Rome and flanked by two standing, black

[19] D. R. Coffin, *The Villa in the Life of Renaissance Rome*, Princeton, N.J., 1979, p. 174.
[20] Huelsen and Egger, *Die römischen Skizzenbücher von Marten van Heemskerck*, I, fol. 25r.

marble barbarians. A portal at the southern end of the eastern garden wall led up to a raised, semicircular terrace whose rear wall was decorated with ancient Latin inscriptions referring to the *gens Caesia*, supposedly ancestors of the Cesi. Statues of Pluto and Heliogabalus stood in columned niches at the ends of the parapet. This raised terrace shaded by a lone mulberry tree and provided with a well of water was also to serve as an outdoor dining room.

Outside the formal garden to the east and south, partly on the slope of Monte di Sto. Spirito, was a large, informal vineyard without any ancient sculpture. A wooden trellised portal guarded by two ancient statues of lions opened into the vineyard at the north end of the eastern garden wall near the palace. Before 1550 Cardinal Federico Cesi added the Antiquarium in the northwest corner of the vineyard on axis with the alley along the eastern edge of the garden. Beside the group of *Roma Triumphans* a steep ramp led up the hill to a terrace behind the garden from which there was a splendid view of St. Peter's. On the terrace was a fountain with a reclining nymph inscribed *Dormio Dum Blandae Sentio Murmur Aquae*, like the famous fountain of the *Aqua Virgo* in

Colocci's garden and versions in other Roman gardens, discussed later. The Antiquarium was a pavilion in the form of a Greek cross whose facade, decorated with stucco work, was opened by a large entrance arch above which was a porphyry bust of Jupiter flanked by portrait busts of Otho and Poppaea. On the interior each of the three arms had several niches for statues and a large niche in the upper lunette for a bust, while a shallow dome decorated with painted stucco covered the center. This garden pavilion with interior walls lined with ancient statues may have resembled the *diaeta statuaria* mentioned by Cardinal Cesarini in the dedicatory inscription of 1500 of his garden. The Cesi garden, particularly after its expansion in the 1540s, differed from earlier statuary gardens not only in the size of its collection of antiquities but also in the variety of its settings, typical of suburban villa gardens of the last half of the sixteenth century. Next to the palace was still the small, walled flower garden or hortus conclusus. The larger, formal garden, also near the palace, was an expanded version of the hortus conclusus with classical statues, fountains, and box hedges replacing the flowers as decoration because of the larger scale and less intimate atmosphere. Here loggias and terraces provided the setting for outdoor dining and conversation. Beyond the carefully designed formal gardens as a foil and frame was the larger, informal, and more utilitarian vineyard undoubtedly planted with vines, fruit trees, and perhaps even a vegetable garden. The garden also partakes of the symbolic expression that will predominate in many of the later gardens. The exhibition of Latin inscriptions commemorating the ancient gens Caesia, presumed ancestors of the Cesi, on the wall of the dining terrace and the figure of *Roma Triumphans* as the principal visual feature of the garden exalt the Roman inheritance of the Cesi family. Nevertheless it is still basically a statuary garden whose major purpose is the exhibition of ancient sculpture or, in the words of one of the inscriptions of the Della Valle garden court, "a living garden of antiquities" (*Antiquarum rerum vivario*).

In addition to the early collection of antiquities exhibited by Cardinal Giuliano Cesarini in the statuary pavilion (*dietam statuariam*) presumably in the garden of his palace on the Via Papale, the Cesarini family possessed a palace and garden just west of S. Pietro in Vincoli at the site of the present church of S. Francesco di Paola. Only the remains of the mediaeval tower of the house still stand behind the church, but an old print preserves a schematic plan of the garden

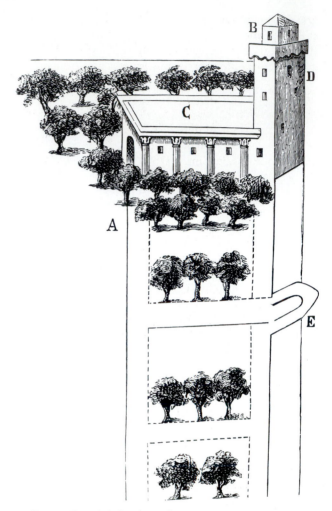

16. Rome, Cesarini Garden, plan

(Fig. 16) and a sixteenth-century drawing of the palace of S. Pietro in Vincoli provides at the right a glimpse of the eastern end of the garden.[21] In his will of 1574 Giangiorgio Cesarini claims that when he inherited the palace and garden about 1564 they lacked any adornment and that he had meanwhile assembled the classical antiquities and furnishings for which the garden and palace were famous.[22] The plan depicts the garden as a long rectangle closed at one end by a casino attached to the old tower and walled in on the other three sides with a garden entrance from the piazza of S. Pietro in Vincoli. Within the walls were apparently three large, square beds with trees planted regularly along their edges. The casino, decorated to-

[21] P. Adinolfi, *Roma nell'età di mezzo*, Rome, 1881, II, p. 105, and H. Egger, *Römische Veduten*, II, Vienna, 1931, pl. 48.
[22] [N. Ratti,] *Della famiglia Sforza*, Rome, 1795, II, pp. 291–92.

ward the garden with Corinthian pilasters, was presumably one story high with a roof terrace, permitting a view into the garden, and was used as a statue gallery containing, according to the notation on the plan, busts of ancient Roman emperors. Other statues, including a satyr carrying the boy Bacchus and an allegory of the Ocean, stood in the garden.[23]

In 1585 Cesarini purchased a gigantic marble column from the Forum of Trajan which, according to a contemporary account, was to be erected in the garden with the addition of a bronze eagle to surmount it and a bronze bear chained to its base, thus reproducing the three symbols of his coat of arms, but his death prevented its completion.[24] This projected monument in association with the gallery of Roman emperors (Caesars) suggests the possible formulation of a program commemorating his family with a possible play on the name Cesarini. An inscription carved at the entrance to the garden, probably on the statue gallery, gave his *Lex Hortorum*, inviting his visitors to contemplate and enjoy the beauties of the garden.[25]

Meanwhile, in the mid-1540s, at the time of the expansion of the Cesi garden, Cardinal Rodolfo Pio da Carpi began a large sculpture garden at his vigna on the Quirinal Hill, the first mention of which is in a poem of Marcantonio Flaminio dated 1547.[26] By the time Boissard visited the garden in the late 1550s, he would assert that there was no garden in Rome, or even in all of Italy, more charming or magnificent than that of Carpi, adding significantly that, although the nearby vigna of the Cardinal of Naples had many gardens, "they have few antique sculptures."[27] In contrast, Carpi assembled at his vigna the largest collection of antiquities then known, including, according to Boissard, some 136 inscriptions.

Set on the northern edge of the Quirinal Hill, a short, steeply ascending alley from the Piazza Grimani in the valley below led along the western side of the vigna to a large forecourt, the Court of the Well, with a huge Medusa head as protectress over the entrance portal (Fig. 17). From the north side of the forecourt another portal with a statue of Mother Nature, the ancient Diana of Ephesus, entered the main court, known from its single, large elm tree as the Court of the Elm, in front of the cardinal's casino. In the north wall of the main court was a loggia with a magnificent view out over the valley to the Pincian Hill beyond, while the walls of the court were lined with ancient herm statues and figures of Minerva, the Muses, Hercules, and Pluto. On the north side in a small piazza below the casino a painted loggia served as entrance into a delightful grotto created in the basement of the casino.[28]

Behind Cardinal Carpi's casino was the usual, walled-in giardino segreto planted with exotic trees and decorated with ancient urns and fragments of ancient reliefs and statues. Beyond the walls of the courts and the casino, stretching across the Quirinal to the road of the Alta Semita, the later Via Pia, was the vigna planted densely with large rectangular areas of elms and cypresses among which were many more ancient fragments, urns, and reliefs, and some statues set in leafy bowers. On axis with the side of the casino, as a slightly formal center for the more naturalistic vigna, was a large ivy circle, and a huge rusticated portal in the wall along the Alta Semita permitted visitors access to the vigna without disturbing the casino. With the creation of a public entrance to the vigna off the Alta Semita, the small enclosed flower garden directly behind the casino became truly a private garden, a giardino segreto, for the personal enjoyment of the owner and his intimate friends residing or dining at his villa.

Insofar as the Vigna Carpi can be reconstructed from literary descriptions and the scanty visual material,[29] its design was extremely casual and informal. Presumably no architect or designer was involved in the overall plan. The gardens as they developed around the casino were probably created from the day-to-day consultation between the cardinal and his gardeners, only calling upon the services of an architect for single features such as the garden portal on the Alta Semita. Undoubtedly the main concern of the cardinal was for the acquisition and exhibition of his

[23] De Navenna, *Rome, le palais farnèse et les Farnèse*, pp. 666–67.

[24] Lanciani, *Storia degli scavi di Roma*, I, p. 134, and C. Huelsen, review of Hübner, *Le statue di Roma*, in *Göttingische gelehrte Anzeigen*, no. 176, 1914, p. 292.

[25] L. Schrader, *Monumentorum Italiae*, Helmstadt, 1592, fol. 217v, and Adinolfi, *Roma*, II, pp. 105–6. See Appendix IV, no. 3.

[26] C. Maddison, *Marcantonio Flaminio, Poet, Humanist and Reformer*, Chapel Hill, N. C., and London, 1965, p. 172.

[27] J. J. Boissard, *Topographia Romana*, Frankfurt, 1627, II, p. 46.

[28] S. Eiche, "Cardinal Giulio della Rovere and the Vigna Carpi," *Journal of the Society of Architectural Historians*, XLV, 1986, pp. 121–22.

[29] The most complete reconstruction is in Huelsen, "Römische Antikengärten des XVI Jahrhunderts," fig. 34, whose reconstruction is partially confirmed by the later publication of the catasto plan of about 1625; see H. Thelen, *Francesco Borromini: Die Handzeichnungen*, pt. 1, Graz, 1967, pl. 26, fig. 47.

17. Rome, Dupérac map of 1577, detail of Vigna Carpi and Vigna Carafa

collection of ancient sculpture. Nevertheless, the emphasis was on a much more naturalistic gardening than previously prevailed, as seen in the placing of the sculpture freely in wooded areas or the imitation grotto.

Two of the features of Cardinal Carpi's gardens existed earlier in other gardens and will occur in later gardens, suggesting that the owners chose to reproduce favorite motifs of horticultural decoration analogous to the classical and Renaissance poet's use of topoi.[30] One was the Court of the Elm, where the principal decoration of the major court of the villa or residence was a single large elm tree. The earliest example at Rome was the one at the Colonna Palace from at least the early fifteenth century. The villa of Giovanni Poggio on Monte Parioli, created probably in the late 1540s just after the villa of Cardinal Carpi, likewise had a huge elm as the focus of its garden. After the Poggio vigna was acquired by Pope Julius III in 1551, he had the base of the elm tree girded with a carved marble relief.[31] The idea of a single tree being the focus of a courtyard or garden is a very simple and natural concept, arising perhaps from the previous existence of the tree at the location. However, the recurrence of the motif with its repeated identification in the documents of the time and the care with which Julius III emphasized and protected his example suggest that it was a particular horticultural feature of Roman landscape design. Marcantonio Flaminio in a poem to Diana speaks of Bocchi dedicating an elm

tree to the goddess in his villa,[32] and at the entrance to the Court of the Elm in the Vigna Carpi stood a statue of the ancient Diana of Ephesus in her role as Mother Nature, as if there were some relationship. Also the classical literary topos of the elm and the vine as a marital allusion was well known to the Renaissance, and Ripa will later use the topos as a symbol for Happiness, Friendship, or Benevolence, but there is no indication of such associations in the Roman gardens.[33]

A much more obvious topos is the grotto of the sleeping nymph in the Carpi vigna. Gradually in the sixteenth century nymphaea and grottoes with attendant waterworks became a dominant and characteristic feature of Roman gardens, but because of the scarcity of water in fifteenth- and early sixteenth-century Rome such water-oriented components remained modest in the context of the Roman garden, whose major attraction, as in the Vigna Carpi, was usually the wealth of ancient sculpture on exhibit. In fact, most of our knowledge of early sixteenth-century Roman gardening results from the lure of the ancient works of art to artists like Heemskerck and Francisco d'Ollanda or to antiquarians like Fra Giocondo, Aldrovandi, or Boissard.

[30] E. MacDougall, "*Ars Hortulorum*: Sixteenth Century Garden Iconography and Literary Theory in Italy," in *The Italian Garden* (First Dumbarton Oaks Colloquium on the History of Landscape Architecture), ed. D. R. Coffin, Washington, D.C., 1972, pp. 37–59.

[31] T. Falk, "Studien zur Topographie und Geschichte der Villa Giulia in Rom," *Römisches Jahrbuch für Kunstgeschichte*, XIII, 1971, pp. 116, 140 (no. 83), 141 (no. 117).

[32] M. A. Flaminio, *Marci Antonii, Joannis Antonii et Gabrielis Flaminiorum Carmina*, Padua, 1743, p. 40. There was likewise a statue of the Ephesian Diana as Mother Nature in the walled garden in front of the Vigna Poggio adjacent to the large garden toward the west where the huge elm stood; see J. J. Boissard, *Romanae Urbis Topographiae, & Antiquitatum*, Frankfort, 1597, pt. 1, pp. 101–2.

[33] P. Demetz, "The Elm and the Vine: Notes toward the History of a Marriage Topos," *Publications of the Modern Language Association of America*, LXXIII, 1958, pp. 521–32; E. Wind, *Pagan Mysteries in the Renaissance*, London, 1958, p. 98; and C. Ripa, *Nova Iconologia*, Padua, 1618, s.v. *Allegrezza, Amicitia,* and *Benevolenza*.

# Waterworks: Fountains, Nymphaea, and Grottoes

Pirro Ligorio, archaeologist, architect, and garden designer, expatiated in the middle of the sixteenth century in obscure philosophical terms on the importance of water, for "fountains are the nourishers and soul of the substance of all plants" and by the end of the century Giovanni Soderini, the Florentine writer on horticulture and agriculture, asserted in direct terms that "since water is the soul of villas, of pleasure gardens [*giardini*], and of kitchen gardens [*orti*], whether natural or artificial, it is needed in abundance."[1] By this time the gardens in and around Rome were particularly notable for the wonders of their waterworks, so that in 1615 the Vicenzan architect Scamozzi would single out the three great villas and gardens of Caprarola, Tivoli, and Bagnaia around Rome in company with the Tuscan villa of Pratolino for their use of water and fountains.[2]

During the fifteenth and much of the sixteenth century, however, the city of Rome lacked the abundance of water sources advocated by Soderini, being reduced to the leaky supply of the ancient Acqua Vergine, the river water of the Tiber, and wells. Even in the late sixteenth century it is significant that the villas identified by Scamozzi for their plenitude of water are in the hill towns surrounding Rome where their owners at great personal expense could tap nearby springs

with aqueducts, which would not only supply their garden fountains but also furnish water to the local communities, which might bear some of the cost.[3] Already in 1525 Andrea Fulvio had noted that the water of the Acqua Vergine was drawn largely from the marshy area of Bocca di Leone just outside the Porta Pinciana instead of its original abundant source at Salone about six miles beyond, and the German Johann Fichard remarked during his visit in 1536 on the scarcity of fountains, necessitating the use of well and river water for drinking.[4] After a disastrously expensive and unsuccessful attempt initiated by Pope Pius IV in 1561 to restore the ancient conduit of the Acqua Vergine to Salone, his successor, Pius V, was able from 1568 to 1570 to complete the work as far as the Trevi Fountain, but it was only under Pope Gregory XIII (1572–1585) that the architect Giacomo della Porta conveyed the water to fountains in other piazze of the city. Although this brought fresh and abundant water to the low-lying portion of the city of the Campo Marzio and adjacent *rioni* near the Tiber, the water pressure was insufficient to impel water to the Monti and hill regions on the eastern side of the city, where in the second half of the sixteenth century huge gardens were expanding around the suburban villas established there by many of the cardinals. In June

---

[1] M. Fagiolo, "Il significato dell'acqua e la dialettica del giardino: Pirro Ligorio e la 'filosofia' della villa cinquecentesca," in *Natura e artificio*, ed. M. Fagiolo, Rome, 1981, p. 178, and G. Soderini, *Il trattato degli arbori*, ed. A. Bacchi della Lega, Bologna, 1904, p. 271.

[2] V. Scamozzi, *L'Idea della architettura universale*, Venice, 1615, pt. 1, pp. 343, 344.

[3] E. B. MacDougall, "*L'Ingegnoso Artifizio*: Sixteenth Century Garden Fountains in Rome," in *Fons Sapientiae: Renaissance Garden Fountains* (Dumbarton Oaks Colloquium on the History of Landscape Architecture, v), ed. E. B. MacDougall, Washington, D.C., 1978, pp. 88–89, with relevant bibliography.

[4] R. Lanciani, *Storia degli scavi di Roma*, III, Rome, 1908, pp. 235–38, and J. Fichard, "Italia," *Frankfurtisches Archiv für ältere Litteratur und Geschichte*, III, 1815, p. 26.

1570 Cardinal Ricci, who presided over the congregation empowered by Pius V to restore the Acqua Vergine, had been granted the right to tap the restored aqueduct for the modest fountains he created at his new villa on the Pincian Hill, but when Cardinal Ferdinando de' Medici purchased the Ricci estate in 1576 he soon discovered that the water pressure was insufficient for the elaborate waterworks planned for the Mount Parnassus to be featured in his addition to the gardens.[5] However, a Milanese engineer, Camillo Agrippa, with new hydraulic devices was finally able to compensate for the lack of water pressure.

Although the major reason for the successive popes' interest in revitalizing the water supply of the city of Rome during the second half of the sixteenth century was the very humane desire to supply the public with safe and abundant water, their interest and that of their advisors, the cardinals at Rome, in creating luxurious garden retreats in the relatively uninhabited region of the Monti undoubtedly augmented their concern for endowing the hills with water. Pope Gregory XIII, soon after his election in 1572, became increasingly enamored with the villa and gardens that Cardinal Ippolito II d'Este had previously laid out on the western headland of the Quirinal Hill. In May 1583, at the moment the pope began to expand the Este casino, the city government of Rome was informed that the pope intended to create an aqueduct to bring water from the Colonna possession of Pantano dei Griffi to the Piazza delle Terme at the eastern end of the Quirinal.[6] The new project, however, was only completed in 1586 by the succeeding Pope Sixtus V with the water pouring in to the great public fountain of the Acqua Felice and allowing the nearby villas and gardens to tap the new source (Fig. 116). Thus, by the last decade of the sixteenth century water was available to most of the city east of the Tiber to supply all the public and garden fountains with that seemingly ceaseless flow of water that was such a dramatic characteristic of baroque Rome.

During the sixteenth century the west bank of the Tiber, including the Trastevere and the Vatican Borgo, had barely sufficient water brought by the ancient aqueduct of the Aqua Alsientina from near Lake Bracciano to the Janiculum Hill, and by 1590 this system began to fail. Finally in 1608 Pope Paul V ordered a complete restoration of the aqueduct, including a huge new fountain on the Janiculum, the Acqua Paola modeled on that of the Acqua Felice on the Quirinal Hill. In the inscription dated 1611, which was proposed to commemorate the building activities of Paul V, the new aqueduct was specifically praised for reviving the gardens in the suburb, thus including gardens within the concept of public welfare.[7] Soon the Pamphili family would be able to tap the aqueduct for the huge gardens of their villa set nearby just outside the Porta San Pancrazio. The water supply, however, was disappointing in both quality and quantity. Even as late as the middle of the seventeenth century this shortage of water had aroused bitter feelings between Queen Christina of Sweden and Cardinal Girolamo Farnese (1599–1668).[8] Farnese, embellishing the gardens at the country house, now called the Villa Aurelia, owned by his relative the duke of Parma on the Janiculum Hill, was granted water from the Acqua Paola by the Camera Apostolica. His diversion of water lessened the supply to the gardens farther down the hill at the Riario Palace rented by Queen Christina from 1659. The queen showed her displeasure by destroying the supports for the palisades that sustained the Farnese gardens. In the late seventeenth century the introduction of water from Lake Bracciano into the aqueduct solved the water shortage, but did not improve its quality.

The magnificent water system of ancient Rome had been indispensable to the papal contribution to the public welfare of Renaissance Rome, since the latter was for the most part merely a restoration of the ancient waterworks. Similarly the ancient Romans contributed ideas for the water devices that enlivened the gardens of Renaissance Rome. The letters of Pliny the Younger, Cicero, and Seneca or the poetry of Ovid and Vergil dwell on splashing fountains and nymphaea or dripping, dank grottoes within groves of plane trees. Thus, Propertius (III, 3, 25) relates how Apollo guided him to a grotto in the Castalian grove, which was "a green cave lined with pebbles and timbrels hung from the hollow pumice stone, also the rit-

[5] D. R. Coffin, *The Villa in the Life of Renaissance Rome*, Princeton, N.J., 1979, pp. 222–23, 230.

[6] Ibid., pp. 209–10.

[7] E. Taramelli, R. Albertazzi, and A. Draghi, "Un documento sulla Roma di Paolo V," *Ricerche di storia dell'arte*, 1–2, 1976, p. 145.

[8] J. Bignami Odier, "Le Casin Farnèse du Monte Janicule (Porte San Pancrazio), maintenant Villa Aurelia," *Mélanges de l'École Française de Rome: Môyen âge—Temps Modernes*, vol. 91, pt. 1, 1979, pp. 507–38, and [Ch. G. Franckenstein,] *Istoria degli intrighi galanti della Regina Cristina di Svezie e della sua corte durante il di lei soggiorno a Roma*, ed. J. Bignami Odier and G. Morelli, Rome, 1979, pp. 39–40.

ual instruments of the Muses and a clay image of Father Silenus and your pipes, O Tegean Pan." There the nine Muses busied themselves gathering ivy for the sacred thyrsus, weaving rose garlands or singing to the lyre. Similarly Pliny the Elder in his scientific encyclopedia, the *Historia Naturalis* (XXXVI, xlii), describes artificial grottoes from whose ceilings hang pumice stones in imitation of natural caves and adds that the Greeks call them "Homes of the Muses" (*musaea*), particularly gratifying to Renaissance poets.

In the mid-fifteenth century Alberti in his architectural treatise (IX, iv) offers Renaissance patrons a detailed image of such ancient grottoes:

> In caves and grottoes the ancients were accustomed to apply ingeniously a rough surface consisting of small lumps of pumice or the foam of Tiburtine stone, which Ovid calls living pumice. And we have seen some overlaid with a green ocher imitating the downiness of mossy caves. Most pleasing was a cave we saw where a stream of water erupted, the wall composed of various sea shells, some upside down, others recumbent, set with a most pleasing skill in a variety of colors.

Some sixteenth-century drawings record lost ancient Roman nymphaea. One drawing, attributed to Peruzzi, depicts an exedra surrounded by a canal of water with a small water stairs in the center, while another of a nymphaeum near Lake Albano is described by its anonymous artist as being "ornamented with shells, pumice and pebbles set in mosaic," somewhat like Alberti's account.[9] There was, however, one renowned example, the so-called Grotto of Egeria off the Via Latina outside the Porta Capena on land owned in the sixteenth century by the Caffarelli family (Fig. 18). Livy in his history of Rome (I, 19 and 21) recounts how Numa Pompilius, the second king of Rome, was accustomed to pay nocturnal visits to the cave of the nymph Egeria, who instructed him to establish the rites of Roman religion and bring peace to the young city-state. Although modern archaeology denies the identification of the grotto in the Valle della Caffarella with the ancient sanctuary of Egeria, the tradition was of long life.[10] Petrarch in the fourteenth

century in a letter to Cardinal Giovanni Colonna identifying the famous sights of Rome lists: "Here [was] the meeting of Numa with Egeria," probably in recollection of the grotto.[11] Much later in 1594, the sculptor Flaminio Vacca in his reminiscences describes the grotto as having

> a fountain under a large ancient vault, which it still enjoys, and the Romans go there during the summer for recreation. In the pavement of this fountain an inscription records that this is the fountain of Egeria, dedicated to the nymphs. Imaginatively the poets say that Egeria had been one of Diana's nymphs, who being in love with her brother far distant from her and wishing to write that he should return, took her pen and, as she wrote, wept so bitterly that Diana moved to compassion converted her into a live spring and this the inscription relates is the same spring into which she was converted.[12]

Several sixteenth-century drawings attributed to Antonio da Sangallo the Younger and Sallustio Peruzzi record the plans of the deep grotto with a transverse, vaulted vestibule and a water channel lining the base of the walls (Fig. 19), and the Portuguese painter Francisco d'Ollanda preserves in his book of drawings at Madrid from his trip to Italy in 1539–1540 a fantastic interpretation of the grotto with a lavish architectural facade decorated with rusticated orders after those of the Porta Maggiore forming tabernacle frames for statues and a reconstruction of the remains of the recumbent figure in the rear niche as an amorous group of Numa and Egeria.[13]

During the fifteenth century the elaborate nymphaea and grottoes of the ancients seem to have had little impact on Roman gardens. Poggio Bracciolini in a letter of June 23, 1425, likens a fountain in the garden at Rome of Antonio Perraro to that of Egeria, but there is no evidence of an actual grotto.[14] For Poggio,

---

[9] N. Neuerburg, *L'Architettura delle fontane e dei ninfe nell'Italia antica*, Naples, n.d., pp. 45, 155, 198–99, and F. J. Alvarez, "The Renaissance Nymphaeum: Its Origin and Its Development in Rome and Vicinity," Ph.D. dissertation, Columbia University, 1981, p. 64.

[10] G. Stara-Tedde, "I boschi sacri dell'antica Roma," *Bullettino della commissione archeologica comunale di Roma*, XXXIII, 1905, p. 222; G. Tomasseti and F. Tomasseti, *La campagna romana*, IV, Rome, 1926, pp. 37–42, 564; and Neuerberg, *L'Architettura delle*

*fontane*, pp. 161–62. Other principal ancient sources in addition to Livy are Ovid, *Metamorphoses*, XV, 482, and Juvenal, *Satire*, III, 12–20.

[11] F. Petrarch, *Le familiari*, ed. V. Rossi, Florence, 1934, II, p. 56.

[12] A. Nibby, ed., *Roma antica di Famiano Nardini*, 4th ed., Rome, 1820, IV, pp. 33–34.

[13] A. Bartolini, *I monumenti antichi di Roma nei disegni degli Uffizi di Firenze*, III, Rome, 1917, pl. CCXXXIII, fig. 403, Uff. 1223Ar, and IV, Rome, 1919, pl. CCCLXXV, fig. 665, Uff. 689Av, and pl. CCCLXXXVIII, fig. 680, Uff. 665Ar; and E. Tormo, ed., *Os desenhos das antigualhas que vio Francisco d'Ollanda*, Madrid, 1940, fol. 33v.

[14] Poggio Bracciolini, *Poggii Epistolae*, ed. T. de Tonelli, I, Florence, 1832, bk. II, letter XXVII, p. 156.

18. Rome, Grotto of Egeria

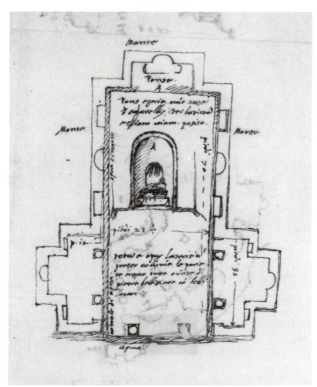

19. Rome, Grotto of Egeria, plan by S. Peruzzi, Uffizi 665A

Perraro's fountain recalls the Egerian grotto for its solitary location appropriate for the contemplative life of the poet or philosopher. It is the mediaeval *hortus conclusus* with its central fountain or well that persists at Rome throughout the fifteenth century. Such garden features demanded no external water supply from the limited sources of the city. The gardens of the Papal Palace, as considered previously,[15] were naturally the most liberally provided with fountains or wells, but nothing specific is known about their form except that there was a water cistern or well in the private garden of Pius II in 1463 into which his dog fell. The building documents of 1467–1469 for the work in the *giardino segreto* of the Palace of San Marco mention the cistern (*cisterna*) or well with its marble wellhead bearing the arms of Cardinal Marco Barbo described in 1523 by the Venetian ambassadors as "a lovely fountain."[16] Thus, the word "fountain" (*fontana* or *fonte*) was also used to describe a "well" or "cistern." Similarly in 1479 Cardinal Gonzaga speaks with approval of the im-

[15] See Chapter 1.

[16] E. Müntz, *Les arts à la cour des papes pendant le XV^e et le XVI^e siècles*, pt. 2, Paris, 1879, pp. 60–62, 65, and E. Albèri, *Relazioni degli ambasciatori veneti al senato*, ser. 2, III, Florence, 1846, p. 106.

provement of the well (*pozzo*) in the garden of his palace at Rome.[17] There still stands at the rear of the lower court of the somewhat later palace of Cardinal Domenico della Rovere, the Palazzo dei Penitenzieri, a well with the cardinal's arms and an arched well-head on tall classical piers from which a bucket drawn from the well can be utilized in the garden on the upper terrace (Fig. 5).

An idea of one of the more elaborate, freestanding fountains used to decorate a hortus conclusus at this time is offered by a drawing by the architect, Baldassare Peruzzi, designer of the Villa Farnesina in Rome (Fig. 20). Drawn on the verso of a letter dated 1523, it is a pedestal fountain of two superimposed basins supported by a polygonal base set in a ground basin.[18] Small jets of water spray from below a bird perched on the apex of the fountain into the upper basin whose overflow fills each of the lower basins. The drawing is carefully dimensioned, suggesting that it is taken from an actual fountain, but there is no information about its location.

Bramante's magnificent concept of the monumental Belvedere Court in the Vatican Palace, begun in 1505, not only introduced a new mode of Roman gardening, discussed later, but was also involved in the revival of the ancient Roman nymphaeum as a feature of gardening. In the center of the rear wall of the middle terrace of the court (Fig. 10) between two flanking ramped stairs to the upper terrace, a deep recess or underground grotto was planned by Bramante to serve as a visual focus on the axis of the view from the papal apartment in the palace that would match the great exedra of the upper level.[19] Coupled pilasters framed the arched entrance to the chamber which was square in plan with a rear apse. Niches cut into the side walls and apse were presumably to contain statues and not jets of water, since, according to the plan, it was decorated with pilasters seemingly inappropriate to a more rustic nymphaeum. Although there is no evidence that Bramante conceived it as a real nymphaeum with fountains or waterworks, in the engraving depicting the tournament that took place in 1565

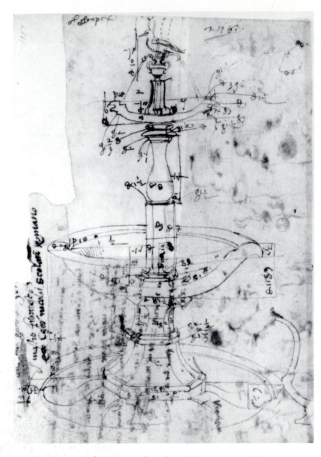

20. B. Peruzzi, drawing of pedestal fountain, Uffizi 1853A

in the Belvedere Court the niche is identified as a "very lovely fountain." It is possible that the transformation to a true nymphaeum or grotto occurred in 1551 when the *fontaniere* Curzio Maccarone was paid for work on the "Fontana grande," as well as the Fountain of Cleopatra in the east wing of the Belvedere Court. Maccarone would not only have introduced water into the nymphaeum, but probably covered the walls with an incrustation of *tartari*, a rough porous stone, suggesting a rustic grotto. Later in the 1560s when the archaeologist-architect Pirro Ligorio was employed to complete the Belvedere Court, he very probably decorated the empty niches with a collection of ancient statues, creating a figured grotto reminiscent of Cardinal Carpi's grotto with which Ligorio may also have been involved. Unfortunately the succeeding pope, Pius V (1566–1572), stripped the grotto of its ancient statuary as he also did elsewhere in the Belvedere Court and the Casino of Pius IV.

In the second half of the sixteenth century the ex-

[17] D. S. Chambers, "The Housing Problems of Cardinal Francesco Gonzaga," *Journal of the Warburg and Courtauld Institutes*, XXXIX, 1976, pp. 57–58.

[18] I. Belli Barsali, *Baldassare Peruzzi e le ville senesi del Cinquecento*, S. Quirico d'Orcia, 1977, p. 17.

[19] J. S. Ackerman, *The Cortile del Belvedere* (Studi e documenti per la storia del Palazzo Apostolico Vaticano, III), Vatican City, 1954, pp. 50, 96, n. 2, and 113; MacDougall, *Fons Sapientiae*, p. 97, n. 40; and Alvarez, "The Renaissance Nymphaeum," pp. 126–32.

21. Rome, Vatican Palace, Belvedere Statue Court, Ariadne, drawing by Francisco D'Ollanda

tensive hillside gardens of the Villa d'Este at Tivoli or the Orti Farnesiani on the Palatine Hill adopted Bramante's terraced gardening of the Belvedere Court to their particular sites and introduced similar nymphaea as central foci for their terraces, but by that time the prevalent naturalism associated with garden features regularly converted the interiors of the nymphaea into naturalistic grottoes, often with pumice stalactites or marine mosaics and shells as described by Alberti and visible in the sixteenth-century drawings of ancient nymphaea.

The concept of the naturalistic grotto, however, may have already been suggested in the setting of an ancient statue of the papal collection exhibited in the Statue Court planned for Pope Julius II by Bramante between the Villa Belvedere and the Belvedere Court. The figure of Ariadne, identified during the Renaissance as Cleopatra, is depicted in the sketchbook of 1539–1540 of the Portuguese artist Francisco d'Ollanda (Fig. 21) as reclining against a rocky grottolike

wall above a water basin formed of an antique marble sarcophagus. Although there is no positive evidence for identifying the grotto setting as original, it has been suggested that an earlier poem by Fausto di Capodiferro celebrating the statue of Cleopatra may hint at such a setting by its echoes of the epigram "Huius Nympha Loci" soon associated with grotto fountains.[20] Ollanda's drawings, however, are often rather fanciful, as already noted regarding the Grotto of Egeria. This is even more apparent in his depiction of the ancient statue of the Nile, also in the Belvedere Statue Court, which was set as a freestanding figure in the court, but which in Ollanda is surrounded by reeds, rocks, and free-flowing water with snakes and snails.

Regardless of its setting, the recumbent statue of "Cleopatra" in the Belvedere Statue Court is certainly related to the most popular fountain topos in Rome in the first half of the sixteenth century, best represented in the fountain in the garden of Angelo Colocci at the Acqua Vergine. Settling in Rome in 1499 as an official at the Vatican, Colocci created a garden on land, probably purchased in 1513, at the foot of the Pincian Hill near the church of S. Andrea della Fratte.[21] Known as the region of Capo le Case, for it marked in the Renaissance the end of the inhabited area where the houses gave way to the open vigne, in antiquity it was the southern end of the gardens of Sallust which spread up over the Pincian Hill. The aqueduct of the Aqua Virgo as it moved on arches down into the Campus Martius crossed this area, and in the garden of Colocci was preserved one of the great rough stone arches from which the garden received its name.

The mid-sixteenth century guide of Mauro to the antiquities of Rome relates that the ancient travertine arch of the Aqua Virgo, about twenty-three meters long, stood opposite the entrance into Colocci's garden and carried an inscription recording its restoration by the emperor Claudius. Nearby was a fountain of a recumbent, sleeping nymph enlivened by two jets of water supplied by the great aqueduct and accompanied by a Latin inscription:

[20] E. B. MacDougall, "The Sleeping Nymph: Origins of a Humanist Fountain Type," *Art Bulletin*, LVII, 1975, p. 357, n. 2. For the Capodiferro poem, see H. Janitschek, "Ein Hofpoet Leo's X über Künstler und Kunstwerk," *Repertorium für Kunstwissenschaft*, III, 1880, pp. 52–56, and H. H. Brummer, *The Statue Court in the Vatican Belvedere*, Stockholm, 1970, p. 221.

[21] F. Ubaldino, *Vita Angeli Colotii Episcopi Nucerini*, Rome, 1673, pp. 22–23.

Huius Nympha Loci, Sacri Custodia Fontis,
　　Dormio, Dum Blandae Sentio Murmur Aquae.
Parce Meum, Quisquis Tangis Caua Marmora, Somnum
　　Rumpere. Siue Bibas Siue Lauere Tace.

(Nymph of this place, guardian of the sacred fountain,
I sleep, while listening to the murmur of the caressing
　　water.
Take care, whoever approaches the marble cave,
Not to break my sleep, either drink or in silence bathe.)

An engraving published in 1602 in Boissard's compendium of inscriptions depicts the fountain (Fig. 22), but, as Boissard notes, the figure was gone at the time of his Roman visit from 1556 to 1559, so that the engraving is probably an imaginary reconstruction of the original.

The Latin inscription, accepted in the Renaissance as an antique inscription, was actually a contemporary invention, created perhaps by the humanist Giannantonio Campano sometime before 1470.[22] By the end of the century the inscription is recorded as being displayed in the garden of Domenico della Rovere, the Cardinal of San Clemente, presumably in the garden of his palace in the Borgo (Fig. 5), although there is no evidence as to the existence of a sleeping nymph or a grotto.

For the Roman humanists the "marble cave" of the nymph evoked the cave of the nymphs in Homer's *Odyssey* (XIII, 102–12) and Vergil's *Aeneid* (I, 166–68), but more especially the grotto of the nymph Corycia on Mount Parnassus, endowing the waters of the grotto with a numinous spirit and equating them with the source of artistic creativity.[23] The appropriateness of this theme for the garden of the Roman humanists and literary coteries of the early sixteenth century is confirmed by the proliferation of fountains and grottoes ringing changes on the motif. Johannes Goritz, a northern official of the Curia, known to the Italians as Giovanni Coricio, whose name could be associated with that of the nymph Corycia or with Vergil's "Corycius senex," had in his garden on the slope of the Capitoline Hill a grotto with a fountain basin inscribed with a shortened version of the Latin epigram: "Nymphis Loci . Bibe . Lava . Tace . Coritius."[24] As the setting for the most famous literary

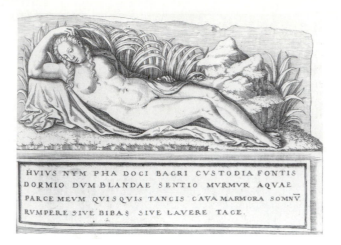

22. Rome, Colocci Garden, Fountain of the Sleeping Nymph, engraving

gatherings of the reign of Pope Leo X, the contemporary references to the garden unendingly evoke the home of the Muses, as Cardinal Egidio da Viterbo does when he likens the "secret grotto of Coricio" (*arcanum Corytium specum*) to the "cave of the Muses" (*antrum Musae*).[25]

Mutations of the topos flourished in early sixteenth-century Rome. On the upper terrace of the garden behind Jacopo Galli's house near the Cancelleria palace surmounting a stubby column was an antique, partially clad nymph leaning on an urn in the semblance of a fountain, but without the inscription or the grotto (Fig. 12).[26] A fountain composed of an ancient statue of a reclining female figure accompanied by one line of the Latin epigram—*Dormio, dum blande sentio murmur aque* ("I sleep, while listening to the murmur of the caressing water")—was recorded by the Frenchman Claude Bellièvre in the house of the Rosci family during the pontificate of Leo X.[27] Somewhat later the same shortened version of the epigram was inscribed on a marble, reclining figure, again presumably a nymph, in the statue garden of the Cesi cardinals in the Borgo.[28]

[22] MacDougall, "The Sleeping Nymph," pp. 357–65.

[23] Ibid., and P. P. Bober, "The *Coryciana* and the Nymph Corycia," *Journal of the Warburg and Courtauld Institutes*, XL, 1977, pp. 223–39.

[24] J. J. Boissard, *V Pars Antiquitatum Romanorum siue III Tomus*, Frankfort, 1600, pl. 78.

[25] Letter of April 1525 in G. P. Valeriano, *Hieroglyphica*, Basel, 1556, p. 123.

[26] C. Huelsen and H. Egger, *Die römischen Skizzenbücher von Marten van Heemskerck*, I, Berlin, 1913, pp. 16–17, pl. 28.

[27] E. Müntz, "Le Musée du Capitole et les autres collections romains," *Revue archéologique*, n.s., XLIII, 1882, pp. 33–35. Giulio Rosci wrote a Latin poem, "In Nympham fontù custodem," celebrating the fountain; see J. Gruter, *Delitiae CC Italorum poetarum*, [Frankfort,] 1608, pt. II, p. 544.

[28] C. Huelsen, "Römische Antikengärten des XVI Jahrhun-

At the same time grottoes and nymphaea were developing independently as garden features. Already about 1510 or 1511 Agostino Chigi had a sumptuous dining loggia erected on the bank of the Tiber River at the end of the garden of his Villa Farnesina. Beneath the loggia was an underground grotto gained by outside stairs. Openings in the river wall of the grotto permitted water to flow into a large basin surrounded by a bench where visitors could seek repose in the dim light from the loggia above filtered through a hole in the vault of the grotto. Again the ancient cave of the nymphs and the home of the Muses is evoked by Egidio Gallo in his contemporary poetic description in Latin of the villa and its loggia when he borrows from Vergil's description of the "cave of the nymphs" (*Aeneid*, I, 166–68: *Intus aquae dulces* and *sedilia Nymphis*) and labels the grotto a "cave fit for poets" (*antrum aptu poetis*).[29] Although the grotto is described as a "cave," there is no evidence of any rustic character associated with it. Of a similar, formal architectural character was the contemporary, or slightly later, large garden nymphaeum of the Colonna family, remains of which still stand built into the hillside below the town of Genazzano.[30] Created for outdoor entertainment and especially dining in the garden, waterworks must have added to the cool relaxing atmosphere of the loggia, which has a water basin with outlet in its rear exedra. An octagonal corner room with a large central pool, resembling the *frigidarium* of ancient Roman baths, may have been for bathing or simply a grotto like that under Agostino Chigi's dining loggia at the Villa Farnesina.

The increasing interest in waterworks, whether fountains or grottoes, is best illustrated in the Villa Madama begun about 1518 on Monte Mario outside of Rome for Cardinal Giulio de' Medici. The cardinal, later Pope Clement VII, was apparently most interested, according to contemporary reports, in the waterworks devised for his villa.[31] In addition to the great fishpool set into the hill below the garden terrace outside the dining loggia at the northwest end of

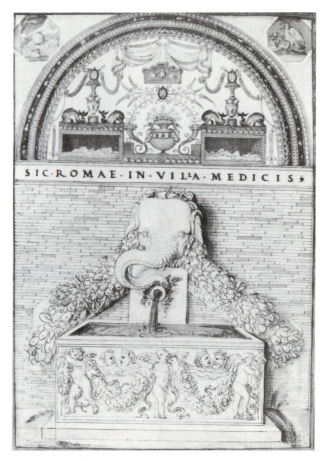

23. Rome, Villa Madama, Fountain of the Elephant, drawing by Francisco D'Ollanda

the villa, the artist Giovanni da Udine designed a grotto fountain with a large elephant's head in the center of the retaining wall at the rear of the garden terrace (Fig. 23). According to the writer Vasari, this grotto fountain was based on the remains of one recently found in the so-called Temple of Neptune on the Palatine. Beyond the garden terrace the architect Antonio da Sangallo the Younger created a terraced nymphaeum set into a cleft in Monte Mario. The grotto cut into the hillside at the end of the nymphaeum was ascribed also to Giovanni da Udine by Vasari, but was contrasted to the Elephant Head Fountain as being "wild" (*salvatica*) with "water dripping and spouting" over rocks and tartari, so as to "appear truly natural." Remains of the nymphaeum and grotto, altered during the later centuries, still exist (Fig. 24).

Giovanni da Udine's naturalistic grotto at the Villa Madama may have been the inspiration for the pop-

derts," *Abhandlungen der Heidelberger Akademie der Wissenschaften: Philosophisch-historische Klasse*, IV, 1917, p. 32, no. 125.

[29] E. Gallo, *De viridario Augustini Chigii*, Rome, 1511, fols. 25v–26r.

[30] C. L. Frommel, "Bramantes 'Ninfeo' in Genazzano," *Römisches Jahrbuch für Kunstgeschichte*, XII, 1969, pp. 137–60, and C. Thoenes, "Note sul 'ninfeo' di Genazzano," *Studi Bramanteschi*, Rome, 1974, pp. 575–83.

[31] Coffin, *The Villa*, pp. 252–53.

24. Rome, Villa Madama, nymphaeum

ularity of this feature in Roman gardens of the first half of the sixteenth century. By 1543, the Sienese writer Claudio Tolomei, when he describes another garden grotto, comments on "the ingenious skill recently rediscovered for making fountains, which is seen used in many places in Rome, where mingling art with nature one does not know how to discern whether it is a work of the former or of the latter."[32] He continues by describing the various water effects that are created:

> But, what pleases me more in these new fountains is the variety of ways with which they guide, divide, turn, conduct, break and at one moment cause water to descend and at another to rise. Since in the same fountain, other waters are seen to descend broken among the roughness of those stones, and with a gentle roar, whitening in different parts, break up among the crev-

ices of various rocks, like a river in its bed falls gently with a slight murmur.

Another rustic grotto and fountain in the vigna of Monsignor Giovanni Gaddi near the Colosseum is described in detail in a letter of 1538 from Annibal Caro to Monsignor Guidiccione at Lucca, who may have been planning a similar fountain for his villa.[33] Caro commences the description by noting:

---

[32] G. Bottari and S. Ticozzi, *Raccolta di lettere sulla pittura, scultura ed architettura*, v, Milan, 1822, p. 103, or E. B. MacDougall,

"Introduction," in *Fons Sapientiae: Renaissance Fountains* (Dumbarton Oaks Colloquium on the History of Landscape Architecture, v), Washington, D.C., 1978, pp. 12–13.

[33] A. Caro, *Lettere familiari*, ed. A. Greco, I, Florence, 1957, pp. 105–9, no. 61, and Guidiccione's reply, p. 108, note 6. Philandrier seems to locate the vigna on the Esquiline Hill in his *In Decem Libros M. Vitruii Pollionis De Architectura Annotationes*, [Rome, 1544,] p. 237: ". . . in esquiliis, vinea hodie Ioannis Gadi, & ei proxima, sunt reliquiae, ut suspicantur aureae domus Neronis." Lanciani, however, publishes part of a document locating the vigna "intro menia urbis prope coliseum in contrada que dicitur septem solum," which he interprets as the lower slope of the Celian Hill

Monsignor has made at the head of his large pergola a rough wall of a certain stone, which is called *asprone* (or *sperone*) at Rome, a type of black and spongy tufa; and there are certain lumps placed one above the other at random, which make some protuberances and some holes planted with grass; and the whole wall looks like a piece of rough and broken antiquity. In the middle of it is opened a door as entrance to a gallery of rooms made indeed with rough stones in the semblance rather to an entrance into a cave than anything else; and on both sides of the portal in each corner is a fountain.

One of the fountains had a statue of a river god with an urn under his arm above a basin like that of the statue of Tigris in the Belvedere Statue Court, while the other one had a gravel-lined pool.

Caro goes on to describe with great admiration the waterworks that supplied the fountains, including a large reservoir. Small canals led water to the top of the niches above the fountains, where the water fell in large drops like rain over bits of white tartari from the cascade of Tivoli, which Alberti in the middle of the fifteenth century had recommended for the decoration of grotto fountains. Other canals shot jets of water to roil the surface of the pool. Every effort was expended to suggest a dripping, humid, naturalistic grotto, even to the artificial roar of water caused by funneling it through terracotta vases. Around the fountains were "in the water, small fish, bits of coral, small stone; in the crevices, shrimp, mother-of-pearl, small snails; on the edges, maidenhair, scolopendra, moss, and other sorts of water herbs."

In the letter referred to earlier, Claudio Tolomei describes a supper he attended in July 1543 in the garden of Agabito Belluomo near the Trevi Fountain fed by the Acqua Vergine.[34] The source of the water from the ancient Aqua Virgo inspired Tolomei to reminisce on the hydraulic wonders of the ancient Romans, most of them lost, but he obviously sees in the new fountain devices of Renaissance Rome a revival of the lost art. After noting that Belluomo's fountain was composed of the "spongy" stone of Tivoli, commented on also by Caro in Gaddi's grotto, Tolomei adds: "But what most delights me in these new fountains is the variety of modes with which they guide, alter, agitate, interrupt, and at one moment make the water go down and at another rise." He then describes a variety of water effects and even tricks for dousing unsuspecting observers, which soon became an important feature in the larger Roman gardens.

As Caro's letter to Monsignor Guidiccione suggests, rustic grottoes, first developed in Rome in emulation of ancient ones, were soon sought eagerly elsewhere in Italy. So Antonio da Sangallo the Younger, who had drawn the plan of the Grotto of Egeria, was asked by Cosimo de' Medici, duke of Florence, to give advice regarding the grottoes being created for him at his favorite villa at Castello. In a letter of March 22, 1546, Sangallo at Rome wrote the duke, noting that the grotto fountains at Castello should be decorated with tartari, which was used to create fountains at a site in Tivoli identified by him as the villa of the ancient Roman poet Manlius Vopiscus.[35] He also sent the duke several baskets and a hamper of samples of tartari.

By the second quarter of the sixteenth century part of the appeal of small Roman gardens apparently lay in their fountains and grottoes and the skill with which water displays were effected. The descriptions of Caro and Tolomei emphasize understandably the new developments, but tell little about the handling of the terrain or the plantings involved, which were presumably no different than that of the traditional hortus conclusus. A description written in 1544 of the garden of Blosio Palladio, however, gives a more complete picture of the relationship of the waterworks to their setting.[36] Since at least 1531 Palladio, who belonged to the early sixteenth-century literary circle of Rome and later was secretary to the popes Clement VII and Paul III and was bishop of Foligno, owned a vigna on the hillside of Monte Ciocci above the Valle dell'Inferno just outside the Vatican. His small villa or casino stood on the summit of Monte

---

where is the present garden of S. Gregorio; see R. Lanciani, *Storia degli scavi di Roma*, II, Rome, 1903, p. 34. The latter would seem to correspond more closely to the mention of the vigna in Pirro Ligorio's manuscripts: ". . . nella sua uigna presso l'Amphitheatro di Vespasiano" (Naples, Biblioteca Nazionale, Ms XIII.B.7, p. 79) and "alle Therme Traiane in la parte doue fu la vigna di monsignore Giovan Gadi" (Rome, Biblioteca Apostolica Vaticana, Ms Ottob. 3373, fol. 38). Cellini in his autobiography claims that during the flood of 1530 he carried the jewels of Pope Clement VII to the house of Giovanni Gaddi on Monte Cavallo, the Quirinal Hill, but this is either a topographical error or another possession of Gaddi.

[34] MacDougall, *Fons Sapientiae*, pp. 12–14.

[35] G. Gaye, *Carteggio inedito d'artisti dei secoli XIV, XV, XVI*, Florence, 1840, II, p. 344, no. CCXXXIX. See E. Mourlot, "'Artifice Naturel' ou 'Nature Artificielle': Les grottes médicéenes dans la Florence du XVIᶜ siècle," in *Ville et campagne dans la littérature italienne de la Renaissance*, II, *Le courtisan travesti*, Paris, 1977, pp. 303–42. Later Antonio Del Re discusses the villa of Manlius Vopiscus at Tivoli in his *Dell'antichità tiburtine capitolo V*, Rome, 1611, pp. 116–23.

[36] G. Rorario, *Quod Animalia bruta ratione vtantur meliùs Homine*, Paris, 1648, pp. 117–19.

Ciocci with the garden on the slope leading up to the building. By 1544 a bridge over a ditch at the foot of the vigna approached the gateway behind which was an opening with two fountains, one encircled by marble benches, the other by a laurel grove. A steep and broad path proceeded part way up the hillside through vines and fruit trees and finally through a small, fragrant wood of citron trees to end between two fishpools. Beyond was another opening in the woods used for outdoor dining. In its center was a spurting fountain enclosed at the rear by a semicircular, vine-covered pergola where Palladio and his friends might dine, since there were nearby small buildings for the preparation of food. Flanking the dining area were two other fountains, both of which had a simulated rocky arch of tartari from Tivoli through which the water fell to irrigate the grove of citron trees below as well as the two fishpools. At the left of the central fountain another path, mounting through a laurel grove, led to the villa at the summit of the hill.

Again the emphasis is on the water basins and fountains that functioned by natural gravity on the hillside, but there is also the image of wooded paths and clearings. Unfortunately the description tells little about the design of the woods, clearings, and paths. Probably they would seem very formal to us with an ascending axis and regularized openings cut through the woods, even to the symmetrical placing of the fishpools and fountains, but for Renaissance Rome the image is rustic. It is, however, a rusticity conditioned by ancient Rome. Pliny, as was noted, had advocated the use of pumice to decorate artificial grottoes and fountains and Ovid's description in the *Metamorphoses* (III, 159–60) of Diana's grotto with a natural arch of pumice is reminiscent of Palladio's fountains. Fifty years later the account by a local historian of the ancient villa of Cassius near Tivoli suggests the type of ancient remains that inspired the Renaissance, for there an "aqueduct led the waters of the Aniene principally into a rustic fountain of Tiburtine tartari whose remains are found even today near a theater with a loggia above . . . which was intended as a magnificent and regal dining room according to the opinion of the excellent Messer Michelangelo Buonarroti."[37]

Although naturalistic fountains and grottoes began to be important in Roman gardens of the second quarter of the sixteenth century, collections of ancient sculpture continued to be the main feature of the most prominent gardens. In the garden of Cardinal Carpi's vigna on the Quirinal Hill, discussed earlier,[38] these two interests blended. On the north side of the basement of the villa, a loggia decorated with "men and women transformed into trees" stood in front of the entrance to a grotto. Above the door to the grotto a relief of a sleeping shepherd accompanied by the Vergilian inscription, *At secura quies, et nescia fallere vitae* ("Now a carefree peace and a life free from deceit," *Georgics*, II, 467) set the mood of the quiet retreat. Within, the walls of the grotto were covered with the usual rough pumice stone, or tartari, to simulate the "frigid cave" described by Marcantonio Flaminio in his poem celebrating the fountain of the villa. At the rear a statue of a nymph lay sleeping above a water basin (Fig. 25) into which water flowed from the beaks of two aquatic birds held by putti as well as from the wineskin of a faun and from the urn of a nymph. Remains of the figure of the sleeping nymph have recently been identified in a large fragment of a marble statue formerly in the Caffarelli garden in the Conservators Palace on the Capitoline Hill, proving that the statue is a Renaissance creation.[39]

Carpi's sleeping nymph is, of course, another version of Colucci's nearby fountain of the Acqua Vergine, but now installed in an underground grotto with a group of ancient statues. Standing guard near the entrance to the retreat was another ancient statue depicting Hercules with the golden apples of the Hesperides. This figure is presumably a clue to the meaning associated with the garden and its grotto. As was seen earlier in the Belvedere Statue Court, where the statue of Commodus as Hercules protected that horticultural retreat in the guise of the mythological Garden of the Hesperides, so Carpi's gardens and quiet cave are also equated with the mythological garden.

The ancient statues that provide the spurts or tricklings of water to the sleeping nymph's basin—the faun, the nymph, and the boys with birds—become standard motifs for sixteenth-century Roman fountains.[40] One, however, the putto with a goose or swan, is particularly interesting, as it is frequently

---

[37] G. M. Zappi, *Annali e memorie di Tivoli di Giovanni Maria Zappi* (Studi e fonti per la storia della regione tiburtina, 1), ed. V. Pacifici, Tivoli, 1920, p. 46.

[38] See Chapter 2. See also Coffin, *The Villa*, pp. 195–200, but for the location of the grotto in the vigna, see S. Eiche, "Cardinal Giulio della Rovere and the Vigna Carpi," *Journal of the Society of Architectural Historians*, XLV, 1986, pp. 121–22.

[39] B. Mocci, " 'Questa pare opera divina non che humana,' " *Bollettino d'arte*, LXXI, 1986, pp. 185–90.

[40] MacDougall, *Fons Sapientiae*, pp. 89–93.

25. Rome, Vigna Carpi, nymphaeum, Sleeping Nymph, engraving

used later as a fountain feature in the gardens and villas associated with the archaeologist and architect Pirro Ligorio.[41] Such a group decorates the fountain in the center of the oval court of his Casino of Pius IV in the Vatican. Another, identified either as an amor or as Ganymede with a swan, was part of the Fontana del Bosco in the Villa d'Este on the Quirinal Hill. Similarly the Grotto of Venus, created in 1568 off the Oval Fountain in the Villa d'Este at Tivoli, had two putti embracing geese, called "ducks" in an inventory of 1572.[42] Ligorio, in fact, reproduced the Carpi

statue in the Neapolitan manuscript of his encyclopedia of antiquities along with another version of the statue, perhaps the one he notes was once in the Cesi collection, and explains that the figure was the boy Amphilocus of Olenus with whom a goose fell in love, as recounted by Pliny the Elder (*Naturalis Historia*, X, xxvi).[43] Certainly Ligorio's concern for the Carpi collection is understandable because of his archaeological interest, but it may not just be coincidental that in November 1549, a few years after the creation of the grotto of the sleeping nymph in the Villa Carpi, when Ligorio was appointed to succeed the deceased Ferrarese architect Jacopo Meleghino as overseer of the fountain in the square of St. Peter's, the document recording the appointment of Ligorio describes him as a member (*familiaris*) of the household of Cardinal Carpi.[44] Ligorio's name is also associated with several of the antiquities that the cardinal possessed in his villa, so that he may have played an important role in the formation of the collection and may have been involved with the design of the cardinal's grotto.

The middle of the sixteenth century marked the beginning of the wealth of great villas and gardens in and around Rome that would eventually compete with the religious sanctuaries and Roman antiquities for the attention of tourists. Earlier only Raphael's ill-fated project for the villa and gardens of the Villa Madama, cut off by the disastrous Sack of Rome in 1527, would have been of a similar scale, but because of its lack of full realization the Villa Madama would fade into obscurity. The first of these great villas was the one begun in 1551 for Pope Julius III at the foot of the Parioli hills just outside the Porta del Popolo.[45] At the end of the theatrical court behind the villa, the sculptor-architect Ammannati created a very unusual nymphaeum fed by the ancient aqueduct of the Aqua Virgo. The nymphaeum, which is completely enclosed by a wall at ground level, is then sunk into the ground on two levels (Fig. 26). A pair of curving stairs opening off the loggia at the rear of the theatrical court descends to the middle level of the nymphaeum, where originally four plane trees shaded the cool retreat, probably inspired by Pliny the Younger's description of the court of the summer apartment

[41] G. Smith, review of *The Italian Garden*, ed. D. R. Coffin, in *Architectura*, V, 1976, p. 80, n. 3.

[42] For the casino, see G. Smith, *The Casino of Pius IV*, Princeton, N.J., 1977, pp. 52–53; for the Villa d'Este at Rome, see Huelsen, "Römische Antikengärten des XVI Jahrhunderts," p. 99, no. 16; and for the Villa d'Este at Tivoli, see D. R. Coffin, *The Villa d'Este at Tivoli*, Princeton, N.J., 1960, p. 34.

[43] E. Mandowsky and C. Mitchell, *Pirro Ligorio's Roman Antiquities* (Studies of the Warburg Institute, 28), London, 1963, p. 84, no. 62.

[44] K. Frey, "Zur Baugeschichte des St. Peter," *Jahrbuch der königlich preuszischen Kunstsammlungen*, XXIII, 1912, Beiheft, p. 150.

[45] See later, Chapters 5 and 8, and also Coffin, *The Villa*, pp. 150–65.

26. Rome, Villa Giulia, nymphaeum

(*diaeta*) at his ancient Tuscan villa (*Letters*, v, 6).[46] On the rear wall of the nymphaeum of the Villa Giulia set into large niches flanking the portals to a grotto were statues of the river gods, Tiber and Arno, from whose urns water poured into basins. The vault of the rear grotto is decorated with a stucco relief illustrating the ancient story, as recounted by Frontinus, of the discovery of the Aqua Virgo, whose waters fed the nymphaeum. At the sides of this grotto were originally hidden spiral stairs leading up to the hortus conclusus behind the nymphaeum. A similar grotto at the front of the nymphaeum between the stairs from the entrance loggia has likewise hidden passages to the lower level of the nymphaeum, which is only visible through a large hole cut through the floor of the middle level, since it is completely surrounded by a balustrade. At the lower level, or sunken grotto, a small paved island set in the water basin was originally decorated with marble putti pouring water from urns on their shoulders and a sleeping nymph with a water urn, another version of the fountain theme made famous in Colocci's garden of the Acqua Vergine and in Cardinal Carpi's grotto. An engraving of 1582 attributed to Dupérac depicts the nymphaeum with the nymph of the fountain in the lower grotto. The nymphaeum was not only a very unusual one—whose splendor the sculptor Ammannati, in his lengthy description of the villa in May 1555 after the death of the pope, indicates he cannot convey in words—but was considered the chief feature of the villa and its gardens, or in the words of Ammannati, "the principal place" (*il luogo principale*) and "one can well say that this is the point of perspective" (*et ben si può dire che questo sia il punto della prospettiva*).

It would be Ippolito II d'Este, cardinal of Ferrara, who would exploit to the fullest fountains, grottoes,

---

[46] T. Falk, "Studien zur Topographie und Geschichte der Villa Giulia in Rom," *Römisches Jahrbuch für Kunstgeschichte*, XIII, 1971, p. 134 and n. 98.

Fontana nel Giardino del Ill<sup>mo</sup> Cardi<sup>le</sup> d'Est nel Monte Quirinale.

27. Rome, Villa d'Este, grotto, engraving, 1618

and various hydraulic devices, as well as the more traditional antique statuary, as decorative features in the great gardens created for him in Rome and at Tivoli after the midcentury. In 1550 the Cardinal rented from the Carafa family their vigna or country residence set on the brink of the Quirinal Hill overlooking the center of Rome and commissioned Girolamo da Carpi to lay out lavish gardens, but it was not until the next decade that extensive waterworks were added to the gardens by the fontaniere Curzio Maccarone.[47] In the loggia of a garden of orange trees near the casino was a nymphaeum of a bathing Venus. To the east of the casino Maccarone fashioned the rustic Fountain of the Woods with a small artificial hill from the top of which water poured from a wineskin held by a reclining Silenus into a basin at the foot of the hill where was a seated figure of Venus and two cupids. Later, in 1565, Maccarone commenced

the Fountain of Apollo and the Muses, using antique figures, in a large niche under the casino toward the west. The most rustic feature, however, was the grotto (Fig. 27) set into the hillside of the adjacent former Vigna Boccacci, now incorporated into the Villa d'Este. Formed as an artificial hill containing grottoes with basins and jets of water, it stood at the rear of one terrace with stairs curving upward around the central grotto to the upper level of the gardens.

Contemporary with the work on his garden at Rome, the Cardinal of Ferrara was developing at Tivoli even more luxurious gardens whose waterworks have overwhelmed visitors from the time of their creation until today.[48] The site of the gardens on a steep hillside at the edge of the town of Tivoli encouraged numerous grottoes set into the hillside with diagonal alleys on each side leading from one terraced level to another (Fig. 66). Thus, on the central axis of the garden there were four such grottoes set above one another up the hillside to the entrance to the villa. These grottoes with their external architectural frames are ultimately derived from Bramante's nymphaeum set at the rear of the middle terrace of the Belvedere Court in the Vatican Palace, but the interior of many of the Tiburtine grottoes were decorated with stalactite forms in the more rustic manner made popular later. The so-called Grotto of Diana or Virtue set under the dining loggia on the terrace of the villa, however, had its walls covered with decorative mosaics. In the wealth of fountains and grottoes enlivening the gardens almost every one of the previous Roman types of fountain statuary was to be found, such as the sleeping nymph or Venus, the boy or cupid struggling with a bird, and the reclining satyr leaning on a wineskin that served as a water source. In 1566 as Curzio Maccarone completed his fountains at the Villa d'Este in Rome, he removed to Tivoli to undertake work there. His major fountains, the Fountain of Tivoli and that of Rome, stood at the ends of an alley running across the hillside part way up the slope. The Fountain of Tivoli, or the Oval Fountain, featured an expansive cascade, alluding to the famous natural waterfalls at Tivoli (Fig. 28). A statue of the winged horse Pegasus perched on the small, artificial hill from which the cascade descends (Fig. 29) identified the hill town of Tivoli with ancient Mount Parnassus, home of the Muses, and a favorite garden theme in sixteenth-century Rome, as will be discussed later. The Fountain of Rome (Fig. 30) in the guise of a theatrical

47 Coffin, *The Villa*, pp. 202–13.

48 Ibid., pp. 311–40.

28. Tivoli, Villa d'Este, Fountain of Tivoli

set at the end of the alley toward the Campagna was composed of small buildings symbolizing the great ancient monuments of Rome, while a small naturalistic cascade gushing from a river god's urn at the left flowed below into the little stream, suggesting the Tiber in front of the podium of the Fountain. Both of Maccarone's fountains incorporate amusing water tricks of unexpected jets of water triggered by paving stones or gates to drench the unsuspecting visitor. There were also benches with weep holes that would stealthily soak the weary spectator.

Perhaps for the first time in Rome since antiquity a new type of garden waterwork appears at Tivoli in the form of hydraulic automata. On the hill above the northeast end of the lower cross axis of fishpools was the Fountain of Nature with a water organ played automatically by the flow of water into large reservoirs (Fig. 31), similar to the water organs described in the ancient texts of Hero of Alexandria and of Vitruvius. Another fountain at Tivoli taken from Hero of Alexandria was the Fountain of the Owl (Fig. 32) with a bronze group of birds motivated by water pressure to

29. Tivoli, Villa d'Este, Fountain of Tivoli, Pegasus

30. Tivoli, Villa d'Este, Fountain of Rome, engraving

31. Tivoli, Villa d'Este, Fountain of Nature

*Fontana à canto la Roma antica nel Giardino di Tivoli*

32. Tivoli, Villa d'Este, Fountain of the Owl, engraving, 1618

sing merrily until the baleful appearance of an owl frightened them into silence. Not only did ancient Alexandria and Rome contribute to the waterworks of Tivoli, but so did Islamic Spain. The water channels that accompany the stairs of the central Fountain of the Dragons (Fig. 33) and the water steps or *scale dei bollori* that mount the hillside must be inspired by similar features in the Islamic gardens of the Generalife at Granada in Spain, which were described in 1526 by the Venetian ambassador Andrea Navagero in a letter first published in 1556.

The quantity and originality of the fountains at Tivoli caught the fancy of several owners of villas, inspiring waterworks at the Villa Lante at Bagnaia and the Villa Medici in Rome. In the gardens at Bagnaia, north of Rome, created for Cardinal Gambara after 1568, the great Fountain of Pegasus with its winged horse set in a large oval basin must be derived from the Fountain of Tivoli at the Villa d'Este (Fig. 71).[49]

Similarly the charming water stair, the *catena d'acqua*, flowing through the upper center of the formal gardens at Bagnaia, may have been suggested by the scale dei bollori at Tivoli (Fig. 73).

Already in June 1570 Cardinal Giovanni Ricci had been granted the right to divert water to the gardens of his villa on the Pincian Hill in Rome from the Acqua Vergine then being restored to increase the supply of water to the public Trevi Fountain. From this supply Ricci fed a traditional jet fountain in the garden behind the loggia of his villa. In 1576 Cardinal Ferdinando de' Medici purchased the villa of Cardinal Ricci and not only revised the building, but also had new plans for the gardens and access to the villa. In preparation for this work the elderly architect Bartolomeo Ammannati was sent from Florence to plan and oversee the revision. During his stay in Rome Ammannati visited the Villa d'Este at Tivoli, attracted by its waterworks.[50] A fresco by Zucchi in the garden study of the Villa Medici depicts a magnificent access to the villa with stairs mounting the hill around a Fountain of Pegasus (Fig. 34). This fresco is presumably a reflection of an Ammannati idea inspired by Tivoli, which was never executed. In the garden, however, to the rear of the villa an artificial hill was created by piling earth upon the ruins of a nymphaeum of the ancient Acilian gardens located there. Tall cypresses covered the hill, which was identified as Mount Parnassus (Fig. 35). A rustic grotto, now gone, stood under the hill and a steep stair climbed to a domed pavilion at the top of the hill. Water gushing from a fountain within the pavilion on the example of Tivoli descended in channels lining the stairs to the woods below. The artificial hill, some fifteen meters high, set already on one of the highest sites in the city of Rome, afforded a magnificent vista from the pavilion on top, but the water supply for the fountain in the pavilion created a difficult hydraulic problem, since the source of the water was the much lower conduit of the Acqua Vergine. A Latin inscription within the pavilion honored the Milanese engineer Camillo Agrippa for solving the problem.[51]

Throughout the sixteenth century the fountains of the gardens within the city of Rome were relatively

[49] D. R. Coffin, "Some Aspects of the Villa Lante at Bagnaia," in

*Arte in Europa: Scritti di storia dell'arte in onore di Edoardo Arslan*, Milan, 1966, pp. 569–75.

[50] G. M. Andres, *The Villa Medici in Rome*, New York and London, 1976, II, pp. 158–61, n. 493.

[51] R. Lanciani, "Il codice barberiniano XXX, 89, contente frammenti di una descrizione di Roma del secolo XVI," *Archivio della R. società romana di storia patria*, VI, 1883, p. 473.

33. Tivoli, Villa d'Este, Fountain of the Dragons

modest as seen rather dramatically in comparing the gardens of the Cardinal of Ferrara on the Quirinal Hill in Rome with his gardens at Tivoli. The water features of the Roman gardens were generally limited to dank grottoes with water dripping over rough pumice stone or to small jets of water spraying into basins. In contrast was the hill town of Tivoli where the Cardinal of Ferrara as governor had an aqueduct built from 1560 to 1561 financed by the commune and himself to bring water from nearby Monte Sant'Angelo to supply both the town and the gardens of the villa he was creating. This supply, however, was considered insufficient, so that two years later the cardinal tapped the river Aniene near the famous cas-

34. Rome, Villa Medici, fresco by Zucchi

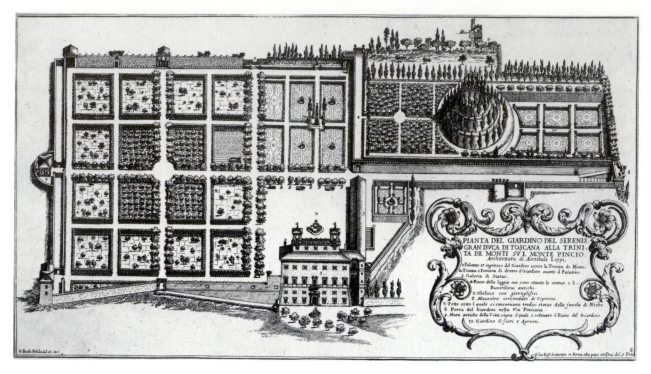

35. Rome, Villa Medici, engraving

cades, bringing water directly to his garden by a conduit excavated under the town of Tivoli (Fig. 65). These water sources entered the garden at the top of the hillside dominating the garden, so that the wealth of garden fountains and jets of water on the hillside and below could be activated by the gravity flow induced by the site.

In a period when major earth movement still had to be conducted by hand labor with picks, shovels, and barrows, rather than by the great mechanical earthmovers of today, the laying on of large networks of water conduits was a time-consuming and expensive process. A plan of about 1630 of the water conduits feeding the fountains of the Villa Borghese offers a visual commentary on such a project.[52]

The increase in the supply of water into Rome of the Acqua Vergine, which the cardinals Ricci and Medici had successively tapped for their villa on the Pincian Hill, would likewise be appropriated by several popes, and particularly Pope Clement VIII, for additional fountains and waterworks to decorate the gardens of the villa, which the Cardinal of Ferrara had developed on the Quirinal Hill, but which had

become a papal possession under Pope Sixtus V. In 1593 hydraulic connections with the Trevi fountain fed by the Acqua Vergine were made from the Quirinal gardens and from 1595 until at least 1597 work was pursued creating a water organ at the Fountain of Apollo and the Muses on the lower terrace of the gardens.[53] The names of several other fountains created at this time, the Cascades or the Fountain of Rain, indicate how the augmentation of water from the Acqua Vergine was changing the nature of the fountains to resemble more those of the hill towns of Tivoli and Frascati.

The other hill town for country relaxation or *villeggiatura*, Frascati, suffered gravely from a water shortage throughout the sixteenth century. Only Cardinal Altemps had provided an appropriate water supply for his Villa Mondragone by tapping the water of Formelle in 1573.[54] This shortage of water at Frascati

---

[52] B. Di Gaddo, *Villa Borghese: Il giardino e le architetture*, Rome, 1985, pp. 24–35, figs. 10–12.

[53] L. Salerno, "La fontana dell'organo nei giardini del Quirinale," *Capitolium*, XXXVI, no. 4, April 1961, pp. 3–9; G. Briganti, *Il Palazzo del Quirinale*, Rome, 1962; and *Il Palazzo del Quirinale*, Rome, 1974, pp. 242–45; for other fountains, see MacDougall, *Fons Sapientiae*, pp. 105–7.

[54] For the water supply at Frascati, see F. Grossi-Gondi, *La Villa dei Quintili e la Villa di Mondragone*, Rome, 1901, pp. 295–99, and K. Schwager, "Kardinal Pietro Aldobrandinis Villa di Belve-

36. Frascati, Villa Aldobrandini, water theater

was dramatically demonstrated when Cardinal Ferreri diverted water for the fountains of his garden at Frascati from the supply of Paolo Sforza's nearby Villa Rufina. The competition led eventually in August 1582 to the vandalizing of Ferreri's fountains and the necessity for Pope Gregory XIII to order their repair by Sforza.[55]

The election of Pope Clement VIII in 1592 gave Frascati its necessary patron in the person of his nephew Cardinal Pietro Aldobrandini, who made every effort to command an extensive water supply for the villa he erected for his own and his uncle's enjoyment. The cardinal himself noted in 1611 that for almost eighty years Frascati had been a popular resort of villeggiatura, although its shortage of water had

prevented the creation of lavish gardens and waterworks—a limitation now overcome by the cardinal at great expense. So in 1604 it had been reported that the pope had given his nephew the sum of fifty thousand scudi to create the waterworks of the cascade, adding "the villa is not worth as much as the water."[56] The major effort from 1600 was, therefore, expended on introducing water from the springs of Molara and beginning the wonderful water theater behind the villa. The architect Della Porta had presumably intended a water display behind the villa, but with his death in 1602 it was his successor Carlo Maderno with the technical aid of the engineer Giovanni Fontana who devised the present water theater, undoubtedly influenced by the Fountain of Tivoli in the Villa d'Este at Tivoli (Fig. 36). At Frascati a steep

dere in Frascati," *Römisches Jahrbuch für Kunstgeschichte*, IX–X, 1961–1962, pp. 334–38.

[55] Coffin, *The Villa*, pp. 51–52.

[56] C. d'Onofrio, *La Villa Aldobrandini di Frascati*, Rome, [1963,] p. 70.

cascade rising between two gigantic columns, the so-called Columns of Hercules, part way up the hill falls thunderously down the hillside through the arcaded *scaenae frons* of the exedra into a basin at the rear of the piazza behind the villa. Although the frieze of the water theater, dated 1619, celebrates the cardinal's introduction of water from Monte Algido as enabling the creation of the "retreat from urban cares," the competition for water at Frascati was still rife.

After the election of the Borghese Pope Paul V in 1605, his nephew, Cardinal Scipione Borghese, purchased the villa of Cardinal Gallo in 1607 and soon created there a magnificent water stair or cascade and theater derived from the nearby one at the Villa Aldobrandini (Fig. 37).[57] Unlike, however, the earlier water theater at the Villa Aldobrandini, that at the Villa Borghese was designed to be completely independent of the building. Rather than being on axis with the casino, it formed a backdrop to the garden on the east side of the building. An *avviso* of 1609 claims that the pope had contracted with an architect to provide two oncie of water to the villa at Frascati, but only half the supply came in. The pope, who was suspicious that the Aldobrandini had succeeded in augmenting their supply at the same time, is reported to swear to have the architect "in his hands to hang him, but did not succeed."[58] The contract in June 1607 for the aqueduct and cascade was made with Maderno and Fontana, who had created the water theater at the Villa Aldobrandini, but the Borghese architect, Flaminio Ponzio, who authorized the payment for the construction of the cascade, may have designed it.[59] Less dramatic than the Aldobrandini cascade, the water stored in a basin in a flat piazza cut into the hillside floods down into three oval basins set below one another with roughened, inclined planes between the basins to roil the water as it descends. Flights of stairs descend on each side of the cascade, curving in and out around the basins. The cascade is a richer, fuller development of the type of water stair or water chain seen more modestly at Bagnaia and Caprarola in the sixteenth century. Later, in 1621, the villa was sold to Cardinal Ludovisi, nephew of Pope

37. Frascati, Villa Borghese, water theater

Gregory XV, and from 1622 to 1625 Maderno oversaw the creation along the base of the hill below the cascade of a wall of twenty-two niches containing basins with water jets and twenty-four vases above the piers with more spouting jets.

That these waterworks, like those of the Villa d'Este at Tivoli, were not only to offer awesome views and thundering sounds to the casual visitor but to dampen them physically is demonstrated by two slightly later travel accounts of visits to the Villa Ludovisi. In 1654 the Dutchman Aerssen van Sommelsdyck remarks that "along an alley which leads to the gardens there are conduits which bathe skirts from below whereby ordinarily one attempts to refresh the ladies; the men who are amused to see them wetted from the side of the garden are also soaked by some water jets which are hidden under the boxwood."[60] Five years later the English visitor Mortoft offers a similar account:

> From thence wee went into the garden, Into which, As wee entered, the water flew up from the ground and wett us before wee could well perceive from whence it came, then wee went to one end of the garden, which is very spatious and large, and there saw a very fine fountaine, which was made with such Art that the water issued al about in potts and vessels in many several places. There was a fine Cascade above this fountaine, from which the water ran down with very great force; wee could not goe up this place without being soundly wett, in regard the man let the water flye out from under the staires, in somuch there could be noe way to avoid it.[61]

[57] For the most recent consideration of the villas at Frascati, see A. T. Mignosi et al., *Villa e paese*, Rome, 1980, and S. Frezzotti, "I teatri delle acque nelle ville di Frascati," *Studi romani*, XXX, 1982, pp. 467–77.

[58] J.A.F. Orbaan, *Documenti sul barocco in Roma*, Rome, 1920, pp. 157–58.

[59] H. Hibbard, *Carlo Maderno and Roman Architecture 1580–1630*, University Park, Penn., and London, 1971, p. 210.

[60] L. G. Pélissier, "Sur quelques documents utiles pour l'histoire des rapports entre la France et l'Italie," *Atti del Congresso Internazionale di Scienze e Storiche*, 1903, III, Rome, 1906, p. 189.

[61] F. Mortoft, *His Book Being His Travels through France and*

38. Frascati, Villa Aldobrandini, Room of Apollo, engraving, 1647

Meanwhile further water devices were being introduced at the water theater of the Villa Aldobrandini. From about 1615 to 1621 the rooms at the ends of the arcaded exedra were decorated, that at the left being a chapel dedicated to St. Sebastian, while that at the right was transformed into a temple to Apollo and the Muses (Fig. 38). At the rear of the "Stanza di Apollo" a small, artificial hill depicted Mount Parnassus with Apollo seated at the summit, the nine muses playing their musical instruments scattered over the hillside, and in the water basin at the foot of the hill the winged horse Pegasus. The wooden statues of Apollo and the Muses were automata activated by the hydraulic power to play their different instruments, while a water organ under the hill, also powered by water, played music, rather like the late sixteenth-century fountain of Parnassus at the Medici villa at Pratolino, except that the figures in the Tuscan garden

were not automata. An organ master, Giovanni Guglielmi, was employed from 1617 to 1621 in creating the musical automata.[62] A lavish banquet set in the Room of Apollo in 1619 indicates that the hall was to serve as a dining room or triclinium, probably in emulation of the ancient villa of Lucullus reputed to have stood here, whose most splendid triclinium, according to Plutarch (*Lucullus*, XLI), was named after Apollo.[63]

In 1613 Cardinal Scipione Borghese, who had previously acquired the old villa of Cardinal Gallo, also obtained the Altemps villa of Mondragone and in the following year also purchased the adjacent Villa Taverna and sold the Villa Gallo, his earlier purchase, thus consolidating his properties. Borghese soon expanded and refurbished the Villa Mondragone under the direction of his architect Vasanzio, although the principal work was devoted to the gardens. On the east side of the villa where there had been a private garden created by Cardinal Altemps for Pope Gregory XIII, a new garden was designed with a large, arcaded loggia closing the south end of the garden and at the opposite end a water theater in the form of a raised exedra with jets of water in the arcaded niches (Fig. 39).[64] The use of a semicircular or semioval exedra as the frame of a display of waterworks, described as a *teatro*, had become standard in early seventeenth-century garden design, as demonstrated in these examples at Frascati.[65] So in 1617 when the Borghese banker Roberto Primo followed his patrons to Frascati and acquired the villa now known as the Villa Lancellotti, he added a nymphaeum or water theater in the shape of an arcaded exedra set into the hill at the end of the central axis of the garden behind the villa.

The earlier water theaters at the Villa Aldobrandini and the Villa Borghese with their great cascades thundering down the hillside had very dramatically exploited the increased water supply at Frascati, but in the later exedras at Mondragone and particularly at the Villa Lancellotti the quantity and activity of the

[62] D'Onofrio, *Villa Aldobrandini*, pp. 138–41.

[63] Alvarez, "The Renaissance Nymphaeum," p. 233.

[64] President De Brosses recounts amusingly the water games he and his youthful companions played with leather water pipes at the theater of Mondragone during their visit in the eighteenth century, but these devices may be the result of later additions; see C. de Brosses, *Lettres familières sur l'Italie*, ed. Y. Bezard, Paris, 1931, II, pp. 296–97.

[65] Schwager, "Aldobrandinis Villa," pp. 379–82, excursus on the meaning and form of the "teatro."

*Italy 1658–1659* (The Hakluyt Society, ser. 2, LVII), ed. M. Letts, London, 1925, pp. 163–64.

39. Frascati, Villa Mondragone, water theater, engraving

water gradually lessened. Similarly in Rome toward the end of the sixteenth century new forms of fountain decoration appear. It has been noted that genre figures began to replace mythological subjects and that heraldic animals and personal or family *imprese* and devices dominated fountains, commencing at the Villa Montalto of Pope Sixtus V in the 1580s.[66] Actually imprese had already played an important role earlier in the decoration of many of the fountains of the Villa d'Este at Tivoli, as at the Fountain of the Owl whose columns were wrapped by festoons of the golden apples of the Hesperides (Fig. 32), but other devices there are actually formed by the movement of the jets of water as in the Este lily in the center of the oval Fountain of Tivoli, whereas at the Villa Montalto the imprese were of carved stone or molded stucco. Similarly after the first quarter of the seventeenth century there is a decrease in the number and types of nymphaea at Rome and a loss of the rusticity that had prevailed in grottoes and fountains for the preceding century.[67] Water was no longer a dominating feature of Roman gardens at the very moment

that it began to be the striking feature of the public piazze of Rome. The wealth of exotic plants that began to invade the different European countries in the late sixteenth and early seventeenth centuries would even penetrate the Roman gardens and become a source of pride and interest of the owners that would replace the hydraulic novelties of the past.[68] In the seventeenth century the gardener came into his own as master of the garden, diminishing the role of the fontaniere.

Two different types of artisans were involved in the creation of the fountains in the sixteenth-century gardens of Rome. The first, who would be described today as a hydraulic engineer, was concerned with the gross water supply to the garden. In the sixteenth century, however, he was generally identified as an architect following the tradition established by Vitruvius and renewed by Alberti in the last chapter of each of their treatises that architects were responsible for the hydraulic problems encountered with ports, aque-

---

[66] MacDougall, *Fons Sapientiae*, pp. 105–8.
[67] Alvarez, "The Renaissance Nymphaeum," p. 110.

[68] G. Masson, "Italian Flower Collectors' Gardens in Seventeenth Century Italy," in *The Italian Garden* (First Dumbarton Oaks Colloquium on the History of Landscape Architecture), ed. D. R. Coffin, Washington, D.C., 1972, pp. 61–80.

ducts, water wheels, pumps, and public fountains. As a result of the breadth characteristic of their interest and work, as well as the generally more public nature of their activity, the names and personalities of these men are often better known than those of the fontanieri, a relatively new craft in Rome related to the role of the plumber and, therefore, identifiable only in building accounts.

The introduction of water to the gardens of Bramante's Belvedere Court at the Vatican was under his direction according to a payment record.[69] Similarly, the architect Antonio da Sangallo the Younger was in charge of the waterworks of the gardens of the Villa Madama. While Raphael was the designer of the villa, Sangallo was his assistant there and certainly directed the project after Raphael's death in 1520 when much of the hydraulic work was undertaken. In this case, the patron Pope Clement VII, who began the villa as a cardinal, was passionately interested in the hydraulic problems. In 1520 he had written precise instructions about some of the features required in the aqueduct supplying the villa and in 1526 the Venetian ambassador reported that, when the pope visited his villa, "his entire pleasure was to discuss hydraulics with his engineers."[70] Because Sangallo was paid in 1524 and 1525 for work on the fountains, it may be supposed that he was a chief figure in these colloquies. At the middle of the century the architect Vignola was to play a similar role at the Villa Giulia. Vasari, who was originally in charge of the building, recounts that Vignola, who had recently returned to Rome and was not yet established there as an architect, was at first busy conducting the water of the Acqua Vergine to the villa and only later served as architect of the building.[71] This seems confirmed by the building records, which list monthly payments to Vignola from February 1551 for unspecified work until August when he is identified as architect.

The Sienese architect Tommaso Ghinucci, whose career is rather obscure, was probably better known for hydraulic accomplishments than for building, although Donato Giannotti described him affectionately in 1545 as *Principe Architectorum*.[72] At that time Ghinucci was in the employ of the Florentine cardinal Niccolò Ridolfi, whose summer retreat was

in the little town of Bagnaia north of Rome, where earlier cardinals had created a hunting park. In March 1549 a contract was let by the cardinal for building an aqueduct to bring water to his residence and to the hunting park.[73] This work under the direction of Ghinucci was celebrated in two poems of Marcantonio Flaminio dedicated to the fountain of Cardinal Ridolfi at Bagnaia.[74] Whether this laying on of water in the park was to be preliminary to more building there is unknown since the cardinal died in the next year.

With the fame of this work at Bagnaia, the Cardinal of Ferrara, who had just rented a villa with gardens on the Quirinal Hill in Rome, took advantage of the death of Cardinal Ridolfi to request Ghinucci to come to Rome to be in charge of the waterworks he wished to develop in the gardens of his new villa. Giannotti, who informs us of this in a letter of August 9, 1550, casts doubts on the success of the invitation, concluding: "I don't know if he [the cardinal] will succeed,"[75] but from at least January 1559 Ghinucci was in the employ of the cardinal at the Quirinal with an annual salary of one hundred scudi.[76]

On July 15, 1561, Giovanni Alberto Galvani, the cardinal's supervisory architect at Rome and Tivoli, was paid for expenses for a trip from Montefiascone to Rome in company with Visdomini, the cardinal's business manager; Girolamo Muziano, the painter; a carpenter Maestro Tommaso; and "messer Tomaso Ghinuzzi."[77] Since several of these men were involved in 1560 and 1561 in the building of the aqueduct conducting water to Tivoli from Monte Sant'Angelo, Ghinucci may have been concerned with the technical problems of the aqueduct. Ghinucci continued on salary through December 1569 when it ceased.[78]

Meanwhile, in September 1568, Cardinal Gambara had plans to convert the old hunting park at Bagnaia into a lovely villa with gardens, the present Villa Lante. Ghinucci then reappears as the supervisory architect of the building and of the waterworks there. His reputation was so well known that when the

[69] Ackerman, *The Cortile del Belvedere*, p. 152, doc. 2.

[70] Coffin, *The Villa*, pp. 250, 252–53.

[71] G. Vasari, *Le vite de più eccellenti pittori, scultori ed architettori*, ed. G. Milanesi, VII, Florence, 1881, p. 107.

[72] G. Milanesi, "Alcune lettere di Donato Giannotti," *Giornale storico degli archivi toscani*, VII, 1863, p. 222.

[73] C. Lazzaro Bruno, "The Villa Lante at Bagnaia," Ph.D. dissertation, Princeton University, 1974, p. 17.

[74] M. A. Flaminio, *Marci Antonii, Joannis Antonii et Gabrielis Flaminiorum Carmina*, Padua, 1743, pp. 39, 79.

[75] Milanesi, "Alcume lettere," pp. 239–40.

[76] ASM, Registro 957, Entrata et uscita de li danari de la Protettione di Francia 1560, fols. 47v and passim.

[77] ASM, Registro delli mandatj . . . dellj Mag.ci Grilandarj 1561, fol. 3r.

[78] ASM, Registro 911, Salariati 1570, loose leaf between fols. 126v–127r.

Frenchman Montaigne visited the Italian gardens in 1581 he noted in his diary that "Tommaso da Siena," presumably Ghinucci, was in charge of the water-works at Bagnaia.[79] Montaigne compares the water effects at Bagnaia with those of the Villa d'Este at Tivoli and of the Medici Villa at Pratolino, awarding the honors to Bagnaia since the water there is fresher and more lively (*viva*) than at Tivoli and more abundant than at Pratolino. He adds that "Tommaso da Siena" had also worked at Tivoli and that the work at Bagnaia "is not finished, and thus, always adding new inventions to the old, he has put into this his last work even more art, beauty and grace." Since several of the fountains at Bagnaia are derived from those at Tivoli,[80] Ghinucci's involvement with their design would seem likely.

Toward the end of the sixteenth century engineering specialists seem to become more prevalent, particularly for military fortifications and hydraulics. So in 1580 when the Medici cardinal wished to have a fountain on top of his artificial Mount Parnassus in the gardens of his villa at Rome, an engineer, Camillo Agrippa of Milan, was engaged to handle the waterworks. The problem of conveying water some fifty meters above its water source in the Acqua Vergine was presumably too difficult for the traditional architectural generalist. Agrippa had already in 1555 published a book on military arms and dueling, the *Trattato di scientia d'armi*, and would during his activity at Rome publish a book on how to transport the obelisk at the Vatican (1583), followed by treatises on the winds (1584) and navigation (1595). A Latin inscription that once was in the pavilion on the top of Mount Parnassus at the Medici villa praised Agrippa's feat by likening him to the ancient Roman Marcus Agrippa who conveyed the Aqua Virgo into the Campus Martius at Rome.[81]

Toward the end of the century Giovanni Fontana, elder brother of Domenico Fontana, the famous architect of Pope Sixtus V, was the chief authority in Rome on hydraulic affairs. Giovanni's major reputation was based on his work in the public sector, for it was he who completed the building of the aqueduct that fed the Acqua Felice after being ordered by Pope Sixtus V to bring abundant water to the Quirinal Hill. Fontana, among other work, would also oversee an aqueduct to supply the papal harbor town of Civitavecchia, regulate the flow of the Teverone River near Tivoli, and later, just before his death in 1614, attempt to ensure adequate water for the west bank of the Tiber River in the area of the Janiculum Hill with the renewal of the ancient aqueduct of Trajan to supply the new Acqua Paola for Pope Paul V.[82] Having completed the renewal of the Acqua Felice, Fontana was employed by Pope Clement VIII from 1595 to 1597 to supervise the hydraulic work necessary to supply the new water organ in the papal gardens on the Quirinal, originally developed by the Cardinal of Ferrara.[83] Because of this and his public works, Giovanni Fontana would also be called upon by the papal nephews when they were faced with similar problems at their villas at Frascati. So in 1604 Fontana and the architect Carlo Maderno, identified as "architetti," subscribed the building account for the aqueduct from Molara that supplied the water theater of the Villa Aldobrandini at Frascati.[84] Presumably Maderno was the designer of the water theater and Fontana was in charge of the more technical hydraulic matters connected with the water theater. Similarly on June 19, 1607, Maderno and Fontana contracted with Cardinal Scipione Borghese to build the aqueduct and waterfall at his recently acquired villa at Frascati, which was in turn revised by Maderno for Cardinal Ludovisi.[85] Later, in the middle of the seventeenth century Luigi Bernini, younger brother of the great sculptor Gian Lorenzo Bernini, served at Rome in a rather analogous capacity to that of Fontana. A mediocre sculptor, Luigi was also a supervisory architect at St. Peter's, assisting his brother in the more technical aspects of work there, and then under Pope Alexander VII (1655–1666) Luigi was appointed papal "architect of waters." Thus, in June 1659 Bernini was listed in the building accounts of the Villa Pamphili inspecting the conduits of the Acqua Paola and in July 1644 he oversaw the introduction into the gardens at the Villa Pamphili of additional water from the Acqua Paola.[86]

[79] M. de Montaigne, *Journal du voyage*, ed. A. D'Ancona, Città di Castello, 1895, p. 527.

[80] Coffin, "Some Aspects of the Villa Lante at Bagnaia," pp. 569–75.

[81] P. Pecchiai, *La scalinata di Piazza di Spagna e Villa Medici*, Rome, 1941, p. 137; see also *Dizionario biografico degli Italiani*, I, Rome, 1960, p. 503, s.v. Agrippa, C.

[82] U. Donati, *Artisti ticinesi a Roma*, Bellinzona, 1942, pp. 77–86, and Thieme-Becker, *Künstler Lexikon*, XII, Leipzig, 1916, pp. 179–80, s.v. Fontana, G.

[83] Salerno, "La fontana," pp. 5–6, and *Il Palazzo del Quirinale*, p. 243.

[84] Schwager, "Aldobrandinis Villa," p. 336.

[85] Hibbard, *Carlo Maderno*, p. 210.

[86] J. Garms, *Quellen aus dem Archiv Doria-Pamphilj zur Kunst-*

The careers of these later "hydraulic engineers" bear witness to the gradual shift in concern regarding water supply from the personal interest of the wealthy and the powerful to the public benefit.

As fountains began to dominate sixteenth-century Roman gardens, the fontanieri, the artisans who crafted the fountains and the plumbing that activated them, constituted an important trade. Already in 1550 in the introduction to the three arts of design in the first edition of Vasari's *Lives*, he devoted a chapter to describing rustic grottoes and fountains, which he then refined in his 1568 edition.[87] As in the writing of the ancients and of Alberti, Vasari's fountains are decorated with marine subjects in mosaic and naturalized with tartari, the rocky congelations famous at Tivoli. In the first edition he notes generally that there are in Rome many fountains imitating antique ones with mosaics of burnt and enameled stones, coral, and other maritime material. In the second edition, however, he adds more specific references, particularly of a Tuscan origin, such as the grotto at Castello created by the sculptor Tribolo, but he also includes Giovanni da Udine's rustic fountain at the Villa Madama.

As the fontanieri were considered merely specialists within the artisan class, their public recognition was very limited and their names remain buried in building accounts. In fact, the most renowned fontaniere of the sixteenth century, Curzio Maccarone, was apparently illiterate, for his contract in 1566 for the Oval Fountain in the Villa d'Este at Tivoli was subscribed by someone else in his name "as he says he does not know how to write."[88] Maccarone's name first appears in the record of payment to him in 1551 for work on the "Fontana grande" and the Fountain of Cleopatra in the Belvedere Court at the Vatican.[89] The account is subscribed by the custodian of the Belvedere, Scipio Perotto il Vignuola, and the architect, Girolamo da Carpi. The "Fontana grande" was, as discussed previously, probably the nymphaeum at the rear of the middle terrace of the Belvedere Court. The Fountain of Cleopatra was designed by Daniele da Volterra as a rustic setting at the north end of the east-

40. Tivoli, Villa d'Este, Fountain of Tivoli, engraving

ern corridor of the Belvedere Court for the ancient statue identified as Cleopatra, which was earlier in the Statue Court of the Belvedere.[90] Maccarone was presumably the artificer of the grotto setting of the statue as well as of the plumbing.

Beginning at least in 1560 Maccarone was active in the employ of the Cardinal of Ferrara, first at his villa and gardens rented from the Carafa family on the Quirinal Hill in Rome and later at his villa and gardens in Tivoli.[91] Maccarone's introduction to the cardinal's service was undoubtedly through the architect Girolamo da Carpi, who had in 1549 been brought to Rome from Ferrara by the cardinal and continued until at least 1552 to supervise the cardinal's villa and gardens on the Quirinal, even while working at the Vatican. Girolamo's major contribution to the gardens on the Quirinal was its wooden pergolas, trellises, pavilions, and other furnishings. Maccarone's principal work at the Quirinal was the rustic Fountain of the Wood, built in 1560 and 1561, which included a small, artificial hill with grottoes and classical statues set in a grove of trees. Slightly later, from 1565 to 1566, Maccarone fashioned in the lower garden on the western side of the casino the Fountain of Apollo and the Muses decorated with mosaic.

Maccarone had no more than completed the major work on the Fountain of Apollo than he was hustled off to the cardinal's other villa and garden at Tivoli, for which on August 22, 1566, in Rome Maccarone contracted to build the so-called Oval Fountain or the Fountain of Tivoli (Fig. 40). His fame as a fontaniere

*tätigkeit in Rom unter Innocenz X* (Quellenschriften zur Geschichte der Barockkunst in Rome, 4), Rome and Vienna, 1972, p. 199.

[87] G. Vasari, *Le vite de più eccellenti pittori, scultori e architettori*, ed. R. Bettarini and P. Barocchi, I, Florence, 1966, pp. 71–74.

[88] F. S. Seni, *La Villa d'Este in Tivoli*, Rome, 1902, p. 121, note a.

[89] Ackerman, *The Cortile del Belvedere*, p. 165, doc. 75.

[90] N. Canedy, "The Decoration of the Stanza della Cleopatra," in *Essays in the History of Art Presented to Rudolf Wittkower*, London, 1967, pp. 71–82.

[91] Coffin, *The Villa*, p. 205.

is signaled at the commencement of the contract where he has himself identified as *Io Curtio Macca-rone delle Fontane*. The fountain at Tivoli still exists, unlike those in Rome, and like the Fountain of the Wood has an artificial hill with grottoes, which the building accounts describe as the "monte di Curzio." Two years later Maccarone undertook the other great fountain, that of Rome, that matches the Tivoli fountain at the opposite side of the garden, but is a much more architectural fountain (Fig. 30).

Maccarone's fame was such that competition for his services began to rise among the wealthy garden patrons. On September 21, 1568, just at the moment Maccarone was beginning his work on the Fountain of Rome, the wealthy and powerful Cardinal Alessandro Farnese, grandson of Pope Paul III, wrote from his summer residence at Caprarola to Paolo Vitelli in Rome:

> I have made every effort that Curzio dalle Fontane should come to Your Lordship and to serve you in whatever you have desired, as I would have done for myself, but in fact there is no remedy to be found so that he could come, since he is at Tivoli in the service of the Lord Cardinal of Ferrara, whence he cannot leave for a while; with all this I will attempt again to see that Your Lordship is served, and if for such you should be content with a young pupil of said Curzio, who is now here, I will willingly send him to satisfy Your Lordship.[92]

The gardens at Caprarola of the Farnese cardinal were, therefore, also delayed in their completion because of the unavailability of Maccarone's services. Only the death of the Cardinal of Ferrara in 1572 would release Maccarone to enter the service of Farnese, just as the death of Cardinal Ridolfi in 1550 had permitted Ferrara to employ Tommaso Ghinucci.

Because of the quantity of water and fountains at Tivoli several other fontanieri were employed there in addition to Curzio Maccarone. So Luca Antonio da Figoli worked on the Alley of the Hundred Fountains and Andrea Romano created one of the ground-floor corridor fountains.[93] The limited scope of their work and their salaries indicate that they did not have the reputation or experience of Maccarone, whose monthly salary of eleven scudi (ten scudi in gold) was similar to that of several of the master painters in charge of the decoration at Tivoli, such as Livio

Agresti and Girolamo Muziano.[94] These craftsmen might be identified as the creative fontanieri, employed solely to fashion the fountains, but there will also be a resident fontaniere, who is responsible for the maintenance and repair of the fountains. This was apparently the role of the fontaniere Giovanni or Giovannino, who was paid a monthly salary of five scudi from 1577 to at least 1586.[95]

There was even a more specialized fontaniere needed at Tivoli because of the amazing hydraulic powered automata used there for fountains. Two of the great wonders of the gardens at Tivoli were the Water Organ (comprising the Fountain of Nature) and the Fountain of the Owl and the Birds (Figs. 31, 32), both the invention of a Frenchman listed in the accounts as Luca Il Clericho, presumably Luc Le-Clerc.[96] From at least 1566 Luc had worked successively at the Fountain of the Birds and then the Water Organ, assisted by his nephew Claude Venard, who on his uncle's death later in 1568 completed the Water Organ.[97] Venard then continued on a regular provision of two scudi a month through 1586, working at both the Este gardens in Tivoli and Rome and even in the Barco at Tivoli where he fashioned a water-wheel in 1585 when Cardinal Luigi d'Este was transforming his uncle's hunting park into a farm.

The idea of the two hydraulic powered automata at Tivoli was derived from ancient sources. The Fountain of the Birds fashioned in bronze had a thicket in which perched artificial birds who sang merrily until an owl appeared slowly to silence the birds in fear, but as the owl withdrew the birds in turn resumed their song (Fig. 41). This was a copy of a fountain described by the ancient Greek engineer Hero of Alexandria in his treatise *Pneumatica*.[98] The fountain particularly appealed to the cardinal's humanist, the Frenchman Marc-Antoine Muret, who in one of his

---

[92] ASP, Carteggio Farnesiano: Estero: Caprarola, Busta 116.

[93] Coffin, *The Villa d'Este*, pp. 28, 55.

[94] Ibid., pp. 29, n. 45; 43, n. 6; and 51, n. 32.

[95] ASM, Registro 1215, Libro di salariati 1579, fol. 127 and Registro 1222, Bolletta de Salariati 1586, fol. 82.

[96] It is possible that the nomenclature "il Clericho" refers to the fact that Luc was actually a priest.

[97] ASM, Registro 1222, fols. 76 and 88, and Coffin, *The Villa d'Este*, pp. 17–19, 22–23.

[98] The Fountain of the Owl and the Birds is no. XVI in Hero of Alexandria, *Opera Quae Supersunt Omnia*, ed. W. Schmidt, Leipzig, 1899, I, pp. 90–99. For the history of Hero's *Pneumatica* during the Middle Ages and Renaissance, see M. Boas, "Hero's *Pneumatica*: A Study of Its Transmission and Influence," *Isis*, XL, 1949, pp. 38–48. Muret's poem regarding the fountain is in M. A. Muret, *Opera Omnia*, ed. C. H. Frotscher, Leipzig, 1834, II, pp. 337–38.

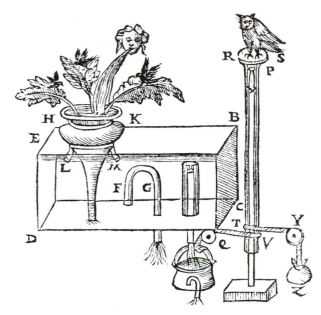

41. G. B. Aleotti, *Gli artificiosi et curiosi moti spiritali dit Herrone*, 1589, Theor. xv

poems composed in 1571 celebrating the gardens at Tivoli singled out the Fountain of the Birds and specifically praised its creator, his countryman the fontaniere Luc, giving conclusive proof of Luc's creation of the fountain.

The Water Organ was housed in the large, very decorative architectural frame of the fountain dedicated to Mother Nature on the terrace above the northeast end of the first cross axis composed of fishpools (Fig. 31). The pipes of the organ stood in the central niche of the fountain behind a statue of the many-breasted Diana of Ephesus, and the great water reservoirs that regulated the air pressure for the pipes were built behind the architectural frontispiece. Both the Roman architect Vitruvius in the last book of his treatise on architecture and the Greek engineer Hero of Alexandria had described a water organ, but their organs had to be played manually by a human operator as the water only provided air pressure for the pipes. At Tivoli the water power also motivated the keys of the organ so that it played a tune like a mechanical piano.[99] The hydraulic engineering problems of the wa-

ter organ were, therefore, capable of solution by the fontaniere Venard, but in 1570 an organist, Giovanni Battista, was called in to tune the organ and in February and March 1573 and again in November Giovanni Ferdinando Portoghese visited Tivoli for several days on each trip for the same purpose.[100]

That the fontanieri responsible for the hydraulic automata at Tivoli were French in origin suggests that the skills and knowledge they had were not yet available in Rome. That Ippolito II d'Este, Cardinal of Ferrara, should employ French craftsmen is not surprising. In 1536, three years before being elected cardinal, Ippolito d'Este was sent to the court of Francis I in France. As cardinal he would then be protector of French interests at the papal court and from 1561 to 1563 was papal legate to France. This French orientation with respect to hydraulic automata may, however, have more significance. During the late Middle Ages and early Renaissance, probably the most famous European example of the use of such automata as garden decoration was at the Franco-Flemish castle of Hesdin. From the very end of the thirteenth century Count Robert II of Artois had begun to develop a great pleasure park outside of his castle at Hesdin, where gradually were fashioned different types of waterworks and automata, perhaps inspired by examples Count Robert may have seen in Sicily of Byzantine or Islamic origin.[101] These amazing devices had been kept in constant repair until the middle of the sixteenth century. It is possible, indeed, that the Cardinal of Ferrara might have seen them during his early years in France. Unfortunately in July 1553, during the siege and eventual razing of the town of Hesdin by Charles V, the park with its hydraulic marvels was

Later Salomon de Caus will offer a thorough description of the mechanics of both the types of automata at Tivoli in his *Les raisons des forces mouuantes*, Frankfort, 1615, fols. 29v–30v and 39v–43r.

[100] ASM, Registro 911, Sallariati in Roma 1571, fol. 79r; Registro 943, Conto dei denari pagati da Marc'Ant. Cambi in Roma 1572, fol. 86r; and Giornale di Scarlatj 1573–1574, fols. 41r and 69v.

[101] M. Charageat, "Le Parc d'Hesdin: Création monumentale du XIIIᵉ siècle," *Bulletin de la Société de l'Histoire de l'Art Français*, 1950, pp. 94–106, and M. Sherwood, "Magic and Mechanics in Medieval Fiction," *Studies in Philology*, XLIV, 1947, pp. 579–91. For more recent consideration of Hesdin, see A. H. van Buren, "Reality and Literary Romance in the Park of Hesdin," and N. Miller, "Paradise Regained: Medieval Garden Fountains," in *Medieval Gardens* (Dumbarton Oaks Colloquium on the History of Landscape Architecture, IX), ed. E. B. MacDougall, Washington, D.C., 1986, pp. 115–34 and 143–44.

[99] Vitruvius, X, viii, and Hero of Alexandria, *Opera*, pp. 192–203. Montaigne in his diary, *Journal*, p. 269, describes the functioning of the organ at Tivoli, but another French visitor, Nicolas Audebert, in 1576 or 1577 gives a much more detailed account; see R. W. Lightbown, "Nicolas Audebert and the Villa d'Este," *Journal of the Warburg and Courtauld Institutes*, XXVII, 1964, pp. 185–87.

destroyed. Although more than a decade passes before Luc LeClerc appears at work at Tivoli, one wonders whether he might have received his training at Hesdin and because of the destruction there sought his fortune with the cardinal in Italy.

The water organ created in 1595 at the Fountain of Apollo for Clement VIII in the papal gardens on the Quirinal was apparently not made by a fontaniere like the one at Tivoli. An actual organ builder, Luca Biagio, called Perugino, was employed to fashion it.[102] His success with that hydraulic wonder caused Pope Clement VIII to grant Biagio in 1600 a twenty-year privilege for the creation of such instruments. He would also continue until at least 1609 to tune and maintain the Quirinal organ, being listed in 1605 as its custodian. Then in July 1616 one Stefano Biagio, presumably a relative, was paid for tuning it.

The activities of the fontanieri will continue into the seventeenth century, particularly at Tivoli and Frascati, where the most lavish waterworks had been developed. So in 1609 the fontaniere Orazio Olivieri was paid for grotto work (*lavori de tartari*) on the Fountain of the Emperor at the Villa d'Este in Tivoli under the direction of the architect Gaspare Guerra and the two may have created the new rustic cascade near the Fountain of Rome.[103] From 1612 to 1620 Olivieri transferred his work from Tivoli to the Villa Aldobrandini at Frascati where he is recorded as creating water tricks (*scherzi d'acqua*). In June 1623, however, he did some work at the nearby Villa Ludovisi, which was probably only a brief diversion, for in accounts in 1647 and 1655 Olivieri is still recorded as fontaniere at the Villa Aldobrandini when it is owned by the Pamphili family. Orazio Olivieri's son Giorgio had meanwhile served as supervisor of the work on the new fountains at the Villa Pamphili at Rome in 1646 and 1647, before joining his father at Frascati with the position there of wardrobe keeper (*guardarobba*).[104] Because of the water organ in the

42. Tivoli, Villa d'Este, Fountain of the Beaker

fountain room dedicated to Apollo and the Muses at the Villa Aldobrandini, the services of an organ master, Giovanni Guglielmi, were required from 1617 to 1621.[105] The date and the length of time of his work suggest that Guglielmi may have been in charge of creating the organ and not merely employed to tune it.

From 1611 until at least 1619 the fontaniere Curzio Donati was in charge of the waterworks of the Villa d'Este at Tivoli, probably succeeding Orazio Olivieri when the latter left for Frascati.[106] Donati's major work was to put back into good repair and to complete the Fountain of Nature with the water organ, which was left incomplete at the death of the Cardinal of Ferrara in 1572. An inscription on the fountain recorded his work there. In 1619 a new fontaniere, Vincenzo Vincenzi, wrote an extended me-

[102] R. Lunelli, *L'arte organaria del Rinascimento in Roma* (Historia Musicae Cultores Biblioteca, x), Florence, 1958, pp. 59–62, and *Il Palazzo del Quirinale*, Rome, 1974, p. 87, n. 56.

[103] ASM, Fabbriche et villeggiature: Tivoli, busta 71, pt. 1, Villeggiatura sotto Alessandro d'Este Cardinale 1606–1614, fol. 7v, and R. W. Berger, "Garden Cascades in Italy and France, 1565–1665," *Journal of the Society of Architectural Historians*, XXXIII, 1974, p. 315.

[104] Schwager, "Aldobrandinis Villa," pp. 353–54; Hibbard, *Carlo Maderno*, p. 132; and Garms, *Quellen*, p. 82, no. 331, and p. 240, no. 1180. For the work at the Villa Ludovisi, see Hibbard, p. 211. For Giorgio Olivieri, see Garms, p. 236, and Schwager, p. 354.

[105] D'Onofrio, *La Villa Aldobrandini di Frascati*, pp. 138–41.

[106] Coffin, *The Villa d'Este*, pp. 105, 107–8, and appendix D, pp. 166–70, with memorial of Vincenzi.

43. Tivoli, Villa d'Este, Fountain of Nature and Cascade, engraving

morial on the condition of the fountains and the work that had been accomplished in four months in cleaning and repairing conduits and in restoring the Fountain of the Birds, which he claims was in such a state of ruin that it had almost to be completely refashioned. After enumerating repairs that still needed to be done, Vincenzi describes at great length new fountain proposals, including automata of arquebusiers to stand one at each side of the entrance shooting streams of water at visitors, a pergola of water across the lower garden, and in the grottoes or rooms of the villa such automata as a satyr playing a pan pipe and a shepherd sounding a bagpipe. Many of these inventions, derived in part from Hero of Alexandria, had already been put into effect in the late sixteenth century at the Medici villa at Pratolino, but by the time

of Vincenzo's memorial were standard features in the various publications on hydraulics, including the Latin and Italian translations of Hero of Alexandria by Commandino, Aleotti, and Giorgi, or the derivative works by Agostino Ramelli and Salomon de Caus. Apparently none of these new inventions was put into effect, for in a letter of November 1624 to the duke of Modena Vincenzo was still involved in restoring fountains, although he complains about the report of the local agent Carandini that the fontaniere was doing nothing, and in another letter of January 1625 he requested money to settle accounts.

The cost of keeping normal fountains of water active, much less the cost of repair of the delicate mechanisms of hydraulic automata, was too expensive to encourage the creation of new garden fountains, and particularly at Tivoli with a nonresident owner. During the seventeenth century only a few prominent water displays were created in the gardens of Rome and its neighborhood. Perhaps the most notable were by the sculptor Bernini: his Fountain of Neptune and Triton, an early work he added in about 1620 to the Villa Montalto in Rome, the figural group of which is now in the Victoria and Albert Museum of London (Fig. 78), his lost Eagle and Triton fountains of the Villa Mattei, or the unnoticed Fountain of the Great Beaker (*Bicchierone*) he set above the Fountain of the Dragons at the Villa d'Este in Tivoli (Fig. 42) or the large cascade he added below the Water Organ there (Fig. 43). It is, of course, Bernini's public fountains, such as that of the Four Rivers in the Piazza Navona or the Fountain of the Triton in the Piazza Barberini, that are still in place attracting public attention.

# The Classicizing of the Roman Garden:
# Form and Association

The Renaissance or revival of classicism began to pervade the arts and culture of Rome in the middle of the fifteenth century. Humanists like the famous writer and architect Leon Battista Alberti were often social reformers who wished to perfect all aspects of their society on the model of classical antiquity, as Alberti's numerous writings demonstrate. The adoption of the classical orders and proportional systems suggested by Vitruvius, the ancient Roman writer on architecture, satisfied their desire to classicize and correct the "mother art" of architecture, as the study of the remains of ancient sculpture brought a greater understanding of the physical form of man for both Renaissance sculpture and painting. In contrast, gardening because of its ephemerality had no physical remains from classical antiquity to aid in any desire to classicize the garden. Even the ancient painted depictions of Roman gardens uncovered later at Pompeii or the House of Livia at Prima Porta were unknown to the Renaissance. The only evidence regarding ancient gardens available to the period was the literary references to gardens in classical poetry, the agricultural writings of the *Res Rusticae Scriptores*, or the letters of Pliny the Younger and of these only Pliny preserved a detailed image of an ancient Roman garden.

A few elements in Pliny's descriptions of his two gardens began to be exploited by Renaissance Roman gardeners during the early sixteenth century. The most striking feature in Pliny's account of his Tuscan villa (*Letters*, v, 6) was a garden to the south of the villa in the shape of an ancient Roman hippodrome or circus (*in modum circi*), which is a familiar ancient

structure of a distinctive form easily replicated in Renaissance gardens. The use by Pliny of particular trees, such as the cypress in his hippodrome garden or the existence of four plane trees nourished by water rising from a basin in their midst set within the small court of a summer casino, will be recreated in some of the Renaissance gardens. Such classical recreations, however, give only a very limited expression to classicism in Renaissance gardening. Perhaps the most influential gardening device of classical antiquity was topiary, the shaping of shrubbery, such as box or cypress, into figural or geometric forms, which was already common in fifteenth-century gardening and was advocated by Alberti in his architectural treatise in the mid-fifteenth century.

The limited information regarding ancient gardening may partly explain the lateness of the appearance of what might be defined as a Renaissance garden based on classical thought, and the persistence into the sixteenth century of the mediaeval hortus conclusus as seen previously in the garden of Pope Paul III in the Vatican. It is during the first two decades of the sixteenth century in the work of the architect Bramante and his younger colleagues Raphael and Peruzzi that the classicizing of gardens began to be realized.

The election in 1503 of Cardinal Giuliano della Rovere as Pope Julius II marks the first important step in the development of the Roman garden, for a year later he commissioned the architect Bramante to design the Belvedere Court and its adjacent Statue Court at the Vatican. The Della Rovere cardinal had previously, as was discussed earlier, a small collection of

Roman antiquities. At the Vatican, Bramante constructed a tremendous, rectangular court on the hillside that climbed up from the north side of the Vatican Palace to the Villa Belvedere on the brow of Monte San Egidio (Fig. 10). The slope of the hill was terraced in three levels, and the east and west sides of the court were enclosed and defined by long corridors of arcaded loggias opening into the court. These loggias have been likened functionally and perhaps formally to the cryptoporticus lining Pliny's hippodrome garden at the Tuscan villa.[1] The stories of loggias at the Vatican diminished in relation to the terraces from three stories flanking the lowest terrace to one at the top. The north end of the court was closed by a one-story wall with a great semicircular exedra in the center at the end of the axis from the palace. An unusual flight of stairs, the lower half convex and the upper concave, was set into the exedra through whose arcaded rear wall one could glimpse the statue garden court behind, as seen in a drawing in Francisco d'Ollanda's sketchbook.[2] The northern wall also masked at the right the old Villa Belvedere set askew to the axis of the new court (Fig. 6). The lowest terrace of the court was the theatrical area, reviving the idea in the fifteenth-century plan of Nicholas V to have a theater at the Vatican set in a garden. The entertainment could be viewed by the pope and his immediate courtiers from the windows of the palace, while the other spectators could use as seats the gigantic flight of steps mounting from the lowest level to the middle level or watch from the side loggias. The upper two terraces were to be formal gardens with box-outlined parterres and fountains. Two double-ramped flights of stairs led from the middle terrace to the upper one with a deep niche set into the center of the retaining wall between the stairs.

For the first time since antiquity an Italian architect was concerned with exterior, spatial organization on a grandiose scale with the additional difficulty of the hillside terrain. It was in comparable examples of ancient Roman planning, as in the "Stadium of Domitian" of the Palace of the Caesars on the Palatine Hill and in the sanctuary at Palestrina, that Bramante found his inspiration. Palestrina contributed the idea of terraces connected by gigantic stairways, but more important was the "Stadium of Domitian," which was apparently a long garden court enclosed by arcaded porticoes. Contemporary visitors realized that Bramante and the pope were emulating one of the main features of the ancient Palace of the Caesars as a propagandistic announcement of the power of the papacy of Julius II, whereby the Vatican Palace of the popes superseded the palace of the ancient Roman emperors.[3] Unlike the ancient garden, Bramante laid out the great architectural space of the Belvedere Court on the basis of the Renaissance invention of linear perspective. Sixteenth-century drawings and prints reveal that the loggias flanking the second terrace were never decorated with classical orders or other architectural detail unlike those of the other two terraces.[4] Those loggias of the second terrace were not visible from the south or palace end of the central axis at the level of the papal apartment because of the two towers flanking the monumental stairs. The entire design was, therefore, conceived in linear perspective like a Renaissance painting from a single viewpoint through a window in the papal apartment of the palace.

At Bramante's death in 1514 the terrain was organized and the long eastern side and northern end completed. For the next half century the work would continue sporadically and slowly. Early in the papacy of Julius III (1550–1555) the first major change was made by raising the northern end wall a second story, closing the rear arcade of the exedra, and substituting for Bramante's unusual stairs a double flight of stairs designed by Michelangelo. With the accession of Pope Pius IV (1559–1565) a concerted campaign to complete the court was undertaken. The palace architect Pirro Ligorio began the work in 1561 with two major changes to the original design of Bramante (Fig. 44). At the south end of the court under the Vatican Palace, Ligorio introduced a semicircular auditorium of stone seats as in a Roman theater. He also vaulted the exedra at the northern end of the court, transforming it into the Nicchione, or great niche, and built on top of the niche a semicircular loggia. As a contemporary print shows, the terrace above the Nicchione was used for the exhibition of spectacular fireworks at any festival. The court was basically completed in time to celebrate the wedding of Annibale Altemps, nephew of the pope, to Ortensia Borromeo, niece of the pope and sister of Cardinal Carlo

[1] J. S. Ackerman, *The Cortile del Belvedere* (Studi e documenti per la storia del Palazzo Apostolico Vaticano, III), Vatican City, 1954, p. 131.

[2] E. Tormo, ed., *Os desenhos das antigualhas que vio Francesco d'Ollanda, pintor portugués (1539–1540)*, Madrid, 1940, fol. 19v.

[3] B. Lowry, review of *The Cortile del Belvedere*, by J. S. Ackerman, *Art Bulletin*, XXXIX, 1957, p. 160.

[4] Ackerman, *The Cortile del Belvedere*, pp. 24–25, 122–25.

44. Rome, Vatican Palace, Belvedere Court, engraving, 1565, Avery Architectural and Fine Arts Library, Columbia University

Borromeo, with a magnificent tournament in the theatrical court on March 5, 1565. Unfortunately the Belvedere Court only survived about twenty more years in its original conception, for the library of Pope Sixtus V was set on the middle terrace, disrupting the great spatial sweep through the court. Many sixteenth-century drawings and prints, however, preserve different stages of the construction and final creation. Already in the Van Cleef engraving of 1550 and the Dosio drawing of about 1561 (Fig. 10), the upper terrace of the court is planted as a formal garden. Cross alleys divide the terrace into four large compartments with a circular fountain basin at the crossing of the alleys. Each of the compartments is in turn composed of four rectangular garden beds with a line of trees along the outer, eastern edge of the garden. The Cartaro engraving of 1574 depicts the completed court with more detail, although the viewpoint from the eastern side does not correspond to the intended perspectival point of view (Fig. 6). Again the upper terrace has the fountain in the center with four large, rectangular garden beds around it. Each bed is outlined by a low hedge, presumably of box, and its innermost corner is cut away by a circular segment to permit a wide, circular alley around the fountain. Within the border each bed is also divided into four rectangular garden beds. None of the prints and drawings can be fully trusted as to the accuracy of the garden details since most artists had an individual formula for such depictions, but the Cartaro print because of its greater detail may be somewhat more accurate.

Actually each of the upper terraces of the Belvedere Court adheres in its garden design to the old formula of the hortus conclusus. In fact, the entire court might be considered as composed of the juxtaposition of a palace courtyard and two such horti conclusi. The totality, however, is entirely different, primarily because the gardens are terraced on a hillside and unified by the perspective point of view. The mid-fifteenth-century Medici garden at Fiesole was likewise terraced on a hillside, but its terraced gardens remained individual, walled-in units. Two other late fifteenth-century gardens began to approach the concept of the architectural garden of the Belvedere Court. Insofar as can be determined from descriptions and scant depictions, the gardens of the Villa at Poggioreale near Naples had a continuity of perspective somewhat analogous to the Belvedere, but it is extremely unlikely that Bramante had ever seen them or knew much about them. The lower court and terraced garden behind the

Della Rovere Palace in the Vatican Borgo (Fig. 5) was undoubtedly known by Bramante and may have played a minor role in his conception of the Belvedere Court, but those terraces remained independent of one another with no physical access between them, and they lacked the breadth of scope and grandeur of space that was so overwhelming in the Belvedere Court. Bramante's concept was determined by the physical terrain where he built and by his assimilation of ancient Roman spatial design. In fact, the architectural garden of the Belvedere Court is really the first Renaissance garden of Rome, and many of the major sixteenth-century gardens of Rome will be influenced by it.

The first Roman garden layout to reflect Bramante's design was that intended to complement the Villa Madama on Monte Mario just north of the Vatican, designed by the painter Raphael for Cardinal Giulio de' Medici, later Pope Clement VII. More important, both villa and gardens have many design elements derived from Pliny the Younger's descriptions of his villas. Begun about 1518, work on the Villa Madama was continued by Raphael's assistants after his death in 1520. In addition to the temporary interruption during the papacy of Hadrian VI, the construction of the villa and its gardens was permanently interrupted by the Sack of Rome in 1527, with completion of only the northern half of the villa and gardens. Raphael in a letter describing his plans for the villa concentrates on the architecture and says very little about the gardens.[5] Next to the entrance court at the southeast end of the villa he planned a small giardino segreto with orange trees (*melangoli*), a central fountain, and a winter loggia at the end next to the building. This garden facing southeast and protected by its enclosing walls would be most suitable for use during cool weather, but like the remaining half of the villa toward the southeast it was never constructed. At the other end of the villa toward the northwest the principal garden (*xystus*) planted with "trees arranged in ordered ranks" opened off the great loggia on that side of the villa. A huge fishpool surrounded by steps for sitting and relaxing ran parallel to the garden at a lower level on the hillside so that one could look down upon it from the garden. This garden with its wonderful prospect across the Tiber and Ponte Milvio toward Mount Soracte was, of course, for summer use. A similar concern for sea-

[5] P. Foster, "Raphael on the Villa Madama: The Text of a Lost Letter," *Römisches Jahrbuch für Kunstgeschichte*, XI, 1967–1968, pp. 307–12.

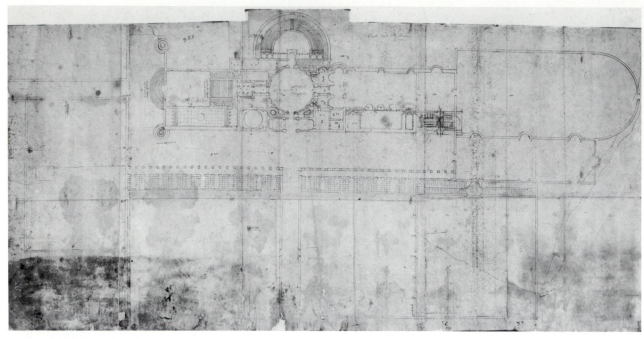

45. Rome, Villa Madama, plan, Uffizi 314A

sonal use of gardens occurs also in Pliny's letters. These are the only gardens mentioned by Raphael in his letter, which he concludes: "Your Lordship can imagine that the grounds of this villa are flanked with trees, such as is suitable for such a building, but I shall not take the trouble to write [about them]."

The design of the principal garden running across the hillside from the main loggia and with the fishpool parallel to the garden at a lower level corresponds rather closely to the design of the gardens of the fifteenth-century Villa Medici at Fiesole except that the fishpool replaces a second garden at Fiesole. To this degree Raphael's garden at Rome may have been suggested by the wishes of the patron and reveals no influence of Bramante's design of the Belvedere Court. In fact, Raphael's letter dating before 1520 suggests that at that stage the only gardens planned for the villa were the giardino segreto and the treed xystus with the fishpool. There are, however, several drawings by Antonio da Sangallo the Younger and his relatives for further gardens related to the villa. At least some of these date after Raphael's death and may correspond to the campaign in 1524 and 1525 when Sangallo was paid for work on fountains there.[6] One early drawing, Uffizi 314A, delineates the entire com-

[6] C. L. Frommel, "Die Architektonische Planung der Villa Madama," *Römisches Jahrbuch für Kunstgeschichte*, XV, 1975, p. 82.

plex (Fig. 45). Beyond the xystus and on axis with it across the hillside, Sangallo adds another square, walled-in garden and then a long hippodrome-shaped garden area in the manner of Pliny's Tuscan villa. Another drawing, Uffizi 789A, which is certainly after 1520, identifies the planting. The hippodrome was to be a wooded area with pines and chestnut trees (*locho p li habeti et castagni*), while a walled garden of orange trees (*aranci*) was to be terraced below the hippodrome, and further down the hillside was to be a large formal garden with numerous square beds, perhaps to contain flowers.

The most impressive drawing for the gardens, Uffizi 1356A, depicts three great terraces of different shapes connected by large flights of stairs (Fig. 46). This drawing must be the project for a monumental entranceway that was to be terraced up the hillside from the road below, which ran across the Prati from the Ponte Milvio to the Vatican Borgo, probably to the great entrance court at the southeast end of the villa. As that portion of the villa was never constructed after Raphael's death, neither was the entranceway. The first terrace is a rectangle, about 134 meters wide (60 canne) by 67 meters deep (30 canne), with great semicircular ends and a long flight of stairs against the inner wall on each side up to the next terrace. At the centers on which the semicircular ends

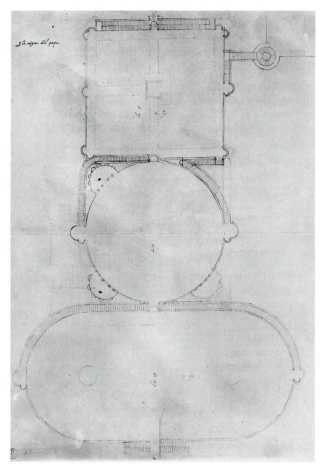

46. Rome, Villa Madama, plan of entrance stairs, Uffizi 1356A

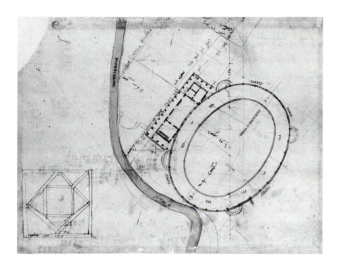

47. Salone, Villa Trivulziana, plan, Uffizi 453A

are constructed were to be round basins or fountains. The middle terrace was circular, about 67 meters in diameter (30 canne), with great niches on the diagonal axes, a circular fountain basin in the center and alternate proposals for stairs along the rear wall to the uppermost terrace, which is square with a double flight of stairs at each side of its rear wall. This last terrace was to contain four garden beds around a square basin. The design of a sequence of terraced gardens in varying forms connected by monumental stairways is obviously derived from Bramante's plan for the Belvedere Court, as are also the smaller stairs just outside of the entrance court of Sangallo's plan for the Villa, Uffizi 314A, which are derived from the unusual stairs in the exedra of Bramante's court. If carried out the project would have provided a most impressive approach to the villa set on the wooded hillside of Monte Mario. The most notable feature of all of the ideas for developing the gardens about the

villa is the skill with which the classical forms have been adapted to the natural terrain and the functions that they were to perform, from the overwhelming entranceway up the hill through the series of architectural and landscaped spaces across the hill to the privacy of the naturalistic nymphaeum.

A contemporary drawing, Uffizi 453A, by the architect Baldassare Peruzzi (Fig. 47) for another cardinalate villa, that of Cardinal Agostino Trivulzio at Salone about six and a half miles outside of Rome on the Via Collatina, may also reflect Pliny's description of his Tuscan villa, although less obviously than at the Villa Madama. A long, narrow casino is set along the northern side of a garden with the casino's central loggia facing south onto the garden, as was Pliny's villa. The garden in front of the cardinal's villa has the very unusual shape of an oval with an alley (*via*) encircling the planted area labeled by Peruzzi as "garden or vineyard" (*giardino o vigna*). A continuous row of trees lines the outer edge of the alley. The river Erculaneo, identified by Peruzzi as the "river of Salone," flows by one end of the garden and casino to empty later into the river Tiber pursuing its course into Rome. So Pliny's Tuscan villa was set above the Tiber "which flows through the middle of the meadows" and was oriented with the principal part of the house facing south. In front of the portico of Pliny's villa was a garden with "an alley in the form of a circus [*in modum circi*] which encircles various figures of boxwood and trimmed dwarf shrubs. . . . Beyond is a meadow no less worth seeing for its nature as those described above are for their art."[7]

7 For Pliny's Latin text, see Pliny, *Letters and Panegyricus* (Loeb

Normally the word "circus" used by Pliny to describe the shape of the garden in front of the villa is understood as a Latin equivalent of the Greek hippodrome or racing stadium. Later in the same letter, however, Pliny actually uses the term hippodrome to describe the form of another garden there. The fact that Pliny seems to use the two words as describing different forms and identifies an alley as encircling the planted area (*gestatio in modum circi . . . circumit*) may have caused Peruzzi to introduce the oval in his project for Cardinal Trivulzio's garden. Some thirty years later the Sienese architect Pietro Cataneo, who was probably a pupil of Peruzzi, noted that for games there could be "some other similar buildings of oval form, which in Rome was the Circus Maximus."[8]

The date 1525 inscribed on the casino may identify the basic completion of the present building, although it seems to be still not fully completed, but the casino differs distinctly from the one in Peruzzi's drawing probably drawn about 1523. There is likewise no evidence that the garden was ever created in the form proposed by Peruzzi.

Another mode of casting a classical aura over Roman Renaissance gardens was by their association with the physical remains of Roman antiquity. Already in the late Middle Ages the Colonna family had apparently planted a garden sometimes known as the "Garden of the Tower of Nero," on the steep slope of the side of the Quirinal Hill among the ruins of the ancient Temple of Serapis behind their palace. The location of their garden was undoubtedly conditioned by the site of their palace with no idea of any significance in their association with the ancient site. By the fifteenth century, however, as noted previously,[9] Flavio Biondo identified the Colonna gardens with those of Maecenas, the great patron of the Augustan era, whose gardens were located in this area.

By the mid-sixteenth century there was a more conscious selection of ancient sites as a frame for gardens. So, in February 1547, Monsignore Euralio Silvestri, chamberlain of Pope Paul III, was granted permission from the city to expand the gardens of his small vigna located on the slope of the Esquiline Hill behind the Basilica of Maxentius (Fig. 48) onto "the upper parts of which are the terrace of the arches of the Temple of Peace [i.e., the Basilica of Maxentius] near to the church of Santa Maria Nova and to his gardens."[10] Bufalini's map of Rome of 1551 offers a rough diagrammatic plan of the L-shaped casino, sometimes attributed to Antonio da Sangallo the Younger,[11] situated on a small hill (*monticello*), composed in part by the ruins of an ancient Roman house and in part by nature, behind the basilica, which at this time was almost half buried. After the death of Silvestri, his nephews and heirs in 1567 sold lifetime rights to the vigna to Alessandro de' Medici, who became archbishop of Florence in 1574, cardinal in 1583, and Pope Leo XI in 1605 for less than one month, but who had already in 1591 given the vigna to the Colonna in exchange for their "Palace of the Elm" behind the church of the SS. Apostoli. The casino has survived many changes, but a good portion of the gardens was destroyed in 1932 when the new Via dell'Impero, now the Via dei Fori Imperiali, was cut through behind the basilica.[12]

The permission granted to Silvestri in 1547 to expand his garden to the top of the Basilica of Maxentius was to permit the half-buried building to serve as a monumental backdrop to the garden and to furnish a terraced garden on the upper part of the basilica with a superb vista over the Forum below. Unfortunately there are no clear accounts or depictions to indicate how much was accomplished during the lifetime of Silvestri. Baglione in his later life of Giacomo del Duca claims that the design of the garden was begun by Del Duca, but this could be either for Silvestri or for Cardinal de' Medici.[13] By 1550, however, when Aldrovandi prepared his survey of ancient sculpture at Rome, Silvestri had a very notable collection in his casino and garden, most of which remained during the occupancy of the cardinal, who also expanded the collection. In 1591 when the Colonna received the vigna an inventory listed a small garden with a "feminine statue lying above the fountain," presumably another example of the fountain of the sleeping

---

Classical Library), London and Cambridge, Mass., 1969, I, pp. 336–54. This interpretation of Pliny's oval garden was made earlier by K. Schwager, "Kardinal Pietro Aldobrandinis Villa di Belvedere in Frascati," *Römisches Jahrbuch für Kunstgeschichte*, IX–X, 1961–1962, p. 365, n. 305. For bibliography on the villa, see D. R. Coffin, *The Villa in the Life of Renaissance Rome*, Princeton, N.J., 1979, pp. 265–67.

[8] P. Cataneo, *I Quattro Primi Libri di Architettura*, Venice, 1554, p. 9 recto as 12 recto.

[9] See Chapter 1.

[10] R. Lanciani, *Storia degli scavi di Roma*, II, Rome, 1903, p. 210.

[11] G. Giovannoni, *Antonio da Sangallo il giovane*, Rome, n.d., I, pp. 291–94.

[12] A. Muñoz, *Via dei Monti e Via del Mare*, 2nd ed., Rome, 1932, pp. 31–32.

[13] G. Baglione, *Le vite de pittori, scultori, et architetti*, Rome, 1642, p. 52, and J. Hess, "Villa Lante di Bagnaia e Giacomo del Duca," *Palatino*, X, 1966, pp. 28–31.

48. Rome, Vigna Silvestri, engraving

nymph.[14] Beyond a staircase led to the larger garden with ancient reliefs set into the back wall of the basilica, several grottoes also with bas-reliefs, and a low stone bench against the wall with more reliefs serving as a back. A statue of Jupiter stood above the garden portal and one area of the garden was wooded. Two sixteenth-century inscriptions at the vigna recorded in the time of Pope Sixtus V (1585–1590) informed the visitor that it was a healthy, quiet retreat where no cares should intrude.[15]

The map of Rome drawn by Falda in 1676 (Fig. 49) and old photographs of the garden before its destruction reveal that there was a smaller, presumably more formal garden directly behind the casino with the larger garden area beyond ending against the southern half of the rear of the basilica. The ground level of this larger garden was about halfway up the height of the partially buried basilica so that the great arched windows at the rear of the building permitted views out into the Forum and across to the Farnese gardens created in the 1570s on the Palatine Hill. The Falda map also depicts a garden on top of the vaults of the basilica, which remained there until 1828, and must have been accessible by a stairway in the garden behind the basilica.[16] Silvestri and the succeeding owners, therefore, took full advantage of the colossal remains of the ancient monument to create a setting for a series of garden terraces with a spectacular vista.

In April 1549, two years after Silvestri was given permission to expand his gardens upon the basilica, another member of the papal court, Monsignore Francesco Soderini, who owned the remains of the

49. Rome, Falda map of 1676, detail with Vigna Silvestri

ancient Mausoleum of Augustus near the Tiber in the area of the Campus Martius, was given permission to excavate there.[17] During the Middle Ages the Colonna family had transformed the massive ruins of the tumulus into a fortress, as the papacy had converted the Mausoleum of Hadrian into the Castel Sant'Angelo, but the Colonna stronghold was dismantled by the papacy in the thirteenth century. Sanuto reports in 1519 that little was left because of the avarice of "the priests and Romans" for antiquities, adding that its present owner, the brother of Cardinal Orsini, had put the final touch to its destruction by removing all the marble revetment.[18] In his pillage he

[14] Lanciani, *Storia degli scavi di Roma*, II, pp. 215–16.

[15] R. Lanciani, "Il codice barberiniano XXX, 89 contenente frammenti di una descrizione di Roma del secolo XVI," *Archivio della società romana di storia patria*, VI, 1883, pp. 473–74, 481–82.

[16] G. Incisa della Rocchetta, "Il Palazzo ed il giardino del Pio Istituto Rivaldi," *Capitolium*, IX, 1933, p. 220.

[17] F. Cerasoli, "Documenti inediti medievali circa le Terme di Diocleziano ed il Mausoleo di Augusto," *Bullettino della commissione archeologica comunale di Roma*, XXIII, 1895, pp. 306–8.

[18] M. Sanuto, *I diarii di Marino Sanuto*, XXVII, Venice, 1890, cols. 470–71.

50. Rome, Soderini Garden, engraving, 1575

had uncovered the foundations and a broken obelisk, which the painter Raphael had suggested might be placed in the Piazza of St. Peter's. Monsignore Soderini's request in 1549 to excavate the ruins then owned by him was not only for the discovery of antiquities, but to prepare a statue garden there. Already on April 6 Busini reports to Varchi: "I am writing this letter to you in the middle of the Tomb of Augustus in the Campus Martius, which my Monsignore has undertaken to redo, and he has transformed it into a rather lovely garden with some rooms there for eating, and this is his pastime. This place, called the mausoleum," he remarks perhaps jokingly, "is now a vegetable garden and there are some fine salad greens there."[19]

Already by 1550 when Aldrovandi made his survey of Roman statues, Soderini had a collection of antiquities in his garden, although not very notable as many of the figural pieces were headless and others were relief fragments built into the wall of the mausoleum; however, Aldrovandi claims that a group of Pasquino embracing Antheus was praised by Michelangelo. Aldrovandi also offers an idea of the location of some of the pieces, noting that a large sarcophagus, presumably with "a triumph of Amor," stood before

the entrance portal and that above the portal was "a large head with open mouth," that is, a theatrical mask. One of the whole statues, a figure of Abundance, stood "in a room of the Mausoleum." A sixteenth-century drawing, Uffizi 1751A,[20] and engravings by Dupérac (1575) and Giovannoli (1619) depict Soderini's garden (Fig. 50). The principal, extant part of the mausoleum was the tall, massive, circular wall of the tumulus, about eighty-eight meters in diameter. On the exterior, flanking the entrance portal toward the church of S. Rocco, were two small dwellings or rooms projecting from the circular wall, one with a terraced roof garden and pergola. In front of the rusticated portal was the large sarcophagus recorded by Aldrovandi, flanked by two freestanding statues. Flights of stairs between the statues and projecting rooms led up to the landing in front of the portal. Above the portal was the large theatrical mask mentioned by Aldrovandi. By this time the idea of a mask or head above a garden entrance as a sort of protective or tutelary goddess had apparently become another garden topos. So at the Vigna Carpi on the Quirinal Hill a gigantic Medusa head stood above the entrance portal to the outer cortile of the vigna and in the Cesi gardens a large, ancient marble mask was over the interior side of the portal leading from the

---

[19] B. Varchi, *Opere di Benedetto Varchi*, I, Milan, n.d., p. 497, no. XX.

[20] H. Egger, *Römische Veduten*, I, Vienna, n.d., pl. 7.

large, formal garden into the giardino segreto. In other examples, Jupiter was the guardian. In fact, at the Cesi gardens, in addition to the mask facing toward the giardino segreto, a bust of Jupiter was placed above the portal facing the larger garden, and at the Vigna Silvestri a full figure of Jupiter with his lightning bolt stood above the garden portal. Theatrical masks, however, had earlier another association with Renaissance Roman gardens. Some time before Fichard's visit to Rome in 1536 thirteen ancient masks were mounted on the walls of the Belvedere Statue Court in the Vatican,[21] and in Cardinal della Valle's sculptural garden five huge, theatrical masks adorned the uppermost level of each of the long side walls of the court alternating with the inscriptions (Fig. 14). These masks must not have served so much as protective, tutelary spirits like the single ones above the portals of the other gardens, but were probably intended to endow the gardens with the spirit of pleasurable recreation also enunciated in the adjacent inscriptions in Della Valle's garden.

Within the great circular wall of the mausoleum Soderini planted a formal garden. The interior surface of the wall was covered with espaliered trees and vines among which were set a few statues or sarcophagi, while a niche at the rear opposite the entrance contained another statue. The garden beds were arranged in two concentric circles with eight beds in the exterior ring and four in the inner one, each bed surrounded by a low hedge with a taller evergreen at the corners as an accent. Other than the exterior edging, the planting of each bed is unknown, but may have contained flowers and herbs.

In the eighteenth century the garden of the mausoleum was completely destroyed when its owners, the Corea family, transformed it into a theater and circus building.[22] Serving as a concert hall in the early twentieth century, the mausoleum was again excavated in the 1930s and left as an archaeological monument.

The most accomplished conversion of an ancient monument into a garden was that of the French cardinal Du Bellay. Jean Du Bellay, bishop of Paris, first arrived in Rome on a brief embassy in the spring of 1534 accompanied by the writer François Rabelais as his secretary. During his brief stay at Rome the bishop purchased a small vigna near the church of S. Lorenzo in Panisperna on the Viminal Hill and became a passionate seeker of classical antiquities as revealed in a letter addressed to him by Rodolfo Pio, the future Cardinal of Carpi, on Du Bellay's return to Paris.[23] In the following year, 1535, Du Bellay was made a cardinal and remained in Rome for most of the rest of his life except for the period 1550 to 1553 when he was in disfavor at the court of Paris and retired to his French chateau at St. Maur whose gardens were decorated with some of his extensive collection of Roman antiquities. Meanwhile, in 1536 Du Bellay's friend, Rodolfi Pio, was also appointed a cardinal and in the 1540s developed his great vigna on the Quirinal Hill with its notable collection of ancient statues, which may have inspired Cardinal Du Bellay after his return to Rome in 1553 to a similar enterprise.

Therefore, in 1554 the cardinal was granted by the friars of Sta. Maria del Popolo the land on the Viminal Hill just southwest of the towering ruins of the main halls of the ancient Baths of Diocletian where were the remains of the exterior precinct walls and secondary rooms of the complex of the baths. These remains consisted primarily of the southwest exterior wall of the complex, about 350 meters in length, with two round towers at its ends and in the center opposite the entrance to the baths a huge, walled exedra about 150 meters in diameter. Of these the cardinal was given the land that included the exedra and the northern tower, which was almost opposite the church of Sta. Susanna on the old street, called the Alta Semita, later the Via Pia, which ran along the crest of the nearby Quirinal Hill, where the cardinal's colleague, Cardinal Carpi, had already laid out his vigna. A drawing attributed to Dosio, Uffizi 2547A, depicts the ancient walls and exedra before they were converted by Cardinal Du Bellay into a garden.[24]

Since the garden is now completely destroyed and only preserved in the slight depictions on maps of Rome, it is impossible to determine with accuracy how much of the garden complex consisted of new construction and how much was merely a refurbishing of the ancient structure. The clearest depiction of

[21] H. H. Brummer, *The Statue Court in the Vatican Belvedere* (Stockholm Studies in the History of Art, 20), Stockholm, 1970, p. 41 and figs. 22–32.

[22] "La trasformazione dell'Augusteo," *Capitolium*, I, 1925–1926, pp. 24–27.

[23] Regarding the vigna, see A. Huelhard, *Rabelais, ses voyages en Italie, son exil à Metz*, Paris, 1891, pp. 34, 74, and R. Scheurer, *Correspondance du Cardinal Jean du Bellay*, I, Paris, 1969, p. 417, letter of Rabelais to Du Bellay, dated August 31, 1534; and for the letter of Pio, see ibid., p. 402, dated July 2, 1534.

[24] A. Bartoli, *Cento vedute di Roma antica*, Florence, 1911, pl. LXXVII, and C. Bernardo Salvetti, "Il sottosuolo delle terme di Diocleziano nel sec. XVI nei disegni della Biblioteca d'Arte nel Museo di Stato di Berlino," *Studi romani*, XVIII, 1970, pl. LXXIII.

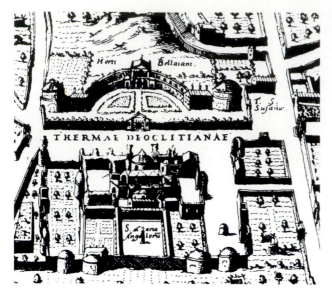

51. Rome, Dupérac map of 1577, detail with Du Bellay Gardens

52. Rome, Du Bellay Gardens, drawing by Dosio, Uffizi 2573A

the garden is on Dupérac's map of 1577 looking from the baths toward the entrance of the gardens (Fig. 51). Projecting from the two round towers at the ends of the complex were two short side walls, which were joined together by a long wall closing the front of the garden. In the center of the front wall was a rusticated portal flanked by windows all topped by a triangular pediment. On the exterior entablature of the entrance portal was the identifying inscription *Horti Bellaiani*, while a dedicatory inscription on the interior of the portal read: *Inchoabat Io. C. Host. E. Sibi Et Amicis. MDLV* ("Cardinal Jean, bishop of Ostia, began this for himself and his friends, 1555"). Along the upper part of the long front wall were set a series of windows visible in another drawing attributed to Dosio, Uffizi 2573A (Fig. 52).[25] In the northern end wall of the complex was a smaller, rusticated portal opening onto the Quirinal. The end round towers were domed and the one at the northern end that was ceded to the cardinal may have served as a chapel, since the tower already contained the cult objects stored there by Don Antonio Lo Duca when he had earlier been forced by Pope Julius III to leave the baths of Diocletian. Duca had long wished to establish a church in the ruins of the Baths, but his desire would only be fulfilled in the papacy of Pius IV who commissioned Michelangelo to transform part of the ancient ruins into the church of Sta. Maria degli Angeli.

At the back of the great exedra on axis with the entrance portal the cardinal built a small, two-story casino, whose facade was apparently flanked by two one-story, domed pavilions. The ground floor of the facade of the casino consisted of a loggia of three arches with another loggia in the form of a *serliana* above it. The exedra was also in two stories, of which the upper one was an ambulatory with small windows opening into the garden. Between the northern end of the exedra and the northern tower was built a small, two-story residence. The ambulatory of the exedra, therefore, furnished interior communication between the central casino and the buildings to the north. The principal garden was planted in the curve of the exedra, although the Dupérac view also shows the tops of trees projecting above the entrance wall.

In the garden and the casino the cardinal assembled a large collection of statues in whose inventory made at his death in 1560 are listed thirty-three life-size statues or statuettes and about one hundred busts or heads.[26] Boissard in his description of the garden made soon after its establishment divides the major pieces of sculpture into two groups. Figures of Jupiter, Apollo, Orpheus, Minerva, Bellona, Vertumnus, and Antinous with other deities and famous men stood on bases in the alleys of the garden or along the exedra wall, while other statues and busts were in the casino and the upper ambulatory.[27] Although there is no mention of fountains, the inventory of 1560 records "two river gods for a fountain for throwing water" and "a Venus for a fountain for throwing water." Boissard also notes that the walls of the exedra and the precinct were espaliered with pomegranate and

[25] Bartoli, *Cento vedute*, pl. LXXVI, and Bernardo Salvetti, *Studi romani*, pl. LXXIV.

[26] A. Bertolotti, *Artisti francesi in Roma nei secoli XV, XVI, e XVII*, Mantua, 1886, pp. 40–44.

[27] J. J. Boissard, *Romanae Vrbis Topographiae*, n.p., 1597, pt. 1, p. 90 and pls. 120–31.

orange trees, with citrons, cypresses, myrtle, and laurel "in the form of a tapestry" and that the garden was provided with every type of plant.

Although the horticultural and decorative features of the garden of Cardinal Du Bellay belong to the traditional *giardino segreto* type of sculptural garden, the setting of the ancient ruins of the exedra imposed a new frame for the garden. Du Bellay's garden may be the first Roman one to have its name, *Horti Bellaiani*, inscribed on its entrance portal.[28] To a sixteenth-century visitor this inscription would recall the names of the ancient Roman gardens, the *Horti Aciliani*, the *Horti Sallustiani*, and the *Horti Luculliani* on the nearby Pincian Hill or *Collis Hortulorum*, which had been embellished by their owners with rich collections of art. It may not be accidental that on Pirro Ligorio's small map of ancient Rome, published in 1553, just before Cardinal Du Bellay began his garden,[29] the *Horti Aciliani* are depicted with a great exedra and wings very like the *Horti Bellaiani*. In this early depiction by Ligorio of the *Horti Aciliani*, he has not depicted the great flights of stairs leading up to the exedra so that its analogy to the Du Bellay gardens is closer than in later depictions.

On February 16, 1560, Cardinal Du Bellay died at his gardens. Immediately his heirs leased the gardens to Cardinal Carlo Borromeo, but as Du Bellay at his death was seriously in debt Cardinal Borromeo agreed in 1565 to purchase the property for 8,000 scudi.[30] Borromeo, however, could not afford the purchase, so in November 1565 his uncle, Pope Pius IV, completed the purchase, giving the property to the Carthusians of nearby Sta. Maria degli Angeli.[31] By 1579 Cardinal Alessandro Sforza was in possession of the gardens. In 1593 his sister-in-law, the countess di Santa Fiora, bought the property for 10,000 scudi and between 1594 and 1596 converted Du Bellay's casino at the rear of the exedra into a small church dedicated to St. Catherine of Alexandria. Between

1598 and 1600 the ancient round tower at the northern end of the property, which may have been Du Bellay's chapel, was transformed into the present church of S. Bernardo alle Terme. Finally in 1885 the Via Nazionale was cut through the center of the exedra at the location of Du Bellay's casino and the church of Sta. Caterina, and the area of the exedra, which had contained his gardens, became the present Piazza dell'Esedra.

The last important Roman garden to rely on antique remains was that created for Cardinal Alessandro Farnese on the Palatine Hill overlooking the ancient Forum. Once the site of the luxurious, sprawling palaces of the Roman emperors, the Palatine Hill had been abandoned in the Middle Ages so that Andrea Fulvio in 1527 could remark that it had reverted to the condition at the time of ancient King Evander, being deserted except for vineyards, orchards, and animals at pasture.[32] As early as January 1542 Marc Antonio Palosci had sold to Cardinal Farnese for 1,200 scudi a vigna on the northern slope of the Palatine, including "grottoes, buildings, figural reliefs, and marble and stone statues."[33] A small casino at the western end of the vigna is seen in several prints and photographs before its destruction in 1883 (Fig. 53). While the upper story of the building is probably seventeenth-century, the ground floor and mezzanine seem early sixteenth-century and presumably predate the Farnese acquisition. In the following year the cardinal presented the property to his brother Ottavio, duke of Parma, and it was so depicted on Bufalini's map of Rome of 1551.[34] Surprisingly, Bufalini's map suggests that the Ducal vigna also covered most of the upper flat plateau of the hill, which according to documents was owned at this time by the Mantaco family and purchased by the Farnese only in 1579. It may be, however, that the documents are missing regarding a temporary, earlier leasing of the property by the Farnese. A road from the Arch of Titus, probably at the location of the present Via di S. Bonaventura, led up the northern slope of the Palatine, and part way up the slope a path at the right gave access to the Vigna Farnese, which on Bufalini's map is a large rectangular area. The northeastern portion of the vigna is depicted by Bufalini as containing a strange pattern of irregular, curvilinear paths, while the remainder is

[28] The nearby vigna of Cardinal Carpi on the Quirinal had its name, *Horti Pii Carpensis*, also inscribed on its gateway on the Via Pia, but the gateway must date after 1560 when Pope Pius IV straightened and widened the old Alta Semita into the Via Pia. The fact that contemporary documents generally describe Carpi's possession as a "vigna" and Du Bellay's as a "giardino" may confirm the different meanings associated with them.

[29] A. P. Frutaz, ed., *Le piante di Roma*, Rome, 1962, II, pl. 25.

[30] S. Merkle, ed., *Concilii Tridentini diariorum, actorum, epistularum, tractatum*, II, pt. 2, Freiburg, 1911, p. 533.

[31] For documentation of the vicissitudes of the gardens after the Cardinal's death, see S. Ortolani, *S. Bernardo alle Terme*, Rome, n.d.

[32] A. Fulvio, *Antiqvitates Vrbis*, Rome, 1527, fol. xxvr.

[33] For most of the documentation, see H. Giess, "Studien zur Farnese-Villa am Palatin," *Römisches Jahrbuch für Kunstgeschichte*, XIII, 1971, pp. 179–230.

[34] Frutaz, *Piante*, II, pl. 203.

53. Rome, Farnese Gardens, engraving

cut up into large, rectangular plots. Certainly the vigna and its gardens were developed sufficiently to offer a pleasant setting for an afternoon outing, since in June 1552 after his return from Florence Cardinal Alessandro Farnese held a banquet there with much "laughter, jests and buffoonry."[35] Similarly there is a payment in December 1554 for food for a small party "at the vigna called La Paloscia."[36] By 1557 a Roman guidebook mentions the "very lovely vigna" owned there by Cardinal Sant'Angelo, that is, Cardinal Ranuccio Farnese, younger brother of Duke Ottavio and Cardinal Alessandro. In 1564 an account for some carpentry work at the vigna offers a slight hint of its condition. There was a small house, presumably the old casino at the northwest end, and stairs up to a *tribuna*, probably a belvedere, covered by a wooden dome. Fourteen wickets (*sportelli*) served as entrances to the small gardens (*orticelli*) and among the trees there was at least one mulberry tree and an elm wood, which had an espaliered pergola.

A year later, in May 1565, just before his death, Cardinal Ranuccio expanded the vigna by purchasing for 400 scudi the small Villa Maddaleni between his property and the Forum on the lower edge of the

north slope of the Palatine Hill. With this purchase the Farnese controlled the entire northern slope west of the Arch of Titus and the Via di S. Bonaventura. With the death of Cardinal Ranuccio, the Palatine vigna reverted to his elder brother, Cardinal Alessandro, who had made the first purchase of land in 1542.

Unfortunately the documentation for the Farnese garden is very scant, and there is no exact evidence as to when the new garden was commenced, except that it occurred in the decade after the acquisition of the Vigna Maddalena in 1565. The earliest record of the garden is a brief glimpse of it on the large Cartaro map of Rome of 1576,[37] depicting the front wall with its entrance portal and tower pavilion in the northeast corner (Fig. 54). A document of July 1577 compares the cost of the travertine for the portal and windows with that of material for work at the Campidoglio, suggesting that the refashioning of the garden was recent and began probably shortly before Cartaro's 1576 map.[38] Although the Cartaro map offers very little evidence regarding the appearance of the new garden, the Dupérac map of Rome a year later (1577) depicts the garden on the slope in its completed form except for the pavilion at the northwest corner (Fig.

[35] L. Romier, *Les origines politiques des guerres de religion*, I, Paris, 1913, p. 298.

[36] Giess, "Farnese-Villa," p. 223.

[37] Frutaz, *Piante*, pl. 238.

[38] P. Pecchiai, *Campidoglio nel Cinquecento*, Rome, 1950, p. 253.

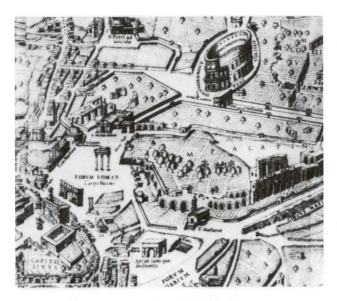

54. Rome, Cartaro map of 1576, detail of Farnese Gardens

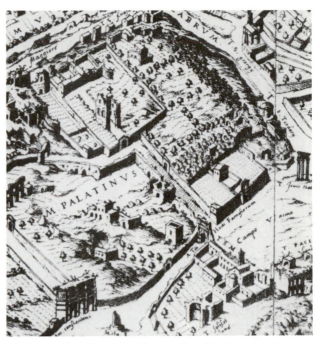

55. Rome, Dupérac map of 1577, detail of Farnese Gardens

55).[39] The problem of the date of commencement involves the more crucial question of the designer. Baglione in his lives of the artists published in 1642 was the first historian to attribute the gardens to the Farnese architect Vignola. The latter, however, died in 1573 and some of the architectural details, particularly the elaborate frames of the horizontal windows in the entrance wall, are not characteristic of his work, but suggest the manner of Giacomo del Duca, who succeeded Vignola as the Farnese architect.

In 1579, two years after most of the design and planting of the hillside was completed, Cardinal Farnese purchased the Vigna Mantaco covering the broad plateau on the western half of the hill adjacent to his hillside garden. This purchase would seem to have been inevitable, as the design of the hillside garden consisted basically of several terraces connected by ramps and stairs climbing up the slope to the Vigna Mantaco and serving, therefore, as a monumental access garden to the plateau above, although as late as the Tempesta map of Rome of 1593[40] the upper vigna was still depicted as an undeveloped, densely wooded area. Therefore, it would seem possible that the cardinal after the acquisition in 1565 of the Vigna Maddaleni at the base of the hill had a project to convert the entire western half of the Palatine into a great garden encompassing the Vigna Man-

taco, which he was only able to purchase in 1579. The fact that the garden on the hillside was actually created before he obtained control of the upper vigna does not preclude such a plan. In fact, the history of the gardens of the Villa d'Este at Tivoli reveals a slightly similar situation. There the Cardinal of Ferrara made a few land purchases in 1550 obviously with the idea of developing a garden. Because of personal difficulties, the major land purchases were effected only from 1560 to 1566, yet already in 1560 the water aqueduct to Monte Sant'Angelo was begun and the underground water conduit to the Aniene was undertaken in 1564. Needless to say, a wealthy and thereby powerful cardinal rarely encountered obstacles to his building projects. In fact, the Cardinal of Ferrara was so ruthless in his land acquisitions that he was charged legally, but in vain, by the magistrates of Tivoli in 1568 with having "ruined the houses of poor citizens against their wish, and if they did not wish to consent to sale, he made them."[41]

If the Farnese cardinal had in mind in the late 1560s to create a great garden on the Palatine Hill, it is possible that the first ideas and general design might have been prepared by Vignola before his death in 1573

[39] Frutaz, *Piante*, pl. 255.
[40] Ibid., pl. 265.

[41] ASM, Archivio Segreto Estense, Casa e Stato, Documenti spettanti a principi Estensi, busta 388, doc. 2038/5, fol. 1v.

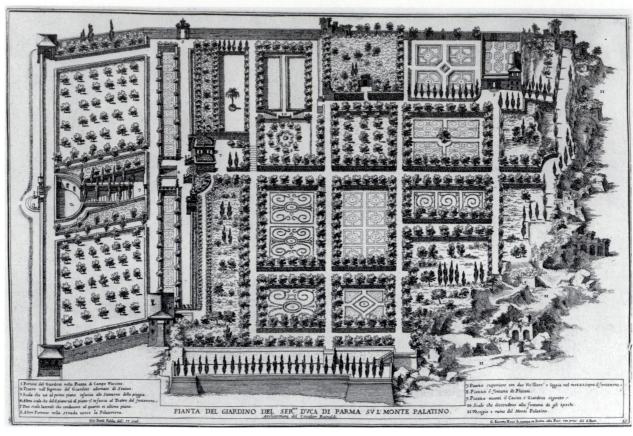

1.*Portone del Giardino nella Piazza di Campo Vaccino.*
2.*Teatro nel Ingresso del Giardino adornato di Statue.*
3.*Scala che uà al primo piano infacia alla Stanzone della pioggia.*
4.*Altra scala che dal 1.piano uà al piano 3.infacia al Teatro del fontanone.*
5.*Altre scale laterali che conducono al quarto et ultimo piano.*
6.*Altri Portoni nella strada uerso la Poluieriera.*

*Gio.Batti Falda delt. et sculp.*

7.*Piazza superiore con due Voĺliere' e loggia nel mezzo sopra il fontanone.*
8.*Piazza è fontana de Platani.*
9.*Piazza auanti il Casino, e Giardino segreto.*
10.*Scale che discendono alla fontana de gĺi specchi.*
11.*Vestigie e ruine del Monte Palatino.*

**PIANTA DEL GIARDINO DEL SER.™ DVCA DI PARMA SV L'MONTE PALATINO.**
*Architettura del Cavalier Rainaldi.*

*G. Iacomo Rossi le stampa in Roma alla Pace con priv. del S.Pont.*

56. Rome, Farnese Gardens, plan, engraving

and that only the architectural detailing of the entrance portal and the windows of the garden wall were Del Duca's contribution.

After the acquisition of the Vigna Mantaco in 1579 some further minor work was carried out at the Palatine. In that same year, however, the cardinal also bought the Chigi Villa Farnesina adjacent to his old vigna outside the Trastevere, thus gaining a garden with the exquisite villa designed by Peruzzi and decorated by him and Raphael. This purchase may have diverted the cardinal from pursuing more intensely the work at the Palatine. In 1582 he obtained one last small parcel of land on the Palatine, the so-called artichoke garden (*orto di carciofi*) at the southwest near Sant'Anastasia, and in 1588, the year before his death, he was granted right to some of the water of the new Acqua Felice. Because of his death the water rights were not utilized and were renewed later for Cardinal Odoardo Farnese.

It is only in the early seventeenth century that Cardinal Odoardo Farnese continued the development of the Palatine gardens (Fig. 56). By 1618 he had converted the plateau of the Vigna Mantaco into a huge formal garden where were planted a variety of exotic flowers and trees. At the edge of the hill marking the transition from the new garden to the sixteenth-century hillside garden was erected a single aviary. Later, but before 1633, a second, matching aviary was built so that the sixteenth-century central ramp and stairway ended on axis with a large fountain set in the retaining wall under the terrace between the two aviaries, and flights of stairs wound around the base of the aviaries up to the new garden. The Falda engravings of the mid-seventeenth century present magnificent views of the Palatine gardens as they were finally completed.

The enthusiasm for archaeology, commencing in the mid-eighteenth century, began the gradual destruction of the Farnese gardens as the Palatine Hill was excavated. Finally in 1880 the long entrance wall separating the hillside garden from the Forum was destroyed, and in 1883 its entrance portal was disman-

tled. The latter, however, was reerected in 1957 at a
new location at the eastern foot of the Palatine on the
Via di S. Gregorio (Fig. 57). Other than the relocated
entrance portal, about all that remains today are the
central entrance ramp and stairs, the cryptoporticus
with its later grotto at the head of the ramp (Fig. 58),
the niche fountain and two aviaries, a few replanted
flower beds on the upper level, and the double-loggia
casino looming like a tower out of the excavations
around it.

Under Cardinal Alessandro Farnese in the 1570s
the northern slope of the Palatine Hill was divided
into three long terraces connected by ramps and stairs
(Fig. 56). At the foot of the hill a very tall wall enclosed the front, and lower walls mounting the hill at
the two ends framed the garden. The lower two-thirds
of the entrance wall, marked by a horizontal molding,
was battered, since it also served as a retaining wall
for the first terrace, which stood behind the wall at
the level of the molding. Above the molding in the
upper third of the wall were ten large, horizontal windows permitting views out into the Forum from the
terraced promenade behind the wall. At the ends of
the entrance wall were corner pavilions, not identical
in size, since the northeast one toward the Arch of
Titus was approximately square, whereas the other
was a deeper rectangle. As both buildings were provided with fireplaces, they presumably served as habitations for the gardeners or custodians and were not
garden pavilions. In the center of the wall was a two-
story, monumental entrance portal about sixteen meters tall (Fig. 57). The lower story, built of tufa except
for the capitals, bases, and entablature carved of travertine, had three bays divided by rusticated Doric orders with pilasters at the ends and half-columns separating the arched entranceway from side niches. The
more elegant upper story was completely of travertine. In its center above the entrance was a tall, arched
opening with balustraded balcony, creating a belvedere looking out into the Forum. Rather delicate,
caryatid herms flanked the balcony and supported the
segmental broken pediment in which stood the arms
of the cardinal. On the entablature was the Latin inscription *Horti Palatini Farnesiorum*. Curved side
pieces formed a transition from the wider lower story
to the single bay above. Single, large windows flanked
the entrance portal at the lower story and lit the entrance vestibule behind.

Passing through the vaulted vestibule that supported the walkway behind the entrance wall, one
came out into a semicircular piazza described on the

57. Rome, Farnese Gardens, entrance portal

58. Rome, Farnese Gardens, cryptoporticus

engravings as the *teatro* with statues set in niches in
the curved back wall as well as portals to two secret,
spiral stairs leading directly up to the terraced promenade. At the rear of the teatro a steep ramp or *cordonata* on axis with the portal led up to the level of
the first terrace where paths went back along the sides
of the cordonata and open teatro to the walkway
along the entrance wall. At the head of the cordonata
was the entrance to the cryptoporticus above which
ran the second terrace. Between the first and second
terraces the sloping hillside was planted with trees,
and ramped alleys joined the two terraces. Originally
the only access from the level of the first terrace at the
top of the cordonata to the second terrace required
the visitor to walk back to the promenade along the
entrance wall and then take one of the ramped alleys
up to the second terrace, which also ran completely
across the hillside. Later Cardinal Odoardo added a
grotto, the Grotto della Pioggia, at the rear of the
cryptoporticus and side stairs hidden within the cryptoporticus with direct access to the second terrace. Behind this terrace were long strips of flower beds. At
the western end of the second terrace set into the hillside was the early sixteenth-century casino to which
an upper story was added probably in the seventeenth
century. A portal at the end of the second terrace gave
access to the ground floor of the building. In the center of the second terrace on axis with the entrance
cordonata was a flight of stairs running from the second terrace to the upper one and set between projecting balustraded terraces. There is no clear evidence
how the sixteenth-century hillside garden was terminated at the rear below the summit of the hill, but an
illustration to the 1588 edition of Bartolommeo Mar-
liani's *Urbis Romae Topographia* suggests that it was
undeveloped with merely the ancient ruins, which
were later incorporated into the seventeenth-century
aviaries, as a backdrop. At the other end of the third
terrace toward the east was a portal entering on the
street that climbed the Palatine from the Arch of Titus
along the outside of the eastern wall of the garden.

Unlike most sixteenth-century Roman gardens the
Farnese garden was oriented primarily outward. It
was organized like the auditorium of a theater with
terraces and balconies from which the visitor was encouraged to look out from the garden onto the stage
of the Forum beyond. On approaching the garden
from the Forum all that could be seen was the great
front wall with the tops of trees growing above it and
the two horizontal lines of the upper terraces cutting
across the hill. After entering the teatro the visitor

59. Rome, view from Farnese Gardens

was immediately aware of the space funneled upward
along the central axis of the cordonata, but the crucial
connection or access between the first and second terraces at the cryptoporticus was missing, forcing a return backward and outward toward the promenade
of the first terrace, so that the garden organization
had some of the ambiguities visible earlier at the Villa
Giulia in the middle of the century. Not only was the
Farnese garden oriented toward the vista of the Forum, it was carefully organized in relation to the towering remains of the Basilica of Maxentius on the far
side of the Forum. The large arched window and balcony over the entrance to the garden were set directly
on axis with the central vault of the basilica, and the
view from within the cryptoporticus through the central opening corresponded to this axial vista (Fig. 59),
so that in the concept of the theater the basilica served
as a backdrop to the stage of the Forum. The only
location from which one could find a splendid, full
view of the Farnese gardens must have been from Silvestri's hanging garden on the top of the basilica,

which was owned at this time by the Medici archbishop of Florence.

As with the earlier garden of Cardinal Du Bellay the Latin inscription on the portal of the Palatine gardens must be a reference to the ancient *Horti Aciliani*, *Horti Sallustiani*, and *Horti Luculliani* on the Pincian Hill. Likewise the rusticated portal of the Farnese gardens with large, horizontal windows along the top of the entrance wall resembled the Du Bellay garden. The Farnese gardens, however, by their use of a terraced hillside were more truly in the mode of the ancient *Horti Aciliani* and may be the last Renaissance Roman garden to reflect the splendors of the Roman gardens of antiquity. On the other hand, the Farnese gardens are almost strictly a garden with little provision architecturally for residence. They offer a setting for the enjoyment of nature and vistas, and thereby foreshadow the great baroque garden parks of Rome in the first half of the seventeenth century.

# The Iconography of the Renaissance Garden

The practice of exhibiting ancient Roman statues, sarcophagi, and reliefs in their gardens presumably promoted the idea among Renaissance Romans to organize iconographical programs, primarily based on classical mythology, for the decoration and classicizing of their gardens. The earliest example of such a program, however, was not concerned with sculpture and it predated the popularity of sculpture gardens in Rome. When Cardinal Francesco Gonzaga decided to decorate the walls of his garden in Rome, the inspiration may have come from the late fifteenth-century tradition of embellishing house facades with painted friezes, often illustrating classical mythological tales.

In October 1467 Pope Paul II granted the youthful Mantuan cardinal a house in the center of Rome near the church of S. Lorenzo in Damaso, which had previously been the residence of the powerful Cardinal Ludovico Trevisan, known usually as Cardinal Scarampo. Trevisan's house had already in 1462 been likened to "paradise," probably because of its delightful garden for which in 1451 its owner had requested pomegranate trees from Onorato Caetani.[1] A letter of the Mantuan agent Arrivabene in June 1472 notes the existence of a loggia in the garden, then owned by Cardinal Gonzaga, where he dined after a recent ill-

ness, but the major changes to the palace and garden apparently date in 1479. At least a series of letters from the cardinal then in Bologna instruct his master of the house at Rome what the cardinal wished done and even more strongly what he disliked. He was outraged to learn that pomegranate trees which "we had planted with our own hands" had been removed, for they were meant to mingle with cypresses, pines, and other trees in a common grove. He was careful to note that some piece of garden architecture, described as the "tempio grande," must not be moved, even if the gardener did not approve of it. The major thrust of the cardinal's letters is that he has left his own design for the garden, which must not "be changed one iota." Thus, it is not surprising to learn by the next letter that the gardener, Master Lorenzo, was replaced.

The most interesting letter, of December 4, 1479, contains suggestions of the cardinal for the decoration of the walls of his garden. On the outer face of the wall of the private garden (*horticello secreto*) was to be painted the battle of the Lapiths and the Centaurs. Since each figure was to be identified, the cardinal suggested that his poet Niccolò Cosmico be consulted for names. On the wall near the labyrinth of the garden was to be the story of Theseus until the moment he was to enter the labyrinth. Then the actual horticultural labyrinth would continue the myth until the killing of the Minotaur, which was to be made within the labyrinth, perhaps in the form of topiary rather than sculpture, although the letter does not specify. On the wall leading to an exit to the well might be depicted the fable of Meleager. Whether

[1] Documents for the Gonzaga residence are in D. S. Chambers, "The Housing Problems of Cardinal Francesco Gonzaga," *Journal of the Warburg and Courtauld Institutes*, XXXIX, 1976, pp. 21–58; for the letter to Caetani, see G. Caetani, ed., *Epistolarum Honorati Caietani*, Sancasciano Val di Pesa, 1925, p. 8. In a previous study, *The Villa in the Life of Renaissance Rome*, Princeton, N.J., 1979, I mistakenly associated the decorative program with the cardinal's suburban garden on the Quirinal Hill.

Hercules should also be represented, as some urged, the cardinal would leave to Cosmico.

The stories suggested for the decoration seem to illustrate the struggle of heroic men with beasts or half-beasts, such as the centaurs, the minotaur, or the Calydonian boar, and, therefore, probably connote the struggle of man with his base passions or the contest of virtue and vice. It may even be significant that the cardinal selected the story of Meleager for the wall near the well, since according to Ovid (*Metamorphoses*, VIII, 456–57) the Fates decreed that Meleager would live only as long as a blazing brand snatched by his mother from a fire was quenched by water. With the emphasis on virtue in the program of decoration, it is understandable that the cardinal had been advised to consider Hercules, the particular Renaissance hero of virtue, for the decoration of the garden.[2]

The most fascinating aspect of the Gonzaga project for classicizing the garden was the incorporation of the actual labyrinth, presumably planted much earlier, even perhaps by his predecessor, Cardinal Trevisan, within the iconographical program devoted to the story of Theseus. There is apparently no further evidence regarding this program of decoration, no surety that it was even pursued. In the early sixteenth century, however, the labyrinth will appear as an impresa of later members of the Gonzaga family and will be visible in the decoration of the Palazzo del Te at Mantua of Duke Federigo Gonzaga.[3] It may be completely irrelevant, but it is tempting to see the importance of the labyrinth as a Gonzaga symbol arising from the prominence of this traditional horticultural form in the garden of the cardinal's Roman residence.

That the mode of classicizing a Renaissance garden with an iconographical program drawn from classical mythology was related to the statuary gardens that prevailed in Rome during the early sixteenth century may be demonstrated by the Belvedere Statue Court in the Vatican Palace discussed earlier. The ancient statues exhibited in the court were chosen only by the chance of discovery of the pieces or their availability for purchase. This had been the origin of the pieces that made up the collection of Cardinal Giuliano della Rovere, which then became the nucleus of the Vatican collection when the cardinal was elected Pope Julius in 1503. The inscription from Vergil (*Aeneid*, VI, 258), "Away, you who are unhallowed" (*Procul Este Profani*), which Albertini, writing in 1509, saw near the statue of the emperor Commodus in the guise of Hercules standing by the entrance to the Statue Court, suggests that the garden court is a sacred precinct guarded by Hercules.[4] The presence of Hercules in a garden richly planted with orange trees, often associated with the golden apples seized by Hercules from the many-headed dragon, guardian of the Garden of the Hesperides, would seem to equate the Belvedere garden court with the garden of classical mythology.

The ancient myth of Hercules and the Garden of the Hesperides was an ideal subject for classicizing a Roman Renaissance garden. Not only was it appropriate as a horticultural theme from classical antiquity, but its hero Hercules was the primary representative of a life of virtue, which the garden patrons of Renaissance Rome, many of whom were churchmen, liked to assume. It has already been noted that the grotto that Cardinal Carpi created in his villa on the Quirinal Hill, perhaps after the design of Ligorio, may have likewise reflected the Garden of the Hesperides, for Hercules with the golden apples stood guardian at the entrance of the grotto.[5] Similarly the theme of the sleeping nymph, which was central to the Carpi grotto, was undoubtedly related to the fountain of the recumbent Cleopatra in the Belvedere Statue Court, suggesting that the Vatican garden court may be the inspiration for some of the garden iconographies in Rome.

The garden of the Villa Farnesina that the very wealthy banker Agostino Chigi had built by 1512 on the bank of the Tiber River just outside the Trastevere walls at Rome apparently was the setting for features illustrating the ancient story of Psyche and Cupid, depicted in part by Raphael slightly later on the vault of the entrance loggia of the villa.[6] The Tiber River, which lined one side of the garden, would recall the

[2] A. Spychatska-Boczkowska, "Diana with Meleagros and Actaeon: Some Remarks on a XV-Century Italian Cassone," *Bulletin du Musée National de Varsovie*, IX, 1968, pp. 29–36. Later Peruzzi will decorate the Sala del Fregio in Agostino Chigi's Villa Farnesina at Rome with the Labors of Hercules and the myth of Meleager, as well as with other Ovidian scenes; see Coffin, *The Villa*, pp. 98–99.

[3] F. Hartt, "Gonzaga Symbols in the Palazzo del Te," *Journal of the Warburg and Courtauld Institutes*, XIII, 1950, pp. 151–88.

[4] H. H. Brummer, *The Statue Court in the Vatican Belvedere* (Stockholm Studies in the History of Art, 20), Stockholm, 1970, pp. 216–51.

[5] See Chapter 3.

[6] J. Shearman, "Die Loggia der Psyche in der Villa Farnesina und die Probleme der letzten Phase von Raffaels Graphischem Stil," *Jahrbuch der kunsthistorischen Sammlungen in Wien*, LX, 1964, pp. 71–74.

mythical river Styx, and the grotto beneath the dining loggia on the river bank could be interpreted as the entrance to Hades; thus, both scenes alluded to the settings for some of Psyche's adventures. In the description of Cupid's palace in the contemporary poetic adaptation by Niccolo da Correggio of the ancient story of Apuleius, the building resembled the Farnesina in having two loggias, one for dining and the other richly painted, and a delightful flower garden before the loggia. Among the few antique statues Chigi possessed was a figure of Psyche and it has even been suggested that in the painted group of Venus and Cupid in the first spandrel of Raphael's loggia Venus was pointing downward to the ancient statue of Psyche, thus tying together the spatial reality of the three-dimensional figure with the illusionistic space of the vault just as the garden trellis frame of the painted ceiling related to the garden setting of the villa.[7]

Another statuary garden in Rome that seems to present a classical iconographical program was that of Antonio del Bufalo, which once was adjacent to the literary garden of Angelo Colocci of the Acqua Vergine. Vasari in his lives of the artists Polidoro da Caravaggio and Maturino relates that they painted in the Bufalo garden "near the Trevi Fountain very beautiful scenes of the Fount of Pegasus." As happened also to the nearby Colocci garden, the creation of the Via del Tritone in 1888 destroyed the Bufalo garden. An eighteenth-century castato map, however, preserves the plan of the garden behind the Palazzo del Bufalo, and old photographs and engravings give some idea of the painted garden decoration that Polidoro and Maturino executed about 1525.[8] Defining the rear of the garden was a shallow casino with a large, central niche fountain whose very elaborate frame must be a seventeenth-century addition (Fig. 60). At the left of the casino, set at an obtuse angle to it, was another casino in whose lower story a three-arched loggia opened onto the garden. The casino on axis with the palace had its loggia on the upper floor

60. Rome, Del Bufalo Garden Casino, engraving

in the center above the wall fountain. On both sides of the ground floor were portals, of which the one at the left communicated by a stair with the upper loggia. Above the left portal was an arched window, while on the right there was only a window feigned in paint, as the casino was too shallow on that side to permit any usable space within it. The entire wall surface of both casinos was then covered with frescoes in grisaille, six of which, now transferred to canvas, are preserved in the Museo di Roma. As a nineteenth-century engraving indicates, the frescoes on the principal garden casino were arranged in three levels (Fig. 60).[9] The upper loggia was flanked by scenes of *Perseus Rescuing Andromeda* and the *Marriage of Perseus and Andromeda*. The middle zone depicted *Perseus Killing Phineus and His Comrades* and *Mount Parnassus*. Flanking the central wall fountain on the lower story were vertical panels with Mars and Venus, the tutelary gods of Rome. On the other casino at the left, a long frieze above the arches of the ground-floor loggia illustrated the transformation of the giant Atlas into a mountain and a view of the Garden of the Hesperides. Above this frieze between the small windows of the second story were scenes of the story of Danae. Later Taddeo Zuccaro emphasized the dedication of the garden by painting a fresco of Apollo and the Muses at the Castalian spring on Mount Parnassus in the small loggia at the left. This too, transferred to canvas, is in a private collection in Rome.[10]

---

[7] E. Schwarzenberg, "Raphael und die Psyche-Statue Agostino Chigis," *Jahrbuch der kunsthistorischen Sammlungen in Wien*, LXXIII, 1977, pp. 117–26.

[8] R. Kultzen, "Der Malereien Polidoros da Caravaggio im Giardino del Bufalo in Rom," *Mitteilungen des kunsthistorischen Instituts in Florenz*, IX, 1959, pp. 99–120, and C. Pericoli Ridolfini, "La mostra delle case romani con facciate graffite e dipinte," *Bollettino dei musei comunali di Roma*, VII, 1960, pp. 1–8. See also H. Wrede, *Der Antikengarten der del Bufalo bei der Fontana Trevi* (Trierer Winckelmannsprogramme, 4), Mainz, 1982; for copies of the frescoes, see L. Ravelli, *Polidoro Caldara da Caravaggio*, Bergamo, 1978, pp. 327–43.

[9] E. Maccari, *Graffiti e chiaroscuri esistenti nell'esterno delle case*, Rome, n.d., pl. 5.

[10] C. Pericoli Ridolfini, "Il 'Parnaso' di Taddeo Zuccaro nel giardino del palazzo del Bufalo," *Studi romani*, XV, 1967, pp. 328–30.

The iconography of the decoration is derived from Ovid's *Metamorphoses* and recounts all the stories as told by Ovid, which come to a climax in the creation of the Hippocrene spring of the Muses on Mount Helicon, or Mount Parnassus as it was identified by other writers. So Perseus, who was born of Danae, first sought rest during his travels in the Garden of the Hesperides owned by Atlas and, when Atlas refused his request, transformed the giant into a huge mountain (IV, 604–62). This is followed by the rescue of Andromeda from the monster and her marriage to Perseus (IV, 663–764). That Polidoro closely followed Ovid is confirmed by the marriage scene where three altars were prominently displayed with their sacrifices, since Ovid relates that Perseus "builds to three gods the same number of altars of turf, the left one to Mercury, the right to you, the warlike virgin, the middle altar is to Jupiter; a cow is sacrificed to Minerva, a calf to the wing-footed god, a bull to you, the greatest of the gods" (IV, 753–56). As Perseus starts to recount his deeds, including the creation of the winged horse Pegasus from the blood of the decapitated Medusa, he was attacked by Phineus, the frustrated suitor of Andromeda, and his followers (V, 1–235). Finally, Minerva, the sister of Perseus, flies to Mount Helicon, the home of the Muses, to view the Hippocrene spring that arises in the mountain in the hoofprints of the winged Pegasus (V, 250–68), as, indeed, Polidoro in the panel of Helicon depicts the waters of the spring gushing from the hoofprints of the rampant Pegasus.

The mythological frescoes in grisaille covering the walls of the Bufalo garden may have resembled those proposed earlier by Cardinal Gonzaga for his garden, but the later garden had a rich collection of ancient statues that may have been related to the fresco decoration. The fountains and antique statuary in the Bufalo garden are described by Boissard and Aldrovandi as of the middle of the sixteenth century.[11] Boissard notes that the garden, planted with a variety of trees, listing myrtle, palm, citron, pomegranate, and orange trees, had scattered among the trees ancient statues, including one of Cerberus, the three-headed dog that guarded Hades, the river god Tigris, Pomona, Diana, and a clothed Venus. More interesting is a fountain described by Aldrovandi as "a fantastic [*bizzara*] and

rustic one handsomely composed as a small, rugged hill [*monticello*] from which water pours forth as from the ground itself, which is trampled, and from every other part." Boissard adds that the artificial rock was strewn with precious, glittering shells and supported trees of laurel, citron, and tamarisk under whose shade were the statues of three Muses and Caracalla. The description of the hill as oozing water from a trampled surface calls to mind the origin of the spring of the Muses in the hoofprints of Pegasus.[12] This similarity, in association with figures of the Muses, suggests that the traditional mount of small mediaeval gardens has here been transformed into the classical Mount Helicon or Parnassus, which has also been depicted in the frescoes of Polidoro and the later one of Taddeo Zuccaro.

The subject of the frescoes in the Bufalo garden may, however, have been chosen as a background for some of the ancient sculpture already in the collection.[13] Drawings of one of the lost frescoes of the story of Danae reveal that the dogs that accompany the guardians of Danae are based on the ancient statue of Cerberus that was in the garden, at least at the time of Aldrovandi's inventory of 1558 and presumably was there when Polidoro painted his fresco. In 1572 there were also in the garden, then owned by Paolo del Bufalo, at least four life-size ancient figures of the Muses, two of which were drawn by Dosio at about the same time.[14] There are, however, no artistic relationships between the figures of the frescoed Muses and the two statues drawn by Dosio. It is, therefore, possible that some of the ancient statues were obtained later by the Del Bufalos as appropriate to the iconography of the garden as determined by the frescoes, but in any event it seems that some of the classical statuary and its setting were to evoke the Garden of the Muses.

Vasari in his life of the painter Perino del Vaga describes a similar situation at the garden on Via Monserrato in Rome of the archbishop of Cyprus, which already housed a collection of ancient statues and other antiquities.[15] The archbishop then engaged his friend Perino to decorate the walls of the garden with

[11] J. J. Boissard, *Romanae Vrbis Topographiae*, I, n.p., 1597, pp. 115–16, and U. Aldrovandi, *Delle statue antiche*, Venice, 1558, pp. 286–90.

[12] E. B. MacDougall, "The Sleeping Nymph: Origins of a Humanist Fountain Type," *Art Bulletin*, LVII, 1975, p. 363.

[13] Kultzen, "Der Malereien Poliodoros," 113.

[14] R. Lanciani, *Storia degli scavi di Roma*, III, Rome, 1907, p. 189, and C. Huelsen, *Das Skizzenbuch des Giovannantonio Dosio*, Berlin, 1933, pl. LXXVIII. Boissard mentions only three statues of Muses in the late 1550s (see previous discussion) and Aldrovandi's inventory of about the same time lists none.

[15] G. Vasari, *Le vite de più eccellenti pittori, scultori ed architettori*, ed. G. Milanesi, Florence, 1906, V, p. 597.

bacchantes, satyrs, and fauns, which would correspond to an ancient group in the garden depicting
Bacchus seated near a tigress.

Although the painting of garden walls was not a
very common practice in the Renaissance, it may have
occurred more frequently than has been previously
considered. Earlier it was noted that in the fifteenth
century the Cardinal of Mantua had proposed to
paint the walls of his Roman garden with the story of
the Battle of the Lapiths and Centaurs,[16] but it is the
pictorial treatises of the late sixteenth century, particularly those concerned with the principle of decorum,
that specifically discuss painted decoration in gardens. Lomazzo, in the sixth book of his treatise of
1584, dedicates a chapter to paintings at springs, in
gardens, and at other places of pleasure.[17] He insists
that paintings on garden walls must be joyful stories
with no trace of melancholy, offering as examples
such classical myths as Mercury and the sleeping Argus, Perseus liberating Andromeda (probably recalling the decoration of the Del Bufalo garden), the hunt
of Meleager or Orpheus taming the beast, as well as
festivals and dances, some featuring nymphs and satyrs. Three years later, in obvious emulation of Lomazzo, Armenini devoted a chapter in his treatise to
the painted decoration of gardens and country
houses.[18] Again the theme is decorum or the appropriateness of the decoration, which Armenini insists
should show more concern "for the form and char-
acteristics of the location than for the rank of the person." He too wishes the scenes to be cheerful, specifying delightful landscapes with distant cities and
castles, scenes of fighting and hunting, or games of
shepherds and nymphs or fauns and satyrs. Both writers are simply following the principles of decorum for
painted decoration in country villas and gardens as
enunciated by the ancient Roman writer Vitruvius

(VII, v, 2) and especially as reiterated in the fifteenth
century by L. B. Alberti (IX, iv). Armenini, however,
not only recalls the painting by Perino del Vaga of the
garden of the archbishop of Cyprus at Rome, but cites
the work of the painter Pordenone in the garden of
Dr. Dal Pozzo in Piacenza, mistakenly identified by
Vasari as in Vicenza, and many other examples in
Lombardy, especially at Milan. Already in an unpublished mid-sixteenth-century treatise on agriculture,
Girolamo Fiorenzuola recommended that small alleys
in perspective radiating out from the wide principal
alley should end in painted or sculpted depictions on
the walls enclosing the garden.[19] Later, in 1600, the
painter Cherubino Alberti was paid for otherwise unknown painting executed by him in the garden of the
papal villa on the Quirinal.[20] In 1674 and 1675 painters were paid to decorate the walls of the grove or
*boschetto* in the Chigi garden at the Four Fountains.[21]
At the same time Mayer in his description of the Villa
Benedetta at Rome, the so-called Vascello, mentions
that a wide alley covered by a large pergola from the
entrance had at its end a fresco of *Roma Triumphans*
by the painter Giovanni Maria Mariani.[22] In the seventeenth century decorative and illusionistic wall
painting will also not be unusual in gardens in northern Europe, especially in France and in the Netherlands.

Pope Julius III gathered together a collection of antique sculpture to decorate his splendid Villa Giulia
and its gardens created for him outside the Porta del
Popolo from 1551 until his death in 1555. Rather like
the earlier Vigna Carpi, the appeal of the landscaping
at the Villa Giulia was its reliance on both formal and
informal planning. The collection of ancient sculpture
was concentrated in and around the casino of the
complex where there were small formal gardens with
fountains and contemporary sculpture. Unlike the
Vigna Carpi, however, the works of sculpture at the
Villa Giulia were completely subservient to the architecture of the villa and, in the tradition of Cardinal
della Valle's sculptural garden, were to be appreciated
not as museum exhibits, but as architectural decoration.

Since all the antiquities have been removed and

[16] Canto XXVI of Boccaccio's *Amorosa Visione*, ed. V. Branca,
Florence, 1944, has been identified as referring to a painted depiction of Hercules with Iole in a garden at Naples in the fourteenth
century and there are remains of extensive fresco decoration, depicting illustrious men, hunting scenes, and tournaments, on the
walls of a small garden in the Castello of Issogne; see N. Gabrielli,
*Rappresentazioni sacre e profane nel castello di Issogne e la pittura
nella Valle d'Osta alla fine del '400*, Turin, 1959. For the decoration of Roman Renaissance gardens in general, see E. B. Mac-
Dougall, "Imitation and Invention: Language and Decoration in
Roman Renaissance Gardens," *Journal of Garden History*, v,
1985, pp. 119–34.

[17] G. P. Lomazzo, *Trattato dell'arte pittura, scoltura, et architettura*, Milan, 1584, pp. 344–48.

[18] G. B. Armenini, *De' veri precetti della pittura*, Ravenna, 1587,
pp. 197–201.

[19] A. Tagliolini, "Girolamo Fiorenzuola ed il giardino nelle fonti
della metà del '500," in *Il giardino storico italiano*, ed. G. Ragionieri, Florence, 1981, pp. 300–1.

[20] A. M. Corbo, ed., *Fonti per la storia artistica romana al tempo
di Clemente VIII*, Rome, 1975, p. 30.

[21] See Chapter 7.

[22] M. Mayer, *Villa Benedetta*, Rome, 1677, p. 8.

61. Rome, Villa Giulia, court

most of the stucco reliefs and even some of the fresco decoration have disappeared, our major source for the original condition of the Villa is a detailed, descriptive letter written in May 1555 by the sculptor Ammannati, who was in charge of the sculptural decoration and the fountain of the nymphaeum, and the inventory of sculpture made in March 1555 after the death of the pope.[23] The great theatrical court just behind the casino of the villa had pieces of ancient sculpture set in niches on the side walls, and the end wall which served as the *scenae frons* of the theater was richly decorated by Ammannati with stucco reliefs (Fig. 61). The stucco decoration related directly to the owner of the villa and the source of the water, which was one of the great features of the villa. Two of the major panels of the rear wall were imprese of

Pope Julius III: an allegory of Justice and Peace and one of Fortune seized by her hair by Virtue. The other two panels depicted Religion and Charity. More interesting were the five reliefs of the attic above. In the center above the entrance into the loggia, which stands above the rear nymphaeum, was the story, according to Pliny (*Historia Naturalis*, XXX, XXV), of the name of the ancient Aqua Virgo whose aqueduct was tapped by the architect Vignola to feed the nymphaeum. In the words of Ammannati, "there is a Hercules seated in the pose of a river and nearby is a woman in the dress of a virgin who flees him. This denotes the water of the secret fountain which running with the Herculean river never mingles with it." Flanking this relief, two on each side, were reliefs of the Four Elements, which are standard decoration for villas, but the depiction of the Elements as described by Ammannati was somewhat unusual. So the Earth was represented by Eve and her children and Fire by the "first fire," presumably the story of the origin of

[23] Both are republished in T. Falk, "Studien zur Topographie und Geschichte der Villa Giulia in Rom," *Römisches Jahrbuch für Kunstgeschichte*, XIII, 1971, appendix II, pp. 170–71, and appendix III, pp. 171–73.

fire in Vitruvius (II, I). The other elements were more traditional in terms of classical deities with Juno for Air and Venus for Water. The emphasis on the origin of the Aqua Virgo will then be repeated in the decoration of the nymphaeum of the villa behind the theatrical court.

Fourteen ancient statues or statue groups enriched the side walls of the theatrical court. Ammannati, who was in charge of the sculptural program, was apparently not aware of the ancient statues contributing any specific meaning to the villa's decoration, since one figure is only identified by him as a "woman in a long dress" and two others are listed simply as "sylvan gods." The contemporary archaeologist and architect Pirro Ligorio, who will later work at the estate, claims, however, that an ancient figure of Aesculapius was recut for Pope Julius III by stripping off its garments "in order to make a nude figure to accompany the other objects at his Vigna."[24] This suggests that there was intended to be a meaningful program to which the ancient statues were to be adapted. The figures as identified by Ammannati do seem to have some collective meaning. Many of the figures, including Bacchus and Pan, Vertumnus and Pomona, are horticultural or woodland deities appropriate as decoration to a country estate. Most of the remaining figures belong to two coherent groups, one centering on the early history of Rome, with the tutelary gods of the city, Mars and Venus, and Lavinia, daughter of King Latinus and wife of Aeneas, whose mother in turn was Venus, and the other group presenting Hercules and his wife Dejanira.[25] A freestanding figure of Venus with her emblem, a swan, stood on the great fountain basin in the center of the court. She is central to the meaning of the decoration, both in her role as patron deity of ancient Rome and as the principal garden goddess.

On the back wall of the nymphaeum sunk into the ground behind the theatrical court are still two large river gods by Ammannati, one of the Tiber, the other the Arno (Fig. 26). The Tiber, of course, refers to the Roman location of the villa, while the Arno presumably alludes to the Tuscan origin of the pope's family. The vault of the grotto under the entrance loggia to the nymphaeum, however, was more original, as it had a relief illustrating the story of the Aqua Virgo as related by Frontinus in his ancient treatise on aqueducts (I, 10), according to which several soldiers seeking water were shown the source of the Aqua Virgo by a young girl. This same scene is also represented in a fresco in the frieze of the main salon of the casino. The Frontinus legend is the more common story of the origin of the Aqua Virgo. The importance of Hercules in the decoration of the court may explain the choice of Pliny's myth of the Aqua Virgo for the stucco relief in the court in contrast to the account of Frontinus in the nymphaeum and casino, where Hercules plays no role. Similarly, the emphasis on Venus in the court decoration may explain why she rather than the more usual classic deity Neptune personifies the element of Water in the stucco reliefs on the rear wall of the court.

In the Villa Giulia even some of the horticulture participated in the classicizing of the villa's grounds. The heart of the complex was the sunken nymphaeum with its waterworks, sculpture, and aviaries. There the only horticultural feature were four large plane trees planted on the middle level of the nymphaeum to shade it (Fig. 62). The plane tree had always been held in great admiration by the ancient Romans; however, a particular classical reference undoubtedly inspired the planting of the four plane trees in the nymphaeum of the Villa Giulia. Pliny the Younger in his description of his villa in Tuscany (*Letters*, V, 6) mentions a small court shaded with four plane trees in the midst of which was a fountain very much like that created in the Villa Giulia.[26]

Until the second half of the sixteenth century the iconographical programs of Roman gardens are somewhat tentative and limited. In fact, the earliest program, that proposed in 1479 by Cardinal Gonzaga for his garden, was one of the most developed, combining several myths with the natural labyrinth of his garden to express presumably a theme of virtue overcoming vice. Gonzaga, however, had no constraints on his ideas other than the existence of the labyrinth, which may have actually provoked his ideas. The other gardens had to cope with the existence of a collection of ancient sculpture, often accidental in its acquisition, governed only by availability. Each figure retained its ancient significance, which only occasionally would adapt to the theme or topos expressed in the particular garden. Certainly Hercules is the principal figure of most of the gardens; only the Del Bufalo garden did not feature him, and

[24] Lanciani, *Storia degli scavi di Roma*, III, p. 159.
[25] MacDougall, "Imitation and Invention," p. 127.

[26] Coffin, *The Villa*, p. 163. The engraving of the nymphaeum in G. B. Falda, *Le fontane di Roma*, Rome, n.d., III, 6 (my Fig. 62), depicts four round holes in the paving of the nymphaeum identified as "Basamenti di alberi."

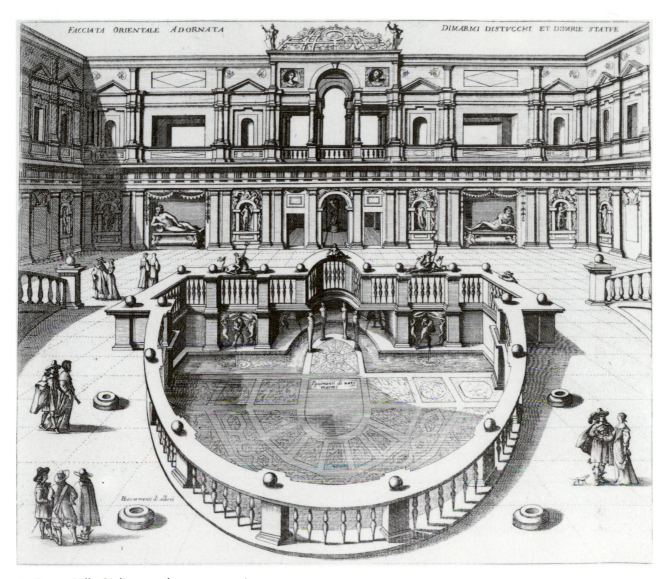

FACCIATA ORIENTALE ADORNATA      DIMARMI DISTVCCHI ET DIVARIE STATVE

62. Rome, Villa Giulia, nymphaeum, engraving

Cardinal Gonzaga was hesitant about his inclusion in his garden. Hercules, as noted previously, was not only the hero of one of the most important ancient horticultural myths, the story of the Garden of the Hesperides, but was the major proponent from classical mythology of the virtuous life.

In the third quarter of the sixteenth century, classical iconographical programs come to a rich climax, particularly in the Villa d'Este at Tivoli and the Villa Lante at Bagnaia. After his disappointment in not being elected pope during the conclave of 1549–1550, Ippolito d'Este, Cardinal of Ferrara, resolved to withdraw to a more leisurely life for which he created two lavish gardens, one in Rome and the other nearby at

Tivoli. In July 1550 he rented the vigna formerly of Cardinal Carafa on the Quirinal Hill and immediately commissioned the painter Girolamo da Carpi to design garden furnishings and pergolas for the new gardens he ordered laid out and provided with water by the architect Tommaso Ghinucci.[27] The work on the new gardens was interrupted by the exile of the cardinal from Rome from 1555 to 1559, but already in 1554 he had begun to assemble there a collection of ancient statues to be used to decorate the garden. In November 1560, a year after his return from exile, the area for the gardens on the Quirinal was ex-

[27] For documentation, see Coffin, *The Villa*, pp. 202–13.

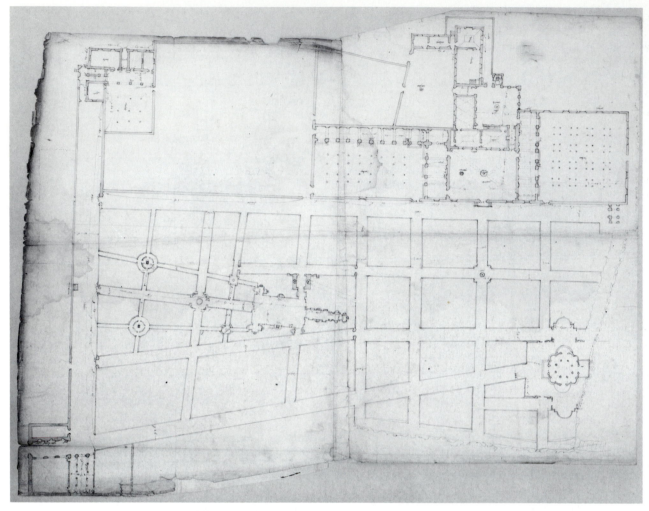

63. Rome, Villa d'Este, plan, Metropolitan Museum of Art

panded by the acquisition of the adjacent Vigna Boc-cacci.

A sixteenth-century drawing preserves the plan of the gardens as they were developed in the early 1560s (Fig. 63). Near the villa were several garden courts, some of which were planted with orange trees and featured loggias, one of which housed a nymphaeum dedicated to Venus. To the east spread the main garden whose northern half toward the edge of the hill was divided geometrically into large flower beds. The densely wooded, southern portion along the street called the Alta Semita, later to be the Via Pia, was cut by a series of great diagonal alleys radiating out from a rustic fountain, the Fontana del Bosco, created by the eminent fontaniere Curzio Maccarone, who would later be employed on the cardinal's fountains

at Tivoli and then go on to work for Cardinal Farnese at Caprarola. The fountain was unusual for Rome in being a small, artificial hill with grottoes, but earlier several of the famous *delizie* or pleasure gardens in the cardinal's native town of Ferrara featured such artificial, wooded hills with grottoes, which may have inspired the cardinal.[28] A long stair and ramp (cordonata) built along the boundary between the cardinal's formal garden and the adjacent Vigna Boccacci led down to a lower garden terrace along the northeastern base of the Quirinal (Fig. 64). There, set into the substructure of the casino and of the northern gar-

[28] E. B. MacDougall, "*Ars Hortulorum*: Sixteenth Century Garden Iconography and Literary Theory in Italy," in *The Italian Garden*, ed. D. R. Coffin, Washington, D.C., 1972, pp. 45–46.

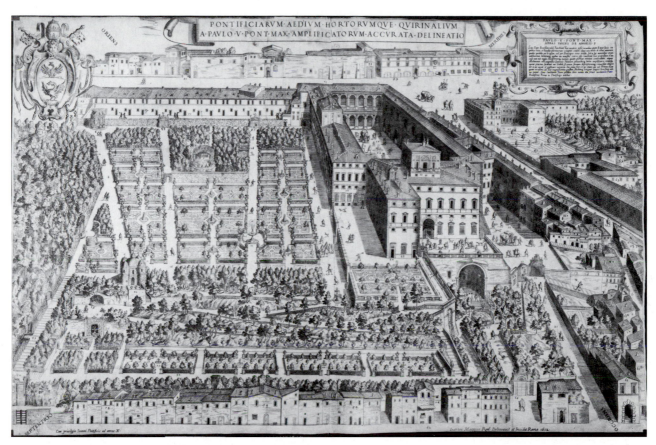

64. Rome, Quirinal, Papal Villa, Maggi engraving, British Museum

den court were several niche fountains, and particularly the great Fountain of Apollo and the Muses built by Curzio Maccarone.

The Villa d'Este at Rome exploited all the sixteenth-century garden features. Only the introduction of the wooded, artificial hill of the Fontana del Bosco marked an innovation for Roman sixteenth-century gardening. All the statues used to decorate the cardinal's gardens were restored antiquities whose names vary so in the several inventories preserved that one cannot determine a specific iconographical program for the Fontana del Bosco or for the entire garden complex, although the Fountain of Apollo and the Muses and the nymphaeum of Venus were common sixteenth-century garden features.

Early in 1550 the Cardinal of Ferrara had been appointed governor of the hill town of Tivoli east of Rome. Although the cardinal had just rented in July the Vigna Carafa at Rome and begun to develop its gardens, he apparently decided to do the same at Tivoli. So in September and October he bought several gardens in the Valle Gaudente that lay to the northwest below the Franciscan monastery attached to Sta. Maria Maggiore, which in the past had served as the palace of the governor of Tivoli and which the cardinal would have architecturally refurbished and redecorated for his villa (Fig. 65).[29] During the next decade, however, little was accomplished there. From the summer of 1560 for a period of six years, more vineyards and houses were bought until the cardinal controlled the entire Valle Gaudente down to the road to the Porta della Colle. Meanwhile a tremendous amount of earth moving was undertaken to reform the topography of the site and an abundant supply of water had to be introduced to activate the numerous fountains, which have always been the particular attraction of the Villa d'Este.

The gardens at Tivoli have, of course, suffered

[29] For documentation, see D. R. Coffin, *The Villa d'Este at Tivoli*, Princeton, N.J., 1960; C. Lamb, *Die Villa d'Este in Tivoli*, Munich, 1966; and Coffin, *The Villa*, pp. 311–40.

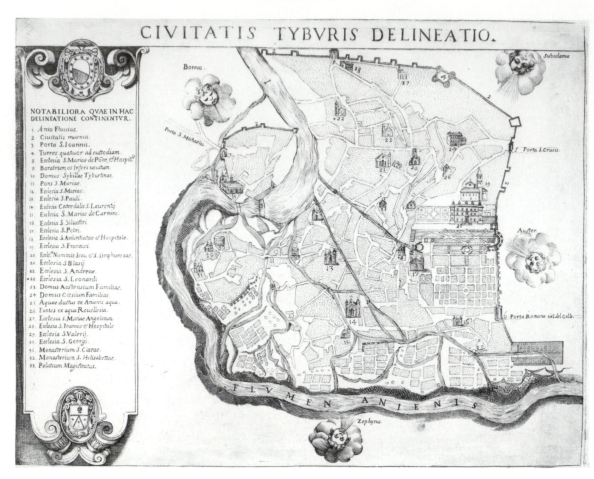

**CIVITATIS TYBVRIS DELINEATIO.**

NOTABILIORA QVAE IN HAC
DELINEATIONE CONTINENTVR.

1. Anio Fluuius.
2. Ciuitatis moenia.
3. Porta S. Ioannis.
4. Turres quatuor ad custodiam.
5. Ecclesia S. Mariae de Pôte, & Hospit.
9. Baratrum os Inferi uocatum.
10. Domus Sybillae Tyburtinae.
11. Pons S. Mariae.
12. Ecclesia S. Mariae.
13. Ecclesia S. Pauli.
14. Ecclesia Catredalis S. Laurentij.
15. Ecclesia S. Mariae de Carmine.
16. Ecclesia S. Siluestri.
17. Ecclesia S. Petri.
18. Ecclesia S. Antiatiae & Hospitale.
19. Ecclesia S. Francisci.
20. Ecle. Nominis Iesu e S. Simphorosae.
21. Ecclesia S. Blasij.
22. Ecclesia S. Andreae.
22. Ecclesia S. Leonardi.
23. Domus Aestensium Familiae.
24. Domus Caesium Familiae.
25. Aquae ductus ex Anienis aqua.
26. Fontes ex aqua Reuellesia.
27. Ecclesia S. Mariae Angelorum.
28. Ecclesia S. Ioannis & Hospitale.
29. Ecclesia S. Valerij.
30. Ecclesia S. Georgi.
31. Monasterium S. Clarae.
32. Monasterium S. Helisabettae.
33. Palatium Magistratus.

65. Tivoli, map, seventeenth century

many changes in the later centuries, but there is extensive pictorial and literary evidence of their sixteenth-century condition. An engraving dated 1573 (Fig. 66), but presumably after a design of about 1568, offers the most complete depiction, although it also represents features never completed, such as the Fountain of Neptune or of the Sea at the lower right, the fourth fishpool at the left, and the belvederes capping the ends of the palace. In addition, a large fresco on one of the walls of the ground-floor *salotto* of the villa itself portrays the gardens from a side angle as of about 1565 (Fig. 67). Finally there is a detailed manuscript description written probably by the designer Pirro Ligorio about 1568,[30] as well as several later printed accounts. Ligorio, who was certainly the programmer and probably the designer of the gardens, had been court archaeologist of the cardinal from 1550 and, although he had been employed as the ar-

chitect of the Vatican Palace in the later 1550s and early 1560s, when among other works he had designed the Casino of Pius IV in the Vatican, he had been again active at Tivoli in 1567 and 1568.

The principal entrance to the garden was at the lower, northwest end where coaches coming from Rome through the Porta della Colle might leave their passengers, who could then walk through the garden up the hill to the villa, while the coaches proceeded into town to the cardinal's stables. The garden itself was divided by alleys and cross alleys into a checkerboard grid that attempted to ignore the irregularity caused by the slope on the east side. The major fountains and waterworks decorated by contemporary sculpture were set at the eastern and western ends of the dominant cross alleys, except for the so-called Fountain of the Dragon part way up the hillside on the central alley from the entrance portal to the villa. A notable collection of ancient sculpture was also ingeniously adapted to the iconography of the entire

---

[30] Coffin, *The Villa d'Este*, pp. 141–50.

86

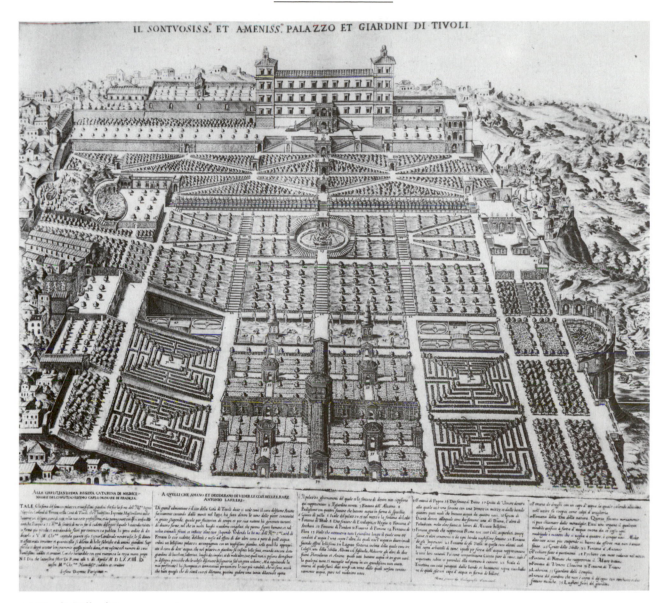

66. Tivoli, Villa d'Este, engraving, 1573

garden, often being used to decorate appropriate grottoes or fountains.[31] The very complicated iconographical program, expressed in a combination of ancient and contemporary sculpture, must have been devised by Ligorio, perhaps with the assistance of the cardinal's court humanist, the Frenchman Marc-Antoine Muret, to honor the cardinal.

Three major interrelated themes composed the iconographical program of the garden with a series of

classical topoi contributing to these themes. The most general theme pervading the entire garden is concerned with the relationship of nature to art, a theme particularly appropriate to a garden and often encountered in Roman gardens, as will be discussed later. Here at Tivoli the two major cross axes are devoted to this theme. The first or lower cross axis marked by a series of fishpools is concerned with nature, the element from which the garden will be created by means of art. On the hill above the northeast end of the line of pools is the Water Organ or Fountain of Mother Nature, *natura naturans*, or the source of nature, identified by a statue of the many-breasted

[31] T. Ashby, "The Villa d'Este at Tivoli and the Collection of Classical Sculptures Which It Contained," *Archaeologia*, LXI, pt. 1, 1908, pp. 219–55.

67. Tivoli, Villa d'Este, Salotto, fresco of Villa d'Este Gardens

Diana of Ephesus, which once was housed in the central niche of an elaborate architectural frame. According to the contemporary manuscript description the fishpools below fed by the Fountain of Nature were to be stocked by a large variety of domestic and exotic fishes and fowl, while nearby were the vegetable forms of flowers and fruit trees. The water of the fishpools was to empty into the Fountain of the Sea identified by a statue of Neptune in his chariot, as depicted in the engraving of 1573, but left incomplete at the cardinal's death in 1572.

The second major cross axis formed by the so-called Alley of One Hundred Fountains running across the upper part of the hillside celebrates art. At the northeast end is the Fountain of Tivoli, now called the Oval Fountain, where statues of the Tiburtine Sibyl and two local river gods are set within grottoes in a small artificial hill above the oval basin (Fig. 28). A boisterous but formal cascade, obviously symbolic

of the great natural cascade at the hill town of Tivoli, flows off of the hill into the water basin. At the top of the artificial hill a statue of the winged horse Pegasus (Fig. 29), originally within a laurel grove, is posed to leap off of the hilltop, equating the hill town of Tivoli with Mount Parnassus, the home of the Muses, the source of art. At the other end of the cross axis is the Fountain of the Rometta, the little Rome, where stucco-covered brick buildings were arranged in seven groups to symbolize the Seven Hills of Rome (Fig. 30). The ancient city of Rome and its architecture was for the Renaissance, of course, the epitome of the artistic manipulation of nature.

Significantly set between the two great cross axes on the west side of the garden was the Fountain of the Owl (Fig. 32). Consisting of a bronze group of automata, now destroyed, several birds, driven by water pressure, sang in a thicket until an owl appeared to frighten the birds into silence. Automata, which are

68. Tivoli, Villa d'Este, Fountain of the Dragons, engraving

works of art so naturalistically contrived in movement and sound as to deceive the spectator with their reality, offer the ultimate twist on the relationship between art and nature that intrigued the Renaissance.

The second or upper cross axis of the garden also expressed in itself a geographical and, therefore, more specific theme. At the left is the hill town of Tivoli identified by the figure of the Tiburtine Sibyl, the local river gods, and the cascade. The three conduits of the Alley of the Hundred Fountains, above which stood originally only a series of boats and Este lilies, represent the three local rivers, the Albuneo, the Aniene, and the Erculaneo, which flow from Tivoli into the Tiber as it enters Rome. So at the right is the Fountain of Rome. This geographical symbolism is, therefore, chosen to honor the cardinal's patronage of the arts.

The last theme at Tivoli is a moral one and associates the cardinal's garden with the mythological Garden of the Hesperides and with the choice of the hero Hercules between virtue and vice. The latter we have seen dominated many sixteenth-century Roman gar-

dens, but his iconography was not so developed as it is here at Tivoli. On the central axis of the garden about halfway up the central staircase is the Fountain of the Dragons (Fig. 68). The sixteenth-century description informs us that the fountain was to be that of the many-headed dragon who, as custodian of the Garden of the Hesperides, was overcome by Hercules. The cardinal, however, took advantage of the sudden visit of Pope Gregory XIII to the gardens in September 1572 to complete the fountain. To honor the pope, whose coat of arms featured a dragon, the central piece was converted to several dragons, thus acknowledging the papal visit but also recalling the original mythological meaning. An ancient statue of Hercules holding the three golden apples he plundered from the Garden of the Hesperides was set above the Fountain of the Dragon. Here in the center of the garden Hercules stood between two grottoes decorated with ancient pieces of sculpture. At the left of the garden, opening onto the piazza in front of the Fountain of Tivoli, was the Grotto of Venus or in the words of the sixteenth-century description, the Grotto of "voluptuous pleasure" (*piacer voluttuoso* or *appetito*). The main feature of the grotto was an antique figure of the Capitoline Venus type, depicted stepping out of her bath. On the other side of Hercules at the top of the hill below the outdoor dining loggia was the Grotto of Diana or "virtuous pleasure and chastity" (*piacer honesto et alla castità*). Within the grotto were four ancient statues, two of Amazons, one of Diana and one of Minerva, the last of which must be a substitute for a figure of Hippolytus, which the sixteenth-century description of the project specified. A figure of the chaste Hippolytus, who rebuffed the advances of his stepmother Phaedra, would have been not only appropriate to the theme of the grotto, but would have also recalled the name of the cardinal, Ippolito. The position of Hercules between the two grottoes alludes to Xenophon's story of the Choice of Hercules who rejected the easy, seductive way of sensuous pleasure and elected instead the steep, hard path up to virtue. By his virtue of mind and body Hercules could overcome the dragon and win the golden apples of the Hesperides, which in the Renaissance were interpreted to be the virtues of temperance, prudence, and chastity, all appropriate to a wealthy, powerful churchman.

The ingenuity with which the ancient sculpture is adapted to the iconographical program, even in minor details, is amazing. So at the northeastern end of the crosswalk along the top of the slope below the terrace on which the villa sits, ancient figures of the medical deity Aesculapius and his daughter Hygeia were set in shallow wall grottoes. Since this walk was particularly associated with the cardinal and was already identified as the Cardinal's Walk in building accounts of 1569, the antique statues should be of some personal significance. The drawings by Pirro Ligorio for a series of tapestries depicting the life of Hippolytus, and probably intended for the villa at Tivoli, explain the reference.[32] It is Aesculapius who as a "physician" (*medicus*) revives the slain Hippolytus in his resurrected form of Virbius. The title medicus then recalls the family name of Pope Pius IV of the Milanese Medici family who recalled the cardinal back to Rome, that is, back to life, after his exile.

The iconographical program of the garden at Tivoli seems to be completely expressed in terms of classical mythology and yet it undoubtedly reflected subtly the Christian faith of the cardinal. In 1557, when the gar-

[32] Coffin, *The Villa d'Este*, pp. 151–59.

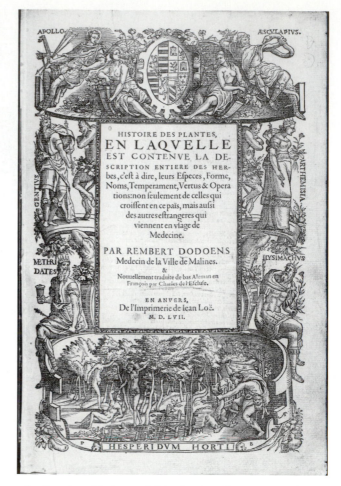

69. Rombart Dodoens, *L'histoire des plantes*, 1557, frontispiece

dens were being commenced, the great Flemish botanist, Rombart Dodoens, published his botanical treatise *L'histoire des plants*. The frontispiece of his book depicts a garden labeled the Garden of the Hesperides (Fig. 69). So Hercules is visible at the right in the act of overcoming the guardian dragon, but then within the garden Eve can be identified plucking the apple of the Tree of Knowledge and in turn offering it to Adam. The classical Garden of the Hesperides is, therefore, equated with the biblical Garden of Eden and it is the importance of apples in both stories that brings them together. A similar association of the figure of Hercules posed above the many-headed dragon might be made with Christ trampling on the beast from Psalm 90. In fact, in 1560 the great French poet Ronsard issued his hymn to "The Christian Hercules" and Ronsard's poetry was well known both to

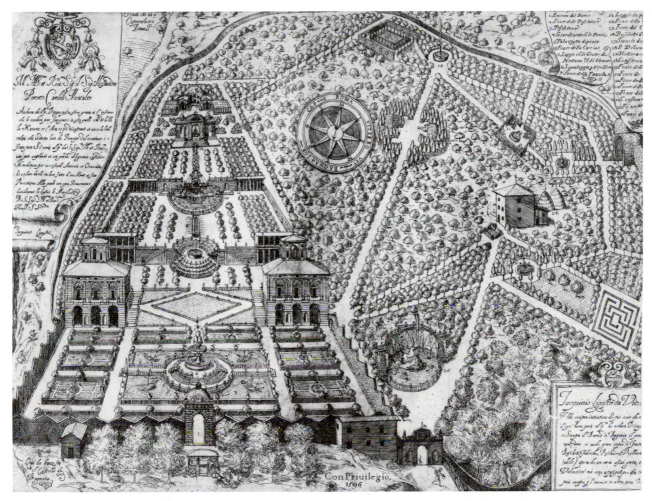

70. Bagnaia, Villa Lante, engraving, 1596, Bibliothèque Nationale, Paris

the cardinal from his legateship in France (1561–1563) and to his court humanist, the French classicist Muret.

In September 1568 as the completion of the gardens at Tivoli was being pursued vigorously for the Cardinal of Ferrara, his colleague Cardinal Gianfrancesco Gambara wrote to his neighbor Cardinal Farnese at Caprarola to send the eminent architect Vignola, then involved in the building there of the cardinal's feudal palace, presumably to aid Gambara in creating a summer residence with lavish gardens in an old hunting park just outside the little town of Bagnaia about three miles east of Viterbo. A small castle in Bagnaia had served as the summer retreat for past bishops of Viterbo to which position Cardinal Gambara had acceded in 1566. Earlier in the century a cardinal-predecessor Raffaele Riario had created a hunt-

ing park by enclosing with a wall a large wooded area on the hillside just outside the town, but the sport of hunting had diminished in popularity in the late sixteenth century.[33] The new summer residence of Cardinal Gambara was to consist of two casinos set in an elaborate terraced garden at one side of the park adjacent to the little town. By 1578 when Pope Gregory XIII visited the villa most of the garden was completed and one casino, that at the right called the Casino Gambara, was erected. The other casino at the left, although planned, was not built until later by a succeeding owner, Cardinal Montalto, who also added fountains in the park and changed the upper

[33] For documentation, see A. Cantoni et al., *La Villa Lante di Bagnaia*, Milan, 1961; C. Lazzaro Bruno, "The Villa Lante at Bagnaia," Ph.D. dissertation, Princeton University, 1974; and Coffin, *The Villa*, pp. 340–63.

71. Bagnaia, Villa Lante, Fountain of Pegasus

part of the large fountain in the center of the formal garden in front of the casinos. However, a fresco in the ground-floor loggia of the Casino Gambara, perhaps from the late 1570s, and an engraving of 1596 offer a complete view of the villa (Fig. 70) presumably as it was originally planned.

The iconographical program was a very subtle one appropriate to the carefully fashioned design and is expressed primarily in the fountains and waterworks. There were no classical antiquities to have to be adapted to the iconography or to raise uncertainties regarding the messages enunciated in the garden. Because of the changes or destruction that many of the fountains, particularly those in the park, have experienced, it is only the 1596 engraving with its identifying inscriptions of the fountains that permits comprehension of the iconographical program.[34] Much of the park was left in its original natural state except that new fountains were scattered almost haphazardly in the grounds around the old hunting lodge. Near the hunting lodge was the Fountain of the Acorns and above the lodge the Fountain of the Duck with nearby a Fountain of the Unicorn. Farther up the hill were the Fountain of Bacchus and the Fountain of the Dragon. The fountains dedicated to the unicorn and to the dragon are suggestive of a virtuous life. These in conjunction with the fountains concerned with nature must associate the naturalistic park with the classic myth of the Golden Age, when, as Ovid relates (*Metamorphoses*, I, 89–112), virtuous men were freely fed by nature's bounty for which they did not have to labor. In Vergil's Golden Age (*Georgics*, I, 132) even the streams ran with wine, the offering of Bacchus. At the same time, just within the great portal near the town by which the public might enter the park, was a prominent fountain with the winged horse Pegasus surrounded by busts presumably of the Muses (Fig. 71). Again the favorite garden topos of the creation of the Fountain of the Muses has been introduced into the broader iconographical program, in this case to associate the park geographically with Mount Parnassus.

To identify the site with Mount Parnassus was important for the continuation of the iconographical program which is actually a narrative as told by Ovid. After describing the Golden Age, Ovid continues with the destruction of most of mankind by a great flood (*Metamorphoses*, I, 262–323) rushing down from between the two peaks of Mount Parnassus. So at Bagn-

[34] C. Lazzaro Bruno, "The Villa Lante at Bagnaia: An Allegory of Art and Nature," *Art Bulletin*, LIX, 1977, pp. 553–60.

72. Bagnaia, Villa Lante, Fountain of the Dolphins, drawing by Guerra, Graphische Sammlung, Albertina, Vienna

aia a Fountain of the Deluge was at the topmost level of the formal gardens introduced at one side of the park. This fountain gushed forth from between two small garden houses identified on the engraving as the Houses of the Muses from their interior frescoed depiction of the Muses. These two houses also symbolized the two peaks of Mount Parnassus where the human survivors, Deucalion and Pyrrha, escaped from the great flood that covered the rest of the world. In front of the Fountain of the Deluge is the Fountain of the Dolphins, which a contemporary drawing depicts as originally covered by an impermanent pergola of lattice work over which shrubs and small trees were once espaliered (Fig. 72). This fountain then reflects Ovid's comment (*Metamorphoses*, I, 302) that the water so covered the earth that dolphins swam among the woods.

The water from the Fountain of the Deluge then plunges in channels and underground conduits down the hillside, activating other fountains on the lower terraces. The water of the so-called water chain (*ca-*

73. Bagnaia, Villa Lante, *catena d'acqua*

74. Bagnaia, Villa Lante, Cardinal's Table

75. Bagnaia, Villa Lante, parterre and casinos

*tena d'acqua*) that bubbles down the hill from in front of the Fountain of the Dolphins issues from the head of a crayfish whose extended arms confine the channel of roiling water (Fig. 73). The crayfish, *gambero* in Italian, is, of course, a punning reference to Cardinal Gambara who is, therefore, identified as controlling the water of his garden. Man, now, because of the destruction of the Golden Age, has to labor for his sustenance. So on the middle terrace the river gods, presumably the Tiber and the Arno, irrigate the cardinal's lands to produce the food, symbolized by the statues of Pomona and Flora, that will sustain him. A huge table stands on the terrace where the cardinal and his friends may dine *al fresco* (Fig. 74), cooling bottles of wine in the water channel cut into the center of the table, as Pliny the Younger describes floating food on little boats in a water basin in the garden of his Tuscan villa (*Letters*, v, 6).

While the middle terrace symbolizes agriculture or

the domination of nature by man's labor to promote food for his sustenance, the lowest level with carefully trimmed parterres and topiary is, of course, representative of horticulture or the transformation of nature into art by man's sense of design (Fig. 75). So here, too, in the architecture of the casinos, the sculpture of the central fountain, the painting of the frescoed loggias of the casinos, and even the reference to the theater in the semicircular Fountain of the Lights, are examples of all the other types of art man creates from nature. As at Tivoli, but perhaps in a subtler manner there is again at Bagnaia a consideration of the relationship between nature and art so essential to the Renaissance theory of art. Like Tivoli also there is obviously at Bagnaia a biblical overlay to the iconography, for the classical story of the Golden Age and its retributive flood can only recall to a Renaissance Christian the Garden of Eden and man's fall from Grace.

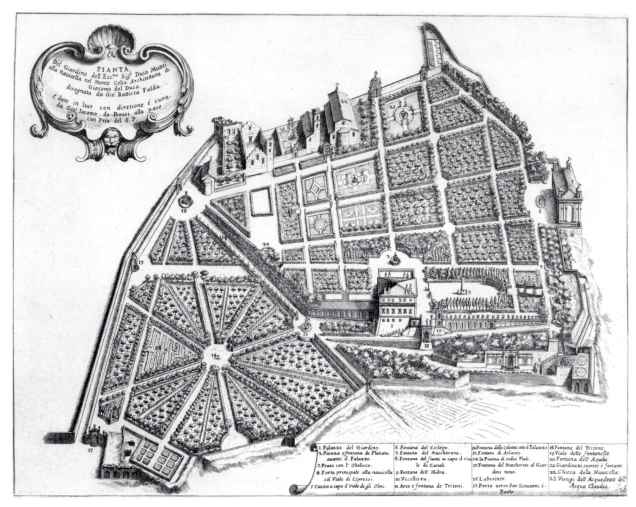

1. Palazzo del Giardino.
2. Piazza e fontana de Platani auanti il Palazzo.
3. Prato con l' Obelisco.
4. Porta principale alla nauicella col Viale di Cipressi.
5. Casino a capo il Viale de gli Olmi.
6. Fontana del Ciclopo.
7. Fontana del Mascherone.
8. Fontana del fiume in capo il Viale de Canali.
9. Fontana dell' Hidra.
10. Vccelliera.
11. Arco e fontana de Tritoni.
12. Fontana delle Colonne sotto il Palazzo.
13. Fontana di Atlante.
14. La Piazza di sedici Viali.
15. Fontana del Mascherone al Giardino nouo.
16. Laberinto.
17. Porta uerso San Giouanni e Paolo.
18. Fontana del Tritone.
19. Viale delle fontanelle.
20. Fontana dell' Aquila.
21. Giardinetti secreti e fontane.
22. Chiesa della Nauicella.
23. Vestigi dell' Acquedotto del Acqua Claudia.

76. Rome, Villa Mattei, engraving

Most of the great gardens in Rome, organized on classical iconographical programs, have been those of churchmen, popes, and cardinals. Toward the end of the sixteenth century, however, one of the old Roman families decorated the gardens of a suburban villa with classical antiquities and contemporary peperino sculpture, which would enhance the reputation of the family. About 1571 the Roman patrician Ciriaco Mattei inherited from his father-in-law, Giacomo Mattei, a vigna on the Celian Hill behind the church of Sta. Maria in Domnica, which Giacomo had purchased in 1553.[35] Between 1581, when the city of Rome had given Ciriaco Mattei an ancient Roman obelisk that had formerly decorated the Circus Flaminius, and 1586, Mattei had built a new casino probably designed by Giacomo Del Duca, within extensive gardens lavishly ornamented by a large collection of Roman antiquities and numerous fountains (Fig. 76). An inventory of the sculpture prepared in 1614 at the death of Mattei forms the only basis for an explanation of the iconography of the gardens, since almost all the sculpture is either destroyed or dispersed.[36] A few of the ancient figures or antiquities, such as the Hercules and Gladiator at the entrance to the Labyrinth of the Dragon, the large head of Alexander the Great and the obelisk in the hippodrome,

[35] E. B. MacDougall, "The Villa Mattei and the Development of the Roman Garden Style," Ph.D. dissertation, Harvard University, 1970, and S. Benedetti, *Giacomo Del Duca e l'architettura del Cinquecento*, Rome, 1972–1973, pp. 308–36.

[36] E. B. MacDougall, "A Circus, a Wild Man and a Dragon: Family History and the Villa Mattei," *Journal of the Society of Architectural Historians*, XLII, 1983, pp. 121–30; the inventory is published in Lanciani, *Storia degli scavi di Roma*, III, pp. 88–97.

were adapted to the iconographical program, but most were apparently merely ornamental figures set in the gardens and the program was basically expressed by the modern peperino sculpture.

The major feature of the grounds was the large hippodrome shaped "meadow" (*prato*), as it is described in contemporary documents, opening immediately south of the casino. In an earlier chapter, the hippodrome shape was noted as a common feature of Roman classicizing gardens inspired by Pliny's description of such a garden south of his Tuscan villa (*Letters*, v, 6). Here at the Villa Mattei, however, the emphasis seems to be more on the original function of the hippodrome form as a location for athletic contests and sports. The erection of the ancient Roman obelisk in the center of the hippodrome corresponds probably to its original location in the Circus Flaminius. The identification of the several dogs in the hippodrome, carved of peperino stone and painted naturalistically, as different hunting dogs—two poodles (*barboni*), two coursers (*corsi*), and two greyhounds (*livirieri*)—introduces sporting associations. Even the two peperino figures in the center of the hippodrome, who are described enigmatically in the inventory as a "good brute" (*brutto buono*) and a "child" (*ragazzo*) may, it has been suggested, be participating in an athletic contest.[37] What seems most unusual is a gigantic bust of the Greek ruler Alexander the Great dominating the end of the hippodrome, but it may be the clue to the introduction of the hippodrome here. Ciriaco Mattei's father, Alessandro—namesake, therefore, of Alexander the Great—had been a leader of the local Roman government. Dying in 1580, the year before the ancient obelisk was given by the city to his son, the gift may, therefore, have commemorated Alessandro's services in the government. Since it was the custom of the ancient Romans to honor prominent citizens with games and athletic contests in the hippodrome or circus, the hippodrome at the villa may be to celebrate Alessandro Mattei and his services on behalf of the city, although it is very puzzling that his name is never inscribed on the obelisk or anywhere in the villa.

At the left of the main entrance to the villa's grounds was the Woods of the Animals (*Boschetto degli Animali*) inhabited by different animals as well as a shepherd. A German visitor toward the end of the century remarked on the naturalism of a stag, goat, swan, doe, and lynx, all life-size and painted in natu-

ral colors, seen there.[38] This bucolic scene must suggest the garden as the setting of a peaceful kingdom, where a variety of domestic and wild animals dwelt peacefully together; in short, another version of the Golden Age. Beyond this setting throughout the garden were numerous fountains and garden ornaments featuring different classical topoi. At the south side of the garden in front of the belvedere known as the Casino of S. Sisto was an oval labyrinth whose entrance was guarded, as the inventory states, by "Two Hercules . . . or rather a Hercules and a gladiator," and a dragon carved of peperino was set in the middle of the labyrinth. This must allude to the Garden of the Hesperides. Several other Herculean labors were presented in fountains such as the Fountain of the Columns with spiral columns recalling presumably the so-called Pillars of Hercules, the Fountain of the Deluge with Hercules and the Hydra, and the Fountain of Atlas.

Hercules was, as we have seen, the predominant dedicatee of Roman gardens. His presence in the gardens of the Villa Mattei is particularly appropriate as Hercules' Roman labor, the killing of Cacus, was supposed to have occurred here on the Caelian Hill. The constant reference to the deeds of Hercules, the man of virtue, is also appropriate to the realm of the Golden Age, the age of peace and virtue, here honoring Alessandro Mattei and his descendants.

The concern for elaborate iconographical programs drawn from classical mythology seems to diminish and even disappear in the seventeenth century. The Villa Montalto built at Rome for Cardinal Montalto, later Pope Sixtus V, almost contemporary with the Villa Mattei, already shows this trend.[39] Two classical statues of Pomona and Flora do dominate the two fountains set in the angles of the *trivium* form of the alleys as they flare out from the main entrance to the villa, but these are merely the traditional garden deities here associated with the lions of the coat of arms of Pope Sixtus V, as signs that one is entering the rustic, garden retreat of the pope (Fig. 77). The common use of imprese and heraldic devices to decorate fountains toward the end of the sixteenth century

[37] MacDougall, "A Circus," p. 126.

[38] H. G. Ernstinger, *Hans Georg Ernstingers Raisbuch* (Bibliothek des litterarischen Vereins in Stuttgart, CXXXV), ed. P.A.F. Walther, Tübingen, 1877, p. 98.

[39] For documentation, see [V. Massimo,] *Notizie istoriche della Villa Massimo alle Terme Diocleziane*, Rome, 1836; J.A.F. Orbaan, "Dai conti di Domenico Fontana (1585–1588)," *Bollettino d'arte*, VII, 1913, pp. 419–24, and VIII, 1914, pp. 59–71; and MacDougall, "The Villa Mattei," pp. 238–262.

77. Rome, Villa Montalto, engraving

has been noted, particularly with respect to the Montalto fountains,[40] although this practice had already occurred to some degree in the villas at Tivoli and Bagnaia. Otherwise the decoration of the Villa Montalto, both in its interior fresco painting and its garden fountains, reflects the virtues of Charity and Justice, particularly valued by Pope Sixtus, who was especially renowned for the severity of his justice in the punishment of the brigands who had previously demoralized the tranquility of the papal states. The decoration of the so-called Torretta or entrance loggia erected by 1587 at the corner of the gardens of the villa near the new Via Felice summed up both these interests. The little fountain within the Torretta had the traditional mediaeval allegory of the pelican tearing its breast to feed its young that was not only a symbol of the sacrifice of Christ, but of Charity in

general. On the vault of the loggia was the punishment of the Elders who had attempted to seduce Susanna while she was bathing. The association of both scenes with water, the water flowing from the breast of the pelican and the water in which Susanna bathed, celebrates the pope's laying on of the Acqua Felice to bring water to the hills, as well as to his own villa. Accounts also speak of a Fountain of a Dwarf (*Fontana del Nanetto*) and a Fountain of a Prisoner (*Fontana del Prigione*). An inventory of 1655 notes that a figure of a prisoner was in the middle of the latter.[41] The fact that this statue was accompanied by antique statues of Apollo, a nude Venus, and a seated Jupiter suggests that the ancient sculpture of the inventory was simply set as decoration in various parts of the garden.

Later the pope's grandnephew, Cardinal Alessandro Peretti Montalto, who also owned and completed the Villa Lante at Bagnaia, commissioned the sculptor Bernini about 1620 to carve the wonderful group of

---

[40] E. B. MacDougall, "*L'Ingegnoso Artifizio*: Sixteenth Century Garden Fountains in Rome," in *Fons Sapientiae: Renaissance Garden Fountains* (Dumbarton Oaks Colloquium on the History of Landscape Architecture, v), ed. E. B. MacDougall, Washington, D.C., 1978, pp. 106–7.

[41] MacDougall, "The Villa Mattei," p. 248.

78. Rome, Villa Montalto, fishpool with Neptune, engraving

Neptune and a Triton, now in the Victoria and Albert Museum at London (Fig. 78). The statuary group, presumably derived from Vergil's *Aeneid* (I, 131–56), illustrates the "Quos ego" theme of Neptune calming the troubled waters. Perhaps inspired by the statue of Neptune of Stoldi Lorenzi created earlier for the Boboli Gardens in Florence, the Bernini group was placed at one end of a large oval fishpool in the western corner of the grounds signifying the peaceful precinct the cardinal rules. Cardinal Montalto's renewal at Rome of a classical topos to decorate his gardens in the seventeenth century was a rather isolated incident compared with the prevalence of classical iconography in sixteenth-century Roman gardens.

There was at Frascati at the turn of the century, however, one elaborate garden layout that depended on classical iconography for its message. In 1601 Cardinal Pietro Aldobrandini, nephew of Pope Clement VIII, commissioned the architect Giacomo della Porta to enlarge a modest country residence set into the hillside at Frascati into the lavish Villa Aldobrandini.[42]

The building with its unusual mammoth broken pediment dominates the hill immediately above Frascati, but its most impressive feature is the huge water theater set into the hill behind the villa (Fig. 36). A large semicircular exedra flanked by long walls masks the foot of the hill forming a rear wall for the terrace behind the building. A rampant cascade pours down the hill and flows through the central niche of the exedra into a water basin. A long Latin inscription on the frieze of the water theater honors Cardinal Aldobrandini for erecting here a country retreat "after restoring peace to Christendom and reacquiring the Duchy of Ferrara for the papal states."[43] Two large spiral columns standing on the hillside at the commencement of the last run of the watery cascade are, of course, the famous Pillars of Hercules reputed to

---

[42] For documentation and analysis, see K. Schwager, "Kardinal Pietro Aldobrandinis Villa di Belvedere in Frascati," *Römisches Jahrbuch für Kunstgeschichte*, IX–X, 1961–1962, pp. 289–382;

C. d'Onofrio, *La Villa Aldobrandini di Frascati*, Rome [1963]; and Fagiolo dell'Arco, "Villa Aldobrandina tusculana," *Quaderni dell'Istituto di Storia dell'Architettura*, ser. XI, fasc. 62–66, 1964, pp. 61–92.

[43] For the iconography of the garden decoration in relation to the inscription, see R. M. Steinberg, "The Iconography of the Teatro dell'Acqua at the Villa Aldobrandini," *Art Bulletin*, XLVII, 1965, pp. 453–63.

stand at the western limits of the world of classical antiquity. Here the columns are to symbolize the expansion in Europe of the power of the Catholic church under Clement VIII by the two deeds of his nephew, the cardinal, enunciated in the inscription. So the cardinal negotiated in 1595 a religious peace with France, his restoration of "peace to Christendom," and he had overseen the seizure of the Duchy of Ferrara for the Church after the death of Duke Alfonso II d'Este in 1597.

The Herculean iconography is also visible in the central niche of the exedra, where Atlas bends under the weight of the celestial globe on his shoulders and Hercules, now destroyed, once reached up to relieve Atlas of the sphere. Hercules was visualized, therefore, actively seeking the celestial sphere which signified divine wisdom, as a lost figure of Tantalus submerged in the water basin depicted the punishment meted out to those who rejected divine wisdom. This scene too was to exalt the cardinal in the guise of Hercules, just as the contemporary poet Marino lauded the virtue of the cardinal in taking onto his own shoulders the heavenly sphere of Atlas.[44] A contemporary account of the villa notes that the Herculean iconography here was derived from two of the fountains at the Villa Mattei dedicated to Hercules: the Fountain of the Column and the Fountain of Atlas.[45] Secondary figures in the side niches of Polyphemus and a centaur, as well as a freestanding group of a lion combating a boar in the center of the parterre of the exedra, all express the struggle of man's reason with his bestial nature. The two rooms at the ends of the water theater, a temple of religion and one of art, finally proclaim man's victory over his baseness. At the left is a chapel dedicated to St. Sebastian, patron of the Aldobrandini family. At the right is the Room of Apollo or of Parnassus, which has at its rear a fountain depicting Mount Parnassus, that favorite topos of Roman Renaissance gardens, while the walls are frescoed by Domenichino with the deeds of Apollo (Fig. 38). So the fresco of Apollo slaying Marsyas conforms to the external theme of reason overcoming the bestial.

Although many more lavish waterworks, fountains, and cascades will be devised at the villas of Frascati in the seventeenth century, the water theater of the Villa Aldobrandini is the last apparently to present an elaborate iconographical program.

Normally the iconographical programs devised for Roman gardens during the Renaissance were chosen from classical mythology, especially Herculean myths, as a means of classicizing the garden suitable to Renaissance culture, although they also may echo the Christian belief, as was suggested at Tivoli. At the very end of the sixteenth century, however, one garden in Rome was created with overtly Christian themes, obviously in conformity with the principles proclaimed earlier by the Council of Trent. This garden, as one might expect, was that of the Jesuit novitiate on the side of the Quirinal Hill between their monastery of S. Andrea al Quirinale and the church of S. Vitale, which later was given to the order by Pope Clement VIII in 1595.[46] The general of the Jesuit order, Father Claudio Acquaviva, apparently formulated the program, which also involved the decoration of S. Vitale with frescoes completed by the painter Tarquinio Ligustri in 1599. Appropriate to the training and meditation of the novices, the frescoes within the church depicted the martyrdoms of early Christian saints, and various instruments of torture were represented in the atrium of the church. In the scenes of martyrdom the human figures are minor and the landscape settings dominate the figures, for the general theme is that nature, which along with mankind is God's handiwork, participates in the suffering of the martyrs.

The garden of the Jesuit novitiate on the hillside below their monastery and above and beside S. Vitale was destroyed in the nineteenth century, but the French Jesuit, Louis Richeome, wrote a spiritual treatise, published in 1611, that described the garden in detail, accompanied by an engraving (Fig. 79), as well as the frescoes of S. Vitale.[47] The garden was organized on the hillside with an upper terrace behind the monastery and a lower terrace at the level of S. Vitale joined by a middle, sloping, wooded area. Above the entrance to the upper garden was depicted the Virgin and on the garden side Christ surrounded by balsam, hyssop, lilies, roses, and other fragrant plants, accompanied by an inscription from the Song of Songs (v, 1): "I am come into my garden, my sister, my spouse: I have gathered my myrrh with my spices." The gar-

[44] M. Menghini, "La villa Aldobrandini, canzone inedita di Giambattista Marino," *Il Propugnatore*, 1, 1888, pp. 440–45.

[45] Schwager, "Aldobrandinis Villa," p. 373.

[46] L. Huetter and V. Golzio, *San Vitale* (Le chiese di Roma illustrate, 35), Rome, n. d.; F. Zeri, *Pittura e controriforma: L'arte senza tempo di Scipione da Gaeta*, Turin, 1957, pp. 92–93; and A. Zuccari, *Arte e committenza nella Roma di Caravaggio*, Turin, 1984, pp. 143–63.

[47] L. Richeome, *La peinture spirituelle ou l'art d'admirer, aimer et louer Dieu en toutes ses oeuvres*, Lyon, 1611, illus. p. 472.

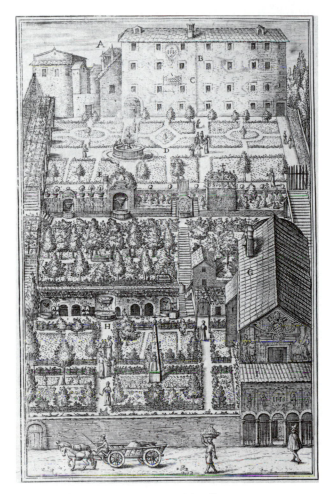

79. L. Richeome, *La peinture spirituelle*, 1611, p. 472

ture define the time of day. Three flights of stairs descended the middle slope planted with cypress and fruit trees, thus connecting the two terraces. Two fountains also decorated the slope. One had two biblical scenes on the back of the wall depicted, as Richeome relates, "without brushes and without color," so probably in relief. Appropriate to a fountain, one scene had *Moses Striking Water from the Rock* and the other *Rebecca at the Well*. The second fountain with water gushing from the jaws of a lion had a representation of the Holy Family resting in the shade of a palm tree on the flight into Egypt. At the end of an alley was a depiction of *Angels Adoring the Cross*.

Several fountains were also set in the lower garden, which because of their location were, according to Richeome, symbols of humility. On the walls of the last alley were pictures of three of the parables of Christ: that of the sterile fig tree, of the sowing of seed, and of the laborers in the vineyard. In the center of the last parterre a large, white marble pyramid had religious scenes on each of its sides appropriate both to their orientation and to garden iconography. On the east face Christ was accompanied by the sun and lilies with Old Testament inscriptions engraved on two ribbons: "The Orient is His Name" (Zacharias, VI, 12) and "I am the flower of the field, and the lily of the valleys" (Song of Songs, II, 1). On the west a crowned Solomon proclaimed: "I built me houses; I planted me vineyards. I made me gardens and orchards . . . and behold, all was vanity and waywardness of spirit" (Ecclesiastes, II, 4, 5, and 11). The north side of the pyramid had the Virgin crowned by myrtle, inscribed: "Awake, O north wind; . . . and blow through my garden" (Song of Songs, IV, 16) and on the south the Virgin crowned with a diadem of flowers, inscribed: "Come, O south [wind]; and blow through my garden, and let my spices flow out" (ibid.).

The garden, therefore, in terms of its horticultural features differed in no way from the other gardens in Rome. Its Christian iconography was conveyed by the decoration of the fountains and other garden furnishings as was true with the classically oriented gardens of Tivoli and Bagnaia. Richeome's treatise, however, also brought a religious, Christian interpretation to what was otherwise a traditional garden. The three stairs joining the two terraces offer "the picture of a triple humility" to those who must descend or mount them, as the fountains on the lower terrace were by their location "a symbol of humility." When Richeome describes the flowers enlivening the upper ter-

den is described as having variegated compartments of colorful flowers, including roses, carnations, lilies, violets, heliotrope, jasmine, daisies, hollyhocks, double poppies, and blue-bottle, all bordered with rue, and the walls were hung with "tapestries of citron and lemon trees," using the traditional sixteenth-century phrase for espaliered walls. All these natural and artificial beauties are "to instruct your soul and to move it to love, praise and thank the author and donor of nature and of art."[48] A fountain in the middle of the parterres shot up a great central jet of water accompanied by smaller jets about the basin. Two sundials, one horizontal, inscribed on a piece of slate supported by a pillar in the corner of one parterre, and the other set vertically on the wall of the monastery, in a good seventeenth-century fashion, had na-

[48] Ibid., p. 475.

race he has a section entitled "Human vanity pictured in the flowers," pointing out that the flowers are never in the same state. Beautiful to see in the morning, they gradually droop and lose their color. "These traits make a picture of the deceitfulness of corporeal beauty and of the vanity of this deceiving World."[49] Not only are the flowers and trees to teach religious lessons to the Jesuit novices, but so do the humblest inhabitants of the garden, the birds, the bees, the ants, the flies, and gnats. So the novices would use their garden as a site of meditation in preparation for prayer in the nearby sanctuary of S. Vitale, where they would be surrounded by depictions of instruments of torture and martyrdom that they might face in their future lives.

[49] Ibid., pp. 490–91.

# Art, Nature, and Illusion

The fifteenth-century humanist and architect Leon Battista Alberti reasserted the dependence of the arts on nature, just as classical antiquity had done. In his treatise on painting he repeatedly directs the artist to learn from nature: "So, let us always take from Nature whatever we are about to paint, and let us always choose those things that are most beautiful and worthy" (III, 56).[1] Even the abstract art of architecture was defined by Alberti in his famous treatise on architecture as an imitation of nature: "We learn from the authorities of antiquity, as I have said elsewhere, that a building is like an animal in which determining the work one should imitate nature" (IX, v).[2] Such imitation goes so far that Alberti could advocate that the columns of garden loggias might be created in imitation of knotty tree trunks (IX, i), as Bramante will actually do in the cloister of St. Ambrogio at Milan.

At the same moment the Neoplatonic philosopher Marsilio Ficino lent the authority of philosophic thought to this concept of artistic imitation, quoting examples from the activity of such ancient artists as Zeuxis, Apelles, and Praxiteles: "And what is quite wonderful, human arts produce by themselves whatever nature itself produces, as if we were not the slaves but the rivals of nature." In fact, this ability to emulate nature was proof to Ficino of Man's immortality, for "man imitates all the works of the divine nature, and perfects, corrects and improves the works

of the lower nature. Therefore the power of man is almost similar to that of the divine nature, for man acts in this way through himself. Through his own wit and art he governs himself without being bound by any limits of corporeal nature; and he imitates all the works of the higher nature."[3]

This adherence to nature as the source of art continues fully into the sixteenth century, whether it is the literary theory of the poet Girolamo Vida, who asserts that "art functions only by imitating nature, and conforms to it closely,"[4] or the architect Palladio claiming that "Architecture (as also all the other arts) is the imitator of Nature" (I, xx).

Alberti earlier had also defined the role of nature as the producer of the physical materials and principles that the artist employed, when he notes in the preface to his treatise on architecture that "we consider a building to be a body which, like other bodies, consists of design and of matter of which one is produced by the mind and the other by nature."[5] This definition of a work of art as the transformation of nature's gifts by man's sense of design was clearly expressed in the programs of two of the most notable sixteenth-century gardens of Rome. Although no theoretical treatises considered the role of gardening as an art, many of the Renaissance gardens were designed by architects or artists who were cognizant of Alberti's ideas and those of the other Renaissance critics. At the Villa

---

[1] L. B. Alberti, *On Painting and On Sculpture*, ed. C. Grayson, London, 1972, p. 101; some other passages where Alberti refers to nature as the source for painting are on pp. 81 and 89.

[2] L. B. Alberti, *L'architettura [De Re Aedificatoria]*, Milan, 1966, II, p. 811.

[3] J. L. Burroughs, translated selections from Marsilio Ficino's *Platonic Theology* in *The Journal of the History of Ideas*, V, 1944, p. 233.

[4] G. M. Vida, *The De Arte Poetica of Marco Girolamo Vida*, trans. R. G. Williams, New York, 1976, p. 73 (book II, 455–64).

[5] Alberti, *L'architettura*, I, p. 15.

d'Este at Tivoli the two major cross axes of the garden layout made explicit reference to such ideas (Fig. 66). The lower cross axis, commencing at the northeast with the Water Organ or the Fountain of Mother Nature, continued with fishpools containing specimens of a variety of fish and fowl and nearby were the vegetal forms of flower gardens and fruit trees, all intended to end on the southwest side in the great Fountain of Neptune or of the Sea. This cross axis thus presented not only Mother Nature or *natura naturans*, but examples of natural life, *natura naturata*, from which a garden is created. The second cross axis, running across the hillside above, denoted art symbolized by the statue of the winged horse Pegasus on the hill above the Fountain of Tivoli, equating the hill town of Tivoli with Mount Parnassus, the home of the Muses, the goddesses of the arts. The Fountain of Rometta at the other end of the cross axis depicts the ancient marvels of Rome that man by his powers of design and art fashioned from nature. Soon the garden and park of the Villa Lante at Bagnaia will present its own version of the theme where the untamed, beneficent nature of the mythical Golden Age symbolized in the park will be fashioned by man's labor and artistic design into the horticultural work of art of the formal garden as a setting for the other arts.[6]

The relationship between art and nature during the Renaissance, however, was not always a simple, straightforward question of imitation. Nature was a tough taskmaster not always conducive to man's conception of beauty. As quoted previously, Alberti in his treatise on painting had qualified the imitation of nature by advising the artist "to choose those things that are most beautiful and worthy." In the sixteenth and seventeenth centuries this selective beauty or the concept of ideal beauty, which is ultimately at odds with the concept of direct imitation, will dominate art criticism.[7] During the Renaissance, art and nature often struggled with one another. The ease with which an artist can overcome the obstacles of nature will enhance his reputation. Daniele Barbaro, the Venetian humanist, in the dedication of his 1567 edition of Vitruvius to the Cardinal of Ferrara, patron of the Villa d'Este at Tivoli, praises the latter in such terms:

> Nature agrees to confess to having been conquered by the art and splendor of your mind, so that in an instant the gardens are born and the groves shoot up, and trees

full of the most delicious fruit are discovered in one night, also hills issue from the valleys and in the hills of the hardest rocks are laid the beds of rivers and stones opened to give place to waters and flood the dry earth, irrigated by fountains and running streams and the choicest fishpools of which men more intelligent than I have given honored judgment.[8]

So Barbaro implies for the cardinal the power of a Moses in bringing water to the Israelites, as the artists will paint on the walls of the Room of Moses in the Villa d'Este at Tivoli.

The uniqueness of a garden as a work of art fashioned from this competition between art and nature will be identified in the sixteenth century as a "nameless third nature." Previously philosophers and critics had identified two "natures": the creative force of nature or natura naturans, and the created substance of nature or natura naturata. In the gardens of the Villa d'Este at Tivoli the fertility statue of the many-breasted Diana of Ephesus, or Mother Nature, standing in a niche in the Fountain of the Water Organ, symbolized the "first nature" or natura naturans, as the various fishes and fowl in the fishpool below accompanied by a wealth of flowers, herbs, and fruit trees exemplified the "second nature" or natura naturata. About 1542, however, Jacopo Bonfadio in a letter notes that at the gardens of Lake Garda there "nature incorporated with art is made a creator and connatural with art, and from both is created a third nature, to which I would not know how to give a name."[9] Bartolomeo Taegio, author of a dialogue on Lombard villas, presumably knew Bonfadio's letter, when he later describes how at the garden of Castellazzo "the industry of a clever gardener who, incorporating art with nature, causes that there issues from both a third nature which is the reason that the fruits are more delicious there than elsewhere."[10]

To confuse further the relationship between art and

---

trans. J.J.S. Peake, Columbia, S.C., 1968, and R. W. Lee, *Ut Pictura Poesis: The Humanistic Theory of Painting*, New York, 1967.

[8] Vitruvius Pollio, *I dieci libri dell'architettura*, Venice, 1567, prologue.

[9] J. Bonfadio, *Le lettere e una scrittura burlesca*, ed. A. Greco, Rome, 1978, p. 96; see also A. Rinaldi, "La ricerca della 'terza natura': Artificialia e naturalia nel giardino toscana del '500," in *Natura e artificio*, ed. M. Fagiolo, Rome, 1979, pp. 154–75; A. Tagliolini, *I giardini di Roma*, Rome, 1980, p. 94; and A. Tagliolini, "Girolamo Fiorenzuola e il giardino nelle fonti della metà del Cinquecento," in *Il giardino storico*, ed. G. Ragionieri, Florence, 1981, pp. 302–3.

[10] B. Taegio, *La villa*, Milan, 1559, pp. 58–59 (p. 59 is given by error as p. 67).

---

[6] For the programs of Tivoli and Bagnaia, see Chapter 5.

[7] See especially E. Panofsky, *Idea: A Concept in Art Theory*,

nature the ancient Roman poet Ovid in his *Metamorphoses* claimed that nature could imitate art as in a grotto of Diana described by him: "In its most secret nook there was a well-shaded grotto, wrought by no artist's hand. But Nature by her own cunning had imitated art; for she had shaped a native arch of the living rock and soft tufa" (III, 157–60).[11] Thus the grottoes and other rock work so common in sixteenth-century Roman gardens particularly confound the spectator's appreciation of this relationship between art and nature. In 1543 Claudio Tolomei, describing the grotto in the garden of Messer Belluomo near the Trevi Fountain fed by the Acqua Vergine, remarks on

> the ingenious skill recently rediscovered for making fountains, which is seen used in many places in Rome, where mingling art with nature one does not know how to discern whether it is a work of the former or of the latter, rather at one moment it seems to be a natural artifact and then an artificial nature. So they try in these things to feign a fountain that should seem made by nature itself, not by accident, but with masterful art.[12]

In the second half of the sixteenth century the introduction of automata into gardens, as at Tivoli in the Fountain of the Owl and the Birds (Fig. 32) or the Water Organ (Fig. 31) and later at the Villa Aldobrandini at Frascati (Fig. 38), brought the relationship between art and nature to its fullest ambiguity. Works of art—that is, pieces of wood or metal sculpture—moved with the life of natural beings and uttered natural and musical or artful sounds. These amazing and often startling "wonders" amused the spectators with their natural semblance just as the waterworks performed amusing and outlandish tricks on the unsuspecting visitors. Alessandro Giorgi concludes his 1592 Italian translation of Hero of Alexandria's *Pneumatica* by noting how "one can derive [from it] the way to make all the most artful fountains blend nature with art, exhibiting groans, sprinklings, garglings, dribblings, bubblings, murmurings, foam, tremors, the music of falling water and a thousand other delightful and unusual caprices."[13]

The element of fantasy in gardening at Rome reached its fullest in the mid-sixteenth century in the Sacro Bosco or Sacred Wood established by Vicino Orsini near his palace at the little hill town of Bomarzo about twelve miles northwest of Viterbo. An inscription cut into the pedestal of one of the two statues of sphinxes that once flanked the entrance to Orsini's garden asked the visitor whether the "many marvels" there "have been made by delusion or merely by art." A little later, in 1579, Alfonso Ceccarelli will remark that Vicino made the garden "where he puts himself in competition with nature, in making things which must astonish anyone who sees them."[14] Unfortunately contemporary information about the Sacro Bosco is very limited, creating a further aura of mystery about it which has recently been exploited by criticism dominated either by nineteenth-century romanticism or twentieth-century Freudianism. Although there has not yet been discovered a fully satisfactory explanation for the program of the Sacro Bosco, and there may never be, as it undoubtedly reflects the very personal expression of its owner, a close examination of the complex indicates that it partakes of many Renaissance features and cannot be considered an anomaly.

In 1542 Vicino Orsini inherited the fief of Bomarzo from his father, Gian Corrado. Vicino himself was not only an eminent military captain, but also a literary figure, who numbered among his literary acquaintances Claudio Tolomei, Annibal Caro, and the poet Molza, according to Betussi, who dedicated his dialogue *Il Raverta* to Orsini in 1544, and it is presumably Orsini who composed the poetic epigrams scattered throughout the Sacro Bosco. Sometime between 1544 and 1546 he married Giulia Farnese, an offspring of the family of Pope Paul III. Her death in the early 1560s will mark a very important moment in the creation of the woods. In 1546 Orsini went north to Germany with the papal troops for a year, and it is probably on his return that he began to create his Sacro Bosco, since an obelisk near the theater-exedra bears the inscription *Vicino Orsini nel MDLII*, perhaps the date of the completion of that area of the garden.[15] Orsini continued to be involved in the Eu-

[11] Ovid, *Metamorphoses* (Loeb Classical Library), trans. F. J. Miller, I, Cambridge, Mass., and London, 1956, p. 135. He offers another example in book XI, 235–36, ibid., II, 1958, p. 137.

[12] G. Bottari and S. Ticozzi, *Raccolta di lettere sulla pittura, scultura ed architettura*, V, Milan, 1822, p. 103; see also E. B. MacDougall, "Introduction," in *Fons Sapientiae: Renaissance Garden Fountains* (Dumbarton Oaks Colloquium on the History of Landscape Architecture, V), Washington, D.C., 1978, p. 12.

[13] Quoted in M. Dezzi Bardeschi, "Le fonti degli automi di Pra-

tolino," in *La fonte delle fonti: Iconologia degli artifizi d'acqua*, ed. A. Vezzosi, Florence, 1985, p. 21.

[14] H. Bredekamp, *Vicino Orsini und der Heilige Wald von Bomarzo*, Worms, 1985, II, p. 91; Bredekamp furnishes all the documentation regarding the Sacro Bosco, unless otherwise noted.

[15] Bredekamp, *Bomarzo*, notes that the creation of the Sacred Wood was *seriatim* over a long period of time and attempts to date

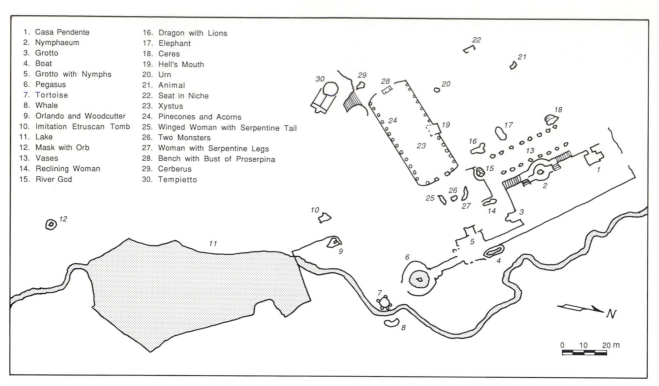

1. Casa Pendente
2. Nymphaeum
3. Grotto
4. Boat
5. Grotto with Nymphs
6. Pegasus
7. Tortoise
8. Whale
9. Orlando and Woodcutter
10. Imitation Etruscan Tomb
11. Lake
12. Mask with Orb
13. Vases
14. Reclining Woman
15. River God
16. Dragon with Lions
17. Elephant
18. Ceres
19. Hell's Mouth
20. Urn
21. Animal
22. Seat in Niche
23. Xystus
24. Pinecones and Acorns
25. Winged Woman with Serpentine Tail
26. Two Monsters
27. Woman with Serpentine Legs
28. Bench with Bust of Proserpina
29. Cerberus
30. Tempietto

80. Bomarzo, plan

ropean wars, being captured in 1553 at the siege of Hesdin, and then in 1556 he defended Tivoli from the invasion of the Spanish. These exploits undoubtedly interrupted the expansion of the garden. By at least 1564, however, much of the work at Bomarzo was completed, since in a letter in October of Annibal Caro to Orsini, Caro refers to the "theaters and mausolea of your Bomarzo."[16] Nevertheless a group of letters of Vicino himself from the 1570s reveals that he continued to work at the Sacro Bosco almost until his death in January 1585.

The Sacro Bosco comprises an irregular-shaped area lying more than 350 meters west of the hill town of Bomarzo. Lacking any clearly defined limits except toward the east where a brook winds across the countryside, the monuments are spread over a tract about 265 meters long and about 120 meters at its widest point (Fig. 80). Aerial photographs suggest that at some time the area of plowed fields lying between the

town and the Sacro Bosco may have been organized as a formal garden.[17] Dimly visible in the photographs is a long, straight alley with three transverse ones running across the fields from the town to the Sacro Bosco. Unfortunately there is no evidence for the date of this lost garden. As none of the sixteenth-century documents mention it, the formal garden is most likely an addition by the Lante family in the seventeenth century or even later. There must have been, however, some access, now lost, in this area between the town and the entrance to the Sacro Bosco, presumably at its northeastern end.

The Sacro Bosco covers a wooded hillock rising to the west of a small brook, which has worn a rather deep valley across the countryside. On the summit of the little hill is a classical *tempietto* oriented roughly east to west more or less on axis with the town (Fig. 81). On the north side of the hill, terraces stepped down to the level of the edge of the brook. Although the original location of the entrance to the woods has been debated, it must have been at the northeast end. The inscriptions on the pedestals of the two sphinxes originally located at that point suggest that the en-

---

the different stages, publishing some four diagrammatic plans (vol. II, pp. 196–97) demonstrating the gradual growth of the complex. His dating, however, is often very insecure for specific monuments.

[16] A. Caro, *Lettere familiari*, ed. A. Greco, III, Florence, 1961, p. 210.

[17] A. Bruschi, "L'abitato di Bomarzo e la Villa Orsini," *Quaderni dell'Istituto di Storia dell'Architettura*, nos. 7–9, April 1955, fig. 5.

81. Bomarzo, tempietto

trance was there and hint at the wonders soon to be encountered. One inscription reads:

> Tu ch'entri qua pon mente
> parte a parte
> e dimmi poi se tante
> maraviglie
> sien fatte per inganno
> o pur per arte

(You who enter here take heed, part by part, and tell me then if so many marvels have been made by delusion or merely art.)

The other inscription likens the monuments to the Seven Wonders of the World:

> Chi con ciglia inarcate
> et labbra strette
> non va per questo loco

> manco ammira
> le famose del mondo
> moli sette

(He who does not walk through this place with raised eyebrows and pursed lips admires even less the famous Seven Wonders of the World.)

The first monument encountered within the entrance at the lower level along the edge of the brook is the leaning house with a dedication to Cardinal Cristoforo Madruzzo of Trent (Fig. 82). In 1561 Cardinal Madruzzo had acquired the hill town of Soriano nel Cimino about six miles south of Bomarzo and there built a one-story country residence with a nymphaeum, the Fontana Papacqua, with figures carved out of the living rock like many of those at Bomarzo. Therefore, it is probably soon after this that Orsini added at Bomarzo his monument honoring the car-

82. Bomarzo, Casa Pendente

83. Bomarzo, Casa Pendente, upper entrance

84. Bomarzo, nymphaeum

85. Bomarzo, Fountain of Venus

dinal. The two-story garden pavilion, like an ancient Roman diaeta, is set close to the edge of the first terrace above the entrance level so that a small bridge at the rear provides direct access from the upper terrace to the entrance portal of the upper story (Fig. 83). Another portal at the rear underneath the bridge admits to the ground floor. The main pavilion, about ten meters tall, has a similar, smaller addition on its northern side, and both are built deliberately out of perpendicular, leaning back toward the northwest, so that on

the interior even the floors slant, causing an insecure feeling for a visitor. The lower story has been carved out of the living rock at the site, while the upper story has been constructed above it. At the base of one corner is carved a bear (*orso* in Italian), the symbol of the Orsini, supporting their coat of arms. An inscription on the pavilion dedicates it to "Christopher Madruzzo, prince of Trent." Another inscription is derived from the so-called Dream of Aristotle formulated by Annibal Caro for the nearby Farnese Palace at Caprarola and published by Vasari in his life of Taddeo Zuccaro.[18] The inscription at Bomarzo reads: "Animus / Qviescendo / Fit / Prvdentior / Ergo." The pavilion, like an ancient Roman diaeta, could also serve as a belvedere, since from the upper story there was a fine view over the countryside to the town.

In a letter of October 1565 Orsini regretfully notes that "the loggia of my fountains has fallen to earth, so that Vignola is wiser than I believed, when he wished for iron clamps for the loggia of Caprarola." It has been suggested that the letter refers to the upper part of the tower dedicated to Madruzzo slipping off its base, but it seems unlikely that the solid-walled pavilion would be described as a loggia.[19]

Beyond the leaning house a large nymphaeum in the form of an exedra with seats and a water basin was cut into the hillside supporting the upper terrace (Fig. 84). The staircase around the fountain, concave at the rear nestling into the exedra wall and convex in front, is perhaps the first example in a garden of stairs derived from those which Bramante created in the exedra at the northern end of the Belvedere Court in the Vatican Palace and which were replaced just at about this same moment by Michelangelo. At the ends of the theater flanking the exedra are stairs leading up to the upper terrace. At right angles to the nymphaeum is a recess, now vaultless, with a female figure, perhaps Venus, goddess of the garden and of love, standing in a niche at the rear (Fig. 85). Nude to the waist, the figure once carried some object, perhaps a basket of roses, in front of her waist, and a hole drilled through the figure at that point suggests that at some time she served as a fountain. Two of the several obelisks that, now fallen, once stood at this level are inscribed. One with Orsini's name and the date 1552 suggests that most of the earlier work was at this level. The other inscription, *Sol per sfogar il core* ("Only to lighten the heart"), enunciates the purpose of at least this area of the woods as a location for carefree repose. A herm with a Pan's head lends an Arcadian spirit to the site. The nymphaeum, comprising Vicino's first gardening, was, therefore, a typical Renaissance garden retreat with none of the fantasy or monstrosity seen elsewhere in the garden and announced in the inscriptions of the two sphinxes at the

[18] G. Vasari, *Le vite de' più eccellenti pittori, scultori ed architettori*, ed. G. Milanesi, VII, Florence, 1881, p. 130.

[19] M. J. Darnell and M. S. Weil, "Il Sacro Bosco di Bomarzo: Its 16th-Century Literary and Antiquarian Context," *Journal of Garden History*, IV, 1984, p. 37, n. 50. The letter is printed in full in Bredekamp, *Bomarzo*, II, p. 18.

86. Bomarzo, grotto

entrance, which must be later in date. The leaning house is similarly a later addition. Standing on the insecure floor of its upper chamber, looking through the out-of-plumb window down onto the nymphaeum beyond, transforms the latter into an eerie world of fantasy.

A walkway continues along between the hill and the brook with several other fountains or monuments. First there is the Fountain of the Boat set alongside the brook where a boat-shaped basin carved with dolphins at either end forms a fountain somewhat like the much later Fontana della Barcaccia in the Piazza di Spagna in Rome. Opposite the Fountain of the Boat is a grotto cut into the hillside with nymphlike figures in niches around the walls and a fragmentary inscription suggesting that the grotto or cave (*antro*) and fountain may offer escape from "any dark thought" (*ogni oscuro pensiero*) (Fig. 86). The walls are cut from the living rock, but they simulate different conditions of construction with rubble walls or fine cut masonry or even plaster walls in a wonderful play on the ambiguity of reality and art. Just to the southeast cut into an adjacent wall is a relief of the Three Graces framed by an arch and flanked by two apsidal niches. These several rock-cut grottoes and niches are very much in the spirit of the nymphaeum.

Soon the path is interrupted by a large, circular water basin set off the perpendicular like the pavilion of the leaning house. In the center of the shallow basin a rustic arched tetrapylon supports a small rocky hill and the remains of a winged horse (Fig. 87). This monument is the Fountain of Pegasus or the Muses illustrating the ancient myth in which the winged horse Pegasus, leaping off the summit of Mount Par-

87. Bomarzo, Fountain of Pegasus

L'ORDINE DEL FONTE CABALINO DI BVONMARTIO
CONTIENE OLTRE ALLE MVSE NELLI QVATRO ANGOLI FVOR
DEL GIRO FIGVRA DI GIOVE APOLO BACCO E MERCVRIO

88. Bomarzo, Fountain of Pegasus, Guerra drawing, Graphische Sammlung, Albertina, Vienna

nassus in ancient Greece, left in his hoofprints the Fountain of the Muses, the wellspring of the arts. Most of the fountains and monuments at Bomarzo are now in ruins, leaving only a very imperfect idea of their original appearance. There are, however, ten drawings in Vienna made by the artist Giovanni Guerra toward the end of the sixteenth century of views of the Sacro Bosco among more than forty drawings prepared of central Italian gardens.[20] In comparison with the figures preserved at Bomarzo, Guerra's renderings are very free, but they do furnish in some cases additional information. According to the drawing of the Fountain of Pegasus, a ring of ten Muses stood on the edge of the circular basin and four freestanding figures with attributes, but identified further by the inscription on the drawing as Jupiter, Apollo, Bacchus, and Mercury, were located around the Fountain (Fig. 88). The depiction of ten Muses on the Guerra drawing instead of the traditional nine is apparently an error by Guerra, as there are remains of only nine pedestals. It is unfortunate that the fountain cannot be dated more accurately as it may represent an early example of a garden fountain topos that was very popular in the neighborhood of Rome in the second half of the sixteenth century with the most famous examples at the Villa d'Este at Tivoli in the late 1560s and soon thereafter at the Villa Lante at Bagnaia near Bomarzo. Orsini's Fountain of Pegasus is obviously meant to allude to the

[20] W. Vitzthum, "Ammannatis Boboli-Brunnen in einer Kopie Giovanni Guerras," *Albertina-Studien*, I, 1963, pp. 75–79. All the Bomarzo drawings are reproduced in Bredekamp, *Bomarzo*, II, figs. 55, 59, 69, 78, 107, 110–11, 123, 133, 141.

woods as a haunt for his literary friends and recalls Ovid's poem, *Amores* (III, 1), in which he meets the Muses of Elegy and Tragedy in an ancient grove with a sacred spring where they berate him for singing of love.

Just beyond the Fountain of Pegasus is the Fountain of the Tortoise (Fig. 89) in which a monstrous tortoise bears on its back a winged female figure of Fame blowing, according to Guerra's drawing (Fig. 90), a pair of long trumpets. Presumably the fountain suggests that Fame comes slowly but inevitably, appropriate to Orsini who, long involved in the northern and Italian wars, could only find ease in his Sacro Bosco. The tortoise is carved as if proceeding slowly down to the stream running along the path. On the opposite side of the stream in line with the tortoise is a gigantic, gaping fish's mouth, perhaps once rising out of the water, and seemingly about to swallow the tortoise.

Further along the path is a group of two gigantic figures cut out of the living rock (Fig. 91). One, a very muscular, bearded colossus, holds the legs of an upturned, more youthful figure who is being torn apart.

89. Bomarzo, Fountain of the Tortoise

90. Bomarzo, Fountain of the Tortoise, Guerra drawing, Graphische Sammlung, Albertina, Vienna

Guerra's drawing identifies the group as the insane Orlando tearing apart a young shepherd from Ariosto's epic poem *Orlando Furioso* (canto XXIV, 5–6): "An immense colossus made of living rock and formed as the insane Orlando tearing to pieces in fury the young shepherd: thirty-five palmi tall."[21] That the colossus is Orlando is confirmed by a letter of April 1, 1578, where Orsini himself speaks of his "Orlando." Likewise a fragmentary inscription on the wall adjacent to the group refers to "Anglante," another name of Orlando. Guerra, however, has apparently misidentified the moment of Orlando's insanity in the poem. Orlando's action in tearing apart the youth is more suitable to his later insane destruction of one of two young woodcutters (canto XXIX, 52–56). Near the group is carved a helmet and armor decorated with the Orsini arms, suggesting a very personal relationship with Vicino, as will be discussed later. In another letter in December 1578 Vicino rec-

ommends highly to his friend Drouet the young sculptor Simone Moschino. The young artist identified only as "my sculptor" in a letter of Vicino in August 1573 to Cardinal Farnese is presumably Moschino. Vicino was then to send him to Caprarola to view its "grandeurs" and to present some sketches of fountains, including one for the piazza below the palace. It has been proposed, therefore, to attribute the Orlando group and several of the other colossal figures to Moschino's activity in the mid-1570s.[22]

Remains of a wall cross the stream that flows under it through an arch just beyond the Orlando group. The wall has recently been identified as a dam which, when closed, would flood the land to the south of the woods, creating a large, artificial lake, probably about 100 meters long.[23] This explains the otherwise mysterious reference to a "lake" by the historian Francesco Sansovino, who, having visited Bomarzo in 1565, writes in the preface to his edition of Sannaza-

---

[21] "Smisurato colosso fatto di grosso sasso et formato come Orlando forsenato sbrana in furor il pastorello alto palmi XXXV."

[22] Bredekamp, *Bomarzo*, I, p. 65.
[23] Ibid., pp. 57–58.

91. Bomarzo, Orlando and the Woodcutter

92. Bomarzo, Orsini Mask

ro's *Arcadia* of the view of a "theater, lake, and temple" from the loggia in the castle at Bomarzo.[24] The lake was completed or in the process of construction, more likely the latter, in the spring of 1561, for in a letter of April 20, 1561, to Cardinal Alessandro Farnese, Vicino Orsini notes that "the embassy from Your Reverend Lordship found me in bed of a fall which I made from the wall of the lake of my little woods." The fashioning of an artificial lake by damming a small stream in the garden recalls the one created in front of the Colonna nymphaeum at Genazzano near Rome earlier in the century.[25] At Genazzano there was a large dining loggia with bathing facilities looking out upon the artificial lake, offering a functional meaning to the lake, which also

may have been a site for other entertainment such as the recreation of an ancient *naumachia* or mock naval battle. At Bomarzo, however, there is no further evidence to explain the function of the artificial lake.

Some 125 meters upstream from the Orlando group, and, therefore, at approximately the end of the artificial lake when dammed up to its fullest, is a colossal mask, over 7.5 meters in height, resembling an animal-form helmet with as its crest a large sphere engraved with the Orsini arms and capped by a small turreted castle (Fig. 92). Guerra's drawing of the mask depicts a man standing in the gaping maw of the face to suggest its monstrous size. Without a more specific knowledge of the physical relationship of the mask to the lake, the monument lacks any comprehensible meaning, except that in its isolation and iconography it seems like a boundary marker or terminus defining the ownership and physical limits of the Sacro Bosco.

The first terrace above the level of the stream, reached originally by stairs near the theater-nymphaeum, is a wide flat expanse with very few trees.

[24] J. B. Bury, "The Reputation of Bomarzo," *Journal of Garden History*, III, 1983, p. 108, quoting the 1578 Venice edition.

[25] C. L. Frommel, "Bramante's 'Ninfeo' in Genazzano," *Römisches Jahrbuch für Kunstgeschichte*, XII, 1969, pp. 137–60; A. Bruschi, *Bramante architetto*, Bari, 1969, pp. 1048–52; and C. Thoenes, "Note sul 'ninfeo' di Genazzano," *Studi Bramanteschi*, Rome, 1974, pp. 575–83.

Two rows each of seven large urns define a wooded xystus directly above the nymphaeum. Several of the urns, each of which differs slightly from the others, bear inscriptions. One simply reads "Night and Day" (*Notte et Giorno*), but another is more expansive: "Night and Day We Are Vigilant and Ready to Guard This Fountain from Any Injury" (*Notte et Giorno Noi Siam Vigili et Pronte a Guardar d'Ogni Iniuria Qvesta Fonte*). A third urn has a fragmentary inscription speaking of "the strangest wild beasts" (*Le Più Strane Belve*). The axis of the xystus runs north-south parallel to the balustrade, which once topped the upper edge of the nymphaeum, and focuses at its southern end on a large fountain basin with a seated river god or figure of Neptune cut out of the rock supporting the next terrace (Fig. 93). To the west of the xystus scattered across the open field are isolated, exotic groups of sculpture. In the northeast corner near the xystus is another fountain basin beside which sits a partially draped female supporting a vase, presumably a flower pot, on her head (Fig. 94). Sometimes identified as Demeter, she has at her back several winged, fish-tailed female figures holding an upended youth.

At the opposite southeast corner a group of a great winged dragon attacked by a lion and a lioness is carved out of a rocky outcrop below the second terrace (Fig. 95). The dragon also has a small animal, perhaps a cub, upside down in its tail. The group resembles quite closely an early sixteenth-century engraving by Lucantonio degli Uberti, which may be its source, but the meaning of the engraving is likewise completely enigmatic.[26] Between the statues of the dragon and the seated female is a life-size statue of an elephant carrying a crenellated castle on its back for a total height of almost 8 meters (Fig. 96). The elephant is guided by a driver seated behind its head, and grasps in its trunk the body of an armored Roman soldier. The blanket on the elephant is decorated with Orsini symbols, which in relation to the castle refer to the Orsini arms as seen previously on the great mask at the end of the lake.

Cut into the hill supporting the upper, second terrace along the southern edge of the first terrace is a grotto whose facade is a tremendous Hell's Mask with the mouth as an entrance (Fig. 97), the eyes as windows, and the tongue forming a table within, for

93. Bomarzo, River God

94. Bomarzo, Demeter

the grotto was a summer dining room as seen in Guerra's drawing with figures seated at the table (Fig. 98). The interior room of the grotto is about 4.25 meters wide and almost 6 meters high. Around the mouth of the mask are the remains of a paraphrase of Dante which can be restored from Guerra's drawing as: "Leave aside all care you who enter here."[27] The inscription obviously relates to the similar theme preserved in the fragmentary inscription of the grotto or cave (*antro*) of the nymphs below near the brook that speaks of freedom from "any dark thought" (*ogni oscuro pensiero*).

Far out in the field stand in isolation a gigantic urn

[26] S. Lang, "Bomarzo," *The Architectural Review*, CXXI, June 1957, p. 428; for the engraving, see A. M. Hind, *Early Italian Engraving*, pt. 1, vol. 1, New York and London, 1938, p. 214, no. 4, and pl. 309.

[27] "Lasciate ogni pensiero voi ch'intrate."

95. Bomarzo, Dragon and Lions

96. Bomarzo, Elephant and Dead Soldier

and the statue of a reclining wild beast with the body of a lion and the rear legs of a horse. Finally, marking probably the end of the open area of the terrace toward the west, there is a large stone bench carved in a freestanding niche on which an inscription speaks of the "marvels" visible here:

> Voi che pel mondo gite errando vaghi
> Di veder meraviglie alte et stupende
> Venite qua, dove son faccie orrende
> Elefanti, leoni, orsi, orche et draghi.

> (You, who wandering through the world make trips
> to see lofty and stupendous marvels,
> come here, where are horrifying faces,
> elephants, lions, bears, orcs and dragons.)

Here the visitor could sit and look back to consider the marvels he has seen, marvels that reflect their announcement on the inscription on one of the sphinx pedestals at the entrance and likened on the other sphinx to the Seven Wonders of the World. Of the marvels most were "the strangest wild beasts" as described on one of the large urns at the other end of the terrace.

At this level much of the iconography of the figures is dominated by an exotic note suggestive of India or China. In fact, toward the end of the sixteenth century the Florentine Soderini in his treatise on agriculture explicitly made this comparison with India:

Nor should one forget to mention that in some of these palaces of India in the meadows which surround them issue out of the ground some lumps of natural rock from which they have carved their idols and some figures of statues of their very fantastic animals. So should there be such rocks in our region, they could be transformed into finely carved statues, colossi, or some other happy idea; as at Bomarzo are seen those carved out of natural rocks of more than a huge pebble which depicts a mask in which the mouth makes the door and the windows are the eyes and within the tongue serves as a table and the teeth are seats, so that when the table is set for supper with lights among the dishes from afar it appears a most frightening mask.[28]

At the southwest corner steps lead up to the second terrace into whose supporting wall is cut the grotto of the Hell's Mask. This terrace too was organized as a xystus oriented east-west and, if the Guerra drawing is reliable (Fig. 99), may have had two large flower beds, which would have transformed it into a hippodrome-shaped garden derived ultimately from that of Pliny the Younger at his Tuscan villa (*Letters*, v, 6). Large carved stone pine cones, alternating with acorns, define the sides of the xystus with those on the south running along the rock-cut wall supporting the third and uppermost terrace (Fig. 100). The pine cones are usually a symbol of immortality, which, as we shall see, is appropriate to the Sacro Bosco. The acorns, however, are normally associated in gardens with the Golden Age of classical antiquity as at the later, nearby Villa Lante at Bagnaia. At the eastern end of the xystus are two stone figures of rampant bears (*orsi*), in reference to the name of the Orsini,

[28] G. Soderini, *I due trattati dell'agricoltura*, ed. A. Bacchi della Lega, Bologna, 1902, pp. 276–77.

97. Bomarzo, Hell's Mask

98. Bomarzo, Hell's Mask, Guerra drawing, Graphische Sammlung, Albertina, Vienna

99. Bomarzo, xystus, Guerra drawing, Graphische Sammlung, Albertina, Vienna

one bearing the Orsini coat of arms and the other with a rose from the arms. Beyond the bears are more fantastic carvings, including two huge female figures, one with wings and a serpentine tail, the other with serpentine legs. A recumbent lion and lioness lie between the harpy and the siren. At the other end of the xystus toward the west, as in the terrace below, stands a large stone bench decorated with a female bust, possibly Persephone, the goddess of the underworld who spends half the year in the underworld and half the year with her mother Demeter above earth (Fig. 101).[29] The bench is at the focus of three stairs: one at the north leads up from the terrace below; another at the rear toward the west heads out to an open, unadorned meadow; toward the south a third stair leads to the uppermost terrace. A stone statue of the triple-headed dog Cerberus, guardian of the underworld, stands at the foot of the stairs mounting to the summit of the hill (Fig. 102).

[29] Bredekamp, *Bomarzo*, I, p. 161.

As one climbs the stairs past Cerberus, there rises into view the little classical temple built of tufa that sits isolated on the crest of the hill. The only other feature at this level is a small, curved stair at the left of the stairs from the lower terrace, which climbs around and up to a small table from which there is a view out over the two lower terraces. The little building, about 6.75 meters by 13.5, imitates an Etruscan temple set up on a podium (Fig. 81). At the rear is a small octagonal cella capped by a prominent dome raised on a drum with oculus windows. Before the cella is a large square pronaos, four columns wide and deep, with Tuscan columns that continue as half-columns around the octagon of the cella. The entrance facade of the pronaos is treated as a *serliana* or Palladian motif with a large arch supported by the two middle columns rising into the triangular pediment of the pronaos. The architectural style is very archaeological with the deep pronaos and columns with strong entasis. Vitruvius, the ancient Roman writer

100. Bomarzo, xystus

on architecture, describes an Etruscan temple in the fourth book of his treatise.[30] Although some features of his account, such as the triple cella and the general proportions, do not agree with the building at Bomarzo, several aspects of it would seem to be derived from Vitruvius. So it is a pronaos temple whose porch is equal in depth to the cella as Vitruvius specifies and the spacing of the columns of the pronaos with three parts for both side aisles compared to four parts for the central aisle agrees with Vitruvius.

Guerra has left a plan of the tempietto on which he has roughly sketched the emblems that once, perhaps in stucco, filled the circular panels in the sides of the podium below the intercolumniations (Fig. 103). The two in the ovals at the ends of the facade of the podium were coats of arms, including that of Orsini at

101. Bomarzo, bench

[30] Vitruvius, *On Architecture* (Loeb Classical Library), trans. F. Granger, London and New York, 1931, I, pp. 238–41.

102. Bomarzo, Cerberus

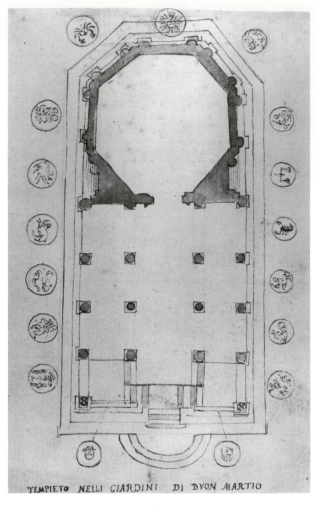

TEMPIETO NELLI GIARDINI DI BYON MARTIO

103. Bomarzo, tempietto plan, Guerra drawing, Graphische Sammlung, Albertina, Vienna

the right. At the front ends of the sides of the podium were two emblems, that on the south probably depicting Adam and Eve flanking the Tree of Knowledge about which was wound the serpent; the one on the north may be the Resurrection, but is too sketchy to be identified with any certainty. If the interpretation of these two scenes is correct they are the only known overtly biblical references in the entire woods. The remaining thirteen symbols in the roundels around the podium have the twelve zodiacal signs plus the sun at the center rear of the cella. The zodiacal signs begin on the south side with the sign of Aquarius and continue around the podium, interrupted by the sun at the center, and ending with the sign of Capricorn on the north.

The historian Francesco Sansovino, who was a personal friend of Orsini, relates that the little temple was built by Orsini as a memorial to his wife, Giulia Farnese, who died sometime early in the 1560s and certainly before October 20, 1564, the date of the letter from Annibal Caro to Orsini mentioning the "theaters and mausolea of your Bomarzo." Sansovino in the preface to his edition of Sannazaro's poem *Arcadia* speaks of the view from the loggia in the Orsini palace in the hill town of Bomarzo, "which reveals

the entire countryside, and leads the eye to look below for that hill at the foot of which is seen the theater, lake, and temple dedicated to the happy memory of the Illustrious Signora Giulia Farnese, your former consort: all of which is done with royal expense and with admirable judgment."[31] The personal character of the tempietto is demonstrated not only by the coats of arms on the podium, but by the roses of the Orsini arms and lilies of the Farnese used to decorate the coffers of the vaulting of the building.

This same personal quality is visible elsewhere at other monuments, which particularly bear the Orsini arms, in addition to the colossal mask or terminus at the head of the artificial lake. The armor that the gi-

[31] Bury, "Bomarzo," p. 108.

gantic figure of the insane Orlando has put aside is decorated with Orsini arms. Just as the insanity of Orlando was provoked by his unrequited love of Angelica in Ariosto's poem, so Orsini in 1574 experienced a similar rebuff for his love of a young woman, Laura. A series of letters from Orsini to his friend Drouet from October 1573 through February 1576 recount Vicino's passion for Laura, who to his despair abandoned him for a younger lover. The group of Orlando and the woodcutter, probably carved by Simone Moschino at this time, is presumably a reflection of Orsini's reaction to this incident.[32] It has likewise been suggested that the war elephant whose blanket was decorated with Orsini roses and which carries a crenellated turret, is a reference to Orsini's involvement in the northern wars when his leader, Orazio Farnese, was killed and Orsini and his brother-in-law, Torquato Conti, were imprisoned.[33]

The unusual feature of the leaning house has also been explained as a possible personal reference of Orsini to his first wife. In 1555 Achille Bocchi published in an emblem book an impresa of Carlo Ruino Antonii depicting a leaning tower and a tree to commemorate the fidelity of his wife taking care of his affairs while he was absent on military service, just as Giulia Farnese Orsini was honored for the performance of her marital affairs while Orsini was at war and in prison.[34] This would seem like a reasonable explanation for the leaning house at Bomarzo. What is puzzling, however, is that there is no overt reference to Giulia Orsini, but that the leaning house is inscribed as dedicated to Cardinal Madruzzo. There would be little point to dedicate to the cardinal a monument honoring Orsini's wife.

There are also frequent references to Etruscan culture in the Sacro Bosco. Not only is the tempietto of an Etruscan form, but some of the ornamental motifs decorating the roundels on the podium of the building have been likened to Etruscan jewelry.[35] Etruscan sources have even been proposed for the winged, snakelike female harpies and sirens, although other critics have noted their similarity to book ornament.[36]

104. Bomarzo, fragment of imitation Etruscan tomb

The similarity of the female monsters to Etruscan sources would seem rather dubious given the scarcity of knowledge of Etruscan art in the mid-sixteenth century. Certainly Etruscan rock-cut tombs were the inspiration for a strange monument carved out of a rocky outcrop on the hillside above the figure of Orlando. About 7 meters long and 2.5 meters high, the block has been carved to resemble the right half of the gabled facade of an overturned Etruscan tomb (Fig. 104). In the fragment of the pediment is carved in relief a winged, fish-tailed figure carrying a ship's rudder over his shoulder.[37]

This area of Latium around Viterbo and of southern Tuscany to the north was once dominated by the ancient Etruscans, who have left rock-cut tombs, particularly in the necropolises of Sovana, Norchi, and Bieda, similar to the imitation ruin at Bomarzo. To use in a garden features that make personal reference to its owner and to the geographical region in which it is created occurs frequently in sixteenth-century gardens as at the contemporary Medici villa at Castello or the Villa d'Este at Tivoli and the later Villa Mattei in Rome. It has been suggested, however, that the Etruscan references at Bomarzo are a reflection of a more interesting idea.[38]

In the late fifteenth century Giovanni Nanni from nearby Viterbo published his *Antiquities*, which popularized an interest in a pseudohistory of the Etruscans. Later it will be Orsini's friend, Francesco Sansovino, who will issue in 1583 an Italian translation

[32] L.M.F. Bosch, "Bomarzo: A Study in Personal Imagery," *Garden History*, X, 1982, pp. 104–5.

[33] J. von Henneberg, "Bomarzo: Nuovi dati e un'interpretazione," *Storia dell'arte*, XIII, 1972, pp. 43–55.

[34] J. von Henneberg, "Bomarzo: The Extravagant Garden of Pier Francesco Orsini," *Italian Quarterly*, XI, no. 42, fall 1967, p. 8, n. 21, and Bosch, "Bomarzo," pp. 102–4.

[35] J. P. Oleson, "A Reproduction of an Etruscan Tomb in the Parco dei Mostri at Bomarzo," *Art Bulletin*, LVII, 1975, p. 411.

[36] Bury, "Bomarzo," p. 109.

[37] Oleson, "An Etruscan Tomb," pp. 412–15.

[38] E. G. Dotson, "Shapes of Earth and Time in European Gardens," *Art Journal*, XLII, 1982, pp. 210–16, and Bredekamp, *Bomarzo*, I, pp. 118–21.

105. Bomarzo, term with head of Pan

battle monument erected by Antiochus Soter.[41] Other identifiable sources are Dante, Ariosto, and perhaps exotic India. From these varied sources Vicino Orsini, perhaps with suggestions from his literary friends, must have gradually developed the complex over a long period of time.

Vicino Orsini himself describes his garden as a "Sacro Bosco" or a "Sacred Wood" in an inscription on the wall below the viewing stand opposite Cerberus:

> Cedan et Memphi e ogni altra meraviglia
> ch'ebbe già il mondo in pregio al sacro bosco
> che sol se stesso e null'altro somiglia.
>
> (Yield both Memphis and every other marvel,
> which formerly the world held in esteem, to the
> Sacred Wood
> which is only itself and resembles no other.)

of Nanni's book.[39] Nanni claimed that during the Golden Age Janus ruled Etruria, where Bomarzo was located. This may explain the occurrence of several large bifrons and quadrifrons heads bearing baskets of fruit, presumably the remains of herms, which once were collected near the nymphaeum. The quadrifrons heads depict the four ages of man, while the Janus heads resemble Pan, the chief figure of Arcadia (Fig. 105). The gigantic acorns that define the upper xystus also refer to the Golden Age so that Bomarzo recalls that pleasurable moment when Nature was beneficial to man, but the references seem to be limited to those areas of the Sacro Bosco, such as the nymphaeum and the upper xystus or garden, which lack the more terrifying features elsewhere in the park.

Much has been written on the meaning of Orsini's Sacro Bosco, but there has never been a completely satisfactory explanation for the whole layout.[40] The individual monuments are drawn obviously from a multiplicity of sources. The majority, of course, come from the western classical tradition as seen in the Fountain of Pegasus, the Fountain with the Graces, the Fountain of the Tortoise, Cerberus, and perhaps the Elephant with the Soldier, which may reflect the

So the emphasis, as in many of the other inscriptions, is on the "marvels" to be seen. Marvels which are to amaze, to startle, even to frighten the visitor, as in the inscription of "horrifying faces, elephants, lions, bears, monsters and dragons." The visitor, entering between the enigmatic sphinxes, was to find himself in an enchanted forest filled with frightening and unnatural images—a leaning house that perverted the principles of building, as also the tipped basin of the Fountain of Pegasus; a monstrous, slow moving turtle; an insane, gigantic Orlando tearing apart a youth—all set in the dank, wooded valley of the brook. As one mounted to the next level the frightening images continued with the great Hell's Mask, the huge elephant bearing a dead soldier, and the dragon combating a lion and lioness. At the third level the element of horror and dread lessens to fantasy with the winged and serpent-tailed harpy and siren. Here is the key to the overall significance, for the three-headed dog, Cerberus, the guardian of classical Hades, sits at the foot of the last stairway. The intrepid visitor, who can finally pass him, arrives at the top to the quiet serenity of the tempietto.

The ancient sacred grove (*lucus*) at Rome, which Vergil in the *Aeneid* (VIII, 342–58) has Evander, king of the Arcadians, show Aeneas might almost be a source of inspiration for Orsini's Sacro Bosco:

[39] Giovanni Nanni da Viterbo, *Le antichità di Beroso Caldeo sacerdote, et d'altri scrittori*, Venice, 1583.

[40] The two most recent analyses are Darnell and Weil, "Il Sacro Bosco di Bomarzo," pp. 1–91, and Bredekamp, *Bomarzo*. Both, I believe, identify the entrance at the wrong location and Bredekamp has the climax of a visit at the figures of Neptune and Demeter before the rows of urns. Darnell and Weil add some interesting references to Ariosto's *Orlando Furioso*, but their interpretation is too dependent upon Ariosto with many unconvincing references.

[41] S. Settis, "Contributo a Bomarzo," *Bollettino d'arte*, ser. 6, LI, 1966, pp. 17–26.

Next he shows him a vast grove where valiant Romulus restored an Asylum, and, beneath a chill rock, the Lupercal, bearing after Arcadian wont the name of Lycaean Pan. He shows withal the wood of Holy Argiletum, and calls the place to witness and tells of the death of Argus his guest. Hence he leads him to the Tarpeian house, and the Capitol—golden now, once bristling with woodland thickets. Even then the dread sanctity of the region awed the trembling rustics; even then they shuddered at the forest and the rock. "This grove," he cries, "this hill with its lofty crown—though we know not what god it is—is yet a god's home: my Arcadians believe they have looked on Jove himself, while oft his right hand shook the darkening aegis and summoned the storm-clouds. Moreover, in these two towns, with walls o'erthrown, thou seest the relics and memorials of men of old. This fort Janus built, that Saturn; Janiculum was this called, that Saturnia.[42]

King Evander's account of the sacred wood at Rome follows closely on the description of the Golden Age enjoyed by the Arcadians. As Vergil notes, Arcadia is particularly associated with the rustic deity Pan, whose head is depicted in one of the bifrons heads that once adorned a herm standing somewhere near the nymphaeum (Fig. 105). The reference by King Evander to overturned walls may then explain the rock carving below the tempietto simulating the ruins of an overturned Etruscan tomb. The most overt equation of Bomarzo to the ancient *locus amoenus* of Arcadia, however, was made by Orsini's friend Francesco Sansovino in his introduction to the 1578 edition of Jacopo Sannazaro's poem *Arcadia*: "reading the present volume, I have found there some descriptions of hills and valleys which, recalling the site of Bomarzo, have awakened in me the greatest longing for it."

So the "sacred wood" (*sacro bosco*) described by Sannazaro in chapter ten of the *Arcadia*, bears features similar to Bomarzo.[43] There the shepherds enter "the revered and sacred wood into which never did any dare enter with any axe or iron, but for many years it had been most religiously preserved inviolate by the country populace for fear of the avenging Gods." It is very likely a complete coincidence, but the shepherds are required to wash their hands "in a tiny spring of fresh water that welled up at the entrance," analogous to the two small basins at the old

entrance to the Bomarzo precinct just before the sphinxes. Sannazaro's "sacred wood" contains a figure of Pan and a "roomy cave—I know not whether naturally or by the handiwork of art hollowed out of the stony mountain." The deities there, in addition to Pan, are the "mightiest Ocean, universal father of all things, and the virgin Nymphs," and gods of the underworld. A stream runs through the deep valley into which a disconsolate lover, throwing ashes from a sacred altar, will have his love borne away to the deep sea peopled by dolphins and swimming whales. Certainly the Sacro Bosco of Bomarzo is not a recreation of Sannazaro's, but there would seem to be enough correspondences between the two to suggest some relationship.

A melancholy, retrospective mood, however, was cast by Sannazaro over his Arcadia when his hero, the shepherd Melisio, recalls the tomb of his beloved Phyllis: "Still I shall make your tomb famous and celebrated among these rustics. And from the hills of Tuscany and of Liguria shepherds will come to worship this corner of the world solely because you once lived here."[44] Vicino Orsini similarly commemorated his beloved wife Giulia by erecting her memorial tempietto in the Arcadian setting of the "sacred wood" of Bomarzo. The concept of a wooded funerary precinct at the edge of town was common in Roman antiquity. So the ancient Roman orator Cicero in an extensive series of letters to his friend Atticus in the spring of 45 B.C. recounts his passionate concern to obtain an appropriate site for funerary gardens for his beloved daughter Tullia.[45] References to death and the afterworld abound at Bomarzo. In addition to the tempietto and the ruin of the Etruscan tomb, the inscription that identifies the site as a Sacro Bosco evokes ancient Memphis in Egypt, perhaps recalling Martial's introduction to his epigram *On Spectacles*: *Barbara Pyramidum sileat miracula Memphis* ("Let barbaric Memphis be silent of the marvels of her Pyramids"),[46] whereas Cerberus and the Hell's Mask bespeak the underworld.

Orsini's Sacro Bosco, however, is peopled in part with frightening images drawn from numerous sources. There is also an overlay of Dantean imagery

---

[42] *Virgil* (Loeb Classical Library), trans. H. R. Fairclough, II, London and New York, 1930, pp. 83–85.

[43] Bury, "Bomarzo," p. 108.

[44] J. Sannazaro, *Arcadia*, ed. M. Scherillo, Turin, 1888, p. 306, lines 257–61.

[45] Cicero, *Letters to Atticus* (Loeb Classical Library), trans. E. O. Winstedt, III, London and New York, 1925, pp. 24–183.

[46] Martial, *Epigrams* (Loeb Classical Library), London and New York, 1919, pp. 2–3.

in the Hell's Mask, bearing an inscription paraphrasing Dante, and Cerberus as the final frightening figure on the terraced levels leading up the hill to the tempietto. The general theme is that only the intrepid and stalwart can endure the trials of the fearsome figures and achieve the summit. The tempietto may even be intended to recall the Temple of Virtue, that quality that permits the visitor to withstand all trials. The garden, therefore, is composed of a group of literary conceits to evoke in Orsini's friends a "pleasurable terror," as well as to commemorate his beloved wife. Its conception is very personal and its appeal limited to a small literary coterie. Like Vergil's description of the sacred wood at Rome, "the dread sanctity of the region awed the trembling rustics."

The personal involvement of Orsini and his friends is clearly demonstrated in the relatively few contemporary letters that mention the Sacro Bosco. In October 1564 Orsini consulted Annibal Caro, the Farnese secretary, regarding a project to paint the story of the Fall of the Giants in a loggia at his palace at Bomarzo. Caro's reply notes that the subject matter is difficult and he must consult his books in Rome, since the "letter found me in Frascati so occupied with alleys and similar novelties at my little vigna as Your Lordship may be with the theaters and mausolea of your Bomarzo."[47] Returning to the same subject in December, Caro again excuses himself with his involvement at Frascati "no less than you may be in your marvels of Bomarzo," using the same word, "marvel," that recurs so frequently in the inscriptions of Bomarzo.[48]

More interesting and illuminating is a series of letters written by Orsini late in his life from 1573 to 1583 to his friend Giovanni Drouet.[49] They reveal that work in the Sacro Bosco continued throughout the latter part of Orsini's life. So in December 1573 he notes that he is passing the time with "either reading or making designs for the grove [*boschetto*]." By the end of 1574 he had decided to color some of the statues, so that in March 1575 he could tell Drouet: "The boschetto when you see it, you will see again in another form. . . . I have already given color to a few statues of the boschetto and I was taught a secret which dilutes the color with milk so that they remain in water and other misfortunes. And now it is already four or five months during which they have had color and they are preserved quite well." In October, how-

ever, he was still seeking another formula to preserve the color, traces of which are still visible on some of the figures.[50] At the same time he reports that he has had "some very fine drawings from Messer Girolamo," but the purpose of the drawings is unknown and the artist Girolamo is uncertain, although both Girolamo Sermoneta and Girolamo Muziano have been suggested. By the summer of 1579 he confesses that "now there remains for me no other comfort except my boschetto, and I bless that money which I have spent and still spend."

Orsini's only preoccupation during the 1570s was his Sacro Bosco and the enjoyment of showing it to his friends and neighbors. In June 1574 the site was visited by the Countess della Sala, members of the Mattei family, and Orsini's neighbor Cardinal Gambara, who at the same time was laying out his splendid garden nearby at Bagnaia. Even when Orsini was about to visit the villa of his neighbor Cardinal Madruzzo in July 1574 he could only think of his own garden where "I am continually in the mud of my boschetto." The following summer in July 1575 the Sacro Bosco was visited by Cardinal Madruzzo and Cardinal Farnese, who later gave Orsini a bear (*orso*), his family emblem, to join the turkey cocks (*galli d'India*) which decorated the garden. His desire for a monkey to join his growing menagerie, however, seems not to have been satisfied. As old age set in, Orsini reminisced of the pleasures "of having here the sweet company of both men as well as women" with "fifers, songs, music and similar things to gladden and exalt the spirits." For him, as he says, the Sacro Bosco is "one of those castles of Atlantis where those paladins and ladies are held by careless enchantments," thus returning to the image of an enchanted forest.

Obviously Orsini was assisted by artists as well as literary consultants in his creation of the figures and architecture of the garden, but the evidence regarding them is very slight. Much of the sculpture is rather crude, even at times primitive, but this is in part owing to the coarseness of the local stone. The variety of styles presented by the figures and the fact that they were probably executed at different times over a span of many years suggests that several different stone-carvers were employed. The recent attribution of the statue of Orlando to the youthful Simone Moschino is quite convincing,[51] but suggestions for other works

---

[47] A. Caro, *Lettere familiari*, ed. A. Greco, III, Florence, 1961, p. 210.

[48] Ibid., p. 213.

[49] Bredekamp, *Bomarzo*, II, pp. 23–65.

[50] A. Bruschi, "Nuovi dati documentari sulle opere Orsiane di Bomarzo," *Quaderni dell'Istituto di Storia dell'Architettura*, ser. x, fasc. 55–60, 1963, p. 36, n. 78, details the remains of color.

[51] Bredekamp, *Bomarzo*, I, p. 69.

of sculpture are less certain. The name of Vignola has often been tentatively proposed for the architecture, although the style of the tempietto seems rather foreign to Vignola. Only the leaning house dedicated to Cardinal Madruzzo and late parts of the palace seem more plausible. With the variety of styles and the uncertainty of dates for the different monuments, it is unlikely that attributions can be very accurate unless more documentation is discovered.

The neglect until recently of the Sacro Bosco has permitted nature to soften the sixteenth-century organization of the garden, destroying stairways and paths, wearing away or partially burying some of the monuments, so that it resembles more an eighteenth-century English garden than it may have in its original form. Even the sequence of viewing of the various pieces of sculpture is now uncertain. Nevertheless its organization must have always been more informal than in other sixteenth-century gardens. In fact, one's experience of the garden is very fragmentary, as it consists of a sequence of isolated monuments with little formal relationship among them. Even the scale of the different figures and monuments is inconsistent, varying from the life-size elephant to the gigantic Orlando to the relatively small leaning house. Part of this fractionalism is, of course, due to the natural locations of some of the great boulders from which the figures are carved and part may be due to the separate campaigns of work carried out over an extended period of time by different artists. This fractionalism, however, enhances the mystery of the complex.

In terms of the history of Roman gardening in the Renaissance, the Sacro Bosco at Bomarzo continues the tradition of endowing the garden with literary associations and symbolic meaning, first suggested in the plans of Cardinal Gonzaga in the late fifteenth century for his garden near San Lorenzo in Damaso in Rome. It is in the latter half of the sixteenth century, however, that this tradition reaches its climax at Bomarzo and the contemporary gardens of the Cardinal of Ferrara at Tivoli and of Cardinal Gambara at Bagnaia. This is the period when the humanistic advisor, such as Annibal Caro, became fully involved with garden plannning.

In fact, in 1563, Torquato Conti, brother-in-law of Vicino Orsini and his comrade-in-arms in the European wars of the period, consulted Annibal Caro regarding the gardens of his castle-villa, the present Villa Catena, near Poli in the Sabine hills about twenty miles east of Rome. Since the twelfth century the area had been a Conti fief and by the early six-

teenth century an old farm on a ridge below Monte Sant'Angelo was converted into a villa visited by Pope Leo X in 1516. It was here that Torquato Conti liked to retire during his free moments from military campaigns, as Orsini did at Bomarzo. Annibal Caro's letter from Rome to Conti on July 6, 1563, gives some idea of the gardens as they existed at the time.[52] Caro urges Conti to complete a water aqueduct since there is no water for the "fountains, the lake, the springs, the waterfalls, the water-jets [*bollori*] which are planned there." He then adds that these "and the hunting parks, the parks, the rabbit warrens, the dovecotes, the woods and the gardens, which are already begun there, are the usual things in comparison to those which could be made. What are needed are extravagances to outdo the boschetto of Signore Vicino." Caro suggests as novelties a windmill with dampened sails to offer a fresh breeze, a rock in the midst of the lake like the one in the Baths of Caracalla, or a water organ like "the beautiful Franceschina which rings the bells in Flanders." Caro's ideas seem in this case to have no literary associations and, as he says, are just novelties "to astonish" (*strabiliar*), although the windmill and the water organ with its reminiscences of Flanders may be chosen as appropriate to a military leader who campaigned in the Lowlands. Interestingly Caro seems to consider the figures at Bomarzo as only "extravagances," just as a year later in his letter to Orsini he refers to them as "marvels." That Caro's ideas were seriously considered is apparent from the fact that he went immediately to Poli whence three days later he wrote his nephew.[53] None of Caro's ideas was carried out because soon afterward Conti was appointed governor of Anagni by Pope Pius IV and his interest in the work at Poli presumably lessened, for in July 1564 Caro wrote him at Anagni to say that the architect Dosio should soon arrive there, adding that "meanwhile I should not like Catena to be neglected."[54] In the seventeenth and eighteenth centuries the gardens of the Villa Catena were extensively revised and enlarged, changing completely their sixteenth-century aspect.

Another Orsini garden, which must have some relationship, though still uncertain, with Vicino Orsini's Sacro Bosco at Bomarzo, contains the mysterious remains of rock-cut figures and furnishings just outside the little town of Pitigliano along the road to Sorano in southern Tuscany. The fief of Pitigliano, long

52 Caro, *Lettere*, III, pp. 163–65, no. 698.
53 Ibid., p. 165, no. 699.
54 Ibid., pp. 196–97, no. 729.

106. Pitigliano, belvedere

107. Pitigliano, bench

a possession of a branch of the Orsini family, came in 1547 into the possession of Niccolò IV Orsini, who had just previously served in the northern wars with Vicino Orsini. In 1562 a popular revolt favoring the Medici overturned the rule of Niccolò, who was only restored to power by the Medici in 1576 and would continue at the discretion of the Medici.[55] The town of Pitigliano was in ancient Etruscan territory, including the necropolis of Sovana, which has been identified as a possible source of the rock-cut version of a destroyed Etruscan tomb at Bomarzo. The fragmentary remains of sculpture at Pitigliano, including those of two colossal, reclining figures, one accompanied by a large cornucopia, are so ruined that no identification can be made of them. Several rock-cut benches, some like those at Bomarzo, line a roughly defined path that leads to a rocky spur on the heights overlooking the Prochio River.[56] There is cut into the hill a level, circular viewing platform (Fig. 106) with rock-cut benches below (Fig. 107) from which is a vast view over the deep river valley to the hills beyond. Nothing further is known regarding the layout.

If the figures at Pitigliano are the work of Niccolò Orsini, as is usually assumed,[57] they would more

likely date from the period 1547 to 1562, when he was first in power. Later the political struggles with the Medici and a growing lack of money would offer a less opportune moment for such activity. One historian notes that the site seems to have been the "prey of a systematic destruction."[58] This damage may be caused by general human vandalism over the centuries, but in the 1570s invading Farnese troops from the Duchy of Castro were reported to have devastated the countryside around Pitigliano and may have caused such destruction.[59] Unfortunately more specific dates are needed for the commencement of both gardens at Bomarzo and Pitigliano to determine

[55] G. Celata, "Proprietà ed economia agricola in un feudo toscano del '500," *Archivio storico italiano*, CXXXIV, 1976, pp. 75–78, and A. Biondi, "Lo stato di Pitigliano e i Medici da Cosimo a Ferdinando I," in *I Medici e lo stato senese 1555–1609*, ed. L. Rombai, Rome, 1980, pp. 75–88.

[56] P. Portoghesi, "Nota sulla Villa Orsini di Pitigliano," *Quaderni dell'Istituto di Storia dell'Architettura*, nos. 7–12, 1955, pp. 74–76, and Bredekamp, *Bomarzo*, I, pp. 152–53.

[57] The garden is attributed to Latino Orsini, another member of the Pitigliano branch, without any demonstrated proof by J. Theurillat, *Les mystères de Bomarzo et des jardins symboliques de la*

*Renaissance*, Geneva, 1973, p. 140, and Darnell and Weil, "Il Sacro Bosco di Bomarzo," p. 73.

[58] Portoghesi, "Villa Orsini," p. 74. Bredekamp, *Bomarzo*, II, p. 139, n. 34, notes that in World War II German troops used some of the coats of arms for target practice.

[59] Biondi, *I Medici*, p. 79.

credit for the revival of Etruscan ideas and the use of colossal rock-cut forms.

Although it is very difficult to envisage the original layout at Pitigliano, the site suggests a completely different atmosphere than that at Bomarzo, where the visitor apparently wound his way along the dark, narrow, sunken valley worn by the slight stream and climbed upward on the level terraces to the open summit of the gentle hill surmounted by the tempietto. At Pitigliano the visitor wandered along the path from the east across the heights above the river valley to come out at the end onto the circular viewing platform with its awesome vista. Man is there overawed and left dwarfed by the vastness of the sky immediately overhead and the deep, wide gorge of the river valley below. Time and possibly man's destruction have returned the work of art back to nature so that rarely can the visitor discriminate between art and nature. The sphinx's question to Bomarzo, whether the "marvels have been made by delusion or merely art," is even more appropriate at Pitigliano.

# CHAPTER 7

# Urban Gardens

Whereas the monks had their cloistered gardens as a location for contemplative retreat, the secular population had their urban horticultural retreats. These urban gardens were scattered throughout the city and their size was usually related to the wealth of their owners. Almost all were lost, as the density of the population thickened, leaving only a few traces. One of the most charming literary remains is offered by Aretino before 1536 when he describes the garden at Rome of the courtesan Nanna.[1] A neighbor remarks that the garden could shame "the garden of Chigi in the Trastevere and that of Fra Mariano on Monte Cavallo."[2] Aretino had previously been in the service of Agostino Chigi and so knew his garden, that of the present Villa Farnesina, very intimately. Nanna's neighbor adds that if her garden had at its central crossing "a small fountain which sprayed water upward or would spill over its edge and gradually water the grass of your paths, you could call it the garden of gardens [*giardino dei giardini*, using the Italian word for a pleasure garden] as well as the kitchen garden of kitchen gardens [*orto degli orti*]." Combining flowers, fruit trees, and vines in a mediaeval mode, the garden was presumably divided into four compartments by paths shaded by pergolas laden with flowers and grapevines, pomegranates and espaliered jasmine. A low hedge of rosemary outlined the flower beds with vases of trimmed box at the corners. Within

the beds was a variety of herbs and flowers, including marjoram, mint and pimpernel, marigolds, stocks and, as the prize feature, late-blooming "roses of September" (*le rose di settembre*).

A drawing by the architect Baldassare Peruzzi (Uffizi 580A) illustrates the plan of a similar, although probably larger urban garden (Fig. 108). As the drawing is usually dated after 1527 it may, therefore, be for a garden of the same type in Siena.[3] The plot of land is defined by two public roads, one along a long side of the garden, the other at the short end set at a slightly obtuse angle to the first road, by an adjacent garden against the parallel long side, and by an unspecified border on the fourth side. Within this slightly irregular plot, the garden is corrected to a rectangle by pergolas outlining all four sides. The main entrance to the garden is at a corner off the angled public road with a secondary entrance at the other end of the garden near the garden house. Like most Roman gardens there are, therefore, two entrances, one more public, primarily for the garden, and the other the private entrance. A two-storied casino or gardener's house flanked by a barrel-vaulted service

---

[3] C. L. Frommel, *Die Farnesina und Peruzzis Architektonisches Frühwerk*, Berlin, 1961, p. 41; I. Belli Barsali, *Baldassare Peruzzi e le ville senesi del Cinquecento*, S. Quirico d'Orcia, 1977, pp. 16–17; and H. Wurm, *Baldassarre Peruzzi: Architekturzeichnungen*, Tübingen, 1984, pl. 264. The Chigi brothers, Agostino and Sigismondo, had a garden (*viridarium*) before 1524 in the Campo Marzio region of Rome, but the size of the garden in the drawing and the angle of the streets would not seem suitable to a site in the Campo Marzio; see P. Pecchiai, "Regesti dei documenti patrimoniali del convento romano della Trinità dei Monti," *Archivi*, ser. 2, XXV, 1958, pp. 136, 143.

---

[1] P. Aretino, *Sei giornate*, ed. G. Aquilecchia, Bari, 1969, p. 352. See G. Masson, "Pietro Aretino and the Small Roman Renaissance Pleasure Garden," *Garden History*, VIII, no. 1, 1980, pp. 67–68.

[2] See Chapters 5 and 10.

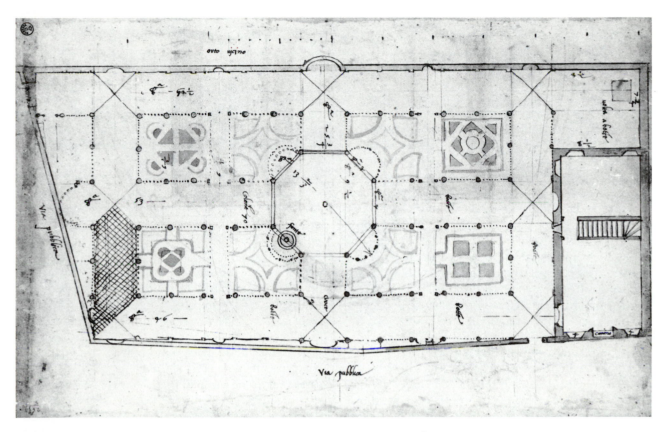

108. B. Peruzzi, plan of garden, Uffizi 580A

court closes one end of the garden. The rectangular garden is laid out on the proportions of 2:1 with the central alley 53 braccia long and the cross alley 25.75 braccia (ca. 31 meters × 15.5 meters, if Sienese braccia). Pergolas 4 braccia wide, consisting of tunnel vaults probably of interwoven wooden slats supported on columns, outline the four sides of the garden and cover the cross alleys with a large octagonal dome at the crossing. Where the pergolas abut or cross one another were cross vaults. A fountain was set in one of the diagonal niches of the central crossing, and it is possible that all four diagonal niches were to contain fountains. In each of the four open compartments outlined by the pergolas were two flower beds. Each of the outermost beds had a different geometrical parterre pattern, while the inner ones, only roughly sketched in, had identical patterns.

In a sketchbook of Giovanni Colonna of Tivoli (Ms Vat. lat. 7721), dating about 1554, are detailed drawings of similar garden pergolas in the otherwise rather obscure garden of the Ghinucci family on the Quirinal Hill off the Alta Semita roughly opposite the Villa Carafa-d'Este.[4] The first identifiable mention of the garden is in the 1527 edition of Andrea Fulvio's *Antiqvitates Vrbis*, where he notes that the Reverend Girolamo Ghinucci, then auditor of the Camera, and elected cardinal in 1535, owned a vigna at the site of the later garden.[5] At the time of the Colonna sketchbook, about 1554, the garden was identified by Colonna as in the possession of Paolo Ghinucci, who still owned it in 1562 according to a tax return.[6] By 1565 the architect and hydraulic engineer Tommaso Ghinucci, who had acquired it, gave the land to the Cardinal of Ferrara as an expansion for his villa across the road.[7] The drawings, however, offer no information regarding the horticultural aspects of the garden or whether there was any habitation; only the cross

[4] M. E. Mitchell, *Giovanni Colonna da Tivoli: 1554* (Xenia Quaderni, 2), Rome, 1982, pp. 39–40.

[5] A. Fulvio, *Antiqvitates Vrbis*, Rome, 1527, fol. xxxiiir as fol. xxiiir.

[6] R. Lanciani, *Storia degli scavi di Roma*, III, Rome, 1907, p. 180.

[7] *Il Palazzo del Quirinale*, Rome, 1974, p. 238.

pergola and the fences that closed two sides of the garden, which will be discussed later, are depicted (Fig. 148).

In April 1562 Alessandro Grandi of Ferrara succeeded his uncle as Ferrarese ambassador at Rome.[8] Like many Ferrarese, Grandi had a passionate interest in gardens as well as classical antiquities. He spent much of his time dealing in antiquities, especially collecting them for his ducal master, but also created his own pleasure garden off the street now known as the Via del Babuino, in the Campo Marzio region of Rome. As early as 1561 Grandi and his neighbor Orazio Naro had paid for a conduit and a supply of water from the Acqua Vergine to supply his "vineyard or habitation and garden." In return for this tapping of the public water supply Grandi was ordered by Pope Pius IV "to make a fountain for public utility on the public street before your said garden." Eventually a public fountain was created with a figure of Silenus, popularly called the "Babuino," reclining above the water basin on the street, which was soon named after the nickname of the statue. By 1567 Grandi must have been laying out his garden, for he informed the duke of Ferrara of having found some seven antique statues in his garden when "we were having to move the earth in one place to accommodate there a compartment of the garden." In 1583, when Grandi leased part of the property to Domenico Capodiferro, the contract noted that there were planted vases and trees in the garden. The contract also lists a dovecote and a henhouse, a fishpool, two fountains, and several marble statues.

On the other side of the Via del Babuino, toward the west, almost directly opposite Alessandro Grandi's garden, was a more elaborate garden created slightly later for Cardinal Flavio Orsini. In the late sixteenth century the Orsini garden was a well-known feature of Rome so that the Frenchman Montaigne in the diary of his trip to Rome in 1581 lists the Orsini garden with those of the Estes, the Farnese on the Palatine, and the Medici as one of the "beauties" of Rome.[9] Early in the 1570s Cardinal Orsini had begun purchasing land in the Campo Marzio until by December 1575 he owned an entire insula or block

bounded on the two short ends by the Strada Paolina or Via del Babuino and the Via Lata or Corso, while one long side bordered the Vicolo degli Orsini, now the Via di S. Giacomo, and the other the present Via di Gesu e Maria.[10] There were several small and partially dilapidated habitations on the southwest corner near the Corso surrounded by large garden areas. As early as 1572 the cardinal, who was in the fortunate position to be a member of the Congregatione d'Acqua in charge of the public water supply for the city, requested that he be granted water rights for his vigna, presumably this garden, and in May 1576 he was given the right to three oncie of water. Roughly at the same time, on December 2, 1575, he paid one hundred scudi to a mason "on account of building the garden." Dupérac's map of Rome in 1577 seems to depict the garden, but it is so schematic that it offers no certainty about the stage of the work.[11] On July 29, 1579, an avviso records that Pope Gregory XIII went to the Collegio de' Greci near the Trinità and then "visited the building and garden of Cardinal Orsini."[12] Such a papal visit would suggest that the work was basically complete, although later evidence indicates that at the cardinal's death in 1581 a few details still remained unfinished. A visitor, slightly later in 1588, notes that the date 1580 was inscribed, probably above the portal, on the Via del Babuino, presumably to mark the completion.[13]

Although the garden has been completely destroyed, several bits of evidence can be assembled to offer a fair image of its layout. The cardinal, dying in 1581, had inscribed in his will a detailed description of the garden, which he left to a nephew, Pietro, bishop of Spoleto. There are also three drawn plans for the garden preserved in the Archivio di Stato at Rome, and one of them corresponds rather closely to the written description (Fig. 111), which suggests that the three drawings represent different projects for the layout.[14] The three drawings have different plantings

---

[8] For Grandi at Rome, see C. d'Onofrio, *Acque e fontane di Roma*, Rome, 1977, pp. 117–18, and E. Corrandini, "Le raccolte estensi di antichità: Primi contributi documentari," *L'Impresa di Alfonso II*, ed. J. Bentini and L. Spezzaferro, Bologna, 1987, pp. 163–92.

[9] M. de Montaigne, *The Complete Works of Montaigne*, trans. D. M. Frame, Stanford, Calif., 1957, p. 960.

[10] For the history, see D'Onofrio, *Acque e fontane di Roma*, pp. 120–21.

[11] A. P. Frutaz, ed., *Le piante di Roma*, Rome, 1962, II, pl. 255.

[12] Rome, BAV, Ms Urb. Lat. 1047, fol. 295r (July 29, 1579).

[13] R. Lanciani, "Il codice barberiniano XXX, 89 contenente frammenti di un descrizione di Roma del secolo XVI," *Archivio della società romana di storia patria*, VI, 1889, pp. 487–88.

[14] The will is published in R. Lanciani, *Storia degli scavi di Roma*, II, Rome, 1903, pp. 17–19. The plans are in the Archivio di Stato, Rome, Disegni e piante, collezione I, cartella 89, no. 637. One of them (my Fig. 111) was published in M. Recci, "La villa e il giardino nel concetto della rinascenza italiana," *Critica d'arte*, II, 1937, pl. 109, fig. 3, without any location identification of the drawing or any information except that it was a Renaissance Orsini

in the garden and different buildings, but all the designs use architecture at each end of the property to
compensate for the angles of the streets, particularly
along the Via del Babuino, and to create a large rectangular garden.

The least detailed drawing (Fig. 109), perhaps representing the earliest project, has very little specific architecture. In the southwest corner, off the Corso, a
large rectangular area is identified as the "site of two
built houses" (*sito dele dui case fatte*) and next to that
another rectangular area is marked as the "site of two
houses to be built" (*sito dele dui case da farsi*). Toward the entrance off the Via del Babuino at the north
side of the entrance passageway was to be a loggia
opening onto perhaps a water basin. The rectangular
garden between the two built-up sections was to be
387.5 palmi (ca. 88.5 meters) long by 230 palmi (ca.
52.38 meters) wide. The only planting indicated consists of six *boschi* or woods, 89.5 palmi (ca. 20 meters) square, each with diagonal cross alleys and probably small fountains at the crossings. The trees were
then to be planted in the triangular plots on a regular
checkerboard pattern. The wider alleys defining the
square boschi would then have been about 17 palmi
(ca. 3.8 meters) wide.

On the second project (Fig. 110) the architecture is
much more fully delineated with measurements for
most of the walls and voids. Like the first project the
houses and stores are concentrated in the southwest
corner. At that location are basically two habitations
each with an entrance off the Corso and a long entrance hall leading back to an open court or garden
area. On each side of the two entranceways is a store
opening onto the Corso and with interior stairs to an
upper floor. There were similarly to be several small
residences along the side street, the present Via di S.
Giacomo. A portal off the center of the Corso side
entered a large entrance court with access at the rear
to the garden and at the north side a small loggia as
well as several rooms. Between the court and houses
along the Corso and the garden was a series of long,
rectangular rooms. From the Via del Babuino an entrance vestibule led to a wide loggia opening into the
garden. Peculiarly, the loggia was asymmetrical with
two piers or columns lining up with the central alley
of the garden, but the open loggia then extended
much further toward the north. In fact, all the architectural planning on this design is very awkward. Several of the small rooms between the loggia and the

garden, although Lanciani had published the will thirty years previously.

109. Rome, Orsini Garden, first project, Archivio di Stato,
Rome

palmi (ca. 78.6 meters). Four rectangular parterres, each with diagonal cross alleys and small fountains at the crossings, compose the main expanse of the garden. Between the parterres and the buildings along the Via del Babuino was to be a multilobed fountain basin set on the central axis and flanked presumably on each side by a small, rectangular grove or *bosco* of some forty trees in a checkerboard pattern. Presumably this planting was to be symmetrical, although only one grove to the north is indicated. At the other end of the garden in the direction of the Corso, two fishpools flank another but more simplified, six-lobed fountain. Lines drawn between the parterres and the fishpools on each side of the central axis probably denote an alley of small trees, offering shade to the pool area. At least, that is the identification for similar lines at that location on the final project.

In the final project (Fig. 111) the architecture is more carefully delineated, although there are not the numerous, detailed measurements of the second project. This third drawing must be the final project as it agrees, except for a few details, with the full description of the garden in the cardinal's will of 1581. On the west side of the design toward the Corso is again a large forecourt (*cortile scoperto*) with a small stable (*staletta*) in the northwest corner. Several buildings next to the court open onto the Corso, one identified as the house of one Pascoli (*habita il Pascoli* and *Site parte fabricato e parte scoperto doue habita il Pascoli*). Between the court and the garden is a symmetrical row of rooms with the central one entered from the court. The area of these rooms is identified as covered with houses, partially in ruins (*case scoperte et ruinate*). They are apparently to be rebuilt as a garden casino with a door into the garden opposite the entrance portal and windows only toward the garden. A spiral stair at each end of the rooms indicates that the casino was to be at least two-storied.

At the opposite end of the garden toward the Via del Babuino were small service buildings, particularly stables and facilities for washing, which corrected the awkward angle of the street. An entrance hall (*andito*) led from the street to a loggia supported on two columns opening onto the garden and with a small fountain set into the north wall of the loggia. The rectangular garden between the two built-up areas is the shortest of all projects, being 348 or 349 palmi (ca. 77.7 meters) long. The garden was to have four parterres with diagonal cross alleys in the shape of the cross of St. Andrew. Two multilobed fountains were to stand at the ends of the central alley with the one

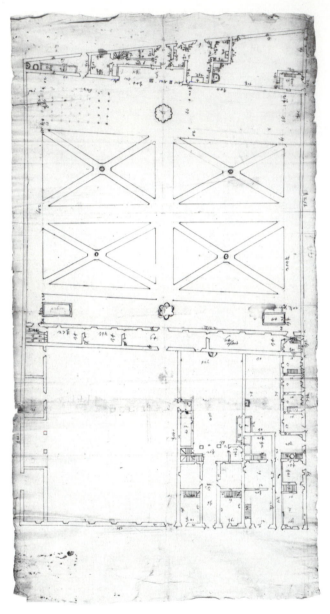

110. Rome, Orsini Garden, second project, Archivio di Stato, Rome

street open into the Via del Babuino. Strangely, four of these rooms have against one of their walls a rectangular piece of furniture inscribed with a cross as if they were altars and the rooms were chapels. In fact, the largest room, which is entered directly from the street, has a small niche cut into the wall next to the presumed altar as if for altar utensils.

The garden in this design is shorter than on the other; the architecture toward the Corso encroaches on the garden area so that its total length is some 352

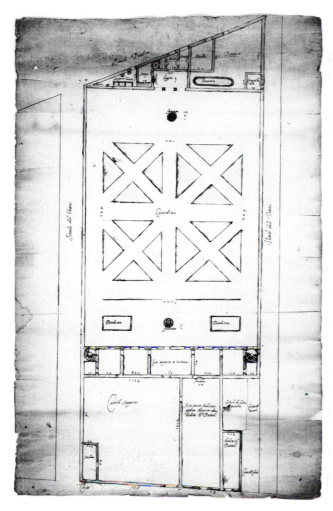

111. Rome, Orsini Garden, final project, Archivio di Stato, Rome

kneeling Venus, and Bacchus pouring water into the basin from a goatskin. On entrance into the garden the visitor first encountered a fountain of mixed African marble with three marine beasts ridden by white marble putti. In the middle of the basin was a black stone vase containing fruit of gilded metal and a large rose. On both sides of the fountain were groves of "forty feet of bitter oranges" (*quaranta piedi di melangoli*) arranged in squares. Although the final drawn project does not indicate the groves or orange trees in the areas provided for them, the second project has a rectangular grove of forty trees. In the cardinal's will the three walls of the garden, but not the casino facade, were espaliered with citron trees (*cedri*). The four parterres or *quadri* according to the 1581 description differed in their planting from the drawn designs. Rather than parterres in the form of the cross of St. Anthony, they were octagonal beds surrounded by wooden pergolas covered with orange trees. The parterres, each containing a simple fountain, were planted with 120 young orange trees. Each parterre had two water conduits with stopcocks to supply little channels outlining the parterres. At the head of the parterres was an alley composed of 11 large apricot trees mingled with 20 young cypress. Beyond the alley were two fishpools, and in the middle of each was a hexagonal marble vase from which four jets of water issued from a lead pipe. Closing the rear of the garden was the latticed facade of the casino broken by three travertine portals and seventeen windows. Even at this date not all the details of the garden were complete. The description notes that some forty-one travertine balusters were piled in the garden, not yet set up, and that fifty marble *quadretti* to serve as drainage lids were not in place.

In 1615 Giovanni Antonio Orsini, duke of Sangemini, sold the garden to the Augustinian monks.[15] Soon the church of Gesù e Maria was begun on the Corso in the corner of the block where there had been the large forecourt. Finally in the nineteenth century all traces of the garden were lost when the Protestant church of All Saints was built on the site opening onto the Via del Babuino and the remainder of the garden was built over.

Although the cardinal's nephew, the bishop of Spoleto, was given the right in the cardinal's will to live at the garden during his lifetime, the garden despite its location in the city was not created to be a princi-

[15] J.A.F. Orbaan, *Documenti sul barocco in Roma*, Rome, 1920, pp. 235–36, and M. Armellini, *Le chiese di Roma dal secolo IV al XIX*, Rome, 1942, I, p. 412.

toward the Corso flanked by fishpools (*peschiera*) and the line of the alley of trees between the parterres and the pools. This final project is obviously a refinement of the second project with changes primarily in the architectural forms and the change in the parterre design from rectangles to squares. In all three designs the public, garden entrance opened off the Via del Babuino, whereas the Corso entrance was the more private, carriage entrance to the casino.

The cardinal's will of 1581 notes that the "large garden" (*viridarium magnum*) is entered from the Via del Babuino through a portal of brocatello marble into a vaulted loggia of three arches painted *alla grottesca* and supported by two variegated columns of black and white marble. A mosaic fountain at the right on entrance into the loggia was decorated with four marble statuettes, including figures of Cupid, a

112. Rome, Aldobrandini Garden

some sort of residence at the vigna for on June 3, 1570, an avviso noted that Giulio Vitelli, who had served as governor of Città di Castello, was sentenced to house arrest at his garden at Magnanapoli under a bond of 20,000 scudi for reputed crimes during his governorship, including threatening the bishop of Città di Castello.[18]

Giulio Vitelli's difficulties may explain an otherwise mysterious transaction on June 5, 1574, when he is recorded as selling for 5,500 scudi the palace and garden of Monte Magnanapoli to his brother Vincenzo. Under the same date, however, there is an affirmation by Vincenzo Vitelli and repeated again in 1600 by the notary that the sale was a simulated one, and that the money stipulated in the contract had been returned to Vincenzo Vitelli.[19]

An old document claims that an inscription dated 1575 on the palace at the Vitelli garden asserted that the building had been restored and decorated by the Vitelli.[20] Later in 1642 Baglione in his lives of artists attributes the restoration of the casino and the decoration of the travertine portal with a superimposed loggia on the side of the garden toward Rome to the Aretine architect Carlo Lambardo. Although the attribution seems right, scholars have questioned it because Baglione claims that Lambardo died in 1620 at the age of sixty-one, which would allow him to be only sixteen years at the time of the work at the Vitelli gardens. Baglione is, however, incorrect regarding Lambardo's age at his death, for his burial inscription in Sta. Maria in Via at Rome reports that he was sixty-six years old at his death in 1620, suggesting that the minor revisions and restoration were the work of a younger man twenty-one years old.[21]

The Tempesta map of Rome dated 1593 gives a glimpse of the Vitelli gardens presumably as of that date (Fig. 113).[22] Roughly triangular in shape, the garden is enclosed by tall retaining walls, which compensate for the sloping site on the hillside so that the garden level raised within the walls can be flat. An irregular habitation is located in the far southeastern

pal residence. Its major purpose was probably to be a place for the cardinal to entertain his friends and colleagues rather like the later Chigi garden at the Four Fountains on the Quirinal Hill. To this extent it was another suburban villa as confirmed by the request in 1572 for water to supply his "vigna."

A similar garden was that of the Aldobrandini family on the slope of the Quirinal Hill in the area called Magnanapoli (Fig. 112). The first secure documentation of the garden was the purchase of the land and buildings in 1566 by Giulio Vitelli for 4,250 scudi from two brothers of the Genoese Grimaldi family, who had inherited it from their uncle, Cardinal Girolamo Grimaldi.[16] Commencing at least with Venuti in the eighteenth century, it has often been suggested that the site had been owned in the time of Pope Leo X by Cardinal Ippolito I d'Este, who died in 1520, but there has not been demonstrated any evidence of the identity of the location.[17] There was certainly

[16] ASF, Fondo Rondinelli-Vitelli, filza 8, inserto 19, contract of sale dated August 19, 1566.

[17] P. C. Lombardi, "La Villa Aldobrandini a Magnanapoli," *Capitolium*, VIII, 1932, pp. 339–40; L. Callari, *Le ville di Roma*,

2nd ed., Rome, 1943, p. 174; and I. Belli Barsali, *Ville di Roma: Lazio, I*, Milan, n.d., p. 395.

[18] Rome, BAV, Ms Urb. Lat. 1041, fol. 283v.

[19] ASF, Fondo Rondinelli-Vitelli, filza 11, inserto 4.

[20] For the history of the garden, see P. C. Lombardi, "La Villa Aldobrandini a Magnanapoli," *Capitolium*, VIII, 1932, pp. 336–49.

[21] V. Forcella, *Iscrizioni delle chiese e d'altri edificii di Roma*, Rome, 1876, VIII, p. 363, no. 865.

[22] Frutaz, *Piante*, II, p. 265.

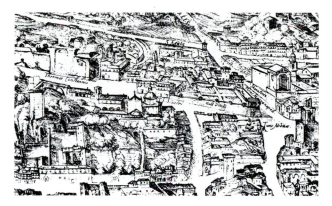

113. Rome, Tempesta map of 1593, detail with Aldobrandini Garden

corner of the garden at the corner of the present Via Panisperna and the Via Mazzarino near the church of Sant'Agata dei Goti. Two tower pavilions are set at the other corners of the triangle. The one toward the center of Rome with a loggia above the rusticated portal must be the entrance pavilion attributed by Baglione to Lambardo. Within the walls the rough sketch of the garden presents the traditional pattern of cross alleys.

The Vitelli brothers led very tumultuous lives. On September 4, 1583, Vincenzo Vitelli left from the center of Rome in a coach to visit the gardens at Magnanapoli.[23] When the coach reached the level of the Tor de' Milizie, shots from several arquebuses rang out, seriously wounding Vitelli. Later, he was also found to have suffered stiletto wounds resulting in his death and on September 10 five servants of Lodovico Orsini, who previously had an altercation with Vitelli, were seized, accused of the murder.

In 1598 the Vitelli property was appropriated by the Camera Apostolica because of transgressions attributed to Giulio Vitelli by the papacy.[24] At the same time Pope Clement VIII must have been interested in the possibility of improving the garden, perhaps in anticipation of its gift to his nephew, for the pope signed a brief authorizing the ample amount of twenty oncie of water of the Acqua Felice to be diverted to the site. An avviso of October 4, 1600, notes the rumor that the pope has given the "palace and garden of the Vitelli on Monte Magnanapoli" to his

nephew, Cardinal Pietro Aldobrandini,[25] and on August 5, 1601, was recorded the act of possession by the cardinal. With the earlier acquisition of an abundant water supply, the cardinal immediately undertook to improve the building and particularly the gardens. On May 1, 1602, an avviso records a visit of Pope Clement VIII on the previous Sunday to the gardens with the glowing account: "Although [the gardens] before were not the worst in the world, still there is no comparison today to what they were before, both for the quantity of fountains made there and for the great abundance of water conducted there."[26]

Soon, however, the cardinal acquired a prize tourist attraction for his garden, when in 1604 a large ancient Roman wall fresco depicting a wedding was discovered on the nearby Esquiline Hill. Known as the Aldobrandini Wedding, the fresco, now in the Vatican Museum, was put on exhibit by the cardinal within the entrance pavilion of the gardens designed by Lambardo. Although there were pieces and fragments of ancient sculpture in the gardens, the rarity of such a large example of ancient painting available at that time became the sole focus of tourist attention and seventeenth- and eighteenth-century travel accounts tell little about the gardens. In 1647 Camillo Pamphili, giving up his cardinalate, married Olimpia Aldobrandini, sister of Cardinal Pietro Aldobrandini, widow of Prince Borghese and heiress of the Aldobrandini family, thus transferring the ownership of the garden to the Pamphili family.

The garden at Magnanapoli served as a rustic retreat for disturbed members of the family, especially the two half-brothers, sons of the domineering Donna Olimpia. On July 7, 1668, it was reported that the Pamphili prince, passionately in love with a French lady, had fled to the garden "not being able to suffer to remain under the care of his mother."[27] By October, the Pamphili prince having moved on to Frascati, his half-brother, Prince Borghese, went to the garden "agitated by this world" (*inquieto di questo Mondo*). When he left on October 20, the avviso amusingly noted that his departure "was not without pleasure of all the gardeners, since by his horrid melancholy he has converted the trees into cypresses."

[23] B. Getta, "Il diario di Lelio della Valle (1581–1586)," *Archivio della società romana di storia patria*, CV, 1982, p. 247.

[24] For Aldobrandini documents regarding the garden, see J. Garms, *Quellen aus dem Archiv Doria-Pamphilj zur Kunsttätigkeit in Rom unter Innocenz X* (Quellenschriften zur Geschichte der Barockkunst in Rom, 4), Rome and Vienna, 1972.

[25] R. Lefevre, "Il patrimonio romano degli Aldobrandini nel '600," *Archivio della società romana di storia patria*, LXXXII, 1959, p. 16.

[26] Orbaan, *Documenti sul barocco in Roma*, p. 66.

[27] Rome, BAV, Ms Barb. Lat. 6401, fol. 134r (July 7, 1668); fol. 311v (October 6, 1668); and fol. 336r (October 20, 1668).

114. Rome, Villa Giulia, Portal of Parioli Hills

By the eighteenth century according to travel accounts, the gardens and house were neglected and deserted. President De Brosses during his visit in 1739–1740 notes the neglect and suggests that the fresco of the Aldobrandini Wedding, which he saw above a door in the entrance pavilion, should be placed in a more honorable location.[28] De Brosse's comment was fulfilled in the early nineteenth century, when in 1814 the fresco was acquired by Vincenzo Nelli, who in turn sold it to Pope Pius VII for the Vatican Museum.[29]

In 1876 the Via Nazionale was cut from the Baths of Diocletian, destroying the garden formerly of Cardinal Du Bellay that had been created in the exedra in front of the baths, to the center of the city, cutting off and destroying more than a third of the Aldobrandini garden toward the north. The street level around the garden was lowered further, so that the entrance pavilion of Lambardo was closed with a blind window. Along the Via Nazionale side of the garden a completely new, tall retaining wall was erected with a tower imitating the sixteenth-century one at each end of the new wall. The garden, although rather shabby as a small public park, still remains a lovely retreat isolated from the city above which it rises and with a superb vista out over the city, especially focused on the monument to Vittorio Emanuele.

Scattered throughout Rome are the relics of lost gardens, relics often moved from their original setting as the city overwhelmed its open spaces. So there is on the Aventine Hill the rustic portal (Fig. 114) from the Villa Giulia across town, which opened onto the path winding up the Parioli hills or the entrance portal of the Farnese gardens on the Palatine Hill (Fig. 57), which originally was on the north side of the hill

overlooking the Forum, and now, reerected, stands isolated on the east side of the hill.[30] At the entrance of the Museo delle Terme in the Baths of Diocletian is the former portal of the garden of the Vigna Panzani (Fig. 115), which was once nearby just north of the baths. The maps of Rome in the second half of the 1570s depict a relatively small, walled-in garden off the Via Pia, the present Via XX Settembre, near the baths, with a portal in the center of the west wall.[31] During the papacy of Sixtus V (1585–1590), a new public fountain, the Acqua Felice, named after the pope, was erected in the corner of the old garden next to the Via Pia. An avviso in June 1586 records that the pope after dining with the imperial ambassadors at his suburban villa, the Villa Montalto, went to hear mass at the church of Sta. Maria degli Angeli in the Baths of Diocletian and "then to see the piazza, which is to be enlarged with the leveling of antiquities, houses, walls, and destruction of the Panzani vigna."[32] Then in December it was noted that the Acqua Felice, the water for a new fountain, had appeared, although not yet very abundantly, in the Via Pia at the portal of the Panzani. A fresco in the new Vatican Library of Sixtus V (Fig. 116) depicts the fountain with a glimpse at the side of the Panzani garden portal and the enclosing garden wall with swallow-tailed crenellations. In the fresco the garden is represented as divided by low hedges into small square compartments, each having in its center a single tree. The portal as it now stands transferred to the Museo delle Terme (Fig. 115) has a polygonal-headed entrance rather like that of Michelangelo's nearby Porta Pia with a large keystone and Doric rusticated pilasters outlined by diamond-faceted square blocks of stone. Vertical scrolls support the sides of the portal. Several features of the gateway are similar to the garden gateway of the Villa Carpi that once opened onto the Via Pia (Fig. 192).[33] The Vatican fresco, which is not very accurate, particularly in proportions, depicts above the Panzani portal an unusual rectangular frame in place of the inscription plaque of the other gateways along the Via Pia.

Cardinal Odoardo Farnese, having ensured the magnificence of the Farnese Palace, which he had in-

[28] C. de Brosses, *Lettres familières sur l'Italie*, ed. Y. Bezard, Paris, 1931, II, p. 313.

[29] B. Nogara, *Le nozze Aldobrandini*, Milan, 1907, p. 4.

[30] For the Farnese gate, see Chapter 4.

[31] Frutaz, *Piante*, II, pls. 240 (1575) and 254 (1577).

[32] J.A.F. Orbaan, "La Roma di Sisto V negli *Avvisi*," *Archivio della società romana di storia patria*, XXXIII, 1910, p. 288, and R. Lanciani, *Storia degli scavi di Roma*, IV, Rome, 1912, p. 159.

[33] For the garden portals along the Via Pia, see D. R. Coffin, *The Villa in the Life of Renaissance Rome*, Princeton, N.J., 1979, pp. 193–201.

115. Rome, Portal of Vigna Panzani, Museo delle Terme, Rome

116. Rome, Vatican Palace, Library of Sixtus V, fresco of Acqua Felice and Vigna Panzani

herited, by the decoration of its gallery by the Carracci, soon revealed a desire for a private retreat at the palace. On the opposite side of the Via Giulia at the rear of the palace in secondary buildings between the street and the Tiber River, a small casino was built from 1602 to 1603.[34] At the rear of the casino a triple-arched loggia on the ground floor opened onto a small garden set between the building and the river. An arch thrown across the Via Giulia permitted the cardinal and friends to reach the garden from his palace. At the same time the setting of the garden was prepared by building a parapet about a meter high along the river and placing in the center of the garden area a large circular water basin for the fountain. Soon Annibale Carracci and members of his school were brought in to decorate the casino. A document of 1626 offers a description of the private garden at that time.[35] The garden was divided into four principal parts, each of which was then subdivided into small beds planted with flowering bulbs and herb roots (*radici di semplici*). Most notable among the beds was a flowering horse chestnut as well as forty-eight tall orange trees. In another part a large fishpool surrounded by a balustrade set among four more small beds contained a fountain decorated with shells, turtles, and four putti. Numerous vases located in many corners of the garden were planted with a variety of flowers and shrubs, including roses, anem-

ones, carnations, and jasmine. In the late nineteenth century with the building of the Lungotevere the garden was destroyed.

A well-documented urban garden is the Pamphili garden created in the Trastevere off the Via dei Vascellari next to the church of Sta. Maria in Cappella for Donna Olimpia Maidalchini, sister-in-law of Pope Innocent X. The first document relating to the garden is probably the gift on May 23, 1653, by the pope to his sister-in-law, identified as the princess of San Martino, of the right to two oncie of water for her garden from the Acqua Paola, the principal source of water for the Trastevere.[36] On June 9 Donna Olimpia bought from the nuns of Sta. Cecilia a canebrake and a mill. On September 30 and December 9 came other purchases, including several small gardens, a house with three caves or grottoes, a granary, and a hay loft. Meanwhile in June the pope had decided that a fountain called the "Lumaca," with three dolphins balancing on their tails a large snail shell (*lumaca*), which the sculptor Bernini had created for the Piazza Navona in front of the church of S. Giacomo degli Spagnoli, was too small for that location. The fountain, therefore, was given to Donna Olimpia for her new garden. If the Fountain of the Snail was ever transferred to the Trastevere garden, its existence there was rather brief, for by the 1680s it was incorporated into the Fontana delle Regina in the gardens of the Villa Pamphili on the Via Aurelia outside the Trastevere as depicted in Venturini's *Fontane di Roma* of about 1684.[37]

[34] F. C. Uginet, *Le Palais Farnèse*, III, 1: *Le Palais Farnèse à travers les documents financiers (1535–1612)*, Rome, 1980, pp. 89–100, and C. Whitfield, "La Decoration du 'palazzetto,' " in *Le Palais Farnèse*, I, 1, Rome, 1981, pp. 313–15.

[35] S. Benedetti, *Giacomo Del Duca e l'architettura del Cinquecento*, Rome, 1972–1973, pp. 479–80.

[36] For the documents, see Garms, *Quellen*.

[37] D'Onofrio, *Acque e fontane di Roma*, p. 506, n. 6.

On January 28, 1654, Donna Olimpia made out her will, leaving the small garden with a granary and grottoes to her grandson, Giovanni Battista Pamphili, for whom she said she had bought them. The inheritance included "all the statues and furnishings of whatsoever sort in said little garden, as well as in the casino which I shall build there, God willing."[38] Already on January 20 payments began for stonecutting for the garden, which would continue until October 1658. Soon Donna Olimpia's garden became the favorite haunt of Pope Innocent X. The avvisi note his frequent visits, even several times a week.[39] On one visit in May 1654 the pope met there the architect Girolamo Rainaldi, who was presumably in charge of the work. On the pope's return to the Quirinal Palace he had the "model" of the garden brought to him for further discussion.

The most devastating plague to torture seventeenth-century Rome even threatened Donna Olimpia's garden. By June 1656 the plague, rampant in Naples, appeared in the Trastevere at Rome, so on the night of June 23 most of the Trastevere was sealed closed by the authority of Cardinal Francesco Barberini.[40] Apparently the cardinal had in mind to use the garden as a burial location for the plague victims rather than transporting their bodies across the river to S. Paolo fuori le Mura, but must have been persuaded not to pursue the idea, for a letter in July notes that "the garden at the Ripa has not been touched, nor will it be used for the burial of the dead as was suggested by Cardinal Barberini."[41]

By 1659 the planting in the garden was probably well established, as some two hundred planting vases were bought in February. A square garden divided into eight flower beds with a central fountain was provided, according to a contemporary account, "with water tricks, fruit trees and rare plants."[42]

Mid-seventeenth-century maps of Rome identify the location of the garden set on the bank of the Tiber River, hence the garden's name as the Giardino a Ripa, opposite the remains of the ancient bridge, the Pons Sublicius.[43] The Falda map of 1676 depicts a

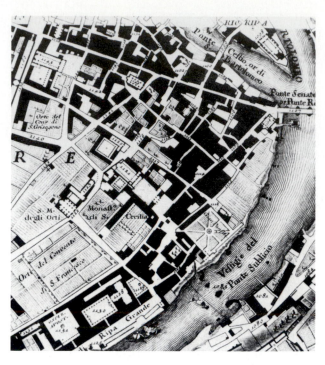

117. Rome, Nolli map of 1748, detail of Giardino a Ripa

roughly square garden with a smaller square area projecting south along the river. The garden is enclosed by walls and buildings and a large pavilion sits on the river bank. Nolli's later map of 1748 is more detailed and depicts a garden at that time square in form with a pattern of eight alleys radiating from the central fountain (Fig. 117).[44] Next to the river in the southern corner of the garden is briefly indicated the plan of a garden pavilion with a colonnade on two sides, the side facing the garden and that toward the river. Brief glimpses of the garden are to be seen in a painting, dating about 1690, by the Dutch view-painter Gaspar Van Wittel of the Tiber River at the Ripa Grande, now in the Accademia di San Luca at Rome, and in an old photograph of that area before the garden was destroyed in the late nineteenth century (Fig. 118).[45] A tall, battered retaining wall supports the garden along the river bank with a walled walk shaded by trees lining the river. At the near corner is a two-story pavilion with an arcaded loggia on the ground floor.

---

[38] I. Ciampi, *Innocenzo X Pamfili e la sua corte*, Rome, 1878, p. 354.

[39] D. Chiomenti Vassali, *Donna Olimpia o del nepotismo nel Seicento*, Milan, 1979–1980, pp. 227–28.

[40] C. d'Onofrio, *Roma val bene un'abiura*, Rome, 1976, pp. 223–59.

[41] J. Garms, *Quellen*, p. 144.

[42] L. Gigli, ed., *Guide rionali di Roma: Rione XIII Trastevere*, pt. III, Rome, 1982, p. 176.

[43] Frutaz, *Piante*, III, pl. 348 (1667) and pl. 354 (1668), and

L. Gigli, ed., *Guide rionali di Roma: Rione XIII Trastevere*, pt. IV, Rome, 1987, p. 15 (1676).

[44] Frutaz, *Piante*, III, pl. 407.

[45] G. Briganti, *The View Painters of Europe*, London, 1970, pl. 5 and a color detail on pl. 4. Two old photographs of the garden, similar to the Van Wittel painting, are published in Gigli, *Rione XIII*, pt. III, p. 191.

118. Rome, Aldobrandini Giardino a Ripa

By at least the late eighteenth century the German guide to Italy of Volkmann remarks that the garden and particularly the house were considered by the Romans to be cursed with evil memories, because they were once the residence of the "power hungry" (*regiersüchtige*) Donna Olimpia.[46] Despite the eighteenth-century comments, the Trastevere garden was not the principal residence of the princess or her grandson, but was meant for the entertainment of friends in a pleasant outdoor locale or for private relaxation at a location not far from the owner's main residence so that extensive moving preparations were not necessary for a daily or weekend outing.

Another urban garden across Rome in the region of the Monti was the scene slightly later in 1668 of an elaborate evening of entertainment demonstrating the use of such urban gardens. In 1660 Prince Mario Chigi, brother of Pope Alexander VII, acquired a casino and garden on the Via delle Quattro Fontane, at the corner of the present Via Nazionale and Via Depretis, which he presented to Abbot Domenico Salvetti.[47] With the death of the Abbot in 1664, the property returned to Prince Mario and was soon the possession of his son, Cardinal Flavio Chigi, who on August 15, 1668, entertained a group of Roman nobility to an operatic banquet organized by the architect Carlo Fontana, whose illustrated book describing the event has preserved some flavor of the occasion.[48] Soon the cardinal resolved to enlarge the garden and on July 13, 1669, signed a perpetual lease for the adjacent kitchen garden of the Carmelite nuns. From

---

[46] J. J. Volkmann, *Historisch-kritische Nachrichten von Italien*, 2nd ed., Leipzig, 1777, II, p. 657.

[47] For the documentation, see V. Golzio, *Documenti artistici sul Seicento nell'Archivio Chigi*, Rome, 1939, pp. 189–200.
[48] See Chapter 10.

1669 until 1675 documents record expenses for the enlargement and beautification of the garden. The sculptor Antonio Fontana furnished several statues of peperino, including one of a lion, and the transportation of two antique statues from the Forum was noted in September 1670. A new Fountain of the Dolphins, first mentioned in August 1671, is described in a later evaluation of Carlo Fontana in 1674 as being decorated with a triton and five dolphins. At the same time the Chigi architect Felice della Greca oversaw the laying on of water conduits and the crafting of "water tricks" (*giochi d'acqua*) in the garden. The last payments in 1674 and 1675 were for painters to fresco the walls of the garden.

A description of the garden in 1683 specifies that the garden was 200 canne long (ca. 447 meters) by 100 wide (ca. 223.5 meters).[49] The main garden near the house had a large fountain in the center with eleven smaller ones scattered throughout the garden, as well as some thirty, another account says thirty-five, water tricks. Beds of flowers, particularly carnations, lent color and fragrance to the setting, as did espaliers of jasmine listed in a description of 1693. Vases of citrus fruit trees decorated the flower beds, while other citrus fruit trees were espaliered on the walls. The upper part of the garden at the rear comprised a grove of laurel and holm oak enlivened by fountains. This part of the garden, called a hermitage (*romitorio*) in an account of 1697, is described in 1683 as having the walls frescoed with a "hermit well disposed and well painted, who teaches temperance in the pleasures of this world. On the other side is seen the figure of a beautiful woman whose too ardent passions are cheated by the fury of water." These are, of course, the figures of a nude Venus and a hermit for which the artist Giuseppe Chiari was paid in March 1675. The scene of a hermit overcoming the temptations of Venus may have been suggested by the fact that the Chigi garden was located directly opposite the church of St. Paul the First Hermit. For visitors to Rome, however, the major attraction of the Chigi garden at the Four Fountains was the museum of curiosities, naturalistic and artistic, exhibited in the cardinal's casino.[50]

As the population of Rome increased dramatically during the late nineteenth century after its selection as the capital of a united Italy, the larger urban gardens, such as that of the Orsini or of the Pamphili, were overwhelmed by building. The modern equivalent of these lost green oases are often the small terraced gardens or balconies of the Romans' apartment buildings which they love to decorate with potted small trees and flowering plants.

---

[49] The several old descriptions of the garden are reprinted by Golzio, *Documenti*.

[50] G. Incisa della Rocchetta, "Il museo di curiosità del Card. Flavio I Chigi," *Archivio della società romana di storia patria*, LXXXIX, 1966, pp. 141–92.

CHAPTER 8

# Garden Parks

On September 11, 1550, Pope Julius III (1550–1555) with several cardinals and his elder brother, Balduino del Monte, went to dine at the villa of the papal treasurer, Giovanni Poggio, set in the Parioli hills outside the walls of Rome just north of the Porta del Popolo.[1] Earlier Julius and his brother had inherited from their uncle Cardinal Antonio del Monte a villa located nearby in the valley at the foot of the Parioli hills. Although Julius had been born in Rome of a prominent Tuscan family of lawyers, he found pleasure and relaxation in the rustic life, enjoying the vintage with the peasants' dances and delighting particularly, as his biographer Onofrio Panvinio relates, "in rural and coarse foods" (*rusticis et crassioribus cibis*).[2] So commencing in February 1551 Julius began to buy in the name of his brother vineyards and plots of land adjacent to their old villa. The major acquisition came on February 26 when he purchased the villa of Poggio. The elevation of Poggio in November during the first creation of cardinals by Julius suggests that the election of Poggio to be a cardinal may have in part been a quid pro quo for the release of the villa. The land purchases continued for the next two years until the pope had expanded his holdings west to the Via Flaminia and north along the road for about 460 meters (Fig. 119).[3] He also ac-

quired a strip of land on the other side of the Via Flaminia between the road and the Tiber River so that a landing stage could be erected on the river bank to accommodate the papal barge.

Already in May 1551 work was underway on revising and expanding the old Del Monte casino into a new, sumptuous villa for the pope. Vasari as architect in charge was joined by the sculptor-architect Ammannati, who was particularly concerned with the addition of the theater court and sunken nymphaeum behind the casino (Fig. 62). The architect Vignola, who was at first charged with the introduction of the water of the nearby aqueduct of the ancient Aqua Virgo to the nymphaeum, soon took over the rebuilding of the casino. The pope for the remainder of his life was completely preoccupied with his villa, or in the words of Panvinio, "he seemed insane with passion for it," going to visit it so often that the Sienese ambassador complained that he was not able to speak to him.[4] By the time of the pope's death on March 23, 1555, most of the villa was completed except for some decoration, as recounted in a letter of May 2, 1555, by Ammannati to his patron Marco Benavides in Padua.[5]

Rather like the earlier Vigna Carpi, but on a larger scale, the charm of the grounds of the Villa Giulia lay in their combination of formal and informal landscaping. The path to the villa from the landing on the river Tiber was laid out formally with pergolas and tree-lined alleys, occasionally accompanied by a se-

[1] S. Merkle, ed., *Concilii Tridentini diariorum, actorum, epistularum, tractatum*, vol. II, pt. 2, Freiburg, 1911, p. 190.

[2] B. Platina, *De vitis pontificum romanorum*, Cologne, 1600, p. 354, and L. Romier, *Les origines politiques des guerres de religion*, I, Paris, 1913, pp. 502–3.

[3] T. Falk, "Studien zur Topographie und Geschichte der Villa Giulia in Rom," *Römisches Jahrbuch für Kunstgeschichte*, XIII, 1971, fig. 2 on p. 106 and pp. 135–38 (nos. 6–31); this study is the most complete consideration of the villa.

[4] Platina, *De vitis*, p. 353, and Romier, *Origines politiques*, p. 299, n. 2.

[5] Published in Falk, "Villa Giulia," pp. 171–73.

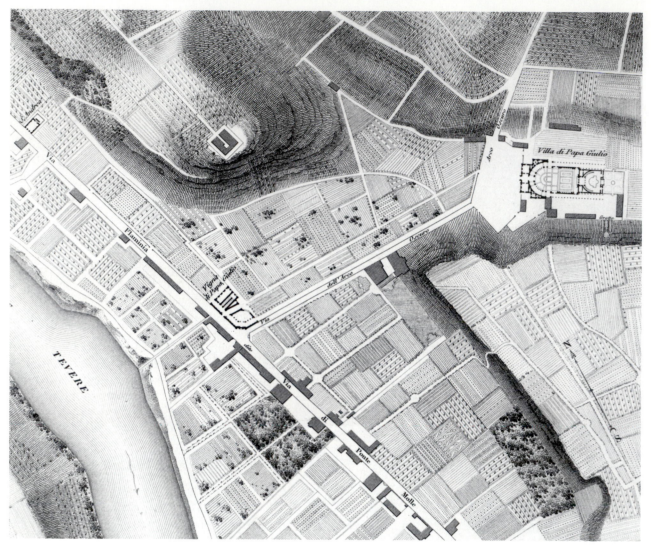

119. Rome, Villa Giulia, site plan

cluded retreat. Behind the wall where a large, ancient head of Apollo spouted water into a basin to serve as a public fountain at the corner of the Via Flaminia and the road up to the villa were three loggias on marble columns surrounding fishpools and fountains "with many water displays." At the casino, the court and nymphaeum had a large grove of orange trees (*naranci*) on each side in which in the center of one boschetto was a statue of a wild boar and in the other a group of a lion crouching over another unidentified wild beast. The heart of the complex was the sunken nymphaeum with its waterworks, sculpture, and aviaries. There the only horticultural feature was the four large plane trees that shaded the nymphaeum.

Behind the nymphaeum was a giardino segreto or private garden visible through the open portico at the top of the back wall of the nymphaeum, but quite literally "secret" in that access to it was by spiral stairs hidden away off the grotto in the back wall.

The Vigna Poggio in the hills had a completely separate planting layout depicted in a later plan (Fig. 120), when it was owned by the Medici. Near the casino (A) were several small, square, formal gardens in the nature of horti conclusi. Before the house was a large greensward (*prato*; B) following the traditional layout of an Italian villa. Beyond the prato were small kitchen gardens (*orticelli*; C). Two areas were set aside for bird hunting. A large grove or *ragnaia* (D) of

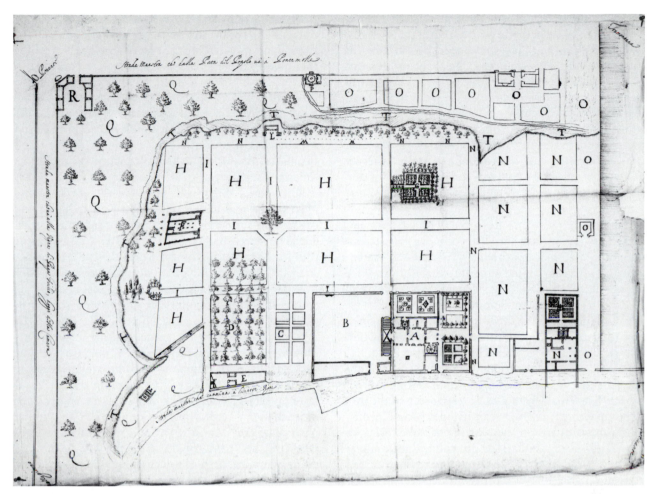

120. Rome, Villa Giulia, plan of Vigna Poggio, Archivio di Stato, Florence

holm oak near the kitchen gardens was for trapping birds with nets and in the midst of the vineyards (H) that composed much of the estate was an *uccellare da tordi* (G), a square blind for hunting thrushes. Farther up the hill was a garden created for Julius III, which featured a pergola supported by eighteen herms with ancient portraits of Greek philosophers and writers from the Villa of Hadrian at Tivoli.[6]

In contrast to the formal areas defined by the architecture in the center of the Villa Giulia and near the Vigna Poggio, the grounds around the edge of the estate, particularly on the hillside toward the north,

were landscaped more informally (Fig. 119). Thousands of trees were brought in to plant woods there. In fact, Ammannati in his letter describing the Villa claims that some 36,000 trees were planted at the Villa Giulia, and in March 1554 alone 1,000 trees were set out.[7] Some trees and plants came from as far away as Naples and Bologna, while others were wild specimens dug up along the coast. The majority of the trees were elms and poplars, but there was also a wide variety of fruit and nut trees, including plums, apricots, chestnuts, pomegranates, quinces, medlars, and arbutus, as well as jasmine. In June and July 1552 an alley or street (*strada* in the documents) was laid out from the semicircular piazza in front of the villa up

[6] C. Huelsen, "Die Hermeninschriften beruehmter Griechen und die ikonographischen Sammlungen des XVI. Jahrhunderts," *Römische Mitteilungen*, XVI, 1901, pp. 123–208, and R. Lanciani, *Storia degli scavi di Roma*, II, Rome, 1903, p. 115. Eleven of the herms are reproduced in A. Stazio, *Illustrum virorum ut exstant in urbe expressi vultus*, 1569.

[7] For planting see documents in Falk, "Villa Giulia"; Lanciani, *Storia degli scavi di Roma*, III, Rome, 1907, p. 16; and I. Belli Barsali, *Ville di Roma: Lazio I*, Milan, 1970, pp. 56–57.

the hill to the Vigna Poggio, passing through a tunnel toward the base where the Arco Oscuro is now. A rusticated gateway that once stood near the Villa was the entrance to this alley (Fig. 114). Near the little church of S. Andrea designed for the pope by Vignola to stand at the edge of the estate on the Via Flaminia was a court decorated with vine-covered pergolas beyond which was a small grove of laurel. These woods and groves were created for the enjoyment of walking, lined with paths and, as Ammannati says, "at every so many paces there are places for repose and for dining in the shade, either loggias of greenery or of masonry."

Officials and servants from the Vatican were employed in laying out the Villa Giulia. Bernardino Manfredi, a former *palafreniere* or groom at the papal court, was appointed superintendent of the work at the Villa Giulia and the gardener was the Belvedere gardener at the Vatican, Scipione Perotto.[8]

The planning of the great park of the Villa Giulia was very casual, conditioned primarily by function and previous architecture. The two major buildings, the Villa Giulia and the Vigna Poggio, had been established before most of the land of their setting was acquired. The Villa Giulia was an expansion of the previous casino of Cardinal Antonio del Monte, which had been set down on the axis of the valley with no consideration of its relationship to the Via Flaminia. The new street that Julius III commissioned to lead from the public fountain on the Via Flaminia to the casino is not lined up with the axis of the building. Therefore, the piazza in front of the villa had to be semicircular to transpose the line of the street to the axis of the casino. The location of the church of S. Andrea was determined by the tradition that the site was where Cardinal Bessarion in the fifteenth century had paused before entering the city with the relic of the head of St. Andrew. Otherwise the landscaping seems to have been determined by the functional necessity of circulation among the various architectural elements of the estate combined with secluded retreats for the quiet enjoyment of dining in nature or for the rustic sport of bird hunting.

In 1910 the city of Rome cut a wide avenue through the valley just north of the villa, reducing the grounds of the villa more or less to the land on which the casino sat. The park portal (Fig. 114) opening to the Parioli hills was dismantled and reerected on the Aventine Hill, as apartment buildings began to occupy the property north of the new avenue. The destruction of the great garden park of the Villa Giulia was the last of several others occasioned by the rapid expansion of the city after its selection as capital of the new Kingdom of Italy.

The rustic, expansive, parklike ambience of the Villa Giulia was rather unusual in Roman gardening of the mid-sixteenth century, when the more formal gardens represented by the Villa d'Este at Tivoli or the Villa Mattei in Rome are prevalent. Even the casual park area of the Villa Lante at Bagnaia in contrast to the formal gardens there is explained by its iconographical program consistent with sixteenth-century Roman gardening. Toward the end of the century, however, in the gardens of the villa of Cardinal Montalto, later Pope Sixtus V, the informal, casual garden park begins to become a characteristic Roman feature. In June 1576 Cardinal Felice Montalto purchased a large plot of land, some 10 pezzi (or more than 6.5 acres), on the Esquiline Hill next to the basilica of Sta. Maria Maggiore; most of the money was furnished from the dowry of the wife of the cardinal's nephew, so that the purchase was made in the name of the cardinal's sister, Camilla Peretti.[9] In January 1578 the purchase was regularized by the cardinal finally purchasing the vigna from his relatives. By late 1580 he had purchased two more adjacent vigne, thus more than doubling his original purchase. In the meantime he had commissioned the architect Domenico Fontana to design and erect a large casino on the first land purchase. By February 1581 the new building had attracted the attention of Pope Gregory XIII who, to the indignation of the cardinal, cancelled the monthly stipend of one hundred golden scudi given to the cardinal as a "poor" cardinal.[10]

The cardinal had his revenge, however, in 1585 when he was unexpectedly elected successor to Pope Gregory XIII as Pope Sixtus V. In August two neighboring vigne were given to him to expand his estate. This presumably inspired him to begin a systematic

---

[8] See Falk, "Villa Giulia," p. 109. The documents in Falk, p. 139, nos. 50 and 59, only identify "Scipione hortolano," which is confusing, as there were two men with the name Scipione employed at the Belvedere: Scipione Perotto, *custode* of the Belvedere, and Scipione Piccio, *hortolano* of the Belvedere (BAV, Ruoli 11, Julius III, 20 December 1551–4 June 1552, fol. 31). One might expect that the gardener at the Villa Giulia was Scipione Piccio, but Lanciani, *Storia degli scavi di Roma*, III, p. 25, quotes as at the Villa Giulia a document that specifically names Scipione Perotto.

[9] Documentation regarding the Villa Montalto is from [V. Massimo,] *Notizie istoriche della Villa Massimo alle terme Diocleziane*, Rome, 1836, and J.A.F. Orbaan, "Dai conti di Domenico Fontana (1585–1588)," *Bollettino d'arte*, VIII, 1914, pp. 61–71.

[10] BAV, Ms Urb. Lat. 1049, fol. 48v, February 4, 1581 and fol. 106v, March 8, 1581.

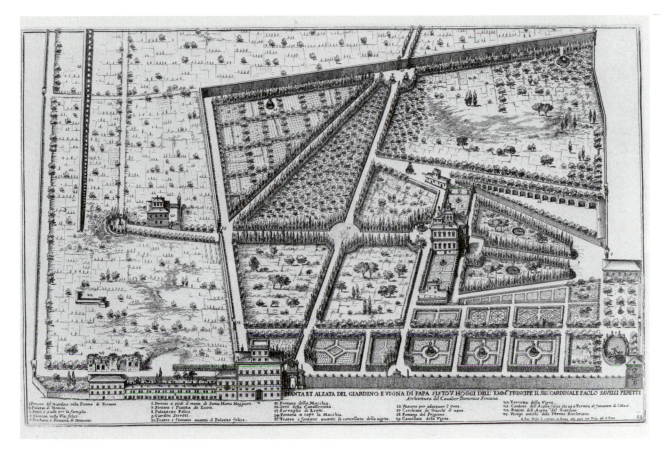

121. Rome, Villa Montalto, engraving of vigna

campaign of land acquisition so that by July 1590 his estate of almost 160 acres extending from the ruins of the Baths of Diocletian to the city gate of S. Lorenzo east of his church of Sta. Maria Maggiore was certainly the largest vigna within the walls of the city (Fig. 121). Old roads and lanes that had divided up the property were destroyed and in July 1587 masons began to enclose the estate with walls interrupted by six prominent gateways. Late in the year a large palace and secondary buildings were begun after the design of Fontana on the northern edge of the vigna facing the ruins of the Baths of Diocletian, part of which had been transformed by Michelangelo into the church of Sta. Maria degli Angeli.

The Villa Montalto resembled the Villa Giulia in its gigantic size, but the relationship between the architecture and the park setting was very different. At the Villa Giulia there was a great contrast, and even conflict, between the regularity of the architecture, outlining and protecting a habitable space in its several courtyards, and the irregularity of its natural setting.

Although the several buildings of the Villa Montalto were physically large, their blocklike character with no interior courts, derived ultimately from rustic farm buildings,[11] made them seem subordinate to their landscaped setting, like the smaller casinos of the Villa Lante at Bagnaia of a similar type. This harmony between architecture and setting is, of course, in part a result of the overall design of the layout, presumably by Fontana, and is unlike the Villa Giulia where, as was noted, function and topography determined the layout. A seemingly minor element of the landscape design at the Villa Montalto enhanced this relationship. The area in front of the casino on the west side of the estate, which had been a triangular-shaped piazza at first, was planted at the accession of Sixtus V as a garden with fountains and espaliered citron trees, which defined three alleys radiating out

---

[11] C. Lazzaro, "Rustic Country House to Refined Farmhouse: The Evolution and Migration of an Architectural Form," *Journal of the Society of Architectural Historians*, XLIV, 1985, p. 355.

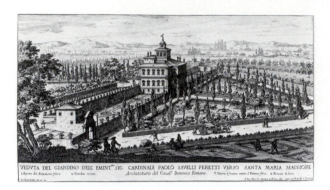

VEDVTA DEL GIARDINO DELL EMINT° SIG. CARDINALE PAOLO SAVELLI PERETTI VERSO SANTA MARIA MAGGIORE
*Architettura del Caual' Domenico Fontana.*

122. Rome, Villa Montalto, view of casino, engraving

into the vigna from the Porta Viminale near the church of Sta. Maria Maggiore (Fig. 122). The central alley led directly from the gateway to the casino, but the outer alleys flared out toward the ends of the giardini segreti flanking the casino where secondary gateways opened onto ramps up to the extensive garden area behind the building. At the entrance these diagonal alleys must have made a visitor aware of the expansive character of the setting in which the casino was located. This pattern of three paths, resembling the urban design element called by the Italians the *trivio*, may have been suggested by the wedgelike shape of the first plot of land purchased by the cardinal, but with the acquisition of adjacent land its expressive potential was realized all the more.[12] The trivio also helped to stabilize the relationship of the casino to its setting. The seriate acquisition of the plots of land after the commencement of the casino occasioned a rather casual design relationship between the architecture and the final landscape setting. The casino was left in the northwest corner of the vigna with its sides oriented in relation to the compass and not to the boundaries of the estate, but this situation was partially masked by the triangular entrance area.

On the northern edge of the vigna next to the palace facing the Piazza delle Terme was the Porta Quirinale. A wide, tree-lined avenue ran from the gateway across the vigna behind the casino, permitting public visitors access to the garden park without disturbing the residents of the papal casino. In the northwest corner around the casino about a quarter of the entire estate was enclosed by walls with the formal gardens, such as the giardini segreti, next to the building. Other areas contained vineyards, olive trees, and

other fruit trees. Sixtus V had a fondness for the rustic life, presumably as a result of his early childhood of poverty when, as he reminisced at the time of his election, he had had to pursue rustic chores, cutting firewood, hoeing the garden, and tending the pigs.[13] According to a contemporary notice soon after his election, when he visited his villa, he was seen walking "among those plants put in by him and weeded many times by his own hands."[14] The remainder of the vigna outside the walls enclosing the casino was left uncultivated. Most of the cost of the new villa must have been in terms of masonry for the walls, portals, and buildings. The architect Fontana in his book published in 1590 describing his feat of moving the ancient Egyptian obelisk at St. Peter's asserts that for the villa "a very great amount of money was spent in this undertaking because the site is full of hills and valleys, which are leveled and filled in to reduce the site to evenness, although it is true that in some places there are left artfully many gentle slopes and most pleasant valleys for greater beauty."[15] His admission of the retention of some of the irregularities of the site "for greater beauty" marks a shift from the prevalent sixteenth-century garden aesthetic with the exception of the Villa Giulia or Bomarzo. In contrast to the great Renaissance villas of the cardinal of Ferrara at Rome and Tivoli or that of the Medici cardinal in Rome, less terrain preparation must have been necessary at the Villa Montalto except for regularizing the slight slope in the neighborhood of the casino, which was built into the hillside so that the front elevation was one story higher than the rear with the giardini segreti at the point of transition.

In 1586 prior to his death on August 27, 1590, Sixtus V had given the villa to his sister Camilla Peretti, who retained possession until her death in 1605. Fontana in his book claimed that the papal villa was not fully completed at the pope's death, for there was to be a third palace erected to the east of the walls surrounding the casino at the highest point in the estate offering a wonderful vista across both the city and the countryside outside the city walls. The pope's grandnephew, Cardinal Alessandro Peretti Montalto, in the early seventeenth century made some notable additions and revisions to the landscape setting. About 1620 the sculptor Bernini was commissioned to carve

---

[12] A lost fresco of the villa of about 1588, once in Fontana's house at Rome, proves that this portion of the landscape design is sixteenth century; see [V. Massimo,] *Villa Massimo*, pl. IV.

[13] L. Pastor, *The History of the Popes from the Close of the Middle Ages*, n.p. [1977], vol. XXI, appendix 1.

[14] BAV, Ms Urb. Lat. 1053, fol. 220r, May 8, 1585.

[15] D. Fontana, *Della trasportazione dell'obelisco*, Rome, 1590, fol. 31v.

the group of Neptune and a Triton Calming the Waters, now in the Victoria and Albert Museum in London, which was set at the head of a large oval fishpool in the northwest corner of the vigna (Fig. 78). It may have been at the same time that a series of formal, square, floral compartments was laid out along the northern border of the estate from the Fountain of Neptune to the Porta Quirinale as visible in the later Falda engravings (Fig. 121). Such floral parterres were always meant to relate to the regularity of architecture and this location at the Villa Montalto was a logical place for them, situated between the casino and the straight, north wall of the vigna. Some of the parterres in the engravings are of the embroidered type originating in France and only accepted in Rome after the midcentury, suggesting that they have been replanted later, but the compartments would seem to be natural companions for the oval water basin. By the time of the 1618 Greuter map of Rome, the network of alleys was expanded, creating new vistas and a more extensive circulation pattern.[16] The Tempesta map of 1593 depicts only the long alley across the vigna from the Porta Quirinale and an open piazza behind the casino, as well as an unusually long pergola south of the building and an entranceway inaccurately indicated as a straight, wide alley instead of the actual trivio. This suggests that the alley extending from the rear of the casino that crosses at right angles the old alley from the Porta Quirinale was added probably at this time. The crossing was designed as a circular water theater with fountains and water tricks. More important, the two long cross alleys were continued through the enclosing wall into the uncultivated lands, enlarging the expansive character of the design. Tall walls of trees or hedges lining the long alleys emphasized the almost unlimited dimension of the vistas. Landscape design was no longer subordinate to architecture. It acknowledged the latter, fitting the architecture into the landscape pattern, offsetting thereby the contrast seen earlier at the Villa Giulia.

The advent of the railroad at Rome brought the destruction of the Villa Montalto, although it had already been dreadfully neglected since the eighteenth century. In 1883 the Villa Ludovisi on the nearby Pincian Hill had been sold to developers, leaving the Villa Montalto as the only remaining extent of undeveloped, level land within the city walls large enough to provide space for the central railroad station and its necessary marshaling yards, which were located

there after the casino and palace were demolished from 1886 to 1888. Only the so-called Fountain of the Prisoner was dismantled and reerected on the Janiculum Hill below S. Pietro in Montorio.[17]

The two great sixteenth-century garden parks of the Villa Giulia and the Villa Montalto in their expanded layouts had been papal possessions, but in the future similar garden parks were sponsored by another, though similar patron, the papal nephew. The two papal villas would seem to have been occasioned by the passion of their two owners, Julius III and Sixtus V, for a rustic life; both had taken advantage of the power and wealth of their position to expand a previous modest possession into a great holding satisfying their love of nature. The motivation of the papal nephews was often quite different and arises from a concern for their social and political image. During the fifteenth century the tradition had arisen that a pope would appoint at least one nephew as a cardinal, someone he could rely on during his pontificate, and who would help guarantee the continuity of power and wealth for the pope's family after his death, even perhaps eligible to succeed his uncle at a later time, since otherwise the power was limited to the usually brief tenure of the pope.

The first of the great villas of the seventeenth century was the Villa Aldobrandini at Frascati commissioned in 1601 by Cardinal Pietro Aldobrandini, nephew of Pope Clement VIII, from the architect Della Porta for the enjoyment of the cardinal and pope. The Latin inscription dated 1619 on the frieze of the water theater behind the villa celebrates the cardinal's feats as secretary of state to his uncle in expanding the power of the Church in France and in the Duchy of Ferrara (Fig. 36). The setting of the villa into the side of the hill with terraces and cascades, as well as a rather complicated iconographical program more like sixteenth-century villas, removes it from the type of garden park discussed here. It is physically on a large scale and uses at its entrance the trivio pattern of alleys, which at the Villa Montalto emphasized the expansive quality of the setting. At Frascati, however, the setting with a densely treed hillside slope at the back of the villa and almost enveloping it pushes forward the tall casino, which dominates the landscape and reduces any vista over the grounds. In fact, like all the villas at Frascati, the vista is out from the building over the *campagna* toward Rome.

[16] A. P. Frutaz, ed., *Le piante di Roma*, Rome, 1962, II, pl. 288.

[17] C. Matthiae, "La Villa Montalto alle Terme," *Capitolium*, XIV, 1939, pp. 139–47, and K. Kerenyi, "Statua di Esculapio in Trastevere," *L'Urbe*, XXIX, no. 3, May–June 1966, pp. 27–29.

123. Rome, Villa Borghese, engraving of vigna

In 1605 Cardinal Camillo Borghese was elected Pope Paul V and reigned until 1621. He immediately appointed Scipione Cafarelli, his nephew by a sister, a cardinal who became known as Cardinal Borghese and flourished as a patron of the arts and particularly the work of the young sculptor Bernini. Earlier the cardinal's grandfather and father of Paul V had obtained a vigna just outside the northern walls of the city in the section called the Muro Torto at the foot of the Pincian Hill.[18] Soon after the election of Paul V, his brothers acquired three additional vigne with which to enlarge their father's Vigna Vecchia and in 1608 their nephew Cardinal Scipione was given a large vigna adjacent to theirs which will eventually become the park of the future Villa Borghese (Fig. 123). In the same year the cardinal bought or was given additional lands where he soon had bosquets planted in front of his villa. In 1609 he acquired another adjacent large plot of land which included a small building. The old structure set at the location of the present villa was incorporated into the new casino, as happens so regularly with sixteenth- and seventeenth-century Roman villas, as at the Villa Giulia and the Villa Medici in Rome or the Villa Aldobrandini, Villa Falconieri, and Villa Vecchia at Frascati, and the land behind it was planted with groves of trees, the boschetti.

The first work commencing in May 1609 was to

[18] For the documentation and history, see especially J. Manilli, *Villa Borghese fuori di Porta Pinciana*, Roma, 1650; Amici dei Musei di Roma, *Villa Borghese: Catalogo*, Rome, 1966; C. H. Heilmann, "Die Entstehungsgeschichte der Villa Borghese in Rom," *Münchner Jahrbuch der bildenden Kunst*, ser. 3, XXIV, 1973, pp. 97–158; and B. Di Gaddo, *Villa Borghese: Il giardino e le architetture*, Rome, 1985.

prepare the grounds of the villa by introducing the water of the Acqua Felice for the fountains and basins decorating the gardens, work that continued until 1611.[19] Also in 1609 the architect Flaminio Ponzio appeared in the records designing and building the main gateway to the villa set just outside the ancient Porta Pinciana in the city walls. By the early summer of 1612 work had begun on the new villa under the direction of Ponzio and by May 1613 the rough masonry and structure was complete, but the stucco and statuary decoration required work for four more years. About the time of the completion of the structure the original architect Ponzio died and was succeeded by Giovanni Vasanzio whose major activity had been more in terms of decoration and, therefore, was very appropriate for the finishing work at the Villa Borghese.

In 1615 the cardinal's uncles ceded to him their vigne near the Muro Torto and by this time, except for some minor purchases of land continuing as late as 1621, the major land acquisitions had been consolidated into one very large estate. On January 28, 1621, the pope died, followed in August by the architect Vasanzio. Although the latter was succeeded by the architect Girolamo Rainaldi, the work on the villa was basically done.

The gardener in charge was Domenico Savino from Montepulciano, listed in the records as *vignarolo* or *giardiniere*, who lived in a small house in the enclosure in front of the villa opposite the Porta Pinciana. Confirming the concern of the cardinal for the early completion of the landscaping, the gardens seem to have been begun to be laid out in 1608, and by 1610 the cardinal had received as a gift from the papal nuncio in Brussels some most desirable tulip bulbs.[20]

In 1650 the *guardarobba* or wardrobe keeper, Jacopo Manilli, published a detailed description of the Villa, which in accompaniment with several earlier plans and the Falda prints of about the same time, offers a complete picture of the gardens and parks. Other than some interior decoration, restoration of statuary, and the laying on of more water from the Acqua Vergine, little change was made in the layout of the Villa Borghese by the time of Manilli's account. He commences by noting that the vigna is divided into three *recinti* or enclosures (Fig. 123). The first recinto is the area of formal bosquets planted in front of the casino. Recinto two consists of the small groves behind the casino that were for the private use of the residents of the casino. The third recinto was then the extensive park with hunting facilities toward the north of the other enclosures.

The entire estate was enclosed for some three miles by a wall about 4.5 meters high broken by several gates. The principal portal, about one hundred paces northeast of the ancient Porta Pinciana in the city walls, entered into a small, semicircular piazza outlined by espaliered laurel trees to form a wall of niches in which were set alternately peperino benches and antique statues. Herm statues by Pietro Bernini of the horticultural deities, Priapus and Flora, once stood flanking the entrance to an alley of elm trees wide enough for carriage traffic that ran some 250 meters across the width of the first recinto to end at the Fountain of the Mask set into the wall separating the first enclosure from the park. This large first garden area was densely planted with evergreen trees and divided by a rectilinear grid of smaller alleys into twenty-three roughly rectangular compartments outlined by espaliers of juniper, laurel, royal laurel, and mezereon. The eleven compartments at the left or south side of the entrance alley comprised a pine forest of more than four hundred pine trees. On the north side was a denser forest of some one thousand fir trees. Beyond the firs and flanking the piazza in front of the casino were four compartments of royal laurel. Manilli also noted that below the trees of the groves were strewn "roses, strawberries and other plants." Hidden in the compartments of firs toward the Via Pinciana is the wine grotto or *tinello*, a domed oval arcade on eight rusticated arches set about 3 meters underground. A double flight of stairs leads down to the sunken piazza, once decorated with eight orange trees, in which the arcade sits and at one end of the piazza is a ramp down to the grotto for wine storage. A large marble table, which stood under the domical ceiling frescoed with a Banquet of the Gods, clearly expressed its purpose as a pleasant retreat for rustic banquets or wine imbibing. Two pedestal fountains, one round, the other oval, stand at secondary crossings of the forest of firs. A jog in the wall separating the first recinto from the park just north of the compartments of fir trees set aside a large area for bird trapping or ragnaia (no. 8 on the Falda map), where a small stream flowed through seven parallel hedges that could support the bird nets.

---

[19] A plan of the landscaping of the Villa datable about 1630 locates the water conduits that feed the fountains and basins; see Di Gaddo, *Villa Borghese*, pp. 24–25.

[20] A.H.L. Hensen, "Nederlandsche Tulpen in de buitenplaats van Kardinal Borghese (thans Villa Umberto)," *Mededeelingen van het Nederlandsch Historisch Instituut te Rome*, III, 1923, pp. 205–8.

The first recinto is, therefore, the public garden park of the Villa Borghese open to the well-behaved general public as a Latin inscription within noted. On entrance the public would not be aware of the cardinal's casino, which would only be visible when a visitor had reached the middle of the rather densely treed precinct and glimpsed the casino at the right at the end of an alley of cypress. A second portal farther north on the Via Pinciana opened directly onto an alley running across the front of the casino to another gateway exiting at the north into the third recinto or park. This alley is obviously the private entrance to the villa for direct access to the residence. Such a circulation pattern with the casino no longer the focus of attention on entrance becomes traditional in the seventeenth-century garden parks, as will be seen soon at the Villa Ludovisi and the Villa Doria-Pamphili, and contributes to the subordination of the architecture to its landscaped setting. At the Villa Borghese, in addition, the densely treed areas increase this effect allowing only occasional glimpses of the casino.

Originally a wall lined the casino side of the alley from the private entrance gateway, thus hiding the giardini segreti that flanked the casino and limiting access to the second recinto or enclosure behind the casino to the residents of the casino. The enclosed private gardens on each side of the building, as at the earlier Villa Montalto, served as outdoor rooms for the casino and were entered directly through doors from the side reception rooms. The longer garden on the south stretching down to the Via Pinciana was the Garden of Orange Trees with citrus fruit trees espaliered along the long walls and 144 freestanding orange trees (*melangoli*) set out in twenty-four ranks. The northern garden was slightly shorter, cut off at the north end by an elaborate aviary. This garden, whose walls were also lined by espaliered citrus fruit trees, was divided into ten flower beds in two ranks. Each bed, outlined by low espaliers of myrtle, contained 6 orange trees and quantities of exotic flowering bulbs, including tulips, anemones, hyacinths, and jonquils. An arcaded passage through the aviary permitted a visitor to the garden to walk through and view the birds fluttering in their copper-netted cages. Beyond the aviary was a court shaded by 8 mulberry trees set about a fountain. At the rear of the court originally stood a rather modest building of four rooms that Manilli identifies as for the "fowl," probably both exotic and domestic. Later in the seventeenth century this henhouse will be refashioned as a

decorative garden building to accompany the aviary and has been called since then the Meridiana because of the large sundial set above the arcaded entrance on the garden side.

The second recinto behind the casino was the private garden sometimes called the Garden of Vistas. Along the wall next to the street were service buildings, including the stables, with access to the street. Directly behind the casino was a broad open area, its center occupied by a large fountain basin of African marble supporting a gilded bronze figure of Narcissus. On each side of the piazza were star-shaped bosquets of laurel with at the center an openwork iron dome supported by eight granite columns over a round stone table. Eight small alleys radiated out from the pavilions to create the star pattern. The plan of the water conduits dating about 1630 shows the major part of the private garden divided by a gridiron of alleys into fifteen large, rectangular groves of holm oaks, planted with more than six hundred trees according to Manilli later. Toward the north end and west side of the enclosure near the giardini segreti were rectangular compartments of laurel trees, which, as seen also at the front of the casino, seem to have been favored in conjunction with architecture. By the time of the Falda engraving (Fig. 123) the planting was consolidated into only six larger groves of holm oak. On the north side of the second recinto a file of cypress trees formed a wall across the garden before entering the laurel groves. Niches in the arboreal wall contained ancient statues, which prepared the visitor for the formal teatro arranged at the north end of the garden. The center of the north wall closing the garden off from the park beyond was richly articulated with elaborate architectural decoration appropriate to the garden and originally decorated with ancient busts in niches and antique inscriptions. In the center of the decorated wall was a large architectural frontispiece surrounding the Latin inscription of the *Lex Hortorum* welcoming visitors to the garden.[21] Two small flights of steps at the sides approached windows in the wall, which offered views to the more casually naturalistic park beyond.

The main entrance to the third recinto or park was at the end of the alley (no. 9 on the Falda engraving) leading from the private gateway to the villa along the west side of the giardini segreti. A large alley of more than ninety holm oaks stretched from the entrance into the park whose irregularity of nature is indicated

[21] See Appendix IV, no. 1.

by Manilli's description of its "valleys, and hills, and plains, and woods, and houses, and gardens."[22] The two miles of wall that enclosed the park were all espaliered with different fruit and nut trees and laurel. A wide variety of animals and birds, according to Manilli, "hares, roebucks [*capriuoli*], fallow deer [*daini*], stags, peacocks, ducks, and other small birds," wandered freely across the park as sport for the huntsmen. Just west of the entrance alley in a small valley was a large, rectangular lake for water fowl enclosed by forty-eight plane trees. Two small, artificial islands each with a pair of plane trees sat in the lake. Beyond the lake on a hillock toward the northern boundary was the *paretaio* (no. 15 on the Falda engraving) or a bower of boxwood within which was a small, two-story round structure where one might wait to net birds.

Along the west side of the valley ran a sustaining wall with several ramps leading up to a pine forest of some three hundred pine trees. Hidden within the *pineta* were two small farmhouses preserved from the original vigne acquired by the cardinal. The larger one toward the north (no. 19 on the Falda engraving), now called the Fortezzuola, was the home of the custodian of the henhouse with exotic birds such as ostriches and peacocks. Parallel to the pine forest on the west was another, but much larger ragnaia (no. 23) or area for bird trapping. This was followed again toward the west by a dense forest of holm oak with more than eight hundred trees according to Manilli (no. 26). A broad alley lined by elm trees commencing near the sustaining wall of the pine forest cut across the several treed areas and ragnaia to exit at a rear portal. At the end of the holm oak forest near the north wall was a semicircular opening with the wild animal house (no. 25) and nearby the underground ice house (no. 16) where during the winter snow would be stored for summer use. In 1620 a merchant from Tunis gave the cardinal a lion, a leopard, and two camels, presumably to be housed here in his menagerie.[23] The Falda print depicts at the northwest corner a fourth recinto or walled-in vigna with a large entrance gateway at the Muro Torto (no. 22). This was not part of Cardinal Scipione Borghese's vigna, but had been owned by his uncles, brothers of Pope Paul V. At the cardinal's death, his heir, Marcantonio II Borghese, also inherited the Muro Torto vigna, which functioned separately for many years as a farm

with a vineyard and several flower gardens, including a large one for tulips and Dutch roses.

The landscaped layout of the Villa Borghese presents the mature design of the Roman seventeenth-century garden park, but its progenitor would seem to be the Villa Montalto of Pope Sixtus V. Like the Villa Montalto, the Villa Borghese was not only vast, but made a clear differentiation between the more formal horticultural areas near the casino and the less regular park, even to separating them by walls. The irregularity of the original terrain of the park at the Villa Borghese seems to have been left rather untouched, although there was a great deal of new planting introduced unlike the park of the Villa Montalto. The care and expense lavished on the planting of the park of the Villa Borghese was undoubtedly in part due to the different function it was to serve in the life of the Villa. The trees, shrubbery, and water features, such as the lake, were to provide a suitable and attractive habitation for the birds and wild animals that might be offered as prey for hunting by the cardinal's guests, which was not true at the Villa Montalto. Unlike some of his predecessors in the fifteenth and early sixteenth century, Pope Sixtus V had no passion for the hunt, which might cause him to flaunt old canonical decrees against hunting by the clergy. Cardinal Borghese, however, must have considered hunting one of the necessary pleasures he should offer his guests at his country retreat. Also like the Villa Montalto, the giardini segreti or private flower and fruit gardens were set on each side of the casino at the Villa Borghese and helped mask some irregularities in the terrain near the building. One feature at the Villa Borghese, however, must have been suggested by the Villa Giulia. That is the location of its lovely Latin inscription of the *Lex Hortorum* in the heart and seemingly most private part of the Villa rather than posted at the gate as at the Villa Medici.

In the late eighteenth and early nineteenth century the setting of the Villa Borghese was drastically revised in the mode of English eighteenth-century landscaping, including the destruction of most of the interior walls so that it was converted into a huge park. Under the severe threat of urban development in the late nineteenth century, when Rome became the capital of Italy, the estate was purchased by the state in 1901 and two years later transferred to the commune of Rome as a public park and art gallery.

Pope Paul V was succeeded in 1621 by Cardinal Alessandro Ludovisi as Pope Gregory XV, who immediately on February 15 selected his nephew Ludo-

[22] Manilli, *Villa Borghese*, p. 161.

[23] J.A.F. Orbaan, *Documenti sul barocco in Roma*, Rome, 1920, p. 270.

vico Ludovisi to be a cardinal. Cardinal Ludovisi had, of course, the notable example of his predecessor Cardinal Scipione Borghese and began almost at once to assemble land for a suburban villa with lavish gardens on the Pincian Hill at the location of the ancient gardens of Lucullus and Sallust.[24] The property was just within the city walls near the Porta Pinciana, so that it was not far from its inspiration, the Villa Borghese, just without the walls. By June 3, 1621, Ludovisi had bought from Cardinal del Monte for 10,000 scudi a vigna with several extant buildings, including a casino of a cruciform plan. The first evidence of this casino dates from Dupérac's map of Rome of 1577 (Fig. 17) where its owner is identified as "Cecchino Del Nero" or Francesco Del Nero, an apostolic secretary. On the map, a treed alley leads up from the Via di Porta Pinciana to a square piazza enclosed by a low fence in which the casino with four equal arms sits at the highest point of the vigna. A month later on July 23 the cardinal expanded his holding by purchasing from Leonora Cavalcanti an adjacent vigna to the northeast. Very soon the painters Guercino and Agostino Tassi were engaged to decorate the casino and in August the papal nuncio at Naples had already sent north some ninety vases of orange trees.

Cardinal Ludovisi's ambition to rival Cardinal Borghese required more land and on February 5, 1622, he was able to purchase from Duke Giovanni Antonio Orsini for 15,000 scudi part of a large vigna adjacent to the east with a Palazzo Grande on the Via di Porta Salaria. At the time of the purchase the architect Carlo Maderno submitted a plan of the vigna showing the palace, gardens, fountains, and woods (Fig. 124). A survey of the property at the time of its sale describes it as "a large most beautiful site within Rome of healthy air with very wide alleys lined on each side by large elm trees and other types, a wood, the garden divided into many compartments."[25] Soon the palace was being refurbished and Maderno added a large frontispiece in the center of its facade. Finally another vigna adjacent to the Orsini property at the east became available in 1623. Known as the Vigna Capponi, the land belonged to the Carmelite monks of Sta. Maria in Traspontina who had ceded it to Cardinal Luigi Capponi for life who in turn offered to cede the property to Cardinal Ludovisi. The confusion of ownership was only settled by Ludovisi's pur-

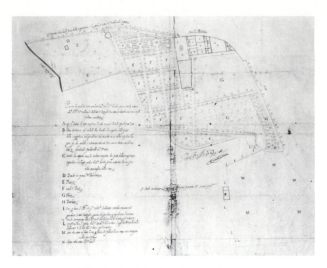

124. Rome, Villa Ludovisi, plan by Maderno, Museo di Roma, Rome

chasing it from the monks. With this purchase the cardinal's vigna reached its fullest extent of about forty-seven acres as depicted in the later Falda engraving (Fig. 125).

Set in the northeast corner of the city, the vigna extended from the Via di Porta Pinciana to the Via di Porta Salaria and was closed at the north by the ancient city walls. The main entrance to the estate was from the Via di Porta Salaria through the old gateway next to the Palazzo Grande of the Orsini property (no. 1 in the Falda engraving). The main house was set with one side along the public road, as were many of the fifteenth-century villas, such as the so-called Casino of Cardinal Bessarion or the Vigna Falcone, so that the entrance portal in an adjacent wall opened into a piazza or court before the building. At the Villa Ludovisi, however, the gateway was at right angles to the Palazzo Grande and a visitor entering through it had before him only a long alley stretching across the entire width of the vigna to end at the city wall (Fig. 126). Turning left at entrance a visitor could proceed into an open piazza with the Fountain of the Triton in the center in front of the main residence and two small, sunken fountain courts separating the piazza from the house (no. 3). On the north side of the piazza opposite the residence were two bosquets or dense groves within which were cut a formal pattern of alleys and openings (no. 5). Called the Labyrinth or the Galleria, the bosquets served as a horticultural setting for the exhibition of many pieces of sculpture from the cardinal's magnificent collection of classical antiquities. In 1622 he had bought the Cesi collection of

---

[24] For documentation, see [G. Felice,] *Villa Ludovisi in Roma*, Rome, 1952, and A. Schiavo, *Villa Ludovisi e Palazzo Margherita*, Rome, 1981.

[25] [Felice,] *Villa Ludovisi*, p. 42.

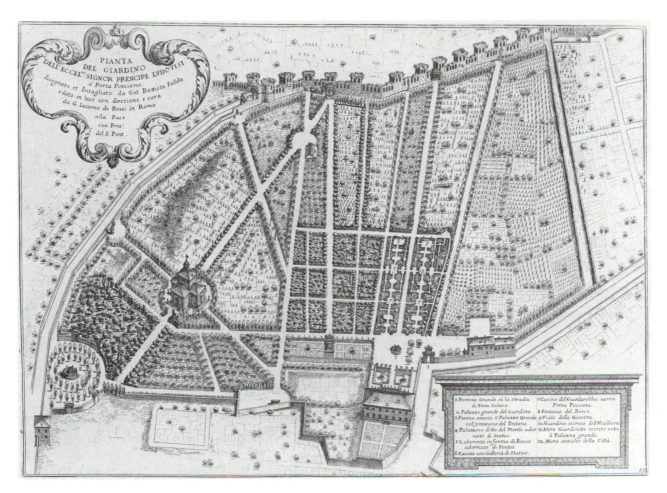

125. Rome, Villa Ludovisi, engraving of vigna

statuary, formerly exhibited in their palace and statuary garden in the Vatican Borgo and in 1623 he acquired the remains of the Cesarini collection. At the right of the entrance portal with its own smaller, open piazza, an extant building of the Vigna Capponi was transformed into a statue gallery (no. 6) and other antiquities decorated the Palazzo Grande and the casino in the park as well as other parts of the gardens.

Another long cross alley ran from the statue gallery at the east along the north side of the main piazza toward the Del Nero cruciform casino on the west side of the park. This alley served as the base line for other alleys stretching northward to end at the city wall. Just west of the main piazza on the south side of the cross alley was the giardino segreto of the aviary (no. 10). Toward the west end of the cross alley was the old cruciform casino, known henceforth as the Casino of Aurora from the famous fresco by Guercino

decorating its interior. Four alleys, one from each side, radiated off diagonally across the property. In the southwest corner of the vigna on the Via di Porta Pinciana was the house of the *guardarobba* or wardrobe keeper (no. 7) with just north of it the Fountain of the Wood with a fountain surrounded by circular files of trees. Again like the Villa Borghese the architectural elements, such as the Palazzo Grande or the Casino of Aurora, are not particularly the center of attention as they would be in sixteenth-century landscaping. The emphasis is on the breadth of the setting expressed by the very long alleys rigidly defined by tall hedges or files of trees. The casual design is very much conditioned by the location of previous buildings to which the landscape is adapted, unlike the prodigious efforts in the sixteenth century at Tivoli, Bagnaia, or the Villa Medici in Rome to regularize the landscape by redoing the topography.

VEDVTA DEL GIARDINO DELL' ECCELLENTIS.<sup>mo</sup> SIGNOR PRENCIPE LVDOVISI. *a Porta Pinciana.*
1. *Palazzo Grande del Giardino.*    3.*Bosco del laberinto.*    5.*Palazzetto detto del Monte adornato di Statue.*    7. *Veduta di Roma.*
2.*Fontana del Tritone nella piazza avanti il Palazzo Grande.*  4.*Vecelliera nel Giardino secreto adornato di Statue.*  6.*Palazzo dell'Eccell.<sup>mo</sup> Sig.<sup>r</sup> Prencipe di Pellestrina fuori del Giardino.*

126. Rome, Villa Ludovisi, view of casino, engraving

Later, in 1672, the writer Bellori in his lives of the artists will assert that "in the Ludovisi Garden the layout of the *Boschetto delle statue*" is after the design of the painter Domenichino.[26] Doubt regarding this attribution is raised by the plan drawn by Maderno at the time of the acquisition of the Orsini property in 1622. The plan depicts a bosquet (D) identified as *Boscho in forma di laberinto* (Fig. 124) opposite the Palazzo Grande. This bosquet, however, does not correspond to the one seen later on the Falda plan (Fig. 125), which is much wider. At another point on the drawing there is definite evidence that the plan incorporates future intentions. So in the lower southeast corner at the letter I is inscribed: "Site where the most illustrious Lord Cardinal Ludovisi intends to enter into the garden." Therefore, it may be reasonable, as has been suggested, to consider that Maderno's drawing is not only a survey of the Orsini property, but also incorporates new features for the cardinal, including the bosquet.[27]

The Villa Ludovisi and its great collection of antiquities remained more or less as created by the car-

dinal until the nineteenth century. The French finance minister Colbert did begin to cast envious eyes on the antiquities in the late seventeenth century as a series of letters from him to several Frenchmen at Rome, including Charles Errard, the director of the French Academy, indicates. Commencing in April 1669 the inquiries and replies regarding the possibility of acquiring at least some of the ancient statues or, in fact, the villa itself with the entire collection continued until November 1671.[28] The cost quoted in October 1671 of 30,000 Roman livres for only five choice statues, or at least 748,000 livres for "the Palace, the Vigna and the art objects" was too daunting for Colbert, who cut off the negotiations. In the nineteenth century Prince Boncompagni-Ludovisi undertook to increase further the land holdings of the Villa, purchasing on September 26, 1825, for 7,200 scudi the huge Vigna Belloni adjacent on the east side of the cardinal's villa and on November 29, 1851, for 4,400 scudi the smaller Vigna Borioni that was farther east. With this final acquisition the Ludovisi owned all the land between the Via di Porta Pinciana and the Via di Porta Salaria along the northern city wall. With this

[26] G. P. Bellori, *Le vite de' pittori, scultori et architetti moderni*, Rome, 1672, p. 350.

[27] H. Hibbard, *Carlo Maderno and Roman Architecture 1580–1630*, University Park, Penn., and London, 1971, pp. 211–12.

[28] A. de Montaiglon, *Correspondance des directeurs de l'Academie de France à Rome*, I, Paris, 1887, pp. 18–33.

expansion of the land the prince soon turned to enlarging the Casino of Aurora and from 1855 to 1858 the architect Nicola Carnevali added additional rooms and a carriageway to the four arms of the building, more or less enclosing the old structure within the new.

When Rome became the capital of the new Kingdom of Italy in 1871, the Villa Ludovisi underwent the same fate that the Villa Montalto would. In 1885 building speculators, having obtained possession of the land, began to cut down the giant ancient trees and to destroy the entrance gateway. On February 12, 1886, they presented to the City Council the urban plan for the development of a new quarter there, which would include the famous Via Veneto winding through the vigna to the Porta Pinciana. All that survived the destruction was the Casino of Aurora, isolated on a small city square, and a fragment of the Palazzo Grande, about half of which was preserved as a wing added to the rear of the huge Palazzo Margherita, now the American Embassy, which the architect Gaetano Koch completed in 1890 on the Via Veneto.

The last great garden park, that of the Pamphili family, will dominate a completely different area of Rome. In October 1630 Pamphilio Pamphili purchased some forty-two pezze, or more than 27 acres, of land with a country house on the ancient Via Aurelia about three-quarters of a mile west of the Porta San Pancrazio.[29] Standing from about forty-six to eighty-six meters above sea level, the site offered a magnificent vista of Rome and a particularly spectacular view of St. Peter's to the north. At the same time the Barberini pope Urban VIII gave Pamphili right to three oncie of water from the nearby aqueduct of the Acqua Paola. Pamphilio having died in 1639, his son Camillo inherited the vigna and in December 1640 enlarged it by acquiring a nearby vigna. On September 9, 1644, Camillo's uncle, Cardinal Giovanni Battista Pamphili, was elected Pope Innocent X and Camillo was elected in November to fill the usual position of cardinal-nephew, although he would be granted in 1647 the unusual permission to resign his cardinalate in order to marry Olimpia Aldobrandini and perpetuate the Pamphili family. Beginning in 1645 there was a concerted campaign to purchase more land along the Via Aurelia with the obvious intent to create another huge garden park that would outdo those of the previous cardinal-nephews. Although land purchases continued until 1673, the last major acquisition was made by Camillo's son in June 1668, resulting in a vigna of about 240 acres. With the increase of the site more water was needed for the fountains and basins foreseen as necessary decoration, so already in January 1645 four additional oncie of water from the Acqua Paola were provided and in the following month three more.

Building activity had begun as early as October 10, 1644, with earth movement and alleys. In 1645 foundations were excavated and plant material purchased for the gardens. From 1645 through 1647 more than 66,000 scudi had been expended to build a new casino at the east side of the park, the giardino segreto enclosed in front of the building and the formal gardens about it. By 1648 the casino with its rich stucco decoration was completed solely to function as an exhibition gallery and a place of entertainment in the park, since it contained no bedrooms. The old house included in the first land acquisition of 1630 remained the dwelling place, called on the Simone Felice plan (Fig. 127) the "Casino for the family with its garden" (no. 14, *Casino per la famiglia col suo Giardino*). In the seventeenth century all sources attribute the design of the new casino and perhaps its attendant gardens to the sculptor Alessandro Algardi, but this attribution has been variously questioned in the twentieth century. A letter of Prince Pamphili in March 1647 indicates that Algardi was in charge of the sculptural decoration of the casino.[30] Later the publisher G. G. de' Rossi in the introduction to his book of engravings of the villa, appearing between 1666 and 1670, clearly identifies Algardi as the architect, as does Bellori in his lives of the artists in 1672.[31] More recently it has been pointed out, however, that the name of the Bolognese painter Giovanni Francesco Grimaldi occurs more frequently in the building accounts overseeing the work or supply of materials. Although he is generally described as painter, in at least one account he is identified as "architetto."[32] Given the strong attributions to Algardi at an early

[29] For documentation, see O. Pollak, "Alessandro Algardi (1602–1654) als Architekt," *Zeitschrift für Geschichte der Architektur*, IV, 1910–1911, pp. 49–79, and J. Garms, *Quellen aus dem Archiv Doria-Pamphilj zur Kunsttätigkeit in Rom unter Innocenz X* (Quellenschriften zur Geschichte der Barockkunst in Rom, 4), Rome and Vienna, 1972.

[30] Pollak, "Alessandro Algardi," p. 57.
[31] Bellori, *Le vite*, p. 395.
[32] Pollak, "Alessandro Algardi," pp. 57–60. Even more confusing is the recent suggestion that the architect might be the aged Girolamo Rainaldi, whose name does not appear in the building accounts, but who might have been on salary as family architect;

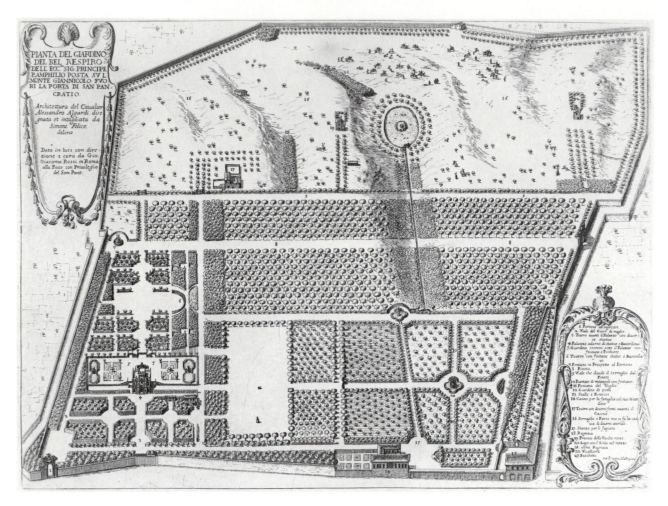

127. Rome, Villa Pamphili, Felice engraving of vigna

date and the favorable position he held as an artist with Pope Innocent X, Bellori's clear claim of "the plan of the villa" for Algardi seems convincing and does not deny the role of Grimaldi as the supervising architect. A letter of Pamphili to Algardi on March 27, 1647, where he notes having received letters from Grimaldi with questions regarding the work, would seem to confirm this relationship.[33]

There are two very important collections of contemporary plans and views of the Villa Pamphili. One is the book entitled the *Villa Pamphilia*, undated but published by G. G. de' Rossi between 1666 and 1670 with a plan by G. B. Falda (Fig. 128); ten perspective views of the villa, including unexecuted projects; and seventy-one engravings of antique sculpture. The

see M. Heimbürger, "Alessandro Algardi architetto?" *Analecta Romana Instituti Danici*, vi, 1971, pp. 197–224.

[33] Pollak, "Alessandro Algardi," pp. 73–74, no. 29.

Pamphili documents record several payments beginning in December 1648 and running on until April 1657 to the French engraver Dominique Barrière for numerous engravings, including an early perspective view of the villa, a depiction of the entrance portal, and numerous views of statuary and fountains. These must have been commissioned by Prince Camillo to present a splendid record of his architectural and gardening accomplishments and which is imperfectly represented in the present volume to which other prints by Falda have been contributed.

About 1670 G. B. de' Rossi published *Li Giardini di Roma*, which depicted the great Roman villas, including a bird's-eye view of the vigna (Fig. 127) and two perspective views of the casino, all by Simone Felice. The Felice plan must postdate that of Falda for the latter has the trees of the *pineto* or umbrella-pine grove (no. 21) planted in the traditional checkerboard

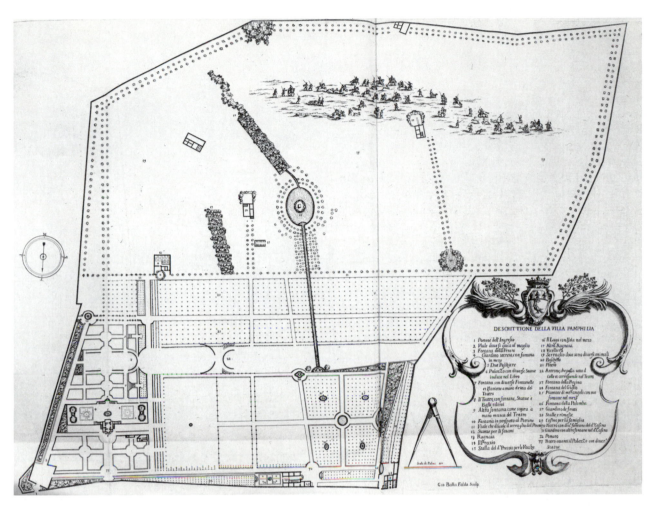

128. Rome, Villa Pamphili, Falda engraving of vigna

pattern rather than in the quincunx pattern derived from antiquity, seen on the Felice view and still extant at the villa today. In addition there are several other major and minor differences between the two plans, suggesting the more tentative, project nature of the Falda plan (Fig. 128). On the latter a broad, open axis (no. 22), corresponding at the left or east with the theater (no. 8) or hippodrome in front of the casino, cuts across the entire vigna; four small fountains are set in the quarters of the garden of bitter-orange trees (no. 25); the small wood (boschetto, no. 20) south of the pine grove is round in the earlier Falda plan, but rectangular in Felice (no. 23); and the canal, which flows south in the small valley in the center of the vigna, does not end at the lake with the island as in Felice (no. 20), but continues into the ragnaia (no. 17 on the Falda plan).

In the Felice plan (Fig. 127) the layout of the Villa Pamphili is the most regular and classic of all the garden parks of Rome. The vigna, set along the ancient Via Aurelia, is roughly rectangular in form, with skewered sides at east and west. Three entrances to the estate on the north side opened off the road and a fourth was in the middle of the west side gained by an alley or small road at right angles to the Via Aurelia. The principal and public portal to the villa was at the northeast corner, thereby nearest to the city of Rome. The gateway next to the old residence of the family (no. 14) was, of course, a private entrance, as was that into the stable court (no. 13) at the northwest corner. The major circulation path for the public presumably ran from the public gateway (no. 1) at the northeast to the western portal at the end of the main cross axis of the park. Entrance was through an arched portal surmounted by the papal arms of Innocent X set in a broken segmental pediment engraved by Barrière as the frontispiece for the book, the *Villa Pamphilia* (Fig. 129). Beyond a small piazza just within the walls was a long alley, entitled the "Alley of the Game of Pall-Mall" (no. 2, *Viale del Gioco di maglio*), running parallel to the east side of the estate. Other alleys opening off the west side of the entrance alley led across the vigna, but were probably for the most part not meant to be public. Certainly the first cross alley leading from the entrance piazza to the family casino with no water displays or features of interest was normally not available to the public, especially when the family was in residence. Similarly, the theater in front of the casino (no. 3) and the giardino segreto (no. 5), which was walled off from the park, were not for public enjoyment.

Like the earlier garden parks of the Villa Borghese and the Villa Ludovisi, the buildings for both recreation and residence at the Villa Pamphili were not centers of visual attention at entrance, but were isolated within the park. The entrance alley focused instead on a fountain at its end and is so identified on the plan as "the fountain in view at the entrance portal" (no. 7, *Fontana in prospetto al portone*). Barrière's engraving of the portal stresses this by telescoping the vista and emphasizing the perspective by lining the alley with hedges taller than man and vertical files of trees that would mask the tall casino. A concerted effort was made, therefore, to limit the public's interest to the entrance alley until a visitor had at least passed by the tall retaining wall of the giardino segreto on which the casino opened (Fig. 130). There the alley running across the garden area in front of the casino and leading to monumental stairs up to the groves beyond must have attracted public attention. Similarly, farther down the Alley of Pall-Mall was a modest opening into the broad, open hippodrome cutting across the garden area of the casino to terminate in the semicircular theater (no. 6) with statuary and fountains. Finally at the fountain at the end of the entrance alley was the major cross axis of the vigna (no. 8). From there the visitor would have a very dramatic view back across the hippodrome and through the gardens to the tall casino. Farther west the gardens cut through the quincunx pattern of the pine grove.

About one-third of the estate south of the umbrella pines was for the most part left undeveloped as a hunting park. At the eastern end of the park was a pheasant house (no. 17). Two large groves for bird netting or ragnaie (nos. 18 and 21) were set in valleys in the undeveloped park. Between them was a cowshed (no. 19). A canal, about a 350 meters long, arose

129. Rome, Villa Pamphili, entrance portal, engraving

from a nymphaeum at the southern edge of the cross alley near the Fountain of the Lily (no. 11) and cut across the pine grove in another valley, ending in an oval lake (no. 20) in the center of the hunting park. A small island stood isolated in the center of the lake, which was enframed by a double file of trees. Out in the southwest corner of the park beyond a small wood or boschetto (no. 23) was an aviary (no. 22). Lines of trees were then planted along the outside edge of the park to mask the walls that enclosed it.

The old family casino (no. 19) on the Via Aurelia had its own walled-in giardino segreto on its east side. The large rectangular area stretching from this casino to the Fountain of the Lily (no. 11) and across to the stable court and western edge of the vigna was quartered by alleys that met in the center at the Fountain of the Queen (no. 24). The four compartments

SECONDO PROSPETTO PER FIANCO DEL PALAZZO CON DIVERSA VEDVTA DEL GIARDINO DEL BEL RESPIRO DELL' ECC.ᴹᴼ SIG. PRENCIPE PAMPHILIO.
*Architettura del Caualier Algardi.*

1. *Fontana di Venere nel primo piano del Giardino.*   4. *Veduta di sotto é per fianco del Palazzo ornato di Statue et bassirilieui*
2. *Scala che porta al secondo, e terzo piano.*   3. *Giardino secreto de fiori et agrumi con fontane éTeatro ornato di Statue nel secondo piano.*   5. *Scale che conducono al terzo piano di sopra del Palazzo e Giardino.*
*Simon Felice del et inc.*   G. Iac. Rossi le stampa in Roma alla Pace cm Priu. del S. Pont.   20

130. Rome, Villa Pamphili, view of casino, engraving

around the fountain were loosely planted in the quincunx pattern with bitter-orange trees (*melangoli*). The entire vigna was, therefore, composed of three somewhat different areas. About a fifth of the land toward the northeast around the pleasure casino was planted very formally with small woods (*boschetti*) and gardens. The casino and its nearby gardens furnished the setting for the Pamphili collection of antiquities. The exterior of the casino was richly covered with antique and contemporary bas-relief sculpture, carrying on the sixteenth-century tradition begun in exterior fresco painting at the Villa Farnesina and translated into stucco relief at the Casino of Pius IV and into ancient marble relief at the Villa Medici, but the most immediate predecessor would have been the Villa Borghese. The interior of the Pamphili casino not only had ancient bas-reliefs set into the walls, but almost every room was an exhibition gallery for ancient freestanding statues and busts. Small spiral stairs led up to the belvedere at the top of the casino where there was a splendid view of Rome, of the Campagna, and of St. Peter's. The rather densely treed area on the northwest side of the estate was the more familial section of the vigna, offering quiet retreat in contrast to the undeveloped park to the south which was the setting for more vigorous, rustic activity.

In contrast to earlier garden parks, and more particularly in contrast to the Villa Ludovisi, the plan of the Villa Pamphili exploited primarily right angles. Unlike the numerous flaring diagonals of the Villa Ludovisi, the only slight diagonal at the Pamphili was offered by the entrance alley running parallel to the diagonal of the east side of the layout. The classicism of the Pamphili design was remarked frequently by early visitors. The guidebook of the Frenchman Misson in 1688 noted that there was at the Villa Pamphili "more Design, more Symmetry, and a more regular Disposition of the Parts than anywhere else," and De Blainville, visiting Italy between 1706 and 1710, will agree, claiming that "There is more Art, Variety, Symmetry, and considerably more Water-works in them [gardens of the Villa Pamphili] than in those of the Villa Borghese."[34] Consistent with this awareness of the classical disposition of the Pamphili gardens is the eighteenth-century tradition to attribute the gardens to the great French gardener André LeNôtre, who vis-

[34] [F. M. Misson,] *A New Voyage to Italy*, 4th ed., II, pt. 1, London, 1714, p. 73, and M. De Blainville, *Travels*, trans. by G. Turnbull and W. Guthrie, London, 1743, III, p. 165.

ited Rome very briefly in 1679, but certainly had nothing to do with the gardens. So the French tourist Lalande in the account of his visit to Italy in 1765–1766 notes: "The garden, as they assure me, has been designed by M. LeNôtre," and Francesco Bettini, who worked for the Doria-Pamphili family, asserts in 1798: "it is certain that LeNôtre . . . was called to Rome by Pope Pamphili to make his famous garden outside the Porta San Pancrazio called the Villa Pamphili."[35]

In the nineteenth century major changes destroyed much of the original character of the Pamphili garden park. Already in the late eighteenth century the general factotum Francesco Bettini, who accompanied Cardinal Giuseppe Doria-Pamphili back to Rome from Paris, made numerous designs for converting parts of the garden park into the new English park style and drew, and sometimes built, new park buildings in the variety of architectural styles introduced by romanticism, including the Chinese.[36] The French invasion of the city of Rome in 1849 brought disastrous damage to the grounds of the villa and the neighborhood, including the destruction of the Porta San Pancrazio and the nearby Villa del Vascello. Prince Andrea V Doria-Pamphili took advantage of the destruction to have the garden park redesigned and replanted in the fashionable English mode, probably urged to the change by having married in 1839 the English Lady Mary Talbot. He also made numerous purchases of adjacent land both to the east and west, more than doubling the original estate and resulting in a vigna of almost 2,000 acres. The most dramatic acquisition came on May 6, 1856, when the Villa Corsini to the east toward the Porta San Pancrazio was bought for 19,000 scudi. With control of the triangle of land between the junction of the Via Aurelia and the Via di San Pancrazio, the public entrance to the villa on the Via Aurelia near the casino was destroyed and the entrance moved farther east to the junction of the two streets. As the suburbs of the city

engulfed the huge open land, the garden park of the Doria-Pamphili, like the earlier ones, was threatened. So in 1957 the broad highway or ring road, the Via Olimpica, was cut through the west side of the estate, isolating a large extent of terrain from the residential portion. Finally in 1967 the government acquired the villa, transforming most of it into a public park.

The ease with which the garden parks of the Villa Borghese and the Villa Pamphili were gradually transformed into English-style parks indicates that with the Villa Montalto a new mode of gardening had been introduced into Rome. Although it is undoubtedly simplistic, one might see an analogy between the development of landscape painting from the *paesi*, or so-called landscapes, of Giorgione and Titian in the sixteenth century to those of Domenichino and Claude in the seventeenth century with the change from the carefully labored topography and horticulture of mid-sixteenth-century gardening, as planned at the Villa Madama or executed at the Villa d'Este at Tivoli and the Villa Medici in Rome, to the expansive, casual landscaping of these garden parks. As the sixteenth-century paintings were dominated by human figures on a large scale, telling stories of significance, and confined their space to the centralized space of linear perspective, the sixteenth-century gardens were generally subservient and adapted to the architecture of man and glorified man in both their designs and their iconography. In the seventeenth-century garden parks man's architecture is dominated by its setting and the significance is more in terms of nature itself, so that the English park landscape of the eighteenth century seems almost a natural development beyond the Roman garden parks. Undoubtedly the huge scale of these garden parks conditions their ultimate character. Each one results from a campaign of multiple acquisitions of smaller, well-established vigne. The final extent of terrain is so large that there is neither time nor money to refashion the topography completely into one homogeneous setting, the way the Cardinal of Ferrara, in more than a decade of work, was able to do at Tivoli. Similarly some of the older buildings supported by the different vigne were kept and incorporated into the new estate, thus forcing parts of the landscape to remain focused on them.

---

[35] [J.J.L.F. de Lalande,] *Voyage d'un françois en Italie fait dans les années 1765 & 1766*, new ed., Yverdon, 1769, v, p. 89, and M. Heimbürger Ravalli, "Progetti e lavori di Francesco Bettini per il parco di Villa Belrespiro," *Studi romani*, XXV, 1977, p. 27, n. 1.

[36] See the Epilogue.

# French Influence

On October 9, 1664, Cardinal Flavio Chigi returned to Rome from France where he had been sent in the spring by his uncle Pope Alexander VII as papal legate on a very delicate mission to King Louis XIV. Earlier, in 1661, the cardinal with his father Mario and his cousin Agostino had purchased great land holdings outside of Rome, including Ariccia and Orsini lands at Campagnano and Formello.[1] Don Agostino would reserve Ariccia, south of Rome, for his country estate and the cardinal would choose for his Formello about twelve miles north of Rome off the Via Cassia. Almost immediately on his return from France the cardinal commissioned the Chigi architect, Felice Della Greca, to design a lavish country residence with extensive gardens. Like the youthful king of France, Cardinal Chigi enjoyed the pleasures of the table, of the theater, and of hunting. During his embassy at Paris he certainly learned of the wonderful entertainment, entitled *Les plaisirs de l'ile enchantée*, organized for the king at his château at Versailles in May 1664 just before the cardinal's arrival. Later, in August 1668, Cardinal Chigi engaged the architect Carlo Fontana to present a similar entertainment, combining feasting and opera in the garden of the Casino of the Quattro Fontane in Rome.[2] It is not surprising, therefore, that an early document for the payment of excavation work and plants supplied in March 1665 at the cardinal's new villa at Formello identifies it as the "Villa Versaglia," the Italian name for the French château at Versailles.[3] The Villa Ver-saglia and its gardens were built from 1665 to at least 1667, with the architect Della Greca in charge until September 1666 when he was succeeded by Carlo Fontana. Beginning in the mid-nineteenth century the villa at Formello was largely neglected, since the Chigi had acquired in 1755 their villa at Castel Fusano. Today there remains only a roofless casino, whose roof was moved to Castel Fusano in 1908; a gutted, three-story entrance tower; and a chapel, whose domical vault is also roofless. No traces remain of the elaborate gardens that accompanied the villa. The architecture of the building is typically Italian and shows no French influence. No determinations in this respect regarding the gardens can be made. The documents indicate a very extensive garden layout, including an orchard and wood (boschetto), with waterworks for which a pump had to be provided in September 1667. Several sculptors carved statues for the garden, including a white marble swan for a fountain and peperino figures of Silenus, Flora, and a dog. Such features were common in Italian gardens of the period and in no way suggest French influence. There was a gardener who specialized in laying out the flower beds (*giardiniere de spartimenti*) and who was provided with some five thousand edging bricks (*pianelle*), but the documents do not specify whether the compartments were laid out as traditional Italian geometric parterres or assumed the more naturalistic, curvilinear forms of the French embroidered parterre. French influence at the Chigi villa was probably only a symbolic one, conveyed by the name of the estate that was

---

[1] R. Lefevre, "Documenti su Villa Versaglia (Formello)," *Archivio della società romana di storia patria*, CV, 1982, pp. 315–44.

[2] See Chapter 10.

[3] For documents for the building and gardens, see V. Golzio, *Do-*cumenti artistici sul Seicento nell'Archivio Chigi, Rome, 1939, pp. 149–54, pp. 163–85.

to associate the Italian villa with the luxurious living that prevailed at the French royal château. The fame of the Chigi villa spread at least to Tuscany, for in 1681 two wooden models of the villa were sent there, one to the Marchese Salviati at Florence and the other to the grandduchess of Tuscany in Siena, the latter made by a pupil of the architect Carlo Fontana. Unfortunately the villa and its gardens seem to have remained private and there are no accounts of visits there by tourists, which might offer more information on the nature of the gardens.

The French formal garden of the seventeenth century was organized along a central axis which, proceeding from the residence, visually unified the variety of the garden and seemed to dominate the entire landscape even to the distant horizon. Near the château elaborate floral displays or turfed patterns composed parterres that encouraged a gentle transition from the geometric, regular forms of the man-made art of architecture to the irregular, natural setting of the landscape surrounding the building. Beyond the parterres, dense groves of trees or bosquets were cut by geometric patterns of alleys, often radiating out on diagonals to encourage the expansive character of the garden. Such gardens for their fullest expression needed the flat terrain of central France, and were more difficult to adapt to the hilly, even mountainous, terrain of central Italy. One feature of the French garden, however, could be easily transported to almost any setting and that was the elaborate embroidered parterre, which could even be created within the limited confines of an urban garden.

During the sixteenth century floral parterres in French gardens were of a strongly geometric character like those of Italy and even occasionally resembling the "knots" of English gardening,[4] but early in the seventeenth century freely flowing, curvilinear, embroidered parterres were introduced, apparently by the French royal gardener Claude Mollet. In his posthumous treatise, *Théâtre des plans et jardinages* (1652), which he probably wrote in a preliminary version in the second decade of the seventeenth century, Mollet asserted that he was the first to devise embroidered parterres using boxwood. Such a date for the appearance of embroidered parterres in France is con-

firmed by two views of the Grand Jardin at Fontainebleau, which in a drawing at the turn of the century is composed of geometric parterres, but in an engraving of 1614 has the geometric compartments replaced by embroidery panels.[5] Soon a series of French garden treatises, commencing with Jacques Boyceau's *Traité du iardinage selon les raisons de la nature et de l'art* (1638), will popularize patterns of *parterres de broderie*. Also the travels and foreign commissions of garden designs by André Mollet, son of Claude, will introduce embroidered parterres to England, as at Wilton House (ca. 1635), and to Holland, as at Honselaersdijk (ca. 1633).

The introduction of French influence, and particularly that of the embroidered parterre, into the neighborhood of Rome seems to come later. In fact, early in the seventeenth century some Romans consciously avoided intricate floral patterns. Vincenzo Giustiniani in an undated letter of about 1615 to 1620 regarding the layout of his gardens at Bassano di Sutri cautions: "It is not a good idea, therefore, to go in for intricate designs of close-cut lawns and flowers which need meticulous care to protect them from the four extremes of weather."[6] Giustiniani, as he notes himself, had been to France and praises there the frequent occurrence of *allées* or "covered avenues in which one can walk in the heat of summer." Similarly Francesco Pona, son of the botanist Giovanni Pona, in his book *Il Paradiso de' fiori*, published in 1622, recommends

> above all a garden composed of four perfect squares, surrounded and divided by spacious avenues. . . . The plots should be marked off by means of divisions and designs of various sorts, and these must above all be striking and elegant, but not very deeply cut. Circles, squares, and ovals are preferable to long strips, star shapes, curves, and other intricate designs, because plants are choked when constricted by acute angles.[7]

The Jesuit Giovanni Battista Ferrari, who wrote the most important seventeenth-century Roman treatise on horticulture, *Flora, seu de florum cultura* (1633), repeats Pona's warnings regarding the constrictive shapes of parterres and even mentions embroidered patterns (*phrygium opus*): "One should, however,

---

[4] This brief survey of French parterre designs is primarily based on S. Karling, "The Importance of André Mollet and His Family for the Development of the French Formal Garden," in *The French Formal Garden* (Dumbarton Oaks Colloquium on the History of Landscape Architecture, III), ed. E. B. MacDougall and F. H. Hazlehurst, Washington, D.C., 1974, pp. 1–25.

[5] Ibid., figs. 5 and 7.

[6] M. L. Simo, "Vincenzo Giustiniani: His Villa at Bassano di Sutri, near Rome, and His 'Instructions to a Builder and Gardener,'" *Journal of Garden History*, I, 1981, p. 266.

[7] L. T. Tomasi, "Projects for Botanical and Other Gardens: A 16th-Century Manual," *Journal of Garden History*, III, 1983, pp. 10–11.

watch lest having imitated embroidery, one breaks the foliate work of the parterres into narrow and very little divisions, unsuitable for planting." Ferrari does commend the imitation of embroidery for parterres in terms of the variety of color used in embroidered work.[8] Following Pona's recommendation of simple geometrical forms for parterres, Ferrari illustrates a series of parterre patterns starting with a square and continuing with an oblong, circle, octagon, oval, as well as a labyrinth and an irregular compartment, which is nevertheless rectilinear in outline (Figs. 143–45). Within the simple, geometrical outlines are very intricate patterns of other geometric forms, but none of the flowing, asymmetrical patterns of French embroidered parterres.

A cursory and random survey of drawings and prints depicting garden parterres during the first half of the seventeenth century confirms the persistence of geometric patterns. Three drawings by several artists for the cloister garden in the Oratorio dei Filippini at Rome over the period 1627 to 1661 are all geometric.[9] The print in Teti's 1642 monograph on the Palazzo Barberini illustrating the garden and rear elevation of the palace has geometric parterres based on circles and squares enclosed by low boxwood hedges (Fig. 142).[10] In a manuscript treatise dated 1644 the architect Felice Della Greca depicts the plan of a small house with a rear, walled-in garden in which two parterres have floral patterns in a St. Andrews cross design closer to the traditional geometric patterns than to the freely curvilinear ones of French *parterres de broderie* (Fig. 131).[11] Later, sometime after 1657, Della Greca drew two alternate projects for the expansion of the Chigi Palace on the Piazza di SS. Apostoli at Rome, which were not executed (Figs. 132, 133).[12] Both projects have two interior gardens with geomet-

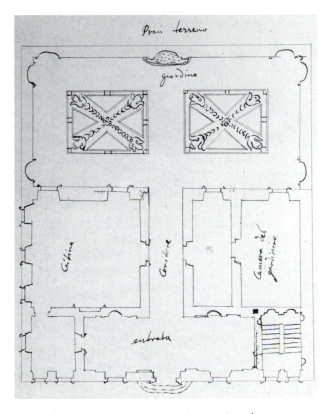

131. Felice Della Greca, manuscript treatise of 1644, house and garden plan, National Museum, Stockholm

ric parterres, although in these cases the geometric designs were encouraged by the desire to incorporate the Chigi device of mounts and eight-pointed stars into some of the parterres. Bernini's drawing after 1662 for the palace at Ariccia contains a large garden apparently with geometric parterres, and a drawing by Bernini's assistant, Mattia de' Rossi, to redo the garden beds in the giardino segreto of the Villa d'Este at Tivoli probably in 1671 uses simple geometric forms of circles and ovals (Fig. 165).[13]

The maps of Rome in the seventeenth century offer rather dubious evidence as they depict such large expanses on a relatively very small scale that the representation of garden parterres is often just a formula. The first map to introduce numerous examples of embroidered parterres in the representations of the gardens at Rome is the map of 1668 of Matteo Gregorio

[8] G. B. Ferrari, *Flora, seu de florum cultura*, new ed., Amsterdam, 1646, p. 22. See also I. Belli Barsali, "Una fonte per i giardini del Seicento: Il trattato di Giovanni Battista Ferrari," in *Il giardino storico italiano*, ed. G. Ragionieri, Florence, 1981, pp. 221–34.

[9] J. Connors, *Borromini and the Roman Oratory*, Cambridge, Mass., and London, 1980, pp. 193–94 (no. 21, 1627), pp. 214–18 (no. 39, 1636–1637), and pp. 284–85 (no. 109, 1702, depicting 1661–1662 garden).

[10] H. Tetius, *Aedes Barberinae ad Quirinalem*, Rome, 1642, plate between pp. 40–41.

[11] G. Curcio, "La 'Breve Relazione' inedita di Felice Della Greca e la trattatisca funzionale fra il Cinquecento e il Seicento," *Ricerche di storia dell'arte*, VIII, 1978–1979, p. 113.

[12] A. Schiavo, *La fontana di Trevi e le altre opere di Nicola Salvi*, Rome, 1956, p. 258 and fig. 147, and H. Hibbard, *Carlo Maderno and Roman Architecture 1580–1630*, University Park, Penn., and London, 1971, p. 213 and pl. 87c.

[13] T. Marder, "La chiesa del Bernini ad Ariccia," in *Gian Lorenzo Bernini architetto e l'architettura europea del Sei-Settecento*, ed. G. Spagnesi and M. Fagiolo, Rome, 1983, I, p. 276, fig. 21, and D. R. Coffin, *The Villa d'Este at Tivoli*, Princeton, N.J., 1960, pp. 118–19 and fig. 133.

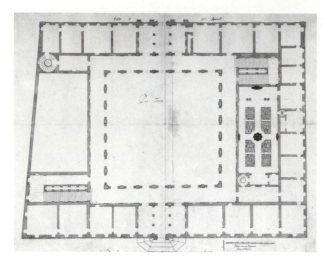

132. Felice Della Greca, project for Chigi Palace, Biblioteca Apostolica Vaticana, Ms Chigi P. VII. 10, fols. 66v–67

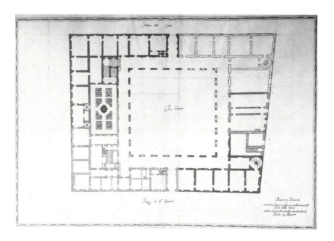

133. Felice Della Greca, alternate project for Chigi Palace, Biblioteca Apostolica Vaticana, Ms Chigi P. VII. 10, fols. 62v–63

De Rossi.[14] The map cannot be trusted as to the accuracy of its depictions of individual gardens. For example, embroidered parterres are indicated near the casino of the Villa Ludovisi. Later maps, such as Falda's of 1676 and Nolli's of 1748, or Falda's engravings and other depictions of the villa do not have such embroidered parterres.[15] De Rossi is, therefore, presumably introducing embroidered parterres as a gen-

eral sign of an ornamental garden, but the fact that he does so is significant as indicating an awareness in Rome of the French designs.

There is a dating problem also regarding several views of embroidered parterres at the Villa Pamphili in Rome in the undated book *Villa Pamphilia* (Fig. 134). The book is dedicated to Giovanni Battista Pamphili, son of Camillo the villa's creator, and its publication, therefore, is presumed to date soon after Camillo's death in 1666. However, the French engraver, Dominique Barrière, was paid variously from 1648 to 1657 for engravings of statues, fountains, the entrance portal, and a perspective view (*prospettiva*) of the villa.[16] The engraving of the entrance portal, signed by Barrière, is the frontispiece of the book and the engravings of statues and fountains are undoubtedly Barrière's, but whether the Barrière "perspective" is one of the several views of the villa with embroidered parterres is less certain. Since these views depict an unexecuted project with long side wings attached to the casino and the engraver is a Frenchman, perhaps more alert to the French garden innovations, it would seem plausible to attribute the idea of embroidered parterres to him. It is less likely, however, that the parterres of the giardino segreto, which were laid out earlier in 1645 and 1646, were of the embroidered type. The documents speak constantly of supplying edging tiles or bricks (*pianelle*) for the compartments (*spartimenti* or *quadri*),[17] which are customary with geometric parterres, and neither the plan by G. B. Falda in the *Villa Pamphilia* nor the later plan by Simone Felice in Falda's *Li giardini di Roma* depict embroidered parterres in the giardino segreto. By about 1670, the generally accepted date of G. B. Falda's *Li giardini di Roma*, most of the great Roman villas illustrated there have at least some embroidered parterres.

The garden of the Riario-Corsini Palace outside of the Trastevere at the foot of the Janiculum Hill showed strong French influence at least in the eighteenth century. Ever since the sixteenth century a large garden spread out behind the palace as far as the hillside, as seen in the Tempesta map of 1598 where

[14] A. M. Frutaz, *Le piante di Roma*, Rome, 1962, III, pls. 350–56.

[15] The 1697 map of Rome by Antonio Barbey is obviously copied from the 1668 map of De Rossi (Frutaz, *Piante*, III, pl. 378).

[16] J. Garms, *Quellen aus dem Archiv Doria-Pamphilj zur Kunsttätigkeit in Rom unter Innocenz X* (Quellenschriften zur Geschichte der Barockkunst in Rom, 4), Rome and Vienna, 1972, p. 72, no. 263; p. 75, no. 284; p. 77, no. 298; p. 88, no. 381.

[17] Ibid., p. 201, no. 984; p. 203, no. 988; p. 217, no. 1059; p. 223, no. 1082; p. 226, no. 1093. Belli Barsali dates the present embroidered parterres to the late eighteenth century ("Il giardino storico italiano: Probleme di indagine," in *Il giardino storico italiano*, ed. G. Ragionieri, Florence, 1981, p. 28).

134. Rome, Villa Pamphili, engraving of casino

a large cross pergola marks the garden.[18] Beginning in 1659, for thirty years the Palazzo Riario was the residence of Queen Christina of Sweden, where she sparked the intellectual activity of Rome, particularly with her Accademia Reale. An anonymous, undated engraving illustrates the palace before the architect, Ferdinando Fuga, began to expand it in the eighteenth century (Fig. 135). The print depicts a French-style garden behind the palace and mounting up the hillside to a casino at the top. The garden has a relatively wide, central alley leading from the middle of the rear of the palace and forming a spine for the garden. Other equally wide alleys run parallel to the central one, weakening the unifying character of the middle alley unlike most French gardens. On either side of the central alley are two long, rectangular parterres with foliate scrollwork in the embroidered mode. Beyond in the middle of the alley is a round fountain basin, and an exedra of bosquets frames the basin except for the continuation of the alley through it. At the right a side alley covered with a barrel-vaulted trellis parallels the central alley. On the first slope of the hill at the left of the main alley is a small, irregular garden house. A series of grotto fountains set into the hillside continues the central axis up to the casino at

the top, but the walkway is a curving, irregular path up the hill to the top.

To date the print and, therefore, the garden with any certainty is difficult. Two drawings attributed to Carlo Fontana's circle are apparently concerned with an unexecuted project to lay out the grounds of the palace as a setting for an Accademia Albana honoring Pope Clement XI soon after his election in 1700.[19] One drawing illustrates the site as it existed before the project would be undertaken and shows no evidence of the French-style garden of the engraving. The most logical time for the print would be after the purchase of the palace in 1736 by Cardinal Neri Corsini and his brother, Prince Bartolomeo, nephews of Pope Clement XII (1730–1740). The French character of the garden would be natural for Cardinal Corsini, who as a young man had lived in Paris from 1716 to 1720 as minister plenipotentiary of Grandduke Cosimo III of Tuscany and was a devotee of French culture. The documentation of activity in the garden early in 1741 may, therefore, mark the work depicted in the print.[20]

[18] Frutaz, *Piante*, II, pls. 262, 272.

[19] A. Braham and H. Hager, *Carlo Fontana: The Drawings at Windsor Castle*, London, 1977, pp. 183–84.

[20] E. Borsellino, "Il Cardinale Neri Corsini mecenate e committente Guglielmi, Parrocel, Conca e Meucci nella Biblioteca Cor-

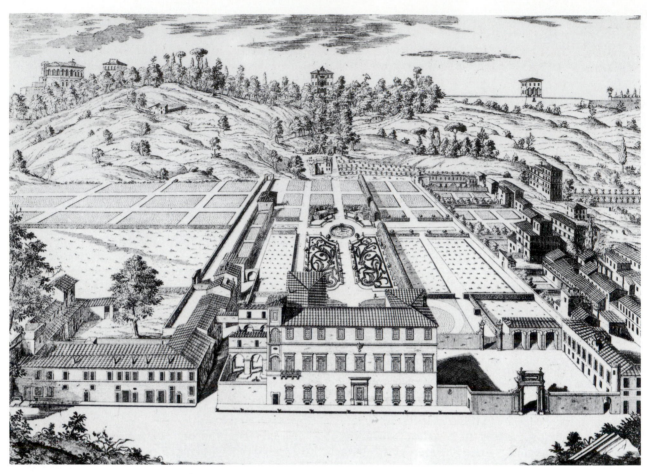

135. Rome, Riario Palace and Garden, engraving, Gabinetto Nazionale delle Stampe, Rome

The principal example of French influence in gardening was that at the Villa Albani, the most famous eighteenth-century Roman villa because of its magnificent collection of antiquities. Alessandro Albani, a nephew of Pope Clement XI (1700–1721), was made a cardinal on July 21, 1721. A passionate collector of antiquities, the cardinal was equally at home with the arts, being elected an honorary member of the Academy of St. Luke at Rome in 1715, and diplomacy, having served in 1720 as papal nuncio to Vienna. On September 27, 1747 Cardinal Albani made his first purchase of land for his future summer residence and supplemented that with three more plots of land in October and November.[21] At the same time on October 7 Pope Benedict XIV granted him three oncie of water from the Acqua Felice to feed the fountains and waterworks of the villa. Although the land purchases in 1747 were the principal ones, the cardinal would continue to expand and fill out his estate until 1764 and would purchase or be granted additional water rights until by 1754 he controlled some eight oncie of water. The land lay just outside the walls of Rome near the Porta Salaria with the Via Salaria, as it proceeded northward, defining the western border of the estate and furnishing the principal entrance to it. From there the terrain eventually stretched toward the east as far as the Via Nomentana. The two principal areas of the final vigna, the large bosco or wood adjacent to the Via Salaria, and the smaller garden

sini," *Bollettino d'arte*, ser. 6, LXVI, no. 10, April–June, 1981, p. 49.

[21] For documentation on the villa, see *Il Cardinale Alessandro Albani e la sua villa* (Quaderni sul neoclassico, 5), Rome, 1980, and S. Röttgen, "Dokumentation zur Villa Albani," in *Forschungen zur Villa Albani* (Frankfurter Forschungen zur Kunst, 10),

ed. H. Beck and P. C. Bol, Berlin, 1982, pp. 153–65; the various purchases of land are plotted by R. Assunto, "Winckelmann a Villa Albani: Il giardino, luogo del rimpatrio," in *Committenze della famiglia Albani: Note sulla Villa Albani Torlonia*, Rome, 1985, fig. 25.

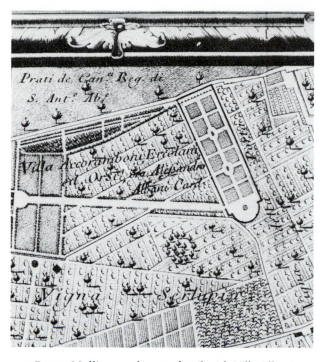

136. Rome, Nolli map of 1748, detail with Villa Albani

area set at right angles to the bosco at a lower level, are already defined on G. B. Nolli's map of Rome of 1748 (Fig. 136). At this time the major alley is shown running diagonally from the Via Salaria down to the exedra at the south end of the garden area, unlike the later layout when this will be a secondary alley with the major one running straight across the bosco from a new entrance on the Via Salaria to the center of the side of the garden. Later the French visitor J. J. de Lalande in 1765–1766 will state that the villa "is, so to say, [the cardinal's] work, as much for the designs as for the taste . . . he has been aided by an architect Carlo Marchionni, who has worked principally after the designs of Nolli."[22] The geometer-architect Giovanni Battista Nolli, who had been in the service of the cardinal since at least 1744, undoubtedly laid out the basic landscape design of the estate,[23] but the publication of the map in 1748 does not determine the date of the commencement of work at the villa, since Nolli may have incorporated into the map a projected

design for the vigna. According to an account of the work of about 1769 a great deal of land movement was required: "here everything is done against the nature of the site. Those many and so beautiful terraces that you see, you should know, are all made by hand. Originally everything was unequal and sloping, whereby it is necessary to take away earth from one part and carry it to another, where to lower the terrain, where to raise it, and then to continue. So imagine the cost."[24]

By the end of 1749 work had commenced on the semicircular portico known as the Caffeeaus, for in the account of a land purchase in November the land is described as contiguous to the "Caffeeaus in order to make his villa always more magnificent and suitable and particularly the new building of the hemicycle begun at the villa."[25] Two years later the architect Marchionni signed and dated a drawing for stairs from "the garden of the two porticoes to the lower site."[26] The account, however, does not specify whether the garden parterre is already planted or merely laid out. The main casino north of the garden will be built between 1755 and 1757, the latter date being inscribed on a portal of the atrium.

The eminent German archaeologist, Abbé Winckelmann, who had followed the creation of the villa since his arrival in Rome in November 1755, reported in a letter of February 1758 for the first of several times that the villa was completed, and in October he was hired by the cardinal to be his librarian and archaeologist, thus offering in his later letters a close record of activities at the villa.[27] In June 1763 Winckelmann notes that a cascade is to be built behind the semicircular portico, which was only completed in the summer of 1766 when a colossal statue of a river god, requiring sixteen oxen for transport, was set at the outlet of the cascade.[28] By August 1766 Winckelmann realized that only death might limit the cardinal's passion for collecting and building: "He [the cardinal] is a Cartesian in building, since he cannot tolerate any empty space, and his villa will appear, if he lives longer, as we must imagine the ancient Capi-

[22] [J.J.L.F. de Lalande,] *Voyage d'un françois en Italie fait dans les années 1765 & 1766*, new ed., Yverdon, 1769, v, p. 122.

[23] F. Noack, "Des Kardinals Albani Beziehungen zu Künstlern," *Der Cicerone*, XVI, 1924, p. 406. Nolli had begun work on his map in 1736; see C. Faccioli, "Gio. Battista Nolli (1701–1756) e la sua gran 'Pianta di Roma' del 1748," *Studi romani*, XIV, 1966, pp. 415–42.

[24] L. Cassanelli, "Nuove acquisizioni documentarie per il giardino della villa Albani Torlonia," in *Giardini italiani: Note di storia e di conservazione* (Quaderni, 3), Rome, 1981, p. 75.

[25] *Il Cardinale Alessandro Albani e la sua villa*, p. 148.

[26] R. Berliner, "Zeichnungen von Carlo und Filippo Marchionni," *Münchner Jahrbuch der bildenden Kunst*, ser. 3, IX–X, 1958–1959, p. 303.

[27] J. J. Winckelmann, *Briefe*, ed. H. Diepolder and W. Rehm, Berlin, 1952, I, p. 326 as p. 226, pp. 426, 428, 435.

[28] Ibid., III, pp. 128, 181, 193.

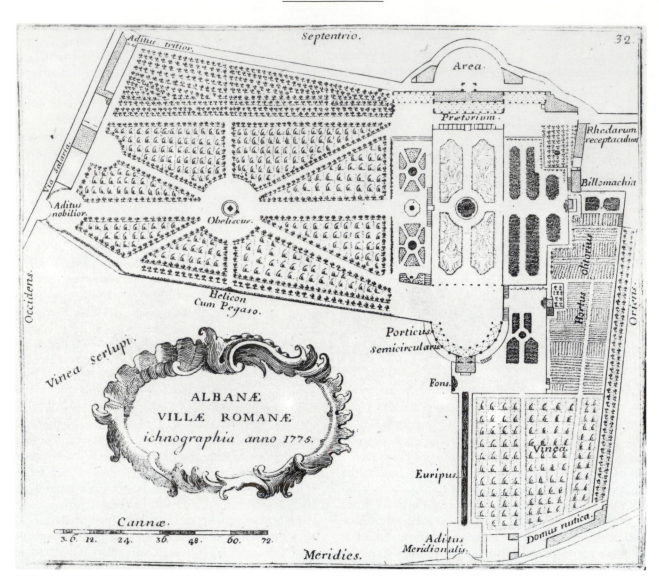

137. Rome, Villa Albani, plan of 1775

tol to have been."[29] Other work is mentioned being undertaken in 1767, but by the time of the Cordara description, presumably about 1769, the villa must have reached its fullest development.

A map of the estate in 1775 (Fig. 137) identifies a new principal entrance portal (*aditus nobilior*) on the Via Salaria.[30] Beyond the entrance was a large, star-shaped bosquet or wood with eight alleys outlined by trees radiating from a *rond-point* in the French manner. The areas between the alleys were planted with vines. The old entrance on the Via Salaria visible in Nolli's map of 1748 (Fig. 136) was closed, although the small house nearby was kept and refurbished as Winckelmann's residence from 1765.[31] In the center of the *rond-point* stood a small obelisk. Along the north side of the bosquet ran a dense grove to protect the vineyard from northern winds. The short alley from the central *rond-point* toward the center of the southern wall focused on a wall fountain of Mount Helicon or Mount Parnassus with the winged horse Pegasus. To the east beyond the bosquet on the terrace above the sunken garden were two flower parterres, each also in a star pattern with eight paths radiating from a central fountain.

[29] Ibid., III, p. 197.
[30] [D. Magnan,] *La città di Roma*, Rome, 1779, I, pl. 32.

[31] Winckelmann, *Briefe*, III, p. 110.

138. Rome, Villa Albani, view of parterre

The basic orientation of the bosquet-vineyard was from west to east, whereas the sunken garden parterre between the casino and the Caffeeaus was at right angles with its orientation from north to south. The terrace with the two flower parterres served as a transition between the two major areas and their contrasting orientations, as the terrace ran parallel to the sunken garden, while the two flower parterres were separated by a fountain basin on axis with the central alley of the bosquet. In the French manner, the ornamental garden parterre was slightly sunken with raised terraces on three sides of it so that the spectator could walk around the parterre and look down on the horticultural patterns (Fig. 138). The 1769 account of the gardens by Cordara describes the sunken parterre as "all embroidered with all sorts of flowers in myrtle,"[32] visible in Magnan's plan of 1775. The English-

man Boswell, visiting the Villa with Winckelmann in May 1765, characterized the parterre as a "spread periwig," obviously sympathetic with the new naturalistic English gardening and disdainful of the French mode.[33] Originally at the center of the four ornamental beds of myrtle was the Fountain of the Atlantes, known popularly as the "Fontana dei Facchini," where four figures of Atlas bore a fountain basin on their shoulders.

At the north end of the sunken parterre is the main casino of two stories with an arcaded ground floor and two long, one-story, arcaded wings. The southern end of the sunken parterre is closed by a semicircular, one-story portico or arcade at the rear of which is the "Coffeehouse," a pavilion with a small apart-

[32] S. Röttgen, "Eine unbekannte Beschreibung der Villa Albani von Giulio Cesare Cordara," in *Forschungen zur Villa Albani*

(Frankfurter Forschungen zur Kunst, 10), ed. H. Beck and P. C. Bol, Berlin, 1982, p. 172.

[33] J. Boswell, *On the Grand Tour, Italy, Corsica, and France, 1765–1766*, ed. F. Brady and F. A. Pottle, New York, 1955, p. 77.

ment for the cardinal. The shape of the parterre garden, therefore, resembles a hippodrome, recalling the hippodrome-shaped garden at the Tuscan villa of the ancient Roman Pliny the Younger (*Letters*, v, 6). The terrain behind the "Coffeehouse" is sunken, so that the pavilion on the south side is in two stories. From the cardinal's apartment in the upper floor was once a magnificent vista oriented directly toward the distant Alban hills. Or as the French artist Pierre-Adrien Paris remarked at the time: "Although this pleasure house is at a location only slightly elevated, there is a delightful view of the area of the Porta Pia, Sant'Agnese and the Temple of Bacchus (Sta. Costanza) seen a little in the distance below the garden."[34] Today the view is gone as the city has grown up around the villa. Below the cardinal's apartment was an open portico, the Porticus Romae, with an ancient statue of Dea Roma in a niche at the rear. In line with the portico was originally a waterway or canal, identified as the Euripus on Magnan's plan (Fig. 137), presumably after the canal at Hadrian's villa at Tivoli. The waterway once ran down to the south or rear entrance off the Via Nomentana, but in the mid-nineteenth century the extent of the villa was restricted, destroying the garden behind the "Coffeehouse." Actually the canal was a gentle cascade of seven levels, the cascade mentioned by Winckelmann in his letters of 1763 and 1766. At the head of the cascade was set a colossal statue of Amphitrite reclining on the back of a bull, which was brought from the gardens of the Villa d'Este at Tivoli.

Flanking the east side of the cascade was a vineyard, probably planted with some of the same Hungarian tokay vines that Cordara noted filled up the eight large triangular compartments of the bosquet at the Via Salaria entrance.[35] North of the vineyard was the kitchen garden (*hortus olitorius*) toward the east of the sunken parterre. Also along the east side were several secondary buildings, including a separate billiard casino and a small ruined temple, which served as an aviary, set at the edge of the kitchen garden. In the garden in front of the billiard casino was a grotto in which was recreated with antique works of sculpture the scene of Odysseus escaping from the blind Polyphemus by clinging to the belly of a ram.

A huge collection of classical antiquities, the largest outside of the Vatican Palace, including among others 150 statues, 176 heads and busts, 161 reliefs, 49 figures of animals, as well as innumerable fountains, basins, urns, altars, columns, and inscriptions, decorated the rooms and porticoes of all the several buildings and were set throughout the gardens. Many of the antique pieces remain, some in their original location, although the collection has been plundered at least twice, once when the French took to Paris almost 300 pieces, of which only 1, a relief depicting Antinous from Hadrian's Villa, was returned, and again when the Torlonia purchased the villa in 1866. It was Winckelmann in close consultation with the cardinal who organized the exhibition of the pieces so that each room or portico had its own particular character, dedicated to emperors or poets, to deities or generals. The personal concern of Winckelmann for the villa and its decoration, both in terms of its antiquities and its gardens, is witnessed by the references repeatedly in his letters after 1766 to "our villa" (*unser Villa*). Like so many northern visitors to Italy, Winckelmann adored the gardens. In May 1756, his first spring in Rome, Winckelmann wrote Franke: "Now is the time to visit the gardens in and around Rome. My friend! one can't describe how beautiful nature is in this land. One walks in shady laurel groves and in alleys of tall cypresses and along trellises of orangeries, to a quarter mile further to several villas, especially to the Villa Borghese."[36]

The great collection of antiquities was not meant to recall a museum. The pieces of art were to adapt to their setting as if they were still playing their original role of architectural decoration. Similarly, in the cardinal's eyes the architecture was considered to be different from contemporary architecture. In 1758 a Swede, having visited the villa in the company of the cardinal, undoubtedly reflected his guide's comments, when he described the casino as "a place in the taste of ancient Rome."[37] He quotes the cardinal as saying "it is not made for eyes accustomed to the marvels of French architecture." Other features of the villa reinforced this concept. The garden set between the casino and the semicircular portico has the hippodrome shape of a garden Pliny the Younger had at his Tuscan villa. Similarly the pavilion with the small apartment for the cardinal and its magnificent view of untouched nature beyond the horticultural enrichment of the garden—despite its eighteenth-century nomenclature, the Caffeeaus—is modeled on an ancient *diaeta*, or

---

[34] A. C. Gruber, "La Villa Albani vue par un artiste du XVIIIᵉ siècle," in *Piranèse et les français*, Rome, 1978, p. 285.

[35] *Forschungen zur Villa Albani*, p. 173.

[36] Winckelmann, *Briefe*, I, p. 221. See also Assunto, "Winckelmann a Villa Albani," pp. 159–165.

[37] P. J. Grosley, *Nouveaux mémoires ou observations sur l'Italie par deux gentilhommes suedois*, London, 1764, II, pp. 256–58.

garden pavilion, which was also a feature of Pliny's villas. In fact, Magnan in the illustration of the Caffeeaus in his book in 1779 labels it a *Diaeta*.[38] All together it is obvious that the cardinal was attempting to recreate an ancient Roman villa as the setting for his collection of antiquities. And so it was considered in its own time. Both the Abbé Richard, who was at the villa in 1762, and the later German Volkmann likened it to Pliny the Younger's description of his Laurentine villa.[39]

The gardening was certainly of French derivation. The two major garden features at the Villa, the bosquet at the entrance and the embroidered parterre of the casino, were French horticultural designs, but the total effect was not. Unlike the French ideal garden designs presented in Dézallier d'Argenville's *La théorie et la pratique du jardinage* (1709), the international handbook for French gardening, at the Villa Albani there is no design relationship between the two features, no unity. The two exist as completely independent entities. This disunity has undoubtedly been occasioned on the one hand by the desire to recreate Pliny's garden in the parterre and on the other hand to locate the bosquet near the Via Salaria so that it would provide privacy for the casino and its garden from the noise and public of the Via Salaria, as was done at the Villa Rufina at Frascati in the mid-sixteenth century.[40] Thus, although the Romans are using French horticultural designs they are being adapted to the native Renaissance traditions.

Contemporary with Cardinal Albani's creation of his villa as a setting for his ancient sculpture, another cardinal, Cardinal Silvio Valenti Gonzaga, secretary of state for Pope Benedict XIV (1740–1758), as if in rivalry, built a new villa to serve as a gallery for part of his outstanding collection of more than eight hundred paintings.[41] Probably shortly before 1748 Cardinal Valenti Gonzaga purchased a triangular piece of land with a casino just within the Aurelian walls next to the Porta Pia (Fig. 139). The land was bounded by the section of wall between the Porta Salaria and the Porta Pia on one side; on the second by the Via Pia, now the Via XX Settembre; and on the third side by

the street to the Porta Salaria, now the Via Piave.[42] Nolli's map of Rome of 1748 identifies the site as that of the "Villa Cicciaporci now Valenti Gonzaga Cardinal." A second, new casino was built for the Cardinal in the center of the grounds about 1749, for in Pannini's painting dated 1749 that depicts the cardinal's gallery of paintings two men are seen studying a plan for the building. Titi in his guidebook of 1763 notes that the cardinal "transformed the greater part of [the vigna] into a garden in the French taste."[43] The gardens were presumably laid out by the French engineer and architect Jacques-Philippe Maréchal, who about a decade earlier had worked at Nîmes on the Jardin de la Fontaine and then had been called to Rome by the pope to work at the port of Anzio.

The gardens at the Villa Valenti Gonzaga existed on two different levels. The higher garden at the rear of the building comprised a small grove of trees and a kitchen garden with fruit trees espaliered along the Aurelian wall, closing it at the rear. An anonymous eighteenth-century painting, formerly in the Maraini collection, depicts the facade of the new villa with its parterre garden in front.[44] Large compartments of presumably boxwood embroidery flank the wide central alley leading to the villa. Large vases planted with shrubbery stand on pedestals at the corners and along the edges of the compartments. Tall, closely trimmed hedges enclosed the parterres at the sides, and in line with the rear wall at each side of the casino were arcaded hedges separating the lower front garden terrace from the rear. A poem of Padre Saverio Bettinelli published in 1758, two years after the cardinal's death, celebrates the unusual, exotic plants, flowers, and trees of the garden and particularly admires a fountain whose hydraulic effects would amaze Hero of Alexandria, the ancient hydraulic engineer, who had taught Italian fontanieri so much.[45] This must be a contribution of Maréchal, who was particularly renowned as a hydraulic engineer.

A very old garden refurbished in the French manner during the eighteenth century was that of the Colonna family on the western slope of the Quirinal Hill behind the Colonna palace. There had been a large garden there decorated with the ruins of the gigantic an-

---

[38] [Magnan,] *La città di Roma*, I, pl. 38.

[39] J. Richard, *Description historique et critique de l'Italie*, Paris, 1766, VI, p. 213, and J. J. Volkmann, *Historische-kritische Nachrichten von Italien*, 2nd ed., Leipzig, 1777, II, p. 885.

[40] D. R. Coffin, *The Villa in the Life of Renaissance Rome*, Princeton, N.J., 1979, p. 43.

[41] C. Pietrangeli, *Villa Paolina*, Rome, 1961, appendix I, pp. 43–71.

[42] For the history, see ibid. and I. Belli Barsali, *Ville di Roma: Lazio I*, Milan, 1970, p. 428.

[43] F. Titi, *Descrizione delle pitture, sculture e architetture*, new ed., Rome, 1763, p. 445.

[44] C. Pietrangeli, *Villa Paolina*, pl. XIII.

[45] The poem is printed in appendix II of Pietrangeli, *Villa Paolina*, pp. 72–80.

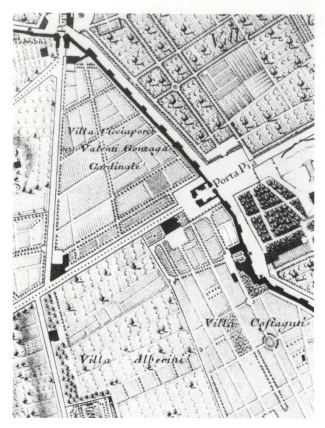

139. Rome, Nolli map of 1748, detail of Villa Valenti Gonzaga

cient Temple of Serapis since the late Middle Ages.[46] In the early seventeenth century the Colonna erected a monumental garden portal, designed by Vincenzo della Greca and bearing the date 1617, at the top of the garden off the lower continuation of the Via Pia, now the Via XXIV Maggio. This was meant to be a public entrance to the garden oriented away from the privacy of the palace at the foot of the garden following the example from the 1560s of several of the great villa gardens along the Via Pia.[47] The clearest record of the garden at this time is the view of it in Maggi's map of Rome of 1625 (Fig. 140). At the base of the hill behind the Colonna Palace, but separated from it by a road, the present Via della Pilotta, was the formal garden with a central alley from the entrance to a wall fountain in the rear wall. Behind that wall the upper part of the hill was left rustic and irregular with densely wooded groves in which were the remains of classic buildings. Finally at the top of the hill was an-

other smaller, formal garden immediately behind the new public entrance.

The public entrance to the garden was no more than established when some of the upper part of the garden was destroyed in order to improve the approach to the Papal Palace on the Quirinal, which had been expanded from the previous Villa d'Este or Vigna Carafa. An avviso of April 12, 1625, records: "His Holiness Our Lord in order to enlarge and embellish the piazza before the Pontifical Palace of Monte Cavallo has had the Camera Apostolica buy for 12,000 scudi that part of the garden of the Lord Constable Colonna which stands opposite said Palace and, therefore, Thursday morning was a beginning by a good number of pioneers to demolish that wall and to level the terrain even with the piazza."[48] Another avviso at the time notes that the Borghese Pope Paul V (1605–1621) had unsuccessfully attempted earlier the same project. This restriction of the upper part of the garden toward the north did not affect the garden portal of 1617. In the late nineteenth century a double flight of steps was added on the exterior side of the portal when the street level was lowered.

In 1713 Filippo II Colonna honored his ancestral hero, Marc Antonio Colonna, the victor of the Battle of Lepanto, by erecting within an aedicula in the garden his statue, depicting him in ancient Roman dress. At this time or earlier two bridges were thrown across the Via della Pilotta, which ran behind the Colonna palace, separating it from the garden on the hillside so as to allow easy access to the garden. The statue of Marc Antonio was set on axis with the bridge that ran from the long gallery of the palace to the garden, so that when the exterior door of the small room at the end of the gallery was opened there was a direct vista from the gallery within the palace to the statue. An engraving published in 1761 by Vasi (Fig. 141) depicts the Colonna garden refashioned in the French mode. By the time of the Vasi print, however, there were four bridges across the Via della Pilotta. A slightly earlier schematic representation of the garden on a map of Rome issued in 1756 seems to portray the garden of the Vasi print except that there are still only two bridges across the street.[49] Presumably the

---

46 See Chapter 1.
47 See Chapter 14.

48 *Il Palazzo del Quirinale*, Rome, 1974, p. 256, where are also gathered together the other documents. For the best summaries of the seventeenth- and eighteenth-century history of the garden, see Belli Barsali, *Ville di Roma*, pp. 410–12, and C. Elling, *Rome*, Boulder, Colo., 1975, pp. 432–34.
49 Frutaz, *Piante*, III, pl. 425; the map is a revision of the late seventeenth-century map by G. B. Falda.

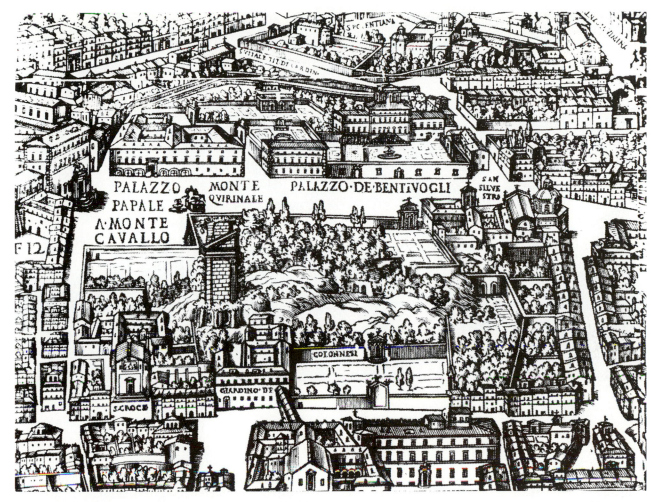

140. Rome, Maggi map of 1625, detail with Colonna Garden

refurbishing of the garden was completed in the early 1750s just before the map of 1756. This is confirmed by two of the identification labels on the Vasi print: "3. New fountains and stairs. 4. New casino erected on the ancient walls." The two additional bridges would then seem to have been erected after 1756, but before 1761.

In the Vasi engraving the bridges are depicted crossing the street to a long, wide terrace decorated with the flowing scrolls of embroidered parterres. Several wall fountains were set in the back wall of the terrace above which were narrower terraces mounting the hillside. A tall wall with statue niches and fountains closed off the rear of the hillside terraces hiding the more informal garden or wooded area entered from the Piazza del Quirinale through the public gateway erected in the early seventeenth century. As in the earlier villas along the Via Pia, there was a more public

garden accessible from the Via Pia and a more formal, private garden or giardino segreto near the residence. In the latter at the Colonna Palace a cascade flanked by stepped ramps flowed down the center of the several hillside terraces. The northern end of the garden was closed by a two-story garden building with windows set in blind arcades. A taller pavilion or belvedere used the roof of the lower building as a lofty terrace from which to look down into the garden or across the city. The French visitor Lalande in 1765 praised especially a long alley of hyacinths and double tulips and "two amphitheaters of live ranks of pots which form the most beautiful effect in the world."[50] Soon, however, Mrs. Miller, accustomed to English gardening, was disdainful. "The Gardens are in a bad

[50] [De Lalande,] *Voyage d'un françois en Italie fait dans les années 1765 & 1766*, III, p. 460.

141. Rome, Colonna Garden, Vasi engraving, 1761, Avery Architectural and Fine Arts Library, Columbia University

taste, having too many parterres formed of box edgings and coloured stucco, which are dignified by the name of English Flower Gardens."[51] Again the French influence is restricted to embroidered parterres. The garden terraces, wall fountains, and cascade flanked by stepped ramps are still Roman. Indeed, the Colonna garden is a simpler, duller version of the late sixteenth-century Farnese gardens on the Palatine.

The influence of French gardening in Rome in general can be reduced really to the acceptance by the Romans of embroidered parterre designs. Also the arcades cut out of verdure at the Corsini and the Valenti Gonzaga gardens are French. Two major factors can probably explain this limited reaction, in addition to that indefinable factor of tradition, which is always resistant to innovation. The most important difference between Roman and French gardening was the topography with which the respective gardening had

to cope. In central France the terrain was primarily flat, inducing broad, level vistas in which man's domination of nature is as obvious as that suggested by the elaborate, intertwining scrolls of the parterres. Most Roman gardens took advantage of a hill terrain to provide ample water for noisy cascades and jets, whereas France was often hampered by a limitation in the water supply and accepted waters in quiet, wide, level lakes and canals. At the same time French gardens were truly descendants of Italian gardening, their difference mainly due to the change in the nature of the terrain. Therefore, the one French innovation that the Romans could accept readily was the use of embroidered designs, which undoubtedly were a welcome change from the less sophisticated geometric patterns familiar to the Romans. The curvilinear scrolls and rinceaux of embroidered parterres would also harmonize better with the decoration of the baroque and rococo buildings, just as the extra skill required of the gardeners in laying out the asymmetrical patterns would redound to the credit of their masters.

[51] [A. R. Miller,] *Letters from Italy . . . In the Years MDCCLXX and MDCCLXXI*, London, 1776, III, p. 93.

# Garden Design and Furnishings

During the late Middle Ages and early Renaissance several treatises, including Crescenzi's *Libri Ruralium Commodorum*, written in the early fourteenth century but first published in 1471 and followed by numerous editions, or the ancient Roman treatises, the *Res Rusticae Scriptores*, edited by Giorgio Merula in 1470, offered sage advice to avid gardeners on agricultural matters, but only very limited information on horticulture and garden design. Crescenzi did differentiate by size and economic level three basic gardens, of which the small garden, planted with herbs, flowers, and trees, was copied from an earlier treatise by Albertus Magnus.[1] The medium-sized garden and the largest garden, suitable for royalty, were protectively enclosed, the medium-size garden by ditches and thorn hedges, the royal and lordly gardens by high walls. Perhaps the most interesting design feature of the large gardens was to ensure that, if any rows of trees were planted close to the palace, "they should run from the palace to the grove but not crosswise so that one can see easily from the palace whatever the animals do in the garden."[2]

In 1546 Luigi Alamanni, having followed his patron Cardinal Ippolito II d'Este to France, published there a poetic treatise, *La coltivazione*, derived principally from Vergil's poem on agriculture, the *Georgics*.[3] Although the first four books are concerned traditionally with the agricultural activities of the four seasons, Alamanni's book five treats the culture of gardens and the last book is devoted to the zodiac and favorable or unfavorable days. In his consideration of the garden, Alamanni defines its form:

Then with carefully reasoned proportions measure the enclosed garden and square it off where Apollo's rays are warmest at midday. . . . Draw the path straight so that it divides the garden vertically down the middle; then bring another from the side to meet it, so exactly aligned that the quarters are equal, and the aspects are equal, so that the eye is not offended by looking at them, and the effects are not more grand here than elsewhere. Where there is plenty of ground, it can be laid out with other paths, but according to the same rules and forms, and leaving a matching space in between, so that they all seem siblings of the same source. . . . Then let the other parts emerge in squares, beautiful to look at, evenly spaced and equal, where the flowers and plants are to be placed.[4]

Contemporary with Alamanni's treatise in the middle of the sixteenth century an unpublished manuscript treatise by Girolamo Fiorenzuola advocates that the garden, "having first been divided into a cross, one ought to put at the head of said garden, in

---

[1] Piero de' Crescenzi, *Trattato della agricoltura*, Milan, 1805, and R. G. Calkins, "Piero de' Crescenzi and the Medieval Garden," in *Medieval Gardens* (Dumbarton Oaks Colloquium on the History of Landscape Architecture, IX), ed. E. B. MacDougall, Washington, D.C., 1986, pp. 155–73.

[2] Ibid., p. 173.

[3] L. Alamanni, *La coltivazione di Luigi Alamanni e Le api di Giovanni Rucellai*, Milan, 1804, and H. Hauvette, *Luigi Alamanni (1495–1556), sa vie et son oeuvre*, Paris, 1903.

[4] L. T. Tomasi, "Projects for Botanical and Other Gardens: A 16th-Century Manual," *Journal of Garden History*, III, 1983, pp. 8–9.

the middle of the principal alley a table of magnificent and fine stone."[5] Fiorenzuola notes that the ancients had used box and laurel for hedges outlining the garden beds, but he strongly advises against box as "a gloomy and stinking greenery," and recommends that, if it is used, it should be mixed with myrtle. He much prefers hedges of the perfumed citrus fruits, such as oranges and lemons, which appeal to the eye as well as the nose.

Another unpublished manuscript treatise of the late sixteenth century, the *Agricoltura teorica* of Agostino del Riccio, asserts that the flower beds or compartments must be enriched with colorful flowers, many of them planted in numerous flower pots so buried as to be invisible to the spectator.[6] The flowers are then to be ordered in the patterns "of pyramids, maps, dragons, stars and other *fantasie* that ingenious and discerning gardeners create."

Although Francesco Pona in his *Il Paradiso de' fiori* of 1622 insists that the form of a garden must adapt to nature and its site, he still suggests that "if there is a choice, I recommend above all a garden composed of four perfect squares."[7] The quartered garden, ideally composed of four equal flower beds or compartments separated by cross alleys or a cross pergola, arising out of the mediaeval hortus conclusus, persists, therefore, into the seventeenth century. Documents and visual evidence support the theoreticians' interest in the quartered garden. So in 1537 the Vatican gardener Lucerta was paid "to make the four little meadows [*praticelli* or grassed compartments] in the Court of the Statues of the Belvedere,"[8] and the sixteenth-century engravings of the Belvedere Court in the Vatican depict the quartered design of compartments also on the upper terrace of the Belvedere Court and in Paul III's large hortus conclusus (Fig. 6). Similarly, a drawing of 1563 of the garden in the Palace of Cardinal Della Rovere, the Palazzo dei Penitenzieri, shows the square garden divided into four square compartments, although the inner corner of each compartment is lopped off to allow an alley around a central fountain basin.[9] The imposition of a quartered pattern upon a rather recalcitrant natural

site is seen clearly at the gardens of the Villa d'Este at Tivoli (Fig. 66). The old monastery, which was transformed into a country residence, stood on the summit of a hill sloping roughly east to west diagonally across the facade of the building, but the new gardens were to be centered on the building. Although a level area could be fashioned by filling in the lower center and right side of the garden with earth pared off the hill at the left, the hill remained. On the lower central plain a cross pergola with its quartered garden set the pattern for the checkerboard design of the entire garden. As if ignoring the hillside at the left, two labyrinths were planted on the slope to match the two labyrinths on the level terrain at the right.

In the sixteenth century, and often in the seventeenth century, the compartments of a garden were outlined by hedges, which might have trees or vases on pedestals intermingled. The seventeenth-century engraving of the Villa Medici (Fig. 35) depicts six rectangular compartments edged with hedges beyond the open piazza behind the villa with four of the compartments centered on the building. Undoubtedly there had been eight such parterres until Cardinal Medici built his sculpture gallery and a terrace at the south or right side, destroying the two parterres on that side.[10] This preference for quartered compartments or multiples thereof is shown also at the Villa Medici in the large garden to the north of the piazza and six parterres, where the area is divided into sixteen compartments. The sixteenth-century Zucchi painting of the villa (Fig. 34) has the garden similarly organized at the time of its creation except that each group of four compartments toward the north was dominated by a cross pergola with a domed crossing. Trees were planted in the hedges along the outer edges of the compartments and along the principal central alley running north and south through the parterres. Statue herms were apparently intended to stand at the corners of the compartments and flanking the entrances to the cross pergolas, but there is no evidence of their existence.

In the project attributed to Cassiano Dal Pozzo of 1627 for the large garden of the Barberini Palace, he suggests that it be divided into two parts, one part sunny and most pleasurable (*amenissima*), the other shady and somewhat rustic.[11] The sunny part, planted with orange trees, was to be a square com-

[5] A. Tagliolini, "Girolamo Fiorenzuola ed il giardino nelle fonti della metà del '500," in *Il giardino storico italiano*, ed. G. Ragionieri, Florence, 1981, p. 306.

[6] Tomasi, "Projects," p. 10.

[7] Ibid., pp. 10–11.

[8] L. Dorez, *La cour du Pape Paul III*, Paris, 1932, II, p. 124.

[9] C. L. Frommel, *Der römische Palastbau der Hochrenaissance*, Tübingen, 1973, III, pl. 191a.

[10] G. Andres, *The Villa Medici in Rome*, New York and London, 1976, II, p. 232, n. 628.

[11] G. Magnanimi, *Palazzo Barberini*, Rome, 1983, codex Barberini Latin 4360, fol. 57.

142. Rome, Barberini Palace Gardens, 1642

The major Roman horticultural treatise, Giovan Battista Ferrari's *Flora, de florum cultura libri IV*, Rome, 1633, is also associated with the Barberini family. A Jesuit from Siena, Ferrari dedicated his first treatise on flowers to Cardinal Francesco Barberini, nephew of Pope Urban VIII.[13] The lavish volume was illustrated with engravings financed by the Barberini after drawings by several of the outstanding painters at Rome, Pietro da Cortona, Andrea Sacchi, and Guido Reni, and illustrations by the botanical artist Anna Maria Vaiani. Ferrari, after the usual admonitions regarding the nature of the site chosen for the garden, assumes that an architect will draw up the plan for the projected garden and will present numerous designs for parterres or flowerbeds (*areolae*). The compartments or parterres must not be so wide that the gardener cannot work as far as the middle of the flowerbed from the surrounding paths. In Ferrari's principles of garden design the compartment is obviously the key feature or module about which the garden design is organized. He warns against too complicated a floral pattern in the compartment, as in a "tapestry" (*phrygium opus*), perhaps with the new French embroidered parterre in mind. He offers illustrations of some six basic parterres and a labyrinth. The parterres include a square, a rectangle, a circle, an octagon, an oval, and an irregular form consisting of a triangular addition to the rectangle (Figs. 143–45). All the exterior frames of the parterres are either square or rectangular. The interior designs are still very geometric, although some are rectilinear and others curvilinear. The interior paths must not be less than 2 palmi (ca. 44.5 centimeters) in width, which seems constricted, but some must be much wider, including those that "meet at the center," reiterating the old quartered garden pattern, and those around the exterior. Like Serlio almost a century earlier in the fourth book of his treatise on architecture, Ferrari compares the design of the garden labyrinth with that of an intricately carved wooden ceiling, but also compares it with geometric floor designs, resulting in a conformity between architectural interiors and the exterior ornamental garden. Ferrari is even more se-

partment, 30 canne (ca. 67 meters) on each side, containing sixteen smaller compartments 6 canne square (ca. 13.5 meters). In each of the sixteen smaller compartments were to be planted sixteen orange trees about 20 palmi (ca. 4.25 meters) apart. In the center of eight of the compartments were to be fountains, four in the center of the group and others in the four corners. In the center of the other compartments were to be floral patterns. The illustrations of the book of 1642 by Tetius on the Barberini Palace (Fig. 142) depict the square flower beds of the garden enclosed by low hedges with busts on pedestals defining the corners along the central alley and pedestals with vases planted with small citrus trees at the outer corners. Similarly in a drawing sometime before 1663 the garden in front of the monastery of S. Lorenzo in Lucina is depicted with twelve parterres, with the front two grassed with large trees at the corners and the remaining ten parterres outlined with hedges whose corners are marked by small trees.[12]

[12] Cassa di Risparmio, Rome, ed., *Via del Corso*, Rome, 1961, fig. 169.

[13] I. Belli Barsali, "Una fonte per i giardini del Seicento: Il trattato di Giovan Battista Ferrari," in *Il giardino storico italiano*, ed. G. Ragionieri, Florence, 1981, pp. 221–34. Barberini payments for drawings and prints for the book are published in M. A. Lavin, *Seventeenth-Century Barberini Documents and Inventories of Art*, New York, 1975, nos. 98, 121, 160. Andrea Sacchi's drawings for some of the engravings are discussed in A. S. Harris, *Andrea Sacchi*, Princeton, N.J., 1977, pp. 101–3. The first Italian translation of the treatise was published in 1638.

143. G. B. Ferrari, *Flora*, 1646, square parterre

144. G. B. Ferrari, *Flora*, 1646, circular parterre

vere than Fiorenzuola against box edging, the "old mode," which is distasteful for its odor and too expensive for its perpetual need of tonsuring. He favors instead the "new invention" of edging with bricks (pianelle). The garden accounts of the Villa Pamphili attest to the popularity in 1645 and 1646 of the use of pianelle for the edging of the garden compartments there.[14] At the Villa Versaglia near Formello of Cardinal Flavio Chigi, nephew of Pope Alexander VII, one Antonio Todeschi, identified at first as a "brick maker," was paid in December 1666 for 2,100 pianelle for the compartments there and by October 1667 Todeschi is designated "gardener of the parterres" (*Giardiniere de Spartimenti*) and paid for 5,000 more pianelle for the gardens.[15]

Among the many notable gardens of Rome in his time Ferrari particularly singles out the garden at Cisterna of the flower collector, the duke of Sermoneta, which Ferrari claims in 1633 was of recent creation, and for which he illustrates a plan (Fig. 146) of a quarter of the layout.[16] Already the various flower beds were separated by the brick pianelle advocated by Ferrari and each bed was planted with two or three kinds of flowers of a similar color. A planting book of the duke, dated 1625, shows the care with which he arranged the colorful compartments with every type and location of bulb or plant identified by a number on his planting diagram.[17] Specializing particularly in anemones, the plants in his planting book are almost

[14] J. Garms, *Quellen aus dem Archiv Doria-Pamphilj zur Kunsttätigkeit in Rom unter Innocenz X* (Quellenschriften zur Geschichte der Barockkunst in Rom, 4), Rome and Vienna, 1972, p. 201, no. 984; p. 217, no. 1059; and p. 223, no. 1082.

[15] V. Golzio, *Documenti artistici sul Seicento nell'Archivio Chigi*, Rome, 1939, p. 177, no. 2507, and p. 180, no. 3232.

[16] G. B. Ferrari, *Flora, seu de florum cultura*, new ed., Amsterdam, 1646, pp. 215–19, and G. Masson, "Italian Flower Collectors' Gardens in Seventeenth Century Italy," in *The Italian Garden* (First Dumbarton Oaks Colloquium on the History of Landscape Architecture), ed. D. R. Coffin, Washington, D.C., 1972, pp. 61–80.

[17] Ibid., fig. 6.

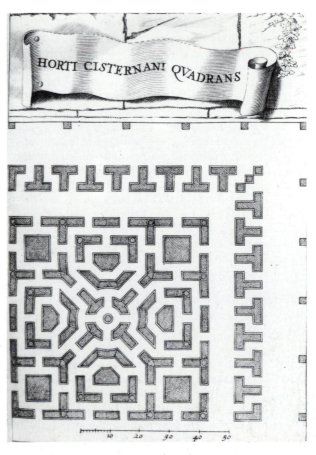

145. G. B. Ferrari, *Flora*, 1646, irregular parterre

146. Cisterna, Sermoneta Garden plan, 1633

all bulbous or tuberous. Ferrari notes that potted tuberoses were buried in the middle of the larger compartments so that they could receive extra water.

There is rather contradictory evidence regarding the surface of the walks that outline the parterres. The Frenchman Montaigne during his visit to Italy in 1581 comments at the Medici Villa of Poggio a Caiano in Tuscany that "in most of the big gardens in Italy they grow grass in the principal walks, and mow it."[18] A century later in 1685 Bishop Burnet, visiting from England, can only complain that the Italians "have no Gravel to give them those firm and beautiful Walks that we have in England, so the constant greenness of the Box doth so much please them, that they preferring the sight to the smell, have their Gardens so high sented by plots made with them, that there is no pleasure to walk in them."[19] Burnet's letter indicates the persistence of the use of box in Italian gar-

dens long after the negative injunctions of Fiorenzuola and Ferrari. Burnet's criticism is occasioned, as he himself notes, by the formal quality of the Italian garden meant to be enjoyed visually as a work of art in contrast to the English recreational attitude toward gardening for walking. Similarly the Frenchman, President de Brosses, later remarks in Rome that "the Italians follow their taste and the nature of their climate; they wish green trees, and grass in the alleys, rather than sand, with long avenues in tall, restricting hedges, which always give shade in a warm country."[20] Shortly after De Brosse's comments, John Northall in 1753 claims that "there is one great defect in the Italian gardens; the want of gravel for the walks, the materials of which are little better than sand," and in 1766 another Englishman complains

---

[18] M. de Montaigne, *The Complete Works of Montaigne*, trans. D. M. Frame, Stanford, Calif., 1957, p. 982.

[19] G. Burnet, *Some Letters Containing an Account of What*

*Seemed Most Remarkable in Switzerland, Italy, &c.*, Rotterdam, 1686, p. 171.

[20] C. de Brosses, *Lettres familières sur l'Italie*, ed. Y. Bezard, Paris, 1931, II, p. 64.

that as the Italians "cannot have either green grass, or fine gravel, they want some of the proper materials to render a garden perfectly beautiful."[21] The latter continues his condemnation of Italian gardening with the same English bias that his countryman Bishop Burnet evinced earlier, saying that

> what is unpardonable and absurd, amongst a thousand other defects in their laying out a garden, is their contrivance to calculate them for winter, when nobody walks, and not for summer, when gardens are agreeable. This absurdity is, the prodigious number of large trees, all of the ever-green kind, with which their gardens abound; it is true, they afford a shade, but of so dismal a hue as is hardly to be imagined, and, at the times they want shade, trees of a beautiful verdure would be stocked with leaves; certainly this vice will be reformed as their taste improves.

Ferrari in 1633 makes no reference to grassed alleys, but rather gives specific instructions of how to surface the alleys of a garden. He recommends covering the alleys with well-beaten clay or clayey earth mixed with the fresh dregs of pressed olives (*morchia*). This paste should be spread on the alley by a cylindrical roller or tamped down by a turf rammer. The surface was then to be strewn again with the dregs of olive pressings and left to dry. Alternate surfaces that he proposes are of lime or sand mixed with gravel or "thin earth" (*terra magra*) mixed with sand. He adds that one could use brick, but that a brick surface is not as good in rainy weather, as it becomes slippery, and in any case soon becomes covered with mold and moss.[22]

## Pergolas

A feature of Roman gardens, which presumably survived from classical antiquity to the present, is the pergola (*cerchiata*) or trellis, a latticework, wooden structure generally covered with vines or espaliered fruit trees to shade an alley or to stand in a corner of the garden as a dining nook or other recreational retreat. Many of the mediaeval documents of the rent or sale of Roman houses cited previously list a garden pergola in their descriptions, so in 958 a house on the road to S. Croce in Gerusalemme had a "pergola and garden and closed-in vineyard and an apple orchard"

and the rental in 1008 of a house near Sta. Maria in Via Lata specifies "a small garden in front in which stands a vine covered pergola and with fruit trees."[23] So Piero de' Crescenzi in his early fourteenth-century treatise identifies pergolas as features of both his medium-sized and his royal garden.[24]

In Roman Renaissance gardens of the fifteenth and sixteenth centuries, such pergolas were a common feature. In 1463 Pope Pius II paid Giovanni di Pietro from Florence for the wood and labor to fashion a pergola (*bergola*) in the papal private garden at the Vatican Palace, presumably the garden below the loggias on the eastern side of the palace.[25] Another lovely garden dominated by a wooden pergola was that attached to the Villa Farnesina designed for Agostino Chigi by the architect Peruzzi, where Blosio Palladio in his poetic description of 1512 speaks of the expanse of wooden pergola over which "plants creep and flowers ramble," and Peruzzi's own drawing (Fig. 108) for an urban garden discussed previously presents a wealth of alleys covered with pergolas or trellises probably like those of the Villa Farnesina.[26] Even the cross pergola, often with a domed crossing, which corresponded to the persistence of the quartered garden noted in the treatises of Alamanni in 1546 and that of Pona as late as 1622, was common in sixteenth-century Roman gardens. One of the finest examples must have been the huge cross pergola dominating the gardens behind the Riario Palace at the foot of the Janiculum Hill, as seen in a panoramic view of about 1540 by Anton van den Wyngaerde.[27]

Drawings by Giovanni Colonna of Tivoli in his sketchbook (Ms Vat. lat. 7721), dating about 1554, offer detailed accounts of the garden pergolas in the Ghinucci garden on the Quirinal Hill discussed previously.[28] A cross pergola and the lattice fences that

[21] J. Northall, *Travels through Italy*, London, 1766, pp. 361–62, and S. Sharp, *Letters from Italy . . . In the Years 1765, and 1766*, London, 1766, p. 240.

[22] Belli Barsali, "Una fonte per i giardini del Seicento," p. 233.

[23] R. Krautheimer, *Rome: Profile of a City, 312–1308*, Princeton, N.J., 1980, p. 312, and L. Cavazzi, *La diaconia di S. Maria in Via Lata e il monastero di S. Ciriaco*, Rome, 1908, p. 247.

[24] P. de' Crescenzi, *Trattato della agricoltura*, Milan, 1805, II, pp. 330, 332; in translation R. G. Calkins, "Piero de' Crescenzi and the Medieval Garden," in *Medieval Gardens* (Dumbarton Oaks Colloquium on the History of Landscape Architecture, IX), ed. E. B. MacDougall, Washington, D.C., 1986, appendix 2, pp. 172–73.

[25] E. Müntz, *Les arts à la cour des papes pendant le XVᵉ et le XVIᵉ siècles*, pt. 1, Paris, 1878, p. 277.

[26] C. L. Frommel, *Die Farnesina und Peruzzis Architektonisches Frühwerk*, Berlin, 1961, p. 39.

[27] H. Egger, *Römische Veduten*, II, Vienna, 1932, pl. 112. For the date of the view, see Frommel, *Der römische Palastbau der Hochrenaissance*, II, p. 69, n. 44.

[28] See Chapter 7.

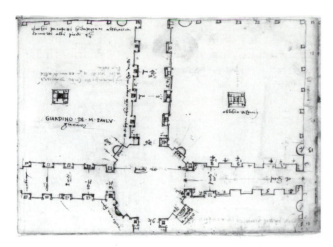

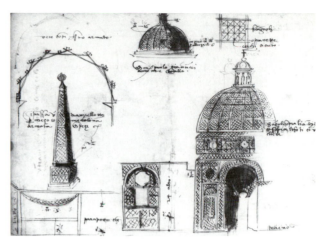

147. Rome, Ghinucci Garden, plan of cross pergola, ca. 1554, Biblioteca Apostolica Vaticana, Ms Vat. lat. 7721, fol. 15r

148. Rome, Ghinucci Garden, cross pergola and parapets, ca. 1554, Biblioteca Apostolica Vaticana, Ms Vat. lat. 7721, fol. 15v

closed two sides of the garden are depicted (Fig. 147). The plan of the cross pergola (fol. 15r) illustrates four arms 30 piedi (ca. 8.9 meters) long and 10.5 piedi (ca. 3.13 meters) wide between the vertical supports except at the entrances into the central octagon, where they are only 9.5 piedi (ca. 2.83 meters) wide. The octagon is 20 piedi (ca. 5.96 meters) wide, with fountains in the diagonal niches. It is noted beside one of the fountains on the plan that an aviary stood above, and undoubtedly this was true also of the other fountains. Between the arms of the cross pergola were four flowerbeds and in the center of each bed was an obelisk of latticework. On the other page of Colonna's sketchbook (fol. 15v) are drawings of elevations and sections of various parts of the garden architecture (Fig. 148), which were made with wooden frames over which were drawn surfaces probably of thick wire in a crisscross lattice pattern. Over the crossing was a large latticework dome with a modest lantern capped by what looks like a cross or an orb, but is more likely a weathervane. A section of the vaults crossing the crossarms depicts a barrel vault composed of wooden or metal bars tied together. Recessed windows were set into each section of the walls of the crossarms and a fence or parapet (*parapetto*) with garlands outlined the outer edge of the flowerbeds. Both the details of the parapet and of the crossing dome are described as "all covered with ivy." The wire netting, therefore, served as a support for the topiary work, creating the impression for the visitor of being surrounded by "green architecture." An-

other detail illustrates one of the obelisks topped by a sphere.

One of the largest cross pergolas with a domed crossing was that built in 1544 in the giardino segreto or hortus conclusus of Paul III at the Vatican, which is still visible in the 1574 Cartaro engraving of the Belvedere Court (Fig. 6). Documents in 1544 list payments to the carpenter, Il Bologna, for 210 chestnut joists and 1,500 pairs of hoops (*cerchi*) for the "espaliers of the bitter oranges in the new garden of the Belvedere."[29] The Cartaro print has a dome raised over the crossing of the pergola and windows piercing the sides of the arms of the pergola, similar to those in the Ghinucci cross pergola. Another monumental example was the cross pergola in the center of the flat garden area at the base of the terraced gardens of the Villa d'Este at Tivoli seen in Dupérac's engraving of 1573 (Fig. 66) and in the contemporary fresco on a wall of the Salotto there (Fig. 67). The engraving shows a tall octagonal drum and dome rising over the crossing and the usual windows cut into the sides of the crossarms. A contemporary description notes that four fountains in the form of giant flowers, presumably the Este lilies, stood in the diagonal sides of the octagonal pavilion.[30] Other elements of the Este coat of arms decorated the crossing pavilion, so eight silver white eagles perched on the corners of the entablature

[29] Dorez, *La cour du Pape Paul III*, I, pp. 282, 296, 304.

[30] V. Pacifici, ed., *Annali e memorie di Tivoli di Giovanni Maria Zappi* (Studi e fonti per la storia della regione tiburtina), Tivoli, 1920, p. 56.

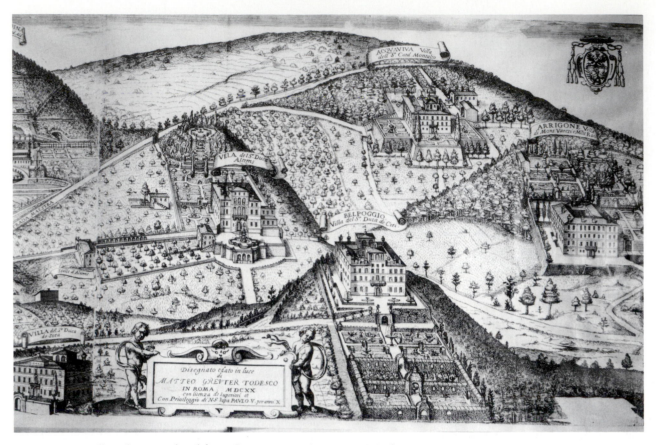

149. Frascati, Villa Belpoggio, detail from Greuter engraving, 1620, British Museum

of the pavilion with a golden lily at the summit of the dome. Shady vines covered the vaults of the arms of the pergola and fruit trees were espaliered along the sides. Each of the four compartments formed by the arms of the cross pergolas were in turn divided up into four smaller compartments with a freestanding, octagonal, domed pavilion at the center. By at least 1610 the cross pergola was gone and soon replaced by the famous circle of cypresses, which is now one of the glories of the garden.

Such cross pergolas were particularly associated with the mediaeval hortus conclusus, hence the prominence of the one in the garden of Paul III at the Vatican. Similarly the garden area on the plain below the Villa d'Este at Tivoli planted with herbs, flowers, and individual fruit trees was the image of an hortus conclusus set down within the wider context of the gardens. In fact, a latticed fence or "parapet," like that at the Ghinucci garden at Rome, outlined this area at Tivoli, closing it off from the rest of the garden. In addition, at Tivoli there was also an actual walled-in giardino segreto attached to one side of the palace

with a freestanding domed garden pavilion decorated with fountains and the Este eagles and lilies in the center of the garden. In the seventeenth century, with the lessening of the importance at Rome of the hortus conclusus, the cross pergola became less prevalent. Nevertheless, in the Greuter print of the villas at Frascati dated 1620, the Villa Belpoggio of the duke of Ceri has still in the center of its garden an octagonal, domed pavilion with two barrel-vaulted pergola arms (Fig. 149).

In the sixteenth century perhaps the most lavish pergolas and other garden woodwork in a Roman garden were those created from 1549 at the Carafa vigna on the Quirinal Hill first rented by the Farnese Pope Paul III and then by the Cardinal of Ferrara. On April 11, 1549, the Farnese architect Jacopo Meleghino was paid for preparing the mulberry garden and a pergola at the Quirinal villa for the pleasure of the pope and in late October, just before the death of the pope, Girolamo, called "Il Bologna," the same carpenter who had earlier created the pergola in the Vatican garden of Paul III, was paid the remainder of his fee for constructing the pergola.[31] By July 1550 Cardinal Ippolito II d'Este, Cardinal of Ferrara, had possession of the Quirinal villa where he soon expanded and improved the gardens. Vasari, the author of the lives of the artists, relates that when the Cardinal of Ferrara returned to Rome from France the Ferrarese artist Girolamo da Carpi accompanied him and there served him "not only in buildings, but also in the truly regal woodwork of the garden in which he worked so well that everyone was amazed by it. And in truth I do not know anyone who could better him in making such beautiful work of wood, which then has been covered by very lovely greenery."[32] It is just at this time that Colonna made his drawings of the elaborate garden furnishings of the Ghinucci garden, which stood across the road from the Quirinal villa and would soon be given to the Cardinal of Ferrara. Even after Girolamo da Carpi left, work continued on pergolas and trellises at the Quirinal gardens. On February 3, 1565, there was a payment for making the hoops (*cerchiade*) above the large pergola of the garden of the bastion, and on March 29 the architect Giovanni Alberto Galvani was paid for measuring and estimating the value of two pergolas there.[33] The extraordinary amount of garden trellis-work at the Quirinal villa is amusingly summed up at the end of the century when Agostino del Riccio, speaking of the princely expenses afforded by the Cardinal of Ferrara for his gardens there, asserts "that I have been told that he spent nine thousand scudi for the nails to make the semicircular hoops [of the pergolas]."[34] The garden woodwork at the cardinal's garden was renowned throughout Italy. Also toward the end of the century Giovan Soderini in his treatise on trees describes the pergolas as

a row of rooms clothed in greenery, and arranged so that the lowest and sunken cool places, shady for summer, resemble a large, spacious palace, as is seen today in Rome at the Este villa. Nor are there lacking there, pilasters, proportioned columns swaddled with ivy, walls covered with laurustinus, jasmine and periwin-

kle, with its chambers, rooms, salons, loggias and kitchens on all sides and covered above with various sorts of greenery, which all can be made according to the judgment of those who understand better this art, which the ancients called *Topiaria*, forming statues, figures, colossi, obelisks and similar fantasies from boxwood and Spanish myrtle and French rosemary which are especially obedient to shears.[35]

## Topiary

One of the most prevalent types of topiary decoration in European gardens was the labyrinth. Although the form of the bewildering labyrinth was central to the ancient classical story of Daedalus and the Minotaur, the labyrinth does not seem to have been used as a garden decoration in classical antiquity. At least by the late Middle Ages the labyrinth began to appear in gardens as well as on church pavements. It is, however, the publication of Colonna's fantastic romance, the *Hypnerotomachia Poliphili*, written in the mid-fifteenth century and first published in 1499, that popularized the labyrinth and other topiary designs as garden ornament.[36] The earliest mention of an actual garden labyrinth at Rome would seem to be the one Cardinal Gonzaga speaks of in his letter of 1479, where he suggests that in the garden of his palace the wall near the labyrinth be frescoed with the story of Theseus and the Minotaur.[37]

At the Villa d'Este at Tivoli, irrespective of the irregularities of the site, as discussed previously, four

[31] A. Bertolotti, *Artisti bolognesi, ferraresi ed alcuni altri del già stato pontificio in Roma nei secoli XV, XVI e XVII*, n.p., n.d., p. 111, and F. Borsi, "Il Palazzo del Quirinale," in *Il Palazzo del Quirinale*, Rome, 1974, p. 36.

[32] G. Vasari, *Le vite de' più eccellenti pittori, scultori ed architettori*, ed. G. Milanesi, VI, Florence, 1881, p. 477.

[33] ASM, Camera Ducale, Amministrazione dei Principi, Registro 991, fol. 14v, February 3, 1565, and fol. 20v, March 29, 1565.

[34] D. Heikamp, "Agostino del Riccio: Del giardino di un re," in *Il giardino storico italiano*, ed. G. Ragionieri, Florence, 1981, p. 85.

[35] G. V. Soderini, *Il trattato degli arbori* (Le opere di Gio. Vettorio Soderini, III), ed. A. B. della Lega, Bologna, 1904, pp. 244–45.

[36] F. Colonna, *Hypnerotomachia Poliphili*, ed. G. Pozzi and L. A. Ciapponi, Padua, 1964, I, p. 116. Regarding the labyrinth, see especially M. Chargeat, "De la maison Dedalus aux labyrinthes, dans l'art des jardins du moyen-âge à la Renaissance," in *Actes du XVIIᵐᵉ congrès international d'histoire de l'art, Amsterdam, 23–31 juillet 1952*, The Hague, 1955, pp. 345–50; also see P. Santarcangeli, *Il libro dei labirinti*, Florence, 1967, and H. Kern, *Labirinti*, Milan, 1981. Giovanni Fontana, the North Italian engineer, wrote early in the fifteenth century an unpublished treatise on labyrinths; see C. Huelsen, "Der 'Liber instrumentorum' des Giovanni Fontana," in *Festgabe Hugo Blümner*, Zurich, 1914, pp. 507–15, and A. Birkenmayer, "Zur Lebensgeschichte und wissenschaftlichen Tätigkeit von Giovanni Fontana (1395?–1455?)," *Isis*, XVII, 1932, p. 44. Filarete's unpublished architectural treatise of the mid-fifteenth century had a water labyrinth in a huge garden.

[37] See Chapter 5. A drawing (Uff. 6769A) attributed to the workshop of Antonio da Sangallo the Younger apparently depicts a garden labyrinth in one of the vigne of Giulio Alberini outside the Porta Portese in the early sixteenth century; see Frommel, *Der römische Palastbau der Hochrenaissance*, II, p. 8, n. 61.

large labyrinths were to frame two sides of the central area dominated by the cross pergola as proposed in the engraving of 1573 (Fig. 66). The description of the projected garden, perhaps written by the designer Pirro Ligorio, indicates that each of the projected four labyrinths was to be created from different plant material, introducing a strong element of variety into the horticulture in contrast to the usual mode of relying on one shrub, such as boxwood. So the description reads: "Labyrinths made of wood, and planted on each side with different types of trees, the first of orange trees [*haranci*] with hedges of myrtle [*mortella*]; the second of arbutus [*cerase marine*] with hedges of honeysuckle [*madre selva*]; the third of pines [*pini*] with hedges of laurustinus [*lentaggine*]; the fourth of firs [*abbeti*] with hedges of privet [*fior fiorella*]."[38] The description indicates that the hedges of the labyrinths were to be constructed of wood upon which the different plants were to be espaliered. As the later accounts in 1576 or 1577 of the local chronicler Zappi or the French visitor Audebert record, only two of the projected four labyrinths were created, but they are inconsistent about the plant material.[39] Zappi notes generally that the labyrinths are forty paces (*passi*) square, each with different shrubs, "myrtle, laurel, and arbutus and other similar trees," whereas Audebert specifies that both labyrinths were of "shrubs called laurustinus [*letaggio*], whose leaf is like that of the laurel." Audebert adds that the hedge or palisade of the labyrinths was the height of a man. The use of wood for the construction of the labyrinths is confirmed by documents of June 8, 1582, which record the cost for "thirty small beams to be used for the labyrinths and espaliers of this garden."[40]

Labyrinths have had a long survival in the art of gardening. Soderini in his treatise on trees at the end of the sixteenth century mentions them briefly and Ferrari in his floral treatise of 1633 reproduces a labyrinth (Fig. 150) at the end of his series of parterre designs.[41] Perhaps one of the longest surviving labyrinths was the one that once stood on the grounds of

150. G. B. Ferrari, *Flora*, 1646, labyrinth

the Villa Altieri on the Esquiline Hill at Rome. In 1698–1699 the antiquarian Bernard de Montfaucon recorded that he went to the Villa Altieri at that time "where there are many Statues, a Labyrinth, and an abundance of Inscriptions."[42] As the villa was erected about 1674, the labyrinth was presumably planted soon after that. The archaeologist Nibby in his account of Rome in 1838 describes "a beautiful labyrinth formed of tall box hedges, in the midst of which towers a pine, to reach which one must study the mass to find the way through the contorted alleys which intertwine and multiply at every moment along

---

[38] D. R. Coffin, *The Villa d'Este at Tivoli*, Princeton, N.J., 1960, p. 143.

[39] Pacifici, *Annali e memorie di Tivoli di Giovanni Maria Zappi*, p. 57, and R. W. Lightbown, "Nicolas Audebert and the Villa d'Este," *Journal of the Warburg and Courtauld Institutes*, XXVII, 1964, p. 187.

[40] ASM, Camera Ducale, Casa Amministrazione, Registri del Card. Luigi d'Este, Pacco 173, Conto generale di Tivoli dell'anno 1582, fol. 46v.

[41] Soderini, *Il trattato degli arbori*, p. 274, and G. B. Ferrari, *Flora, seu de florum cultura*, new ed., Amsterdam, 1646, p. 37.

[42] B. de Montfaucon, *The Antiquities of Italy*, 2nd ed., London, 1725, p. 76. Other references are A. Nibby, *Roma nell'anno MDCCCXXXVIII*, IV, Rome, 1841, p. 905; Belli Barsali, "Una fonte per i giardini del Seicento: Il trattato di Giovan Battista Ferrari," p. 231, and H. Kern, *Laberinti*, Milan, 1981, p. 341. For photographs, see C. Pietrangeli, "La raccolta fotografica presso X ripartizione A.B.A. del Comune e musei dipendenti," *Bollettino dei musei comunali di Roma*, XII, 1965, p. 39, and *Rome in Early Photographs: The Age of Pius IX*, Copenhagen, 1977, no. 200.

151. Rome, Villa Altieri, labyrinth, ca. 1852, Kongelige Bibliotek, Copenhagen

the circular path." A calotype, dated about 1852, in prints in the Royal Library at Copenhagen, Denmark, and in the Museo di Roma at Rome, preserves an image of a wide, circular labyrinth leading into a single, gigantic, umbrella pine at its center (Fig. 151).

More unusual and rarer at Rome was topiary cut in the form of representational figures—human, animal, or merely geometrical. Such figures existed in mid-fifteenth-century gardens, for there are several such topiary images described in Colonna's romance, the *Hypnerotomachia Poliphili*, and later illustrated in its first edition of 1499. At the same time that Colonna was imagining such monstrous forms, the well-to-do Florentine Giovanni Rucellai describes in his *Zibaldone* the extraordinary topiary figures he had in his garden at Quaracchi outside of Florence, but there is no evidence for such figures in Rome, unless Cardinal Gonzaga had intended that the figure of the Minotaur, which was to be in the midst of the labyrinth in his garden at Rome, was to be a work of topiary and not a stone statue.[43] The French naturalist Pierre Belon in the mid-sixteenth century, however,

claims that there was in the Roman gardens topiary of cut privet representing animals and ancient Roman triremes, particularly identifying the garden of Stefano Del Bufalo as one location.[44] Another example of such Roman topiary he cites depicted a horseman with a lance.

Certainly the most famous example of a garden with elaborate topiary work was the one owned by Fra Mariano on the Quirinal Hill next to the church of S. Silvestro. In a letter of 1519 Fra Mariano himself describes his garden to Isabella d'Este as a "labyrinth where you may see small groves and sylvan ornaments in a homely hodgepodge of one hundred varieties and a thousand caprices."[45] A little later in a letter of November 15, 1524, Giovanni Battista Sanga, once secretary of Cardinal Bibbiena, mentions "the caves of ivy of Fra Mariano at San Silvestro on Monte Cavallo," and Girolamo Rorario in a visit in 1544 speaks of "topiary dining rooms, walkways, intercolumniations, all swathed in ivy."

Toward the middle of the sixteenth century there appears an occasional hint of distaste for such representational topiary. So the writer Paolo Giovio likens his youthful experiments in the convoluted styles of Quintus Curtius Rufus and Tacitus to topiary scenes whereas his later adoption of Roman classicism is compared by him to the clearer, sunny gardens of Sallust.[46] In his dialogue on the villa of 1559 Taegio has Partenio assert that he "cannot praise an art that teaches us to offend nature."[47] When he is asked to explain his position, he speaks of the "many monstrous fabrics of plants, queer grafts and metamorphoses of trees" and, emulating Horace's attack in the *Ars poetica* on unnatural combinations, demands: "Whence have we learned to join horses with asses, and wolves with bitches, whence have mules and illicit things been born against the law of nature, if not from this art?"

[43] F. Colonna, *Hypnerotomachia Poliphili*, ed. G. Pozzi and L. A. Ciapponi, Padua, 1980, I, pp. 296–97; G. Rucellai, *Giovanni Rucellai ed il suo Zibaldone* (Warburg Institute Studies, 24), I, London, 1960, pp. 21–22.

[44] P. Belon, *De neglecta Stirpium Cultura atque earum cognitione Libellus*, Antwerp, 1589, p. 56.

[45] A. Luzio, "Federico Gonzaga ostaggio alla corte di Giulio II," *Archivio della R. società romana di storia patria*, IX, 1886, p. 574. Other contemporary references are in a letter of Sanga published in D. Atanagi, *De le lettere facete et piacevoli di diversi grandi huomi, et chiari ingegni*, Venice, 1561, p. 214, and G. Rorario, *Quod Animalia bruta ratione vtantur meliùs Homine*, Paris, 1648, p. 120.

[46] T. C. Price Zimmerman, "Renaissance Symposia," in *Essays Presented to Myron P. Gilmore*, ed. S. Bertelli and G. Ramakus, Florence, 1978, I, p. 365.

[47] B. Taegio, *La villa*, Milan, 1559, p. 54.

### Sundials and Vases

Although sundials became a traditional ornament of North European gardens, especially in the seventeenth century, the evidence for such ornaments in Roman gardens is scarce and limited to the seventeenth century. So in 1628 there is an account of payment to two master stonecutters, Agostino Radi and Francesco Castelli, for work in making a "sun clock" for the middle of the "new garden" at the papal villa on the Quirinal.[48] In one case the sundial is actually a horticultural feature, for in Barrière's plan of the Villa Aldobrandini at Frascati published in 1647 he locates with the number four in front of the fountain at the left of the Villa a "sundial of myrtle" (*Horologia è myrto*) enclosed in a low enframing hedge (Fig. 152). The evergreen sundial can also be seen earlier on Greuter's engraved view of Frascati of 1620.[49]

The principal ornamental feature of Roman gardens, particularly in the seventeenth century, was vases or urns planted with flowers, shrubs, or small ornamental trees and set primarily at the corners and along the edge of flower compartments interspersed within the low hedges outlining the compartments or posed on walls or balustrades along terraces, ramps, and stairs. Already early in the sixteenth century Aretino imagined the garden of his courtesan Nanna as having vases planted with boxwood at the corners of the rosemary hedges that framed the flower beds.[50]

When Pope Julius III began to build and plant his villa at Rome just outside the Porta del Popolo, many well-wishers sent gifts of plants, so early in 1552 the bishop of Tivoli presented the pope with some 270 pomegranate plants and 70 quinces, and Lelio Orsini added more pomegranates and a bundle of jasmine, while the viceroy of Naples sent him as decoration for the villa 50 vases containing unspecified plants.[51] It was, however, at the Villa d'Este at Tivoli that the use of large numbers of vases with plants was common to decorate the parapets and walls of the terraces and stairways. The description of the project of the villa and its garden written probably before 1568 specifies that the "parapet of the thirteenth alley [will be] full of vases and greenery" and an undated document

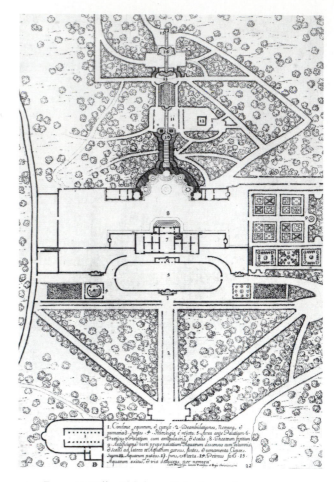

152. Frascati, Villa Aldobrandini, plan, 1647

from the decade 1573 to 1583, when the villa was owned by Cardinal Luigi d'Este, lists 268 vases being used "to decorate the walls of the Garden," with 72 set around the fishpools, 30 along the main alley under the palace, 24 on the wall with the Fountain of the Swans, and smaller numbers scattered elsewhere.[52] At least some of the vases for Tivoli were made at Nepi, for on January 24, 1571, Giovanni Paolo d'Ambrosij and his brother Baldo, "vasemakers [*vasellari*] at Nepi," were paid twenty-five scudi to make 72 vases for Tivoli. At the same time, in 1576, the chronicler Zappi notes that on the balustrade above the oval basin at the Fountain of Tivoli vases 3

[48] *Il Palazzo del Quirinale*, Rome, 1974, p. 258.

[49] D. Barrière, *Villa Aldobrandini, siue Uarij illius hortorum et fontium prospectus*, Rome, 1647, pls. 5 and 22. For a detail of the Greuter view, see C. d'Onofrio, *La Villa Aldobrandini di Frascati*, Rome, [1963], pl. 13.

[50] P. Aretino, *Sei giornate*, ed. G. Aquilecchia, Bari, 1969, p. 352.

[51] I. Belli Barsali, *Ville di Roma: Lazio I*, Milan, 1970, p. 56.

[52] Coffin, *The Villa d'Este*, p. 144. The list of vases is at ASM, Camera Ducale, Fabbriche e Villeggiature, Tivoli, Busta 70, pte. 6, Villeggiatura sotto il Cardinale Luigi d'Este 1573–1583, fasc. 5, fol. 1r. For the payment in 1571 for vases, see ASM, Camera Ducale, Casa Amministrazione, Registri del Card. Ippolito II, Pacco 122, Protetione di Francia 1571, fol. 10r. See also Pacifici, *Annali e memorie di Tivoli di Giovanni Maria Zappi*, p. 60.

palmi high (ca. 67 centimeters) were planted with "carnations, lilies and other similar, both beautiful and pleasing flowers." More often the vases ornamenting a garden were planted with citrus trees, as an inventory dated 1597 for a small garden within the Palace of Monte Giordano identifies "seven large vases with large, green plants, two citron, one lemon, and four oranges."[53]

It is, of course, the large gardens and garden parks of the seventeenth century that required a great variety of planted vases. The accounts for the renewal of the papal garden at the Quirinal under Pope Paul V (1605–1621) particularly contain payments for garden vases. In 1614 the stonecarver Agostino Naldini was paid for work "on the large vases of the garden of the palace of Montecavallo," but in January 1615 a kiln worker was paid for different sized vases, that is, for 50 vases one soma in weight, and 50 of half a soma in weight. An account of June 8, 1612, lists 50 vases of Seville-orange trees; on May 5, 1615, there is recorded a payment for 39 vases of jasmine, 4 vases of carnations, and 50 vases of hyacinths and narcissuses "for use in a compartment of a new parterre in the garden"; on March 31, 1616, 24 more vases of carnations and on July 30, 110 vases of Catalonian or Spanish jasmine.[54] The appeal of such planted vases as the decoration of a garden is suggested by the Dutchman Aerssen van Sommelsdyck, when he visited the Villa Aldobrandini at Frascati in 1654. He pointed out that while they had entered the grounds from above, one must, if one wishes "to see it in its splendor, ascend from below." He then adds:

When one has ascended to the fountain where all the seven alleys by which one ascends meet, one can continue, if you wish to go up in a carriage, by two types of stairs without steps [i.e., ramps], one at right, the other at left, each of which makes a semicircle to arrive above on the terrace. Along this ramp, in spring and in summer, are a quantity of vases with flowering trees of orange and jasmine which, in addition to the pleasing greenery, divert the curious by the excellence of their fragrance.[55]

A century later President de Brosses, who was less favorable to the hydraulic automata at the Villa Aldobrandini, recalls with pleasure "the avenues below decorated with orange trees and hedges of laurel, terraces in steps, balustrades loaded with vases full of myrtle and pomegranates." Later at Cardinal Chigi's lavish Villa Versaglia near Formello, the accounts indicate that the planting vases were regularly painted or gilded, for in December 1666 the architect Carlo Fontana approved the payment to the gilder (*indoratore*) and the painter Basilio Onofrii for painting the vases of citrus fruit and a decade later 16 vases of jasmine were painted.[56]

In a contract with the gardener of the Villa d'Este at Tivoli in 1629, to be discussed later, item six specifies that the gardener "is obligated at the suitable time to put out and in the vases of Seville oranges [*melangoli*], being helped as usual," and in the foreground of a plate depicting the Casino Pio at the Vatican in Falda's illustrations of the most notable seventeenth-century gardens in Rome (Fig. 153), two gardeners are shown pulling a tubbed tree on a four-wheeled dolly.[57] Falda's garden views indicate the prevalence of vases of shrubs or trees at the time.

## Orangeries and Pavilions

At Rome in the fifteenth and sixteenth century the citrus trees (*agrumi*)—citron, lemon, or Seville oranges—were the primary fragile greenery, which planted in the ground required protection during the cold season. Since most of these trees were espaliered against the walls of the garden, they could be protected with cane matting. The gardener's contract at Tivoli of 1629, already mentioned, specified that he was "to cover and will uncover at the suitable time the espaliers of citrons," but that the Este stewards were to provide the materials for the protective covering. In the early seventeenth century when the Roman plant collectors began to import large quantities of exotic plants and wished to have large planted groves of citrus fruits, their protection during the cold season became increasingly a difficult problem. G. B.

[53] S. Eiche, "Towards a Study of the Palazzo di Monte Giordano in Rome: A Plan by Orazio Torriani," *Mitteilungen des Kunsthistorischen Institutes in Florenz*, XXIX, 1985, p. 195.

[54] The payments for the sculptor and for the kiln worker are in *Il Palazzo del Quirinale*, Rome, 1974, pp. 250, 251. The vases are in ibid., pp. 252, 254, and J.A.F. Orbaan, *Documenti sul barocco in Roma*, Rome, 1920, pp. 309, 317.

[55] L. G. Pélissier, "Sur quelques documents utiles pour l'histoire des rapports entre la France et l'Italie," in *Atti del Congresso Internazionale di Scienze Storiche, 1903*, III, Rome, 1906, pp. 189–90.

For de Brosses's comments, see C. de Brosses, *Lettres familières sur l'Italie*, ed. Y. Bezard, Paris, 1931, II, p. 295.

[56] V. Golzio, *Documenti artistici sul Seicento nell'Archivio Chigi*, Rome, 1939, p. 177, no. 2506, and p. 185, no. 2870.

[57] For the gardener's contract see ASM, Camera Ducale, Fabbriche e Villeggiature, Busta 71, Tivoli, no. 6, Villeggiatura sotto Francesco d'Este, fasc. 2, 1629–1630, and see G. B. Falda, *Li giardini di Roma*, Rome, n.d., pl. 3.

VEDVTA DEL GIARDINO DI BELVEDERE DEL PALAZZO PONTIFICIO IN VATICANO
*Architettura di Carlo Maderno.*

153. Rome, Vatican, Casino Pio, engraving

Ferrari, who had written his very important flower treatise in 1633, followed it with an equally important study of arboriculture, and particularly the growing of citrus trees, under the title *Hesperides sive De Malorum Aureorum Cultura et Vsv Libri Quatuor* (Rome, 1646). He describes in detail the wooden winter housing prepared to cover a grove of orange trees (*mala medica*) planted in the "royal orchard of the [Farnese] duke of Parma" on the Palatine Hill and illustrates both a plan combined with a section (Fig. 154) and a perspective view (Fig. 155) of the protective house.[58] Since the engraving of the plan and section is inscribed as drawn by the architect Girolamo Rainaldi, it can be presumed that he was the designer of the housing. Surrounded by a wall espaliered with citron, lemon, and orange trees, each freestanding tree was planted in the center of four wooden supports, forming a quincunx pattern that permitted the trees to be viewed in freestanding ranks. The grove is protected by a temporary roof on which hay might be spread, when cool autumn arrives, certainly by the end of September. With the beginning of May the trees are freed to the sun. Ferrari also illustrates the

long wooden shed that was erected in cold weather over a magnificent arched pergola covered with orange trees in the garden of Cardinal Carlo Pio (Fig. 156).[59]

It is at Frascati, however, at the Villa Aldobrandini that the traditional solution to the problem was offered as described and illustrated (Fig. 157) by Ferrari.[60] On the east side of the villa, as depicted in Barrière's engraving of the complex (Fig. 158) at number four, was a large building with a vaulted room some 270 palmi long (ca. 60.3 meters), roughly north and south, by 30 palmi wide (ca. 6.7 meters) and 35 palmi tall (ca. 7.8 meters). The west wall was opened with a large door flanked on each side by three tremendous windows barred with iron gratings. Seven smaller windows above pierced the barrel vault. All the windows had wooden shutters to control the elements. The floor of this large orangery or hothouse consisted of soft soil in which the orange trees could be planted during their hibernation, so that Ferrari could liken the chamber of greenery to an Elysium. This orangery

[58] G. B. Ferrari, *Hesperides*, Rome, 1646, pp. 459–60; on p. 461 is the plan and on p. 463 the perspective view.

[59] Ibid., p. 145, illustrated on p. 147.

[60] Ibid., pp. 454–56, illustrated on p. 457. See also K. Schwager, "Kardinal Pietro Aldobrandinis Villa di Belvedere in Frascati," *Römisches Jahrbuch für Kunstgeschichte*, IX–X, 1961–1962, p. 353.

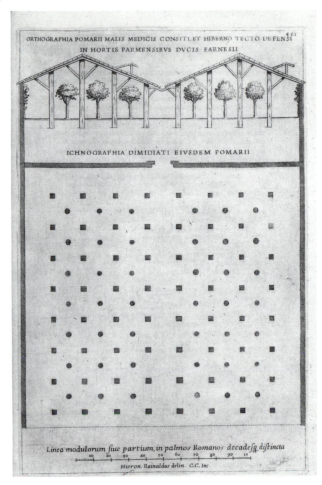

154. Rome, Farnese Gardens, plan and section of hot-house, 1646

155. Rome, Farnese Gardens, perspective view of hot-house, 1646

156. Rome, Cardinal Pio's Garden, winter protective cover, 1646

was probably a later addition to the villa as it first appears in Ferrari in 1646 and in Barrière's view of 1647, but is not in Greuter's 1620 engraving of Frascati. It is at this time, early in the seventeenth century, that orangeries of this type began to become frequent in northern gardens, where the possibility of wintering citrus trees was more difficult. The French hydraulic engineer and garden designer, Salomon de Caus, published in 1620, for example, his design for a portable wooden orangery that he had used at the Palatine gardens at Heidelberg and also a design for a proposed permanent orangery of stone.[61]

Pavilions, whose main purpose was as a secluded retreat for dining and conversation within a garden, but which on occasion might be used in inclement weather as temporary orangeries, were common in

[61] S. de Caus, *Hortus Palatinus*, Frankfurt, 1620, pls. 9 and 10.

157. Frascati, Villa Aldobrandini, hothouse interior, 1646

caded pavilion with pilasters engaged to the piers, the loggia stood above an underground grotto reached by outside stairs. A large basin of water fed by the Tiber River and surrounded by a bench enhanced the damp, dank atmosphere of the grotto, dimly lit by an oculus in the vault.

The ancient Roman writer Pliny the Younger in his descriptions of the gardens at his Laurentine and Tuscan villas (*Letters*, II, 17, and V, 6) repeatedly mentions a type of garden pavilion or apartment called the *diaeta*, which will appeal to the Renaissance Romans' attempt to classicize their own gardens. They will adapt both the concept and name of the diaeta to different functions in their gardens. Diaetae were built, as noted previously, to house small antiquities, such as portrait busts, in the statuary gardens of Cardinal Cesarini on the Via Papale at the beginning of the sixteenth century or slightly later in the Cesi gardens in the Borgo (Fig. 15). Raphael in the description of his project for the Villa Madama (Fig. 45) planned a winter garden house or diaeta at the east corner of the villa near the secluded winter garden with a glazed room at the top of the pavilion offering magnificent views over the countryside, and a corresponding tower at the northern corner served as a chapel. The very unusual Casa Pendente or the Leaning House in Vicino Orsini's garden at Bomarzo (Fig. 82) is certainly derived from the Roman idea of a diaeta, although its tilted character has nothing to do with the ancient concept.

One of the most impressive garden pavilions was the domed, octagonal structure (Fig. 159) erected in 1561 for the Cardinal of Ferrara on the edge of the Quirinal Hill in his villa at Rome, which later became the papal Quirinal villa. The pavilion had an interior colonnade supported on eight columns above which rose the drum with eight oculi and a dome capped by a lantern on which posed the Este eagle of the cardinal's coat of arms. Within the building an ambulatory encircled the colonnade, and the balustrade that marked the ambulatory on the outside was decorated with Este lilies on each corner of the octagon. In the interior, fountains played in niches set in the four diagonal sides of the octagon, offering a refreshing air when the cardinal dined there. The pavilion also served as a belvedere with a wonderful view out from the edge of the hill over the valley to the Pincian Hill beyond. In the private garden, the giardino segreto, at the cardinal's other villa at Tivoli, a smaller kiosk or

Roman gardens from at least the fifteenth century. In June and July 1461 several payments were made to stonecutters and carpenters for work building a new pavilion for Pope Pius II in the vineyard next to the Vatican Palace.[62] A little later in 1479 Cardinal Gonzaga remarked on the "tempio grande" in his urban garden at Rome, which he insisted must be left untouched by the gardener and which would seem most likely to have been some sort of a garden pavilion.[63]

Probably one of the most delightful dining pavilions, the dining loggia erected at the edge of the Tiber at the end of the garden of the Villa Farnesina, had unfortunately a very short life, being seriously damaged by a flood in 1530, and thus leaving as evidence only the limited descriptions in the Latin poems of Gallo (late 1511) and Palladio (1512).[64] An open ar-

[62] E. Müntz, *Les arts à la cour des papes pendant le XVᵉ et le XVIᵉ siècles*, pt. I, Paris, 1878, p. 276.

[63] D. S. Chambers, "The Housing Problems of Cardinal Francesco Gonzaga," *Journal of the Warburg and Courtauld Institutes*, XXXIX, 1976, p. 57.

[64] Frommel, *Die Farnesina und Peruzzis architektonisches*

*Frühwerk*, pp. 32–33, 42–43, and D. R. Coffin, *The Villa in the Life of Renaissance Rome*, Princeton, N.J., 1979, pp. 96–97.

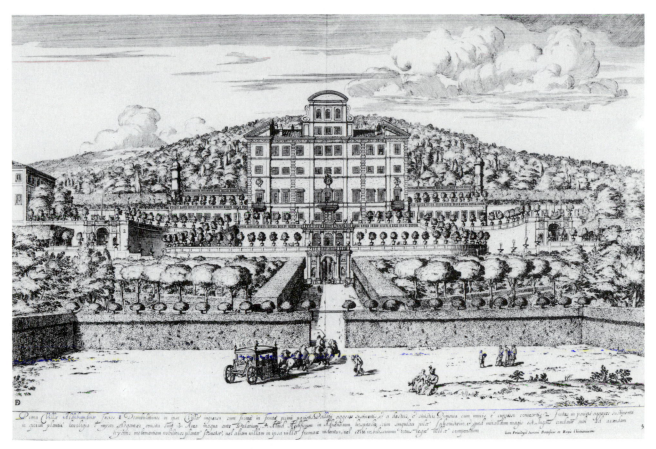

158. Frascati, Villa Aldobrandini, 1647

pavilion stood in its center as barely visible in the engraving of 1573 (Fig. 66). Created in 1565–1566,[65] the Janus-arched pavilion resembled the domed crossing of a cross pergola with its crossarms removed. Fountains stood in the four corners of the mosaic pavement that lined the interior.

A totally different type of garden pavilion is found at the Villa Lante at Bagnaia in the two so-called Houses of the Muses (Mansiones Musarum) at the top of the formal garden flanking the Fountain of the Deluge. Each of the miniature rectangular houses (Fig. 160) has a tiny room at the rear lit by a small window on the side of the Fountain of the Deluge and a larger front portico open toward the facade by a Palladian motif or an arch flanked by colonnaded openings. While the two identical pavilions may be used for recreation, their main purpose is to further the iconographic program of the garden by representing the twin peaks of Mount Parnassus between which poured forth the Ovidian deluge.

[65] Coffin, *The Villa d'Este*, pp. 36–37.

The only characteristic that pavilions in sixteenth-century Roman gardens have in common is variety. The range of different types they present is controlled generally by the different functions they satisfy.

The most important seventeenth-century Roman location for garden pavilions or dining loggias was Cardinal Scipione Borghese's garden palace on the Quirinal Hill across the Via Pia from the papal villa.[66] Begun in 1611 for the cardinal as a summer residence near the papal villa then inhabited by his uncle, Pope Paul V, the incomplete palace was sold in 1616 to Duke Altemps, as the cardinal began to center all his attention on his Villa Borghese just outside the Porta Pinciana. Owned later by the Rospigliosi family and now by the Pallavicini, the garden palace survives with many changes and some destruction. Laid out originally as a series of rather independent gardens set

[66] H. Hibbard, "Scipione Borghese's Garden Palace on the Quirinal," *Journal of the Society of Architectural Historians*, XXIII, 1964, pp. 163–92, with later slight revisions in H. Hibbard, *Carlo Maderno and Roman Architecture 1580–1630*, University Park, Penn., and London, 1971, pp. 193–94.

159. Rome, Villa d'Este, garden pavilion, view and section, engraving

at different levels, the complex once included three garden pavilions or dining loggias. One, the Casino of Psyche, built in 1611, probably after the design of the Florentine artist Cigoli, stood in the lower garden, but was destroyed in the nineteenth century. The interior was decorated by Cigoli with frescoes depicting the story of Psyche, which have been preserved in the Museo di Roma. At the same time a larger recreational loggia, the Casino of the Muses, was erected at one side of a garden area where later in 1611 and 1612 was created a large water basin and a theater of waterworks. The casino, whose name came from the interior frescoes depicting the Muses by the artists Agostino Tassi and Orazio Gentileschi, was probably designed by the Borghese architect Flaminio Ponzio as a freestanding loggia opening onto the garden by three arches supported on coupled columns. The most imposing garden pavilion of the Borghese gardens is the Casino of Aurora (Fig. 161), so-called from the famous painting of Aurora by Guido Reni decorating the vault of the central loggia. The casino dominates the west end of the upper or so-called hanging garden near the entrance to the grounds. Be-

160. Bagnaia, Villa Lante, House of the Muses

161. Rome, Villa Borghese-Pallavicini, Casino of Aurora

gun early in 1612, the casino, based on ideas of either Carlo Maderno or Cigoli, was executed with changes under the direction of Vasanzio. The casino consists of three rooms with the large central loggia opening onto the garden by a tripartite Palladian motif flanked by two enclosed rooms which project to protect the open center. Large pilasters separate the three components of the Palladian motif with freestanding marble columns supporting the side colonnades and freestanding colorful columns of *rosso antico* bearing the central arch. Quoins mark the corners of the projecting end bays and relief sculpture on the walls presents a decorative gay face to the garden appropriate to its principal function as a recreational retreat for dining, music, and conversation.

Giovanni Vasanzio, who succeeded Ponzio as the Borghese architect and had carried out the building of the Casino of Aurora, was soon called on by Cardinal Borghese to make garden additions at the Villa Mon-

dragone at Frascati, which the cardinal acquired late in 1613.[67] From 1616 to 1618 Vasanzio, with the aid of Giovanni Fontana for the waterworks, laid out on the east side of the villa a new large garden to replace the smaller private one created there earlier for Pope Gregory XIII. At the south end of the garden an elaborate water theater (Fig. 39) was created of the type erected just earlier for the cardinal in his gardens on the Quirinal. Closing the garden at Frascati at its northern end opposite the water theater was a large arcaded portico or loggia, five bays long, and each bay had an arch supported by freestanding Ionic columns as if compressed Palladian motifs (Fig. 162). The bays are separated by Ionic pilasters whose shafts are covered with very regular, smooth blocks of *bugnato*. Like the Casino of Aurora in Rome, it is a very decorative architecture with garlands hanging be-

67 A. T. Mignosi et al., *Villa e paese*, Rome, 1980, pp. 109–13.

162. Frascati, Villa Mondragone, portico

tween the Ionic volutes and Borghese eagles carved in relief on the spandrels of the arches. The portico lacks the precise structural expression one senses in the facade of the Casino of Aurora and is more chaotic in its contrast of surface movement and light and shade. Although the Latin inscriptions adorning the interior of the portico suggest that the garden is the equal of the ancient Garden of the Hesperides or the classical valley of Tempe, offering relaxation from the cares of the world, the portico no longer offers the pleasure of a secluded retreat for entertainment, but is rather the necessary monumental foil to the tempestuous water theater at the other end.

In 1741, however, when Pope Benedict XIV commissioned the architect Ferdinando Fuga to design a pavilion for his garden on the Quirinal Hill (Fig. 163), Fuga took as his model the early seventeenth-century

163. Rome, Quirinal Palace, coffeehouse

164. G. P. Pannini, *Reception of King Carlo III of Naples by Pope Benedict XIV*, Museo di Capodimonte, Naples

Casino of Aurora (Fig. 161) which stood nearby across the Via Pia in the former gardens of Cardinal Scipione Borghese.[68] The account of the commencement of the building on July 14, 1741, describes the structure as "a closed portico or rooms in the English mode called in that language a Coffeehouse [Caffeeaus] with seats and sofas on the interior." The Englishman Northall, who visited the Quirinal in 1752, made the amusing comment that the pavilion has been furnished "after the English taste, even to the hearth brush, and bellows, which are English commodities; and his holiness has given it the name of 'The Coffee-house.' "[69] Although the layout of the

building and its massing in terms of an open loggia between two protruding bodies is similar to the Borghese pavilion, the detailing and spatial expression are completely different. The central loggia is very shallow and is not very expressive of an interior chamber, but is rather just a corridor between the two end rooms. The exterior detailing is very sober and precise, lacking any of the sense of gaiety and rich decorativeness expressed in the earlier Borghese pavilion. Only the interiors of the two side rooms, decorated by a group of painters including Ghezzi, Batoni, and Pannini, suggest the rococo spirit of early eighteenth-century art. In the earlier Casino of Aurora (Fig. 161), the Palladian motif of an arched bay flanked by lintels helped centralize the facade composition, unifying somewhat the open bays of the loggia and even the protruding end bays. At the Quirinal casino the emphasis is on the repeat of identical in-

[68] G. Matthiae, *Ferdinando Fuga e la sua opera romana*, Rome, n.d., pp. 39, 78; R. Pane, *Ferdinando Fuga*, Naples, 1956, pp. 94, 127–28; G. Briganti, *Il Palazzo del Quirinale*, Rome, 1962, pp. 62–65, 81–82; and F. Borsi in *Il Palazzo del Quirinale*, Rome, 1974, p. 134.

[69] J. Northall, *Travels through Italy*, London, 1766, p. 161.

dependent bays in the manner of sixteenth-century architecture. The very staid and decorous exterior style of the architecture is perhaps meant to express the dignity of the position of the owner. The official notification of the laying of the cornerstone by the pope on August 1, 1741, describes the building as "a portico with some rooms most adaptable to benefit with air those private audiences and business meetings in which for the help of the Holy Seat and of the public His Holiness is all the time and even now occupied untiringly."

The decoration of the interior of the Coffeehouse was scarcely completed when Pope Benedict used it as the setting for his reception of King Carlo III of Naples on November 3, 1744. There the pope welcomed the king as his liberator because of the king's temporary victory at Velletri in August over the Austrian troops. The artist G. P. Pannini, who had contributed two large paintings of *vedute* of Benedict's Rome for the decoration of the left or west room of the Coffeehouse, painted presumably for the king the scene of him being received on the terrace in front of the pavilion (Fig. 164). Pannini apparently did not care for

the taut, linear quality of Fuga's architecture and loosened the architectural style by inaccurately doubling the pilasters and the sculpted busts set above the pedestals and introducing five instead of three triglyphs over each arch. Almost thirty years later in March 1772 the pavilion would also be the location of a very private meeting of Pope Clement XIV with the duke of Gloucester, brother of King George III of England.[70] According to Cardinal Bernis, the meeting was part of the pope's policy to meet Protestant princes so that he might encourage them to greater tolerance for their Catholic subjects. Bernis describes the first twenty-minute meeting on March 9 as the pope recounted it to him: "He [the pope] had him sit in the pavilion of his garden opposite him on an armchair, but lower than that which he [the pope] occupied. He did not wish the masters of ceremonies to meddle in this audience, so that no one was witness of what took place the doors were closed and the curtains of the windows drawn."

Over the centuries the use of the papal gardens has remained basically unchanged when one recalls how Pope Pius II in his autobiography described in the middle of the fifteenth century holding audiences for ambassadors in his private gardens at the Vatican. Only the architectural style of the garden pavilion has changed.

[70] A. Theiner, *Histoire du pontificat de Clément XIV*, trans. P. de Geslin, Paris, 1852, II, pp. 155–56, and H. Walpole, *Horace Walpole's Correspondence*, ed. W. S. Lewis, XXIII, New Haven, Conn., 1967, pp. 388–89.

# CHAPTER 11

# *Flora et Pomona*

The architecture of old gardens—the terraces, stairs, and walls—preserves their basic structure, as the carved pieces of fountains and statuary, if still in place, may conserve some of the charms of the setting, but the essence of a garden was its horticulture, its living plants, which gave color, form, and fragrance to it. Unfortunately the existence of the plants, shrubs, and most of the trees, except the largest, was very ephemeral, a life that lasted often only a season or even a few days. The garden and building accounts that help date the architecture and sculpture and frequently identify their designers offer very limited information on the horticulture, generally using generic terms such as plants or seeds. There are, however, a few descriptions of gardening lists that aid the necessary determination of what was or might be planted in the gardens of Rome.

The most prevalent horticultural feature of Roman gardens during the Renaissance were the *spalliere*, the trees, shrubs, or vines trained to cover walls or trellises, often for ornament, but also to encourage early blooming or to give protection from the wind. The term spalliere could also include hedges, more often called *siepi*, which were frequently trained on fences or palisades. An undated document, preserved from the period 1572 to 1586 when Cardinal Luigi d'Este possessed the Villa d'Este at Tivoli, lists the plants, shrubs, and trees best suited for growing there in different capacities, including spalliere.[1] The first group on the list are evergreens appropriate for groves (boschetti) or hedges (siepi), including holly, box, pyramidal cypress, juniper, holm oak, laurel, cherry lau-

rel, mastic, privet or buckthorn, and myrtle of several types. The low growing evergreens for the hedges of parterres or compartments are hyssop, lavender, rosemary, privet, daphne, and ruscus hypoglossum. For other hedges laurustinus and privet may be used. Plants that can be found in gardens but, according to the list, are not suitable for espaliers or compartments are aloe, belladonna, the Indian fig, and the Indian yucca. The writer adds that all types of Seville or bitter oranges and lemons are good to make groves and hedges in temperate locations, pointing out that in the garden of Carlo Pio there are some forty-four different types, but the writer warns that no type of jasmine is appropriate at Tivoli. The remainder of the document continues with detailed recommendations for plantings at specific locations in the garden at Tivoli.

The anonymous written project for the gardens at Tivoli, perhaps written by their architect Pirro Ligorio sometime before 1568, adds a few other shrubs and trees: arbutus, honeysuckle, pines, and firs to be in the espaliered labyrinths and citron, pomegranates, and oleanders espaliered on several of the walls.[2] Certainly the plants listed in the two accounts for Tivoli would have been used in other gardens in Rome and Latium. It is also likely that the plants recorded by the Florentine horticultural writer Soderini at the end of the sixteenth century would have been suitable for Roman gardens, so he offers a large list of plants for the creation of low hedges (*spallierette basse*), many of which are herbs not in the Tiburtine lists: common and garden thyme, hyssop, calamint, pen-

[1] See Appendix I.

[2] D. R. Coffin, *The Villa d'Este at Tivoli*, Princeton, N.J., 1960, pp. 143–44.

nyroyal, avocado pears, marjoram, rosemary, lavender, sage, violets, lavender cotton or santolina cha-
maecyparissus.[3]

Early in the next century, probably about 1615,
Vincenzo Giustiniani, who had just completed a
lovely villa and gardens at Bassano di Sutri north of
Rome, wrote a friend an extensive account of how
one should pursue such building and gardening. The
plants he advises for spalliere in a chilly climate where
there is the threat of frost and snow are juniper, box,
royal laurel, arbutus, and perhaps common laurel or
laurustinus. In a hot, dry location the citrus plants are
desirable.[4]

The role of boxwood as a plant suitable for hedges
seems to have been rather debatable, with contradictory information coming both from garden accounts
and garden theorists. The treatise by Girolamo Fiorenzuola, written in the mid-sixteenth century, but
not published until recently, advised against using
only box because of its odor.[5] If box is to be used, he
recommends that myrtle, because of its fragrance and
color, be interspersed with it. He prefers for hedges
the citrus fruits, the *agrumi*, or other perfumed plants.
Similarly Soderini in a treatise at the end of the century mentions "box planted densely and thickly as
hedges, or laurustinus, myrtle, rosemary, rosebushes,
holly and similar plants, but among these boxwood is
seriously injured and drenched particularly by the
drizzle which comes from the seashore. In places
more exposed to the sun there could be used Spanish
myrtle and of these the Catalonian types."[6] Soderini's
warning of the ill effect of the seashore atmosphere
on boxwood, which does not seem particularly appropriate to the experience of a Florentine horticul-
turist, may be derived from Pliny the Younger's comment on the box hedge at his Laurentine villa set on
the seashore (*Letters*, II, 17). Nevertheless, the inventory of plants in 1588 at the Villa Lante at Bagnaia
lists "low hedges" (*spaglierette*) of box on the slope
behind the lower formal garden, although the com-

165. Tivoli, Villa d'Este, drawing for compartments of
giardino segreto, Archivio di Stato, Modena

partments of the parterre itself had edging of laurustinus.[7]

Myrtle and laurustinus frequently served for
hedges or edging in Roman gardens. Boissard, who
visited Rome in the mid-sixteenth century, speaks of
myrtle and lemon hedges in the Belvedere Statue
Court at the Vatican, edging probably for the four
*praticelli* created by the gardener Lucerta in 1537,
and accounts of planting at the Villa d'Este at Tivoli,
in the project written before 1568 and in Del Re's description of 1611, mention both myrtle and laurustinus hedges.[8] A drawing for the replanting in the late
seventeenth century of the giardino segreto at Tivoli
(Fig. 165) has myrtle hedges enclosing the compart-

[3] G. V. Soderini, *Il trattato della cultura degli orti e giardini* (Le
opere di Gio. Vettorio Soderini, II), ed. A. B. della Lega, Bologna,
p. 14.

[4] G. Bottari and S. Ticozzi, *Raccolta di lettere sulla pittura, scultura ed architettura*, VI, Milan, 1822, pp. 99–120; translated in
M. L. Simo, "Vincenzo Giustiniani: His Villa at Bassano di Sutri,
near Rome, and His 'Instructions to a Builder and Gardener,'"
*Journal of Garden History*, I, 1981, pp. 253–70.

[5] A. Tagliolini, "Girolamo Fiorenzuola ed il giardino nelle fonti
della metà del '500," in *Il giardino storico italiano*, ed. G. Ragionieri, Florence, 1981, p. 301.

[6] G. V. Soderini, *I due trattati dell'agricoltura e della coltivazione
delle viti*, ed. A. B. della Lega, Bologna, 1902, p. 251.

[7] See C. Lazzaro, *The Italian Renaissance Garden*, New Haven,
Conn. and London, 1990, pp. 328–32.

[8] J. J. Boissard, *Romanae Vrbis Topographiae*, Frankfort, 1597,
I, p. 12. For the 1637 planting, see L. Dorez, *La cour du Pape Paul
III*, Paris, 1932, II, p. 124. The Tiburtine accounts are in Coffin,
*The Villa d'Este*, p. 143, and A. Del Re, *Dell'antichità tiburtine
capitolo V*, Rome, 1611, pp. 64, 70.

ments between pedestals bearing vases and similar hedges outlining ovals and circles within the compartments with instruction that the myrtle hedges are not to be permitted to grow higher than three-quarters of a palmo (ca. 17 centimeters).[9]

G. B. Ferrari in his treatise on flowers of 1633 says that a garden should not be enclosed by boxwood or any of the evergreens, but rather with thorn bushes, which are "hardier and less expensive," and the garden accounts often confirm this use.[10] So in March 1536 the gardener Lucerta at the Vatican was paid for furnishing "thorn bushes and the work to set the hedge of the Via di Belvedere," and in 1560 and 1561 there are several payments for thorn bushes for hedges in the Cardinal of Ferrara's garden on the Quirinal Hill, one payment on June 5, 1560, being made, in fact, to a man identified as a *spinarolo* or specialist in procuring thorn bushes. Later in 1582 eighteen bundles of thorn bushes and 250 stakes were supplied by another spinarolo to make a hedge in the kitchen garden (*orto*) for the cardinal in his garden at Tivoli. In the seventeenth century a spinarolo Loreto will for almost two years, from December 1644 to July 1646, repeatedly supply thorn plants, specified as *spine arabbiate* and *spini brugnoli*, for planting the new gardens at the Villa Pamphili.

In 1633 Ferrari admits that the "old art" of edging parterres or compartments with fetid boxwood and similar plants was not yet completely out of date, although it remained a troublesome habit. Because they had to be so frequently tonsured and ran to wood readily so that they had to be repeatedly renewed,[11] he recommended the "rather new invention" of pianelle or edging bricks.

Almost everyone agreed, however, that boxwood was preferable for topiary work. There they had the authority of the ancient Romans. Pliny the Elder (*Historia Naturalis*, XVI, xxviii) had remarked on how valuable the box was for ornamental gardening (*topiario opere*), and his nephew, Pliny the Younger, described the garden of his Tuscan villa (*Letters*, V, 6) as having "box cut in the form of beasts facing each other" and in another location box "cut into a thousand different forms, sometimes into letters, which spell the name of the master or that of the creator." So when Colonna in his mid-fifteenth-century romance, the *Hypnerotomachia Poliphili*, describes a fantastic piece of topiary of a man balancing on his hands two towers, he claims that it was cut of boxwood, and at the end of the century Grapaldi in his treatise on the house asserts that boxwood "is worthy of praise for topiary work."[12] Myrtle, however, also had its supporters, if the climate was suitable. When G. B. Sanga offers advice in 1524 for replanting a garden, he advises for topiary "to plant myrtle trees, but if they do not grow because of the cold put boxwood in their place."[13] Soderini, who as the writer of a general treatise is, as usual, more flexible when he says that "this art, which the ancients called topiary (forming statues, figures, colossi, obelisks and similar fantasies, from boxwood and Spanish myrtle and French rosemary which are so very obedient to the shears) is no longer favored."[14]

For the wall espaliers of Roman gardens the citrus trees and pomegranates were certainly the predominant plants. Boissard during his visit to Rome in the middle of the sixteenth century describes the walls of the Quirinal villa of the Cardinal of Ferrara as "hidden under pomegranates, oranges, citrons, and lemons in the manner of tapestries," and at the same time records that the walls of Cardinal Du Bellay's garden are planted with pomegranates, oranges, citrons, cypress, myrtle, and laurel "like a coverlet."[15] Later Soderini will recall seeing the walls of the papal villa on the Quirinal, formerly that of the Cardinal of Ferrara, espaliered with laurustinus, *perploca*, and jasmine, although the list of recommended plants for the cardinal's villa at Tivoli warned that jasmine was not suitable at Tivoli.[16] There it was planned to espalier the walls around the Fountain of Tivoli with oranges and citrons, pomegranates along the wall lining the rear of the Cardinal's Walk, and pomegranates and oleanders on the walls of the giardino segreto

---

[9] Coffin, *Villa d'Este*, p. 177.

[10] G. B. Ferrari, *Flora, seu de florum cultura*, new ed., Amsterdam, 1646, p. 19. For garden accounts, see Dorez, *La cour du Pape Paul III*, p. 36; ASM, Camera Ducale, Amministrazione dei Principi, Registro 957, fol. 58v, June 5, 1560, fol. 71, October 9, 1560, and fol. 76, November 23, 1560; Registro 958, fol. 23, March 23, 1561, and fol. 25, April 5, 1561; and Registro 1320, fol. 35, December 31, 1582; and J. Garms, *Quellen aus dem Archiv Doria-Pamphilj sur Kunsttätigkeit in Rom unter Innocenz X* (Quellenschriften zur Geschichte der Barockkunst in Rom, 4), Rome and Vienna, 1972, p. 205, no. 998; p. 216, no. 1053; and p. 226, nos. 1092, 1095.

[11] Ferrari, *Flora*, p. 39.

[12] F. Colonna, *Hypnerotomachia Poliphili*, ed. G. Pozzi and L. A. Ciapponi, Padua, 1980, I, pp. 296–97, and F. M. Grapaldi, *De Partibus Aedium*, Parma, 1516 (first edition probably in 1494).

[13] D. Atanagi, *De le lettere facete et piacevoli di diversi grandi huomi, et chiari ingegni*, Venice, 1561, p. 214.

[14] G. V. Soderini, *Il trattato degli arbori* (Le opere di Giov. Vettorio Soderini, III), ed. A. B. della Lega, Bologna, 1904.

[15] Boissard, *Romanae Vrbis Topographiae*, I, pp. 90, 94.

[16] Soderini, *Arbori*, p. 245.

where the French visitor Audebert saw later in 1576–1577 pomegranates, citrons, and oranges.[17]

Such espaliers, particularly the citrus trees, would require protection during the cold season so that in November 1560 there is a payment for the "forked branches [*forcini*] which have been cut at Pantano di Gripta to cover the bitter-orange trees of the new garden of Monte Cavallo," the Cardinal of Ferrara's villa on the Quirinal Hill, and in January 1561 three bundles of "cartica" were purchased for the same trees.[18]

The basic principle of Renaissance garden design was, of course, regularity in which symmetry and repetition were essential, but this orderly approach, especially in a large garden with constant repetition, could often run the risk of dullness and monotony. Although statuary in the garden might alleviate the danger, it was the variety of the planting that particularly enlivened the design. In the proposed planting for the Villa d'Este at Tivoli or the actual planting in the Villa Borghese almost a century later, it is obvious that a very conscious choice of different and even contrasting plants was to achieve some variety.[19] At Tivoli each of the four identical labyrinths flanking the central parterre with the cross pergola was to be planted differently: orange trees with a hedge of myrtle; arbutus with a hedge of honeysuckle; pines with a hedge of laurustinus; and firs with a hedge of privet. At the Villa Borghese the planting of the alleys differed: the wider alleys were accented by an alternation of cypresses and elms, whereas the narrow alleys were planted with holm oaks. The compartments of groves at the left of the main entrance alley were composed of pines contrasted with firs at the right. The two giardini segreti flanking the casino also had different planting patterns: the southern garden had a bitter-orange tree grove of 144 trees ordered in twenty-four rows, whereas the northern garden was divided into ten flower beds outlined with myrtle hedges and accented by six bitter-orange trees in each bed at whose feet grew tulips, anemones, jonquils, and hyacinths.

The two huge giardini segreti attached to the rear sides of the pentagonal Farnese Palace at Caprarola in the last quarter of the sixteenth century offered different designs and plant material, although both still preserved the traditional basic quartered design of a giardino segreto (Fig. 166). Here, however, the differences between the two gardens were not only occasioned by an aesthetic desire for variety, but were to meet differing seasonal functions. The summer garden at the north had a large circular opening at the center of the cross alleys, promoting a feeling of broad open expanse suitable for warm weather.[20] Each quarter of the garden was divided into nine smaller flowerbeds, principally planted with rosebushes appropriate to Venus, the subject of the major fountain. If one can believe the poetic description of Ameto Orti, who may rather be pursuing the traditional classic literary device of a "flower garland," a variety of other colorful flowers, including lilies, marigolds, violets, and narcissi, augmented the roses. The winter garden at the west, on the other hand, was traversed by a single, long pergola from its entrance stretching back toward the rear, all to offer protection in windy weather, as there was also a sheltered, terraced walkway across the rear of the garden. Here Orti in his Latin poem only emphasizes the orange, pomegranate, and citron fruit trees.

## Trees

In Roman Renaissance gardens trees were a vital element, primarily because of their shade, but also for color and fragrance, and even to provide homes and traps for birds and other small game, which the Romans loved to pursue. Three types of trees, however, were notable in Roman gardening and landscaping, and received the most comment: two shade trees, the plane tree (*platano*) and the elm (*olmo*), and one ornamental tree, the bitter- or Seville-orange tree (*melangolo*).

The plane tree had always been held in great admiration by the ancient Romans. Pliny the Elder (*Historia Naturalis* XII, iii–iv) discoursed at length on how the plane tree was imported into Italy merely for the magnificent shade it offered. In fact, he claims that it was held in such esteem by the Romans that they poured wine on its roots to encourage growth. He then records some of the most notable examples of the plane tree in antiquity whose fame accrued from their tremendous size, including one in the walks of

[17] Coffin, *The Villa d'Este*, p. 144, and R. W. Lightbown, "Nicolas Audebert and the Villa d'Este," *Journal of the Warburg and Courtauld Institutes*, XXVII, 1964, p. 189.

[18] ASM, Camera Ducale, Amministrazione dei Principi, Registro 957, fol. 76 and Registro 958, fol. 13v.

[19] Coffin, *The Villa d'Este*, p. 143, and J. Manilli, *Villa Borghese fuori di Porta Pinciana*, Rome, 1650.

[20] L. Gambara, *Caprarola*, Rome, 1581; F. Baumgart, "La Caprarola di Ameto Orti," *Studj romanzi*, XXV, 1935, pp. 77–179; and J.A.F. Orbaan, *Documenti sul barocco in Roma*, Rome, 1920, pp. 365–472.

166. Bagnaia, Villa Lante, fresco of Farnese Palace, Caprarola

Plato's Academy at Athens and two, one in Lycia and the other at Velletri in Italy, so large that banquets for fifteen to eighteen guests were held in the tree branches. With this classical background it is understandable that the Renaissance also admired the plane tree. Soderini at the end of the sixteenth century recounts at length in his treatise on arboriculture not only Pliny's notices, but those of other ancient authors, such as Pausanias and Theophrastus, and many contemporary wonders.[21]

Grapaldi, when he considers the garden in his treatise on the nomenclature of parts of the ancient house, first published probably in 1494, recalls that Pliny the Younger in the description of his Tuscan villa (*Letters*, V, 6) has a garden in the form of a hippodrome encircled by plane trees.[22] Grapaldi then adds that the "plane tree is now almost unknown in Italy." About the same time the humanist Ermolao Barbaro, who died in 1493, in his commentary on Dioscurides, published later, noted that the plane tree was rare in Italy, but that it was visible at Rome and in the village of Fogia near Bassano in the Veneto.[23] Lorenzo de' Medici, who died in 1492, had in the gardens of the Villa Careggi outside of Florence unusual specimens of trees, herbs, and other plants, and Alessandro Bracci in his poetic description of the gardens at the end of the century claims that there was a "plane tree so rich with broad branches which cover the ground with vast shade."[24]

By the second quarter of the sixteenth century more sightings of plane trees in Rome and its vicinity were noted. So in August 1534 the French writer François Rabelais reported to his master Cardinal Du Bellay that "we saw a single plane tree at Lake Nemi," and later the French naturalist Pierre Belon, having visited Rome in 1546 and 1549 during his travels in the Near East, commented on the very tall plane trees he had seen in Asia Minor, which were not to be seen in France or Italy "except for some cultivated at Rome and other cities for their unusualness."[25] Another French scholar, Guillaume Philandrier, the commentator on the treatise on architecture by the ancient Roman Vitruvius, identifies the location of some of the plane trees in Rome in his book written at least by 1541. After mentioning the famous plane trees in the ancient Academy at Athens, Philandrier adds "we have seen many not without pleasure in the vigna of Cardinal Salviati at Rome and at other places," and slightly later the Spanish doctor-botanist Andres de Laguna in his commentary on Dioscurides also claims to have seen them "in the vigna in the Trastevere of the Very Reverend Cardinal Salviati."[26]

The Sienese architect Cataneo in his architectural treatise published in 1554 lists the trees prized by antiquity, including the holm oak, laurel, olive, myrtle, and white poplar, "but the plane tree was not only prized by all, but even worshiped," adding, "today there are some in Florence in many gardens, as also in Rome."[27]

After the middle of the sixteenth century plane trees appear quite commonly in the great gardens of Latium, although their planting indicates the deep respect with which they were held. Sometimes it was the particular use of plane trees in antiquity that governed their use in the Renaissance, as was seen previously at the Villa Giulia where four plane trees were planted on the second level of the nymphaeum around the sunken fountain (Fig. 62) in emulation of a court in Pliny the Younger's Tuscan villa.[28]

In the project for the planting of the Villa d'Este at Tivoli the open piazza before the Fountain of Tivoli was to be shaded by ten plane trees.[29] As there were also to be statues of ten water nymphs to decorate the rear arcade of the fountain (Fig. 40), the number of trees was probably chosen to relate to the number of water nymphs, for it appears that, plane trees were particularly associated with water during the Renaissance. If this were true, the significance of the numbers was soon lost as both Zappi in 1576 and Del Re in 1611 identify fourteen plane trees in the piazza of the fountain. Zappi also asserts that twenty plane

---

[21] Soderini, *Arbori*, pp. 568–72.

[22] F. M. Grapaldi, *De partibus Aedium*, Parma, 1516, fol. 31r.

[23] E. Barbaro, *In Dioscoridem Corollariorū libri quinque*, Cologne, 1530, fol. 10r.

[24] A. Bracci, *Alexandri Braccii Carmina*, ed. A. Perosa, Florence, 1943, p. 76.

[25] P. Delaunay, *L'aventureuse existence de Pierre Belon du Mans*, Paris, 1925, p. 92; see also P. Belon, *De neglecta Stirpium Cultura atque earum cognitione Libellus*, Antwerp, 1589, p. 51.

[26] G. Philandrier, *In Decem Libros M. Vitruuii Pollionis De Architectura* [Rome, 1544], p. 175, and A. de Laguna, *Pedacio Dioscurides Anazarbeo, Acera de la Materia Medicinal, y de los Venenos morteferos*, Salamanca, 1566, p. 66 [dedication dated 1555 at Antwerp].

[27] P. Cataneo, *I quattro primi libri di architettura*, Venice, 1554, fol. 30r.

[28] See Chapter 3, and D. R. Coffin, *The Villa in the Life of Renaissance Rome*, Princeton, N.J., 1979, p. 163.

[29] Coffin, *The Villa d'Este*, p. 144. For other and later planting of plane trees, see G. M. Zappi, *Annali e memorie di Tivoli di Giovanni Maria Zappi* (Studi e fonti per la storia della regione tiburtina), ed. V. Pacifici, Tivoli, 1920, pp. 57, 60, and Del Re, *Dell'antichità tiburtine capitolo V*, p. 46.

167. Bagnaia, Villa Lante, fresco of Barco at Caprarola

at nearby Caprarola where the account of his visit describes an artificial lake just created previously in the hunting park as being encircled with plane trees (Fig. 167).[31]

Plane trees are mentioned at several prominent locations in the 1650 description of the grounds of the Villa Borghese by its gardener Jacopo Manilli.[32] In the entrance garden or *primo recinto*, sixteen plane trees stood at the theatrical entrance piazza ranged in order behind the curved laurel hedges whose niches embraced statues. Pairs of plane trees also flanked the rustic fountain at the end of the principal entrance Alley of the Elms. Repeatedly during the sixteenth and seventeenth centuries, plane trees were planted in Roman gardens in association with water and fountains, as seen in the nymphaeum of the Villa Giulia, the Fountain of Tivoli, and the fishpool at the Villa d'Este at Tivoli, the "water chain" and Cardinal's Table at Bagnaia, and at the hunting park at Caprarola. So also in the park or *terzo recinto* at the Villa Borghese, a large artificial pond created as a sanctuary for water fowl was encircled (*coronato*), according to Manilli, by forty lovely plane trees. Two more large plane trees stood on each of two islands in the lake "as a pleasing refuge [*albergo*] for the water birds that sojourn there."

The elm tree during the sixteenth and seventeenth centuries was particularly notable in Roman gardens for defining alleys or creating windscreens. The tree was familiar as a public feature in the city since at least the Middle Ages, for documents of the fifteenth and sixteenth centuries still speak of the "Piazza degli Olmi," the "Contrada degli Olmi," or the "Strada dell'Olmo di Treio."[33] In the seventeenth century the elm tree was especially chosen to line, and thereby define, public ways. Paul V, who was concerned with public works in the Trastevere, in addition to building there the Acqua Paola with its aqueduct to Lake Bracciano, had planted by 1611 the Olmata or elm way between the churches of S. Francesco a Ripa and S. Callisto. Later threatened by destruction, it would be saved much later by Pope Alexander VII who pursued a much more extensive campaign of beautifying the city with elm-lined streets and ways.[34] By April 1656

trees mingled with a grove of elms near one of the large fishponds.

The doctor-botanist Durante in his herbal first published in 1585 claims in his article on the plane tree that "the most beautiful are to be seen today in the very lovely park of Bagnaia, that famous possession of the Most Illustrious and Magnanimous Lord Cardinal Gambara, my Lord."[30] The account of the visit of Pope Gregory XIII in 1578 then specifies that many very lovely plane trees shaded the middle terrace of the garden where was the cardinal's great outdoor dining table (Fig. 74), as well as on other levels. This is confirmed by the inventory of 1588 at the death of the cardinal, which also mentions that just above the level of the cardinal's table in the "Meadow" (Prato) or the slope with the "water chain" were five plane trees on each side of the "water chain." When Pope Gregory XIII visited Bagnaia in 1578 he also stopped

30 C. Durante, *Herbario nuovo di Castore Durante medico, et cittadino Romano*, Venice, 1636, p. 379. Other references to plane trees at Bagnaia are found in the description of Pope Gregory XIII's visit published in Orbaan, *Documenti*, p. 390, and in the inventory of 1588 in Lazzaro, *The Italian Renaissance Garden*, pp. 328–32.

31 Orbaan, *Documenti*, p. 367.

32 Manilli, *Villa Borghese*, pp. 5, 9, 165–66.

33 See, for example, P. Adinolfi, *Roma nell'età di mezzo*, Rome, 1881, II, pp. 99–102, and R. Lanciani, *Storia degli scavi di Roma*, III, Rome, 1907, pp. 200–3.

34 For Paul V, see A. Menichella, *San Francesco a Ripa*, Rome, 1981, p. 49, and for Alexander VII, R. Krautheimer, "Roma verde nel Seicento," in *Studi in onore di Giulio Carlo Argan*, Rome,

168. Rome, Elm Alley in the Forum, drawing attributed to Van Wittel, Gabinetto Nazionale delle Stampe, Rome

a new way or avenue lined on each side by double files of elm trees had been created running across the ancient Roman Forum from the Arch of Septimus Severus to the Arch of Titus (Fig. 168). The public purpose of the elm-sheltered way was to encourage those riding carriages to visit the numerous churches around the Forum on festive days and still have the side alleys available for pedestrians, a plan like the great colonnade Bernini would soon erect at St. Peter's for the same pope. The avenue in the Forum was, however, only a small, but prominent, portion of the pope's plan to beautify the city, which according to the plan's preliminary proposal would require about 5,500 trees, mainly elm, although mulberry trees were also used where suitable.

With the expansion of villa landscaping commencing in the mid-sixteenth century, elm-planted alleys were frequent in Roman gardens. As discussed previously, formal gardens played a minor role at the Villa

Giulia of Pope Julius III, but the vast expanse of grounds around the villa and into the Parioli hills was laced with walkways and alleys. The hundreds of elms and poplars that were purchased late in 1551 and early 1552 were undoubtedly to define these alleys.[35] The project in the 1560s for the planting of the Villa d'Este at Tivoli specified that the Cardinal's Alley, the walkway running across the top of the gardens just below the palace, where the cardinal was later to be seen exercising, was to be planted with elm trees for shade.[36] In 1576 Zappi described a wood of 270 elm trees between the labyrinths and the outer wall toward Rome, visible also in the 1573 engraving (Fig. 66) and presumably identified in the earlier written project simply as *Boschi* under the letter *I*. Zappi explains that this elm grove on the Roman side of the garden was to protect it from the "marine air." He also identifies a prominent alley running across the

1984, II, pp. 71–82, and R. Krautheimer, *The Rome of Alexander VII, 1655–1667*, Princeton, N.J., 1985, pp. 110–13, 186.

[35] Lanciani, *Storia degli scavi di Roma*, III, p. 16, and I. Belli Barsali, *Ville di Roma: Lazio I*, Milan, 1970, p. 56.
[36] Coffin, *The Villa d'Este*, pp. 143, 144, and Zappi, *Annali e memorie di Tivoli di Giovanni Maria Zappi*, pp. 57–58.

slope of the garden from the Fountain of the Owl and Birds to the church of S. Pietro as "covered by eighty elm trees 22 piedi [ca. 6.55 meters] distant from one another as is the width of this alley." Similarly at the Villa Lante at Bagnaia the inventory of 1588 records three prominent alleys of elms. One planted with 7 elm trees on each side led from town to the main gate entering the formal gardens; the other two alleys were in the park, both also planted with vines in the ancient Roman tradition of using elms as supports for vines. In the seventeenth century at the Villa Borghese, the major entrance alley proceeding across the entrance garden or *primo recinto* was defined by elm trees interspersed with columnar cypresses and was crossed by a similar alley of elms and cypresses leading to the casino.[37] Another broad alley lined by elm trees cut across most of the park or *terzo recinto*, commencing at a pine forest in the middle of the park and running through it, then through an area for bird trapping or a ragnaia, and finally through a holm oak wood to a rear entrance.

The bitter- or Seville-orange tree (*melangolo*), which was probably the most popular ornamental tree in Roman gardening, had a long history in Italy. Known to the ancient Romans, the tree was particularly propagated after the prolonged cultural contact with the Near East promoted by the Crusades. On the other hand, the sweet or Chinese orange, also known by the Italians as the Portuguese or Lisbon orange from their source for it, was a sixteenth-century import to Rome. Its relative rarity is indicated in the middle of the seventeenth century when G. B. Ferrari notes especially that sweet oranges or oranges of Lisbon had been sent "to the Pio and Barberini gardens."[38]

By at least the fifteenth century bitter-orange trees were common in secular gardens of Rome. A document of sale of a house in 1448 to Berardo Franciosi describes it as having a terrace and cloister or court with orange trees and in 1451 Cardinal Scarampo wrote to Onorato Caetani to ask for some orange trees (*pomeranzi*), if he had any, to plant in his garden at Rome.[39]

The most famous garden of orange trees in sixteenth-century Rome was the papal Statue Court of the Belvedere in the Vatican. The Venetian ambassador in 1523 described the court as "paved in squares of terracotta laid on edge and from each square of the paving issues a very lovely orange tree [*arancio*] of which there is quite a number arranged in perfect order."[40] This planting, of course, immediately prompted the antiquarian Andrea Fulvio in his *Antiqvaria Vrbis* (1513) and the writer Baldassare Castiglione in his poem *Cleopatra*, dedicated to a statue in the garden, to liken the garden to the ancient mythological Garden of the Hesperides.

Other prominent gardens throughout Rome in the first half of the sixteenth century were planted predominantly with orange trees. The private garden in the Castel Sant'Angelo prepared by Pope Leo X in honor of Bianca Rangone is described later by Trissino in his dialogue *Il Castellano* as "that lovely little garden of orange trees, which is above the river," or the cloister garden attached to the Palace of San Marco was planted with orange trees mingled with cypress and laurel according to the Venetian ambassador in 1523.[41] The large hortus conclusus created for Pope Paul III at the Vatican had an extensive planting of orange trees.

With the expansive gardens of the later sixteenth century, the smaller, more private gardens, the giardini segreti, near the habitation, were particularly embellished with orange trees as at the villa of the Cardinal of Ferrara on the Quirinal where there were several such enclosed, private gardens around the casino, of which the largest on the bastion behind the house was identified in an inventory of 1572 as the "private garden of orange trees."[42] The garden was created in 1560, for there are documents for the purchase of orange trees and for masonry at "the loggia of the garden of orange trees at the fountain of Monte

---

[37] Manilli, *Villa Borghese*, pp. 8–9, 12, 168.

[38] G. B. Ferrari, *Hesperides sive De Malorum Aureorum Cultura et Vsv Libri Quatuor*, Rome, 1646, p. 425. The Pio garden is presumably the old Silvestri-Medici garden behind the Basilica of Maxentius, which Cardinal Carlo Emanuele Pio of Savoy acquired in 1626. See the previous discussion, in this chapter, of the winter protection for the cardinal's orange trees.

[39] P. Adinolfi, *La Via Sacra o del Papa*, Rome, 1865, p. 80, and G. Caetani, ed., *Epistolarium Honorati Caietani*, Sanscasciano Val di Pesa, 1926, p. 8.

[40] E. Albèri, *Relazioni degli ambasciatori veneti al senato*, ser. 2, III, Florence, 1846, p. 115; see also H. H. Brummer, *The Statue Court in the Vatican Belvedere* (Stockholm Studies in the History of Art, 20), Stockholm, 1970.

[41] G. G. Trissino, *Il Castellano di Giangiorgio Trissino ed il Cesano di Claudio Tolomei*, ed. G. Antimaco, Milan, 1864, p. 7, and E. Albèri, *Relazioni degli ambasciatori veneti al senato*, ser. 2, III, Florence, 1846, p. 106. For the Paul III garden, see Dorez, *La cour du Pape Paul III*, II, pp. 148, 199, 296.

[42] C. Huelsen, "Römische Antikengärten des XVI Jahrhunderts," *Abhandlungen der Heidelberger Akademie der Wissenschaften: Philosophisch-Historische Klasse*, IV, 1917, p. 97; documents are in ASM, Camera Ducale, Amministrazione dei Principi, Registro 957, fols. 48v and 49v.

Cavallo." In smaller gardens, such as the urban one of Cardinal Orsini near S. Giacomo degli Incurabili, as we saw, the entire garden was dominated by orange trees with some 120 trees in the central parterres as well as groves near the entrance. Variety was introduced by an alley of apricot trees and cypress at the head of the garden and by having the walls espaliered with citron trees.

In the seventeenth century the orange tree remained equally, if not more, popular than before. So in a long memorandum to Cardinal Francesco Barberini of about 1627 generally attributed to his secretary Cassiano dal Pozzo, it is recommended that the open, sunny part of the main garden of the Barberini Palace should contain "the most noble plants, which much love the sun and the heat, and such are the orange trees [*melangoli*]."[43] So there were to be sixteen compartments each with 16 orange trees for a total of 256. Like the earlier Villa d'Este on the Quirinal, the wealth of orange trees that decorated the extensive grounds of the Villa Borghese were always kept closely associated with the buildings. The orange tree is in particular an ornamental plant that needs to relate to man-made objects and has nothing to do with the more rustic park areas. Manilli in his description of 1650 notes that the wine grotto near the house, which was also a location for outdoor dining, was flanked by 8 large orange trees and that the two private gardens flanking the casino were dominated by orange trees.[44] The southern garden was solely a garden of orange trees with 144 trees ordered in twenty-four files, whereas the northern garden was to exhibit rare, particularly bulbous, flowers, but also had orange trees as vertical accents within the flower beds. Even a minor outlying lodge for the porter set down within the edge of the park had its own small gardens, one of orange trees and the other of flowers.

A tree that was particularly remarked on by visitors because of its rarity in Rome was the palm tree. The eminent botanist Matthioli in his commentary on Dioscurides in 1550 claimed that "although in many, and even more, cities of Italy in the kitchen gardens, in the pleasure gardens, in the cloisters of friars, are seen palm trees . . . none of the palms produce fruit for us."[45] In Rome, however, even the trees seem to have been scarce and in the sixteenth century almost always limited to the gardens of monastic cloisters.

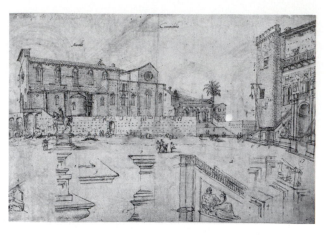

169. Rome, Capitoline Piazza with Fig Tree, drawing by Heemskerck, Herzog Anton Ulrich Museum, Brunswick

The German visitor Fichard noted in the account of his trip to Rome in 1536 that a palm tree grew in the garden of the monastery of Sta. Maria d'Aracoeli on the Capitoline Hill and a later anonymous drawing from after 1549 depicts the tree looming over the triple-arched loggia on the north side of the Capitoline piazza (Fig. 169).[46] Boissard, visiting Rome in the late 1550s, said that palm trees are seen many places in Rome, but in contradiction of Matthioli, the only ones that bear fruit are trees in the monastic gardens of Sta. Maria del Popolo and of Sta. Maria in Trastevere.[47] Another monastic cloister sheltering a palm tree was that of S. Francesco a Ripa in the Trastevere. Visible first on the Dupérac map of 1577, the tree apparently survived until the cold of 1689 killed it.[48] These palm trees in the monastic gardens were hidden away sufficiently to escape the notice of most tourists. So the Englishman Fynes Morison in 1594 claims to have seen a palm tree near the church of S. Alessio "whereof I remember not to have seene any other at Rome" and the anonymous Harleian account of about 1610 remarks at the church of S. Pietro in Vincoli that "without in the cloisters, it is very pleasant winter and summer, being planted with orange-trees and in the midst a mighty date-tree, like to which there are none found, neither in Rome, nor in all Italy."[49] A secular setting for palm trees was the Villa

[43] G. Magnanimi, *Palazzo Barberini*, Rome, 1983, Ms Barb. Lat. 4360, unpaginated.

[44] Manilli, *Villa Borghese*, pp. 22, 115, 117, 165.

[45] A. Matthioli, *Il Dioscuride*, Venice, 1550, p. 187.

[46] J. Fichard, "Italia," *Frankfurtisches Archiv für ältere deutsche Litteratur und Geschichte*, III, 1815, p. 31, and H. Egger, *Römische Veduten*, II, Vienna, 1931, p. 10 and pl. 3.

[47] Boissard, *Romanae Vrbis Topographiae*, I, p. 115.

[48] A. Menichella, *San Francesco a Ripa*, Rome, 1981, p. 117, and M. Escobar, *Le dimore romane dei santi*, Bologna, 1964, p. 68.

[49] F. Moryson, *An Itinerary*, Glasgow, 1907, I, p. 286, and "A True Description and Direction of what is most worthy to be seen

Borghese where Manilli notes in 1650 that in the small piazza before the porter's lodge were "two trees of the feminine palm which have between them a larger masculine tree of the same species."[50] The variety of tree planting at the Villa Borghese almost resembled that of an arboretum, for Manilli indicates that on the other side of the porter's lodge in another small square were "two large trees, one a sycamore [*sicomoro*] and the other a lignum vitae [*legno santo*]." Soon after this in the Falda prints, probably from the 1670s, depicting the sixteenth-century Casino Pio in the Vatican (Fig. 153), there appear a few palm trees in several of the formal, ornamental parterres before the casino.[51] As this is the location where much earlier Michele Mercati laid out a botanical garden, discussed later, these trees may be remainders from the old garden.

The association of palm trees with monastic locations persists into the nineteenth century when Mrs. Hinde in her travel journal in 1820 writes: "Drove to the Aventine Mount and from thence, at a Villa belonging to the King of Spain. . . . In the garden is the only one of the two Palm Trees which can be seen by a Woman, the other being in the Garden of a Convent of Monks where no Woman may enter, the Gardener has three seedlings he is endeavouring to raise. That mentioned in 'Corinne' near St. John Lateran is dead."[52] *Corinne* was a novel by Mme. de Stael, which claimed that only two palm trees were in Rome, both in monastic gardens.

### Fruit Trees

Many of the Roman villas had orchards of fruit trees along with their recreational gardens. These fruit trees were domestic trees, valued for their fruit as well as their flowers, and are not the more ornamental citrus fruits or *agrumi*. A letter dated 1578 from the Villa Rufina at Frascati relates that on the west side on terraces below the building (Fig. 170) were several gardens (*orti*) that were not ornamental, but furnished vegetables and fruit, one being planted with pear and apple trees.[53] So in December 1582 accounts

170. Frascati, Villa Rufina, detail from Greuter engraving, 1620

record the purchase of 75 fruit trees for the kitchen garden (*orto*) at the Villa d'Este at Tivoli and in January of the following year peach and plum trees were specified as among the different types of fruit trees planted there.[54] Early in 1585 more extensive planting of fruit trees, including peach, cherries, and pears, created orchards in the Barco or hunting park at Tivoli down in the plain near the river below the town and villa. One of these purchases involved 1,830 fruit trees. At Cardinal Chigi's Villa Versaglia north of Rome at Formello a separate fruit orchard (*pometo* or *pomaro*) was planted late in 1665 and early 1666 where were planted at least apple and mulberry trees.[55]

In some of the extensive parks, fruit trees were planted intermingled with shade trees. For example, at the Villa Giulia in November 1551 apricot trees were being brought for planting at the same time as numerous elm and poplar trees were sought, and in January 1552 it was noted that several of the alleys laid out in the park were lined with elm, chestnut, egriot, plum, pomegranate, and quince trees mingled with "forest

in all Italy," in *The Harleian Miscellany*, XII, London, 1811, p. 107.

[50] Manilli, *Villa Borghese*, pp. 16, 18.

[51] M. L. Gothein, *A History of Garden Art*, London and Toronto, 1928, I, p. 265.

[52] C. A. Hinde, *Journal of a Tour Made in Italy in the Winter of the Years 1819 and 1820*, ed. M. Merlini, Geneva, 1982, p. 63.

[53] A. T. Mignosi et al., *Villa e paese*, Rome, 1980, pp. 83–88;

A. Tanillo, "Un complesso di giardini romani tra '500 e '700: Le ville del Tuscolo. Storie di una immagine di paesaggio," in *Giardini italiani*, ed. M. L. Quondam and A. M. Racheli, Rome, 1981, pp. 54–55; and L. Devoti, *Campagna romana viva: Le ville tuscolane: La Villa Rufina-Falconieri*, Frascati, 1986, pp. 20–22.

[54] ASM, Camera Ducale, Amministrazione dei Principi, Registro 1320, fol. 35; for the Barco, see ASM, Casa Amministrazione, Registri del Card. Luigi d'Este, Pacco 182, Registro de mandati 1585, fols. 62r and 75r.

[55] V. Golzio, *Documenti artistici sul Seicento nell'Archivio Chigi*, Rome, 1939, p. 168, nos. 1620 and 1626; p. 169, nos. 1659 and 1680; p. 170, nos. 1717 and 1736; p. 171, nos. 1756 and 1832.

trees" (*arbori salvatichi*) and vines.[56] It was, however, in the grounds of the Villa Lante at Bagnaia that fruit trees were most abundantly planted both in the formal garden and along alleys and in groves of the park. The account of the visit of Pope Gregory XIII to the villa in 1578 describes the park, "which, as it is empty of animals, only retains the name of park [*barco*], being now an exceedingly beautiful and delightful garden with very lovely alleys covered by the shade of different sorts of trees, for the most part fruit-bearing, in addition to the groves, in part rustically produced by nature and in part planted with industry and art."[57] The inventory of 1588 offers the most complete picture of the intermingling of different fruit trees in the planting of the garden and the park. Even the formal parterre garden in front of the casino had eight different fruit trees within each of the twelve compartments hedged about by laurustinus (Fig. 70). Above at the back entrance at the left of the so-called street of Rome (*strada di Roma*) were two groves of pomegranates and quinces. Beyond the quinces were a series of oak and olive groves among which was a slope covered with peach trees. Beside the reservoir at the top of the park was a fig grove. In the park the inventory repeatedly speaks of avenues lined with various types of fruit trees. So on the alley to the Fountain of the Meadow was a plantation of peaches with below it one of plum trees "where in other times there was the labyrinth," which oddly is still depicted, although in an unusual diagrammatic presentation, on the 1596 engraving, suggesting an older source for the engraving. Finally below the Fountain of Pegasus near the entrance to the park was a plantation of apricots.

### Plant Procurement

From at least the sixteenth century on there is some evidence at Rome of a slowly evolving trade in plant material, occasioned probably by the development there of large pleasure gardens, but the evidence is meager. For five years from early 1561 one Rosso da Cassia was paid frequently by the Cardinal of Ferrara for supplying a great variety of plants and trees for the gardens of his two villas, one on the Quirinal Hill in Rome and the other in the nearby hill town of Tiv-

oli, and also for his palace in Rome.[58] Rosso furnished, among other plants, elm trees, myrtle, laurel, laurustinus, ivy, honeysuckle, jasmine, and periwinkle. Throughout 1568 there are numerous payments for plants to Giovanni Agnollo da Cassia, who is probably a relative of Rosso and may have succeeded him.[59] On June 5, 1560, as noted before, one Pandolfo, identified as a *spinarolo* or supplier of thorn bushes, was paid for work at the Quirinal.[60] Similarly the descriptive term *piantarolo* or plant seller appears in 1615 attached to the name of Tommaso, who supplied material to protect the orange trees at the papal villa on the Quirinal, formerly that of the Cardinal of Ferrara.[61]

By the middle of the seventeenth century in the accounts for planting the Villa Pamphili at Rome, Evangelista Cortegiano piantarolo provides from 1644 to 1646 a great variety of plants, including laurel, holm oak, bitter-orange and citron, myrtle, and fir trees.[62] Several payments in 1645 are to Arcangelo Corteggiano, presumably also a relative of Evangelista, as another account speaks of Evangelista Cortegiano "and companions, plant sellers" (*e compagni piantaroli*). Cortegiano is certainly not a nursery man, but an intermediary purchasing agent, as the accounts list various geographical sources for his material. So to obtain the fir trees necessary for the landscaping of the Villa Pamphili he brought trees from Sta. Sabina, Sta. Fiora, Piano Cartagnare, and a thousand from Tuscany. At the same time several other piantaroli, Parentio Carbone, Biagio di Leonardo, and Giovanni di Francesco, were filling smaller orders for the villa. Again there is a specialist in thorny plants, Loreto spinarolo, who furnished black thorn and other thorny plants.

As for the geographical sources of plant material for Roman gardens, the scant accounts available offer little in the way of any pattern. Certainly one of the sources of material was determined by personal relationships, so in 1552 the bishop of Tivoli sent Pope Julius III 270 pomegranate trees and 70 quince, while the Viceroy of Naples dispatched 50 vases of plants, for the Villa Giulia at Rome, and in 1561 the Cardinal of Ferrara sent back to his native city for plants,

---

[56] R. Lanciani, *Storia degli scavi di Roma*, III, p. 16.

[57] Orbaan, *Documenti*, p. 389. For the inventory of 1588, see Lazzaro, *The Italian Renaissance Garden*, pp. 328–32.

[58] The documents are in ASM, Camera Ducale, Amministrazione dei Principi, Registri 895, 897, 898, 958, 991, 993.

[59] Ibid., Registro 995.

[60] Ibid., Registro 957, fol. 58v.

[61] *Il Palazzo del Quirinale*, Rome, 1974, p. 252.

[62] All the Pamphili accounts are published in Garms, *Quellen*.

which were forwarded by way of Pesaro.[63] In August 1584 Cardinal Farnese requested the general of the monastery at Camaldoli to furnish "four hundred young fir trees for a grove" he wished to plant at his Barchetto or summer casino just built at Caprarola.[64] The request, of course, was granted, but he was informed that because of the heat he would have to wait until mid-October for the plants.

Naples was the major source of delicate plants. In 1537 Pope Paul III dispatched his head gardener to Naples to purchase 1,500 orange and citrus trees for his new garden at the Vatican, and in the next year the trip was repeated for more orange trees and myrtle.[65] Pope Julius III will similarly obtain from Naples in March 1555 30 peach trees for his villa among other unspecified plants from there, and in 1621 90 vases of potted orange trees will be forwarded by the papal nuncio from Naples to the Villa Ludovisi.[66]

Bitter-orange trees, being the most desirable ornamental trees, were sought all over Italy. In 1566 they came along with citron trees from Corneto for the Cardinal of Ferrara's villas, while by 1609 and 1611 one Don Pompeo Pietromenico was paid for hundreds of *melangoli* brought to the papal villa on the Quirinal from Gaeta.[67] To satisfy the needs of the Villa Pamphili the trees were brought in 1645 from Florence, Longara, and apparently Genoa, since at least 650 trees were supplied by one Luca Ranta of Genoa.[68] In some cases of native plants, however, expeditions were simply sent out to the natural woods along the shore, as one in 1554 for medlar trees and arbutus for the Villa Giulia.[69] In the case of purchase, there is very limited information in the accounts for the cost of plant material.[70]

[63] For the Villa Giulia, see Belli Barsali, *Ville di Roma*, p. 56, and for the Cardinal of Ferrara, see ASM, Camera Ducale, Amministrazione dei Principi, Registro 895, fol. 7v, December 30, 1561.

[64] S. Benedetti, *Giacomo Del Duca e l'architettura del Cinquecento*, Rome, 1972–1973, p. 484.

[65] Dorez, *La cour du Pape Paul III*, II, pp. 148, 161, 162, 189, 199.

[66] Belli Barsali, *Ville di Roma: Lazio I*, pp. 56–57, and A. Schiavo, *Villa Ludovisi e Palazzo Margherita*, Rome, 1981, p. 122.

[67] ASM, Camera Ducale, Amministrazione dei Principi, Registro 993, fol. 65, April 25, 1566; Registro 897, May 25, 1566; and Orbaan, *Documenti*, p. 303, June 3, 1609, and p. 307, May 28, 1611.

[68] J. Garms, *Quellen*, p. 201, no. 984; p. 205, no. 998; p. 226, no. 1092.

[69] Lanciani, *Storia degli scavi di Roma*, III, p. 16, and Belli Barsali, *Ville di Roma: Lazio I*, p. 57.

[70] See Appendix II.

## Flowers

It has been pointed out that flowers played a more consequential role in Italian gardens than was once considered.[71] It is, however, more difficult to identify the types of flowers used than for trees and shrubs. For one reason, in financial accounts the generic terms "seeds" or "bulbs" are commonly used without specifying their types. Also, many of the descriptions of gardens during the Renaissance were poetic and there was a strong literary tradition of "the flower garland," revived by the Renaissance from antiquity, which lists specific flowers in a poetic series conditioned by the verse and not reality in the case of an actual description.[72] So Blosio Palladio's poetic description of 1512 of the garden of Agostino Chigi at his villa, the later Farnesina, mentions apples and flowers, laurel, myrtle, boxwood, cypress, and citron trees with violets, roses, and lilies or Benedetto Lampridio's poem dedicated to the Villa Mellini on Monte Mario at Rome lists narcissi, lilies, pale crocuses, and ruddy violets, red spring roses, and "an abundance of yellow marigolds."[73] It is very probable that all these specific plants were there, but because of the poetic tradition one cannot be sure.

By 1524 G. B. Sanga, the former secretary of Cardinal Bibbiena, was recommending his friend Mentebuona to replant Bishop Giberti's garden not only with trees and topiary, but "with roses and all sorts of fragrant and beautiful flowers."[74] Roses, of course, remained as always one of the most favored flowers for gardening, as was noted earlier with Aretino's imaginative description of the courtesan Nanna's garden, where he listed the herbs, marjoram, mint, and pimpernel with the flowers, marigolds, and stocks, but was particularly enthused by the September roses (*rosa bifera*). So in the gardens of the Farnese Palace at Caprarola roses dominated the summer garden, although Orti's poetic description also mentions

[71] G. Masson, "Italian Flower Collectors' Gardens in Seventeenth Century Italy," in *The Italian Garden* (First Dumbarton Oaks Colloquium on the History of Landscape Architecture), ed. D. R. Coffin, Washington, D.C., 1972, pp. 63–64.

[72] C. Ruutz-Rees, "Flower Garlands of the Poets, Milton, Shakespeare, Spenser, Marot, Sannazaro," in *Mélanges offerts à M. Abel Lefranc*, Paris, 1936, pp. 75–90.

[73] I. Belli Barsali, *Baldassare Peruzzi e le ville senesi del Cinquecento*, S. Quirico d'Orcia, 1977, p. 131, and J. Gruter, *Delitiae CC Italorum Poetarum* [Frankfort], 1608, pt. 1, pp. 1311–29.

[74] D. Atanagi, *De le lettere facete et piacevoli di diversi grandi huomi, et chiari ingegni*, Venice, 1561, p. 214.

"snowy" white lilies, marigolds, violets, crocuses, purple hyacinths, and narcissi, and at least in 1578 a rose garden (*odora rosaria*) stood at the entrance to the Villa Rufina at Frascati (Fig. 170).[75]

The Cardinal of Ferrara incorporated flower beds and flower gardens in the extensive grounds of his villa on the Quirinal in Rome and in that at Tivoli. In April 1564 the cardinal complained to his brother, the duke of Ferrara: "I had given an order to Baletti to provide me with many narcissus bulbs and seeds of other flowers to use in my garden of Monte Cavallo. ... Now all of them have been stolen along with other household property."[76] At the Villa d'Este at Tivoli the project written in the late 1560s identifies two "compartments of simples" (*appartamenti di semplici*) as decorating the giardino segreto or private garden, and the engraving of 1573 (Fig. 66), which is derived from the drawing accompanying the earlier written project, labels the parterres in the quarters defined by the cross pergola as *Giardini delli Semplici*. The Italian word *semplici* or its English equivalent "simples" in most modern literature is equated with the English word herbs. This is a modern limitation of the old word, which included both flowers and herbs, following the mediaeval tradition that most flowers like herbs had medicinal or culinary values. Therefore, the Frenchman Audebert in his description of the gardens in 1576–1577 at one time speaks of "two flower parterre gardens and compartments" (*deux Jardins de Parterre a fleurs et compartments*) and later of "two gardens of rare and foreign simples" (*deux Jardins de Simples rares & estrangers*).

The mention by Audebert at Tivoli that the parterres contained rare and foreign simples indicates the increasing interest at Rome toward the end of the sixteenth century in exotic flowers and plants, especially from the Middle East and eventually from the Americas. So Paolo Giordano Orsini, for whom a new garden was being prepared at his castle at Bracciano, received a letter in August 1584 from Leonardo Neri at Ancona informing him that there has been "sent some sea objects," presumably shells and the like, "which I have obtained for your fountain and I shall obtain others along with the flowering plants for which I have written to the Levant."[77]

The major location in Rome for the propagation and exhibition of unusual, exotic flowers and plants was the extensive Farnese garden developed on the plateau of the Palatine Hill early in the seventeenth century (Fig. 56). Later, in 1625, Pietro Castelli, writing under the pseudonym Tobias Aldinus and describing himself as "Doctor of Cardinal Odoardo Farnese and Prefect of his gardens," published a lengthy catalogue of all the rare plants growing in the garden.[78] One of the earliest exotic plants he notes there is identified by him as "Acacia Indica Farnesina" (*Acacia farnesiana*), whose seeds, coming from the West Indian island of Sto. Domingo, were a gift to the cardinal from the grand duke of Tuscany and bloomed first at the Palatine gardens in 1611.

Among the famous flower amateurs mentioned by Castelli in his catalogue was the Scotch Catholic writer John Barclay, who settled in Rome in 1616 with a pension from Pope Paul V.[79] Barclay rented a house near the Vatican until his death in 1621 and is reported to have bought unusual flower bulbs from the "highest Alps" at a great cost. Other gardens, relatively small but notable for their exotic flowers, were that of Cardinal Sannesio along the Tiber River across the road from the Villa Giulia, where according to the botanist Fabio Colonna in 1616, the *Muscari comosum plumosum*, identified as *Hyacinthus Sannesius paniculosa coma*, first grew, or the garden of Monsignore Acquaviva, also on the bank of the Tiber River, behind the present Sacchetti Palace on the Via Giulia owned by the Acquaviva family in 1620.[80]

G. B. Ferrari in his treatise *Flora* particularly singles out the flower garden at Cisterna, south of Rome, of the passionate plant collector Francesco Caetani, duke of Sermoneta, as one of the loveliest such gardens in his time and illustrates a quarter of its planting plan (Fig. 146).[81] Almost all the plants there were

---

[75] F. Baumgart, "La Caprarola di Ameto Orti," *Studj romanzi,* XXV, 1935, p. 105; for Frascati, see Mignosi et al., *Villa e paese,* pp. 14–15, and Devoti, *La Ville Rufina-Falconieri,* p. 21.

[76] V. Pacifici, *Ippolito II d'Este, Cardinale di Ferrara,* Tivoli, n.d., p. 152. For Tivoli, see Coffin, *The Villa d'Este,* p. 144, and Lightbown, "Nicolas Audebert and the Villa d'Este," pp. 187–88.

[77] S. Benedetti, "Nuovi documenti e qualche ipotesi su Giacomo

Del Duca," *Palladio,* n.s., XX, 1970, p. 29.

[78] T. Aldino, *Exactissima descriptio rariorum quarundam plantarum que continentur Rome in Horto Farnesiano,* Rome, 1625. See also S. Coggiatti, "Tra giardini e piante nel rinascimento," in *Rinascimento nel Lazio* (Lunario romano, IX), ed. R. Lefevre, Rome, n.d., pp. 33–45.

[79] Aldino, *Horto Farnesiano,* p. 56. See also [G. V. Rossi,] *Pinacotheca Imaginum illustrium,* new ed., Leipzig, 1692, and A. Dupond, *L'Argénis de Barclai,* Paris, 1875, pp. 2–12.

[80] Ferrari, *Flora,* p. 165, and G. Masson, "Italian Flower Connoisseurs," *Apollo,* LXXXVIII, 1968, p. 168. For the location of the Sannesio garden, see Lanciani, *Storia degli scavi di Roma,* III, pp. 17, 30. For the Acquaviva garden, see Masson, "Flower Collectors' Gardens," p. 80.

[81] Ferrari, *Flora,* pp. 90, 216–19. See also Masson, "Flower Col-

bulbous or tuberous flowers; the exceptions, some bitter-orange trees and white broom, presumably are to offer vertical accents within the flower beds. In an incomplete manuscript describing his garden the duke claims his plants came from all over Europe and the Near East, naming Constantinople, Paris, Avignon, Brussels, Amsterdam, Vienna, and Frankfort, and his correspondence confirms this. His specialty among flowers, however, were double or plush anemones. So Sir Thomas Hanmer, a great fancier of flowers in England, notes in his garden book of 1659 that "Paris hath some very good [Plush Anemones], but Rome exceeds all places for this sort of Anemones."[82] Hanmer then identifies three anemones he particularly favors, all bearing names associating them with the duke of Sermoneta—"Cazertane," "Gayetan," and "Sermonetta."

In addition to his favorite anemones, the duke of Sermoneta had many notable tulips in his garden, for this is the period when throughout Europe tulips began to rival roses as the gardeners' favorite flower, culminating in the fever of "tulipomania" in France and particularly in the Netherlands in 1634 to 1637. Already in September 1610 Guido Bentivoglio, the papal nuncio at Brussels, sought favor with the papal nephew, Cardinal Scipione Borghese, by sending him two boxes of tulip bulbs "as ornament of your vigna," the Villa Borghese, which was only just begun.[83] Ferrari in his chapter on bulbous plants, such as crocuses and tulips, in his floral treatise, first published in 1633, calls attention to the expert knowledge regarding tulips offered by Fabrizio Sbardoni, whom he identifies as the "very learned explorer for the gardens of Cardinal Carlo Pio" of Savoy, once the Silvestri-Medici gardens behind the Basilica of Maxentius.[84]

In 1627 when presumably the Barberini secretary, Cassiano dal Pozzo, composed his memorandum to Cardinal Francesco Barberini regarding the gardens that might be created at his summer palace on the Quirinal Hill, he specifically recommends the preparation of a "private flower garden."[85] The location chosen was particularly private "since no one will ever have any need to enter there for any other reason, nor without the gardener or the owners will one be able to do so, whereby the plants will remain secure." The passion for rare, exotic plants, of course, awakened a need for their security. Later Ferrari will identify some of the notable and rare plants there, including purple narcissi, jasmine, and "Indian" flowers.

Ferrari in his two treatises mentions several other smaller Roman gardens of the early seventeenth century that featured exotic flowers and plants. That of Tranquillo Romauli near the Colosseum, which Pietro Castelli in his catalogue of the Farnese gardens also commended, was renowned especially for the propagation of American plants.[86] From at least 1622 Romauli was exchanging plants with the duke of Sermoneta, and according to Ferrari by 1633 Romauli had been able to induce to bloom in his garden two varieties of narcissus that had failed northern collectors. Ferrari also singles out Giovanni Battista Martelletti, whose garden was on the Janiculum Hill, for the culture of anemones, and Sir Thomas Hanmer in 1659 lists in his garden book a plush anemone "the Marguerite of Martilletti, all flame color."[87] Ferrari in his later treatise, the *Hesperides* of 1646, also confers the name Martelletti on a lemon tree propagated by the gardener. Another small flower garden in Rome identified by Ferrari in the *Flora*, for which other information is lacking, was that of Marcantonio Specchi.[88]

As was noted earlier, the Villa Borghese had two walled-in private gardens to flank the casino, entered directly from the building. That at the north was the bitter-orange tree garden, but the one at the north also contained, according to Manilli in 1650, ten flower beds in two rows outlined with low hedges of

lectors' Gardens," pp. 70–80, and I. Belli Barsali, "Una fonte per i giardini del Seicento: Il trattato di Giovan Battista Ferrari," in *Il giardino storico italiano*, ed. G. Ragionieri, Florence, 1981, pp. 223–33.

[82] Thomas Hanmer, *The Garden Book of Sir Thomas Hanmer Bart.*, London, 1933, p. 61.

[83] A.H.L. Hensen, "Nederlandsche Tulpen in de buitenplaats van Kardinaal Borghese (thans Villa Umberto)," *Mededeelingen van het Nederlandsch Historisch Instituut te Rome*, III, 1923, pp. 205–8.

[84] Ferrari, *Flora*, p. 146; Ferrari in his later treatise, the *Hesperides* of 1646, p. 251, identifies Sbardoni as prefect of the garden of the Pio family.

[85] Magnanimi, *Palazzo Barberini*, Ms Barb. lat. 4360, unpaginated, and Ferrari, *Flora*, pp. 136, 195, 389.

[86] Ferrari, *Flora*, pp. 125, 194, 214, 328, 401; Aldino, *Exactissima descriptio . . . plantarum . . . in Horto Farnesiano*, p. 83; see also Masson, "Flower Connoisseurs," p. 169; Masson, "Flower Collectors' Gardens," pp. 78–79; and Belli Barsali, "Una fonte per i giardini del Seicento: Il trattato di Giovan Battista Ferrari," pp. 222, 229.

[87] Hanmer, *Garden Book*, p. 59. For the Martelletti garden, see Ferrari, *Flora*, pp. 337, 407; Ferrari, *Hesperides*, p. 231; and Masson, "Flower Collectors' Gardens," p. 73.

[88] Ferrari, *Flora*, p. 40.

myrtle and planted with "Tulips, Anemones, Jonquils, Hyacinths, and other of the rarest flowers that can be found."[89] Later, when Misson visited the villa in 1688, he was shown there "a double white *Hyacinth*, the Root of which, [the gardener] assured us, cost Five hundred Crowns, a Year before."

In 1678 Benedetto Pamphili, who would be elected a cardinal in 1681, was appointed grand prior of the Order of Malta, whose house was on the Aventine Hill. There the passion of the young prior for flowers was satisfied in the gardens developed under his care at the priory.[90] A document of 1680 mentions anemones, "jonquils of Spain and of Lorraine," narcissi, and "rose double violets." In the private garden the gardeners composed floral pictures for the pleasure of their master.

By the eighteenth century the travel account of the Frenchman Lalande in Italy in 1765 and 1766, after the usual description of the gigantic remains of a classical pediment, the "frontispiece de Néron," in the Colonna gardens on the slope of the Quirinal Hill, notes there particularly a long avenue of potted hyacinths and double tulips flanked by "two amphitheaters of five rows of pots which form the most beautiful effect in the world."[91] Lalande adds that "until the first of April these pots are only covered by straw mats with a little air through an opening above which they can close with cloths." At the same moment, however, that the gardeners were taking such care to safeguard the flowers, the ladies of Roman society were evincing a strong distaste for floral fragrances. The English Marquis of Kildare wrote his mother in May 1767: "Don't you pity the Roman ladies not being able to bear any sweet smells? They can't so much as suffer flowers of any kind, though they have charming ones. Whenever I go into their villas I must own I envy them their fine orange trees out of doors."[92] President de Brosses already in 1740 remarked that the ladies of Rome "have an invincible horror of odors" and recounts his visit to the Borghese with two lovely citron fruits in his pocket

that he had obtained at Cardinal Passionei's residence. When he remarked on the citrons to a Borghese daughter she replied in dismay: "Ah, monsieur, hide them and take them away, if mother saw them, she would be ill." Similarly, Mrs. Piozzi toward the end of the century claims that "a drop of lavender water in one's handkerchief, or a carnation in one's stomacher is to throw them all into convulsions." The solution for the Roman ladies was artificial flowers. So Lalande during his visit commends the artificial flowers produced at Rome, especially those made by the nuns of the convent of S. Cosimato or those sold by "the renowned Virginia Massi in the Piazza of St. Peter's opposite the custom house."[93]

## Botany

The city of Rome has never been renowned for botanical studies like Padua, Pisa, or Bologna in Italy, Montpellier in France, or Leiden in the Netherlands. This is disappointing considering the promise of interest evinced there in botany in the late fifteenth and early sixteenth century. The first well-illustrated herbal published in Italy was the herbal of Pseudo-Apuleius, *Herbarium Apulei*, printed by Giovanni Filippo de Lignamine, physician to Pope Sixtus IV, at Rome probably in 1481 based on a ninth-century manuscript in the monastery at Monte Cassino.[94] The Venetian humanistic scholar, Ermolao Barbaro, having studied at Rome with Pomponio Leto, returned there in 1491 to be appointed patriarch of Aquileia and died there in 1493, having published at Rome in 1492 his famous critical study of Pliny's *Historia Naturalis* under the title *Castigationes Plinianae et Pomponii Melae*. It will also be at Rome in the university that the first chair for the teaching of botany will be established by Pope Leo X on November 5, 1513, when he issued a reformed papal constitution for the institution.[95] In the university faculty roll of 1514 one

[89] Manilli, *Villa Borghese*, p. 117; see also [F. M. Misson,] *A New Voyage to Italy*, 4th ed., II, pt. 1, London, 1714, p. 70.

[90] L. Montalto, *Un mecenate in Roma barocca*, Florence, 1955, pp. 355–56.

[91] [J.J.L.F. de Lalande,] *Voyage d'un françois en Italie fait dans les années 1765 & 1766*, Yverdon, 1769, III, pp. 459–60.

[92] Duchess of Leinster, *Correspondence of Emily, Duchess of Leinster*, ed. B. Fitzgerald, III, Dublin, 1957, p. 468. See also C. Elling, *Rome*, Boulder, Colo., 1975, pp. 438–39; C. de Brosses, *Lettres familières sur l'Italie*, ed. Y. Bezard, Paris, 1931, II, pp. 207–8; and Mrs. Piozzi, *Glimpses of Italian Society in the Eighteenth Century*, London, 1892, pp. 209–10.

[93] [De Lalande,] *Voyage*, V, pp. 35–36.

[94] V. Capiabili, *Notizie circa la vita, le opere, e le edizioni di messer Giovan Filippo La Legname*, Naples, 1853; A. Arber, *Herbals: Their Origins and Evolution*, 2nd ed., Cambridge, 1953, p. 16; University of St. Thomas, Houston, Texas, *Builders and Humanists: The Renaissance Popes as Patrons of the Arts*, Houston, Tex., 1966, pp. 234–35; and W. Blunt and S. Raphael, *The Illustrated Herbal*, London and New York, 1979, p. 113.

[95] F. M. Renazzi, *Storia dell'Università degli Studj di Roma*, II, Rome, 1804, pp. 65–66, 235, 239; L. von Pastor, *The History of the Popes*, VIII, St. Louis and London, 1913, pp. 272–74; A. Chiarugi, "Nel quarto centenario della morte di Luca Ghini 1490–1566," *Webbia*, XIII, 1957, p. 2; and M. Catalano and E. Pellegrini,

Master Giuliano da Foligno was listed with an annual salary of eighty florins "for the teaching of medical simples" (*Ad declarationem Semplicium Medicinae*).

By 1568, however, the eminent Ferrarese physician and botanist Alfonso Panza wrote the naturalist Ulisse Aldrovandi at Bologna: "The plants that one can have in Rome are *Baccharis, hemionite storace, molidene, rubia marina, Thimelae*, and other things, which we already have; no garden there I would consider unusual; the most full is that of [Ippolito] Salviano."[96] The failure for the study of botany to flourish at Rome, as it will at some other Italian cities, can in part be explained by the destructive nature of the Sack of Rome in 1527, which temporarily closed the university, but in the end the sack did not curtail, except momentarily, other aspects of culture, especially the arts. Botany and anatomy were definitely neglected until about 1539 when their teaching was reestablished under Doctor Giuseppe Cenci, who normally taught medicine, but on festive or holidays was charged to expound on botany. Cenci must be the "mastre Josepho" mentioned by the Spanish physician-botanist Andres de Laguna as physician of Madama Margarita of Austria and as having at Rome his own garden of unusual plants.[97] Botany in the sixteenth century was closely allied to medicine—all the early botanists were either physicians or apothecaries—and medicine was not a particularly strong or eminent faculty at Rome. As one might expect in the city of the pope and the Curia, the outstanding faculties were in philosophy, theology, and law.[98]

After the Sack of Rome in 1527 several gardens of unusual plants flourished there, although, as Panza noted, none was of particular eminence. Panza did single out the garden of Dr. Ippolito Salviani, professor of medicine at the university from 1551 to 1568, as "the most full."[99] Already in 1558 Salviani had been asking Aldrovandi at Bologna to send him any rare seed Aldrovandi might have that he thought Rome did not have. The French naturalist Pierre Be-

lon, who was in Rome during the pontificate of Paul III, identifies one Scipio as the papal botanist (*Pontificis simplicista*) at the Vatican. This is probably Scipione Perotto, who was supervisor (*soprastante*) of the Belvedere garden in the Vatican from at least 1528 to 1552 and may be the gardener Scipio whom the German botanist Gesner claimed had a "noble garden" at the monastery of the SS. Apostoli. Gesner also identifies a garden with many notable plants in the monastery of Sta. Maria d'Aracoeli kept by two friars, Angelo Palea and Bartolommeo of Orvieto, whose names are listed in the title of a book on herbs published in 1543.

The close association of monks with botany continues into the late sixteenth century when the chief botanist for the members of the Este family in Rome and Ferrara was the Augustinian friar Fra Evangelista Quattrami.[100] In 1587 Quattrami published a book entitled *La vera dichiaratione di tutte le metafore* with a dedication to Duke Alfonso II d'Este of Ferrara in which he claims

> I have served about twenty years with your uncle the Very Illustrious and Reverend Lord Ippolito d'Este, Cardinal of Ferrara, of happy memory, and with your brother the Very Illustrious and Reverend Luigi d'Este, Cardinal d'Este, as botanist and distiller, out of obedience for my Father, the Very Reverend General as also for the commission of the most happy recollection of Our Lord Pope Pius V and Pope Gregory XIII. Therefore, while the Very Illustrious Cardinal of Ferrara, of happy memory, lived, I continued to search for four continuous years as botanist in different parts of Italy to bring back to his gardens on Monte Cavallo at Rome and in Tivoli different types of plants [*Semplici*]. And then in the time of the Very Illustrious Lord Cardinal d'Este of happy memory I have been until the present day superintendent of said garden of Monte Cavallo in Rome, nor have I also ceased studying (to flee boredom and for the public benefit) different authors who show the way as a distiller to make potable Gold, the Elixir of Life, the Fifth essence, and the Stone of the Philosophers.

In 1598, much later in his life, he will exaggerate the length of his service with the Estes when he claims in

*L'Orto botanico di Roma*, Rome, 1975, pp. xxi–xxii.

[96] [G. Fantuzzi,] *Memorie della vita di Ulisse Aldrovandi*, Bologna, 1774, p. 236.

[97] A. de Laguna, *Pedacio Dioscorides Anazarbeo, Acerca de la materia Medicinal, y de los Venenos mortiferos*, Salamanca, 1566, pp. 227, 258, 335, and R. Pirotta and E. Chiovenda, *Flora romana*, Rome, 1900, p. 40.

[98] V. de Caprio, "Intellectuali e mercato del lavoro nella Roma medicea," *Studi romani*, XXIX, 1981, esp. pp. 42–46.

[99] For the history of gardens of botanical interest at Rome at this time, see Pirotta and Chiovenda, *Flora romana*. The Gesner references are in Valerius Cordus, *Annotationes in Pedacij Dioscuridis Anazarbei de Medica materia libros V*, n.p., 1561, pp. 239v, 276.

[100] F. Ranghiasca Brancaleoni, "Quatrami Fra Evangelista," *L'Album*, XXVII, distribuzione 26, August 11, 1860, pp. 201–3; G. B. De Toni, "Il carteggio degli italiani col botanico Carlo Clusio nella Biblioteca Leidense," *Memorie della Reale Accademia di scienze, lettere ed arte in Modena*, ser. III, vol. X, pt. I, 1912, *Memorie della sezione di lettere*, pp. 113–269; and G. B. De Toni, "Notizie bio-bibliografiche intorno Evangelista Quattrami semplicista degli Estensi," *Atti del Reale Istituto Veneto di scienze, lettere ed arti*, LXXVII, pt. 2, 1917–1918, pp. 373–95.

one letter to Duke Cesare d'Este of Modena, successor of Duke Alfonso II, that he served the cardinals and Duke Alfonso for about thirty-seven years and in the letter of the following month to the duke reduced the service to about thirty-five years. The Este accounts show that he entered the service of the Cardinal of Ferrara in the middle of October 1569.[101] The documents confirm his activity as a distiller for in June 1572 he was reimbursed for distilling utensils (*orinali et capeli di vetro per stilare, vno bagno marin' di Ramo et altre robbe comprate per seruitio suo e per stilatori*). After the death of the Cardinal d'Este in 1586 Fra Evangelista remained in charge of the gardens on the Quirinal and was present on April 11, 1589, when the representatives of Cardinal Serbelloni came to take possession of the Este gardens at Rome and Tivoli in accordance with the will of the Cardinal of Ferrara.[102] They, however, returned the keys to the garden at Rome to him since he was to continue to guard the gardens. By March 1593 the friar was in Ferrara to serve the Este duke of Ferrara as botanist.

On the 1574 Cartaro engraving of the Belvedere Court at the Vatican there is depicted before the Casino Pio a series of small rectangular and square planting beds (Fig. 6) identified as the "Botanical Garden of Pope Pius V" (*Horto di semplici*) and in a book published in 1590 the papal physician Michele Mercati asserts that an ancient Roman measurement stone was "in the botanical garden formerly established by me in the Vatican Palace on the order of Pius the Fifth of sainted memory."[103] The botanical garden planted in front of the Casino Pio, therefore, must date after 1566 when Pius V was elected pope, and more likely about 1570 when Mercati succeeded Doctor Ajola as papal physician, but with the title "botanist" (*Semplicista*).[104] He will continue in papal service into the papacy of Clement VIII, devoting his later days to the study of metallurgy with the hope of establishing a papal museum of natural history. His major interest in plant collecting was in the 1570s, as on March 10, 1571, Cardinal Bonelli issued orders

that the labors of Mercati in searching throughout Italy for plants for the Vatican garden should not be disturbed and there are several letters regarding plant exchanges between Mercati and Aldrovandi in Bologna in 1573.

Pope Alexander VII, who had shown such great concern for beautifying the streets of the city of Rome with shade trees in 1656, soon showed interest in providing a proper botanical garden for the teaching of botany for physicians at the university. In his personal diary on March 6, 1659, Alexander VII records giving the design of the botanical garden to Father Virgilio Spada, his advisor on architectural commissions.[105] Earlier two botanically interested Franciscan friars of S. Pietro in Montorio on the Janiculum Hill had planted there a large garden. Since part of the land for the garden situated behind the public fountain of the Acqua Paola was owned by the Camera Apostolica, the pope resolved to transfer that terrain to the ownership of the university for their garden, but the university at first showed little enthusiasm for a location so far from the university and one situated on a windy hill. Finally on September 15, 1660, the pope signed the chirograph authorizing the garden and mounted an inscription dated 1660 on the university chapel of Sant'Ivo alla Sapienza commemorating the perfection of the university library and the establishment of the "Medical Garden." The Falda map of Rome of 1676 offers a slight glimpse of the layout of the garden, suggesting that the only built structure at the garden was a large circular pool at its center.[106] Commencing in 1668 the Bolognese botanist G. B. Trionfetti was appointed director of the garden, serving for the next thirty years. A pentagonal building containing a lecture hall on its upper floor by the architect G. B. Contini was erected in 1703 at one corner.[107] A detailed engraving of the garden by Andrea de Rossi was published at Rome in 1772 in the book *Hortus Romanus* by G. Bonelli and L. Abbate (Fig. 171). The engraving depicts the garden after it was enlarged to the south

[101] ASM, Camera Ducale, Amministrazione dei Principi, Registro 908, fol. 51v; for distilling utensils, see ibid., Registro 943, fol. 48.

[102] *Il Palazzo del Quirinale*, Rome, 1974, pp. 241–42.

[103] M. Mercati, *ConsIderationi di Monsig. Michele Mercati sopra gli avvertimenti del sig. Latino Latini Intorno ad alcune cose scritte nel libro de gli Obelische di Roma*, Rome, 1590, p. 68.

[104] [G. L. Marini,] *Degli Archiatri pontificj*, Rome, 1784, I, pp. 451, 459. See also Pirotta and Chiovenda, *Flora Romana*, p. 52, and [G. Fantuzzi,] *Memorie della vita di Ulisse Aldrovandi*, Bologna, 1774, pp. 249–51.

[105] R. Krautheimer and R.B.S. Jones, "The Diary of Alexander VII," *Römisches Jahrbuch für Kunstgeschichte*, XV, 1975, p. 210. For other information on the botanical garden, see L. Gigli, ed., *Guide rionali di Roma: Rione XIII Trastevere*, pt. 1, 2nd ed., Rome, 1980, pp. 182–83, and Catalano and Pellegrini, *L'Orto botanico di Roma*, pp. xxviii–xxxi.

[106] A. M. Frutaz, ed., *Le piante di Roma*, Rome, 1962, III, pl. 362.

[107] L. Pascoli, *Vite de' pittori, scultori, ed architetti moderni*, Rome, 1736, II, p. 554. Pascoli says Contini "organized" the garden as well as planned the casino; this is probably a replanning of the garden at the time of the building and not the original design.

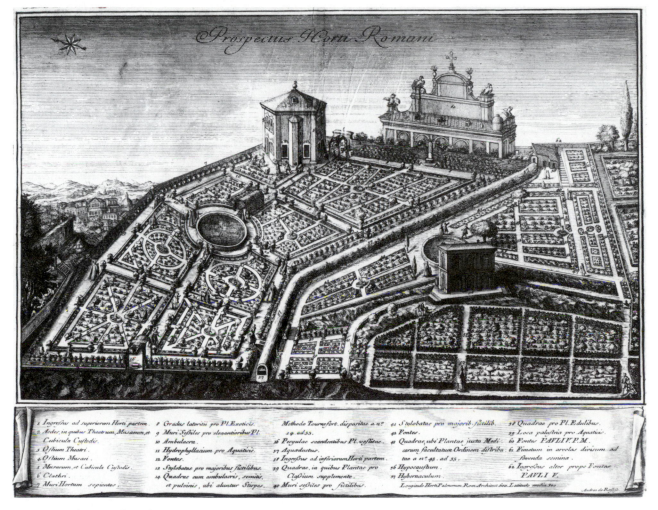

171. Rome, botanical garden, engraving, 1772, Archivio di Stato, Rome

beyond the aqueduct. The original Alexandrian garden was bounded on the east by the rear of the large frontispiece of the Acqua Paola, the public fountain erected by Pope Paul V, on the north and west by walls, and on the south side by the aqueduct that fed the Acqua Paola, as was still visible in Nolli's great plan of Rome of 1748.[108] In the northeast corner of the original garden is the two-story lecture hall and in the center of the garden the large pool that the print identifies as for the growing of water plants. The planting beds in the old garden are still laid out in a rather formal, ornamental style, several parterres having circular paths around a central circular fountain or eight alleys radiating from such a fountain. Each compartment is outlined by low hedges with potted plants at the corners. In the center of the "lower garden," the new garden south of the aqueduct, is a hothouse (*Hypocaustum*). The planting beds in this area are more utilitarian in their layout and less ornamental than the others. This difference in design may suggest that the original garden was more ornamental in its design. Visitors to Rome in the late eighteenth century tended to denigrate the botanical garden. Herr Volkmann, who visited Rome in 1758, remarked that the gardens were in "wretched condition," but the Englishman Smith in 1787 was even more severe:

We visited the botanic garden, near the Fontana Paolina, and never examined one more indigent. Not a new or interesting plant to console us. There was indeed plenty of the two species of *Melianthus* in flower,

[108] Frutaz, ed., *Piante*, pl. 409.

and *Potentilla anserina* was shown us in a pot as a very curious and beautiful plant. The latter quality certainly cannot be denied, but it grows as commonly on all the waste ground and ditch banks in Italy as in England, and everywhere else. The gardener appeared very ignorant, and seemed to know nothing of either Tournefort or Linnaeus, but the names he used were chiefly those of the former; and when we inquired if botany was taught here on the Linnaean principles, he thought we were asking for some species of *Linum*.[109]

Although Goethe in 1788 admitted that the garden was "neglected and uninteresting," he claims that he learned from the garden.

In 1800 Francesco Bettini, the Pamphili factotum who introduced the English style of gardening to Rome, created a botanical garden at the Villa Pamphili, which was opened to the public in April. In a letter of May 1, Bettini explains the reason for its creation:

> The Botanical Garden, which is made at your villa of Belrespiro behind the little garden of the old villa, is now finished . . . and already some youth have begun

to come to study here. The Botanical Garden of S. Pietro Montorio [the Sapienza garden founded by Alexander VII] is half in ruins, since the guardian is not being paid, he neglects it and this year the public lessons are not being given.[110]

The Pamphili garden was still in existence in 1820 when the university botanical garden was revived.

In the nineteenth century the Roman botanical garden became rather peripatetic. The need to provide space for the wealth of "new introductions" coming from the explosion of plant collecting in the late eighteenth and early nineteenth century caused Pope Pius VII to decide in 1820 to organize the botanical gardens in the gardens of the former Salviati Palace at the foot of the Janiculum Hill, which was inaugurated in 1823 and remained there with later enlargements until 1873, when the gardens were transferred for a decade to the Via Panisperna.[111] Finally in 1883 the botanical gardens were established on the Janiculum Hill below the Villa Lante and behind the Corsini Palace at the foot of the hill, where in the eighteenth century there had been very elaborate ornamental gardens in the French mode.

---

[109] J. J. Volkmann, *Historisch-kritische Nachrichten von Italien*, 2nd ed., Leipzig, 1777, II, p. 655, and J. E. Smith, *A Sketch of a Tour on the Continent*, 2nd ed., London, 1807, II, pp. 313–14. For Goethe's comments, see J. W. Goethe, *Italian Journey (1786–1788)*, trans. W. H. Auden and E. Mayer, New York, 1968, p. 490.

[110] M. Heimbürger Ravalli, "Progetti e lavori di Francesco Bettini per il parco di Villa Belrespiro," *Studi romani*, XXV, 1977, p. 35.

[111] L. Gigli, ed., *Guide rionale di Roma: Rione XIII Trastevere*, pt. 1, 2nd ed., Rome, 1980, pp. 28–32, 114–17.

# CHAPTER 12

# The Gardener

In May 1585, after Pope Sixtus V, formerly Cardinal Montalto, had ceremoniously taken "possesso" of the ancient basilica of S. Giovanni in Laterano, he immediately proceeded to the villa on the Esquiline Hill that he had begun as a cardinal and there relaxed from the ceremonies before returning to the Vatican at dusk. The avviso describing his visit relates that at the villa he strolled in the gardens "among those plants put in by him and weeded many times by his own hands."[1] It was certainly unusual for a prince of the Church to dirty his own hands with gardening, but Cardinal Montalto, unlike most of the cardinals, came from a rustic and relatively poor background in which, according to contemporary accounts, he took pride and probably even exaggerated the menial labors of his childhood.

There was, however, a tradition well known during the Renaissance that ancient kings and emperors had personally cared for their own gardens. The most famous account was that of Xenophon (*Oeconomicus*, IV, 20–25) regarding the great Persian king Cyrus, who had claimed to plant with his own hands parts of his gardens. So Renaissance writers on agriculture or villas, such as the Florentine Tanaglia in the late fifteenth century or Taegio in Lombardy in the mid-sixteenth century, will quote the story of Cyrus to ensure the nobility of gardening.[2] In the same way the Roman emperor Diocletian, after he had abdicated and retired to his country residence, was reputed to have planted his garden with his own hands, as Vicino Orsini, who had a similar personal care for his garden at Bomarzo, wrote his friend Drouet in 1573, when the latter was about to purchase a vineyard.[3]

Because of this classical tradition of the nobility of gardening, it is more often the humanist-scholars of the fifteenth century who worked their own gardens rather than the princes of the Church or other nobility. Nevertheless, there is one rather surprising example of personal gardening by a cardinal in the person of the Cardinal of Mantua, Francesco Gonzaga, who, in contrast to the rustic and relatively menial background of Cardinal Montalto, was born of a very wealthy ruling family. It was Cardinal Gonzaga himself in a letter of November 18, 1479, who asserted in anger that some pomegranate trees removed from his garden at Rome by the gardener "we had planted with our own hand."[4] Another such incident offered of the early life of Pope Paul III is very dubious, when Celio in his guidebook to painting in Rome reports the tradition almost a century and a half after the fact that Paul III had planted a cypress tree still visible in the court of the Vigna Farnese in the Trastevere on the day "he had achieved his doctorate."[5] This tradition is very much in the same spirit as the slightly earlier legends of St. Dominic and St. Francis personally planting orange trees at their monasteries at Rome.

[1] BAV, Ms Urb. Lat. 1053, fol. 220r, May 8, 1585.
[2] M. Tanaglia, *De Agricultura*, ed. A. Roncaglia, Bologna, 1953, p. 13, and B. Taegio, *La Villa*, Milan, 1559, pp. 49–51.
[3] H. Bredekamp, *Vicino Orsini und der Heilige Wald von Bomarzo*, Worms, 1985, II, pp. 26–27.
[4] D. S. Chambers, "The Housing Problems of Cardinal Francesco Gonzaga," *Journal of the Warburg and Courtauld Institutes*, XXXIX, 1976, p. 57.
[5] G. Celio, *Memorie delli nomi, dell'artefici delle pitture che sono in alcune chiese, facciate, e palazzi di Roma*, Naples, 1638, pp. 128–29.

Already in the middle of the fourteenth century Petrarch, as he revolutionized the world of literature, found his recreation in gardening and urged his readers to do the same. For more than twenty years, from 1348 to 1369, Petrarch kept his own gardening journal, reporting occasionally the weather and his own gardening activities.[6] A century later Pomponio Leto, the founder of the Roman Academy and teacher of Roman history and literature at the university, published in about 1480 with his own commentary the tenth book of the ancient Roman writer Columella's treatise on agriculture, which was a poetic treatment of how to take care of a garden. In his commentary Leto urges princes and scholars (*studiosi homines*) to devote time to the care of their gardens, and he himself attempted to offer an example by tending a vineyard on the Pincian Hill as well as the garden of his small house on the Quirinal Hill.[7] The vineyard, however, was not very successful in terms of cultivation as two anonymous poems of about 1479 soon after Leto's marriage speak of the land as sterile, lacking trees and vines. At the same time Leto's friend and neighbor, the Vatican librarian Bartolommeo Platina, recommended in his book, *De honesta voluptate*, of 1475 that the hoeing, harrowing, and grafting necessary to tending a garden was good for one's health as well as recreational.[8] Later, in the sixteenth century, Marc Antonio Flaminio in his poem celebrating the gardens of the humanist and writer Blosio Palladio says that Palladio sowed and tilled with his own hands the plants there, which is confirmed in a letter of Girolamo Negro.[9]

Because of their other activities, some knowledge of the lives and personalities of such amateur gardeners is preserved, but the only knowledge we have regarding most paid gardeners during the Renaissance is their names and occasionally salaries, as these are recorded in the papal accounts, such as the *ruoli di famiglia*, or among the account books of major, wealthy cardinals or of noble families. The gardeners at Rome will remain in the artisan class of manual laborers with only a few exceptions, particularly where unusual and exotic plants were concerned, and

most of those gardeners, such as Fra Evangelista Quattrami for the Estes or G. B. Ferrari for the Barberini, belonged to religious orders.

In November 1365 when Pope Urban V was preparing to return to Rome from Avignon in France, word was sent to the Vatican Palace to replant and renew the gardens there that had been neglected during the pope's absence in France.[10] Records of work begin, however, only late in 1367 just after the pope's arrival at the Vatican. The work was very extensive, continuing through 1369, and was apparently under the direction, as head gardener, of a French Dominican friar Guillaume Peyrer.

With the return of the popes to Avignon the Vatican gardens were probably neglected again, although Pope Gregory XI, successor to Urban V, sent a letter from Avignon on May 21, 1371, confirming a Franciscan friar, Giovanni Chambaret, as custodian of the Vatican Palace and its vineyards and garden, which was an important administrative position, but not a gardening position.[11] By the early fifteenth century the accounts regularly list an overseer or custodian of the palace and gardens or soon just of the gardens. So in 1410 Giacomo Tedallini was named by Pope Alexander V to be "custodian and governor of the palace and pontifical gardens," and in 1433 Beltramo Lombardo is recorded as "governor of the garden of the sacred palace," receiving twenty-five florins for his men.[12]

By the mid-fifteenth century papal documents begin to preserve with some regularity the names of the gardeners working at the Vatican Palace and occasionally record their salaries.[13] So in February 1447 at the death of Pope Eugenius IV two gardeners, Jaquemin *ortulano* and his associate (*eius socio*) Giovanni Bernardo, are listed with monthly salaries of eight florins and in 1453 the prefect of the garden at a monthly salary of twelve florins was again a Domin-

[6] P. de Nolhac, *Pétrarque et l'humanisme*, new ed., Paris, 1907, II, pp. 260–68.

[7] V. Zabvghin, *Giulio Pomponio Leto*, Rome, 1909, I.

[8] M. Stokstad and J. Stannard, *Gardens of the Middle Ages*, Lawrence, Kan., 1983, p. 66.

[9] M. A. Flaminio, *Marci Antonii, Joannis Antonii et Gabrielis Flaminiorum Forocorneliensium Carmina*, Padua, 1748, p. 54. See also J. L. de Jong, "De Oudheid in Fresco," Ph.D. dissertation, University of Leiden, 1987, p. 456.

[10] The documents for the activity under Urban V are in A. Theiner, *Codex Diplomaticus Dominii Temporalis S. Sedis*, II, Rome, 1862, p. 430, no. CCCCVIII, and p. 473, no. CCCCLXXVII; J. P. Kirsch, *Die Rückkehr der Päpste Urban V und Gregor XI von Avignon nach Rom*, Paderborn, 1898; and F. Ehrle and H. Egger, *Der Vaticanische Palast in seiner Entwicklung bis zur Mitte des XV. Jahrhunderts* (Studi e documenti per la storia del Palazzo Apostolico Vaticano, II), Vatican City, 1935, pp. 74–76.

[11] M. Catalano and E. Pellegrini, *L'Orto Botanico di Roma*, Rome, 1975, p. xvi.

[12] P. Pagliucchi, "I castellani del Castel S. Angelo di Roma," *Miscellanea di storia e cultura ecclesiastica*, III, 1904, p. 278, and G. Bourgin, "La famiglia pontificia sotto Eugenio IV," *Archivio della R. società romana di storia patria*, XXVII, 1904, p. 213.

[13] See Appendix III for lists and documents.

ican friar, Giacomo di Giovanni from Gaeta. The first complete papal *ruolo di famiglia* or household roll is that of Pope Pius II in 1460, where three gardeners are named: Roberto, in charge of the private garden (*vernherus hortulani secreti*), presumably the garden below the loggias of the Vatican Palace; Giovanni (*hortulanus*); and Matteo Cardinale, guardian of the vineyard (*custos vineae*). In the roll of Pope Pius III in 1503 are two custodians of the private garden, two gardeners for the private garden, and a vineyard keeper. On the roll of Leo X from 1514 to 1516 are three gardeners (*ortolani*).

From the sixteenth century on, therefore, there is a regular pattern of employment at the Vatican of one custodian or supervisor of the gardens and three gardeners, usually differentiated as one *hortulanus* and two *giardinieri*. These, of course, are not the only people employed to work the garden. They are the regular, full-time gardeners, who by being listed on the papal rolls are also entitled to food allowances and housing. The remainder of the labor force in the gardens was often casual labor dependent upon the season. The differentiation between *orto* or *hortus* and *giardino* or *gardinum/giardinum* is very uncertain as they are frequently used interchangeably. *Hortus* was a classical word primarily connoting a kitchen garden in contrast to the later classical word *viridarium* for a pleasure or flower garden. The Latin word *gardinum* is of mediaeval origin when there was not a clear differentiation between a pleasure garden and a kitchen garden. When there is, however, a careful distinction made in the papal accounts between *hortulano* and *giardiniere*, it would seem that the *hortulano* is a kitchen gardener and the *giardiniere* is concerned with ornamental gardening. So in the papal accounts during the renewal of the gardens at the Vatican for Urban V there are frequent references to the *viridarium*, but in November 1368 there are several accounts for "laborers in the kitchen garden" (*in orto*) along with the cost of cabbage plants (*pro plantus caulium*).[14] Similarly, at the Villa d'Este at Tivoli the pleasure gardens are regularly identified as *giardini*, although in 1582 the same gardener may in one account be labeled *giardiniero* and in another *ortolano*. When in 1582 the documents, however, list the planting of artichokes and peas along with fruit trees, the planting is described as in the kitchen garden (*nell'orto*).[15] So the architect Vincenzo Scamozzi

notes in 1615: "The kitchen gardens [*horti*] should be convenient to those who have charge of the service rooms of the house and of the family, and hidden there at one side rather than in front and under the view of the owner, as are the gardens [*giardini*] which are made only for recreation and beauty."[16]

In 1528 there first appears in the papal accounts the name of Scipio Perotto da Benevento as supervisor of the Belvedere gardens, who is certainly one of the most famous gardeners in Rome in the sixteenth century, mentioned admiringly by several of the foreign botanists or plant collectors who visited Rome.[17] Both the Spanish botanist Andres de Laguna and the French naturalist Pierre Belon identify Scipio as the papal gardener or botanist (*simplicista*) at the Belvedere gardens, who had shown them unusual plants he had there. The Scipio whom the German botanist Conrad Gesner mentions as having his own "noble garden" at the SS. Apostoli is possibly Perotto, although Gesner identifies this Scipio as a Roman citizen and, as noted below, there was even at least one other Scipio employed for a while at the Vatican. The last reference to Perotto is in the *ruolo di famiglia* of Julius III from December 20, 1551, to June 4, 1552, where he is recorded as "Custode in Belueder" with Paolo Salvatore and Guido Bandelot.

The building accounts for the new *giardino segreto* of Pope Paul III list the names of other gardeners and their salaries. In 1535 there are accounts in the name of Fioretto *giardiniere* and Lucerta *hortulano*. Lucerto or Lucertola, according to baptismal accounts from 1541 to 1547, was a Florentine whose actual name was Romolo.[18] According to the same baptismal records a Frenchman Luca was also a *giardiniere* in the Belvedere. In 1537 the papal accounts identify in addition to Lucerta two *giardinieri*, Don Joanni Aloysi, who was sent at least twice to Naples to ob-

[14] Kirsch, *Die Rückkehr*, pp. 129–30.

[15] ASM, Camera Ducale, Amministrazione dei Principi, Registro 1320, fols. 15–18, 35.

[16] V. Scamozzi, *L'idea della architettura universale*, Venice, 1615, p. 328.

[17] For Perotto's activity at the Vatican, see J. S. Ackerman, *The Cortile del Belvedere* (Studi e documenti per la storia del Palazzo Apostolico Vaticano, III), Vatican City, 1954, p. 157, and BAV, Ms Ruoli 11, December 20, 1551–June 4, 1552, fol. 31. For the foreign writer references, see A. de Laguna, *Pedacio Dioscurides Anazarbeo, Acerca de la Materia Medicinal, y de los Venenos mortiferos*, Salamanca, 1566, p. 402; P. Belon, *De neglecta Stirpium Cultura atque earum cognitione Libellus*, Antwerp, 1589, p. 53; and Conrad Gesner in Valerius Cordus, *Annotationes in Pedacij Dioscuridis Anazarbei de Medica materia Libros V*, n.p., 1561, pp. 239v, 276.

[18] C. De Dominicis, "Immigrazione a Roma dopo il sacco del 1527 (1531–1549)," *Archivio della società romana di storia patria*, CIX, 1986, pp. 165, 179.

tain plants for the new garden, and Don Antonio, who is also recorded in 1538 as aided by his nephew Luca, who may be the French gardener listed in the baptismal accounts. As late as 1544 Lucerta was still working at the Vatican when he paid a giardiniere Domenico for trimming the hedges of the new garden. Lucerta's salary until November 1537 was four and a half scudi per month. Then salaries for several gardeners are mingled, resulting in uncertainty about individual salaries. So commencing in November 1537 through September 1538 six and a half scudi are paid Lucerta each month for his salary and those of Don Aloysi and Don Antonio. There is a gap in the salary records until November 1543 when Lucerta was paid monthly through November 1544 ten and a half scudi for his own salary and that of other, unspecified gardeners.

In the ruolo di famiglia from December 20, 1551, to June 4, 1552, where Scipio Perotto is still listed as custodian of the Belvedere, the two giardinieri were Antonio Massuli and Nicolo Ramerio with Scipio Piccio as hortulano, which can cause confusion because in most accounts only the first name Scipio is given. In other accounts one Francesco Veniens is identified as a distiller (*distillator*) in May 1552 preparing rosewater from rose petals furnished by Scipio Perotto, but in November Veniens was working as a gardener providing winter covering for the bitter-orange trees at the Belvedere.[19] Under Pope Paul IV the position of distiller was officially recognized on the papal rolls with the appointment of Messer Desiderio as *stillatore* on the roll of June 30, 1558, to August 13, 1558, but as was noted on a later roll in a revision in March 1559 the position was terminated, although again with Pope Pius IV in 1562 Messer Bastiano Manzoni was listed briefly as stillatore.

With the papacy of Pope Pius V (1566–1572), the appointment of a botanist on the papal ruolo di famiglia became standard. Already on the roll of December 1, 1569, one Messer Costantino Pietrasanta was listed as druggist (*speziale*) of the palace and as most drugs at the time were herbal, the druggist was probably a botanist. By 1570 Michele Mercati had been enrolled as the papal botanist and began to collect plants and create a botanical garden in front of the Casino of Pius IV, as discussed previously (Fig. 6). The engraving of 1574 depicting the garden also identifies with the letter *S* the "rooms of Pius IV where the officials and gardeners of the Belvedere are." This was

the new building begun by Pope Pius IV to furnish facilities for papal conclaves, but which during its construction had been converted to house the papal archives, as the papacy began to be inundated by paper. The last record of Mercati as papal botanist was in November 1587. Another later eminent occupant of the post was the German botanist Johannes Faber from Bamberg, who in 1600 had been appointed to the Chair of Botany at the Sapienza in Rome. In April 1609 Faber was reimbursed by the papal treasurer for a trip to Ostia to collect plants for the Belvedere garden and was still listed on the ruolo di famiglia of December 31, 1627, under Pope Urban VIII.[20] A later employment roll of Urban VIII on November 5, 1637, has Pietro Castelli, known as Tobias Aldini, the former prefect of the Farnese gardens on the Palatine, as papal simplicista.

The records indicate that many of the gardeners were not of local origin, but came from distant localities, such as Benevento, Florence, or even France. Often they were probably hired because of personal contacts among their patrons. Undoubtedly there were many such requests as that seen in a letter of June 9, 1451, from Cardinal Scarampo to Onorato Caetani, regarding Scarampo's new country residence at Albano.

> On that account we beg Your Magnificence to search your lands that two men may be found who should be skilled and experienced in hoeing and making gardens and in scything and stacking hay and straw and doing everything necessary in such a place and will be faithful. And we shall be happy, whatever the cost, to give them that pay that would seem to you suitable; and being able to have two, as we have said, we shall wish that you send them here and as soon as possible the better.[21]

The salary listed in fiscal accounts often does not fully convey the actual income of a gardener, who may also receive food and residence or separate monetary allowances for them and may also be awarded gratuities for special services. So in March 1536 Matheo, who was serving as gardener at the papal hunting lodge at La Magliana on the way to Ostia, was given one scudo and sixty baiocchi "for his salary

---

[19] R. Lanciani, *Storia degli scavi di Roma*, III, Rome, 1907, pp. 25, 38.

[20] J.A.F. Orbaan, *Documenti sul barocco in Roma*, Rome, 1920, pp. 303, 350 and BAV, Mss Ruoli 147, December 31, 1627, fol. 18v and Ruoli 158, November 5, 1637, fol. 12v.

[21] G. Caetani, ed., *Epistolarium Honorati Caietani*, Sancasciano Val di Pesa, 1926, pp. 9–10.

and food allowance for all of the past January."[22] The money seems extraordinarily slight to cover both a monthly salary and food, but then in July 1537 Francesco, another gardener or a successor at La Magliana, was given three scudi "for his gratuity for having brought melons to His Beatitude."

The accounts of the Cardinal of Ferrara, Ippolito II d'Este, for his two gardens, one on the Quirinal Hill or Monte Cavallo, which later became a papal villa, and the other at Tivoli, give additional information regarding gardeners in the second half of the sixteenth century, and especially in respect to salaries.[23] At the Quirinal from June 2, 1559, through October 1572, just before the death of the cardinal, the gardener Menicuccio, described regularly as *giardiniero*, except for an occasional odd reference as *ortolano*, and twice in February and March 1565 as *erbarello* furnishing herbs to be planted there, was paid at an unchanging salary of five scudi per month. He was joined from February 1560 by two *ortolani*, Francesco and Maurelio or Morella, each normally receiving five scudi a month.[24] Later from 1566 to 1572 there is only one *ortolano* listed at a salary of five scudi with Vincenzo da Modena filling the position through at least 1569.

Late in 1569 a new position appeared on the employment rolls at the Quirinal gardens. From September 20 through December 1569 one Messer Giovanni Ambrogio Vergerio was paid a monthly salary of seven scudi to serve as botanist (*semplicista*). His service was very brief, but in the middle of October 1569 Padre Evangelista Quattrami was hired as botanist and continued in that position with a monthly salary of three scudi until at least 1589, serving both cardinals Ippolito and Luigi d'Este.[25] Born in Gubbio in Umbria in 1527, Quattrami entered the Augustinian order and was sent to Rome where he received a doctorate in theology. He soon, however, became interested in botany, plant collecting, and alchemy. In

1560 he was on a plant-collecting expedition in the mountains of Norcia with Luigi Anguillara, the eminent first prefect of the botanical garden at Padua from 1546 to 1561, and several other herbalists. Joining the staff of the Quirinal gardens, Padre Evangelista was not only employed to collect unusual plants for the gardens, but to serve as distiller. While in the Este service he continued his scholarly contacts, sending plants and letters to the naturalist Aldrovandi at Bologna as the latter notes in 1579. Later the padre wrote three scientific studies, two while at Rome. The first, a small, rare treatise on the plague, is dated from his rooms on Monte Cavallo, or the Quirinal, August 10, 1586. During his residence at the Quirinal Padre Evangelista must have also served as director of the cardinal's gardens. This is suggested by a strange, inexplicable entry in the Quirinal accounts of 1579, which reads: "Luca gardener at Monte Cavallo is owed on February 3 twenty scudi in coin for his salary in the garden of said location [for] the recent past month of January according to the agreement made with him for 240 scudi per year as appears by a writing from the hand of Padre Fra Evangelista botanist of the month of July 1578."[26] Then for the first six months of 1579 there are monthly payments of twenty scudi to the gardener Luca, which are very high payments for a gardener. Thereafter the payments to Luca resume at the normal gardener's salary of five scudi per month with the notice that "the agreement made with him of twenty scudi per month finishes on the last day of the recent past June." Although the reason for the unusual payments cannot be explained, the fact that the accountant would pay the sums of money on the authority of a written statement of Padre Evangelista suggests that he is at least in charge of the garden personnel. So in 1589, long after the death of Cardinal Luigi d'Este, the representatives of Cardinal Serbelloni took possession of the Quirinal garden, once owned by Boccaccio, in the presence of its custodian Fra Evangelista to whom the keys were returned as he was to continue to guard it and had his residence in the area of the old Vigna Boccaccio.[27] In 1593 Fra Evangelista was at Ferrara in the service of Alfonso II d'Este.

One minor account at the Quirinal when it was a papal garden indicates that at that time at least in addition to food and residence there was a clothing allowance, for on July 12, 1610, twenty-five scudi were

[22] L. Dorez, *La cour du Pape Paul III*, Paris, 1932, II, pp. 34, 136.

[23] The documents regarding both Este villas are in the following Registri in the ASM, Camera Ducale, Amministrazione dei Principi, nos. 957 (1559–1560), 895 (1561–1562), 958 (1561), 991 (1564–1565), 828 (1566), 897 (1566), 898 (1566), 993 (1566), 907 (1567–1568), 995 (1568), 908 (1568–1569), 909 (1570), 911 (1570–1571), 943 (1572–1573), 1215 (1579), 1320 (1582), and 1222 (1585–1586).

[24] Until 1561 the two ortolani were each listed as being paid five and a half scudi per month and in 1561 Maurelio was listed as a giardiniero.

[25] For bibliography on Quattrami, see Chapter 11, n. 100.

[26] ASM, Camera Ducale, Amministrazione dei Principi, Registro 1215, fol. xvi.

[27] *Il Palazzo del Quirinale*, Rome, 1974, pp. 241–42.

paid to Silvio Sigismondi giardiniere "for the customary clothing [*vestito*] which he should have made for the summer of the present year 1610."[28]

Later in 1644, when the English traveler John Evelyn visits the garden, in addition to praising it lavishly, he informs us: "I am told the Gardner is annually alow'd 2,000 scudi for the keeping it."[29]

The financial accounts for the Cardinal of Ferrara's garden at Tivoli offer some additional information. So in February 1568 the gardener Cecco, listed as giardiniero, was paid four scudi and forty baiocchi for a month's salary ending January 21, whereas in 1571 the giardiniero Francesco was paid twelve scudi for the three months of July, August, and September, and Marco, assistant to Cecco, received three scudi per month for September and October. These wages at Tivoli seem to have been slightly less than comparable wages of the same time at Rome. This may be due to less competition for labor at Tivoli or to differences in unspecified allowances. In 1579, however, the giardiniero Battista at Tivoli received on January 18 five scudi "in coin on account of his salaries and provisions." His further wages were sporadic with four scudi on March 4 and five on May 24. Later in 1583 Giovannino giardiniero and Piero Antonio his helper (*garzone*) are paid together six scudi and twenty baiocchi for each of the two months of January and February.

In the early seventeenth century, because of the increasing interest in exotic plants and botany, the names of several gardeners at Rome became well known. Probably the most eminent was Pietro Castelli, known as Tobias Aldini, who as prefect of the Farnese garden on the Palatine published a catalogue of its exotica in 1625, and in 1637 was botanist at the Vatican gardens. Others were the Jesuit Giovan Battista Ferrari, associated with the Barberini gardens and author of two important books on horticulture and arboriculture, and Fabrizio Sbardoni, whom Ferrari mentions in 1646 as prefect of the gardens of the Pio family behind the Basilica of Maxentius.[30] The gardener Domenico Savini da Montepulciano, whose name is listed as giardiniere or *vignarolo* in the building accounts of the Villa Borghese and whose name, with another gardener Andrea Speciale, is recorded still there in 1626, will be identified later by Fiora-

vente Martinelli in his guide to Rome as having "designed, laid out and planted the vigna and garden in the pontificate of Paul V."[31] This is the first time in Rome apparently that a gardener was also identified as a garden designer.

The Pamphili accounts for their gardens, including several of Donna Olimpia Aldobrandini, also contain information on gardeners' salaries.[32] At the new Villa Belrespiro and its gardens outside the Porta di S. Pancrazio, Andrea Calenne giardiniere, who was employed there at least from November 1645 to December 1647, was paid nine scudi per month without any indication as to whether this amount also included his food allowance. At the same time an entry for March 1647 lists a food allowance of four scudi a month for the gardener at the Aldobrandini garden on Monte Magnanapoli in Rome. Later the ruolo di famiglia of 1660 to 1661 of Don Camillo Pamphili records Tomaso di Antonio Iacomo giardiniero at the Aldobrandini garden on Monte Magnanapoli with a monthly salary of five scudi and a food allowance of three scudi and Giovanni M. Pelle giardiniero at the Villa Aldobrandini at Frascati with the same provisions, although the ruolo specifies that the food allowance for Pelle is only for the first month of employment. In the ruolo di famiglia of 1665–1666 the head gardener at the Villa Pamphili or Belrespiro, Silvestro Sabatini da Monte Falco, has a salary of six scudi a month and the undergardeners (*sotto giardinieri*) were also paid six scudi. On that same ruolo Francesco Benigrassi, gardener at Donna Olimpia's *Giardino a Ripa* in the Trastevere, received six scudi and Ettore Brasco da Cesena, gardener at Monte Magnanapoli, eight scudi, without specifying whether the amounts also included a food allowance as in the previous ruolo of 1660–1661 for his predecessor Tomaso. By March 1672 Silvestro Sabatini, the head gardener at the Villa Pamphili, was still employed there with a presumably increased monthly salary of eight scudi.

The financial accounts, therefore, limited as they are, indicate that at least throughout the sixteenth century the salary of a head gardener was regularly

[28] Ibid., p. 246.

[29] J. Evelyn, *The Diary of John Evelyn*, ed. E. S. de Beer, II, Oxford, 1955, p. 287.

[30] G. B. Ferrari, *Hesperides sive De Malorum Aureorum Cultura et Vsv Libri Quatuor*, Rome, 1646, p. 251.

[31] C. d'Onofrio, *Roma del Seicento*, Florence, 1969, p. 299. See also C. H. Heilmann, "Die Entstehungsgeschichte der Villa Borghese in Rom," *Münchner Jahrbuch der bildenden Kunst*, ser. 3, XXIV, 1973, p. 109, and for the 1626 account, *Regio Tribunale Civile di Roma in grado di appello: Nella causa in punto di reintegrazione o manutenzione di preteso uso di pubblico passeggio nella Villa Borghese: Documenti*, Rome, 1885, p. 39.

[32] See J. Garms, *Quellen aus dem Archiv Doria-Pamphilj zur Kunsttätigkeit in Rom unter Innocenz X* (Quellenschriften Geschichte zur Barockkunst in Rom, 4), Rome and Vienna, 1972.

set at five scudi a month with the addition usually of a food allowance and residence. During the seventeenth century there may be a little more fluctuation in the pay, but not a radical difference. The salary of the head gardener was the same as that of a master cook. For example, at the same time in 1566 when the Cardinal of Ferrara's two gardeners at the Quirinal Hill, Menicuccio and Vincenzo da Modena, were each receiving five scudi a month and Giovanni the water carrier (*acquarolo*) two scudi, the cardinal's head cook, Francesco, was paid five scudi a month and the undercooks and pastry chef only two scudi.[33]

A couple of gardener's contracts prepared and signed at the moment of employment offer a detailed breakdown as to the duties of the gardener (although whether such contracts for important gardening positions were common practice is unknown). On August 8, 1525, the *majordomo* of Cardinal Farnese, later to be Pope Paul III, signed a contract with Antonio Longo of Naples confirming the latter to continue for another year as gardener at the Vigna Farnese in the Trastevere between the walls of the Trastevere and the Chigi villa, later purchased by the Farnese and thus known as the Villa Farnesina. The gardener was thereby required to plant all the bitter-orange trees and every other type of tree in the gardens and kitchen gardens (*in detti giardini et orti*) and to sow and to transplant every sort of vegetable, herb, root, melon, and any other type of kitchen plant at his own expense.[34] All the bitter-orange espaliers were to be maintained, cleaned, and fertilized and all the alleys cleaned as many times as was necessary. Second, the gardener was to furnish for the household all sorts of salad greens, herbs, roots, and vegetables as needed. All this produce was to be supplied every day in sufficient amount for the table of the cardinal and his prelates. For the household and servants' hall he should furnish such greens every vigil of a holy day and every Monday, Wednesday, Friday, and Saturday, and all Lent. The vegetables for the latter will be supplied on every vigil, Lent, and all year on the three weekdays desired. All roses, flowers, and fruit at all seasons were to be for the cardinal. The gardener Antonio was also to have an annual expense budget of sixty ducats and was responsible for the irrigation systems, pay for casual labor, and maintenance of a mule.

The other gardener's contract dates about a century later and was signed on December 29, 1629, between Camillo Molza, as governor of the Este garden at Tivoli, with the gardener Domenico Severini for a period of three years.[35] The contract consists of eighteen items. It commences with the obligation of the gardener to maintain all the espaliers and to replant them where they are lacking, with the Ducal ministers, when they are in residence, furnishing the plants. He is also obliged to plant cherry laurel, cypress, and myrtle for the maintenance and improvement of the garden, the plant material being supplied as before. He is forbidden, however, to plant kitchen herbs (*herbaggi*) on the inner side of the espaliers or to put dung around the trees without it being dug in. At the appropriate time, the gardener is obliged to cover and to uncover the citron espaliers with cane covering provided by the ministers and to exhibit or to store the vases of orange trees that are to be in his care. All the alleys and the water courses in the different gardens and in the wood are to be kept clean. He is forbidden to cut anything in the wood and garden without permission of the ministers, and when any fruit trees are removed the small branches belong to the gardener and the large ones to the palace. The gardener is then obliged to replant wherever needed with material supplied as before. All kitchen produce needed by the ministers, when they are in residence at Tivoli, is to be supplied by the gardener, and he is obliged to obey them in all things regarding the garden and these terms. The small, private garden is to be maintained by the gardener, but when it is in bad condition and necessary to be dug up, the ministers are obliged to dig it up at the cost of the garden. The gardener must not introduce anyone into the garden except for those necessary for work, and he must not bring manure into the garden during the month of May or from the Madonna's feast day of September (September 8) up to All Saints Day (November 1).

For the above duties it is agreed that the gardener will be paid five and a half scudi a month and housing "with bed as customary." If the gardener should leave or be dismissed, the Ducal ministers or whoever replaces the gardener are obligated to pay for all the produce based on the evaluation of appraisers. In case the gardener should not observe these conditions or should not make corrections after being warned, he may be dismissed and replaced by another gardener.

[33] ASM, Camera Ducale, Amministrazione dei Principi, Registro 872, fol. xxxi.

[34] C. L. Frommel, in *Le Palais Farnèse: École française de Rome*, Rome, 1981, I, pt. 1, p. 127, n. 1.

[35] ASM, Camera Ducale, Fabbriche e Villeggiature, Busta 71, Tivoli, no. 6, Villeggiatura sotto Francesco d'Este, fasc. 2, 1629–1630, A. Nomina del giardiniere.

The contract is then signed by Camillo Molza for the duke and by one Francesco Mantovani, who writes that "I have seen said Domenico, who does not know how to write, make the cross."

Several comprehensive payment accounts for work at the Villa Borghese also cover some of the gardener's activities there. In 1626, for example, the gardeners (giardinieri) Domenico Savini and Andrea Speciale were paid "to cultivate, to dig up, to break up, and to fertilize, to dig out stones, to pickax the compartment of bitter-orange trees where strawberries are planted with myrtle hedges about it" and in September 1631 there are expenses "to trim the hedges, woods, to clean the alleys, to pick flowers and fruits, to water and mow for the second time the grass of the compartments, alleys and plain of holm oak at a cost of ten scudi, to pile up and to burn said grass."[36]

Financial accounts also indicate that normally the gardener's tools were furnished or bought by the owner of the garden. For example, in 1535 a smith was paid in the papal accounts for two billhooks and two hatchets to be used in the Belvedere gardens and in 1536 shovels, pickaxes, and mattocks were purchased to enable leveling the terrain for the new garden created at the Vatican for Pope Paul III with more shovels, hoes, and handbarrows bought in successive years.[37] Such tools, especially small handtools, were the essential aids of the gardener who could not perform his duties without them; G. B. Ferrari at the beginning of his chapter five on garden tools (*arma hortensia*) likens them to the soldier's weapons.[38] Unlike today all the earthwork necessary for the creation of a garden was done by hand with shovel and pick and moved by hand in wheelbarrows, handbarrows, or occasionally small carts drawn by horse or mule. Most suitable, therefore, is the lavish rhetoric of Daniele Barbaro in the dedication of his 1567 edition of Vitruvius to the Cardinal of Ferrara for the creation of his gardens at Tivoli, where "nature agrees to confess to having been conquered by art."

The tools with which the Roman gardeners labored until the nineteenth century were very little different from those of their ancestors or even those of ancient Romans, any differences being limited to refinements

172. M. Bussato, *Giardino di Agricoltura*, 1590, tools

in the design or materials of construction. During this period there are a few collections of illustrations of horticultural or agricultural tools that identify the tools with which the gardener had to work.[39] Agostino Gallo's treatise on agriculture, *Vinti giornate dell'agricoltura et de' piaceri della villa* (Venice, 1569), offers depictions of a broad range of agricultural tools, and Marco Bussato in his *Giardino di agricoltura* (Venice, 1590) illustrates many hand tools, including a pick, a hoe, a round shovel and spade, a sickle, rake, ax, knife, and several billhooks (Fig. 172). A different type of illustration is in Bartolommeo Taegio's dialogue, *La Villa*, where he describes how to level land with a water level and depicts its use (Fig. 173).[40]

[36] *Regio Tribunale Civile di Roma in grado di appello: Nella causa in punto di reintegrazione o manutenzione di preteso uso di pubblico passeggio nella Villa Borghese: Documenti*, Rome, 1885, pp. 38, 40. Other accounts are on pp. 45–49.

[37] L. Dorez, *La cour du Pape Paul III*, ii, pp. 4, 41, 104, 169, 196.

[38] G. B. Ferrari, *Flora, seu de florum cultura*, new ed., Amsterdam, 1646, p. 57.

[39] For bibliography on horticultural tools, see I. Belli Barsali, "Una fonte per i giardini del Seicento: Il trattato di Giovan Battista Ferrari," in *Il giardino storico italiano*, ed. G. Ragionieri, Florence, 1981, p. 222, and L. T. Tomasi, "Projects for Botanical and Other Gardens: A 16th-Century Manual," *Journal of Garden History*, iii, 1983, pp. 1–34.

[40] B. Taegio, *La Villa*, Milan, 1559, p. 162.

For Roman gardening of the seventeenth century the most interesting information is presented in the fifth chapter of G. B. Ferrari's *Flora*, devoted to more specialized horticultural tools. While the basic gardening tools remained the same, the growing interest in exotic plants encouraged some new tools to handle them. Unlike the previous descriptions and depictions of tools, Ferrari's are those needed by the flower gardener maintaining flower beds and alleys. In fact, the first tool he describes is a well-sharpened double mattock that can dig around in the narrow areas of the floral compartments without damage. Ferrari describes a variety of tools, often giving their dimensions and use, but he only illustrates three somewhat unusual tools, two of which seem to be of foreign origin. The first is the Gallic rake (Fig. 174), or slightly dentated garden scraper, which was very convenient for the removal of grass from alleys. Another is the *Imbrex ferreus extractorius* (Fig. 175), or iron extractor trowel, which is also a French tool for uprooting and transplanting living plants. It has a twin in function, but of different form, in an iron tube (Fig. 176) used for transplanting, which is presumably the more traditional Italian tool. Another instrument for digging out around dried roots, Ferrari relates, was invented by the Flemings, but bears a French name. He also describes more common tools, such as spades, a dibble, watering jugs, brooms, and brushes

173. B. Taegio, *La Villa*, 1559, water level

174. G. B. Ferrari, *Flora*, 1646, Gallic rake

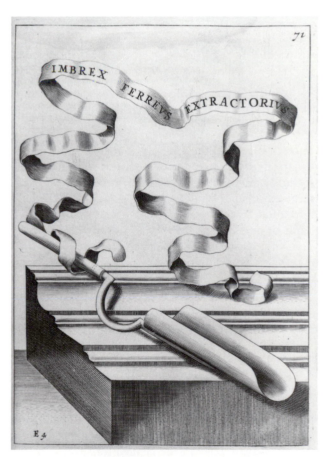

175. G. B. Ferrari, *Flora*, 1646, extractor trowel

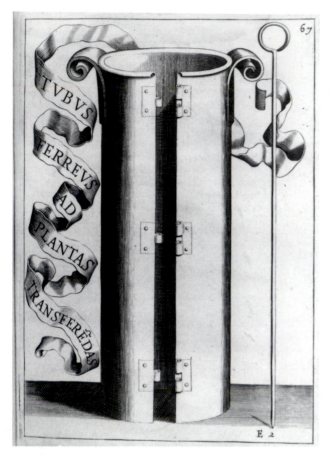

176. G. B. Ferrari, *Flora*, 1646, transplanter

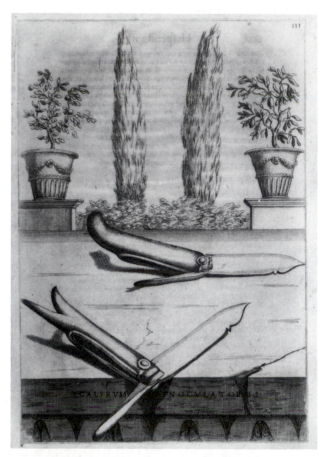

177. G. B. Ferrari, *Hesperides*, 1646, grafting knives

to clean off the pianelle or brick edging of the flower beds, sieves, saws, and even an oil or whetstone. Ferrari in his later treatise on trees, *Hesperides* (1646), includes other tools with which the gardener should be familiar. So there is an illustration of two different kinds of grafting knives (Fig. 177), and in the depictions of the interior of a garden loggia he shows on a table at one side billhooks, grafting saws, and pruners (Fig. 178).

Several of the prints of about 1670 from Falda's collection of engravings of the most famous Roman gardens depict gardeners employed with their basic tools. For example, in the foreground alley of the view of the gardens of the Villa Borghese toward the center is a man raking, while behind him another gardener trudges along pushing a wheelbarrow (Fig. 179); in the foreground alley of the depiction of the Casino Pio in the Vatican, as noted previously, two men move a large potted shrub on a four-wheeled dolly (Fig. 153). Similarly in the central foreground of the prospect of the gardens of the Villa Medici (Fig. 180)

178. G. B. Ferrari, *Hesperides*, 1646, loggia with tools

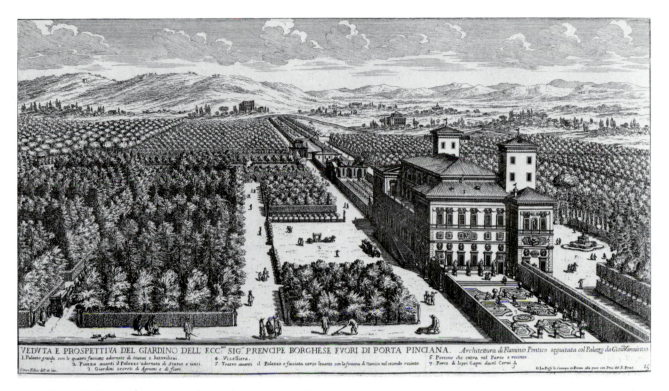

VEDVTA E PROSPETTIVA DEL GIARDINO DELL' ECC.<sup>MO</sup> SIG.<sup>R</sup> PRENCIPE BORGHESE FVORI DI PORTA PINCIANA.    *Architettura di Flaminio Pontico seguitata col Palazzo da Gio.Vansaintio.*

1.Palazzo grande con le quatro facciate adornate di statue e bassirilieui .    4.Vccelliera .    5.Portone che entra nel Parco e recinto .
2. Piazza auanti il Palazzo adornata di Statue e uasi .    5.Teatro auanti il Palazzo e facciata uerzo leuante con la fontana di Narciso nel secondo recinto .    7.Parco di lepri Capri daini Cerui.&
3. Giardini secreti di Agrumi e di fiori .
Simon Felice del' et inc.    G.Iac.Rossi le stampa in Roma alla pace con Priu' del S.Pont.    15

179. Rome, Villa Borghese, engraving

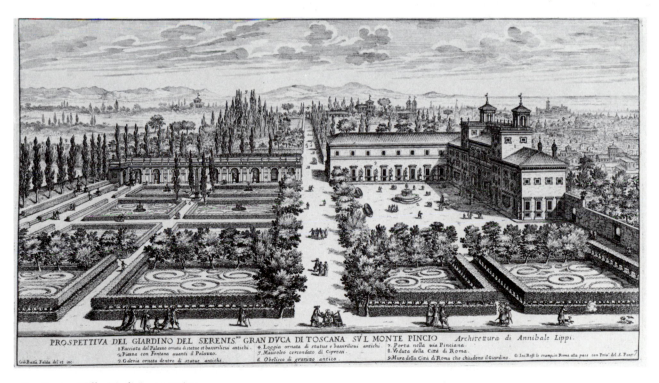

PROSPETTIVA DEL GIARDINO DEL SERENIS.<sup>mo</sup> GRAN DVCA DI TOSCANA SVL MONTE PINCIO    *Architettura di Annibale Lippi.*

1.Facciata del Palazzo ornata di statue et bassirilieui antichi .    4. Loggia ornata di statue e bassirilieui antichi .    7. Porta nella uia Pinciana .
2.Piazza con Fontana auanti il Palazzo .    5.Mausoleo cercondato di Cipressi .    8.Veduta della Cittd di Roma .
3.Galeria ornata dentro di statue antiche .    6. Obelisco di granito antico    9.Mura della Citd di Roma che chiudono il Giardino    G.Iac.Rossi le stampa in Roma alla pace con Priu' del S.Pont.
Gio.Batti Falda del' et inc.

180. Rome, Villa Medici, engraving

is a gardener with a wheelbarrow and shovel, being addressed apparently by a visitor in the gardens. The significance of these engravings is not for the everyday activities of the gardeners, but the time of day when they are shown working. As the gardeners work at their daily duties they are surrounded by visitors walking or even riding in coaches in the alleys of the gardens. There is a natural casualness about the different activities taking place in the Roman gardens, which would not be encountered even earlier in the French gardens. So John Evelyn when he visits the gardens of the Luxembourg Palace in Paris in 1644 remarks: "What is most admirable, you see no Gardners or people at Worke in it, and yet all kept in such exquisite order, as if they did nothing else but worke; It is so early in the mornings that all is dispatch'd and don without the least confusion."[41] For the French the transience of nature must never be considered. Insofar as it is possible the garden must remain in perfection, seemingly untouched by man. So it is not sur-

prising that in about 1680 after the replanting of the gardens of the Tuileries in Paris Colbert proposed closing the public out of the gardens lest they be ruined by the people and only strenuous arguments by Perrault and the gardeners themselves, who assured Colbert of the people's care, preserved the traditional public right to visit the garden.[42] As will be considered later, in Rome there was a strong tradition of the right of public access to all gardens. At the same time there was an almost fatalistic acceptance of the transience of nature and of life. So earlier Lorenzo de' Medici had nostalgically sung: *Quant'è bella giovinezza, che si fugge tuttavia* ("Oh, how lovely is youth that flees us forever"). Hence the Roman gardeners will labor away, revealing their attempts to stave off the transience of nature, as the elegant men and women wander in relaxation among the natural wonders.

[41] Evelyn, *The Diary of John Evelyn*, II, pp. 130–31.

[42] C. Perrault, *Mémoires de Ch. Perrault*, ed. P. Lacroix, Paris, 1878, pp. 121–22.

# CHAPTER 13

# Entertainment

In January 1519 the Ferrarese representative at Rome, Alfonso Paolucci, wrote the duchess of Ferrara a brief account of his visit with Marc Antonio Colonna to the latter's vigna on the Capitoline Hill, where "his Lordship showed me a lovely alley made there for racing and for horsemanship, and another alley, which looks in the direction of the Ripa [the bank of the Tiber at Trastevere], where ivy and laurel have been planted to prepare a place to walk and to philosophize."[1] The range of activities from boisterous horse racing to the quiet, contemplative mode of philosophy provided in Colonna's garden was typical of the types of entertainment often found in Roman Renaissance gardens. Already in the middle of the fifteenth century Alberti in his treatise on architecture (v, xvii) had recommended that there be a large space in front of the entrance to a country residence for "chariot" (curriculus) or horse racing. The recommendation may reflect Pliny the Younger's identification of part of the gardens of his Tuscan villa (Letters, v, 6) as in the form of a hippodrome or ancient racecourse. This association of horse racing or jousting with the villa is repeated in 1566 by Anton Francesco Doni in his treatise on villas where he notes that the villa of a king or lord should have an open space two hundred braccia square for "horse racing,

breaking the lance or a ball court."[2] So in the anonymous account of the Villa d'Este at Tivoli written about 1571, perhaps by the architect Ligorio, the thirteenth alley of the garden immediately in front of the villa is described as being "large enough so that one might joust there."[3]

That this tradition of horse racing and jousts in the grounds of a villa is not merely a literary one is demonstrated by Claudio Corte in his treatise on horsemanship, published in 1572, where he recalls that "we came to sport many times in the delightful garden of Agostino Chigi [the Farnesina at Rome], to break lances, to drill horses in its lovely, delightful and shady alleys in order to flee the wicked heat."[4]

The period for the most exuberant public celebration was naturally during carnival each year. Dependent upon the enthusiasm or strictures of the reigning pope, bullfights and jousts were the major events offered as public entertainment, while lavish banquets and performances of comedies were of a more private nature. The great physical encounters required large, open spaces for their settings. So during the sixteenth century the avvisi repeatedly report the performance of bullfights and tournaments in the major squares of the city, such as the Piazza of St. Peter's, the Piazza Navona, or the Piazza of the SS. Apostoli.[5] The creation from 1505 by the architect Bramante of the great

[1] ASM, Cancelleria Ducale, Ambasciatori a Roma, busta 25, January 26, 1519: ". . . trovai el Sr Marco ant.o [Colonna] quale volea andare a la vigna; dove accompagnai sua s.ria. . . . Giongemo á la vigna, che e de sopra in campidoglio, et sua s. me fece vedere una bella strada li fa da corere, et manegiare cavali, et una altra strada, che guarda á la dritura del Ripa; dove fa seminare edere, et lauri per far uno loco da pasegiar, et staresi a filosofare." John Shearman very kindly furnished me with the material.

[2] U. Bellocchi, ed., Le Ville di Anton Francesco Doni, Modena, 1969, p. 33.
[3] D. R. Coffin, The Villa d'Este at Tivoli, Princeton, N.J., 1960, p. 144.
[4] C. L. Frommel, Die Farnesina und Peruzzis Architektonisches Frühwerk, Berlin, 1961, p. 40.
[5] F. Clementi, Il carnevale romano, Rome, 1899.

Belvedere Court next to the north side of the Vatican Palace offered an ideal setting for such entertainment in the context of horticulturally decorated spaces, as the upper two terraces of the court were planted as gardens. Already in February 1509 the lower court of the Belvedere was leveled by order of the pope in preparation for a bullfight,[6] but the climax of this type of entertainment in the Belvedere Court was the tournaments held there during the papacy of Pius IV.[7] In February 1561, when the architect Ligorio had just renewed work at the court, a splendid carousel "in the Spanish mode" took place in the lower court where several squadrons of knights led by papal nephews and their friends battled "at the barricade." Earlier in the century there had been occasional jousts at Rome during the carnival season, but the more popular entertainment had been the bullfight, which was a form of joust in which the wounding and killing of the animals involved appealed to the bloodlust of the populace. The second half of the sixteenth century was marked by a renewal of feudalism and chivalry represented dramatically in architecture by the country palace of the Farnese at Caprarola with its moat, bastions and domineering presence over the contiguous town. Similarly jousting then began to replace bullfights as a major feature of carnival. With the near completion of the Belvedere Court at the Vatican and the wedding of a papal nephew, Count Annibale Altemps, to a papal niece, Ortensia Borromeo, an even more splendid tournament was held in the court on March 5, 1565 (Fig. 44). The audience began assembling at dawn until all the loggias, balconies, great stairs, and windows were jammed with spectators—one contemporary account estimated some thirty thousand people. The fire from two batteries of artillery, one in the upper garden and the other in the lower court near the Borgia Tower, announced the commencement of the joust in the afternoon. After twelve squadrons of knights had battled, the festival ceased at nightfall with a burst of fireworks from the upper terrace of the huge niche at the end of the court.

The carnival seasons of 1576 and 1578 were likewise celebrated with jousts in the city and in 1579 the Medici cardinal offered his company a great feast at the hunting lodge of La Magliana with both a traditional bullfight and the "breaking of many lances." This use of the grounds of La Magliana for a joust may be the inspiration later in the carnival for the cardinal to set another joust of fifteen horses "in his gar-

den of the Trinità," that is, at the Villa Medici on the Pincian Hill.[8] Although the splendor of the event was dampened by rain, the Marchese di Riano, who participated faithfully in all the Roman jousts, won particular acclaim for his dexterity in "lancing the ring." The avvisi unfortunately do not specify the location of the games at the villa. Carnival, however, did not have to be the only inducement for tournaments, for on June 19, 1579, less than four months after the carnival joust at the Villa Medici, another similar encounter of tilting at the ring was held there with some of the same participants.[9]

Occasionally the less genteel entertainment of bear baiting and bullfights surfaced at some of the gardens. In July 1583 bear baiting was presented at the Villa Medici for the company honoring the visit of the duc de Joyeuse before sitting down to a lavish banquet, and during the carnival of 1584 an even fiercer event was planned at the garden of Giangiorgio Cesarini, consort of Clelia Farnese, the daughter of Cardinal Alessandro Farnese.[10] Cesarini scheduled a bullfight with a lion and dogs, but the lion, after two gorings by the bull, disgraced himself by turning to scuffling with the dogs. Undoubtedly the bullfight did not take place in the actual formal garden of the Cesarini, but they owned also several other less cultivated gardens there, since an old plan (Fig. 16) mentions "orti e giardino," where the entertainment may have occurred, or the piazza of S. Pietro in Vincoli next to the garden might have formed the bullring as happened elsewhere at Rome in the sixteenth century.

Giangiorgio Cesarini took great pride in his inherited position as Gonfaloniere, or standard bearer, of the city of Rome, so that the historian Francesco Sansovino could describe him as "having a reputation as a Knight inclined to the profession of arms, occupying himself in continuous military or knightly exercises."[11] His garden at S. Pietro in Vincoli was apparently to further this image. In 1585 he purchased a gigantic marble column from the Forum of Trajan which, according to a contemporary account, was to be erected in the garden with the addition of a bronze eagle to surmount it and a bronze bear chained to its base, thus reproducing the symbols of his coat of

[6] R. Lanciani, *Storia degli scavi di Roma*, I, Rome, 1902, p. 145.

[7] M. Tosi, *Il torneo di Belvedere in Vaticano*, Rome, 1946.

[8] BAV, Ms Urb. Lat. 1047, fol. 71r, last February 1579; published in F. Clementi, *Il carnevale romano*, p. 253.

[9] Ibid., fol. 232v, June 20, 1579.

[10] Ibid., Ms Urb. Lat. 1051, fol. 298r, July 9, 1583, and Ms Urb. Lat. 1052, fol. 56v, February 15, 1584; the latter published in E. Rossi, "Roma ignorata," *Roma*, VII, 1929, p. 517.

[11] F. Sansovino, *Della origine et de' fatti delle famiglie illustri d'Italia*, Venice, 1582, fol. 333r.

arms.[12] Although his death prevented the completion of the commemorative monument, it, in association with the gallery of Roman emperors (Caesars), suggests the formulation of a program celebrating his family and lordly position with a possible play on the name Cesarini. This would then furnish the appropriate setting for the almost ritualistic entertainment Giangiorgio offered his fellow nobility. The account of a banquet in August 1584 conveys a picture of this lordly life.

Wednesday morning, Lord Giangiorgio Cesarini gave a dinner at his garden of S. Pietro in Vincoli for one hundred princely gentlemen of this city and for other foreign nobility, almost as if in his position as King Ahasueris and his wife Queen Vashti, since Lady Cleria also did the same that afternoon for many ladies, this, however, being their custom almost every year for the festival day [of the church] near his garden [i.e., August 1, Festival of S. Pietro in Vincoli], and for his being Gonfaloniere of the Romans.[13]

Jousts continued to take place at the Villa Medici into at least the early seventeenth century. During the morning of November 24, 1609, Prince Peretti and the ambassador of Spain put on a manege demonstration at the villa followed by a banquet, and in the late afternoon tilting at the ring for prizes. Similarly in January 1612 the same hosts had another demonstration of horsemanship in the garden before dinner.[14] At the Villa Ludovisi the Falda plan (Fig. 125), dating from after the middle of the seventeenth century, identifies an alley on the west side of the layout (no. 9) as the Viale della Giostra and depicts two posts erected in the alley, presumably for "lancing the ring."

There are records of payment in 1627 totaling twenty-two scudi to the sculptor Domenico de Rossi for having cast a lifesize tilting horse evaluated by Bernini to stand in the gardens of the Barberini Palace.[15] One document describes the horse for jousting as made of papier-mâché (*carta pista*). Although an earlier document notes the payment for a horsehide to cover the "wooden horse," it also records payment for molding hooves of papier-mâché (*piedi di car-*

*tone*) for the same horse, as well as for metal fittings or rings for the horse's gear.[16] And as late as 1756 a payment was made at the Villa Pamphili for horsehair forelocks, tails, and manes for two artificial jousting horses.[17]

Later in the seventeenth century some of the plates of Gian Battista Falda's *Li giardini di Roma* illustrate the variety of games that took place in the Roman gardens.[18] There on the plan of the Villa Pamphili (Fig. 127) the uncultivated park at the rear is identified as "16. Serraglio o Parco oue si fa la caccia di diuersi animali" ("Enclosure or Park where the hunting of different animals takes place") and a stag hunt is depicted in that area. The long straight alley leading from the entrance portal past the side of the casino is labeled "2. Viale del gioco di maglio" ("The Alley of the Game of Pall-Mall") and in a later view of the casino two men stand in the alley holding the long mallets and a ball used in this primitive form of the game of croquet (Fig. 130). Similarly the Dutchman Sommelsdyck during his visit in 1654 notes running down the center of the garden of the Villa Medici "a large and beautiful alley, which they use for the game of Mall" and five years later the Englishman Mortoft will comment on the long walks of the Villa Medici making "a very convenient place to play at Mall."[19] Falda, however, in his view of the Villa Medici depicts in the foreground cross alley a young huntsman with a dog firing a musket at some birds (Fig. 180).

An unexecuted project for the Villa Pamphili by Virgilio Spada, friend and colleague of the famous architect Borromini, demonstrates the ingenuity shown by seventeenth-century designers for villa entertainment:

All the alleys and theaters of the garden should have masonry parapets so that after having enjoyed the garden during the morning by promenading there, while the guests are eating, the alleys and theaters can be inundated from the convenience and abundance of water from the nearby conduits. On notice to rise from the table one could with small boats go everywhere that a little before one went dry footed.[20]

[12] Lanciani, *Storia degli scavi di Roma*, I, p. 134, and C. Huelsen, review of *Le statue di Roma*, by P. G. Hübner, in *Göttingische gelehrte Anzeigen*, no. 176, 1914, p. 292.

[13] BAV, Ms Urb. Lat. 1052, fol. 275v, August 4, 1584.

[14] J.A.F. Orbaan, *Documenti sul barocco in Roma*, Rome, 1920, pp. 158, 197.

[15] M. A. Lavin, *Seventeenth-Century Barberini Documents and Inventories of Art*, New York, 1975, p. 38.

[16] Ibid., p. 47.

[17] A. Schiavo, *Villa Doria-Pamphilj*, Milan, 1942, p. 121.

[18] A. Tagliolini, *I giardini di Roma*, Rome, 1980, pp. 189–90.

[19] L. G. Pélissier, "Sur quelques documents utiles pour l'histoire des rapports entre la France et l'Italie," in *Atti del Congresso Internazionale di Scienze Storiche, 1903*, III, Rome, 1906, p. 181, and *Francis Mortoft: His Book*, ed. M. Letts, Hakluyt Society, ser. 2, no. LVII, London, 1925, p. 121.

[20] M. Heimbürger, "Alessandro Algardi architetto?" *Analecta Romana Instituti Danici*, VI, 1971, p. 219.

The essential aspect of entertainment in a Roman garden was always eating. In a letter of 1501 Agostino Vespucci wrote Machiavelli in despair of the Roman July heat, which prevents sleep, relating how the Romans

are continuously in the garden with women, and others similar to them, where they awaken the silent muse with their lyre, giving themselves pleasure and amusement. But, good God, what means they have, to my mind, and how much wine they guzzle after they have poetized! The Roman Vitellius and Sardanapalus of olden times have come to life again, nor would they be anything here. They [the Romans] have players of various instruments and they dance and leap with these girls in the manner of the Salii or rather the Bacchantes.[21]

The saints' feast days were, of course, one of the principal provocations for banquets in the Roman gardens during fair weather. In August 1606 for the feast of S. Pietro in Vincoli, which Giangiorgio Cesarini and his wife had honored previously with repasts, the titular cardinal after the church observances gave in his garden "a most sumptuous banquet to fourteen prelates who court him, and for which with music, decorations, hangings, and food, he had to spend one thousand scudi and he complained how much they had from him, since the merchant creditors meanwhile have stopped the payments from his investments (*Monti*)."[22] Similarly in August 1615 for the feast of S. Rocco, which was traditionally celebrated with boat races on the Tiber, Cardinal Caetani, whose palace had a garden overlooking the river, invited several cardinals to view the races. To entertain them

he gave a most regal banquet in the loggia of the garden, seating all of them at one side and at the ends of the table so as to enjoy fully the view of the gardens and fountains, which are there. He is praised for the abundance of food and the silence with which it was served whereby the splendor of the house of the Caetani is apparent and the skill of his servants who were able to serve at the different tables all at once the cupbearers, gentlemen, and grooms of the guests coming all day long with drink for all those who wished it. In addition to the boat races there was tightrope walking by a French acrobat with other worthwhile diversions of sound and song.[23]

Later in the century Cardinal Flavio Chigi, nephew of Pope Alexander VII, emulated the lavish banquets that their ancestor Agostino Chigi had offered Pope Leo X and his cardinals early in the sixteenth century at the Villa Farnesina or its riverside dining loggia,[24] with a magnificent feast accompanied by an elaborate operatic spectacle in the garden of his Villa alle Quattro Fontane on the Quirinal Hill at the corner of the present Via Nazionale and the Via Agostino de Pretis. In March 1668 the architect Carlo Fontana had signed a receipt for the delivery from Terni of some seven loads of "tartari," the spongy rock formation used for garden grottoes and waterworks, and in April there was a payment for vases to decorate the garden of the Quattro Fontane.[25] On August 4 avvisi speak of the preparation of a sumptuous banquet in the Chigi garden to honor the Rospigliosi, relatives of Pope Clement IX, but a week later the banquet was postponed until August 15.[26] An account of August 18 describes the guests received by a musician in rustic habit who provided them with a table of cheese and other country foods. Soon four wood nymphs appeared to reprimand the gardener for permitting entrance to their home and overturned his table. The rustic setting was then suddenly replaced by a regal garden where the guests dined after a deluge of perfumed water and confetti accompanied by music, including birdsongs. According to this notice everything "had been arranged by the Cavalier Bernini."

The attribution of the entertainment to Bernini and some details of the account seem to be inaccurate rumor. The architect Carlo Fontana, who had been in charge of the earlier work in the garden, published in November a long, detailed description of the banquet with illustrations of several settings.[27] The noble guests, all identified by Fontana, descended from the casino into the garden by torchlight, the time being "twenty-four hours" or sunset. A wide avenue through the garden, divided into flower beds and enlivened by fountains, led to the raised stage at one end, which was seemingly completely wooded except for a small opening in the center (Fig. 181). Two small semicircular flights of stairs in the center led up

[21] P. Villari, *Niccolò Machiavelli e i suoi tempi*, 2nd ed., Milan, 1895, I, p. 574.

[22] Orbaan, *Documenti*, p. 74.

[23] Ibid., pp. 236–37.

[24] D. R. Coffin, *The Villa in the Life of Renaissance Rome*, Princeton, N.J., 1979, pp. 107–8.

[25] The documents and old descriptions of the garden are published in V. Golzio, *Documenti artistici sul Seicento nell'Archivio Chigi*, Rome, 1939, pp. 189–200.

[26] BAV, Ms Barb. Lat. 6401, fols. 181v, 193v, 209.

[27] [C. Fontana,] *Risposta del Signor Carlo Fontana alla lettera dell'Illustriss. Sig. Ottavio Castiglioni*, Rome, 1668.

181. Rome, Villa Chigi at the Four Fountains, woodland setting for feast, 1688

to a table set with sausage, cheese, and wine and overseen by the gardener, Ciarmaglia, who greeted the guests with song. Three nature deities, Bacchus, Flora, and Pomona, then appeared to scold the gardener for such rustic fare. Flora promised a wealth of flowers, Pomona all the fruits, and Bacchus, touching the gardener's table with his thyrsis, completely changed the setting. Amid thunder and lightning followed by a shower of scented water and hail of confectionery, the table disappeared and was replaced by a fountain of water between the stairs. Simultaneously the woods vanished, revealing a richly appareled dining set framed by a huge *credenza* or sideboard with seven levels of plate at the right or west and a similar *bottiglieria* or buttery at the left. The rear of the dining stage was closed by a wall with a central wall fountain and niches with floral vases (Fig. 182). The three gods reappeared in new costumes to sing to the guests. Finally, two huge tables lavishly set with food, which stood temporarily at the sides in the large arches of the credenza and the bottiglieria, slid into the center of the stage to feed the guests (Fig. 183).

Similarly Queen Christina, who abdicated her Protestant throne of Sweden to be converted to Catholicism, entertained her new subjects in Rome both intellectually and musically, often using the gardens of the rented Palazzo Riario at the foot of the Janiculum Hill as the setting for her entertainment (Fig. 135). In September 1688 the Marchese Del Monte persuaded the queen to mount a musical *serenata* at his nearby rented Casino del Cipresso.[28] In an amphitheater set within a small garden of jasmine "the most famous musicians of Rome sang there together with two of the better songstresses of the Queen, who were Georgina, or as she is known, Angelica, and Mariuccia, daughter of the Marchese del Monte."

Another time the queen held a musical collation in her own garden.[29] After a concert by the singer Angelica in the woods, the crowd of visitors entered a "cabinet of verdure" where was presented a wonderful collation of the "most beautiful and exquisite fruit in the world and with most exquisite wines and waters." While they dined, a band of trumpeteers on a hill above the garden serenaded the guests with the popular tune, "Le Flon, le Flon," whose last words echoing in the garden were sung gaily by all the guests, including the queen.

For a short time after the queen's death in 1689 the

[28] [Ch. G. Franckenstein,] *Istoria degli intrighi galanti della Regina Cristina di Svezia e della sua corte durante il di lei soggiorno a Roma*, ed. J. Bignami Odier and G. Morelli, Rome, 1979, p. 140.
[29] Ibid., p. 171.

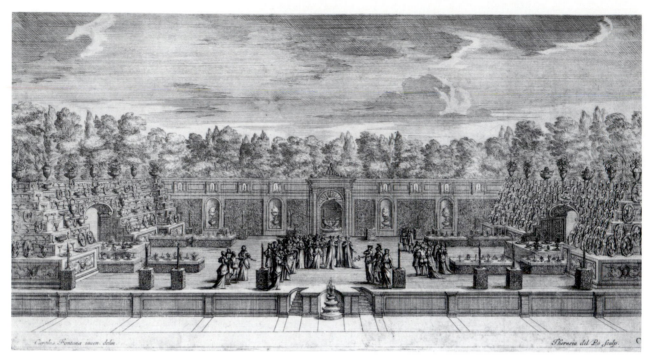

182. Rome, Villa Chigi at the Four Fountains, dining setting, 1688

183. Rome, Villa Chigi at the Four Fountains, banquet, 1688

gardens of the Palazzo Riario would be the home of the famous Arcadian Academy, which, succeeding the Royal Academy established by the queen, would reestablish the idea of a sylvan or garden setting for intellectual gatherings. During the Renaissance gardens had been especially associated with the intellectual meetings of poets and philosophers. We have already noted that in the Colonna garden on the Capitoline Hill there was an alley planted with ivy and laurel, the latter sacred to Apollo, the god of the arts and particularly of poetry, and the alley was for meditative walking and "to philosophize." Similarly the favorite topos expressed in the iconography of many Roman Renaissance gardens was Mount Parnassus, home of the Muses, the goddesses of the arts.[30] The most famous sixteenth-century literary gatherings were those held in the gardens of Johannes Goritz (died 1527), known to the Italians as Giovanni Coricio or Corycius, and of Angelo Colocci (1467–1549).[31] Goritz, a northerner whose name first appears in Rome in 1497 as a notary of the Rota in the Vatican, was devoted to St. Anne. He commissioned the sculptor Andrea Sansovino to carve the group of the Madonna and St. Anne dedicated in 1512 in Sant'Agostino and had Raphael paint the prophet Isaiah on the pier above the statue in its original location in the church. Every year Coricio invited the poets of Rome and the literati of the Vatican to celebrate the festival of his patron saint at her statue and then to banquet in his garden near the Capitoline Hill. For this annual occasion those present composed poems, which were published in 1524 by Blosio Palladio under the title *Coryciana*. In the foreword to the anthology Blosio likens Coricio in humanistic fashion to the "Corycium senem" of Vergil's *Georgics* (IV, 125–48), whose land was no longer fertile, but who lived out a happy life content with the modest fruits of his garden. It is a similar literary theme to that called "Beatus ille," which, derived from Horace's second epode, pervades English gardening in the seventeenth and eighteenth centuries.[32]

The garden of Coricio stood on the slope of the Capitoline Hill near the Forum of Trajan. Some time ago the Roman historian, Domenico Gnoli, searching for Coricio's house and garden, found on the Via dei Carbonari the remains of a sixteenth-century house incorporated into a later rebuilding and an old inscription, "I. Coritius. Trevir. MDXVII." Of the old building there was a loggia of three arches open onto the area presumedly of the renowned garden. Unfortunately the creation of the Via dell'Impero destroyed the entire site.

The poems describe a garden of lemon and citron trees among which were fragments of ancient statues, sarcophagi, and inscriptions. The major feature was a grotto with a Latin inscription: *Nymphae Loci. Bibe, lava, tace. Coricius* ("To the nymph of the place. Drink, wash, be silent"). Here, as Blosio Palladio asserts, "the Muses, brought down from Mounts Helicon and Parnassus, are transferred to your gardens near the Tarpeian and Quirinal Hills. . . . In all the world, I dare say, no gathering nor banquet is more noble or illustrious than yours on that day [of St. Anne]." With a company numbering Bembo, Sadoleto, Castiglione, Giovio, Vida, Flaminio, Colocci, and Beroaldo, the claims of Blosio are not too exaggerated, for these are the literary figures of the Rome of Leo X. In the Vergilian metaphor of the age, Goritz was a very modest Maecenas whose devotion to St. Anne lent a Christian aura to the gatherings, but it was a bucolic spirit that prevailed. In the words of one guest, "our happy host, Corycius, runs meanwhile here and there among all the tables and fills the cups of wine with a liberal hand, arousing raucous laughter," all in contravention of the admonition of his grotto to "drink, wash, and be silent."

More informal and, therefore, more typical were the literary and convivial gatherings in the garden of Angelo Colocci, who arrived in Rome in 1497. By 1513 Colocci had purchased a garden at the foot of the Pincian Hill in which stood a large arch of the ancient aqueduct of the Aqua Virgo. Near the arch was a fountain with the image of a reclining water nymph (Fig. 22) and a famous inscription dedicated to the nymph, ending with the phrase, *Sive Bibas Sive Lavere Tace*,[33] similar to the brief inscription on Coricio's grotto. As in Coricio's garden, there were stones with classic inscriptions or reliefs and groups or frag-

[30] See the discussion in Chapter 5.

[31] D. Gnoli, "Orti letterari nella Roma di Leon X," *Nuova Antologia*, CCCXLVII, 1930, pp. 3–19, 137–48. For Goritz, see U. Gnoli, "Ceramiche romane del Cinquecento," *Dedalo*, II, 1921, pp. 199–202, and D. Gnoli, *La Roma di Leon X*, Milan, 1938, pp. 151–58. A drawing in the Uffizi (989A) attributed to one of the Sangallos is inscribed as of Goritz's garden; see G. Giovannoni, *Antonio da Sangallo il Giovane*, Rome, n.d., I, p. 26.

[32] See M. Rostvig, *The Happy Man*, Oxford and Oslo, 1954.

[33] See Chapter 3. For Colocci, see especially F. Ubaldini, *Vita di Mons. Angelo Colocci*, ed. V. Fanelli (Studi e testi, 256), Vatican City, 1969; G. F. Lancellotti, *Poesie italiane, e latine di Monsignor Angelo Colocci*, Jesi, 1772; and V. Fanelli, *Ricerche su Angelo Colocci e sulla Roma Cinquecentesca* (Studi e testi, 283), Vatican City, 1979.

ments of ancient sculpture. One inscription (*CIL*, VI, 22) was particularly appropriate, since it records the Sallustian gardens in which Colocci created his retreat. The collection of sculpture was quite impressive. In 1527 Andrea Fulvio lists a group of Socrates embracing Alcibiades, which was probably Silenus with Bacchus, figures of Jupiter Ammon, Proteus, and Aesculapius, a calendar bas-relief with the tutelary gods of five of the months (*CIL*, VI, 46), and a measure of the Roman foot. In every respect the garden of Colocci was on a larger scale than that of his contemporary Coricio; even its literary coterie was more famous, in part because of the longer period of its activity, which was renewed after the Sack of Rome in 1527.

Angelo Colocci's arrival in Rome in 1497 coincided with the death of Pomponio Leto, the leader of the Roman Academy, thus encouraging Colocci to continue Leto's role. From 1486 to 1491 Colocci had lived in Naples where, in company with the poet Sannazaro, he was a member of the famous academy of Giovanni Pontano. In Colocci's Roman garden there gathered, in addition to the participants in Coricio's banquets, poets and literary figures such as Tebaldeo, Molza, Navagero, Inghirami, Valeriani, and Casanova. For all of them the nymph of the Aqua Virgo was inspiration and a flood of lyric poetry, good and bad, honored her. Some of the poetry is preserved in a manuscript in the Vatican (Ms Vat. Lat. 3388), gathered together by Cardinal Marcello Cervini, who was later to reign briefly as Pope Marcellus II (April 1555). In one poem Giambattista Casalio, referring to Colocci under his academic name Bassus, has Apollo beg the Muses to return to Mount Helicon, which they have deserted for Colocci's garden.[34]

The best picture of the activities of these literati is given in a letter of 1529 written to Colocci by Sadoleto from Carpentras in France, where the latter had retired to his episcopal duties dissatisfied with the actions of the papal court at Rome. The letter describes their life under Leo X before the Sack of Rome in 1527, which vividly confirmed the fears that inspired Sadoleto's retreat. So Sadoleto recalls

the past when many of us were accustomed to get together and our age was rather disposed to joy and merriment. How many times do you think there come to my mind those gatherings and banquets which we were repeatedly accustomed to hold? When either in your

suburban gardens, or in mine on the Quirinal, or in the Circus Maximus, or on the bank of the Tiber at the temple of Hercules, and indeed at other times in other localities of the city, there were held meetings of very learned men, who were graced with especial virtue and the universal praise of all. Where, after an intimate banquet not so much dependent on many delicacies as on many witty sayings, either poems were recited or orations proclaimed to the greatest pleasure of all of us who listened, since both praise of the noblest things appeared in these and there were those who, nevertheless, offered much mirth and beauty.[35]

The good spirits and informality of the relations among these men is borne out by an undated letter to Colocci, probably written between 1524 and early 1527 while Giberti was datary, in which Blosio Palladio invites himself and comrades to Colocci's garden.

Messer [Battista] Sanga, Messer Lorenzo Grana and I, being yesterday at dinner with Monsignore the Datary [Giammatteo Giberti], resolved to come to dinner today with you at the Aqua Virgo; and so, relying upon your courtesy and kindness, we will come at twenty-three hours [an hour before sunset]. So that we may not be accused of presumption, with two sausages and seven pounds of veal. You may add the rest, that is all, especially Pisones and Agrestones. The names now of your invited guests are, namely, Master Giovanni Coricio Edentulus [the toothless one], with Pylius that enemy of ceremony, Testudo [the tortoise], Pietro Corsi, Lutius.[36]

That these spontaneous dinner gatherings are inspired by the meetings of the academy is seen in another similarly undated but later note written to Colocci by Paolo Giovio: "Vigil [Fabio], Blosio [Palladio] and Maffei [Bernardo] will lunch tomorrow with me in my park [*in paradiso*], so that the delightful friendship of the old Academy will be renewed. We expect you the most learned of all. We repeatedly and urgently beseech that you favor us if you can because of your gout."[37]

At this time or earlier Giammatteo Giberti, who was at first secretary to Cardinal Giulio de' Medici and then datary (1524–1528) in the Vatican when the cardinal was elected Pope Clement VII, presumably founded an academy associated with a garden at

---

[34] F. Ubaldini, *Vita Angeli Colotii Episcopi Nucerini*, Rome, 1673, p. 42.

[35] J. Sadoleto, *Epistolarum libri sexdecim*, Lyons, 1560, p. 188.

[36] V. Cian, "Gioviana," *Giornale storico della letteratura italiana*, XVII, 1891, pp. 293–94.

[37] P. de Nolhac, *La bibliothèque de Fulvio Orsini*, Paris, 1887, p. 134, n. 6.

Rome. The only evidence is the much later claim of Cardinal Federigo Borromeo that "Matteo Giberti also founded another Academy whose inscription I recall seeing in a garden in Rome along with Cardinal Aldobrandini, who later was Clement VIII. In fact, we had entered there by chance and we both looked at that inscription."[38]

With the death of Leo X and election of Hadrian VI in 1521 the revival of Vergilian Rome was suspended. Colocci lost his office in the Vatican court and six years later with the disastrous Sack of Rome his coin collection and library were destroyed or scattered. Already in 1531 Colocci and his neighbor Antonio del Bufalo had traded contiguous property and one of Colocci's damaged houses was incorporated into the magnificent gardens that Del Bufalo possessed next to that of Colocci.

Jacopo Sadoleto, who first gained fame as one of the Latin secretaries of Pope Leo X, bought in May 1518 the vigna mentioned in his letter to Colocci. Situated on the Quirinal Hill on the southeastern side of the Alta Semita, later the Via Pia and now the Via del Quirinale, roughly in the area of public gardens northeast of the church of S. Andrea al Quirinale, the location was a superb one for a suburban villa as is demonstrated by the later purchases of neighboring tracts by the wealthiest of the cardinals at Rome.

For Sadoleto his vigna, in addition to being a center for gay dinners topped by poetic improvisations, was a retreat where he could concentrate quietly on his philosophical writings. One of his dialogues, the commentary on Paul's Epistle to the Romans, is introduced as occurring at the vigna: "Once during the festival of Pentecost when I was in my gardens at Rome which are on the Quirinal Hill at the Alta Semita . . . my brother Giulio approached me."[39] Since Giulio Sadoleto died in 1521, the date of the three days of discussion is presumed to be before that time. Later in the dialogue the two brothers were joined by Cardinal Trivulzio and Guillaume du Bellay.

Another dialogue, one in praise of philosophy, *De Laudibus philosophiae*, of which Sadoleto completed the first part, the *Phaedrus*, while in retirement in late 1522 and early 1523 at his Quirinal vigna, is set at the suburban villa of the Roman Jacopo Gallo, near the Castel Sant'Angelo.[40] Early in the morning during spring Sadoleto says that he went "to the gardens which Gallo had created for himself and for his learned friends in a field of fennel near Hadrian's tomb." There Sadoleto met Cetrari, Fedra, and Gallo and, after "complimentary exchanges in the hippodrome (for such was the name of the western edge of the field)," they walked together, while Fedra attacked the contemplative life. Gallo adds a little more information about the vigna and garden when he is made to remark that his "villetta . . . will certainly then become more famous because of this discourse of yours than for the exotic plants gathered here from everywhere or for the beautiful paintings that adorn the portico." By the end of the *Phaedrus* Gallo urged the participants to retire into the villa where there was a shady court with a "lovely exedra." The second part of the dialogue, entitled the *Hortensius*, written later by Sadoleto as a reply to the accusations of Fedra in the *Phaedrus*, takes place as they sit in a garden path near the portico of the villa. The end of the dialogue finds them passing "the remainder of that happy and pleasant day at the table in various discussions accompanied by the congenial witticisms of Fedra."

By the sixteenth century it was a standard literary device to depict a garden or villa as the *locus amoenus* for a philosophical dialogue. Roman antiquity, and particularly the dialogues of Cicero, gave the authority for this custom. Even those early fifteenth-century Florentine dialogues, which had found in Aristotle's *Nicomachean Ethics* and Cicero's letters and dialogues support for the active life, were set in the solitude of the villa or garden and not the bustling city, which was advocated as a citizen's arena of activity. However, Sadoleto in a letter of 1536 to Mario Maffei Volterrano, to whom Sadoleto dedicated his dialogue, suggests that for his dialogue the location is not merely a question of literary tradition, since he is publishing "the defense of philosophy which I sustained some years ago in the suburban villa of Jacopo Gallo against the eloquent, but rather unjust, accusation uttered by your relative Tommaso Fedro." The fact that the letter is addressed to Mario Maffei, who was a member of the literary circle at Rome in the time of Leo X, indicates that the location of the dialogue and even, perhaps, the actual discussion existed, although the details of the discussion are purely the literary production of Sadoleto. As Tommaso Inghirami, the Fedro of the dialogue, died in 1516, the suburban villa and gardens of Gallo must have been frequented by his friends from at least the early reign of Leo X

[38] L. A. Muratori, ed., *Caroli Sigoni Mutinensis Opera omnia*, I, Milan, 1732, p. XI.

[39] J. Sadoleto, *In Pauli epistolam ad Romanos commentariorum libri tres*, Lyons, 1535, p. 11.

[40] J. Sadoleto, *Elogio della Sapienza (De Laudibus philosophiae)*, trans. A. Altamura, Naples, 1950.

(1513–1521). In terms of the history of villa and garden architecture the most interesting aspect of Sadoleto's description is his comment that the western portion of the vigna was called the hippodrome. As was noted previously, in Roman antiquity Pliny the Younger had likewise used the word hippodrome to describe part of the gardens attached to his Tuscan villa (*Letters*, v, 6) and very soon after the presumed date of the discussion at Gallo's villa, Raphael designed in a hippodrome form one of the terraces of the Villa Madama, which work was overseen by Maffei, Sadoleto's correspondent, for Cardinal Giulio de' Medici, the future Pope Clement VII.[41]

Not far from Gallo's suburban villa another garden became famous as a meeting place for the Roman intellectuals. Lelio Giraldi set the first dialogue of his *De poetis nostrum temporum* in the garden of the Castel Sant'Angelo, which Pope Leo X created for Bianca Rangone in partial repayment for the help she had given him as a cardinal in 1512 after his capture by the French at Ravenna.[42] Her further reward was the election of her son Ercole as a cardinal. As Bianca Rangone was in Rome from September 1513 to September 1515, the garden in the castle must have been prepared at this time. In fact, throughout the papacy of Leo X a gardener for the castle was paid regularly a monthly salary of three ducats and the pope himself found the castle a pleasant retreat, particularly in the summer.[43] In a letter of July 1520 the Ferrarese ambassador reported that Leo lunched at the castle and that he remarked that he could sleep better at night in the castle, avoiding the flies that infested the Vatican Palace.[44] As one of the participants in Giraldi's dialogue was again Giulio Sadoleto, brother of the cardinal, the presumed date of the dialogue must be before his death in 1521 during the papacy of Leo X.

The location of the castle garden is visible in later engravings. One by Lafreri in the middle of the sixteenth century depicts at the right of the great, round,

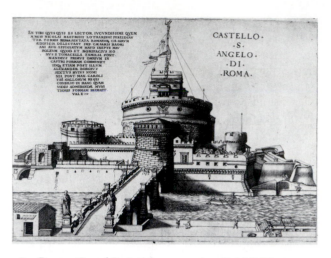

184. Rome, Castel S. Angelo, engraving, British Museum

entrance tower facing the Tiber River a crenellated wall with fireports below the crenellations and the tops of trees looming over the wall (Fig. 184). Another engraving by Lafreri looking down into the garden reveals a three-arched loggia facing the garden on the ground floor of the structure that rises between the entrance tower and the garden wall. Despite the claim of Giraldi that Leo X "prepared" (*paraverat*) the garden for Bianca Rangone, there is earlier evidence for a garden at the castle. In 1486 and 1487 Pope Innocent VIII paid for the reconstruction of "the wall of the lower garden on the side of the Tiber."[45] This fifteenth-century garden, however, was presumably outside the walls of the castle between it and the river. Historians of the fortress have assumed that the walled garden was built by Pope Alexander VI at the time he created the entrance tower, since the garden loggia was decorated with stories of the pope. The reference in Giraldi, therefore, must only mean that Leo X planted or rearranged the garden for Bianca Rangone. The entrance tower of Alexander VI and the garden wall were destroyed in the seventeenth century by Pope Urban VIII in order to widen the river bed and thereby eliminate the disastrous floods that plagued sixteenth-century Rome. Although the protecting garden walls were leveled, the garden itself remained as can be seen in Nolli's map of Rome of 1748. Eventually the gardens too gave way for the Lungotevere.

When Clement VII came to the papacy in 1523 he appointed his cousin Giovanni Rucellai governor of the Castel Sant'Angelo. Although Rucellai only lived

[41] Coffin, *The Villa*, pp. 246–56.

[42] L. G. Giraldi, "De poetis nostrum temporum," in *Lateinische Litteratur-denkmäler des XV und XVI Jahrhunderts*, 10, ed. K. Wotke, Berlin, 1894, p. 8, and V. Rossi, "Per la cronologia e il testo dei dialoghi 'De poetis nostrorum temporum' di Lilio Gregorio Giraldi," *Giornale storico della letteratura italiana*, XXXVII, 1901, pp. 246–77.

[43] Regarding the castle, see E. Rodocanachi, *Le Château Saint-Ange*, Paris, 1909; M. Borgatti, *Castel Sant'Angelo in Roma*, Rome, 1930; and C. d'Onofrio, *Castel S. Angelo e Borgo tra Roma e Papato*, Rome, 1978, pp. 266–67.

[44] A. Ferrajoli, "Il ruolo della corte di Leone X (1514–1516)," *Archivio della R. società romana di storia patria*, XXXV, 1912, p. 488, n. 1.

[45] E. Müntz, *Les arts à la cour des papes Innocent VIII, Alexandre VI, Pie III*, Paris, 1898, pp. 50, 280.

about eighteen months longer, he devoted such attention to embellishing the garden that it soon attracted the Roman literati.[46] The humanist Giangiorgio Trissino, who was in Rome at the same time, later wrote a dialogue, entitled *Il Castellano* in honor of Rucellai, with the garden of the castle as its setting.[47] The tradition of literary-philosophical gardens was dear to Trissino, who earlier participated in the philosophical and political discussions of the Rucellai gardens, or Orti Oricellari, in Florence.[48] Trissino commences the dialogue when Giovanni Rucellai

> taking his leisure, went down and entered that lovely garden of orange trees which is above the water, and having sat down to talk with me (who was very familiar with him), he was told that Messer Jacopo Sannazaro and Antonio Lelio had come to visit him. Immediately going to meet them, he gaily received them and, having them sit with him under that loggetta, which is there, they began to discuss together things of beauty and of virtue worthy of them.

As a garden, that of the Castel Sant'Angelo is the end of a long tradition of walled-in, castle gardens provided with fruit trees and the protection of a small *loggia* for repose out of the sun, but where one can enjoy a glimpse of nature in flower.

A more interesting garden, which later may have served as the location for learned dialogues, is the garden of Fra Mariano, Leo X's favorite table companion and jester, at the Dominican monastery and church of S. Silvestro al Quirinale. Fra Mariano dwelt, as he notes in 1519, in the imprisonment of the Vatican Palace, but occasionally he could seek freedom with his fellow Fratri in the garden of S. Silvestro, only to return each evening to the Vatican.[49] The garden originally stood behind the church on the upper slope of the Quirinal overlooking the Colonna gardens. According to the Portuguese artist, Francisco d'Ollanda, it was at S. Silvestro al Quirinale that he heard Michelangelo discuss art with Vittoria Colonna and Lattanzio Tolomei in October 1538. Publishing these dialogues ten years later, Francisco locates the third dialogue in the garden where Michelangelo and Tolomei "pass the siesta hour in the midst of trees, ivy and running water." They sit "at the foot of a laurel tree on a stone bench where, leaning against the green ivy that covered the wall, we all found a comfortable position from which we could view a good part of the city." The authenticity of these dialogues has been doubted, as some of the statements attributed to Michelangelo do not seem creditable and the character of the discussions suggests a literary creation. Nevertheless, the garden of S. Silvestro existed, and Francisco's dialogues represent another example of the garden topos for a dialogue in which the choice of an actual site lends reality to the discussion.

The Sack of Rome in 1527 temporarily disrupted the literary gatherings, which had begun to flourish in the time of Leo X. When these gatherings are revived, particularly after the election of Paul III in 1534, they are truly more academic in spirit with names for the academies, humanistic pseudonyms for the participants, and occasionally even specific programs for discussion rather than the more improvisatory nature of the earlier meetings.

Biagio Pallai, called Blosio Palladio (died 1550), was one of the most active academicians of the first half of the sixteenth century. He first acquired literary fame in 1512 when he wrote a Latin poem lauding and describing the magnificent Villa Farnesina of Agostino Chigi. Against the wishes of his friend Coricio, Palladio published in 1524 the poems celebrating the feast of St. Anne. At the election of Clement VII, Palladio became a papal secretary and Paul III rewarded him in 1540 with the bishopric of Foligno. By at least 1531 Palladio had acquired a suburban villa near the Vatican, since in that year Sadoleto wrote from Carpentras that he had heard often how much Palladio enjoyed his vineyards and buildings.[50] The tone of the letter suggests the recent acquisition of the property by Palladio. Several poems by his friend Marc Antonio Flaminio (*Carmina*, I, 55–65) dedicated to Palladio or his mistress identified as Turunda, the classical name for the ball of suet fed to fattening geese, refer to the gardens of the villa. In one poem (*Carmina*, I, 55) Flaminio praises the gardens

[46] On August 15, 1524, thirty-three ducats were spent on order of Rucellai for "repair" of the garden; see E. Müntz, "Les monuments antiques de Rome à l'époque de la Renaissance," *Revue archéologique*, ser. 3, V, 1885, pp. 361–62.

[47] G. G. Trissino, "Dialogo del Trissino intitolato Il Castellano," in *Tutti le opere di Giovan Giorgio Trissino*, II, Verona, 1729, p. 222.

[48] F. Gilbert, "Bernardo Rucellai and the Orti Oricellari: A Study of the Origin of Political Thought," *Journal of the Warburg and Courtauld Institutes*, XII, 1949, pp. 101–31.

[49] A. Luzio, "Federigo Gonzaga ostaggio alla corte di Giulio II," *Archivio della R. società romana di storia patria*, IX, 1886, pp. 574–75.

[50] A. Ferrajoli, "Il ruolo della corte di Leone X (1514–1516)," *Archivio della R. società romana di storia patria*, XXXVIII, 1915, p. 444.

as one of the literary centers of Rome dedicated to fostering the Muses and speaks of sparkling fountains and dark caves. Another poem (*Carmina*, I, 57) alludes to grapes, apple, pear, and lemon trees, and emphasizes the abundance of the pure, cold water of the fountains. In 1541 a mandate of Paul III records the payment to Palladio of fifty scudi for work in his vigna "below the Belvedere in the location called Valle dell'Inferno."[51] It may be at this time that Palladio widened the old road through the Valle dell'Inferno at the foot of the Belvedere and paved it with rubble and gravel up to his vigna, as is mentioned in a later letter of the Cardinal Camerlingo.[52] Palladio also built then a bridge over the ditch at the gate to the vigna to escape the winter torrents that rushed from the hills down into the Prati. Palladio's casino stood, therefore, on the top of Monte Ciocci just outside the northeastern wall of the Vatican. Unlike most of the contemporary vigne of Rome, there is preserved a detailed, Latin description of Palladio's garden written in 1544 by Girolamo Rorario:

When we are in Rome, I led some German nobles to the gardens of Blosio, where I showed them at the base of the valley the marble fountain surrounded by marble benches behind which verdant laurels shaded another sunny fountain. I led them among the dense vines along the wide path planted with fruit trees of all kinds. Having mounted the steep alley through the small wood of very fragrant lemon trees to the stone fishpools, one on each side, we arrived at the open area where my friend Blosio Palladio of the captivating city of Rome, whose name alone revives me, is accustomed to dine. Near the clear fountain murmur small streams of water led through the simulated rock of the arch of rough stone clotted by the falling drops of the Tiburtine river. I showed them another fountain opposite, falling gently through a similar rock, both of which watered the lemon trees, and between them buildings erected for the preparation of food, in the midst of which shot up a third fountain with superimposed columns in the form of a theater bearing an arbor of vines, all lightly suspended. As we entered the ascending path at the left near the fountain, I pointed to the laurel grove provided so that berries would not be lacking to feed the birds. Thus, they said, the pine is born in Germany, just as in the Roman land of the lemon tree the laurels are born; whoever has not seen a pine should

no less admire it. Having arrived at the house of Blosio, I showed them in the rear the henhouse with brick walls where they admired the Indian peacocks basking in the wide court at the rear; they were less interested in the hens huddled together, the geese, and the steward enjoying their company. We entered the wine cellar set between both buildings big enough at the most for two hundred vessels.[53]

Early in this century Domenico Gnoli found remains of Palladio's casino and gardens.[54] A small bridge still led into the lower gardens of which only the two fishpools were preserved. At the level of the dining theater there were traces of the brick colonnade which once carried the vine arbor, and fragments of the Tiburtine stone rockery stood in one of the fountains. On the summit of the hill was Palladio's casino, used then as a customhouse. By 1938 the slope in front of the casino was completely torn away, destroying the remains of the garden and leaving the casino perched precariously on the edge of the hill. The extant casino, which is now a pathetic wreck, has undoubtedly undergone many changes.[55] Thus, the inexorable expansion of the city has finally destroyed Palladio's suburban villa.

During the reign of Pope Paul III (1534–1550) a succession of academies became the center of intellectual life in Rome. The first of these groups, the Accademia dei Vignaiuoli, was formed soon after 1532 when Umberto Strozzi, a nephew of Castiglione, came to Rome from Naples. According to Marco Sabino, the accademici, including Berni, Mauro, Della Casa, Lelio Capilupo, Abbot Firenzuola, Gian Francesco Bini, and Giovio da Lucca, met almost daily at Strozzi's house for literary improvisation and music under the direction of the two censors of the Academy, Pietro Ghinucci and Federigo Paltroni. A letter of Francesco Berni to Gianfrancesco Bini in April 1534 indicates that the academy was flourishing by that time, as in it Berni sends greetings to Molza, Della Casa, "and all that divine Academy."[56] The letter continues with horticultural metaphors in which Berni wishes that Bini's garden should be productive all year under a benign Priapus. Antonfrancesco Doni in his *La seconda libraria* (1551) and his *Mondi ce-*

---

[51] L. Dorez, *La cour du Pape Paul III*, Paris, 1932, I, p. 216, n. 10. Its location, identified as Vigna Colonna, is visible on Nolli's 1748 plan of Rome; see A. P. Frutaz, *Le piante di Roma*, Rome, 1962, III, pl. 412.

[52] [G. L. Marini,] *Degli archiatri pontificij*, II, Rome, 1784, p. 274.

[53] G. Rorario, *Quod Animalia bruta ratione vtantur melius Homine*, Paris, 1648, pp. 117–19.

[54] Gnoli, *La Roma di Leon X*, p. 161.

[55] I. Belli Barsali, ed., *Per le ville di Roma e del Lazio*, Rome, 1968, figs. 73, 74, and I. Belli Barsali, *Ville di Roma: Lazio I*, Milan, 1970, p. 382, with a plan of the present ground floor.

[56] D. Atanagi, *De le lettere facete et piacevoli di diversi grandi huomi, et chiari ingegni*, Venice, 1561, p. 320.

*lesti, terrestri, et infernali degli Academici Pelegrini* (1563) describes the program of the Accademia dei Vignaiuoli. He claims that the academicians, all of whom bore horticultural pseudonyms, such as the Quince (*cotogno*), Billhook (*pennato*), or Fig (*fico*), met to discuss the cultivation of vines, the planting and drying of fruits, or horticultural tools. Several burlesque poems by members of the group in honor of the bean, of figs, or of Priapus suggest the activities of the academy.[57] The Accademia del Vignaiuoli, which was merely a gathering of kindred spirits, continues the burlesque joviality of earlier literary groups and does it still within the world of the vigna and of the garden, but as the sixteenth century progressed the numerous academies that proliferated often became more dignified and less interested in an outdoor setting. So the Accademia della Virtù led by Claudio Tolomei eventually turned from its burlesque offerings, such as the *Naseide* of Annibal Caro on the nose of Giovan Francesco Leoni, to the study of the ancient Roman architect Vitruvius and his ideas.[58] At the end of the seventeenth century, however, with the foundation of the Arcadian Academy, there was a renewed interest in literary matters conducted within a sylvan or garden ambience.

In 1674 a group of intellectuals interested in philosophy and poetry had founded the Accademia Reale under the patronage of the queen of Sweden at her Palazzo Riario. Among the principles of the academy the last was concerned with improving the Tuscan tongue by imitating the writers of the time of the Roman emperor Augustus and at the time of Pope Leo X, since contemporary writing was too "turgid and bombastic."[59] On October 5, 1690, a year and a half after the death of the queen, fourteen writers gathered in a meadow in the gardens of the Monastery of S. Pietro in Montorio on the Janiculum Hill to form the Accademia dell'Arcadia.[60] Their goal was likewise to reform literary style. One of the founders, the official "custodian" (*custode*) Crescimbeni, noted that sci-

ence had flourished in Italy in the seventeenth century, but letters had deteriorated and the academy was founded "to exterminate bad taste" in literature.[61] As the name of their society indicates, they were inspired by the epic poem *Arcadia* of the Neapolitan poet Sannazaro, who had helped to revive the pastoral mode of poetry in the early sixteenth century. So each member of the academy was given as his pseudonym an ancient shepherd's name combined with the name of one of the regions of ancient Arcadia. The eminent jurist Gianvincenzo Gravina defined the rules of the new academy and in 1696 read his *Oratio pro legibus Arcadum*, asserting that they should return "to the simplicity of nature" and "having washed away the stain of citizenly ambition, they should bring back spontaneously the law of nature."[62] Their society should shepherd in another Golden Age. The insignia of the academy, therefore, was the shepherd's pan pipe of seven reeds crowned by sprigs of laurel and pine.

The early history of the academy described in 1719 by Crescimbeni in his history of the church of Sta. Maria in Cosmedin is one of constant movement from one garden to another in Rome, seeking an appropriate home for their poetic contests or orations. From May 1691 the academicians began to meet around a "large round ditch" in the gardens of the Palazzo Riario, the former home of the Accademia Reale of the queen of Sweden. Although the Arcadian Academy had not been founded by the queen's academicians, many of them soon swelled the growing membership of the new group. The "round ditch," serving as an amphitheater, exemplified the ideals of rustic simplicity of the life of shepherds. In 1693 an academician, Cavalier Felini, Roman agent of the duke of Parma, gained permission from the duke for the academy to transfer to his renowned garden on the Palatine Hill. As the legendary home of Evander, the king of the Arcadians, the Palatine gardens were most appropriate for a permanent seat of the academy. In June 1693 the academicians inaugurated in the woods a round theater with two ranks of earthen seats planted with laurel (Fig. 185). The center of the theater was planted with myrtle topiary in the form

[57] L. Campana, "Monsignor Giovanni della Casa e suoi tempi," *Studi storici*, XVI, 1907, pp. 47–52.

[58] M. Maylender, *Storia delle accademie d'Italia*, V, Bologna, 1930, pp. 479–80, and L. Sbaragli, *Claudio Tolomei*, Siena, 1939, pp. 49–53.

[59] R. Stephan, "A Note on Christina and Her Academies," in *Queen Christina of Sweden: Documents and Studies* (Analecta Reginensia, I), ed. M. von Platen, Stockholm, 1966, pp. 365–71.

[60] See especially G. B. Crescimbeni, *Stato della basilica diaconale, collegiata, e parrocchiale di S. Maria in Cosmedin di Roma*, Rome, 1719, pp. 110–33; E. Portal, *L'Arcadia*, n.p., 1922; and C. d'Onofrio, *Roma val bene un'abiura*, Rome, 1976, pp. 263–90. A sociological study of the academy is offered by A. Quondam,

"L'istituzione Arcadia: Sociologia e ideologia di un'accademia," *Quaderni storici*, VIII, 1973, pp. 388–438.

[61] Crescimbeni, *S. Maria in Cosmedin*, pp. 110–11.

[62] G. Costa, *La leggenda dei secoli d'oro nella letteratura italiana*, Bari, 1972, pp. 157–58, and M. Werner-Fädler, *Das Arkadienbild und der Mythos der goldenen Zeit in der französischen Literatur des 17. und 18. Jahrhunderts*, Salzburg, 1972, p. 106.

185. Rome, Farnese Gardens, Arcadian Academy

186. Rome, Aventine Hill, Ginnasi Gardens, Arcadian Academy

of a panpipe, the insignia of the academy. In 1696 there were also set up in the theater marble tablets inscribed with the laws of the society. Soon, however, the academy was to lose what they had expected to be their permanent home. In 1698 violent dissension arose among the members over several satires read at their meetings. Cavalier Felini, fearing the anger of the duke of Parma when he learned of the scandalous comments, ordered the academicians in May 1699 to leave their Palatine home.

Duke Salviati offered the academy a new home in his garden where an oval theater was excavated into the slope of a small hill with three ranks of seats in the upper part of the theater and one below, but with the death of the duke in 1704 the academy moved on. By 1705 they had a round theater with benches covered with green tapestries in the Giustiniani gardens outside the Porta del Popolo. Then from 1707 until 1712 the academy had its seat in the Ruspoli gardens on the Esquiline Hill. When Prince Ruspoli proposed to the duke of Parma in July 1712 that the marble tablets inscribed with the laws of the academy, which had been left in the Farnese gardens on the Palatine, be moved to the Ruspoli gardens, the duke pointed out that the stones were a conspicuous indication of how his house had aided the first efforts of the group and suggested that Prince Ruspoli have copies made for his garden. Still later in 1712, however, the academy moved to the gardens on the Aventine Hill in a vigna formerly of the Savelli family, but then owned by Cardinal Ginnasi. The architect, Giovanni Battista Contini, who was an academician, was then commissioned to build there an amphitheater of three levels of seats with a *platea* carefully restricted to 68 palmi (ca. 15.19 meters) in diameter so that the voice of any shepherd declaiming his poetry could be heard by an audience of about three hundred seated and more

than one hundred standees (Fig. 186). Four aisles led into the theater, the two on the south flanking a broad throne with seats for twelve cardinals. Opposite the cardinals were seats for a discussant and for a poet, separated by a marble statue of a seated Apollo, his right hand resting on a lyre and holding in his left hand a gilded pipe of seven reeds, the symbol of the Arcadians.

The peregrinations of the academy from one temporary horticultural home to another ceased when in 1724 King John V of Portugal, elected an academician, gave four thousand scudi to create a permanent seat. A building committee of academicians led by the architect Antonio Canevari visited many sites in and around Rome. They finally chose a large, partially cultivated garden on a rather steep slope of the Janiculum Hill below the Acqua Paola and near to the gardens of the Palazzo Riario, where they had earlier resided, purchasing it for one thousand scudi. In 1725 Canevari with the assistance of another academician, the architect Nicola Salvi, designed an intriguing garden obviously inspired by the famous Spanish Stairs on the Pincian Hill of Rome just begun by the architect Francesco De Sanctis (Fig. 187).[63] A short wide stair from the entrance gateway leads to two curving staircases that, embracing two fountains dedicated to the rivers Tiber and Arno, mount the hillside among laurel groves appropriate to Apollo (Fig. 188). The diverging staircases come together at a second level

---

[63] M. Loret, "La Scalinata della Trinità de' Monti vista dal suo autore," in *Atti del V Congresso Nazionale di Studi Romani*, Rome, 1942, III, pp. 456–62. Actually the plan of an unrealized project for the Spanish Stairs by the architect Alessandro Specchi is so similar to that of Canevari's garden that one can only suspect a specific relationship; see L. Salerno, *Piazza di Spagna*, Naples, 1967, fig. 102.

187. Rome, Arcadian Academy, project, Accademia di S. Luca, Rome

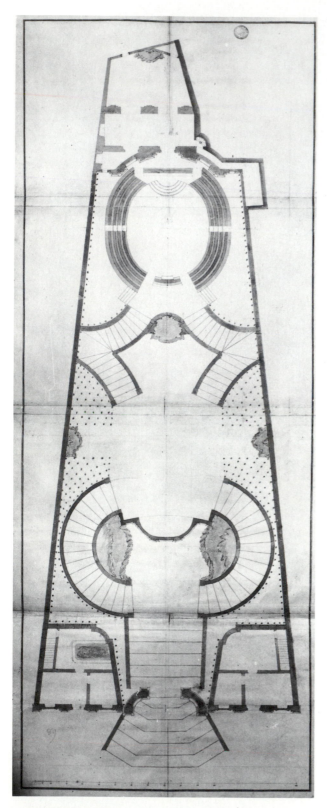

188. Rome, Arcadian Academy, plan, Accademia di S. Luca, Rome

where a visitor looking back can view the city of Rome. Again, two stairs flare out around a central grotto and then return to the central axis where one comes out into the opening of the oval amphitheater with four ranks of seats. Like Contini's amphitheater in the Ginnasi garden, there is a broad throne for the cardinals and a seat for the reciting shepherd. The concave, classic facade of a small building, serving as backdrop for the auditorium, contains a room for private recitals and service rooms, including space for the archives of the academy, which are now in the Biblioteca Angelica.

The similarity of the design of the Spanish Stairs to that of the Arcadian Academy cannot be accidental or merely the result of a lack of inventiveness on the part of Canevari, the designer of the garden. Canevari was an academic architect, not only a member of the predominantly literary academy of the Arcadians, but also a recent member of the Academy of St. Luke, the old artistic academy of Rome. To any academician, whether literary or artistic, imitation was one of the principles of good art and contributed to the meaning of the work of art. The Spanish Stairs offered a magnificent urban transformation of a site that in Roman antiquity was known as the Hill of the Gardens, particularly as the home of the lavish gardens of Lucullus. The urban starkness of the present Spanish Stairs was not the original intention of its designer De Sanctis, who in a contemporary memorandum noted that there were to be planted along the sides of the stairs double files of trees that should shade the stairs from the summer sun.[64] Any Roman would have been conscious of the allusion to the Spanish Stairs made by Canevari in the garden of the Arcadian Academy, as he was subtly ringing a change on what was basically urban design by using it as the model for a garden design. There may even be suggested an Arcadian association for the city of Rome as two of its hills are brought together by a similar artistic design.

It was proposed to lay the foundation stone of the new theater on October 5, 1725, as appropriate to the first meeting of the society on October 5, 1690, but because of rain the ceremony had to be postponed to October 8. The official inauguration of the new home of the academy was held on September 9, 1726, with such a crowd that even the platea of the amphitheater was occupied. A description of the amphitheater, published in 1726 before it was fully completed,[65] claimed that on the summit of the building, as seen

[64] Loret, "La Scalinata," p. 460.
[65] D'Onofrio, *Roma val bene un'abiura*, pp. 273–74.

also in Canevari's design (Fig. 187), was to be a statue of the winged horse Pegasus, relating the site to the ancient Mount Parnassus, home of the Muses.

This home of the Muses became the center of attention for many of the aspiring poets and intellectuals of western Europe. Actually the meetings of the academy were often more social affairs than intellectual meetings. A letter of Mme. du Bocage from Rome in November 1757 relating her attendance at a meeting of the academicians conveys well the social atmosphere.[66] She notes that the meeting was held to receive her, for unlike most seventeenth- and eighteenth-century academies, the Arcadian Academy welcomed women to their meetings. After Mme. du Bocage offered her thanks in verse, which she claimed she "stammered out," and several of the academicians had praised her in verse, a young Orsini prince proclaimed a Latin poem in her honor and was followed by his sister, the sixteen-year-old Duchess d'Arcé, who did the same in Italian.

> I was the saint of the day. . . . When the assembly was over, I took the liberty to tell her father, the cardinal *Orsini*, that his daughter was the goddess of *Rome*. I was overheard by that beauty, who immediately replied, "no, madam, the *Romans* borrowed their Gods from foreign countries." I was as much at a loss, as

[66] Mme. du Bocage, *Letters concerning England, Holland and Italy*, London, 1770, ii, pp. 114–17.

tennis-players, who seldom throw back the ball at the proper time. I am inclined to think that the incense of flattery is highly salutary; I am supported by it, and find myself the better in health.

Even the great German writer Goethe became a member of the academy. In his *Italienische Reise* Goethe gives a somewhat reluctant account of his admission to the society.[67] "At the end of 1786 I was besieged on all sides by people trying to persuade me that I should allow myself to be admitted into Arcadia as a distinguished shepherd." His inauguration was held in the meeting room of the academy within its building at the rear of the garden or as his diploma noted, "Dato alla Capanna del Serbatojo dentro il Bosco Parrasio" ("Given at the shepherd's hut of the archives within the Parrhasian Wood").

At the time Goethe joined the Arcadian Academy Marie Antoinette of France was completing her *hameau*, or rustic village, in the grounds of the Petit Trianon at Versailles. Both offered a rather pale and almost trivial reflection of the pastoral spirit that had revived in fifteenth- and early sixteenth-century Italy, but both created wonderful garden settings in which contemporary society could assemble and be entertained.

[67] J. W. Goethe, *Italian Journey (1786–1788)*, trans. W. H. Auden and E. Mayer, New York, 1968, pp. 441–45.

# The Public and the Roman Garden

On May 12, 1885, Prince Marcantonio Borghese ordered the gates of the park of his villa at Rome to be closed to the public, which had been accustomed to ride or walk freely in the grounds.[1] Rumors had already begun to circulate in Rome that Borghese was planning to sell about two-thirds of his estate for some 8 million lire, or 20 million according to other reports, to building speculators, retaining only the casino and its immediate gardens for his own use. With the establishment of Rome as the capital of the new Kingdom of Italy in 1871, the city was undergoing rapid expansion, endangering the undeveloped portions of the city. Earlier in 1885, on April 6, the prince of Piombino had sold the huge Ludovisi villa park on the Pincian Hill, just within the city walls outside of which lay the Borghese park, and the Ludovisi gardens were being transformed into the urban development now centered around the Via Veneto. So on May 8, 1885, Duke Leopoldo Torlonia, mayor of Rome, heeding the rumors regarding the Borghese holdings, wrote to Borghese that before he should alienate any of his property, Torlonia would like to discuss it with him

on behalf of the commune of Rome, adding "independent of eventual rights that the municipality might itself point out." The latter phrase alarmed Borghese, who in his reply of May 11 announced his decision to close the park to the public, thus ensuring his legal ownership of the estate.

On June 26 the city, having appealed to the courts, won the right of public access to the property four afternoons a week, as was the previous custom, and Prince Borghese was fined court costs. The appeal of the prince to a superior court was disallowed in February 1887 with confirmation of the previous decision. Finally the controversy was resolved in 1901 when the State purchased the park and the casino with its works of art for 3.6 million lire, and presented them in 1903 to the city of Rome as a public park and museum.

The previous decisions of the courts had been very difficult, since it was acknowledged that the Borghese family legally owned the property, but that the Roman public had right of access for public *passeggiata*. The Roman legal code provided no laws or decisions exactly relevant, but the courts could cite a few analogous examples, such as access to fountains provided for public use on private property. Also in forming the decision, the courts took into account that some of the land had belonged to the Camera Apostolica before Pope Paul V gave it to his nephew, Cardinal Scipione Borghese, that the cardinal had been provided with water from the public aqueducts, that an old public road had been incorporated within the grounds of the villa, that some of the ancient statues used to decorate the villa had come from public loca-

[1] Among the wealth of documentation regarding the nineteenth-century controversy, see especially P. S. Mancini, L. Meucci, and C. Rebecchini, *Il diritto del popolo romano sulla Villa Borghese in giudizio di reintegrazione in grado di appello: Memoria*, Rome, 1885; A. Gennarelli, *La Villa Pinciana fuori della Porta Flaminia ed i diretti del Popolo Romano e dello Stato sulla medesima: Memoria*, Rome, 1885; P.L.D.V. (pseudonym for Ludovico Passarini), *La questione di Villa Borghese*, Rome, 1885; L. Vicchi, *Villa Borghese nella storia e nella tradizione del popolo romano*, Rome, 1886; and G. Biroccini, *Dissertazione sul Villa Borghese letta in Arcadia*, Rome, 1886.

tions, and that there were numerous records confirming the tradition of public access.

In the evidence cited by the courts and all discussions on the problem, reference was particularly made to a Latin inscription that once stood in the garden behind the casino (Fig. 123). The text of the inscription, which is now presumably lost, was first printed in Manilli's mid-seventeenth-century guide to the villa:

> I, custodian of the Villa Borghese on the Pincio, proclaim the following:
> Whoever you are, if you are free, do not fear here the fetters of the law.
> Go where you wish, pluck what you wish, leave when you wish.
> These things are provided more for strangers than for the owner.
> As in the Golden Age when freedom from the cares of time made everything golden, the owner refuses to impose iron laws on the well-behaved guest.
> Let proper pleasure be here as the law to a friend, but if anyone with deceit and intent should transgress the golden laws of hospitality, beware lest the angry steward break his token of friendship.[2]

The Villa Borghese inscription, which has been suggested as the possible creation of Cardinal Maffeo Barberini, later Pope Urban VIII, who composed for Cardinal Borghese the distychs inscribed on the base of Bernini's group of *Apollo and Daphne* in the Villa Borghese,[3] still retains the association of a garden with the mythical Golden Age of classical antiquity when man was nourished by nature without labor and was free from turmoil and laws. This association, revived by fifteenth-century poets, had during the sixteenth century even inspired the iconographical planning of gardens, as at the Villa Lante at Bagnaia. At the same time the inscription was one of the finest and latest examples of what has become known as the *Lex Hortorum*, the principle that gardens are created not only for the personal enjoyment of their owners, but to afford pleasure to their friends and even to strangers and the public, diminishing the concept of private property.

Probably the earliest example in Renaissance Rome of the *Lex Hortorum* was an inscription in the grounds of the Villa Carafa or Vigna di Napoli, the suburban residence of Cardinal Carafa of Naples on the northwest edge of the Quirinal Hill, where the present Quirinal Palace of the president of Italy stands (Fig. 17). The cardinal's Quirinal villa may date before 1476 and certainly was in existence in 1483, when the Cardinal of Aragon spent the night there.[4] The first mention of inscriptions at the Villa is in Albertini's guide to Rome of 1510 where he mentions that the vigna and garden were decorated "with many epigrams."[5] The inscriptions in the Villa Carafa, which presumably date from the late fifteenth century, were only published in 1592 by Schrader, who had made several trips to Italy in the mid-sixteenth century. All the pithy epigrams in Greek and Latin are derived from the classical poets and agricultural writers, including Vergil (*Georgics*, I, 338–39), Pliny the Elder (*Historia Naturalis*, XVIII, viii, 43), Cato, Varro, and Columella (all quoted by Pliny), and Hesiod (*Works and Days*, 354). A longer, contemporary inscription offered Cardinal Carafa's interpretation of the *Lex Hortorum*:

> The dutiful Cardinal Oliviero Carafa, illustrious offspring of learned Naples, dedicates this villa of continuous salubrity, set on the suburban Esquiline Hill, to all his friends, come guests.[6]

Later in 1522–1523 Cardinal Sadoleto in his dialogue *Il Fedro*, which he locates in the vigna of Jacopo Gallo set in the Prati of Rome outside the walls of the Castel Sant'Angelo, conveys the same sentiment when he begins the dialogue: "During the floral holidays, early in the morning, I took myself to the gardens which Gallo had created for himself and for his learned friends in a field of fennel near the Hadrianic tomb."[7]

As the Roman gardens in the late fifteenth and early sixteenth centuries began to amass large collections of ancient sculpture and inscriptions as their particular decorative feature, the concept of the *Lex Hortorum* began to spread, since the owners took pride in showing their treasures as evidence of their cultural heritage. Cardinal Giuliano Cesarini at the turn of the

---

[2] See Appendix IV, 1.

[3] P. della Pergola, *Villa Borghese*, Rome, 1962, p. 13.

[4] Dr. Andrea Brenzio in an introductory letter to a book dedicated to Pope Sixtus IV says it was written at Cardinal Carafa's vigna where the physician had withdrawn during the plague, which has been suggested as the plague of 1476; see [G. L. Marini,] *Degli archiatri pontificj*, Rome, 1784, I, p. 215. For Cardinal Aragon's visit, see P. Paschini, *Il carteggio fra il Card. Marco Barbo e Giovanni Lorenzi (1481–1490)*, Vatican City, 1948, p. 94.

[5] F. Albertini, *Opusculum de mirabilibus novae & veteris urbis Romae*, Rome, 1510.

[6] See Appendix IV, 2.

[7] J. Sadoleto, *Elogio della Sapienza (De laudibus philosophiae)*, trans. A. Altamura, Naples, 1950, p. 13.

century possessed such a collection in the garden behind his palace on the old Via Papale in Rome. An inscription on the statuary garden house (*diaeta statuaria*) read:

> Giuliano Cesarini, Cardinal Deacon of Sant'Angelo, has dedicated this statuary pavilion to his own studies and to the decorous pleasure of his countrymen on his thirty-fourth birthday, the thirteenth Kalends of the eighth year of Pope Alexander VI, the year 1500, and the 2,233rd year of the founding of Rome.[8]

Somewhat later the several Cesi cardinals assembled in the garden of their palace in the Borgo near St. Peter's a large collection of Roman antiquities. Although the first collection was formed in the early 1520s, it was sold and then replaced by another collection during the fourth and fifth decades of the century. A garden portal, probably dating from the period of the later collection, bore the inscription: "The Garden of the Cesi and of Their Friends," as recorded in a drawing attributed to Ammannati.[9] Still later the French cardinal Jean Du Bellay, who had a collection of antiquities in the lovely garden he arranged in part of the ruins of the Baths of Diocletian, had the entrance portal inscribed on the exterior with the name of the garden, *Horti Bellaiani*, and on the interior face of the portal a similar dedicatory inscription: "Jean, Cardinal Bishop of Ostia, founded [these gardens] for himself and his friends, 1555."[10]

The fullest exposition of the *Lex Hortorum* was in the garden statue court of Cardinal Andrea della Valle, designed by Lorenzetto probably in the 1520s as a "hanging garden" above the stables at the cardinal's palace in the center of Rome. The visual appearance of the garden is preserved in Cock's engraving of 1553, probably after a drawing by Heemskerck made during his Roman trip from 1532 to 1535, and in a drawing in Francisco d'Ollanda's manuscript in the Escorial of 1537 or 1538 (Fig. 14). The court, created as a setting for the cardinal's collection of ancient sculpture, has the sculpture set into the walls or in niches. Low garden beds along the walls were planted with small trees and flowers, and vines and fruit trees were espaliered against the walls. At the top level on each of the long side walls were five large antique masks alternating with four modern inscriptions in which the cardinal defined the purposes of his sculpture court:

Right Wall

- I. For the restoration of damaged statues and the decoration of the hanging gardens.
- II. For the enjoyment of friends and for the delight of citizens and strangers.
- III. Not for pleasure, but for the sake of the people and their prosperity.
- IV. For the enjoyment of life as a retreat of taste and beauty.

Left Wall

- V. For his own enjoyment and the pleasure of posterity.
- VI. For a garden of antiquities as an aid to painters and poets.
- VII. For the enjoyment of proper leisure and for the convenience of the house.
- VIII. In memory of our ancestors and for the emulation of their descendants.[11]

It was Cardinal della Valle, therefore, who expanded the concept of the *Lex Hortorum* to include not only his friends, but all Romans and visitors, as well as specifically noting the contribution of the garden collection to artists. Unfortunately the Della Valle Sculpture Court, later owned by his nephew Camillo Capranica, was dismantled toward the end of the sixteenth century, and its ancient sculpture, sold to Cardinal Ferdinando de' Medici, was used to decorate the Villa Medici at Rome.

The Villa Giulia, built from 1551 to 1555 for Pope Julius III off the Via Flaminia just north of the Porta del Popolo, still preserves *in situ* the inscription of its *Lex Hortorum*. The casino of the villa is set in a valley south of the Parioli hills and was originally surrounded by the extensive land holdings that constituted the vigna (Fig. 119). The main casino was designed with a horizontal axis running from its entrance portal through the theater court behind the casino to a sunken nymphaeum or fountain court. On the interior side walls of the nymphaeum are two large, inscribed plaques. The plaque on the left or north wall describes the history and ownership of the villa, forbidding alienation of the property by the pope's heirs. The opposite plaque on the south wall (Fig. 189) preserves a very lovely, extended version of the *Lex Hortorum*, noting that the garden is for seemly pleasure and establishing the laws by which it is to be enjoyed.[12] Like the *Lex Hortorum* of the Villa Borghese, visitors are permitted to walk freely or rest

---

[8] See Appendix IV, 3.
[9] See Appendix IV, 4.
[10] S. Ortolani, *S. Bernardo alle Terme*, Rome, n.d., p. 14.

[11] See Appendix IV, 5.
[12] See Appendix IV, 6.

189. Rome, Villa Giulia, nymphaeum, *Lex Hortorum*

190. Rome, Villa Medici, portal with *Lex Hortorum*

Having entered, guest, these gardens that Ferdinando de' Medici created at great expense, may it satisfy you seeing and enjoying them; may you wish nothing more.[13]

The Villa Mattei on the Caelian Hill behind Santa Maria in Domnica had a long history of public enjoyment and is now fittingly a public park like that of the Villa Borghese. Purchased in 1553 by Giacomo Mattei, it was his son-in-law, Ciriaco Mattei, who began to transform it into a magnificent villa park with richly decorated gardens. Given an ancient obelisk, which once stood on the Capitoline Hill, Mattei erected the obelisk in the *prato* before the casino with an inscription, dated 1582, recording the gift of the "Roman people" as a monument to public goodwill (Fig. 76). Four years later he inscribed on the main gate to the villa the following:

Ciriaco Mattei dedicated in 1586 to his enjoyment and that of his friends the Caelian gardens, given by Giacomo Mattei, his father-in-law, to him and his descendants, developed more magnificently with many decorations.[14]

In his will, dated July 26, 1610, Mattei claimed that the "garden has been of great recreation and entertainment to me and of enjoyment of *virtuosi* and men of reputation, the house being seen often and being

where they wish as long as they harm nothing. It then elaborates on the pleasures of the garden—the spurts of the Acqua Vergine, the playfulness of the fish and the song of the birds, the statuary and painting.

In 1576 Cardinal Ferdinando de' Medici purchased the villa of Cardinal Ricci on the Pincian Hill and soon began to expand and revise his new possession, including work on the gardens behind the villa. A long, straight alley was laid down from the gardens out to the Via di Porta Pinciana, where the architect Ammannati designed an impressive, rusticated gateway (Fig. 190) to permit public entrance to the gardens without disturbing the residents of the villa. Two Latin inscriptions carved on plaques above the side niches of the public gate welcomed visitors:

On entering, guest, into these gardens planted as you see, on the summit of the Hill of Gardens, may it ever please you to praise them; you should know that they are open to the master and all the master's friends.

[13] See Appendix IV, 7.
[14] S. Benedetti, *Giacomo Del Duca e l'architettura del Cinquecento*, Rome, 1972–1973, pp. 308–36, and E. B. MacDougall, "The Villa Mattei and the Development of the Roman Garden Style," Ph.D. dissertation, Harvard University, 1970.

247

visited daily not only by persons of note and people of Rome but by foreigners."[15]

Unlike some of the examples of the *Lex Hortorum*, which were inscribed on the public portal of the gardens, the location of the inscription at the Villa Giulia addressed to the general visitor, but set within the innermost and seemingly most private area of the vigna, would suggest that either the concept of the *Lex Hortorum* was hypocritical or that there was a broadly observed and well-understood tradition of free access to the gardens by most of the public. This was also true at Cardinal della Valle's statue court, which was set within the palace at an upper level over the stables.[16] The wealth of sixteenth-century artists' sketchbooks and drawings depicting antique sculpture in Roman gardens suggests the freedom of access offered them and confirms the intent of the Della Valle inscription that his garden was to be an aid to artists.[17]

Understandably it is foreign visitors who remark on the accessibility of the Roman gardens. So in March 1554 the German monk, Matthäus Rot, records in his account of his Roman trip visiting the Villa Giulia when "Balduino del Monte, brother of the Pontifex, was driven to the vigna in a carriage and carried to the fountain in a litter; I was admitted with him so that I could contemplate perfectly the fountain from every part."[18] This custom of free access, however, is most clearly expressed by the Frenchman Michel de Montaigne:

> Among the most beautiful vineyards are those of the Cardinal d'Este at Monte Cavallo, Farnese on the Palatine, Orsini, Sforza, Medici: that of Pope Julius, that of Madama, the gardens of Farnese and of Cardinal Riario at Trastevere, and of Cesi outside the Porta del Popolo. These are beauties open to anyone who wants to enjoy them, and for whatever purpose, even to sleep there, even in company if the masters are not there, and they do not like to go there much.[19]

One cannot, of course, interpret this right of access in a modern, democratic context. The Latin language of the inscriptions alone indicates the limitation of this concept. Undoubtedly the outcasts of sixteenth-century Roman society, such as the beggars or the Jews, might not be accorded that privilege, as an incident at the Villa Medici reported in an avviso of April 1581 notes:

> This week some Jews having gone to see the Garden of the Cardinal de' Medici under the Trinità, the day being last Saturday, were against their will put to work with a wheelbarrow moving earth and then given a good meal as recompense.[20]

Nevertheless, the avviso does indicate the ease of access into these gardens.

During the eighteenth and early nineteenth centuries in Rome the freedom of public access continued, although Volkmann in his guide to Italy of 1770–1771, based on his trip of 1757–1758, claims that only the Villa Medici was freely open and then "only to people of the middle class," while a gratuity of a couple of "Groschen" to the porter was required at other gardens.[21] Lady Miller, however, claims in 1771 that at the Corsini gardens: "The public are allowed to walk in these gardens; a very great convenience, and an instance, amongst others, of the Italian hospitality." Similarly she notes the freedom of access to the Borghese gardens, although limited to twice a week, where the English play cricket and football watched by the Roman ladies with "their fine *Abba-*

[15] R. Lanciani, *Storia degli scavi di Roma*, III, Rome, 1907, p. 84.

[16] Nolli's magnificent eighteenth-century plan of Rome presents diagramatically the areas of public access then and undoubtedly earlier. The urban palaces and buildings of private ownership are depicted as solid black blocks, and those areas freely open to the public are in white, as are the streets, the interiors of churches, and the courtyards of palaces with their accesses from the streets; see F. Ehrle, ed., *Roma al tempo di Benedetto XIV: La pianta di Roma di Giambattista Nolli del 1748*, Vatican City, 1932.

[17] Some of the most notable sketchbooks are those of the Bolognese painter Aspertini (P. P. Bober, *Drawings after the Antique by Amico Aspertini*, London, 1957), the Dutch painter Heemskerck (C. Huelsen and H. Egger, eds., *Die Römischen Skizzenbücher von Marten van Heemskerck*, Berlin, 1913 and 1916), the Portuguese painter Ollanda (E. Tormo, ed., *Os desenhos das antigualhas que vio Francisco d'Ollanda, pintor portugues*, Madrid, 1940), the Italian sculptor-architect Dosio (C. Huelsen, ed., *Das Skizzenbuch des Giovannantonio Dosio*, Berlin, 1933), and the French sculptor Pierre Jacques (S. Reinach, ed., *L'album de Pierre Jacques sculpteur de Reims dessiné à Rome de 1572 à 1577*, Paris, 1902). See also P. P. Bober and R. O. Rubinstein, *Renaissance Artists and Antique Sculpture*, London, 1986.

[18] Gmelin, "Die Romreise des Salemer Conventuals und späteren Abtes, Matthäus Rot, 1554," *Zeitschrift für die Geschichte des Oberrheins*, XXXII, 1880, p. 249.

[19] M. de Montaigne, *The Complete Works of Montaigne*, trans. D. M. Frame, Stanford, Calif., 1957, p. 960.

[20] BAV, Ms Urb. Lat. 1049, fol. 175r, April 29, 1581.

[21] J. J. Volkmann, *Historisch-kritische Nachrichten von Italien*, 2nd ed., Leipzig, 1777, II, pp. 764–65.

*tis.*"[22] The most prominent exception to public access seems to have been the Villa Ludovisi, which never exhibited a welcoming inscription nor had a public gateway. So in 1779 the English Lord Herbert commented in his diary at Rome: "In the Evening we went to the *Villa Ludovisi* belonging to Prince Piombino, his Mother a ficklesome old Lady has the Key, and seldom permits any body to see it."[23]

In the early nineteenth century James Forsyth observed the continuation of the tradition by remarking when he arrived at the Villa Ludovisi: "This is the only place in Rome where a ticket of admission is required at the gates: not that Prince Piombino reserves the sacred retreat for himself; but his porters and gardeners take advantage of his absence and his order, and are only the more exacting from those strangers whom they admit without his leave."[24] At the Villa Borghese the inscription of the *Lex Hortorum* inspired Forsyth to an amusing panegyric:

> A few cardinals created all the great villas of Rome. Their riches, their taste, their learning, their leisure, their frugality, all conspired in this single object. While the Eminent founder was squandering thousands on a statue, he would allot but one crown for his own dinner. He had no children, no stud, no dogs, to keep. He built indeed for his own pleasure, or for the admiration of others; but he embellished his country, he promoted the resort of rich foreigners, and he afforded them a high intellectual treat for a few pauls, which never entered his pocket.

In contrast Forsyth condemns his countrymen for their materialistic egotism:

> How seldom are great fortunes spent so elegantly in England: How many are absorbed in the table, the field, or the turf; expenses which centre and end in the rich egotist himself! What English villa is open, like the Borghese, as a common drive to the whole metropolis?[25]

Since the relationship of the public to European private gardens has a confusing and changing history dependent upon local laws and traditions often related to the psychology of the individual owner, it would seem particularly significant that many Roman gardens in the sixteenth and early seventeenth centuries not only permitted free access to the public, but proclaimed that right in the *Lex Hortorum* inscribed on their walls. This custom of publicly dedicating gardens to the pleasure of friends and even strangers seems to be a particular sixteenth-century Roman idea and reflects a change from the earlier attitude toward the villa and its garden.

Early in the fifteenth century the great Italian humanist and architect, Leon Battista Alberti, in a little treatise on the villa asserted: "You will buy the villa to nourish your family, not to give pleasure to others."[26] Alberti's treatise is modeled, therefore, on those of the ancient agricultural writers, the *Res Rusticae Scriptores*, such as Cato and Varro, who extol the agricultural and productive aspect of the country residence during the Roman Republic and are uneasy, as Varro certainly was, about the increasing association of luxury and idle pleasure with the Roman villa, but Alberti's dictum was as in vain as the desires of Varro.

The change in the purpose of the Roman villa and garden came about toward the end of the fifteenth century, possibly as a result of several factors. Certainly the collecting of Roman antiquities and their exhibition in Roman courts and gardens, commencing in the late fifteenth century, encouraged access to their gardens, as evidenced by the dedicatory inscriptions in the statuary gardens of Cardinal Giuliano Cesarini in 1500 and of Cardinal della Valle. Similarly the humanists and antiquarians must have been aware of the public nature of some of the ancient Roman gardens. So Julius Caesar bequeathed his garden on the right bank of the Tiber to the Roman people and Agrippa left the Romans the gardens in the Campus Martius near the baths he created for the people. In fact, it is probable that he built the gardens for the public, but had not completed them before his death.[27] To my knowledge, however, none of the contemporary accounts of Renaissance Roman gardens make reference to these precedents, which is understandable, as the ancient examples were concerned

[22] A. R. Miller, *Letters from Italy*, London, 1776, III, pp. 79, 152–55.

[23] [Henry Herbert, Earl of Pembroke,] *Henry, Elizabeth and George (1734–80)*, London, 1939, p. 278.

[24] J. Forsyth, *Remarks on Antiquities, Arts and Letters during an Excursion in Italy in the Years 1802 and 1803*, 4th ed., London, 1835, pp. 230–31.

[25] Ibid., pp. 219–20.

[26] L. B. Alberti, *Opere volgari*, ed. C. Grayson, I, Bari, 1960, p. 359.

[27] For Caesar, see Suetonius, *Caesar*, LXXXIII; Cicero, *The Philippic Orations*, II, 109; and Dio Cassius, XLIV, 35; and for Agrippa, Dio Cassius, LIV, 29, 4, and P. Grimal, *Les Jardins romains*, 2nd ed., Paris, 1969, pp. 179–80.

with public ownership and not public access. Whether private gardens of ancient Rome were regularly open to the public is difficult to determine. The gardens of Sallust between the Quirinal and Pincian Hills, later owned by the emperors, may have been accessible at least by the fourth century to some of the public. The first of the fourth-century Pseudo-Seneca letters to St. Paul claims that Seneca and his friend Lucilius "retired to the gardens of Sallust," where they were presumably joined by several disciples of St. Paul, and an anonymous panegyric of Constantine in the early fourth century remarks on the fearful reluctance of Maxentius to visit the gardens.[28] As these seem to be the only ancient references to the accessibility of the gardens of Sallust, they may have inspired the comment of Michele Mercati in the late sixteenth century that the gardens of Sallust were "filled with delights made for the amusement of the Roman people," but it is equally possible that he viewed the ancient gardens from the perspective of a sixteenth-century Roman garden.[29]

A more likely source of the concept of public access to gardens in Rome in the early sixteenth century may be offered by the writings of the Neapolitan humanist and statesman, Giovanni Pontano. Two of his treatises written after 1494 and published in 1498 discuss the role of architecture and its furnishings for the image of its owner. In the treatise on Magnificence Pontano praised Cosimo de' Medici for building churches, villas, and libraries and for renewing "the custom of using private money for the public good and for the ornament of his native country."[30] The accompanying treatise on Splendor then differentiates between the two virtues:

> It is not unjustified to relate splendor closely to magnificence, since the former also involves great expense and has money in common with it as its material. Magnificence, however, assumes its name from magnitude and is involved in buildings, public shows, and gifts. Splendor, on the other hand, which is resplendent in domestic ornament, in care of the person, in furnishings, in the disposition of different things, then takes its name from being showy. So as the word magnifi-

cence is derived from making large things, then the latter virtue comes from showy things. Moreover magnificence is more involved in public works and those things of more permanence, while splendor is concerned rather with private things and does not slight more transient or smaller things.[31]

So the last chapter of Pontano's treatise on Splendor is entitled "On Gardens and Villas,"[32] in which he notes that gardens are for walking in and as settings for banquets. Therefore, they should contain exotic and rare plants, "for the reason for gardens for the thrifty and profit-seeking father of a family should not be the same as for those for a splendid man." In contrast to Alberti's earlier dictum that the villa and its garden should be a source of nourishment for the family and not for the pleasure of others, Pontano asserts that the splendid man "should not only feed his family well and sumptuously, but will have to his table many, as they say, fellow citizens and strangers [*cives peregrinosque*]," which is echoed later in the dedicatory inscription of Cardinal della Valle's statuary garden at Rome "for the delight of citizens and foreigners [*civium et advenarum*]."

Obviously Pontano's association of splendor with pleasure gardens and villas is a reaction to the old tradition that a private garden denotes possession of natural resources that can bring material profit and sustenance, as well as pleasure, to its owner. That a garden should be open to friends and strangers as a sign of personal splendor is, therefore, merely an earlier enunciation of Thorstein Veblen's concept of "conspicuous consumption," or the idea that people may be more interested in the status conferred by their possessions than in their utilitarian value. It is understandable that this concept will be realized with the gardens at Rome in the early sixteenth century where the social leaders and patrons of pleasure gardens were primarily cardinals of the Church who lived off church benefices and family wealth—men not concerned with making money, but with promoting an image of power through the splendor of their possessions. As many of these gardens at Rome also contained great collections of antiquities, they also satisfied Pontano's belief that appropriate statues, paintings, and other rich furnishings should decorate the house of a man of splendor because "their appearance is pleasing and lends prestige to the owner,

---

[28] *Epistolae Senecae ad Paulum et Pauli ad Senecam*, ed. C. W. Barlow (Papers and Monographs of the American Academy in Rome, x), Rome, 1938, pp. 139–40 and [Oratores Panegyrici,] *Panégyriques latins*, ed. E. Galletier, Paris, 1952, II, p. 135.

[29] M. Mercati, *De gli obelischi di Roma*, Rome, 1589, p. 255.

[30] G. Pontano, *I trattati delle virtù sociali*, ed. F. Tateo, Rome, 1965, p. 101.

[31] Ibid., p. 126.

[32] Ibid., pp. 136–37.

as long as many people frequent these houses so that they may see the objects."[33]

It may not be coincidental then that perhaps the first villa complex in Rome to exhibit an inscription dedicating the garden to the enjoyment of the friends of the owner was that created during the late fifteenth century for Oliviero Carafa, Cardinal of Naples, on the Quirinal Hill. Born of one of the oldest and most powerful Neapolitan families, Carafa was not only a dominant figure in the papal court, but played a leading role in Neapolitan affairs, being a particular favorite of King Ferdinando who engineered his cardinalate in 1467. As an important patron of art and architecture in both Rome and his native city, Carafa was a living embodiment of those qualities exemplified in Pontano's image of a man of magnificence. Giovanni Pontano, on the other hand, was not only one of the great fifteenth-century humanists and director of the academy at Naples but, in the earlier fifteenth-century tradition of civic humanism, served as one of the chief ministers of the Neapolitan court and was entrusted with some of the most delicate embassies of the period, including several to the papal court at Rome. It is possible then that Pontano's concept of splendor may have induced the cardinal to display in his garden at Rome the dedicatory inscription to his friends. In fact, in 1498 when Pontano's treatises appeared at Naples, Cardinal Carafa made a triumphal visit to his native city, but unfortunately the exact date of the inscription in the cardinal's garden cannot be determined other than before Albertini's guide of 1510.[34]

Outside of Rome the only garden of the early sixteenth century known to me with an inscribed *Lex Hortorum* was at Naples.[35] In the early sixteenth century Colantonio Caracciolo, marquis of Vico, created outside the eastern walls of the city a lavish suburban villa called the Garden of Paradise, and displayed on the portal of its palace a Latin inscription dated 1543,

which dedicated the house and gardens with its fountains and woods "to the pleasure of life and to the withdrawal and perpetual enjoyment of his friends."[36] Caracciolo's inscription may, of course, be inspired by the Roman gardens, but it would seem just as readily of Neapolitan origin.

The idea that Roman gardens are open to public access will, therefore, have consequences for garden design—if nothing else, the question of entrance and circulation within the garden. During the Middle Ages and early Renaissance the garden had been basically an enclosed piece of land protected by walls or thorn hedges, the hortus conclusus of the Song of Solomon that permeated the religious writings and iconography of the period. So when the Medici country estate at Trebbio was refurbished in the early fifteenth century, a completely walled-in garden stood at one side of the old castle with a single entrance at the corner nearest the residence (Fig. 191). Although the Utens view of the villa dates from the late sixteenth century, enough of the structure of the original garden is still extant, including the entrance pergola supported on early fifteenth-century brick columns, to confirm the painting as a reasonably accurate depiction of the fifteenth-century garden.[37] The location of the entrance gate indicates that it is a garden meant only for the owner and his family, a private garden or outdoor living room. The same idea was incorporated into the magnificent new palace in Florence built for Cosimo de' Medici, which had at its rear a garden enclosed by crenellated walls, a truly outdoor living room meant primarily for the activities of the family. It has been suggested that the garden of the Medici Palace was a reincarnation of the peristyle garden of an ancient house as "a pleasurable retreat, probably intended for family use in contrast to the public formality of the first courtyard."[38] Similarly the Piccolomini Palace at Pienza built in the mid-fifteenth century by Pope Pius II had a garden at its rear above the stables set into the hillside on which the palace was erected. The walls enclosing the garden, however, were pierced by great windows offering vistas out of the garden to match the vistas from the loggias lining the rear elevation of the palace over the garden, but

---

[33] Ibid., pp. 131–32.

[34] The building activity of Alfonso II at Naples in the late fifteenth century has been related to Pontano's writings in G. L. Hersey, *Alfonso II and the Artistic Renewal of Naples 1485–1495*, New Haven, Conn., and London, 1965.

[35] The Botanical Garden at Padua had inscribed in Latin on its entrance gate rules for the use of the garden by the public; see T. Coryate, *Coryat's Crudities*, Glasgow and New York, 1905, I, pp. 292–93. However, these differ from the *Lex Hortorum* in disciplining the public in its use of a public area. Regarding the *Lex Hortorum* later in the Netherlands, see M. Morford, "The Stoic Garden," *Journal of Garden History*, VII, 1987, pp. 151–75.

[36] See Appendix IV, 8.

[37] G. Masson, *Italian Gardens*, New York, [1961,] pp. 71–73 and fig. 29.

[38] I. Hyman, *Fifteenth Century Florentine Studies: The Palazzo Medici and a Ledger for the Church of San Lorenzo*, New York and London, 1977, p. 186.

191. Trebbio, Villa Medici, painting by Utens

because of the topography of the site the windows were set high above the exterior ground plane, thus preserving the privacy of the garden from exterior visual intrusion.

The idea at Pienza of loggias running across the rear of the palace and looking down upon the pope's garden probably derived from the same idea at the mediaeval Papal Palace of the Vatican in Rome. Since the late thirteenth century a three-story loggia had covered the eastern facade of the Papal Palace, later replaced by Bramante's and Raphael's loggias, now forming one side of the Cortile di San Damaso (Fig. 2). Presumably the loggias opened onto a small, private garden for the pope, the small garden (*viridarium parvum*) whose crenellated walls were built or repaired a century later, after the neglect induced by the Avignon papacy.[39] By its location near the papal apartments, the garden was obviously intended as the pope's private garden, although some of his activities

might open it up occasionally to more public use. Throughout the fifteenth century this garden will be identified in documents as the "private garden" (hortus secretus or giardino segreto).

When Pope Paul II began in the 1460s to expand his cardinalate palace next to the church of San Marco at Rome into the huge Palace of San Marco, he too built a completely walled-in giardino segreto at the southeast corner of the palace (Fig. 3). On the exterior there were entrances to the basement stables under the garden, like that at the Piccolomini Palace in Pienza, but the only major access to the garden was a door into the upper portico from the pope's private apartment in the southeast corner of the palace, as it too was designed to be a private garden for the owner of the palace. So during the fifteenth century, except for the occasional incorporation of pieces of ancient sculpture or inscriptions, the Roman garden was no different from the hortus conclusus that prevailed throughout Northern Europe and the rest of Italy in the late Middle Ages and early Renaissance.

Soon the exhibition of ancient sculpture in garden areas at Rome provoked the concept of public access

[39] F. Ehrle and H. Egger, *Der Vaticanische Palast in seiner Entwicklung bis zur Mitte des XV Jahrhunderts* (Studi e documenti per la storia del Palazzo Apostolico Vaticano, II), Vatican City, 1935, p. 76.

and its control. At the Vatican Palace in the early six-teenth century Bramante added his famous spiral stairway at the eastern end of the Villa Belvedere as a public access to the new statue garden court in which Pope Julius II exhibited his collection of antiquities, including the Apollo Belvedere and the Laocoön. This stairwell permitted the public to reach the Statue Court without penetrating the Belvedere Court or the Vatican Palace (Fig. 6). By the second half of the six-teenth century when the privilege of public access to Roman gardens had become a local tradition, provi-sion for a separate public entrance was often made. In 1564 Cardinal Giovanni Ricci purchased in the name of his nephews the old Crescenzi villa on the Pincian Hill, now the Medici Villa, soon rebuilding the old residence and purchasing adjacent land until he controlled most of the summit of the hill.[40] Behind the villa, whose entrance was on the western brow of the hill, Ricci laid out expansive gardens which, with his additional purchase of land toward the south, would border on the Via di Porta Pinciana, allowing another access to the garden running behind the church of SS. Trinità dei Monti. With the death of the cardinal the villa and its grounds were purchased in 1576 by Cardinal Ferdinando de' Medici, who in turn made extensive changes in the building and gardens. An avid collector of Roman antiquities, the Medici cardinal converted this suburban retreat into a mu-seum of statuary, covering the garden facade of the building with the ancient bas-reliefs from the disman-tlement of the Della Valle statue court, erecting a long sculpture gallery above the stables attached to the south side of his villa, and scattering other pieces and groups of sculpture in niches and pavilions around the garden (Fig. 35). During the first year of work the alley to the Via di Porta Pinciana was straightened, and for the street end Ammannati, the Florentine ar-chitect who was handling the redoing of the villa, de-signed a large rusticated portal on which, above the two side niches, were plaques with the Latin inscrip-tions of the *Lex Hortorum* noted previously (Fig. 190). While the introduction of ancient sculpture into the gardens of the Villa Medici may have caused the cardinal to emphasize so prominently the public en-trance to his garden, the inscriptions make no refer-ence to the statuary, and the topographical layout that permitted public access from the Via di Porta Pinciana had been prepared by the previous owner,

Cardinal Ricci, who did not exhibit a collection of an-tiques in his garden. The passageway from the street debouched directly into the central alley of the garden so that there was a continuous long promenade from the street to the northern end of the garden and the public could frequent that alley and most of the gar-den without disturbing the cardinal and his friends, if they were in residence at the villa. On the western side of the end of the public alley just before it entered the large garden was a small, square, walled-in garden next to the sculpture gallery, which in turn was acces-sible from the cardinal's private apartment in the villa. This garden, which apparently did not contain any ancient sculpture, was the giardino segreto, the private garden, normally reserved for the personal en-joyment of the owner.

The provision of a separate, prominent, public por-tal to gardens, as seen at the Villa Medici, was partic-ularly prevalent at Rome beginning in the 1560s as a result of the urban development of the area of the Quirinal Hill. The hill at the western side of the city had remained deserted throughout the Middle Ages and early Renaissance with only vineyards and an oc-casional neglected or abandoned church scattered around and among the ruins of the ancient Baths of Constantine and of Diocletian. An old road, the Alta Semita, wandered along the spine of the hill from the inhabited portion of the city to the Porta Nomentana. In the late fifteenth and early sixteenth centuries sub-urban villas with expansive gardens lined the north-ern side of the street, commencing with the Vigna di Napoli of Cardinal Carafa nearest the city (Fig. 17). In each case the residence was built on the brow of the northern edge of the hill, offering magnificent views out over the city or over the valley between the Quirinal and Pincian Hills, and extensive gardens stretched back from the villa to the street. In 1561 as part of the continuing papal plan to encourage resi-dence in the more healthy, but deserted, hill regions of the city, Pope Pius IV widened and straightened the old street of the Alta Semita, diverting it from the Porta Nomentana, so that the street, renamed the Via Pia, would end at the new Porta Pia designed by Mi-chelangelo (Fig. 116). By this time the old Vigna di Napoli of Cardinal Carafa at the western end of the Via Pia was leased by Ippolito II d'Este, Cardinal of Ferrara, who had begun extensive building at the villa and had particularly expanded the gardens in part as a setting for the magnificent collection of antiquities he was assembling. In February 1561 is the first of

---

[40] D. R. Coffin, *The Villa in the Life of Renaissance Rome*, Princeton, N.J., 1979, pp. 219–32.

several payments to a builder for "the gate that he has to make in the garden of Montecavallo [the Quirinal garden of the Cardinal of Ferrara] on the new street."[41] This must be the gate seen in the Dupérac map of 1577 (Fig. 17) entering directly into the garden on axis with a long alley that ran across the garden between the older Carafa property on the west and the new land toward the east, which had been the old Vigna Boccacci or Bertina given to the cardinal in 1560 to be incorporated into his expansive new garden. As there was already more direct access to the original Villa Carafa from the old Alta Semita at the southeast corner of the property, the new garden portal must have been meant for public access. Like the later Villa Medici, which had a small, private garden near the building, the Villa d'Este had several such walled-in *giardini segreti* clustered around the residence, two of which had loggias opening onto the gardens planted with bitter-orange trees (*merangoli*) for the relaxation of the owner.

Beyond the villa of the Cardinal of Ferrara toward the east along the Via Pia were three more magnificent villa garden complexes, those of Cardinal Grimani, Cardinal Pio da Carpi, and the Cardinal of Sermoneta. Each of these had a rather similar layout to the Villa d'Este with the residence toward the northern brow of the Quirinal or, in the case of Sermoneta's, in the valley beyond so that personal access to the villa for the owner and his friends would be directly from the valley, leaving the summit of the Quirinal open for the extensive gardens that ran back to the Via Pia. The Villa Carpi, like the Villa d'Este, had several walled-in courts near the building and directly behind the villa was a *giardino segreto* of exotic trees carefully walled off from the more casual, larger garden. Each garden also had an elaborate, often rusticated, portal inscribed with the owner's name, opening onto the Via Pia. Engravings of these three portals, which survived longer than the one to the Villa d'Este, are preserved in later editions of Vignola's book on the orders, where they are mistakenly attributed to Michelangelo.[42] There is evidence to date all three portals at the time of the revision of the Via Pia in the early 1560s. The inscription on the portal of the Cardinal of Carpi (Fig. 192), who died in 1564, proclaims that this is the portal of "the gardens of Pio da Carpi" (*Horti Pii Carpensis*), thus associat-

192. Rome, Vigna Carpi, portal, engraving

ing it with the famous ancient Roman Horti Sallustiani or Horti Luculliani, as was done about this time at other gardens in Rome, such as those in the remains of the Baths of Diocletian of Cardinal Du Bellay (*Horti Bellaiani*) or of Cardinal Farnese on the Palatine Hill (*Horti Palatini Farnesiorum*). Again these portals on the Via Pia were to serve as the public entrances to the gardens. So in 1561 when Pope Pius IV laid the cornerstone of Michelangelo's Porta Pia, the Mantuan ambassador described the Via Pia as "now a most beautiful street, as almost all who dwell there have built lovely high walls with most attractive gateways, which lead into those vigne."[43] These lavish public garden portals then served as signs along the walled street identifying the location of the gardens.

The tradition of a conspicuous garden portal permitting public access to the gardens without interfering with the residential life of the owner, established so prominently in the 1560s along the Via Pia, then became a regular feature at most of the later Roman gardens, as seen previously at the Villa Medici.[44] For

[41] ASM, Camera Ducale, Amministrazione dei Principi, Registro 958, fol. 15, February 4, 1561.

[42] G. B. da Vignola, *Li cinque ordini di architettura . . .*, Venice, 1603 and 1648.

[43] L. von Pastor, *The History of the Popes*, XVI, London, 1928, p. 465, no. 11.

[44] The Farnese gardens on the Palatine, dating from the 1570s and early 1580s, had only a public entrance, but this is understand-

example, Cardinal Montalto in the late 1570s had begun a very charming villa with gardens on the Esquiline Hill near the Via Pia with a single major entrance at the west side of the property oriented toward his church of Sta. Maria Maggiore. After his election as Pope Sixtus V in 1585, he acquired a tremendous amount of additional, adjacent land until he possessed the largest vigna within the walls of Rome and expanded the gardens around his suburban residence (Fig. 121). At the same time he transformed the area between the northern boundary of his newly enlarged vigna and the remains of the Baths of Diocletian into a new public piazza with a large palace, service buildings, and some eighteen shops along the northern edge of his estate. Adjacent to the new Palazzo di Termini was erected a large entrance portal to the gardens, the Porta Quirinale, which opened onto a long alley running completely across the garden at some distance behind the villa. This is obviously then a public portal entered from the public space of the new piazza, while the Porta Viminale on axis with the villa and near to his favorite church became a more private access for the pope or visitors to his villa. Similarly the Villa Borghese, whose *Lex Hortorum* was discussed at the beginning, was created from 1605 to 1613 on the Pincian Hill just outside the Aurelian walls of the city (Fig. 123) with its public garden portal set just opposite the Porta Pinciana of the city so that the public could enter the gardens in front of the villa directly from the city gateway, while another portal farther east communicated with the villa proper.

At Rome during the sixteenth century the circulation pattern within a garden was generally determined loosely by the topography of the site and eventually with the development of the tradition of a public portal, by the relationship among the several entrances to the garden. Within the garden the order of the paths and alleys leading away from the entrances limited, of course, the circulation path of the visitor, and the different elements composing the garden—plants, shrubs, trees, garden seats and pergolas, fountains or statues—might determine his path relative to his personal interests. During the second half of the sixteenth century, however, several of the great

gardens near Rome were created with extensive iconographical or symbolic programs usually founded on classical mythology. It was one way by which the Renaissance could classicize gardens analogous to the adoption of the classical orders of architecture for their building or the depiction of classical subject matter in their painting. With an iconographic program, often of a narrative mode, the circulation pattern within a garden had to be more strictly controlled in order that the program might be read correctly.

From about 1550 to 1572 the Neapolitan archaeologist and architect, Pirro Ligorio, laid out extensive gardens for Ippolito II d'Este, Cardinal of Ferrara, in one corner of the hill town of Tivoli just within the old city walls near the Porta Romana. As seen in a contemporary painting decorating an end wall of the *salotto* of the villa itself (Fig. 67), the gardens were set on a steep hillside leading up to an old monastery, revised by the cardinal as his villa, perched on top of the hill. Today when visiting the Villa d'Este one first enters directly into the villa proper by a portal opening off a small piazza in front of the adjacent church of Sta. Maria Maggiore and then, after traversing the building, exits into the garden below the villa. This approach to the villa and its gardens was obviously the private entrance for the cardinal or residents of the villa. The principal and, therefore, public portal was at the bottom of the hill at the foot of the garden on axis with the building atop the slope and on the road from Rome that entered the town at the west through the Porta Romana. An anonymous account of the projected form of the garden, dating about 1568 and written perhaps by Ligorio himself,[45] describes the garden in accordance with its circulation pattern, which can be followed on the Dupérac engraving of 1573 of the garden (Fig. 66). The written description starts with the "principal portal" opening into a narrow "vestibule" covered by a pergola. Although the engraving cuts off both the portal and vestibule, they still exist at Tivoli. The description then continues with the identification of the central alley that runs through the garden and the cross pergola that covers the lower part of this alley. The large garden is designed in a checkerboard pattern running across the lower, flat area of the site and then continuing up the hillside beyond. In addition to the major alley corresponding to the central axis from the public

---

able as there was no residential villa requiring privacy. On the other hand, the gardens of Cardinal Du Bellay at the Baths of Diocletian, which had likewise only one major entrance, did have a small summer residence, where, in fact, the cardinal died in 1560, but the creation of the garden in 1554–1555 predates the development of the Via Pia entrances.

[45] D. R. Coffin, *The Villa d'Este at Tivoli*, Princeton, N.J., 1960, pp. 141–50.

portal to the villa, there are introduced into the design two major, very dominant cross axes.

Although there is a central axis from the entrance portal to the building, the checkerboard pattern, dramatically defined by the cross pergola immediately after the entrance, and the two powerful cross axes diminish the impact of the central alley as the path for circulation. A visitor would undoubtedly pause under the vast dome over the center of the cross pergola, tantalized by vistas down the side tunnels. If he could resist those contradictory attractions and continue toward the villa, he would emerge from the confinement of the pergola onto the wide cross axis of the fishpools, drawing his attention equally right and left. At this point of his tour of the garden, a visitor must have been sorely tried in his decision as to the direction in which to proceed.

If the visitor persisted in his desire to reach the villa above by mounting the hillside, after climbing around the central Fountain of the Dragons, he was faced with an even more frustrating choice at the next major cross axis, the Alley of the One Hundred Fountains that cut across the middle of the slope. Although the Dupérac engraving depicts a slight break in the alley before being diverted right or left by the diagonal paths covering the upper part of the hillside, this momentary continuation of the central alley was omitted during the creation of the garden so that there is an unbroken wall of fountains running along the alley.

All the major features of the garden were arranged along the sides of the garden at the ends of cross axes with the one notable exception of the Fountain of the Dragons on the central alley halfway up the hill just before the visitor was left with the inescapable choice of turning left or right along the Alley of the Fountains. Originally an ancient statue of Hercules, to whom the garden was dedicated, stood above the central Fountain of the Dragons, which according to the written description was meant to represent the many-headed dragon guardian of the mythical Garden of the Hesperides. At the left end of the Alley of the Hundred Fountains on Hercules' right was the Grotto of Venus or "voluptuous pleasure" in the words of the sixteenth-century description and on his other side, but at the top of the hill, was the Grotto of Diana or "virtuous pleasure and chastity." Thus, the central motif of the garden illustrated the famous Choice of Hercules, when he elected the steep, hard way of Virtue. The cross axes and the diagonal paths of the circulation pattern of the garden, therefore, compelled a visitor to choose between diverting interests that prepared him for the symbolism of the Choice of Hercules dominating the upper portion of the garden.

While the Cardinal of Ferrara was completing his gardens at Tivoli, Cardinal Gambara began the gardens of his villa, the present Villa Lante, in 1568 within an old hunting park at Bagnaia north of Rome, probably after the design of the architect Vignola. An engraving, dated 1596, of the Villa Lante (Fig. 70) is very helpful for the identification of many of the fountains, which are now lost, particularly in the park. At Bagnaia there are two portals into the grounds of the villa, both at the front toward the little town of Bagnaia. The left-hand portal leading directly into the formal gardens and the two casinos is the private entrance for the owner and his immediate friends coming to the casinos. The larger, right-hand gateway opening into the adjacent park is, therefore, the public portal. Immediately on entrance into the park one encounters, cut into the gentle hillside, a large oval fountain basin in which stands a figure of the winged horse Pegasus, associating this area with the ancient Mount Parnassus.[46] The engraving then presents a very haphazard organization of alleys cut through the park. Only the diagonal alley proceeding from the public entrance directly to the old hunting lodge, erected earlier in the century in the center of the park, demonstrates a logical circulation pattern. The other fountains in the park, now lost or transformed, but identified by the engraving, are associated with the world of nature, such as the Fountain of the Acorns and the Fountain of the Duck, or are symbolic of virtue, as in the Fountain of the Unicorn and the Fountain of the Dragon. This combination of associations suggests that the naturalistic, wooded hillside of the park is meant to recall the classical myth of the Golden Age when virtuous men and women lived off the simple offerings of nature and did not have to labor for a living. The identification of the park with the Golden Age explains the irregular pattern of the alleys and their lack of clarity from a circulation point of view, since the inhabitants of the Golden Age lived a life of unfettered freedom, as the *Lex Hortorum* of the Villa Borghese expressed so eloquently, in an uncultivated and untouched nature. The random pattern of the alleys is, therefore, the Renaissance mode

[46] See D. R. Coffin, "Some Aspects of the Villa Lante at Bagnaia," in *Arte in Europa: Scritti di storia dell'arte in onore di Edoardo Arslan*, Milan, 1966, pp. 569–75, for the probable influence of garden ideas and garden features from the Villa d'Este at Tivoli.

193. Bagnaia, Villa Lante, *catena d'acqua*

of expressing the irregularity of nature in contrast to the geometrically organized checkerboard pattern of the gardens of the Villa d'Este at Tivoli or those of the Villa Medici at Rome and is really no more artificial than the serpentine windings that the eighteenth-century English landscapist used for the same expression.

The geometrical regularity of the formal garden at Bagnaia in contrast to the adjacent park then underscores the development of the iconographical program. A visitor after exploring the park would cross over into the upper part of the formal garden, as he does today, and view from the top the series of garden terraces organized along the central axis to the private portal below. On the uppermost terrace the Fountain of the Deluge gushing forth between the two little houses dedicated to the Muses recalled Ovid's account in the *Metamorphoses* (I, 89–112 and 262–323) of the destruction of the Golden Age by a great flood that covered the earth except for the twin peaks of Mount Parnassus where the only human survivors, Deucalion and Pyrrha, landed. The carefully manicured terraces below then represent the different stages of man's shaping of untamed nature by labor

and art after he lost the free bounty of the Golden Age. Thus, the formality of the garden and the naturalism of the park reinforce the iconographical program.

In contrast to the program of the Villa d'Este at Tivoli, that at Bagnaia is a narrative, requiring a continuous linear circulation pattern that can be read from either entrance portal. From the public portal into the park, the circulation path follows the story recounted by Ovid. That this reading was taken into account in the design of the gardens is confirmed by the vista down the terraces of the formal garden from the uppermost level (Fig. 193). From that point the semicircular recession of the Fountain of the Lights cuts into the retaining wall behind the lower terrace, permitting a clear glimpse of the circular island in the center of the lower terrace.

From the cardinal's portal into the formal garden, one moves up the terraced slope, which is the more usual approach to an Italian Renaissance garden, since one thereby is clearly aware of the wall fountains and grottoes set into the retaining walls of the terraces. This reading then expresses the favorite Renaissance theme of man's desire to return to the freedom and leisure of the Golden Age, associated so often with gardens.

The designers of Roman Renaissance gardens have, therefore, created them with different levels of comprehension and attraction. Open to a very broad and diverse public, it is understandable that the average visitor might not fully comprehend the involved, symbolic meaning conveyed by the fountains and statues, whose enjoyment might only be available to the intelligentsia or the friends of the owner. The average public, however, might enjoy the formal elements of the garden design and certainly would be attracted by the lavishness of water, statuary, and floral displays. These were to endow the owner, as Pontano noted, with the image of being a "Splendid Man." To gain the fullest benefit of this concept, however, the Roman gardens had to be open to the general public with concatenated consequences for circulation and design.

# Epilogue

In May 1792 Francesco Bettini, who was the first to introduce the English naturalistic mode of gardening to Rome, wrote his patron Cardinal Giuseppe Doria-Pamphili that this gardening style was not favored at Rome "because the Roman lords are taken by regularity and the new English taste cannot offer them any pleasure."[1]

Certain aspects of French formal gardening, particularly embroidered parterres and occasionally radiating bosquets, had been accepted by the Romans and incorporated into their own tradition of gardening, as seen for example at the Villa Albani. The principles of naturalistic landscaping as developed in England in the mid-eighteenth century, based on the new assumption that the irregularities of nature were beautiful in their own right, were radically different from classical gardening. The advent of the English mode would, therefore, be only destructive to formal gardening on the Continent and in England itself, so that the history of Roman gardening will cease by the end of the eighteenth century.

Francesco Bettini, born at Maderno in northern Italy, accompanied the Venetian ambassador to Paris in 1772 as a general factotum. Remaining in Paris for some twelve years, except for the two years from 1776 to 1778 when he was in service in England with Lord Lucan, Bettini gradually developed a passion for English gardening, which he had seen in England, and more particularly for the Anglo-Chinese manner of gardening that had just become fashionable in France. In 1778 Bettini entered the employ of the papal nuncio to Paris, Giuseppe Doria-Pamphili, who being made a cardinal in 1784, returned to Rome with Bettini in the following year. Immediately the cardinal's brother, Prince Andrea IV Doria-Pamphili,

consulted Bettini about possible improvements at the Villa Pamphili. Over the next some thirteen years Bettini churned out a series of projects to refashion in the new English mode a formal lake in the park, none of which came to fruition, although he did create later both a botanical garden and an agronomical garden at the villa and designed several service buildings. The major transformation of most of the Pamphili grounds into an English landscape park, however, occurred after 1849 when French troops, invading Rome, created great destruction in the Pamphili park.

Cardinal Doria-Pamphili, who was a more enthusiastic supporter of the new fashion in gardening, bought the Vigna Crivelli near the park of the Villa Borghese and the adjacent Vigna Olgiati with the so-called Casino of Raphael, a small, rustic, sixteenth-century building mistakenly associated with the painter Raphael. Beginning in November 1786 Francesco Bettini began to transform the two vigne into an Anglo-Chinese garden with serpentine walks, an irregular lake, buildings and bridges in the Chinese style, a Dutch flower garden, a hermitage, and a large assortment of rare and exotic trees, shrubs, and plants.[2] First called the "Orti di Raffaello" and later the "Villetta," the completion of the new garden, although almost finished in 1788, dragged on until 1793. According to a letter in April 1788 from Bettini to the cardinal, who was away from Rome, the garden had the approval of foreign visitors, even if the English complained about its small scale, but not the support of the Romans. With an amusing characterization of the different national personalities, Bettini remarks:

The true applause is that of the English and of the French. An Englishman tells me "it isn't bad, it doesn't displease me, one day it will make a fine effect, the site is lovely, the house is proper for that great artist [Raphael] who lived there," etc. The French then give out

---

[1] M. Heimbürger Ravalli, "Progetti e lavori di Francesco Bettini per il parco di Villa Belrespiro," *Studi romani*, XXV, 1977, p. 32. The major source of information on Bettini's activity is M. Heimbürger Ravalli, *Disegni di giardini e opere minori di un artista del '700 Francesco Bettini*, Florence, 1981.

[2] Ibid., fig. 55.

freely with "charment, joli, agréable, tableau superbe," etc. The Romans then make me lose courage when they ask me if I shall level these elevations of earth, I answer yes, then they say, "oh, it will not be bad"; they ask me if I shall level the Chinese mountain, I answer yes, then they say, "oh, you will do well since it is unsuitable in a garden" and other such ridiculous and stupid questions.[3]

The cardinal's garden or the "Orti di Raffaello" had, however, only a very brief life. During the French Republic the Doria-Pamphili were forced in 1798 to sell the garden to "citizen" Ottaviano Bevilacqua. Bettini, the creator of the garden, took the opportunity to dig up the more unusual trees and plants, which he transferred to the Prince's Villa Pamphili. In 1831 the land was bought by the Borghese, who incorporated it into the park of the Villa Borghese and in 1849 the Casino of Raphael was destroyed by French cannon fire.

Because of its brief life the cardinal's garden would be forgotten in the history of gardening, but indirectly it left a mark. Just before the cardinal had begun his garden his neighbor Prince Marcantonio Borghese had commissioned the young neoclassical architect Mario Asprucci to design and build the so-called Temple of Aesculapius in the southwest corner of the park of the Villa Borghese.[4] In the summer of 1786, before Cardinal Doria-Pamphili began his garden nearby, Borghese ordered the excavation of a rectangular lake in the formal manner in front and around the new temple. By March 1787 Borghese had changed his mind and called in the Scotch landscape painter Jacob More to redesign the lake in the new English style. It was certainly not coincidental that in the meantime, in December 1786, Bettini had begun the cardinal's garden with a naturalistic lake not far from the new Borghese temple and its lake. Soon, in fact, Bettini was offering advice on the plants for the new English garden planted around the Borghese lake. By March 1789 Bettini could write his master: "I went to see the Borghese gardens where a great deal of work has been done and they copy all that Your Eminence does."[5] It was, therefore, Prince Borghese and the painter More who received credit for the introduction of English landscaping to Rome.

About the same time a few other isolated examples of English gardening had appeared earlier elsewhere in Italy. As early as 1782 Senator Lomellini of Genoa was developing an English garden at his suburban residence at Pegli,[6] and Queen Maria Carolina of Naples, probably on the instigation of her friend Sir William Hamilton, the English ambassador, had begun in 1786, almost exactly contemporary with Cardinal Doria-Pamphili's garden at Rome, an English garden in the northeast corner of the park of the royal palace at Caserta.[7] The idea for the garden at Caserta, however, occurred in 1785, when Sir William sent back to England for a gardener, John Andrew Graffer, who arrived at Naples only in the spring of 1786. These random, scattered examples of English gardening probably had little impact on the introduction of the new style into Italy. It will be the writings of two North Italians at the end of the eighteenth century and early in the nineteenth century that gave a strong motivation for the acceptance of the English mode. In 1792 the Veronese poet and writer, Ippolito Pindemonte, after an extended trip from 1788 to 1791 to England and France, including a visit to the tomb of Jean-Jacque Rousseau in the English-style park at Ermenonville, read his *Dissertazione su i giardini inglesi e sul merito in ciò dell'Italia* at the Accademia di Scienze, Lettere, ed Arti at Padua, which was then published in the fourth volume of the *Atti* of the academy.[8] This was followed by another memorial, *Saggio sopra l'indole dei giardini moderni*, read at the same academy four years later. Meanwhile the Milanese Count Ercole Silva, after a four-year tour in the north, began probably soon after his return to Milan in 1787 to refashion in the English manner the formal garden at his villa at Cinisello north of Milan. More important, the count published in 1801 a treatise on the new gardening, *Dell' arte dei giardini inglesi*, in which he asserted that Italy could only reassert its previous primacy in the art of gardening by understanding and adapting the new style. So in 1811 he published a detailed description of the new mode of gardening he had achieved already at his own villa and in 1813 reissued a second edition of his treatise. By this time the resistance to the new gardening was dissipated and it was enthusiastically adopted, as were the foreign architectural styles of neoclassicism and romanticism.

[3] M. Heimbürger Ravalli, "Francesco Bettini e l'introduzione del giardino romantico a Roma," in *Studia romana in honorem Petri Krarup septuagenarii*, Odense, 1976, p. 222, n. 60.

[4] P. R. Andrew, "An English Garden in Rome," *Country Life*, CLXIX, April 23, 1981, pp. 1136–38, and Heimbürger Ravalli, *Disegni di giardini*, pp. 76–81.

[5] Heimbürger Ravalli, *Disegni di giardini*, p. 79, n. 43.

[6] S. Rotta, *Documenti per la storia dell'illuminismo a Genova: Lettere di Agostino Lomellino a Paolo Frisi*, Genoa, 1958, p. 206.

[7] C. Knight, *Il giardino inglese di Caserta*, Naples, 1986.

[8] I. Pindemonte, *Il giardino inglese*, Verona, 1817, and N. F. Cimmino, *Ippolito Pindemonte e il suo tempo*, 2 vols., Rome, n.d.

# APPENDIX I

# Plant Materials

ASM, Camera Ducale, Fabbriche e villeggiature, Busta 70, Tivoli, no. 6, Villeggiatura sotto Card. Luigi d'Este, fasc. 5, Documenti e carteggi diversi relativi alla Villa di Tivoli, fols. 19r–20v.

Arbori e piante qle son sempre vestite de fogli
   p boschetti e p siepe
      Aquifoglio
      Busso
      Cipresso maschio
      Ginepro
      Lecce
      Lauro domestico
      Lauro Regio
      Lentisco
      Oliuella seu alaternus
      Mortella
      Mortella essotica
      Mortellone
   p siepe di compartimenti
      Formichella
      Isopò
      Lauanda ouero spico
      Rosmarino
      Ligustro ouero fior fiorella
      Laureole
      Ippoglosso ouero bislunga
Piante che vogliano appoggio senza alora cura
      Ederà comune
      Ederà frutaj aureo
      Gelsomino Indico } perdeno le foglie l'inuerno
      Vita canadensis }

   p boschetti oltre li detti
      Abeti
      Cipresso femina
      Lauro americano
      Leandro
      Palma
      Palma stellara
      Pini
      Sabina
   p siepe oltre le d^te
      Camelia oricocos
      Lentagine
      Ligustro

Piante che si vengano ne giardini ma no son buone ne p spalliere ne p compartimenti
      Erba filo ouero Aloe
      Bella donna
      Fico Indico
      Iucca Indica
   p coprire doue e spogliato sotto il bosco
      si pol piantare della bislingua e della Prouenza a due ci qualche poca di aria sementati di lauri
Tutte sorte di Merangoli e Limoni son buoni da far boschetti et siepe ne luoghi alquanto temperadi e di d^te nel giardino del sig.^re Don Carlo Pio ui si ritrouano 44 sorte.
Tutte sorte di gelsomini nō son appreposite p Tiuoli (fol. 19r)

### p Il Giard^n di Tiuoli

Il vialone che si uol far di nuouo la spalliera o siepe uerso la ualle sarebbe assai apreposito di Agrifogli p respetto che riempe bene et e forte e seruira p muro in essa piantarci di pini 40 palmi discosto d'un d'al'altro e tra detti pini piantarsi tre cipressi qllo di mezo lasciarlo uenire alto al possibile e gli altri due de lati nº fargli uenire piu che 12 p^mi sopra la spalliera osia siepe di Agrifoglio, il che farra molto uago alla uista.

L'altra spalliera canto li muri della Città tutti cipressi p coprire tutti le falzi, Auanti di d^ti una spaliera bassa di lauri Reggij, e in d^ta delli Arbori diuersi tra meza di 15 p^mi di stante l'un dall'altro, come sarrebbe lauro comune Aquifoglio, cirasa marina, Alaternus, Agrifoglio eseguisa, ouero altro che sarra giudicato più al preposto.

Nel giardin grande nel uiale che e dalla porta d^ta San Pietro, alla fontana d^ta ciuetta doue mancha la spalliera o siepe si pol piantarci et è il migliore Alaternus e lauro comune con qualche cipresso doue è più aria tramezzato.

Nell'altri uiali più umbrosi Mortella spinosa seu Ruscus, et bislingua seu Ippoglosso.

Le siepe dalla bande della pischiere q̄ll doue al presente son le Nocciole e ben piantarci un spallerone di Lauro Reggio q̄l facci 2 siepe una bassa e l'altra in aria, dietro detto cioè dentro il quadro una fila di Abeti e il resto di quadri Pini.

Dall'altra parte cioe incontro, son più quadri il p.º la spalliera basso lauro regio, l'altra Agrifoglio 2º quadro Agrifoglio nella bassa nell'alta lauri comuni 3º quadro nella bassa lauro Regio nell'alta cirase marine. (fol. 20r)

Nelli siti che son spogliati da lato doue capa l'acqua della fontana dell'organo ne muri che confinano con d^to sito cioe doue cascha l'acqua da tutte due le parte due file di Abbetti.

Auanti di essi più costo d^ti muri una spalliera di cipressi alti n^o più di p^mi 15, Il resta del sito diuersi Arbori boscharecci
  cioe cirasa marina
  Alaternus
  Agrifoglio
  Lauro comune
  Lauro Reggio
  Cipresso femina
  con qualche altro maschio tramezzato

E la spalliera o siepe di un di d^ti boschetti cioe q̄ll a man dritta che confinera co la spalliera de zampilli de Acqua tutta cipressi alti 15 p^mi.

Il resto da terminarlo sù il sito. (fol. 20v)

# Plant Costs

1. 1561 March 16

   ... sei olmi grossi à 7 b. ½ l'uno, 50 vite saluatiche, e 50 vite Albe à b. 2½ l'una, 300 piante di lauro à 4 quattrini la pianta et b. 40 p una soma d'edera

   1561 March 18

   ... p il prezzo di olmi 172 à un carlin l'uno

   ASM, Camera Ducale, Amministrazione dei Principi, Registro 958, fols. 21v and 22.

2. 1562 February 14

   olmi n.° 70 a b. 6 l'uno

   Piante dj Zafronj n.° cento a b. 2 l'uno

   n.° 264 cerase marine a q$^{tri}$ 4 l'una

   28 ridalpe a b. 2 l'una

   Ibid., Registro 895, fol. 9.

3. 1566 March 14

   lauri 763 a b. tre luno ... lentaginea n° 1300 a b. 40 il cento ... olmi 75 a carlino luno ... Matriselua rose in mazziero a b. 15 luno ... ellera fassi 10 a b. 10 luno ... Melacci 13 a b. 6 luno ... cianfron piedi 20 a b. 2½ luno ... Gielsomini some una b. 17

   Ibid., Registro 898, unfoliated.

4. 1568 January 26

   a coto dellj 300 olmj ... sc. 12

   Ibid., Registro 995, fols. 11 and 15.

5. 1568 February 18

   102 castagni for 4.74 sc.

   1568 March 13

   per il prezzo de 51 Abbetti sc. 11.50

   per prezzo d'olmi 70 a 7 b. luno, lauri 380 a b. 25 il c.° ... sc. 17.40

   See D. R. Coffin, *The Villa d'Este at Tivoli*, Princeton, N.J., 1960, p. 20, n. 19.

6. 1608 March 20

   p n.° 56 piante di melangoli ... sc. 19.50

   ASM, Camera Ducale, Fabbriche e Villeggiature, Busta 71, Tivoli, no. 1, Villeggiatura sotto Alessandro d'Este, Libro di spese 1606–1614, fol. 5r.

7. 1616 March 18

   piante n. 90 di melangole a baiocchi 45 l'una, e piante n. 10 della china [chinchona tree] a baiocchi 35 l'una

   See *Il Palazzo del Quirinale*, Rome, 1974, p. 253.

8. 1645 June 25

   piante 65 di cedro a b. 10

   1645 November 12–December 17

   sc. 30 for 100 melangoli

   1645 December 17–31

   sc. 6 ... per arra de mortella

   sc. 10 ... a conto di piante 200 di mortella

   sc. 2.40 ... per some 6 di spini

   See J. Garms, *Quellen aus dem Archiv Doria-Pamphilj zur Kunsttätigkeit in Rom unter Innocenz X*, Rome and Vienna, 1972, p. 208, no. 1015, and p. 226, nos. 1092 and 1095.

9. Undated, but ca. 1650–1670

   Nota di quello si puote spendera nelle piantate il più alto prezzo

   Piante buone, e mezzane di celsi, delle quali se ne trouerà quante se ne uuolo di buone, e mezzane à dieci sette baiochi la pianta.

   A piantarse à fosse aperto à terra soda un giulio la canna.

   A fossette di cinque palmi per ogni uerso à piantarle, e ricanzarle due carlini l'una.

   A spinarle, e ligarle tre baochi l'una.

   A darle à tutte sue spese à pianta uiua per tre anni cinque giuli la pianta.

   L'olmi la pianta un giulio l'uno.

   Le fosse et altre spese come li celsi.

   A dar l'olmi à pianta uiua quatro giuli la pianta.

   E credo che di questi ci auantaggiaremo.

   BAV, Chigi Ms M.VIII.LX. fol. 205.

# APPENDIX III

## Gardeners and Their Salaries

### A. Papal Gardeners

1. Eugenius IV (1431–1447):

    1447 February 27
    Iaquemino ortulano
    Iohanni Bernardi, eius socio

    See G. Bourgin, "La familia pontificia sotto Eugenio IV," *Archivio della R. società romana di storia patria*, XXVII, 1904, p. 213.

2. Nicholas V (1447–1455):

    1453 August–September
    Fra Giacomo di Giovanni from Gaeta [prefect of garden, 12 florins per month]

    See M. Dykmans, "Du Monte Mario à l'escalier de Saint-Pierre de Rome," *Mélanges d'archéologie et d'histoire*, LXXX, 1968, p. 571.

3. Pius II (1458–1464):

    1460
    Robertus, Vernherus Hortulani secreti
    Cardinalis, Matthias Custodes Vineae
    Johannes Hortulanus

    See [G. L. Marini,] *Degli archiatri pontificj*, Rome, 1784, II, p. 155.

4. Pius III (1503):

    1503
    Dominus Iohannes Solanes et ⎱ ortolani secreti
    Magister Iohannes ⎰
    Francis de Briscia, vignarolus antiquus
    Iacobus Vualdech, ortolanus, qui servit in palatio

    See P. Piccolomini, "La *famiglia* di Pio III," ASRSP, XXVI, 1903, pp. 158–59.

5. Leo X (1513–1521):

    1514 May 15–1516 September 17
    3 ortolani

    See W. Friedensberg, "Ein Rotulus Familiae Papst Leo's X," *Quellen und Forschungen aus Italienischen Archiven und Bibliotheken*, VI, 1904, p. 61.

6. Paul III (1534–1549):

    1535 November 6–1537 February 25
    Fioretto giardiniere di Belvedere

    1535 November 14–1544 December 3
    Lucerta, hortolano, 4.50 scudi per month

    1537 September 22–1538 March 21
    Don Joanni Loysi, giardiniere di Belvedere

    1537 December 2–1538 October 14
    Don Antonio, giardiniere

    1544 January 4
    Domenico, giardiniere

    See L. Dorez, *La cour du Pape Paul III*, Paris, 1932, II.

7. Julius III (1550–1555):

    1550 November–1552 January

    *Officiali*

    1 Custode a Belueder cu' 3 et 1
    1 Hortulano a belueder' cu' 1
    1 Giardiniero a beluedere cu' 1
    1 Hortulano alla Malliana
    Bernardino Manfredi fattore alle vigne cũ 1 (added February 1, 1551)

    BAV, Mss Ruoli 5, fol. 9v and Ruoli 6, fols. 11v and 25v.

    1551 December 20–1552 June 4

    *Officiales palatini*
    Antonius Massulus ⎱ Iardinerij ad Bel^re
    Nicolaus Ramerius ⎰
    Scipione piccio, Hortulano di Bel^re
    Scipione perotto, Custode in Belueder cum
    Paulus Saluatoris
    Guido Bandelot

    BAV, Ms Ruoli 11, fol. 31.

8. Marcello II (1555):

    1555 April 13
    Filippo Zoboli, Soprastante di Belueder'

    ASF, Carte Cerviniane, filza 52, fol. 20, letter of Filippo Zoboli to Alessandro Cervini.

9. Paul IV (1555–1559):

    1557 April 8–1557 August 1

    *Officiali Minori*

    1 Suprastante a Belueder con 2 fam. et 1 caual. [crossed out]
    1 Hortulano con 1 fam.

1 Giardiniero con 1 fam.

BAV, Mss Ruoli 29, fol. 14v and Ruoli 30, fol. 17v.

1558 June 30–1559 March 1

*Diuersi minori*

Messer Bernardino Manfredi [not on January 1, 1559 roll]

Messer Desiderio stillatore in Belueder [crossed out in March 1, 1559 revision]

*Officiali minori*

1 Superstante a Belueder cõ 1
1 Hortulano cõ 2
1 Giardinero cõ 2

BAV, Mss Ruoli 32, fol. 14v; Ruoli 33, fol. 12v; and Ruoli 34, fol. 9.

10. Pius IV (1559–1565):

1559 December 25–1565 November 30

*Officiali minori*

1 Suprastante a Belueder con 1 fam.
1 Hortulano con 2 fam. [Giouan added on March 19, 1560]
1 Giardinero con 2 fam.

BAV, Mss Ruoli 36, fols. 13v and 24v and Ruoli 37, fol. 28.

1562 January 1–1564 July 20

*Diuersi minori*

Messer Bastiano Manzoni, Stillatore con 1 [omitted January 1, 1564]

Messer Thomasso del giardin di Magnanapoli con 1 [omitted January 1, 1564]

Barnaba giardinero a Magnanapoli [added on June 1, 1562]

*Officiali Minori*

1 Soprastante à Belueder con 1
1 Hortulano con 2
1 Giardinero con 2

BAV, Mss Ruoli 44, fols. 9v, 12 and 28; Ruoli 45, fols. 11v and 14v; Ruoli 46, fols. 11v and 14v; Ruoli 48, fols. 12v and 15v; Ruoli 49, fols. 12v and 15v; and Ruoli 50, fols. 11v and 14v.

1564 April–1564 September 3

*Diuersi Minori*

Barnaba giardiniero a Magnanapoli

*Officiali Minori*

1 Soprastante [crossed out] a belueder Mantua [added] con 1 [crossed out]
1 Hortulano Giuliano [added] con 2
1 Giardinero Ottaviano [added] con 2

BAV, Ms Ruoli 51, fol. 13v.

1564 August 1–1565 November 30

*Diuersi Minori*

Barnaba giardiniero a Magnanapoli

*Officiali Minori*

Giuliano Hortolano in beluedere con 2
Ottaviano Giardiniero in beluedere con 2

BAV, Mss Ruoli 52, fol. 11v and Ruoli 53, fol. 13.

11. Sede Vacante (1565):

1565 December 9

*A tutto uitto*

1 Hortolano in belueder con 2
1 Giardinero con 2
Messer. Antonio soprastante a beluedere con 1 et 1

BAV, Ms Ruoli 55, fol. 3v.

12. Pius V (1566–1572):

1566 January 7

*Officiali Minori de Seruitio*

1 Soprastante à beluedere
1 Hortolano in detto con dui Aiutantj
1 Giardinero con dui Aiutantj
Giuliano Giardinere in belueder domanda esser Confirmata

BAV, Ms Ruoli 57, fol. 7.

1566 January 31–1568 July

*Diuersi Minori*

Messer Bastiano Stillator in beluedere con 1 et 1 [only on April 10–September 1566 roll]

*Officiali Maggiori*

Messer Antonio Soprastante de beluedere con 1 et 1

*Officiali Minori*

Giuliano Hortolano in beluedere con 2 [Giuliano crossed out and Bast.º added in margin by September 1566, later called Bart.º]
Niccolo Giardinero in beluedere con 2

BAV, Mss Ruoli 58, fols. 10v and 11; Ruoli 59, fols. 7v, 9, 10, and 10v; Ruoli 60, fols. 10 and 11v.

1569 December 1

*Officiali minori*

Cecchino Giardiniere in Beluedere con 2

BAV, Ms Ruoli 63, fol. 11.

13. Sixtus V (1585–1590):

1587 November–1590 July 1

*Medici Fisici A tutto Vitto*

Messer Michele Mercati, semplicista, scudi 6 companatico

*Diuersi Minori*

*Vigna di N. S$^{re}$ a S$^{ta}$ Maria Magg.$^{ri}$*

Claudio Modenese (Montonesi) Vignarolo ò giard.ro no' ha parte ma solò salario ogni mese dal Thes.r sec.to in scudi 5 (obijt die 25 Julij 1590)

*Beluedere*

Sopranzo giardiniero hà di salario scudi 3.50 ogni mese dal Thes.ro Sec.to, scudi 2.20 companatico [not on 1590 roll]

Valerio giardiniero alla Vignola et Peschiera hà da salario scudi 6 ogni mese dal Thes.re sec.to, scudi 3 companatico [in July 1590 named as Giardiniero in Beluedere at 10 scudi per month]

Doi lauoranti al giardino de semplici, che no' han parte, ma solo salario ogni mese dal Thes.r secreto in scudi 10 trà tutti doi [in July 1590 reduced to one laborer at six scudi]

BAV, Mss Ruoli 66, fols. 3v and 4v; Ruoli 82, fol. 6; and Ruoli 98, fol. 5v.

14. Gregory XIV (1590–1591):

1590 December

*Officiali Minori*

Mattheo Giardin.re Alla spalliera e Giardino sec.to

BAV, Ms Ruoli 101, fol. 11v.

15. Clement VIII (1592–1605):

1592 February 22–1593

*Officiali Minori*

Mantreo [crossed out and Grillo written above]— Giard.o alla spalliera et Giard.to sec., scudi 1.50 companatico in denari [Grillo listed in position in 1593]

Visdomini sop'nte in Beluedere, scudi 2 [all crossed out]

Messer Giouanni Custode de M.te Cauallo, scudi 3

BAV, Mss Ruoli 110, fol. 11 and Vat. lat. 7956, fol. 19.

1603 April 19–November 6

Carlo, giardiniere, venuto da Francia

See J.A.F. Orbaan, *Documenti sul barocco in Roma*, Rome, 1920, p. 4.

16. Paul V (1605–1621):

1605 April 8

Silvio Sigismondo, custode del giardino di Monte Cavallo [later called giardiniere, see below]

See *Il Palazzo del Quirinale*, Rome, 1974, p. 244.

1606 January 19–1614 December 6

Cristoforo Ramuschi, custode di Belvedere

See J.A.F. Orbaan, *Documenti*, pp. 296–315.

1609 April 4

Giovanni Fabro, 5 scudi per andare a Ostia a pigliar diversi semplici per piantar nel giardino di Belvedere

See ibid., pp. 302–3.

1610 July 12–1612 January 11

Silvio Sigismondo, giardiniero di Monte Cauallo

See *Il Palazzo del Quirinale*, p. 308.

17. Sede Vacante (1621):

1621 January 20–February 9

Giovanni Fabro, semplicista

See J.A.F. Orbaan, *Documenti*, p. 350.

18. Urban VIII (1623–1644):

1623

Rocco Sisto, giardiniero di Monte Cavallo e di Belvedere

See *Il Palazzo del Quirinale*, p. 255.

1627 December 31

*Elemosine*

frate Indiani con il Giardiniero n.º 3

*Officitiali Maggiori*

Bonifatio Angelini soprastante al giard.º

Gio. fabbri semplicista

Custode di Monte Cauallo

*Diuersi della Corte*

Rocco Giardiniero di Monte Cauallo

felice Giardiniere di Beluedere

BAV, Ms. Ruoli 147, fols. 9v, 10v, 12v, and 18v.

1637 November 5

*Offitiali Minori A Tutto Vitto*

Tubia Aldini semplicista, 2 Ser.ri

Sopast.e à Belued.re

Custode di m.t Cauallo

Bonifatio Angelini, sopast.e al Giard.no, 2 Ser.r, 1 Caualli

*Diuersi della Corte A Pane e Vino*

Bart.º fior.no Giard.o di m.t Cauallo

Ant.º di fatio Altro Giard.ro

Egidio Giard.ro com à Belued.re

Gio. Giard.ro a Belued.re

*Diuersi della Corte A Pane solo*

Vignarolo della Vig.a Giulia

Iac.º Boccarini Custode della Vignia Giulia

BAV, Ms. Ruoli 158, fols. 12v, 18v, 22v, and 25v.

### B. Miscellaneous

1. Vigna Farnese in Trastevere:

    1525 August 8
    Antonio Longo of Naples [gardener]

    See C. L. Frommel, in *Le Palais Farnèse: École fran-çaise de Rome*, Rome, 1981, I, pt. 1, p. 127.

    1544 May 31
    Bertino, giardiniere in Trasteuere

    See R. Lanciani, *Storia degli scavi di Roma*, II, 1903, p. 156.

1554 August 1
Bertino  }
Don Guido } giardinieri
Giacomino dalla Spalliere el prete

See F. Benoit, "Farnesiana," *Mélanges d'archéologie et d'histoire*, XL, 1923, pp. 203–4.

2. Villa Medici:

    1581 July 4
    Marentio [gardener]

    See G. M. Andres, *The Villa Medici in Rome*, New York, 1976, I, p. 298.

# APPENDIX IV

## *Leges Hortorum*

1. I. Manilli, *Villa Borghese fuori di Porta Pinciana*, Rome, 1650, p. 159:

> Villae Burghesiae Pincianae
> Custos Haec Edico
> Quisquis Es Si Liber
> Legum Compedes Ne His Timeas
> Ito Quo Voles Carpito Quae Voles
> Abito Quando Voles
> Exteris Magis Haec Parantur Quam Hero
> In Aureo Saeculo Vbi Cuncta Aurea
> Temporum Securitas Fecit
> Bene Morato Hospiti
> Ferreas Leges Praefigere Herus Vetat
> Sit His Amico Pro Lege Honesta Voluptas
> Verum Si Quis Dolo Malo
> Lubens Sciens
> Aureas Vrbanitatis Leges Fregerit
> Caveat Ne Sibi
> Tesseram Amicitiae Subiratus Villicus
> Advorsum Frangat.

The Manilli transcription of the inscription is obviously inaccurate in a few places, so that the version given here is taken from later, corrected versions. L. Passarini, *La questione di Villa Borghese*, Rome, 1885, p. 11, claims to have seen the original inscription, while L. Vicchi, *Villa Borghese nella storia e nella tradizione di popolo romano*, Rome, 1886, p. 288, mentions that the stone was then in fragments, but exhibited to the public. Recently P. della Pergola, *Villa Borghese*, Rome, 1962, p. 46, noted that she was informed by Professor Pietrangeli that the inscription may be in the Vatican Museum. For a complete history of the creation of the Villa, see C. H. Heilmann, "Die Entstehungsgeschichte der Villa Borghese in Rom," *Münchner Jahrbuch der bildenden Kunst*, ser. 3, XXIV, 1973, pp. 97–158.

2. L. Schrader, *Monumentorum Italiae*, Helmstadt, 1592, p. 218:

> Villam Perpetuae Salubritatis
> Suburbi Modo Montis Esquilini
> Oliverius Ille Cardinalis
> Doctae Clara Neapolis Propago
> Hanc Caraffa Pius Suis Amicis
> Dicat Omnibus, Hospites Venite.

The reference to the villa set on the Esquiline Hill, rather than its actual location on the Quirinal Hill, is evidence of the fifteenth-century date of the inscription, when the Quirinal Hill was regularly misidentified as the Esquiline.

3. Rome, Biblioteca Angelica, Ms 1729, fol. 12v:

> Julij S. Ang. Diac. Car. Caes.
> Dietam hanc statuarium
> Studijs suis
> Et gentil. suor. uolup. honestas
> Dicauit suo natali die XXXIIII
> XIII kal. Junij
> Alex. VI Pont. Max. An. VIII
> Sal. MD.ab V. C. MMCCXXXIII

See also C. Huelsen, review of *Le statue di Roma*, by P. G. Hübner, in *Göttingische gelehrte Anzeigen*, no. 176, 1914, p. 292, and C. Huelsen, "Römische Antikengärten des XVI. Jahrhunderts," *Abhandlungen der Heidelberger Akademie der Wissenschaften: Philosophisch-historische Klasse*, IV, 1917, p. VI.

Later the Cesarini family had an even more impressive garden with classical sculpture near the church of S. Pietro in Vincoli. It is Schrader (*Monumentorum Italiae*, p. 217v) again who preserves a record of the inscription in the garden addressed to each visitor:

> Hosce hortos anni quacunq̄ intraueris hora,
>   Et domus haec pulcri rustica quid quid habet,
> Inspicias lustresq̄ oculis licet hospes, & oris
>   Ista tibi in primis esse parata putes.
> Vt si quid fuerit quo tu oblectare voluptas,
>   Quae nunc vna mea est iam geminetur oro.
> Sin autem nulla his animum re pascis, abito,
>   Et patiare alios his sine lite frui.

4. C. Pietrangeli, *Il Museo di Roma*, Bologna, 1971, p. 40:

> Caesiorum Atque E[o]r[um] Amicorum Viridarium.

5. The inscriptions are first recorded in Fichard's account of his trip to Rome in 1536; see "Italia, Auctore Ioanne Fichardo," *Frankfurtisches Archiv für ältere deutsche Litteratur und Geschichte*, III, p. 69:

> I. Ad collabentium [collabeatum in Fichard] statuarum instaurationem pensiliumque hortorum ornamentum.
> II. Ad amicorum iucunditatem civium advenarumque delectationem.

III. Non ad voluptatem sed ad census fortunarumque favorem.

IV. Ad delicium vitae elegantiarum gratiarumque secessum.

V. Sibi et genio posterorumque [posterisque in Fichard] hilaritati.

VI. Antiquarum rerum vivario pictorum poetarumque subsidio.

VII. Honesti otii oblectamento domesticaeque commoditati.

VIII. Maiorum memoriae nepotumque imitationi.

See also C. Huelsen and H. Egger, *Die Römischen Skizzen-bücher von Marten van Heemskerck*, Berlin, 1916, II, pp. 56–66.

6. T. Falk, "Studien zur Topographie und Geschichte der Villa Giulia in Rom," *Römisches Jahrbuch für Kunstgeschichte*, XIII, 1971, p. 170:

### Deo Et Lodi Dominis Volentibus

Hoc in suburbano omnium si non quot in orbis at quot in urbis sunt ambitu pulcherrimo ad honestam potissime voluptatem facto, honeste voluptuarier cunctis fas honestis esto, set ne forte quis gratis ingratus siet, iussa haecce ante omnia omnis capessunto

Quovis quisq. ambulanto, ubivis quiescunto verum hoc citra somnum circumsepta illud

Passim quid libet lustranto, ast nec hilum quidem usquam attingunto

Qui secus faxint quidquamve clepserint aut rapserint non iam ut honesti moribus set ut furtis onusti in crucem pessumam arcentor

Ollis vero qui florum frondium pomorum olerum aliquid petierint, villici pro anni tempore pro rerum copia et inopia proq. merito cuiusque largiuntor.

Aquam hanc quod virgo est ne temeranto, sitimq. fistulis non flumine, poculis non osculo aut volis extinguunto

Piscium lusu oblectantor, cantu avium mulcentor, at ne quem interturbent interim cavento

Signa statuas lapides picturas et caetera totius operis miracula quamdiu lubet obtuentor dum ne nimio stupor in ea vortantur.

Sicui quid tamen ita mirum videbitur eorum caussa quae nemo mirari sat quivit, aequo potius silentio quam sermonibus iniquis praeterito

Dehinc proximo in templo deo ac divo Andreae gratias agunto, vitamq. et salutem Iulio III. pont. max. Balduino eius fratri et eorum familiae universae plurimam et aeviternam precantor.

Huic autem suburbano speciem atq. amplitudinem pulchriorem indies maioremq. ac in eo quicquid inest felix faustum perpetuum optanto hisce actis valento et salvi abeunto.

7. G. M. Andres, *The Villa Medici in Rome*, New York and London, 1976, II, n. 585:

Aditurus hortos, hospes, in summo, ut vides,
    Colle Hortulorum consistos, si forte quid
    Audes probare, scire debes hos hero,
    Heriq. amicis esse apertos omnibus.
Ingressus, hospes, hosce quos ingentibus
    Instruxit hortos sumptibus suis Medices
    Fernandus, expleare visendo licet
    Atq. his fruendo plura velle non decet.

8. L. de la Villa sur-Yllon, "Il Palazzo degli Spiriti," *Napoli nobilissima*, XIII, 1904, pp. 97–100, and B. Croce, *Galeas Caracciolo, Marquis de Vico*, Geneva, 1965, pp. 6–11:

Nic. Ant. Caracciolus Vici Marchio
Et Caesaris A Latere Consiliarius Has
Genio Aedes, Gratiis Hortos, Nymphis
Fontes, Nemus Faunis, Et Totius
    Loci Venustatem
Sebeto Et Syrenibus Dedicavit
Ad Vitae Oblectamentum Atque
Secessum Et Perpetuam Amicorum
Jucunditatem. M.D.XXXIII.

# BIBLIOGRAPHY

## Abbreviations

ASF     Archivio di Stato, Florence
ASM     Archivio di Stato, Modena
ASP     Archivio di Stato, Parma
ASR     Archivio di Stato, Rome
*ASRSP*     *Archivio della R. società romana di storia patria*
BAV     Biblioteca Apostolica Vaticana, Rome

## General

Borsi, F., and G. Pampaloni. *Ville e giardini.* Novara, 1984.

Chatfield, J. *A Tour of Italian Gardens.* New York, 1988.

Comito, T. *The Idea of the Garden in the Renaissance.* New Brunswick, N.J., 1978.

Cruciani Boriosi, M. T. "La realizzazione barocca del giardino italiano e la sua parziale discendenza dalla contemporanea scenografia." *Antichità viva,* II, 2, February 1963, pp. 15–28.

Dami, L. *Il giardino italiano.* Milan, 1924.

Florence, Pal. Vecchio. *Mostra del giardino italiano: Catalogo.* Florence, 1931.

Gothein, M. L. *A History of Garden Art.* 2 vols. London and Toronto, 1928.

Gromort, G. *Jardins d'Italie.* Paris, 1922.

Masson, G. *Italian Gardens.* New York, [1961].

Miglio, M. "Immagine e racconto: Note sul giardino in qualche manoscritto italiano (XII–XIV secolo)." In *Il giardino storico italiano,* ed. G. Ragionieri, pp. 279–93. Florence, 1981.

## Waterworks

Alvarez, F. J. "The Renaissance Nymphaeum: Its Origins and Its Development in Rome and Vicinity." Ph.D. dissertation, Columbia University, 1981.

Bober, P. P. "The *Coryciana* and the Nymph Corycia." *Journal of the Warburg and Courtauld Institutes,* XL, 1977, pp. 223–39.

Fagiolo, M. "Il significato dell'acqua e la dialettica del giardino: Pirro Ligorio e la 'filosofia' della villa cinquecentesca." In *Il giardino storico italiano,* ed. G. Ragionieri, pp. 192–210. Florence, 1981.

MacDougall, E. B. "The Sleeping Nymph: Origins of a Humanist Fountain Type." *Art Bulletin,* LVII, 1975, pp. 357–65.

———. "*L'Ingegnoso Artifizio*: Sixteenth Century Garden Fountains in Rome." In *Fons Sapientiae: Renaissance Garden Fountains* (Dumbarton Oaks Colloquium on the History of Landscape Architecture, V), ed. E. B. MacDougall, pp. 85–113. Washington, D. C., 1978.

Maggi, G. *Fontane diverse che si uedano nel'Alma Città di Roma.* Rome, 1618.

Onofrio, C. d'. *Acque e fontane di Roma.* Rome, 1977.

Varming, J. C. "Fontane romane." *Analecta romana,* III, 1965, pp. 85–137.

Venturini, G. F. *Le fontane ne' palazzi e ne' giardini di Roma.* Rome, n. d.

## Botany and Horticulture

Aldino, T. *Exactissima descriptio rariorum quarundam plantarum quę continentur Romę in Horto Farnesiano.* Rome, 1625.

Belli Barsali, I. "Una fonte per i giardini del Seicento: Il trattato di Giovan Battista Ferrari." In *Il giardino storico italiano,* ed. G. Ragionieri, pp. 221–34. Florence. 1981.

———. "Il giardino storico italiano: Problemi di indagine." In *Il giardino storico italiano,* ed. G. Ragionieri, pp. 19–29. Florence, 1981.

Bonelli, G. *Hortus romanus,* I. Rome, 1772.

Catalano, M., and E. Pellegrini. *L'orto botanico di Roma.* Rome, 1975.

Coggiatti, S. "Tra giardini e piante nel rinascimento." In *Rinascimento nel Lazio* (Lunario romano, IX), ed. R. Lefevre, pp. 33–45. Rome, n. d.

Ferrari, G. B. *Flora, seu de florum cultura,* new ed. Amsterdam, 1646.

———. *Hesperides sive De Malorum Aureorum Cultura et Vsu Libri Quatuor.* Rome, 1646.

Lanzara, P. "Storia degli orti botanici romani." *Capitolium,* XLII, July–December 1967, pp. 318–20.

Masson, G. "Italian Flower Connoisseurs." *Apollo,* LXXXVIII, 1968, pp. 164–71.

———. "Italian Flower Collectors' Gardens in Seventeenth Century Italy." In *The Italian Garden* (First Dumbarton Oaks Colloquium on the History of Landscape Architecture), ed. D. R. Coffin, pp. 61–80. Washington, D. C., 1972.

Pirotta, L. "Nuovo contributo alla storia del R. Giardino Botanico di Roma." *Capitolium,* XVI, 1941, pp. 377–84.

Pirotta, R., and E. Chiovenda. *Flora romana.* (Estratto dal vol. X dell' R. Istituto Botanico di Roma). Rome, 1900.

## Rome

Ackerman, J. S. *The Cortile del Belvedere* (Studi e documenti per la storia del Palazzo Apostolico Vaticano, III). Vatican City, 1954.

Amici dei Musei di Roma. *Villa Borghese: Catalogo*. Rome, 1966.

Andres, G. M. *The Villa Medici in Rome*. 2 vols. New York and London, 1976.

Bafile, M. *Il giardino di Villa Madama*. Rome, 1942.

Baggio, C., and P. Zampa. "Le fontane del Quirinale nel codice barberiniano latino 4409 alla Biblioteca Apostolica Vaticana." *Bollettino d'arte*, LXX, 1985, pp. 85–94.

Barosso, M. "Il portale palatino farnesiano del Vignola: La porta senza pace." In *Atti del V Convegno nazionale di storia dell'architettura*, pp. 347–52. Florence, 1957.

Belli Barsali, I. *Ville di Roma: Lazio I*. Milan, 1970.

Belli Barsali, I., and M. Grazia Branchetti. *Ville della campagna romana: Lazio II*. Milan, 1975.

Beck, H., and P. C. Bol. eds. *Forschungen zur Villa Albani* (Frankfurter Forschungen zur Kunst, 10). Berlin, 1982.

Benedetti, S. *Giacomo Del Duca e l'architettura del Cinquecento*. Rome, 1972–1973.

Berliner, R. "Zeichnungen von Carlo und Filippo Marchionni." *Münchner Jahrbuch der bildenden Kunst*, ser. 3, IX–X, 1958–1959, pp. 267–396.

Bernardi Salvetti, C. "La porta degli 'Horti Bellayani' e quella dei giardini dei Panzani." *Strenna dei romanisti*, XXVII, 1966, pp. 41–45.

Boni, G. "L'Arcadia sul Palatino." *Bollettino d'arte*, VIII, 1914, pp. 369–80.

Boyer, F. "La construction de la Villa Médicis." *La revue de l'art ancien et moderne*, LI, 1927, pp. 3–14, 109–20.

Bresciani, C., and G. Sacchi. "Rome—Villa Doria Pamphili." *Bollettino del Centro di Studi per la Storia dell'Architettura*, no. 24, 1976, pp. 60–66.

Briganti, G. *Il Palazzo del Quirinale*. Rome, 1962.

Brummer, H. H. *The Statue Court in the Vatican Belvedere* (Stockholm Studies in the History of Art, 20). Stockholm, 1970.

*Il Cardinale Alessandro Albani e la sua villa* (Quaderni sul neoclassico, 5). Rome, 1980.

Casanova, E. "La Villa Celimontana." *Capitolium*, I, 1925–1926, pp. 15–23.

Cassanelli, L. "Nuove acquisizioni documentarie per il giardino della villa Albani Torlonia." In *Giardini italiani: Note di storia e di conservazione* (Quaderni, no. 3), pp. 73–80. Rome, 1981.

Coffin, D. R. *The Villa in the Life of Renaissance Rome*. Princeton, N.J., 1979.

———. "The 'Lex Hortorum' and Access to Gardens of Latium During the Renaissance." *Journal of Garden History*, II, 1982, pp. 201–32.

Colonna, G. B. "La Villa Albani." *Capitolium*, VIII, 1932, pp. 283–95.

Crescimbeni, G. M. *Stato della basilica diaconale, collegiata, e parrocchiale di S. Maria in Cosmedin di Roma*. Rome, 1719.

Dami, L. "Il giardino Quirinale ai primi del '600." *Bollettino d'arte*, XIII, 1919, pp. 113–16.

Davico, A. "La ricostruzione del portale degli ex Orti Farnesiani ed il nuovo ingresso al Palatino." *Bollettino d'arte*, XLIV, 1959, pp. 272–75.

Debenedetti, E., ed. *Committenze della famiglia Albani: Note sulla Villa Albani Torlonia*. Rome, 1985.

De Feo, V. *La Piazza del Quirinale*. Rome, 1973.

Di Gaddo, B. *Villa Borghese: Il giardino e le architetture*. Rome, 1985.

Dorez, L. *La cour du Pape Paul III*. 2 vols. Paris, 1932.

Eiche, S. "Cardinal Giulio della Rovere and the Vigna Carpi." *Journal of the Society of Architectural Historians*, XLV, 1986, pp. 115–33.

Fagiolo, M. "Idea degli Horti Farnesiani: 'Roma Quadrata' e il 'Foro della Pace.'" In *Giardino: Storia e conservazione*, pp. 217–27. [Rome, 1984].

Falda, G. B. *Li giardini di Roma*. Rome, n. d.

Falk, T. "Studien zur Topographie und Geschichte der Villa Giulia in Rom." *Römisches Jahrbuch für Kunstgeschichte*, XIII, 1971, pp. 101–78.

[Felice, G.] *Villa Ludovisi in Roma*. Rome, 1952.

[Fontana, C.] *Risposta del Signor Carlo Fontana alla lettera dell'Illustriss. Sig. Ottavio Castiglioni*. Rome, 1668.

Frommel, C. L. *Die Farnesina und Peruzzis Architektonisches Frühwerk*. Berlin, 1961.

Gallo, E. *De viridario Augustini Chigii*. Rome, 1511.

Garms, J. *Quellen aus dem Archiv Doria-Pamphilj zur Kunsttätigkeit in Rom unter Innocenz X* (Quellenschriften zur Geschichte der Barockkunst in Rom, 4). Rome and Vienna, 1972.

Giess, H. "Studien zur Farnese-Villa am Palatin." *Römisches Jahrbuch für Kunstgeschichte*, XIII, 1971, pp. 179–230.

Gioja, C. *Gli orti Colocciani in Roma*. Foligno, 1893.

Gnoli, D. "Il giardino e l'antiquario del Cardinal Cesi." *Mitteilungen des kaiserlich deutschen archäologischen Instituts: Römische Abteilung*, XX, 1905, pp. 267–76.

———. "Orti letterari nella Roma di Leon X." *Nuova Antologia*, CCCXLVII, 1930, pp. 3–19, 137–48.

Golzio, V. *Documenti artistici sul Seicento nell'Archivio Chigi*. Rome, 1939.

Gombrich, E. H. "The Belvedere Garden as a Grove of Venus." In *Symbolic Images*, pp. 104–8. Oxford, 1978.

Heilmann, C. H. "Die Entstehungsgeschichte der Villa Borghese in Rom." *Münchner Jahrbuch der bildenden Kunst*, ser. 3, XXIV, 1973, pp. 97–158.

Heimbürger, M. "Alessandro Algardi architetto?" *Analecta Romana Insituti Danici*, VI, 1971, pp. 197–224.

Heimbürger Ravalli, M. "Progetti e lavori di Francesco Bettini per il parco di Villa Belrespiro." *Studi romani*, XXV, 1977, pp. 27–37.

———. *Disegni di giardini e opere minori di un artista del '700 Francesco Bettini*. Florence, 1981.

Hibbard, H. "Scipione Borghese's Garden Palace on the

Quirinal." *Journal of the Society of Architectural Historians*, XXIII, 1964, pp. 163–92.

Huelsen, C. "Römische Antikengärten des XVI Jahrhunderts." *Abhandlungen der Heidelberger Akademie der Wissenschaften: Philosophisch-historische Klasse*, IV, 1917.

Incisa della Rocchetta, G. "Il palazzo ed il giardino del Pio Istituto Rivaldi." *Capitolium*, IX, 1933, pp. 213–34.

———. "Il museo di curiosità del Card. Flavio I Chigi." *Archivio della società romana di storia patria*, LXXXIX, 1966, pp. 141–92.

Krautheimer, R. "Roma verde nel Seicento." In *Studi in onore di Giulio Carlo Argan*, Rome, 1984, II, pp. 71–82.

Kultzen, R. "Die Malereien Polidoros da Caravaggio im Giardino del Bufalo in Rom." *Mitteilungen des kunsthistorischen Institutes in Florenz*, IX, 1959, pp. 99–120.

Lombardi, P. C. "La Villa Aldobrandini a Magnanapoli." *Capitolium*, VIII, 1932, pp. 336–49.

MacDougall, E. B. "The Villa Mattei and the Development of the Roman Garden Style." Ph.D. dissertation, Harvard University, 1970.

———. "*Ars Hortulorum*: Sixteenth Century Garden Iconography and Literary Theory in Italy." In *The Italian Garden* (First Dumbarton Oaks Colloquium on the History of Landscape Architecture), ed. D. R. Coffin, pp. 37–59. Washington, D. C., 1972.

———. "A Circus, a Wild Man and a Dragon: Family History and the Villa Mattei." *Journal of the Society of Architectural Historians*, XLII, 1983, pp. 121–30.

———. "Imitation and Invention: Language and Decoration in Roman Renaissance Gardens." *Journal of Garden History*, V, 1985, pp. 119–34.

Magnanimi, G. *Palazzo Barberini*. Rome, 1983.

Manilli, I. *Villa Borghese fuori di Porta Pinciana*. Rome, 1650.

[Massimo, V.] *Notizie istoriche della Villa Massimo alle Terme Diocleziane*. Rome, 1836.

Masson, G. "Pietro Aretino and the Small Roman Renaissance Pleasure Garden." *Garden History*, VIII, no. 1, 1980, pp. 67–68.

Matthiae, G. "La Villa Montalto alle Terme." *Capitolium*, XIV, 1939, pp. 139–47.

Meulen, M. van der. "Cardinal Cesi's Antique Sculpture Garden: Notes on a Painting by Hendrik van Cleef III." *Burlington Magazine*, CXVI, 1974, pp. 14–24.

Michaelis, A. "Geschichte des Statuenhofes im Vaticanischen Belvedere." *Jahrbuch des königlich deutschen archäologischen Instituts*, V, 1890, pp. 5–72.

Mignosi, A. T. "Boschi sacri e barchi nei paesi feudali del Lazio." *Ville e parchi nel Lazio* (Lunario romano, XIII), ed. R. Lefevre, pp. 3–15. Rome, 1984.

Montani, C. "Villa Borghese." *Capitolium*, I, 1925–1926, pp. 657–73.

Morcelli, S. A., C. Fea, and E. Q. Visconti. *La Villa Albani descritta*. 3rd ed. Rome, 1869.

Onofrio, C. d'. *Roma val bene un'abiura*. Rome, 1976.

Ortolani, S. *S. Bernardo alle Terme* (Le chiese di Roma illustrate, 8). Rome, n. d.

*Il Palazzo del Quirinale*. Rome, 1974.

Palladio, B. *Suburbanum Augustini Chisii*. Rome, 1512.

Pecchiai, P. *La scalinata di Piazza di Spagna e Villa Medici*. Rome, 1941.

Pergola, P. della. *Villa Borghese*. Rome, 1962.

Pietrangeli, C. *Villa Paolina*. Rome, 1961.

Pollak, O. "Alessandro Algardi (1602–1654) als Architekt." *Zeitschrift für Geschichte der Architektur*, IV, 1910–1911, pp. 49–79.

Portal, E. *L'Arcadia*. n. p., 1922.

Quondam, A. "La crisi dell'Arcadia." *Palatino*, XII, 1968, pp. 160–70.

———. "L'istituzione Arcadia: Sociologia e ideologia di un'accademia." *Quaderni storici*, VIII, 1973, pp. 388–438.

Romanelli, P. "Horti palatini Farnesiorum." *Studi romani*, VIII, 1960, pp. 661–72.

Sacripanti, M. *La Villa Borghese in Roma*. n. p., 1953.

Salerno, L. "La fontana dell'organo nei giardini del Quirinale." *Capitolium*, XXXVI, no. 4, April 1961, pp. 3–9.

Sartorio, G. P. "Una *domus* sotto il giardino del Pio Istituto Rivaldi sulla Velia." In *Città e architettura nella Roma Imperiale* (Analecta romana Instituti Danici, Supplementum X), pp. 147–68. [Odense], 1983.

Schiavo, A. *Villa Doria-Pamphilj*. Milan, 1942.

———. *Villa Ludovisi e Palazzo Margherita*. Rome, 1981.

Tagiolini, A. *I giardini di Roma*. Rome, 1980.

Tetius, H. *Aedes Barberinae ad Quirinalem*. Rome, 1642.

Vicchi, L. *Villa Borghese nella storia e nella tradizione del popolo romano*. Rome, 1886.

Weiermann, H. "Bemerkungen zur Villa Madama und ihr Gartenanlagen." In *Festschrift Luitpold Dussler*, pp. 299–316. n. p., 1972.

Westfall, C. W. *In This Most Perfect Paradise*. University Park, Penn., and London, 1974.

Wrede, H. *Der Antikengarten der del Bufalo bei der Fontana Trevi* (Trierer Winckelmannsprogramme, 4). Mainz, 1982.

Zippel, G. "Paolo II e l'arte: Il giardino di San Marco." *L'arte*, XIII, 1910, pp. 240–52.

### Bagnaia

Arnoldi, F. N. *Villa Lante in Bagnaia*. Rome, 1963.

Boni, L. "La villa di Bagnaia residenza estiva dei Vescovi di Viterbo." *Capitolium*, XXXV, no. 2, February 1960, pp. 3–9.

Bruschi, A. "Bagnaia." *Quaderni dell'Istituto di Storia dell'Architettura*, no. 17, 1956, pp. 1–15.

Cantoni, A., et al. *La Villa Lante di Bagnaia.* Milan, 1961.

Coffin, D. R. "Some Aspects of the Villa Lante at Bagnaia." In *Arte in Europa: Scritti di storia dell'arte in onore di Edoardo Arslan*, pp. 569–75. Milan, 1966.

Durm, J. "Die Villa Lante bei Bagnaia und das Kloster S. Maria della Quercia." *Zeitschrift für bildende Kunst*, XI, 1876, pp. 292–98.

Fritelli, V. "La Bolla delle Gabelle, le 'Delizie' di Bagnaia e i Cardinali Gambara e Borromeo." In *Rinascimento nel Lazio* (Lunario romano, IX), ed. R. Lefevre, pp. 137–57. Rome, n. d.

Hess, J. "Villa Lante di Bagnaia e Giacomo Del Duca." *Palatino*, X, 1966, pp. 21–32.

———. "Entwürfe von Giovanni Guerra für Villa Lante in Bagnaia (1598)." *Römisches Jahrbuch für Kunstgeschichte*, XII, 1969, pp. 195–202.

Lazzaro Bruno, C. "The Villa Lante at Bagnaia." Ph.D. dissertation, Princeton University, 1974.

———. "The Villa Lante at Bagnaia: An Allegory of Art and Nature." *Art Bulletin*, LIX, 1977, pp. 553–60.

Natilj, M. *Cenno storico e compendiosa descrizione della Villa di Bagnaia com'era avanti al 1820.* Rome, 1864.

Pinzi, C. *Il Castello e la Villa di Bagnaia già Signoria dei Vescovi Viterbesi* (extract from *Bollettino storico archeologico viterbese*, III). Viterbo, 1908.

Ridolfi, R. "Alcune notizie inedite sulla Villa di Bagnaia." *Rivista storica degli archivi toscani*, I, 1929, pp. 203–5.

## Bomarzo

Battisti, E. *L'Antirinascimento.* Milan, 1962.

Bosch, L.M.F. "Bomarzo: A Study in Personal Imagery." *Garden History*, X, 1982, pp. 97–107.

Bredekamp, H. *Vicino Orsini und der Heilige Wald von Bomarzo.* 2 vols. Worms, 1985.

Bruschi, A. "L'abitato di Bomarzo e la Villa Orsini." *Quaderni dell'Istituto di Storia dell'Architettura*, nos. 7–9, April 1955, pp. 3–18.

———. "Nuovi dati documentari sulle opere Orsiane di Bomarzo." *Quaderni dell'Istituto di Storia dell'Architettura*, ser. x, fasc. 55–60, 1963, pp. 13–58.

———. "Il problema storico di Bomarzo." *Palladio*, n. s., XIII, 1963, pp. 85–114.

Bury, J. B. "Some Early Literary References to Italian Gardens." *Journal of Garden History*, II, 1982, pp. 17–24.

———. "The Reputation of Bomarzo." *Journal of Garden History*, III, 1983, pp. 108–12.

Calvesi, M. "Il Sacro Bosco di Bomarzo." *Scritti di storia dell'arte in onore di Lionello Venturi*, Rome, 1956, I, pp. 369–402.

Darnell, M. J., and M. S. Weil. "Il Sacro Bosco di Bomarzo: Its 16th-Century Literary and Antiquarian Context." *Journal of Garden History*, IV, 1984, pp. 1–91.

Dotson, E. G. "Shapes of Earth and Time in European Gardens." *Art Journal*, XLII, 1982, pp. 210–16.

Jensen, S. S. "Lucubratiunculae: Reflections on the Sacro Bosco at Bomarzo." In *Studia romana in honorem Petri Krarup septuagenarii*, pp. 204–12. Odense, 1976.

Kretzulesco-Quaranta, E. *Les jardins du songe*, pp. 275–89. Paris, 1976.

Lang, S. "Bomarzo." *The Architectural Review*, CXXI, January–June 1957, pp. 427–30.

Miller, N. "The Secret Garden of Vicino Orsini." *Daidalos*, III, 1982, pp. 38–49.

Nicoletti, M. "Il Bosco Sacro." *FMR: Mensile di Franco Maria Ricci*, no. 12, April 1983, pp. 56–62.

Oleson, J. P. "A Reproduction of an Etruscan Tomb in the Parco dei Mostri at Bomarzo." *Art Bulletin*, LVII, 1975, pp. 410–17.

Quaranta, E. *Incantesimo a Bomarzo.* Florence, 1960.

Quartermaine, L. "Vicino Orsini's Garden of Conceits." *Italian Studies*, XXXII, 1977, pp. 68–85.

Recupero, J. *Il Sacro Bosco di Bomarzo.* Florence, 1977.

Settis, S. "Contributo a Bomarzo." *Bollettino d'arte*, ser. 6, LI, 1966, pp. 17–26.

Theurillat, J. *Les mystères de Bomarzo et des jardins symboliques de la Renaissance.* Geneva, 1973.

Von Hennenberg, J. "Bomarzo: The Extravagant Garden of Pier Francesco Orsini." *Italian Quarterly*, XI, no. 42, Fall 1967, pp. 3–19.

———. "Bomarzo: Nuovi dati e un'interpretazione." *Storia dell'arte*, XIII, 1972, pp. 43–55.

Zander, G. "Gli elementi documentari sul Sacro Bosco." *Quaderni dell'Istituto di Storia dell'Architettura*, nos. 7–9, April 1955, pp. 19–32.

Zolla, E. "Il Sacro Bosco." *FMR: Mensile di Franco Maria Ricci*, no. 12, April 1983, pp. 42–51.

## Caprarola

Baumgart, F. "La Caprarola di Ameto Orti." *Studj romanzi*, XXV, 1935, pp. 77–179.

Benedetti, S. "Sul giardino grande di Caprarola ed altre note." *Quaderni dell'Istituto di Storia dell'Architettura*, nos. 91–96, 1969, pp. 3–46.

Gambara, L. *Caprarola.* Rome, 1581.

Labrot, G. *Le Palais Farnèse de Caprarola: Essai de lecture.* Paris, 1970.

Liberati, G. *La Caprarola.* Ronciglione, 1614.

Partridge, L. W. "Vignola and the Villa Farnese at Caprarola." *Art Bulletin*, LII, 1970, pp. 81–87.

Tagliolini, A. "Il Cardinale Alessandro Farnese e il giardino del Cinquecento." In *Ville e parchi nel Lazio* (Lunario romano, XIII), ed. R. Lefevre, pp. 17–35. Rome, 1984.

Trasmondo-Frangipane, C. *Descrizione storico-artistica del R. Palazzo di Caprarola.* Rome, 1869.

## Frascati

Barrière, D. *Villa Aldobrandina*. Rome, 1647.

Del Re, N. "Villa Sora a Frascati." In *Ville e parchi nel Lazio* (Lunario romano, XIII), ed. R. Lefevre, pp. 311–22. Rome, 1984.

Devoti, L. *Campagna romana viva: Le ville tuscolane: La Villa Rufina-Falconieri*. Frascati, 1986.

Fagiolo dell'Arco, M. "Villa Aldobrandina tusculana." *Quaderni dell'Instituto di Storia dell'Architettura*, ser. XI, fasc. 62–66, 1964, pp. 61–92.

Franck, C. L. *Die Barockvillen in Frascati*. Munich and Berlin, 1956.

Frezzotti, S. "I teatri delle acque nelle ville di Frascati." *Studi romani*, XXX, 1982, pp. 467–77.

Grossi-Gondi, F. *La Villa dei Quintili e la Villa di Mondragone*. Rome, 1901.

Mignosi, A. T., et al. *Villa e paese*. Rome, 1980.

Onofrio, C. d'. *La Villa Aldobrandini di Frascati*. Rome, [1963].

Schwager, K. "Kardinal Pietro Aldobrandinis Villa di Belvedere in Frascati." *Römisches Jahrbuch für Kunstgeschichte*, IX–X, 1961–1962, pp. 289–382.

Tantillo, A. "Un complesso di giardini romani tra '500 e '700: Le ville del Tuscolo. Storia di una immagine di paesaggio." In *Giardini italiani*, ed. M. L. Quondam and A. M. Racheli, pp. 51–62. Rome, 1981.

## Tivoli

Ashby, T. "The Villa d'Este at Tivoli and the Collection of Classical Sculptures Which It Contained." *Archaeologia*, LXI, pt. 1, 1908, pp. 219–55.

Barisi, I. "Anticipazioni sul restauro del verde storico di Villa d'Este." *Bollettino del Centro di Studi per la Storia dell'Architettura*, no. 24, 1976, pp. 55–59.

Coffin, D. R. *The Villa d'Este at Tivoli*. Princeton, N.J., 1960.

Lamb, C. *Die Villa d'Este in Tivoli*. Munich, 1966.

Lightbown, R. W. "Nicolas Audebert and the Villa d'Este." *Journal of the Warburg and Courtauld Institutes*, XXVII, 1964, pp. 164–90.

Madonna, M. L. "Il Genius Loci di Villa d'Este: Mito e misteri nel sistema di Pirro Ligorio." In *Natura e artificio*, ed. M. Fagiolo, pp. 192–226. Rome, 1979.

———. "Pirro Ligorio e Villa d'Este: La scena di Roma e il mistero della Sibilla." In *Il giardino storico italiano*, ed. G. Ragionieri, pp. 173–96. Florence, 1981.

Pacifici, V. *Ippolito II d'Este, Cardinale di Ferrara*. Tivoli, n. d.

Seni, F. S. *La Villa d'Este in Tivoli*. Rome, 1902.

Venturini, G. G. *Le fontane del Giardino Estense in Tivoli*. Rome, n. d.

Zappi, G. M. *Annali e memorie di Tivoli di Giovanni Maria Zappi* (Studi e fonti per la storia della regione tiburtina, 1), ed. V. Pacifici. Tivoli, 1920.

## Miscellaneous

Calabrese, F. "Il recupero delle ville Colonnesi a Marino." In *Ville e parchi nel Lazio* (Lunario romano, XIII), ed. R. Lefevre, pp. 283–98. Rome, 1984.

Lefevre, R. "Le rovine di 'Villa Versaglia' a Formello." *Colloqui del Sodalizio*, ser. 2, VII–VIII, 1980–1984, pp. 199–205.

———. "Documenti su Villa Versaglia (Formello)." *Archivio della società romana di storia patria*, CV, 1982, pp. 315–44.

Milone, M. F. "Il Casino del Cardinale Madruzzo a Soriano nel Cimino." *Quaderni dell'Istituto di Storia dell'Architettura*, nos. 17–19, 1970–1972, pp. 71–94.

———. "La triplice allegoria dell' 'Acqua di Papa': La fonte del Cardinal Madruzzo a Soriano nel Cimino." *Psicon*, III, nos. 8–9, July–December 1976, pp. 121–31.

Portoghesi, P. "Note sulla Villa Orsini di Pitigliano." *Quaderni dell'Istituto di Storia dell'Architettura*, nos. 7–12, 1955, pp. 74–76.

———. "Il Palazzo, la villa, e la chiesa di S. Vincenzo a Bassano." *Bollettino d'arte*, XLII, 1957, pp. 220–40.

Simo, M. L. "Vincenzo Giustiniani: His Villa at Bassano di Sutri, near Rome, and his 'Instructions to a Builder and Gardener,'" *Journal of Garden History*, I, 1981, pp. 253–70.

## English Gardening

Andrew, P. R. "An English Garden in Rome." *Country Life*, CLXIX, April 23, 1981, pp. 1136–38.

Angioletti, G. B., ed. *Le più belle pagine di Ippolito Pindemonte*. Milan and Rome, 1933.

Cimmino, N. F. *Ippolito Pindemonte e il suo tempo*. Rome, n. d.

Graf, A. *L'Anglomania e l'influsso inglese in italia nel secolo XVIII*. Turin, 1911.

Heimbürger Ravalli, M. "Francesco Bettini e l'introduzione del giardino romantico a Roma." In *Studia romana in honorem Petri Krarup septuagenarii*, pp. 213–25. Odense, 1976.

Pindemonte, I. *Sui giardini inglesi e sul merito in ciò dell'Italia*. Padua, 1792.

———. *Il giardino inglese*. Verona, 1817.

# INDEX